EXAM✓PREP

D1315134

PHR

Professional in Human Resources

Second Edition

Cathy Lee Gibson

PHR Exam Prep: Professional in Human Resources, Second Edition

ISBN-10: 0-7897-3677-2

ISBN-13: 978-0-7897-3677-2

Library of Congress Cataloging-in-Publication data is on file.

Printed in the United States of America

Fifth Printing: August 2010

Trademarks

Warning and Disclaimer

Bulk Sales

Que Publishing offers excellent discounts on this book when ordered in quantity for bulk purchases or special sales. For more information, please contact

U.S. Corporate and Government Sales
1-800-382-3419
corpsales@pearsontechgroup.com

For sales outside of the U.S., please contact

International Sales
international@pearsoned.com

ASSOCIATE PUBLISHER
David Dusthimer

ACQUISITIONS EDITOR
Betsy Brown

DEVELOPMENT EDITOR
Dan Young

MANAGING EDITOR
Patrick Kanouse

PROJECT EDITOR
Seth Kerney

COPY EDITOR
Barbara Hacha

INDEXER
Ken Johnson

PROOFREADER
Water Crest Publishing

TECHNICAL EDITOR
Bob Prescott

PUBLISHING COORDINATOR
Vanessa Evans

MULTIMEDIA DEVELOPER
Dan Scherf

BOOK DESIGNER
Gary Adair

Contents at a Glance

Table of Contents

About the Author

Cathy Lee Gibson (SPHR) is the Director of Human Resource Management Programs at Cornell University's School of Industrial and Labor Relations in New York City. Cathy has more than 20 years of progressively responsible generalist, specialist, and management experience in the field of human resources and has worked at small and large organizations, in educational settings, in for-profit, and in not-for-profit sectors.

Cathy leads professional development programs for managers and human resources professionals on interviewing and performance management—and how to ensure that those functions have a more strategic impact on organizations. In that spirit, in 2004 Cathy wrote *Performance Appraisals*, for Silver Lining Publications, a division of Barnes & Noble. In 2006, Cathy also wrote *Mission Driven Interviewing: Moving Beyond Behavior Based Questions* for PTI Publishing. She has also co-authored online workshops titled "Effective Interviewing," "Performance Management and Appraisal," "Managing Performance," and "Fundamentals of Compensation." Cathy also spoke at the SHRM National Conference and Exposition in 2006 and 2007 and is slated to speak again in 2008.

You can reach Cathy at Cathy@CathyLeeGibson.com

Dedication

Acknowledgments

I've learned many things from writing this book—one of which is that I'll never again skip past the "Acknowledgments" section of a book that I'm reading. I've come to realize that an author—at least this author—is a person fortunate enough to be surrounded by a team of talented and committed individuals without whom there would be no book—and therefore without whom there would be no authorship.

So, in recognition of those who wove together the tapestry that you now hold in your hand, I would like to express my appreciation to the following individuals:

- Bob Prescott, Technical Editor: For his guidance, perspective, discernment, and insight—along with his willingness to be a sounding board—all of which yielded far better ideas and results than I could have generated on my own. Drawing on his decades of experience as a practitioner, academic professional, and author, Bob kept me on the technical straight and narrow.

- Betsy Brown, Acquisitions Editor: For her leadership, expertise, and sound advice throughout the editorial transition and the actual publication of this book.

- Seth Kerney, Project Editor, and Dan Young, Development Editor: For their eagle-eyed scrutiny and for their simultaneous—yet single-minded—attention to the "forest" as well as to the "tree."

- Patrick Kanouse, Managing Editor, and Barbara Hacha, Copy Editor for their individual and collective contributions.

- The many family members, friends, and colleagues who, in myriad ways, have made a difference in my personal and professional life and who thus helped make this book possible.

- Philicia and Leah, the lights of my life: For their love, their support, their genuine interest and inquisitiveness, their patience and understanding, and for reminding me how important it is to keep the chairs at the same height.

We Want to Hear from You!

As the reader of this book, *you* are our most important critic and commentator. We value your opinion and want to know what we're doing right, what we could do better, what areas you'd like to see us publish in, and any other words of wisdom you're willing to pass our way.

As an associate publisher for Pearson Education, I welcome your comments. You can email or write me directly to let me know what you did or didn't like about this book—as well as what we can do to make our books better.

Please note that I cannot help you with technical problems related to the topic of this book. We do have a User Services group, however, where I will forward specific technical questions related to the book.

When you write, please be sure to include this book's title and author as well as your name, email address, and phone number. I will carefully review your comments and share them with the author and editors who worked on the book.

Email: scorehigher@pearsoned.com

Mail: Dave Dusthimer
           Associate Publisher
           Pearson Education
           800 East 96th Street
           Indianapolis, IN 46240 USA

Reader Services

Visit our website and register this book at www.examcram.com/register for convenient access to any updates, downloads, or errata that might be available for this book.

Introduction

Welcome to the *PHR Exam Prep*, second edition. Whether this is the first Exam Prep book you've ever picked up, or whether you've used our exam prep resources before, you'll find that this book will provide valuable information and perceptive insights, as well as helpful suggestions as you prepare to take the Professional in Human Resources (PHR) examination.

This introduction will explain the PHR exam in a general sense and will explore ways in which this Exam Prep can help you as you prepare to take the exam. It will also begin to give you an idea of the various topics that you'll be exploring in greater detail in the book, as well as important information about how the book is structured.

About the Exam

Performing HR-related transactions well is important—but, by itself, it's not enough. Those of us who truly want to succeed in the ever-evolving HR profession must thoroughly understand the HR body of knowledge and be well equipped and well prepared to apply that knowledge in effective, meaningful, impactful, and appropriate ways. Passing the PHR exam is one way that HR professionals can demonstrate to themselves, their employers, and their potential employers that they do, in fact, possess this fluency and knowledge.

It also serves to establish a foundation of credibility with other HR colleagues—in a sense, even before one is personally acquainted with them. Separate and apart from how others might perceive this accomplishment, earning the PHR certification also represents a level of professionalism and will inspire a measure of self-confidence that is uniquely attainable through this achievement.

The PHR exam is administered by the Human Resource Certification Institute (HRCI), an affiliate of the Society for Human Resource Management (SHRM). SHRM is one of the most—if not *the* most—preeminent professional organizations with which HR professionals can align themselves, and HRCI enjoys the full measure of respect that comes along with its close affiliation with SHRM. Since 1976, HRCI has certified more than 85,000 HR professionals and in so doing has contributed immeasurably to the advancement of the profession.

> **NOTE**
>
> For more information on HRCI and SHRM, visit www.hrci.org and www.shrm.org.

The PHR exam constitutes an important part of what makes our profession a *true* profession. A well-recognized, well-respected credential, it is also a near-universal indicator of achievement. By purchasing this book, you have taken an important first step toward earning the distinction that accompanies the PHR designation.

About This Book

Most of the exam preparation materials on the market today don't distinguish exam prep for the PHR exam from exam prep for the Senior Professional in Human Resources (SPHR) exam. We do. Why? First, because the exams are different (see Chapter 1, "The HR Profession and the PHR Exam"). It's our belief that because the PHR and SPHR exams are designed and constructed differently, your preparation should be different as well. By tailoring your preparation to more closely reflect what will be covered on the PHR exam, you are positioning yourself to focus on those areas that matter most to you.

Like so many other factors, elements, and experiences that make up our profession, however, this isn't necessarily as clear cut as it sounds. Certain questions that you'll encounter on the PHR exam will seem quite "senior" or "strategic" in nature—almost more like what you would expect to see on the SPHR exam instead of on the PHR exam. As such, we're not going to limit our questions in this book only to those that represent what the PHR exam is "supposed to" contain, because this exam—like our profession—can be anything but typical at times.

Specifically, we've taken the following approach in this book: Although it's true that the PHR exam contains more fact-based questions than scenario-based questions, the reality is that it's impossible to know exactly which topics will be covered in terms of "just the facts" and which will be placed in the context of a workplace scenario. We're committed to helping you to prepare for whatever you might encounter on the PHR exam, which is why we've included more scenario-based questions than you might encounter on the actual exam. (It's also why we will use the Exam Alerts to suggest specific topics that you might want to seek additional information about—topics that extend beyond the scope of what we can explore in this book.)

We believe that if you can answer a scenario-based question correctly, it's almost certain that you understand the raw facts behind it (assuming you haven't guessed at the answer, that is). Answering a strictly fact-based question successfully, however, doesn't necessarily mean that you could answer a scenario-based question that has been built around those same facts. And on the PHR exam, you might be called upon to do exactly that.

In short, we hope to test your limits (if you will pardon the expression), and to help you prepare as thoroughly as possible, even if that means that some people might find the exam prep to be a bit more challenging than the actual PHR exam. In a way, in fact, we would consider that to be very good news.

Chapters

Chapter 1 covers everything you need to know about the exam—how to apply for it, suggestions relative to how to prepare to take it, and what you can expect before, during, and after you take the actual exam. We'll also provide you with the information you'll need to determine whether you qualify to take the PHR exam or whether you might want to consider taking the SPHR exam instead.

Chapter 2 explores the underlying knowledge and principles of HR—important building blocks that you'll need to understand and interpret in a myriad of ways across the six functional areas of HR. Each of the six remaining content-based chapters (Chapters 3–8) of this book are devoted to one of the specific functional areas covered on the PHR exam:

- ▶ Chapter 3: Strategic Management

- ▶ Chapter 4: Workforce Planning and Employment

- ▶ Chapter 5: Human Resource Development

- ▶ Chapter 6: Total Rewards (formerly known as "compensation and benefits")

- ▶ Chapter 7: Employee and Labor Relations

- ▶ Chapter 8: Risk Management (formerly known as "occupational health, safety, and security")

At the end of the book, there are two practice PHR exams, as well as an answer key and explanations about why each choice was—or wasn't—the best answer. But let us be clear about one very important point: This book is neither designed nor intended to teach you everything you need to know to pass the PHR exam. Instead, we've brought together as much information as possible to help you prepare for the PHR exam—as well as lists of resources where you can get more information about particular topics. We'll also give you more practice, and lots of it.

In addition to reading this book cover-to-cover, you can use it to brush up on particular areas in which you want a bit more review or practice. To do this, use the index or the table of contents to go straight to the specific topics, sections, and questions you want to reexamine. We've structured the book according to headings and subheadings to facilitate the process of providing straightforward, outlined, easy-to-reference information about each specific topic. In fact, after you've taken the PHR exam, you can use this book as a tightly focused reference tool that will serve you well as a day-to-day resource for HR-related information.

Chapter Formats

Each Exam Prep chapter follows a regular structure and includes graphical cues about especially important or useful material. The structure of a typical chapter is as follows:

▶ *Objectives List*—Each chapter begins with a listing of the PHR objectives the chapter covers. A short, descriptive paragraph also sheds some light on what's expected for that objective.

▶ *Chapter Outline*—Next you'll find an outline of the chapter's topics complete with the page number of where that topic is found. This is a handy feature that can help you quickly locate the topics that interest you most.

▶ *Study Strategies*—This section offers you some helpful tips and hints as to how you can effectively study and interact with the chapter's content.

▶ *Topical Coverage*—After the opening items, each chapter covers a variety of topics, all of which are related to the chapter's primary subject.

▶ *Exam Alerts*—Throughout the topical coverage section, we highlight material most likely to appear on the exam by using a special Exam Alert layout that looks like this:

EXAM ALERT

This is what an Exam Alert looks like. An Exam Alert stresses concepts, terms, or activities that will most likely appear in one or more exam questions. For that reason, we think any information found offset in Exam Alert format is worthy of particular attention on your part.

We'll also use Exam Alerts to bring your attention to information that is likely to be covered on the exam that goes beyond the scope of what is specifically explored in the chapter. Use this type of an Exam Alert as an indicator that you need to seek out additional sources of information about the particular topic that is being referenced.

Please note, however, that even if material isn't flagged as an Exam Alert, *all* of the content in this book is associated in some way with exam-related material, and any of it could appear as part of a question on the PHR exam.

▶ *Notes*—This book provides an overarching examination of many of the topics covered on the PHR exam. As such, we'll present information that relates in a variety of ways to different dimensions of each functional area. But we can't touch on everything—the reality is that the HR body of knowledge consists of more information, knowledge, and wisdom than any single book could meaningfully impart. Where the body of knowledge runs deeper than the scope of the book, we'll also use notes to indicate areas of concern or specialty training. The following is an example of a note.

NOTE

Passing the PHR exam will help you earn a valuable credential, but that alone won't make you a competent HR practitioner. Although you could choose to simply memorize the facts you need to know in order to pass the PHR exam, you'd be much better off spending time understanding the underlying concepts and reconciling those concepts with your own professional experiences.

▶ *Tips*—We provide tips that will help you to build a better foundation of knowledge or that will help you to focus your attention on an important concept that appears elsewhere in the book. Tips are intended to remind you of the context surrounding a particular area or topic under discussion.

TIP

The intent of a tip is to provide you with alternative ways of looking at and approaching some of the situations and challenges that HR professionals encounter in the real-world. Tips may suggest quicker ways of performing tasks or new methods or techniques that are not particularly well known. Tips help us bring real-world HR content into the boundaries of this Exam Prep book.

▶ *Review Breaks and Chapter Summaries*—At the end of each chapter, and at other transitional points within each chapter, we've included review breaks and summaries. Specifically, we've included lists of key points you need to know and remember, brief summaries of preceding content, and transitional "turn signals" to let you know what you'll be studying next. In addition, at the end of each chapter you'll find a comprehensive summary of the material covered in that chapter.

▶ *Key Terms*—A list of key terms appears at the end of each chapter. As part of your review, make sure you understand and can recognize, define, and/or explain each of those terms and that you are prepared to apply each of them within the context of a specific scenario, if you're called on to do so.

▶ *Exercises*—Located at the end of each chapter in the "Apply Your Knowledge" section, the exercises include additional tutorial material and more chances to apply the knowledge and practice the skills that were presented earlier in the chapter.

▶ *Review Questions*—These open-ended, short answer/essay-type questions will elicit your explanation of important chapter concepts.

▶ *Exam Questions*—This section presents a short list of exam questions based on a sampling of the content that was covered in the chapter.

▶ *Review and Exam Question Answers and Explanations*—The next two sections will include the Review Questions and Exam Questions answers and explanations.

▶ *Suggested Readings and Resources*—Each chapter concludes with a listing of suggested books, websites, or other resources through which you can explore the topics covered in that particular chapter in greater detail.

The bulk of the book follows this chapter structure, but there are also a few other elements that we would like to point out:

▶ *Objectives Quick Reference*—This jump table is found at the beginning of the book. This organizes the important PHR objectives and puts them alongside the page numbers where each objective can be found in the book. This is a great tool to help you quickly find items you want to review immediately.

▶ *Study and Exam Tips*—This section helps you develop study strategies. It also provides you with valuable exam-day tips and information. We suggest that you read it early on in your study process, which is why we placed this resource near the front of this book.

▶ *Practice Tests*—The two practice tests, which are included toward the end of this book, provide you with the opportunity to prepare for the exam by answering a full set of sample test questions (225, to be exact) that are representative of what you're likely to encounter on the PHR exam. Use these tests as a way to test your knowledge and understanding and to map out areas in which you want to invest additional study time.

▶ *Answer Keys*—The answer keys provide the answers to the practice exam, complete with an identification of the "best answer," as well as detailed discussions and explanations of all the choices you could select for each question.

▶ *Glossary*—This is an extensive glossary of important terms used in this book and covered on the PHR exam.

Contacting the Author

On a personal note, please know that the highly talented team of Exam Prep editors and I have worked diligently to create a real-world tool that you can integrate into your overall personalized PHR study strategy. We take this responsibility seriously and would greatly appreciate hearing back from you about your experiences with this book, along with any feedback you have—positive as well as constructive. For instance, let us know the degree to which you found this book to be helpful in your preparation efforts. We'd also like to know how you felt about your chances of passing the exam *before* you used the book, and then *after* you used the book.

We also recognize that—despite our best efforts—there's always room for improvement. In that spirit, each of us is keenly interested in hearing your suggestions for changes or additions that could enhance the value of this book for future PHR candidates. We'll consider everything you say carefully and will respond to all reasonable suggestions and comments.

And, of course, we love good news. So, even if you just want to tell us that you passed your PHR exam and share the story of your success, let us know.

Whatever the nature of your comment, I invite you to reach out to me at Cathy@CathyLeeGibson.com, and thank you in advance for doing so.

Last, let me offer a word of thanks for including us in your exam prep strategy. Enjoy the book and your experiences with it. We would wish you luck on the exam, but we don't think you really need it. Using this book as part of a larger test-prep plan, we know you'll do well on the strength of your knowledge, skills, and your ability to apply those skills to real-life workplace situations—and with all that going for you, there's no need for luck.

Study and Exam Prep Tips

Close your eyes and imagine yourself in this situation (well, first read this paragraph, *then* close your eyes): It's the day before you're scheduled to take the PHR exam. Your legs, arms, and fingertips tingle as you experience a rush of adrenaline. Beads of sweat dot your forehead. If you've scheduled the exam on a workday, or on a day that follows a workday, you may find yourself dreading the tasks you normally enjoy because, in the back of your mind, you're wishing you could read just a few more pages, or review your notes one more time, or complete a couple more practice questions.

Now, read through the following scenario, then close your eyes and visualize this image instead: It's the day before you're scheduled to take the PHR exam. You're going about your daily routine—either at work or at home—calmly and confidently looking forward (yes, we said *looking forward*) to taking the PHR exam the next day. You're confident in your knowledge that you did everything you set out to do when you made your PHR study plan months earlier. A slight smile plays about your lips as you relax in the knowledge that you are well prepared to take the PHR exam.

If you like the second scenario more than the first, you're not alone. And it doesn't have to be just a dream. In fact, you have already taken one of the first steps toward creating that reality, and you're holding it in your hands right now.

With this book, along with your other prep materials, you can develop an evenly paced study plan that will help you avoid most of these pretest jitters. Although no one book or product (including this one) should ever serve as your only preparation tool, know that your commitment to buying this book—and, especially, to using it to prepare for the PHR exam—brings you one step closer to attaining your objective of passing the PHR exam.

This section of the book provides you with some general guidelines for preparing for any certification exam, and for the Professional in Human Resources (PHR) exam in particular. It's organized into three sections. The first section addresses learning styles and how they impact how you should prepare for an exam. The second section covers exam-preparation activities as well as general study and test-taking tips. This is followed by a closer look at the PHR certification exam, including PHR-specific study and test-taking tips.

Learning Styles

To best understand the nature of test preparation, it is important to understand the learning process. You're probably already aware of how you best learn new material; if you're not, right now would be a great time to figure it out. For instance, if you're more of a visual learner, you might need to "see" things for them to "sink in." If so, you might find that creating outlines works well for you. If you're a kinesthetic learner, a hands-on approach will likely serve you well, so you might prefer to work with homemade flash cards. Auditory learners may want to create their own audio recordings of key facts and information that can be listened to on a cassette or digital voice recorder.

Whatever your preferred learning style, test preparation is always more effective when it takes place over a period of time. It goes without saying (well, perhaps it does need to be said) that it's not a good idea to study for a certification exam by "pulling an all-nighter" the night before the exam, nor is it advisable to postpone your study until the week before the exam. But solid preparation means even more than that. It requires *consistent* preparation—at a steady pace over a period of months, not days or even weeks. As you begin your preparation, it's important to keep in mind that learning is a developmental, evolving process. Taking a planned, deliberate approach to studying and learning material that will be on the exam will help you recognize what you already know well, what you need to know better, and what you still need to learn—in other words, what you don't know very well at all, at least not yet.

Learning takes place when you incorporate new information into your existing knowledge base. And remember—even if this book is the first PHR study tool you've looked at so far, you already *do* have an existing knowledge base. How can you (and, for that matter, how can *we*) be so certain of that? Because you're required to have at least two years of exempt-level (according to the FLSA, see Chapter 6, "Total Rewards") experience in order to sit for the PHR exam. That represents two years of knowledge, skills, and experience, which means you're already on your way to passing the PHR.

> **CAUTION**
>
> Don't rely on any single resource—even this book—to prepare for the PHR exam. No matter how good a resource might be, it provides only one perspective, and it can provide only a limited amount of material. *PHR Exam Prep* should serve as a *supplement* to your other study resources, *not as a replacement for them*. There is more knowledge and information required to pass the PHR exam than could ever be included in this book, or any other single resource. So, in short, don't put all your eggs in one basket—even this one.

As you prepare for the PHR exam, this book, along with many of the other study materials you'll use, will serve three purposes:

- ▶ It will add incrementally to your existing knowledge base.

- ▶ It will facilitate the process of drawing meaningful connections between the test content and your own professional experience.

- ▶ It will enable you to restructure and translate your existing knowledge and experience into a format that's consistent with the PHR exam.

Perhaps without even realizing it, you'll be adding new information into your existing knowledge base—all of which will then be organized within the framework of the six functional areas of HR around which the PHR exam is designed. This process will lead you to a more comprehensive understanding of important concepts, relevant techniques, and the human resources profession in general. Again, all this will happen only as a result of a repetitive and self-reinforcing process of study and learning, not as the product of a single study session.

Keep this model of learning in the forefront of your mind as you prepare for the PHR exam. It will help you make better decisions about what to study and about how much more studying you need to do.

General Study Tips

There's no one "best" way to study for any exam. There are, however, some general test-preparation strategies and guidelines that have worked well for many test takers, and that might work well for you, too.

Study Strategies

Although each of us learns and processes information somewhat differently, certain basic learning principles apply to everyone. You might find these principles helpful to keep in mind as you develop your own personal study plan. For instance, one important principle is that learning can be broken into various depths:

- ▶ Recognition (of terms, for example) represents a somewhat superficial or "surface" level of learning in which you rely on a prompt of some sort to elicit recall.

- ▶ Comprehension or understanding (of the concepts behind the terms, for example) represents a deeper level of learning than recognition does.

- ▶ Analysis of a concept, along with the ability to apply your newly expanded understanding of that concept, represents an even deeper level of learning.

This is not to say that recognition isn't important. It is—particularly for multiple-choice exams, and particularly for the PHR exam.

> **NOTE**
>
> This is in large part a function of the level of knowledge that PHR candidates are expected to have mastered, which is not as advanced or complex as what is expected of SPHR candidates. As such, recognition (by itself) is a somewhat less-relevant level of learning on the SPHR exam because the SPHR exam focuses on more complex and strategic applications of the same body of knowledge.

In addition to ensuring that you are able to recognize terms, you should build a study strategy through which you will develop the ability to process, digest, and absorb the material at a level or two deeper than that. In this way, you'll know the material so thoroughly that you'll be able to perform well on a variety of types of questions—for instance, on questions that require you to apply your knowledge to specific problems, as well as on questions that only require you to be able to recognize and identify the correct (meaning, the "best") answer from among a series of possible answers. The PHR contains questions of both types, along with a variety of other types of questions.

Macro and Micro Study Strategies

One strategy that can enhance and support learning at multiple levels is outlining (especially for visual learners, as we mentioned earlier). Creating your own study outline that incorporates concepts covered on the PHR will support your efforts to absorb and understand the content more fully, to make connections between related topics, and to map together information that you have gleaned from a variety of study sources. For instance, it will help you make connections between the six functional areas, the 23 core areas of knowledge, and the HR-related responsibilities and knowledge associated with each of those six functional areas. Your outline will also help you dig a bit deeper into the material if you choose to include a level or two of detail beyond what you might find on most generic, summary-style study tools. You can add more value to your outline, for instance, by expanding it to include information such as definitions, details, analyses, examples, related laws, related cases, key historical events, key thinkers, and the like.

An outline such as this can support your study efforts in a variety of ways. For instance, as you build the points and subpoints of your outline, you'll be able to better appreciate how they relate to one another. You'll also gain a better understanding of how each of the main objective areas outlined in this book is similar to—and different from—the other main objective areas. If you do the same thing with the subobjectives; you'll also gain a fuller understanding of how each subobjective relates to its objective, and how those subobjectives relate to one another. It's also important to understand how each of the HR-related responsibilities is similar to—or different from—other HR-related responsibilities, which an outline can also help clarify. The same holds true for the 23 core areas of knowledge that span the six functional areas and for the HR-related knowledge required for each of the functional areas—each of which is identified within each chapter.

Next, work through your completed outline. Focus on learning the details. Take time to refamiliarize yourself with—and, in some cases, memorize—and understand terms, definitions, facts, laws, cases, and so forth. In this pass-through of the outline, you should attempt to focus on learning detail rather than just an overview of the big picture (on which you already focused your attention as you built your outline).

It's not a good idea to try to accomplish both of these strategies at once. Research has shown that attempting to assimilate both types of information (macro and micro) at the same time interferes with the overall learning process. If you consciously separate your studying into these two approaches, you are likely to perform better on the exam.

Active Study Strategies

The process of writing down and defining objectives, subobjectives, terms, facts, and definitions promotes a more active learning strategy than you'd experience by just reading study materials. In human information-processing terms, writing forces you to engage in more active encoding of the information. Conversely, simply reading the information results in more passive processing. Using this study strategy, focus on writing down (or typing out) the items that are highlighted in the book's bulleted or numbered lists, Exam Alerts, Notes, Cautions, and review sections.

EXAM ALERT

At various points, we'll offer suggestions about when to seek more information on topics that aren't directly or thoroughly explored in this book. Please take those suggestions seriously and consider incorporating the additional information you research and collect into the written study tools that you create.

Consider doing the same for your other study sources as well. Try to merge your notes whenever possible to take an integrated approach to your test prep.

Another active study strategy involves applying the information you have learned by creating your own examples and scenarios. Think about how or where you could apply the concepts you're learning. You could even try your hand at writing your own questions, which you could then consider sharing with a study partner or group. Again, write everything down to help you process the facts and concepts in an active fashion.

The multiple review and exam questions at the end of each chapter provide additional opportunities to actively reinforce the concepts you are learning, so don't skip them.

Commonsense Strategies

As you study your test prep materials, use good common sense. For instance, study when you are alert. Reduce or eliminate distractions. And take breaks when you get tired. "Pushing through" when your body really needs a break can sometimes result in frustration, anxiety, and physical exhaustion—none of which will enhance your performance on the exam.

Design Your Own Personal Study Plan

And do it now. There is no single best way to prepare for any exam. Different people learn in different ways, so it's important to develop a personal study plan that's right for you. As you do so, establish long-term and short-term goals for yourself. Know exactly what you will accomplish, and by what date. You'll experience a sense of accomplishment each time you reach a milestone—so allow yourself the opportunity to celebrate! You will have earned the right to revel a bit—plus, taking a little celebratory break will help you feel more refreshed as you move into the next stage of your prep.

Questions to Ask Yourself

As you develop your personal study plan, ask yourself the following questions:

- How much time do I have to invest in preparing for the exam?
- How much money do I have to invest in preparing for the exam?
- Do I learn better on my own or when I have the chance to interact with others? Or, does some combination of both work best for me?

► Am I comfortable with an online study environment, or do I prefer a traditional classroom setting?

► Does my schedule afford me the opportunity to attend regularly scheduled classroom-based exam prep workshops?

► What is/are my preferred learning style/s?

► If I've taken this test before and didn't pass, what have I learned? What was effective about my original study plan? What was ineffective? What could I have done differently?

> **NOTE**
>
> If you didn't pass the PHR exam the first time around, let the experience go—take the lessons that you learned, and put them to good use now. It's your time to shine.

Pretesting

One of the most important aspects of learning is what has been called *meta-learning*. Meta-learning has to do with realizing when you know something well, and/or realizing when you need to study some more. In other words, you assess and recognize the degree to which you have learned the material you've been studying.

For most people, this can be a difficult assessment to make independently, in the absence of study tools. Pretesting is one tool that can help you in this way, by establishing a baseline of what you already know before you start your study regime and as you proceed through different phases of your study plan. Pretesting tools can include review questions, practice questions, practice tests, and the like.

You can then use the insights you obtain from these pretesting assessment tools to guide and direct your studying, because developmental learning takes place as you cycle (and re-cycle) through your study plan. So, begin by assessing how well you already know, or have learned, a particular topic. Use that assessment to decide what you need to continue studying. Then, conduct another assessment, followed by more review. Repeat this process until you feel confident in your knowledge and understanding of the topic.

You might have already noticed that there are two practice exams included in this book. We strongly suggest that you consider incorporating these into your study plan. The test-simulation software included on this book's CD-ROM also provides you with a tool you can use to assess your knowledge.

See Appendix A, "CD Contents and Installation Instructions," for further explanation of the test-simulation software.

General Test-Taking Tips

▶ Taking exams can be stressful. This is especially true if it's been a while since you've been in school or have taken tests. There are, however, steps you can take to reduce the level of stress you are experiencing as you prepare for—and take— the exam. As you prepare—and answer lots of practice questions—your comfort level with test taking will likely increase. Be patient with yourself; your "rustiness" will fade away. In addition, consider other stress-reducing techniques, such as visualization. Just as Olympic athletes visualize themselves performing in their events as part of their preparation, visualize yourself progressing comfortably and confidently through the questions on the PHR exam.

▶ The structure, format, and style of the exam may be unfamiliar to you. Test taking is a skill all on its own—separate and apart from the material that the test covers— and every test is different. This is why so many individuals and organizations offer test-preparation services. You've probably seen the advertisements for test-prep services for the SAT, LSAT, GRE, GMAT—the alphabet soup of test taking goes on and on. The specific attributes of each exam, however, are unique, as is the quality and worth of various test prep services and resources. Collect as much information as possible and choose wisely before availing yourself of test-prep services.

PHR-Specific Information, Study, and Test-Taking Tips

We've all heard of "the fear of the unknown." Well, knowledge dispels fear (or at least it helps to do so). Knowing as much as you can about how the PHR exam is designed, formatted, administered, and delivered will help you as you prepare to take the exam.

How Is the PHR Exam Administered?

HRCI contracts with the Professional Examination Service (PES) to handle a variety of administrative responsibilities related to administration of the PHR exam, including

▶ Determining whether PHR, SPHR, and GPHR candidates meet exam eligibility requirements.

▶ Handling payments.

▶ Issuing "Authorization to Test" (ATT) letters after a candidate's eligibility to take the test and earn the credential has been confirmed. (You'll need to bring this letter with you to the test site, so put it in a safe place after you receive it.)

▶ Tabulating and communicating (in writing) PHR, SPHR, and GPHR test scores.

HRCI contracts with Thomson Prometric for exam delivery services. These services include scheduling, administering, and proctoring exams.

How Is the PHR Exam Put Together?

It's helpful to understand how the PHR exam was developed—and how it's updated. This information can help you maintain your focus on what's most important to study.

Since 1976, HRCI (known at the time as the "ASPA Accreditation Institute") has defined the HR body of knowledge for the PHR exam. This body of knowledge has evolved and changed over time, and the PHR exam has evolved and changed with it. This body of knowledge also translates directly into the PHR exam test specifications.

EXAM ALERT

Since 1976, the HR body of knowledge has been completely revised four times. At other times, however, other less-comprehensive modifications have been made to the PHR exam, reflecting the evolution of our profession.

CAUTION

In 2007, HRCI updated the body of HR knowledge. This update will, in turn, be reflected on the PHR exam.

CAUTION

Be sure to periodically check the HRCI website to monitor whether—and how—the PHR exam test specifications have changed or evolved, and then modify your preparation content and strategy accordingly.

PHR Exam Format

In addition to studying the actual content within each of the six functional areas, you also need to be familiar with the format of the PHR exam.

The PHR exam is a computerized test consisting of 225 multiple-choice questions. You'll have four hours to complete the exam, which is administered by a computer at a testing center.

Of the 225 test questions, only 200 will count toward your overall score. The other 25 questions are being tested for possible use in future exams, and your answers to these questions will not count toward your overall score. The catch is, however, that you won't know which questions will count toward your overall score and which won't—so your best bet is to assume that every question is a scored question, and to approach every question with focus and attention.

Each question has four possible answers. Often, more than one answer will make some degree of sense or may initially seem correct. You must, however, choose the "best answer."

CAUTION

It has been said that "close only counts in horseshoes and hand grenades." Close doesn't count on the PHR exam, either. Take your time and evaluate all four options before selecting the "best answer."

CAUTION

Be particularly careful not to automatically default to the response that most closely approximates how your employer would handle a particular situation, or how you've handled a similar situation in the past. Every organization has its own way of handling HR-related situations; however, your employer's way of handling a situation isn't necessarily the best way, or the way that HRCI has deemed "the best."

Examples of multiple-choice questions appear at the end of each chapter in this book.

PHR Preparation Options

You can choose from many options as you prepare for the PHR exam. Here is a sampling of some of those options:

▶ *College/University Preparatory Courses*—Hundreds of colleges/universities have partnered with SHRM to offer the "College/University SHRM Training System" preparatory course. Visit www.shrm.org to find a college/university program offered near you. This program is offered in classroom, online, and blended formats (check with the colleges/universities in which you're interested to see what specific versions they offer).

▶ *PHR/SPHR Certification Preparation Course*—SHRM sponsors intensive three-day preparatory courses throughout the country. This "immersion" program affords test takers with a condensed training opportunity, which may represent a valuable option for those who cannot attend a semester-long college/university-based program.

▶ *Chapter-Level Courses*—From time to time, some SHRM chapters offer PHR/SPHR preparatory courses. (A "chapter" is a SHRM-affiliated local or regional-based group of SHRM members who benefit from the opportunity to network and collaborate on a regular basis.) A list of SHRM-affiliated chapters can be found at www.shrm.org. If this option is of interest to you, contact your local SHRM chapter to find out if it offers a preparatory course.

▶ *In-House Corporate Courses*—If there are enough individuals at your employer who are interested in earning PHR or SPHR certification, your employer may decide to bring SHRM onsite to facilitate a preparatory course. Normally, only individuals within the sponsoring organization can participate in these programs. (The sponsoring organization is the one that has brought SHRM onsite to conduct the prep course.)

▶ *Online Courses*—As referenced previously, you may want to consider a college/university-based online prep course instead of a traditional classroom program. Through the Internet, you'll become part of a "virtual class" that prepares together for the PHR exam.

> **CAUTION**
>
> Check out online college/university programs carefully before signing up, to ensure that you choose a format that's right for you. Be particularly alert to real-time ("synchronous") participation requirements if you have limited time availability or if you are available to study only during nontraditional classroom hours (in which case you might find "asynchronous" participation to be a better option).

▶ *Self-Study*—If being part of a cohort group isn't the best choice for you, you might want to consider a "self-study" option. SHRM offers a self-study learning system, which contains preparation materials and tools on each functional area and on the entire HR body of knowledge.

The self-study format allows you maximum flexibility to prepare for the PHR at a time and a place that's most convenient for you. It also contains an online component, which offers lots of additional questions in a computerized format, thereby more closely replicating what you will experience during the actual PHR exam.

▶ *Study Buddies*—Whether you're preparing for the PHR using a classroom, online, or self-study format, you may find it helpful to find another test taker with whom you can partner as you prepare for the test. Ideally, you'll want to find someone whose schedule is similar to—and whose learning style is compatible with—your own. Even more important, look for a buddy who has strengths in those functional areas in which you need the most development and who would benefit from the assistance of someone who is well versed in those functional areas in which you are strongest. You may want to look for a buddy with whom you'll study in person, or someone with whom you can confer online. Buddies can be found through colleagues at work, through a prep course, or through other reputable sources.

▶ *Online Study Groups*—Be open to the idea of forming an online study group. Multiple online study groups, for instance, are registered with www.groups.yahoo.com. (As always, of course, be prudent and cautious when creating any online relationships.)

PHR-Specific Test Preparation Tips

Make no mistake: The PHR exam challenges your knowledge, your HR skills, *and* your test-taking abilities. Here are some tips to help you as you prepare for the PHR exam:

▶ Be prepared to combine your skill sets with your experience, and to identify solutions using that combined insight, because the PHR exam tests your knowledge as well as your skill. You will be called on to resolve problems that may draw on different dimensions of the material covered. For example, you could be presented with a realistic workplace scenario about a layoff that requires you to understand when—and how—the Age Discrimination in Employment Act (ADEA) needs to be taken into consideration. Why is this type of question likely to appear? In this particular example, it's one thing to know the provisions of the ADEA, but it's something else entirely to understand its application and relevance to a layoff situation. More broadly, these types of scenario-based questions are reflective of real life. And, to be an effective HR professional, you'll need to be able to successfully make these kinds of connections and applications.

▶ Get used to delving into minute details. Each exam question can incorporate a multitude of details. Try thinking of each detail as a potential clue. Some of these details will prove to be ancillary. Some of them will help you rule out possible answers, but not necessarily enable you to identify the best answer. Other details will provide you with a more complete picture of the situation being described. The reality is that you may be called on to combine this information with what you know and what you have experienced in order to identify the best answer. If you don't pay attention to how the information that you're given helps you to eliminate certain responses, the best answer might elude you.

▶ Hold yourself to time limits when taking practice tests. The PHR exam must be completed within four hours. To get used to this time constraint, use a timer when you take practice tests. Learn to pace yourself.

▶ Peruse the HRCI (www.hrci.org) and SHRM (www.shrm.org) websites for valuable information and materials, such as the *PHR/SPHR/GPHR Handbook*.

▶ Talk with others who have already taken the PHR exam—*whether or not they passed*. Although PHR test takers are prohibited from divulging specific types of information about the exam, they can tell you about their overall test-taking experience. You may find that their insights, ideas, and suggestions might hold great value for you as you prepare to take the test. Be careful, however, not to let yourself feel anxious on the basis of anything that you might hear. Just use it as a way to make better choices relative to developing your own exam-prep plan, and relative to taking the actual exam.

Strategies and Tips for PHR Exam Day

Your studying is done, you've familiarized yourself with the test center (online virtual tours are available), you're wearing comfortable clothing, and you've arrived at least 30 minutes early with ID in hand. Now what? First, breathe. Remember that you have thoroughly prepared yourself for the PHR exam. You are ready for this.

Now, prepare yourself mentally. Focus on your feelings of confidence. There's no one "right" way to do this. Some people, however, find it helpful to consider one (or perhaps both) of the following two mindsets:

"If you can see it, you can be it." As discussed earlier, continue to visualize yourself confidently answering test questions—just as you did during your test preparation. Start by writing your name with the letters "PHR" after it on the mini whiteboard you've been given to use as a scratch pad. You're self-assured, relaxed, and ready to demonstrate what you know. Then see yourself leaving the test center, a smile on your face, having just learned that you have passed the exam.

"What's the worst that can happen?" Remind yourself that the worst thing that could possibly happen is that you do not pass the PHR exam. If that does happen, many choices are available to you, the most obvious of which is retaking the test. So, even if the worst possible thing happens, you'll get through it, and you will have learned valuable lessons along the way—lessons you can use to help you pass the test the next time.

Here are some additional suggestions to consider as you sit down to take the PHR exam:

- *Take your time*—Determine how much time you can spend on each question while still allowing yourself time to check your responses afterward. Most importantly, read every question—and every answer—deliberately and completely. Don't skip over even one word. Remember that you will need to identify the best answer, not just a good answer.

- *Collect yourself*—When you actually sit down at the computer terminal, take a few moments to collect yourself before you jump right into the test. Again, breathe. Set aside any internal distractions and focus on the exam. You're ready for this—so take a moment or two to remind yourself of that.

- *Take a break if you need one*—You have four hours to complete the exam, so give yourself some time to get some air, stretch your legs, and reenergize yourself.

- *Remember that you might be audiotaped or videotaped*—Don't allow this to distract you; instead, remember that taping test takers is "business as usual" for Prometric testing facilities. Don't take it personally. Just let it go. You have more important things to focus on than a camera or microphone.

- *Don't rush, but don't linger too long on difficult questions, either*—The questions will vary in their degree of difficulty and complexity. Don't let yourself be flustered by one particularly difficult, wordy, or (seemingly) tricky question.

- *Read every word of every question*—Just like in real life, one word or one minute detail can make all the difference in selecting the "best answer."

- *Don't look for patterns in answer selections*—There aren't any.

- *Don't assume the longest answer is the best answer*—Don't assume the shortest answer is the best answer, either.

- *Answer every question*—Unanswered questions are 100% likely to be wrong. If you make a wild guess, you have a 25% chance of getting it right. If, however, you can narrow down your choices to two or three possible responses, you can double or triple your chances of answering the question correctly.

- *Take advantage of the fact that you can "mark," return to, and review skipped or previously answered questions*—When you reach the end of the exam, return to the more difficult questions. You may even want to deliberately skip some of the more difficult questions along the way, knowing that you can return to them after you have successfully answered many, many other exam questions.

▶ *Try to build in time to review your answers after you have answered all the questions—* Pay particular attention to questions that contain a lot of detail, or those that seemed particularly straightforward the first time around (it's possible you might have initially overlooked something important).

▶ *When rechecking your responses, you may be tempted to question every answer you've made, but be careful not to fall into the trap of second guessing yourself too much—*If you read the question carefully and completely the first time through, and you felt like you knew the right answer, you probably did. If, however, as you check your answers, a response clearly stands out as incorrect, change it. You also might want to consider changing a response if you missed, misread, or misinterpreted details in the questions the first time around, or if you jumped to a clearly incorrect conclusion. If you are left feeling completely unsure whether you should change your original response, however, it's usually a good idea to go with your first impression.

And, last—but perhaps most important—believe in yourself: now, when you study, and when you sit down to take the test. It's your turn. So roll up your sleeves—you're about to complete the process of earning your PHR designation.

PART I
Exam Preparation

The HR Profession and the PHR Exam

Study Strategies

This chapter contains information that will enable you to deepen your understanding of the human resources (HR) profession and the value of professional certification, as well as understand the rich history of its flagship professional association. This chapter will also present multiple certification options, which may, for some readers, mean *not* taking the PHR exam at this time.

As you work your way through this chapter, you'll notice that it doesn't include specific knowledge-based or skill-based content that will be on the PHR exam; however, the information that it does contain will be important to you as you prepare to embark on your journey toward certification as a PHR. We look forward to journeying with you.

Introduction

The HR profession is a respected and accredited field. Within the HR profession, there is an immense amount of opportunity to grow professionally while contributing meaningfully to attaining the objectives of the organizations for which we work. Nowadays, it's a respected and recognized profession; however, it hasn't always been viewed that way. For well over 50 years, Human Resources (HR) practitioners have struggled with how to define and establish themselves as members of a true—and recognized— profession. (Of course, we weren't always called "HR professionals," or even "HR practitioners"—or, for that matter "HR" anything.) In 1948, Herbert Heneman, Jr., Ph.D., opened the discussion of certification for our professional ancestors when he wrote an article titled, "Qualifying the Professional Industrial Relations Worker." The discussion was picked up by the American Society for Personnel Administration (ASPA), which was renamed Society for Human Resource Management (SHRM) in 1989.

In 1967, ASPA cosponsored a conference with Cornell University's School of Industrial and Labor Relations ("Cornell-ILR"). The purpose of this conference was to define "personnel" as a profession and to identify HR's "body of knowledge." One year later, Cornell-ILR and ASPA reconvened and identified the following five defining criteria of a profession:

- A profession must be full time.

- Schools and curricula must be aimed specifically at teaching the basic ideas of the profession, and there must be a defined common body of knowledge.

- A profession must have a national professional association.

- A profession must have a certification program.

- A profession must have a code of ethics.

ASPA felt that personnel (as it was called) already met three of the five criteria. Two critical elements were yet to be accomplished—identifying a body of knowledge and establishing a certification program.

By 1975, that body of knowledge had been identified, and the certification exam was not far behind; it was administered by AAI (ASPA Accreditation Institute) less than a year later. Exam exemptions were granted to 2,100 individuals—the first of whom was the very same Herbert Heneman, Jr., Ph.D., who had begun the discussion around certification more than a quarter of a century earlier.

The Professional in Human Resources (PHR) and Senior Professional in Human Resources (SPHR) certification exams have been modified many times since, reflecting a continuous commitment to quality, relevance, and the ever-evolving nature of our profession. These exams are administered by the Human Resource Certification Institute (HRCI), the modern-day version of AAI. HRCI is a separate organization from SHRM, which is the largest HR professional association in the world. The two organizations are, however, closely affiliated.

The PHR certification exam will test your knowledge of the HR body of knowledge—the sum total of information and insight with which each HR professional should have fluency. It will also test many of the HR-specific skills you'll need to perform successfully as an HR professional. In addition, the PHR exam will go well beyond what you know and what you can do; rather, it's specifically designed to determine how well you can actually apply that knowledge and those skills to the workplace. It's this ability to integrate and apply knowledge and skills (along with solid preparation and relevant professional-level experience) that will enable you to pass the PHR exam and to perform successfully as an HR professional.

What Is SHRM?

As you prepare for the PHR exam, it's important to have a general understanding of SHRM (nicknamed, and pronounced, "sherm"). More than 210,000 HR professionals in more than 100 countries make it the largest professional association for HR practitioners in the world. In addition to being the largest, SHRM is considered by many to be one of the foremost professional organizations with which HR professionals can affiliate themselves.

Membership Information

Although you're not required to be a SHRM member to take an HRCI certification exam, membership will prove to be of invaluable assistance as you prepare for the exam and as you grow professionally in your career. Visit the Join/Renew section at SHRM's website (www.shrm.com) for guidelines that will help you determine the type of membership that's most appropriate for you.

> **NOTE**
>
> SHRM membership is individual, not corporate. Wherever you go, your SHRM membership will go with you, and you'll keep receiving the benefits of being a member (as long as you remember to renew it each year, that is).

Benefits of Membership

SHRM's membership benefits are many and varied and include the following:

- *Professional resources*—Tools, directories, forums, webcasts, chats—even an online job listing service.

- *Publications*—Weekly, monthly, and quarterly updates on a variety of critical HR issues, including legislative updates, workplace issues, and a host of other HR-related topics.

- *Research*—Original surveys, reports, and analyses on a wide spectrum of emerging workplace issues.

- *Professional development*—SHRM provides a wide array of online, classroom, and self-study resources.

- *Conferences*—Regional, state, and national conferences provide virtually limitless learning and networking opportunities. Although nonmembers can attend conferences, SHRM members enjoy discounted prices on conference fees. Be sure to visit SHRM's website to keep up to date on when and where its conferences will be held.

> **CAUTION**
>
> Because membership in SHRM is individual and nontransferable, only SHRM members can avail themselves of designated member benefits. Many portions of the website, for instance, are accessible to members only. Access by nonmembers is considered an ethical violation—and it could also constitute theft.

What Is HRCI?

HRCI is the current-day version of AAI. Although closely affiliated with SHRM, HRCI and SHRM are two separate entities and their mission statements are as follows:

- ▸ SHRM's mission statement, as articulated on its website (www.shrm.org), is "to serve the needs of HR professionals by providing the most essential and comprehensive resources available. As an influential voice, the Society's mission is also to advance the human resource profession to ensure that HR is recognized as an essential partner in developing and executing organizational strategy."

- ▸ HRCI's mission statement, as articulated on its website (www.hrci.org), is as follows: "The Human Resource Certification Institute develops and delivers credentialing programs to validate mastery in the field of human resource management and to promote organizational effectiveness."

The number of individuals seeking—and attaining—certification in the HR profession has increased dramatically, particularly during the past five years. HRCI offers three core certification exams: PHR, SPHR, and GPHR (Global Professional in Human Resources). Later in this chapter ("Which Exam Should You Take?"), we'll provide you with information and suggestions to help you decide which—if any—of these certifications might be appropriate for you to pursue at this time.

Why Is Certification Important?

Successfully passing an HRCI certification exam (and thereby becoming a certified HR professional) constitutes a significant professional and personal accomplishment. An HRCI credential speaks volumes about you to your current—and to your potential—employers.

> **NOTE**
>
> More and more organizations are beginning to indicate a strong preference in job postings and advertisements for HRCI certification, particularly the PHR or SPHR designations. Earning this credential, therefore, can enhance your appeal to potential employers while increasing your value to your current employer.

Certification affirms that

- ▸ You have, at minimum, two years of exempt-level HR work experience.

- ▸ You are committed to your profession, to your professional development, and to your career.

- ▸ Through testing, you have demonstrated mastery of the HR body of knowledge and understand how that body of knowledge is applied in the workplace.

- ▸ You've demonstrated your commitment to maintaining currency in our ever-changing profession through the recertification process.

NOTE

HRCI requires certified HR professionals to recertify every three years. More information on recertification is available on the HRCI website.

You'll work hard to earn your PHR certification, so don't let it lapse! Make recertification a priority—in part because it is part of the commitment that certified HR professionals make to their profession, and in part because if you do let your certification lapse, you'll probably have to take the PHR exam again. And although successfully passing the PHR exam will hopefully constitute a largely positive experience for you, it's not necessarily an experience that you would choose to repeat.

Should You Go for Certification Now?

There's no doubt that HRCI certification has value. This alone, however, doesn't automatically mean that taking the PHR exam at this time is the best choice for you. There are any number of reasons you may choose to wait until a different time to seek HR certification. On a practical level, perhaps you don't have the required HR exempt-level experience and therefore don't meet HRCI's minimum qualifications. Perhaps you simply don't have sufficient time right now to prepare adequately to take the exam. Taking the exam—and preparing to take it—also requires commitment of financial resources, which may not be realistic for you at this time.

Another consideration worth pondering is this: Test taking requires risk taking. If you take the exam, you are opening yourself up to the possibility that you will pass the exam and earn an HRCI credential. You are also, however, opening yourself up to the possibility that you may *not* pass the exam and may *not* earn an HRCI credential—*at this time*. Before you commit to taking the exam, be sure that is an outcome you are prepared to accept.

NOTE

Becoming a "certified HR professional" through HRCI is completely different from earning an "HR certificate," and it's critical to understand the differences between the two. HR certificates—such as those offered through the Extension Division of Cornell University's School of Industrial and Labor Relations—are earned by completing required workshops and courses. The PHR certification can be earned only by successfully passing the PHR exam. In addition, the PHR exam has an experiential requirement, whereas most certificate programs (including Cornell-ILR's) do not.

CAUTION

The only way to become a certified HR professional is to successfully pass the PHR exam or the SPHR exam. Completing a prep course of any type does not equate to passing the exam, nor does it equate to earning HR certification. In addition to being the only way you can become certified, passing the PHR exam is the only way you earn the right to use the "PHR" or "SPHR" designation after your name.

Overcoming Gaps in Employment—Certification Can Help

Many of us, at one point or another, will experience a gap in employment. Whether your gap in employment is planned or unplanned, and whatever the reason for that gap in employment may be, you can use this gap in your employment to fill a gap in your credentials. For example, for many HR professionals, the time between two jobs may present an ideal opportunity to prepare for—and take—an HRCI certification exam.

The most obvious benefit of taking an HR certification exam is that you will earn an HRCI credential and will be eligible to enjoy all the benefits that come with earning that credential. There are, however, less immediately obvious benefits to earning HRCI certification while you are experiencing a gap in employment:

> ▸ *"I want to do something for myself, too."*—Whatever the reason is that you're experiencing a gap in employment, chances are that it demands either a lot of your time or a lot of your energy, or both. At times like that, it can be beneficial, and even healthy, to do something for yourself. Working toward a goal may also help you to focus your attention on your own positive growth and development from time to time—regardless of whatever else is happening around you.

> ▸ *"What did you do while you were on leave?"*—When you decide to return to the workplace and are asked that seemingly inevitable question about what you did while you were on leave, you'll be able to respond in a professional context, with an impressive deliverable to show for your efforts.

Earning an HRCI certification is an investment in yourself and an investment in your future. It validates your commitment to return to the workplace, both to you as well as to potential employers.

Getting to Know the Exams

After you decide to work toward HRCI certification, the next step is to familiarize yourself with HRCI's certification exams:

> ▸ PHR exam
> ▸ SPHR exam
> ▸ GPHR exam

PHR and SPHR Exams

We'll start by taking a look at the PHR and SPHR exams—together, because both of them are targeted toward the same population of HR professionals: those who are primarily responsible for domestic HR-related responsibilities.

Exam Similarities

The PHR and SPHR exams share a number of common characteristics. First, both exams focus on the same six functional areas:

- *Strategic Management*—Strategic HR management speaks to HR's overall commitment, in both word and deed, to meeting the ever-evolving short-term, long-term, and strategic objectives of the organization.

- *Workforce Planning and Employment*—Workforce planning and employment speaks to HR's responsibility to ensure integrated, seamless, and effective recruitment, hiring, orientation, and exit processes that support the short-term, long-term, emerging, and strategic objectives of the organization.

- *Human Resource Development*—Human resource development employs effective training, development, change management, and performance management functions and initiatives to ensure that the skills, knowledge, abilities, and performance of the workforce will meet the short-term, long-term, emerging, and strategic objectives of the organization.

- *Total Rewards*—Total rewards (formerly referred to as Compensation and Benefits) speaks to HR's responsibility to ensure that an organization's total rewards programs, policies, and practices support the short-term, long-term, emerging, and strategic objectives of the organization.

- *Employee and Labor Relations*—Employee and labor relations encompass every dimension of relationships at the workplace, with the overall objective of balancing employee's needs and rights with the employer's need to attain short-term, long-term, emerging, and strategic objectives.

- *Risk Management*—Risk management promotes employees' physical and mental well-being while maintaining a safe and nonviolent work environment, all in support of the employer's short-term, long-term, emerging, and strategic objectives—and all the while protecting the organization from liability.

Other similarities exist between the PHR and SPHR:

- Both require two years of exempt-level HR experience.

- Both constitute valuable, well-respected credentials that speak to your knowledge and skill as an HR professional.

- Both will garner respect from your current employer.

- Both represent an increasingly important "preferred" credential by many potential employers.

Exam Differences

A number of key differences exist between the PHR and SPHR exams:

> ► *Relative weights of functional areas*—One of the most important differences between the two exams is the relative emphasis that each exam places on the six previously listed functional areas (and, consequently, the number of questions that are asked about each of these areas). Table 1.1 highlights these differences.

TABLE 1.1   Relative Weight of Functional Areas for the PHR and SPHR Exams

Functional Area	PHR	SPHR
Strategic Management	12%	29%
Workforce Planning and Employment	26%	17%
Human Resource Development	17%	17%
Compensation and Benefits	16%	12%
Employee and Labor Relations	22%	18%
Occupational Health, Safety, and Security	7%	7%

Source: Human Resource Certification Institute. www.hrci.com. Accessed August 2007.

NOTE

Note that these weightings are accurate as of the date on which this book went to print, and are subject to change. Please check www.hrci.org for updated information.

> ► Because the SPHR exam places a significantly stronger emphasis on the more strategic areas of HR, those test takers with less experience, or who have been siloed in one particular discipline of HR, might want to consider taking the PHR exam instead.

EXAM ALERT

No amount of study can replace practical experience. Even if you take a course, engage in self-study, join a study group, and complete every practice PHR question that has ever been written, taking either of these exams without sufficient experience is strongly discouraged. In this case, "sufficient" doesn't just necessarily equate to the two-year minimum requirement established by HRCI. Only you can truly know the depth and richness of the jobs you have held, and whether *your* "two years" (or however many you have under your belt) really have prepared you for an exam that assumes exposure to a variety of HR disciplines.

Exam Candidates—The Differences

You've explored how the PHR and SPHR exams are similar and different. Now let's take a look at some of the key differences between the people who take those exams. Table 1.2 highlights some of the more important differences.

TABLE 1.2 Key Differences Between PHR and SPHR Candidates

Difference	Explanation
Length of Experience	HRCI recommends that PHR candidates should ideally have two to four years of exempt-level HR experience and that SPHR candidates should ideally have six to eight years of exempt-level HR experience.
Breadth of Experience	PHR candidates are more likely to have experience in only one or two HR disciplines, whereas SPHR candidates are more likely to have held positions in a variety of HR disciplines. SPHR candidates are also more likely to have served in a generalist capacity.
Depth of Experience	PHR candidates are more likely to hold jobs that requires a transactional or tactical "hands on" approach, whereas SPHR candidates' jobs are more likely to have a broader, more strategic focus.
Level of Responsibility	PHR candidates are more likely to hold positions that are at a lower level in the HR departmental hierarchy, whereas SPHR candidates are more likely to have greater overall responsibility and accountability.
Sphere of Impact	PHR candidates are likely to hold positions that allow them to have an impact within the HR function and on the overall performance of the HR department, whereas SPHR candidates are more likely to hold jobs that enable them to have broader impact across various segments of the organization—HR, as well as operational.

GPHR Exam

The Global Professional in Human Resources (GPHR) exam is designed for HR professionals whose work has a decidedly global focus. Typical job responsibilities for GPHR candidates might include developing and implementing global strategies, overseeing international assignments, or managing an overseas HR function. If your responsibilities don't include these sorts of functions, the GPHR exam probably isn't the right choice for you. If your role does have a decidedly international focus, however, you might want to consider the GPHR exam, perhaps in addition to either the PHR or SPHR exams.

Which Exam Should You Take?

So now that you're familiar with each of the exams, deciding which one to take should be a *conscious* decision. Unless you have an international focus, chances are that you'll be taking the PHR exam or the SPHR exam. Like any decision, it needs to be made carefully, logically, unemotionally, and in an informed manner. The following sections will help you in determining which exam is more appropriate for you to take at this point in your career.

Making an Informed Decision

As you ponder whether you should take the PHR exam or the SPHR exam, you should take many factors into consideration. It is natural—and in many ways a good idea—to seek input from others whom you respect as you work to make this decision. However, it's also important to be cognizant of whom you choose to allow to influence your decision.

Yes, we said *choose*. When many of us were teenagers, our elders told us to choose our friends carefully because they will a big impact on what you become in life. We face the same reality now, albeit in a professional sense—and specifically, in this context, with respect to which certification exam (if any) to take. For instance, be careful not to allow the decisions of others who are opting for the PHR or SPHR to have a disproportionately strong influence on you. For example, many test takers have shied away from the SPHR exam because they have allowed themselves to be unduly influenced by the lack of confidence, anxiety, or fear expressed by people at work, in their study groups, or in their prep classes. Similarly, many individuals who weren't ready to take the SPHR exam opted to take it anyway (and haven't always passed) because of undue—and largely irrelevant and unhelpful—peer pressure.

In short, although the opinions of your family and friends are important, they shouldn't be the deciding factor for *you*. Listen to what others are suggesting, hear and understand their words. Then, step back from those words, and look inward, for it's time to do some soul searching. Ask yourself the following questions, and answer them honestly:

▸ Have I compared myself to typical PHR and SPHR candidates? To which group am I more similar? To what degree do I differ from the characteristics of those who have taken the exam that I'm currently considering taking?

▸ Am I confident that I have enough exempt-level HR experience, both in terms of *how much* experience I have and also in terms of the *relative value* of that experience?

▸ Is my experience professionally diverse? Have I been "siloed" in one or two particular HR disciplines, or have I had exposure to multiple disciplines within HR?

▸ Have I experienced exposure to different HR philosophies, approaches, and practices, or am I primarily familiar with the philosophies, approaches, and practices espoused by my past educators and/or employers?

▸ Am I confident that my organization employs "best practices," and have I had a chance to work actively within those? Can I honestly and candidly assess the degree to which my organization employs best practices? Am I comfortable going beyond those practices with which I have experience, and those practices with which I am most familiar?

▸ Have I sought the advice of a trusted mentor(s), or an objective "outsider(s)"? What did that person(s) suggest in terms of HRCI certification?

▸ Have I allowed my decision-making process to be overly, or inappropriately, influenced by those around me?

▸ Have I allowed my desire to "shoot for the stars" to lead me away from setting a more realistic goal for myself? In other words, do I want to take the SPHR examination because "it is there," because it represents the pinnacle of professional achievement with respect to the HR profession, or because *it is really the best choice for me at this time*?

▶ Am I leaning toward taking the SPHR exam because I just want to "get it over with," rather than take the PHR now and subsequently take the SPHR at some point in the future? (This can be a tough one to answer honestly.)

▶ Have I explored the HRCI website and other available materials for current statistics and information on the exam and on the test takers?

▶ With what degree of risk am I comfortable? Would I be able to accept not passing the exam (the first time)?

You know yourself better than anyone else knows you—so dig deep and add any other questions that you feel are relevant to your particular situation. Even if it feels a bit odd or uncomfortable, write your responses down. This technique can help you to candidly and objectively assess where you stand as you decide whether to seek PHR or SPHR certification. You may even want to consider sending yourself an email and looking at it in a couple of days after you've allowed yourself a bit of time to reflect on this important decision.

Perhaps it is most important to remember that deciding to take the PHR exam instead of the SPHR exam would not necessarily constitute a less-desirable choice (just as deciding to take the SPHR exam instead of the PHR exam would not necessarily constitute a *more*-desirable choice). You would not be "settling." This decision would not reflect personal or professional inexperience, incompetence, or any other sort of deficiency. It would reflect only a prudent, honest assessment of where you are today, compared to where you'd like to be on the day you sit down to take the PHR exam.

In addition, consider this: If you *do* decide to take the PHR exam instead of the SPHR exam, you wouldn't be saying "no" to the SPHR exam. In reality, all you'd be saying is "not right now."

> **NOTE**
>
> Don't assess your readiness to take the PHR or SPHR exams solely on the basis of your knowledge, skills, education, or formal training. Having an MBA doesn't mean you'll pass the exam, and not having a bachelor's degree doesn't mean you won't. Instead, ascertain the degree to which you possess and have successfully applied relevant knowledge and practiced relevant skills in the workplace.

Assessment Exam

It's often suggested to HRCI candidates that they may want to take an assessment exam. Without a doubt, you can certainly benefit from taking an assessment exam before beginning—or even planning out—a full study strategy. Taking an assessment exam and reviewing the results can also help you determine whether to take an HRCI certificate exam, or which exam to take. However, your performance on the assessment exam should not be the only factor—or even necessarily the most important factor—to take into consideration when deciding whether to take an HRCI certification exam (or which one to take). Why? In short, how well you perform on the assessment exam may *or may not* be an accurate indicator of how you will perform on the actual exam. This can be especially true for those PHR/SPHR candidates who haven't taken a test in years.

(continues)

(continued)

Here's another way to look at the assessment exam: In some ways, test taking is similar to interviewing. Just because a candidate doesn't perform well on an interview doesn't mean that he or she isn't the best-qualified candidate for the position, because the skills that are required to perform well during an interview can be (and usually are) very different from the skills that are required to perform the job for which the candidate is interviewing. So, too, poor performance on an assessment exam doesn't necessarily mean that you shouldn't take an HRCI certification exam, nor does it necessarily mean that you wouldn't pass it.

In summary, be patient with yourself. If you decide to take the assessment exam, consider your results as one of many pieces of information you'll use to make your own decisions pertaining to testing. Finally, whatever you decide, know that your comfort with and performance on the exam will increase with study, familiarity, and time.

Going Forward with the PHR Exam

If, at this point, you have decided to take the SPHR exam, congratulations! You may want to also consider purchasing *SPHR Exam Prep*, by Larry Phillips. The *SPHR Exam Prep* was designed specifically with the SPHR candidate in mind, and reflects more strategic and policy-level focus than what you'll find in this book.

If, on the other hand, you have decided to take the PHR exam, congratulations! You've engaged in one of the most challenging activities of all—self-scrutiny. You haven't allowed either your desire to attain the "highest" level of recognition or a desire to "get it over with once and for all" to deter you from making a decision that's right for *you*.

As a PHR candidate, you'll find that this book will help you in a number of ways as you prepare for the exam. For instance, it will help you to identify those areas where you're already strong and those areas in which you need additional preparation. It will also provide you with a series of suggestions, tips, study tools, and ideas, all in an effort to increase the likelihood that you will successfully pass the PHR examination. And, perhaps most important, it will direct you toward other resources that will help you dig more deeply into each of the six HR functional areas.

EXAM ALERT

As you read this book, you'll come across the following warning several times because it bears repeating: To pass the PHR exam, this book should be used in addition to—*not instead of*—other PHR test prep resources. We simply can't state it strongly enough—no one source, including this one—can offer you everything you'll need to prepare to take the PHR exam. Undoubtedly, each resource will help you become more prepared than you otherwise would have been.

Registering for the PHR Exam

Now that you've decided to take the PHR exam, the next step is to register for it. The following sections describe eligibility requirements and timetable considerations you need to be aware of when registering.

> **NOTE**
>
> The following information was accurate when this book went to print. Because guidelines, requirements, and other information is subject to change, visit www.hrci.org to view the most up-to-date exam registration information.

Eligibility Requirements

U.S. PHR candidates must have at least two years of HR exempt-level experience to qualify to take the PHR exam and to subsequently earn the PHR credential. Specific requirements for U.S.-based and non-U.S.-based PHR candidates can be found at www.hrci.org.

> **NOTE**
>
> What's meant by the term *exempt-level* work experience? Exempt level can be loosely defined as "professional level." In reality—and in practice—however, there's nothing "loose" about the phrase "exempt-level." "Exempt" and "non-exempt" refer to the overtime provisions of the Fair Labor Standards Act (FLSA) and its amendments. The FLSA is an involved and complicated law. Various provisions of it are also the subject of much public, political, and legislative debate and discussion (for example, the federal minimum wage). It's also an important part of the Total Rewards HR functional area, so now is as good a time as any for you to refresh your understanding of this law. In addition to reviewing Chapter 6, "Total Rewards," in this book, you can learn more about exempt and non-exempt status at the U.S. Department of Labor's website at www.dol.gov/elaws.

> **NOTE**
>
> Special requirements and opportunities also exist for students and recent graduates. If you are currently an undergraduate student, or if you have earned your bachelor's degree within the past year, please review the information available "For Students or Recent Grads" at www.hrci.org.

Registration Timeframes

Timetables for registering for the exam, and for actually taking the exam, can be found at www.hrci.org. Applications for the PHR exam can be completed online or submitted on paper.

> **CAUTION**
>
> Whether you are applying online or on paper, be sure to provide all the requested information, particularly relative to documenting your exempt work experience. Failure to do so can result in being ruled ineligible to take the exam—and determinations of ineligibility are final.

What to Expect the Day of Your Exam

In "the old days," the PHR exam was administered at a particular time, on a particular day, in a particular place. Rows of test takers, #2 pencils in hand and heads bent low, diligently filled in rows of bubbles under the watchful eye of test proctors. Today, however, the PHR exam is administered in a computerized format, during particular time frames (May 1–June 30, and December 1–January 31) at hundreds of testing locations. This format represents a significant improvement over the former test-taking protocol in that it affords test takers far more flexibility with respect to when and where they can choose to take the PHR exam.

Test Centers

PHR testing is conducted at Thomson Prometric test sites, located in all 50 states and throughout the world. Currently, there are more than 250 test sites conveniently located throughout the United States, U.S. territories, and Canada. For more information on Prometric testing centers, visit www.prometric.com.

> **CAUTION**
>
> Thomson Prometric testing centers provide testing services for many, many organizations—ranging from A (Air Conditioning Contractors of America) to Z (well, actually to W—the State of Wyoming). To allow yourself maximum choice and flexibility with respect to the time, date, and place of your exam, be sure to schedule your exam as early as possible.

First and foremost, be sure you bring an unexpired, government-issued, signature-bearing photo ID with you. Just as important, make sure you bring the Authorization to Test (ATT) letter you received after your eligibility to take the PHR exam was reviewed and approved by the Professional Examination Service (PES), HRCI's testing vendor. Also, be sure to arrive at least half an hour before you are scheduled to begin your exam.

The more you know about what to expect after you arrive at the test center, the more comfortable you'll be when you actually get there and the less anxious you'll be when it's time to take the exam. To take a test drive of the test experience, visit www.prometric.com. The test drive will actually re-create (or, to be more accurate, "pre-create") the exam experience, beginning to end, including check-in, ID confirmation, biometric identity capture, image capture, seating, tutorial, a sample exam, candidate survey of the experience, an end-of-test report, and check out. You can also see a list of frequently asked questions and their answers.

Exam Results

One of the best things about taking the PHR exam at a computerized Thomson Prometric Testing Center is that you'll receive preliminary exam results (in other words, you'll know whether you passed the exam) before you leave the center.

> **NOTE**
>
> These preliminary results are just that—preliminary, and therefore unofficial. As such, you may want to wait until you receive official notification (two or three weeks later) from HRCI before you formally notify others of the exam outcome.

So, although you'll still have to wait for official notification, there's no more running to the mailbox to see if that long-awaited letter has arrived yet. No longer do PHR candidates need to wonder (and worry) about the results for up to six weeks, as candidates had to do years ago. Instead, you'll have your preliminary answer immediately.

The minimum possible score on the PHR exam is 100, and the maximum possible score is 700. The passing score is 500, based on a scaled score.

"What If I Don't Pass the Exam?"

Okay, it's not a positive thought—but it happens. And it happens a lot. And it can even happen to you. Test taking requires risk taking, and failing the PHR exam is a possibility.

Realistically, it's important to keep in mind that a considerable number of individuals don't pass the PHR exam. According to HRCI, approximately one-third of the individuals who take the PHR exam don't pass it. After all, if it were that easy to earn the PHR credential, it wouldn't be nearly as valuable.

There's no shame in not passing the PHR exam. It's important to remember that not passing the PHR exam does not in any way preclude you from taking it again. There's always the second time around. In fact, it might just turn out that the knowledge, insight, and experience you gain from taking and not passing the PHR exam the first time could equip you with what you need to know to pass the exam the next time around.

So now that you have worked your way though this chapter, you should be able to proceed with a greater degree of confidence relative to whether taking the PHR exam is the right choice for you at this time, and with a better understanding of what the exam actually entails. If so, excellent! We'll see you in Chapter 2, "HR: A Body of Underlying Knowledge and Principles." If not, then we suggest that you take some time—time to do some additional readings and research in HR, time to round out your HR experience through cross-training or other opportunities, and time to deepen the depth and breadth of your current knowledge and understanding of the HR profession. You might just find that the resources cited in the book might provide an excellent starting point. You might also want to consider an HR certificate program, as a "warm-up" to your HR certification process.

Chapter Summary

In this chapter, you learned about HR as a profession. You also learned about two important organizations that exist to support our profession—SHRM and HRCI. You also considered why it is so important to become (now, or at some point in the future) a certified HR professional and to enjoy the credibility and respect (from others, as well as from yourself) that accrues from this earning this distinction.

You also reviewed information that helped you determine whether this is the right time for you to take an HR certification exam. If it is, you reviewed information that helped you decide which exam is right for you. Last, you were provided with information that will assist you with registering for the exam and detailed information about what will happen on the day of your exam.

Key Terms List

- ASPA
- SHRM
- PHR
- SPHR
- HRCI
- Strategic Management
- Workforce Planning and Employment
- Human Resource Development
- Total Rewards
- Employee and Labor Relations
- Risk Management

Suggested Readings and Resources

Human Resource Certification Institute. www.hrci.org, 2007.

Society for Human Resource Management (SHRM). www.shrm.org, 2007.

Prometric. www.prometric.com, August 2007.

CHAPTER TWO

HR: A Body of Underlying Knowledge and Principles

Study Strategies

This chapter explores the HR body of knowledge, which consists of six functional areas. Specifically, these areas encompass 23 core areas of knowledge that HRCI has identified as essential for all HR professionals.

To help with learning, understanding, and remembering the core areas, try the study following tips:

▶ On small index cards, write down the names of each of the 23 core areas of knowledge. Then, on separate index cards (ones that are either different colors or different sizes), write down key notes about each of these functional areas. Ensure that your notes are general enough that they describe or define the core area of knowledge in a way that does not limit it to just one or two specific functional areas. Then, to see how well you're able to make those connections, match up the descriptive cards with the card on which the core area of knowledge is indicated.

▶ Practice matching the core areas of knowledge to the various functional areas to which they are related.

▶ As you review each functional area, create running lists of the ways in which each of the core areas of knowledge (as appropriate) applies to that area.

Introduction

As discussed in Chapter 1, "The HR Profession and the PHR Exam," HRCI has identified and classified the HR body of knowledge, which consists of the following six functional areas:

- ▶ Strategic management
- ▶ Workforce planning and employment
- ▶ Human resource development
- ▶ Total rewards
- ▶ Employee and labor relations
- ▶ Risk management

Underlying these six functional areas are 23 areas of core knowledge that HRCI has identified as essential for all HR professionals. Many of these core areas of knowledge have relevance, application, and impact across multiple functional areas within HR. Possessing knowledge in each of these areas is mandatory for successful performance on the PHR exam. Even more important, being able to readily recall that knowledge and apply it to a wide variety of workplace situations is foundational to being an effective HR professional.

Although our profession spans many critical areas of responsibility, we cannot (nor should we try to) break our function down into a finite list of tasks and duties. Nor can we limit ourselves to memorizing definitions, models, or fact patterns and outcomes of relevant legal cases. Instead, we must establish a backdrop—an infrastructure, in one sense—within which we can knowledgeably approach the intricacies of our multifaceted and multidimensional profession.

As one way to begin looking at these intricacies in a more holistic manner, this chapter will provide a brief overview of each of the 23 core areas of knowledge required for HR professionals. Although this chapter will not provide you with all the information you will need as you prepare to take the PHR exam, it will help you identify those areas in which you could benefit from additional preparation and study. This chapter also will encourage you to approach the HR profession with a more integrated perspective and to think more broadly about the potential impact that each of us can have as an HR professional.

Each of these core areas of knowledge will be addressed to varying degrees in subsequent chapters. At this point in your PHR exam preparation process, however, you may want to consider using this chapter as a way to begin to frame out and make connections between the six functional areas of HR.

Core Area of Knowledge: Needs Assessment and Analysis

Needs assessment and analysis is the first step in ADDIE, a process model often used in the area of instructional design. ADDIE is actually an acronym that stands for

- ▶ A: Needs Assessment/Analysis (cited differently in different sources)

- ▶ D: Design

- ▶ D: Development

- ▶ I: Implementation

- ▶ E: Evaluation

We're going to take a much closer look at ADDIE in Chapter 5, "Human Resource Development," but for now, let's address the idea of needs assessment and analysis. Needs assessment and analysis is a way of defining problems. Taking this a step further, a *problem* could be defined as the difference between a situation or condition as it currently is compared to what that situation or condition needs to be.

Ask Questions and Listen to the Answers

Managers—and even other HR professionals—may come to you with definite ideas of how to resolve a particular problem. When this happens, pause, ask questions, and—above all—listen. It's critical at this point in the process to collaboratively identify the actual—rather than the perceived—problem, and to ascertain the underlying causes of that problem. Therein lies an important difference between *assessment* (identifying the problem) and *analysis* (identifying the causes of that problem). Skipping either of those steps is likely to impact the effectiveness of the remaining steps in the ADDIE process.

CAUTION

Solutions that are predicated on faulty needs analysis and assessment are, by definition, likely to be faulty, as well.

Core Third-Party Contract Management, Including Development of Requests for Proposals (RFPs)

More and more organizations are deciding to have certain services performed by individuals or entities that are external to the organization, rather than by employees. Welcome to the ever-expanding world of third-party contracts.

Third-party relationships are no longer a phenomenon; rather, they are progressively becoming a standard—and even expected—way of conducting business. Some services that are outsourced represent new initiatives or projects. At other times, work that is currently being performed by employees is outsourced to individuals or entities outside the organization.

Functions Often Outsourced

Different organizations may choose to outsource different functions. Many functions (and some people would argue that almost any function) within an organization can be outsourced.

Many HR departments outsource significant functions, as well. Some of the HR functions that are often partially—or fully—outsourced include the following:

- 401(k) or 403(b) programs
- Pensions/benefits
- Stock option administration
- Health and welfare benefits
- Learning and development
- Payroll
- Safety and security

Strategic Outsourcing

Decisions about outsourcing should be made within a broader strategic context. This context should extend beyond those considerations that relate specifically to the HR function that is being considered for outsourcing. Instead, that function must be looked at from a more holistic perspective that encompasses the entire HR function—as well as the organization as a whole. For instance, before outsourcing the training function, an organization should weigh many factors, just one of which could be perceived credibility:

> ▶ *Possible disadvantage to outsourcing*—Would an outside trainer be perceived as having diminished credibility because he or she does not have prior experience within the organization?

> ▶ *Possible advantage to outsourcing*—Would an outside trainer be perceived as having added credibility because he or she is less subject to organizational dictates? In other words, since "no one is a prophet in his or her own town," could an outsider's message—even it is the same message that is being promulgated by someone within the organization—be more highly valued because of his or her external status?

Request for Proposal (RFP)

The Request for Proposal (RFP) is a written document that invites contractors to propose written solutions that address the organization's needs—all within a price that the customer is willing to pay. Developing a solid and carefully constructed RFP is critical; a poorly designed or overly vague RFP may yield proposed solutions that do not address the organization's actual problems. Worse yet, those solutions may appear to be workable and appropriate—until they have been implemented.

Communication Strategies (For Example, Presentation, Collaboration, Influencing, Diplomacy, and Sensitivity)

In the course of performing our jobs, HR professionals need to possess and demonstrate a wide variety of skills and abilities—analytical, problem solving, decision making, interpersonal, intrapersonal, conflict resolution—just to name a few. Underscoring all these is the ability to communicate effectively and strategically. Again, this concept spans all six areas of HR. Doing our jobs well just isn't enough—we have to ensure that the work that we do is appropriately communicated to and understood by the people with whom we partner. For instance, we might design a compensation program that is designed to lead the market (see Chapter 6, "Total Rewards," for more information on what this means). We might accomplish that posture by establishing competitive base-pay rates, along with an incentive program that is—potentially—very lucrative for employees who meet or exceed certain goals. If we don't communicate with managers and employees about how we designed the program, however, and about how the incentive program really puts us ahead of our labor market competitors in terms of compensation, the impact and power of our design might be unappreciated or, even worse, misunderstood or misapplied.

One way to look at this is to consider the five Ws and one H that news reporters traditionally seek to answer:

▸ *Why communicate*—First, think about why you are communicating this message. If you don't clearly convey a reason for the message, others within the organization will undoubtedly ascribe a reason. Not surprisingly, that reason will not always be accurate or positive.

▸ *What to communicate*—Balancing employees' "need to know" (and some would say "right to know") against the organization's legal and/or ethical obligations relative to the dissemination of information presents a delicate and precarious situation. If you find yourself in a situation like this (and it is likely that sooner or later you will), be truthful. Lies or half-truths will always surface. And, once lost, credibility can rarely be regained. Even then, it must be earned—a slow and costly process. Sometimes, telling the truth means that you can't reveal every detail of every situation—and that you might need to acknowledge this.

CAUTION

Confidential information is just that—confidential! This may especially true if you have "friends" within the organization who may come to you looking for "the inside scoop." Reminding employees (regardless of the nature of your personal relationship with them) of your commitment to maintaining confidentiality is part of truth telling, as well.

▸ *When to communicate*—Timing may not be everything when it comes to communication, but it is critically important. First, consider the content of the message you will be communicating. How much urgency is there for communicating the message? Is there a benefit to waiting? Think about other considerations, as well. In a micro sense, be aware of the day of the week and the time of the day when you choose to communicate a message. In a macro sense, consider what's going on in the organization, in the industry, in society, and even in the world before you share critical information.

▸ *Where to communicate*—Think about where you want people to be when they receive the message: Attending a face-to-face meeting, which is largely presentation driven? Or participating from a satellite location in teleconference that permits questions and answers? Or alone, behind their computers, reading an email? There is no one right approach or solution for all situations, so it's important to consider the totality of the exact situation in which you find yourself.

▸ *Who will communicate, and to whom*—Sometimes HR professionals prepare messages that they will communicate directly. At other times, HR professionals will collaborate with managers to put together a particular message that the managers will deliver personally. Or, HR professionals deliver messages that—in some form or fashion—others have created for us. And of course, there are times when we ghost write information that someone else will actually communicate.

There's no one right answer for any situation, so think through the cast of characters—those who will construct the message, deliver the message, and receive the message—thoroughly and carefully.

▶ *How to communicate*—It's not enough to rely on one method of communication. Identify multiple ways to communicate important messages. Different media are available to you, including in person, print, email, teleconference, and live streaming video, to name just a few.

How to communicate addresses another important consideration: the directional flow of communication. Are methods in place within the organization to ensure that information can flow up, as well as down? Can individuals across different units or divisions of the organization communicate with each other? And are meaningful feedback mechanisms in place to enable you to accurately gauge the impact and effectiveness of your communication efforts?

"I'm a People Person"

The answers to why, where, when, who, and how can convey just as powerfully as "what" the message is. HR professionals must be keenly aware not only of what they communicate, but that how one communicates, by itself, constitutes another level of communication. You must be keenly aware of the nuances of these underlying messages and approach them in a strategic manner.

This approach constitutes a significant departure from the stereotypical image of the HR professional as a "people person." That image evokes, in part, the idea of a "touchy-feely" person, armed and ready with a shoulder to cry on.

In reality, there is nothing soft or natural about communicating in your role as an HR professional, and there is much justification for HRCI to identify it as a core area of knowledge. With respect to the ways in which you communicate as an HR professional, you must be an ear to listen, not a shoulder to cry on.

Core Area of Knowledge: Organizational Documentation Requirements (to Meet Federal and State Requirements)

Within an organization, maintaining documentation is dreaded by many, enjoyed by few, and viewed suspiciously by others. HR's role in establishing and maintaining legal and effective documentation practices is particularly pivotal.

Some documentation basics that HR professionals need to think about include

▶ *Knowing what needs to be documented*—This includes federal, state, and local requirements—as well as documentation mandated by collective bargaining agreements, employment contracts, and/or performance management programs.

▶ *Knowing how to document*—Many forms must be completed in accordance with specific, detailed, and mandatory guidelines. Those specific requirements can also impact the ways in which documents are maintained, stored, retrieved, and distributed.

▸ *Knowing what not to document*—Documentation takes two main forms—documentation that pertains to collecting and maintaining legally mandated record keeping, and documentation that pertains to performance management (in the broadest sense of that term). For purposes of the core areas of knowledge, this discussion will focus on the first type of documentation.

CAUTION

There's an old joke that goes something like this:

Question: "What's the difference between true love and employment litigation?"

Answer: "Employment litigation is forever."

In truth, there is nothing funny about employment litigation. However, there's a valuable reminder that can be taken away from this quip: Any written or electronic communication you create, in any form, is—for all intents and purposes—forever subject (potentially) to subpoena. This is particularly true for electronic communications—emails, and even instant messages. Our most contemporary communications are, in some ways, even more permanent than the stone tablets of ages gone by—so be extremely prudent and careful about the documentation you maintain. You may one day have the opportunity to review it again—in a courtroom, in front of a jury, or on the front page of a newspaper.

Core Area of Knowledge: Adult Learning Processes

Two realities: First, organizations continually change and evolve, thereby demanding more and different things from the people they employ. Second, those employees must be willing and able to learn new skills to perform their expanding roles in a fully proficient manner. With respect to an employee's performance within the organization, maintaining a current level of performance often equates to stagnation, or even atrophy.

This is true for employees who want to grow into higher-level positions within the organization, as well as for employees who want to continue successfully performing in their current positions. Even the "Steady Eddies" and "Steady Bettys" within organizations will find that they must learn and grow within their jobs to keep them. Few individuals can say that they are performing their current job in the same way they performed it 10, or even 5, years ago. During those years, much has been learned, and most likely more will be learned as they remain employed with the organization. This requires the organization to understand adult learners and the realities of teaching adults new skills.

Adults learn very differently, however, from children (see Chapter 5). HR professionals must understand these differences and incorporate them into the instructional design of training programs. Training, like documentation and so many other areas of core knowledge, is more than just a function. How you carry out your role with respect to training will have a tremendous impact on how you are perceived and on how you are defined within the organization—both individually and as a member of HR. Treat a roomful of employees or managers like children and you'll have a captive audience—but not in a good sense. They'll be looking for ways to duck out early for breaks, surreptitiously answer emails on a handheld wireless device under the table, or—worse yet—just leave and not return.

Every training session provides you with an opportunity to partner. But be cautious—don't unintentionally patronizing your participants. Training can help define you as an inspiring and motivating facilitator, or it can reinforce the negative adage that "those who can't do, teach."

Core Area of Knowledge: Motivation Concepts and Applications

Motivation cuts across all six functional areas. Motivation, for instance, is often associated with why—and how—employees learn. It's also highly relevant, however, to how employees perceive and value salaries, wages, and benefits, and to establishing and sustaining positive relationships in the workplace.

Motivation theory directly impacts employee performance in the workplace. As such, HR professionals need a keen understanding of the various motivation theories to incorporate them—in a practical sense—into their initiatives and into their consulting relationships with managers. Some of the key theories in which HR professionals must be well versed are the following:

- Maslow's Hierarchy of Needs
- B.F. Skinner—Operant Conditioning
- Frederick Herzberg—Motivation-Hygiene Theory
- Douglas McGregor—Theory X and Theory Y
- David McClelland—Acquired Needs Theory
- J. Stacy Adams—Equity Theory
- Victor Vroom—Expectancy Theory

The following subsections will describe each of these theories to help you build your knowledge of these critical theories.

Maslow's Hierarchy of Needs—1954

Maslow's theory presents five levels of need experienced by humans. People move into higher levels of need as lower levels of need are sufficiently satisfied. Those levels, from most fundamental to most evolved, are

- *Basic physical needs*—Basic physical needs include food, water, shelter, acceptable working conditions, and other fundamental, foundational needs.

▶ *Safety and security*—Safety and security needs speak to the need to live and work in an environment that feels—and is—safe.

▶ *Belonging and love*—In the workplace, this need can manifest itself through membership in a department, a profession, a division, clubs, affinity groups, or simply through friendships and relationships.

▶ *Esteem*—Esteem manifests in two dimensions: *self* and *others*. Self-esteem refers to valuing one's own self, personally and/or professionally. Esteem from others relates to receiving recognition and approval from others.

▶ *Self-actualization*—Through self-actualization, individuals want to, and strive to, reach their full potential. Self-actualization is, very often, its own reward.

Maslow at Work

HR professionals need to look for creative ways to address the motivational needs identified by Maslow— even though employees may not be fully aware of them.

Addressing needs doesn't mean trying to move everyone to the next level. It is important not to impose expectations on employees that they do not want to embrace. It is equally important to afford workplace-appropriate opportunities for those who do.

On that note, be sure to keep all applications of Maslow's theory firmly grounded in the workplace. Link it clearly and unambiguously to performance—of the organization, the department, and the individual. Always maintain your focus on the organization's goals, and always be prepared to articulate job-related reasons for motivation-based initiatives.

Last, as you focus on creating opportunities that enable employees to move to higher-level needs, don't lose track of whether and how well employee's lower-level needs are being met. A compensation system, for instance, that allows employees to meet their basic physical needs at one point in time may eventually become problematic and fall well below what labor market competitors are paying. How can this happen? Try "taking your eye off the balls," even for a short period of time, of range movement, merit budgets, and the like, and watch what happens.

EXAM ALERT

Be prepared to match to which of Maslow's needs to the different workplace situations, rewards, opportunities, and/or conditions to which they most closely relate.

B.F. Skinner, Operant Conditioning—1957

B.F. Skinner's theory of operant conditioning assumes that the ways people choose to behave in the future are a function of the consequences that have resulted from their past behavior. Skinner identifies four types of consequences:

▶ *Positive reinforcement (praise)*—Demonstrating desired behavior results in a desirable outcome or consequence. This may encourage the individual to choose to engage in desired behaviors again.

Workplace example: A customer service supervisor observes a customer service representative skillfully resolve a complaint from an irate customer, and praises that person for successfully defusing a potentially volatile situation.

▶ *Negative reinforcement*—When an individual believes that specific behaviors will result in a specific undesirable outcome or consequence, he or she may choose to demonstrate more desirable behaviors, instead. In this way, the individual will behave in a way that prevents that undesirable consequence from happening.

Workplace example: An employee chooses to use his or her own personal email address and computer—rather than the company's email system—for jokes and/or other correspondence that could potentially be viewed as inappropriate for the workplace.

▶ *Punishment*—Demonstrating undesirable behavior results in an undesirable outcome or consequence. This may encourage the individual to choose not to engage in that undesired behavior again.

Workplace example: An employee who continues to answer incoming personal cell phone calls during a training session, even after being asked to stop, is asked to leave the training session and is not permitted to register for a make-up program for at least three months.

▶ *Extinction*—An individual's behavior—whether desired or undesired—elicits *no* outcomes or consequences at all. The individual may choose not to demonstrate that behavior again.

Workplace example: An employee persists in trying to engage co-workers in counterproductive conversations about other co-workers (that is, gossip). If the co-workers do not join in, the employee might choose not to initiate these sorts of (undesired) conversations in the future.

Frederick Herzberg, Motivation-Hygiene Theory—1959

Herzberg identified two separate and distinct types of needs:

▶ *Motivation factors*—Motivation factors relate specifically to the job itself—for instance, the nature of the work, the challenge inherent to the work, and/or the perceived or real value of the work.

▶ *Hygiene factors*—Hygiene factors relate to everything else an employee might experience in the workplace—everything associated *with* the work, but *not the work itself*. This includes—but is not limited to—pay, benefits, nature of supervision, relationships with co-workers, and so forth.

Dubbed "The Father of Job Enrichment," Herzberg distinguished between factors that can generate positive feelings about work (the motivation factors) and factors that can result in negative feelings about work (hygiene factors). So, although unacceptable motivation factors won't cause an employee to be unhappy at work, unacceptable hygiene factors could. Conversely, acceptable or positive motivation factors will cause an employee to be happy at work, but acceptable or positive hygiene factors won't. However, motivation factors will have a positive impact on an employee's motivation level *if, and only if*, hygiene factors are acceptable.

Herzberg's theory challenged employers—and personnel departments—to look at employees' satisfaction at work in a completely new and different way. No longer was job satisfaction viewed as existing along a single continuum. Herzberg transformationally defined it as a function of two related, but wholly different, factors—both of which warranted attention.

Douglas McGregor, Theory X and Theory Y—1960

Building on Maslow's work, Theory X and Theory Y refers to two approaches to management:

▶ Theory X managers manage in accordance with the general belief that employees are uncommitted, uninterested, hesitant to assume any additional responsibility, and essentially lazy.

▶ Theory Y managers manage in accordance with the general belief that employees will take on—and even look for—additional work if the employee perceives that the work is satisfying and rewarding.

David McClelland, Acquired Needs Theory—1961

McClelland's theory identified and focused on one particular need—*achievement*. According to McClelland, achievement is not a universal motivator for everyone, and the degree of need varies from individual to individual.

Individuals who experience—or, perhaps more appropriately, possess—the need for achievement are neither risk averse nor risk embracing. More frequently, they take a middle-of-the-road approach when it comes to risk—calculated, and conscious. Those motivated by the need for achievement, therefore, will assume an acceptable and tolerable level of risk that allows the opportunity for upside potential, confident all the while that their skills, abilities, and contributions will have the greatest impact in determining the outcome of a situation. Interestingly, individuals with a high achievement need are less concerned with the rewards of achievement than they are with the actual attainment of that achievement.

With respect to performance management, individuals who have a high need for achievement may gravitate toward stretch goals, which are explored further in Chapter 5. They would also be more likely to focus on the goals portion of a performance management system or form than the competencies portion.

J. Stacy Adams, Equity Theory—1963

Equity theory, as the name implies, is predicated on the assumption that people want to be treated fairly, particularly when compared to how others around them are treated. It also purports that such comparisons will be made frequently.

In the context of employment, equity theory asserts that employees will compare their *inputs* (everything they bring to the job and invest in the job) and *outputs* (how they are rewarded—both intrinsically and extrinsically—for what they invest in the job) to others' inputs and outputs. If employees come away from this process feeling as though they are being treated fairly in comparison to others, they will continue to put forth effort. Conversely, employees who come away from this process with the belief that they are being treated unfairly will seek to make a change. That change might include trying to change their own inputs, trying to change their own outputs, or trying to change the inputs or outputs of others. Any of these options could manifest themselves in either productive or unproductive ways. And, of course, that same employee could quit—the most dramatic way that an employee can change inputs.

Victor Vroom, Expectancy Theory—1964

Vroom's expectancy theory is all about weighing options and making choices. It asserts, in essence, that people will put forth effort when they believe that such effort will result in an outcome, and that that outcome is worthwhile. This theory is composed of three key elements and resulting questions that individuals (in this case, employees) ask themselves:

▶ *Expectancy*—"How likely is it that I'll be able to attain a particular goal (in this case, a certain level of performance) if I put forth the required effort?"

▶ *Instrumentality*—"Assuming that I do attain this level of performance, how likely it is that I'll be recognized or rewarded in some way?"

▶ *Valence*—"Assuming that I am recognized or rewarded, what is that recognition or reward really worth to me?"

Core Area of Knowledge: Training Methods (For Example, Computer-Based, Classroom, On-the-Job)

HR professionals, in collaboration with the clients we serve, can choose from a variety of training approaches (see Chapter 5). Having familiarity with as many of these methods as possible will enable the HR professional to develop a training solution that is most appropriate for each unique problem while taking into account individual, departmental, and organizational considerations.

TIP

Not every situation requires a training solution. However, HR professionals (particularly those with a background in learning and development) often default to a training solution before exploring all possible options. It's critical for HR professionals to develop a solution that addresses each particular problem, not a solution that seems most readily available or that most closely matches one's own background and skill set.

EXAM ALERT

Be prepared to identify, describe, and address case-study issues regarding both active and passive training methods and techniques, including (but not limited to)

▸ *Passive*—Conference, lecture, presentation, and so on.

▸ *Active*—Case studies, demonstrations, facilitated discussions, exercises, role play, self-paced study, and so on.

EXAM ALERT

Be familiar with the advantages and disadvantages of each, as well as different situations in which each approach would be most effective.

Core Area of Knowledge: Leadership Concepts and Applications

Developing leaders within the organization is a key objective for HR professionals, especially for those who are involved in organizational development.

Leadership is difficult to define, as many different individuals have set forth just as many different definitions. Leadership is also very different from management, although those terms are often used (or misused) interchangeably. In simplest terms, leadership can be defined as the ability to encourage "followership" to attain specific objectives.

Followership, in this sense, does not refer to unthinkingly submissive imitators; rather, it speaks to highly dedicated devotees who are passionately and wholeheartedly committed to the vision of someone else. That someone else, in this case, is the leader. For without followers, there can be no leaders. Without effective leaders, there will be no followers, and there will be no organized, implemented strategy for attaining organizational objectives.

Over time, the following four theories have emerged on the subject of leadership, each evolving from the prior:

▸ Trait Theories

▸ Behavioral Theories

▸ Situational Leadership Theories

▸ Contingency Theories

Trait Theories

Trait theories support the idea that leaders are born, not made. Being a great leader, then, was more a function of nature than nurture. It had to do with being a great person—and being born that way. Research in support of this theory, however, was neither consistent nor complete. For instance, no one set of leadership traits could be identified. Additionally, different leaders using very different approaches in different situations could all effect a successful outcome. Enter behavioral theories.

Behavioral Theories

Beginning in the 1940s, a new school of thought on leadership began to emerge: Leadership can be taught. All it would take to develop nonleaders into leaders would be a willing student who would receive proper instruction relative to essential and appropriate leadership behaviors.

Ohio State University and the University of Michigan both conducted considerable research on behavioral management theories. Their research yielded similar results by identifying two critical dimensions of leadership behavior:

- ▶ *"Consideration" (Ohio State) or "Employee-Centered" (University of Michigan)*—Refers to the interpersonal, trust, respect, and social dimensions of leadership.

- ▶ *"Initiating Structure" (Ohio State) or "Job-Related" (University of Michigan)*—Refers to factors related to the work itself—specifically, what employees need to do, and how they need to do it, to attain objectives.

As with trait theories, questions about leadership still remained unanswered by the behavioral theory approach. Situation leadership theories represented the next evolution of thought.

Situational Leadership Theories

Situational leadership theories demonstrate a greater appreciation for the complexity of the leadership role. They suggest that no single leadership approach is right for every situation. Situational leadership theories also suggest that part of what is required to be a good and effective leader is having the ability to select and utilize the most effective leadership approach for each specific situation.

The following sections will present three key situational leadership theories.

Paul Hersey and Ken Blanchard's Situational Leadership Theory

How does a leader encourage followership? According to Paul Hersey and Ken Blanchard, "it depends." Hersey and Blanchard's theory of situational leadership suggests that leaders must use different approaches, at different times, with different employees. These approaches will depend on each employee's maturity and proficiency at performing specific functions. Maturity or proficiency relate to the technical skills required to perform a particular task, as well as the nontechnical skills (or behavioral competencies) required to bring a task to its successful conclusion.

Hersey and Blanchard identify four approaches:

▶ *Telling*—Leaders must provide the employee with precise instruction and fairly close supervision while the employee is learning to perform the new task. Feedback must be specific and frequent.

▶ *Selling*—As the employee begins to develop proficiency at the new task, an effective leader will begin to provide additional background information and/or explanation relative to the nuances of the task. At this stage, the employee has moved beyond the basics and can function with a bit less supervision.

▶ *Participating*—By now, the employee has developed a certain level of skill at performing the task and can comprehend many of the underlying principles of the task. The employee still, however, requires support, encouragement, and reinforcement. In this phase, leaders need to make the employee more aware of what he or she *can* do, and encourage the employee to perform the tasks in an increasingly confident, independent, and self-sufficient manner.

▶ *Delegating*—By now, in addition to being able to perform the technical aspects of the task, the employee possesses the behavioral characteristics and competencies required to bring the task to a successful conclusion. The leader needs to communicate the goal (ideally, after collaboratively developing it with the employee) and must allow the employee to accomplish it independently. In short, at this point, an effective leader lets go.

See Figure 2.1, which describes directive and supportive behaviors.

BLANCHARD SITUATIONAL LEADERSHIP MODEL	
LEADER BEHAVIOR CATEGORIES	
DIRECTIVE BEHAVIOR	**SUPPORTIVE BEHAVIOR**
• One-way communication • Followers' roles spelled out • Close supervision of performance	• Two-way communication • Listening, providing support & Encouragement • Facilitate interaction • Involve follower in decision making

FIGURE 2.1 Examples of directive and supportive behaviors.

In addition to Figure 2.1, Figure 2.2 illustrates the Hersey-Blanchard Situational Leadership Model.

The Hersey-Blanchard Situational Leadership Model also represents a different relationship between task and relationship. As described previously, each of these considerations will be "low" or "high" depending on the maturity and proficiency of the employee. In other words, the emphasis that a leader should place on task and relationship considerations will be different for each quadrant.

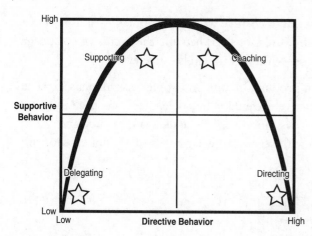

FIGURE 2.2 The Hersey-Blanchard Situational Leadership Model.

> **NOTE**
>
> It is important to note that—at any one point in time—the same employee can function in different quadrants relative to different tasks/responsibilities. An employee should not be assigned to or identified as performing in any one particular quadrant (in other words, don't pigeon-hole your employees). Instead, recognize that each individual task performed by the employee may fall into a different quadrant and would therefore warrant a different leadership approach.

Robert R. Blake and Jane S. Mouton's Situational Leadership Theory

Blake-Mouton's situational leadership theory depicts leadership behavior along a two-axis grid:

- ▶ Concern for people (vertical axis)
- ▶ Concern for task/production (horizontal axis)

Each axis uses a one-to-nine scale on which to chart the degree of concern that leaders demonstrate for each dimension (see Figure 2.3).

Unlike Hersey and Blanchard's model, there is room for gradations within each of the four quadrants in this model. Looking at the extremes, however, does afford insight into the leadership style that each of the four quadrants (to one degree or another) represents:

- ▶ *Authority-Obedience* (Task Management) (nine on production, one on people) are demanding and authoritarian. They rarely, if ever, admit to being wrong. They shift blame away from themselves. They focus entirely on what needs to be attained, with little concern for the human dimensions that speak to how the task will be attained.

- ▶ *Team Management* (nine on production, nine on people) focus on attaining tasks as well as maintaining and enhancing relationships with those who will be performing those tasks.

- ▶ *Country Club Management* (one on production, nine on people) are more like cheerleaders than coaches. They focus almost exclusively on cultivating positive relationships with employees—within a positive work environment—and pay little if any attention to the tasks at hand. Relationships become the exclusive goal; organizational objectives become almost—if not completely—irrelevant.

▶ *Impoverished Management* (one on production, one on people) take the laissez-faire management style to an unproductive extreme. They delegate work (the task), and are often not seen again until there is more work to be delegated. They are absentee leaders in every sense—with respect to what needs to get done, who will do it, and how it will get done.

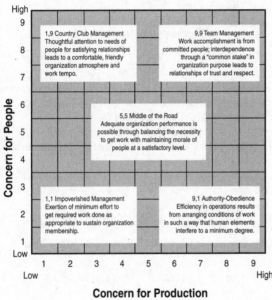

From Blake, R.R., and J.S. Mouton, The Managerial Grid. Gulf Publishing, Houston, 1964. RMW 2/10/02

FIGURE 2.3 The Blake-Mouton Situational Leadership Model.

In the center of the grid is "organization man management" (five on production, five on people). This is a more middle-of-the-road (or middle of the grid, to be precise) approach that balances concern with production for concern for people, and for morale.

Contingency Theories

Evolving out of situational leadership theory, the fourth stage in this evolutionary process involves contingency theories, the best known of which was developed by Fred Fiedler. Like some of the earlier theories, Fiedler devised a method of ascertaining the degree to which leaders were concerned with tasks and the degree to which leaders were concerned with people. Fiedler then used that measure to determine situations in which different leaders would be most effective or, in other words, the situations that would be most favorable for specific leadership styles.

The factors that determine that level of favorableness are

▶ *Leader-members relations*—How strong, and how significant, are the relationships between the leader and the team members? To what degree will those relationships make the leader more, or less, effective and influential?

▶ *Task structure*—How structured is the work that the team members are performing?

▶ *Position power*—How much power or influence does the leader's position hold, or how much can it exert? To what degree can the leader ensure accountability for performance and authority to delegate?

A leader's effectiveness will be impacted by the relative strength or weakness of these three factors. In general, the higher the factors, the more effective the leader will be.

Core Area of Knowledge: Leadership Concepts and Applications

Though leadership styles vary widely, they can be grouped into two primary categories—transactional leadership and transformational leadership:

▶ *Transactional leadership*—The transactional leadership style is characterized by the possibility of rewards and the threat of punishment. This is a "no news is good news" approach to leadership—leaders get involved only when goals are not met or when employees are not adhering to stated rules.

▶ *Transformational leadership*—Transformational leaders are coaches, not enforcers. They model the behavior they expect the group to emulate, and they focus on relationships as well as tasks. These two concerns are not mutually exclusive; rather, they coexist and are complementary. Both are essential, and neither is expendable.

EXAM ALERT

Be prepared to speak to the differences between leadership and management as each pertains to specific organizational roles, functions, and activities. More information about this is available in Chapter 5. In addition, be familiar with the differences between dictatorial (authoritarian), democratic, and laissez-faire leadership styles, and appropriate applications of each.

Core Area of Knowledge: Project Management Concepts and Applications

In the vernacular of project management, a *project* is a special and temporary undertaking designed to accomplish a specific goal and yield a specific output. The management portion of this term speaks to the overall process required for ensuring the successful accomplishment of this goal, rather than the goal itself.

Projects are usually deadline driven. Though the project timeline may be demanding, it is not uncommon for projects not to have additional resources devoted to their accomplishment.

As HR professionals, it is likely that we will undertake projects in addition to our regular responsibilities, rather than being afforded a temporary hiatus from those responsibilities. Balancing day-to-day workload, therefore, while working to complete a special project can be challenging and requires a unique skill set—one that is often separate and distinct from the skills needed to execute the project itself.

Like HR, project management is a profession. Although HR managers may not be members of the project management profession, we still must develop many of the unique skills associated with project management to successfully accomplish our objectives—which, again, will span all six functional areas of HR. Some of those skills will include the following:

▶ Clarifying goals

▶ Analyzing a project and developing a workable plan to complete it on time

▶ Managing the project according to the plan

▶ Ensuring that other work expectations are still met

Core Area of Knowledge: Diversity Concepts and Applications

Diversity is a workplace issue. Diversity is also a performance issue. Creating a workplace that recognizes and values diversity is essential for organizational health, growth, and (often) survival.

Diversity is sometimes bundled—and confused—with affirmative action or equal-employment opportunities. Although it falls on the same spectrum, diversity is *not* the same thing.

Diversity is in no way limited to the protected classes that are identified in EEO law—categories such as gender, age, religion, national origin, sexual orientation, color, veteran status, or disability status. Diversity also reaches out to recognize differences in communication styles, thought patterns, and a wide range of other factors that make each of us, as humans, unique.

EXAM ALERT

Be aware of the benefits that can accrue to an organization that embraces diversity, offers diversity training, and/or launches diversity initiatives. Also be well versed in the differences between equal-employment opportunity (EEO), affirmative action, and diversity. See Chapter 4, "Workforce Planning and Employment," for more information on EEO and affirmative action.

Core Area of Knowledge: Human Relations Concepts and Applications (For Example, Interpersonal and Organization Behavior)

Workplaces are composed of people, with all the unique attributes and foibles that humans possess. Although this may seem obvious to us today, it wasn't until the establishment of the Industrial Relations Association of America (later renamed the American Management Association) in the 1920s that any real legitimacy was granted to the study of workplaces as social—as well as economic—organizations.

This concept touches on all six functional areas and all HR disciplines. It relates directly to the topics of motivation, productivity, and a host of other issues, and will be addressed throughout this book.

Core Area of Knowledge: HR Ethics and Professional Standards

SHRM has developed and published standards for ethical behavior for the HR profession. The six dimensions of this code can be summarized as follows:

▶ *Professional Responsibility*—As HR professionals, we serve as more than just individual contributors to our organizations. Instead, we are representatives of and ambassadors for our profession. In that spirit, we must demonstrate personal and professional accountability for every decision we make and for every action we take. We must behave in a manner that consistently demonstrates personal and professional credibility and that creates organizational value.

▶ *Professional Development*—As HR professionals, we must commit ourselves—both formally and informally—to learning about and contributing to our profession's ever-expanding knowledge base. We must never allow ourselves to stagnate professionally.

▶ *Ethical Leadership*—As HR professionals, we must "walk the walk" of ethical leadership. We must always hold ourselves to the highest standards of ethical behavior and, through this, serve as role models of ethical behavior for current, emerging, and future leaders.

▶ *Fairness and Justice*—As HR professionals, we must promote fairness and ensure justice for all employees within the organizations in which we work. This commitment extends beyond adhering to specific legal mandates; rather, it encompasses cultivating workplaces that foster dignity, respect, diversity, and inclusion.

▶ *Conflicts of Interest*—As HR professionals, we must ensure that we avoid any and all situations where a real or perceived conflict of interest could exist. This includes any situation in which we have benefited—or in which it appears as though we could benefit—materially or financially from the positions we hold within our organizations.

> ▶ *Use of Information*—As HR professionals, we have an obligation to protect the proprietary organizational and personal information with which we are entrusted on a regular basis.

Core Area of Knowledge: Technology to Support HR Resource Information Systems (HRIS) to Support HR Activities (For Example, HRIS, Employee Self-Service, E-Learning, ATS)

An organization's human resource information system (HRIS) is both a repository of vast amounts of data and a tool for extracting, manipulating, and deriving information from that data. How that information will ultimately be used will be a function of the system itself, as well as of the individuals who are responsible for its initial implementation and ongoing maintenance.

Core Area of Knowledge: Selecting an HRIS

Selecting an HRIS is a critical business decision that will have long-term implications for the business—not just for the HR department. HR issues must reflect organizational business issues, so the HRIS must be designed to store, retrieve, summarize, and report information in a way that enables HR professionals to address the organization's needs.

As with any other business decision, the process of selecting an HRIS must start with conducting a needs assessment and analysis (the "A" in ADDIE). In the IT field, this step is also referred to as a *requirements assessment* or *requirement gathering*. An early step in that analysis will include identifying the functions that the HRIS will be expected to support, such as the following:

▶ Affirmative action reporting

▶ Applicant flow

▶ Benefits administration and enrollment

▶ Candidate database

▶ Compensation administration

▶ EEO reporting

▶ Payroll administration

▶ Skills database—employees

▶ Training programs administration

61

Core Area of Knowledge: Qualitative and Quantitative Methods and Tools for Analysis, Interpretation, and Decision-Making Purposes

In addition to identifying the ways in which your organization will use an HRIS (applications that should, ultimately, support its organizational objectives), other considerations need to be taken into account, as well. These should include, but are not necessarily limited to, questions such as:

- ▸ What are the system requirements?

- ▸ What limits are, or will be, in place within the system?

- ▸ What are the key data security concerns, and how must the system address those concerns?

- ▸ How much organizational growth do you anticipate?

- ▸ What financial resources can you commit to process of purchasing and implementing the system?

- ▸ What human and capital resources will be required to support implementation of the system?

- ▸ What financial, human, and capital resources will be required to support and maintain the system?

- ▸ How will cutover from the existing HRIS, if any, be handled?

- ▸ How will the new system interface with other existing systems, such as payroll?

- ▸ Is the system easily upgradeable?

- ▸ Is Internet-based employee self-service one of the organization's objectives?

Conducting a needs analysis is one step, and selecting an HRIS is another. A third key step is implementing the system. The most carefully selected and technologically advanced HRIS system can devolve into a nightmarish fiasco if the implementation phase of the project is underestimated or poorly executed.

Core Area of Knowledge: Qualitative and Quantitative Methods and Tools for Analysis, Interpretation, and Decision-Making Purposes (For Example, Metrics and Measurements, Cost/Benefit Analysis, Financial Statement Analysis)

As stated throughout the chapter, and as is true for our profession, HR decisions are business decisions. As such, they mandate a structured and deliberate businesslike analysis.

An early part of any analysis is identifying the problem that needs to be solved. This is not always as easy as it seems, because symptoms often disguise themselves as problems. From there, careful data collection and data analysis is undertaken, and conclusions are drawn.

Different types of analyses can be clustered into two categories:

- Quantitative Analysis
- Qualitative Analysis

Quantitative Analysis

Numeric, mathematical models are utilized in conducting quantitative analysis. Historical data is measured and scrutinized to extract objective and meaningful insights. Correlation and measures of central tendency are two types of quantitative analysis with which you will want to be familiar.

Correlation

Quantitative analysis involves measuring *correlation*. Through measurement and comparison, correlation mathematically determines whether a demonstrated relationship exists between two factors or entities. A positive correlation or negative correlation indicates that a relationship does exist. The *correlation coefficient* is a number between –1 and +1 that defines the strength of that relationship. The closer that coefficient is to zero, the weaker the relationship between the two factors.

EXAM ALERT

Understand and be able to articulate the difference between a positive correlation and a negative correlation. In addition, become familiar with scattergrams and be able to indicate whether a particular scattergram represents a positive correlation, a negative correlation, or no correlation.

Measures of Central Tendency

When it comes to quantitative analysis, it's important to look beyond—and even within—what we commonly think of as an average. Three measures of central tendency with which HR professionals need to be familiar are

- *Mean—Mean* most closely corresponds to what people usually imply when they use the word "average." The mean of a set of numbers is calculated as follows:

  The total of all the values (or numbers) in a set divided by the number of values that are in that set.

63

Core Area of Knowledge: Qualitative and Quantitative Methods and Tools for Analysis, Interpretation, and Decision-Making Purposes

EXAMPLE: For the set: 57, 64, 15, 37, 11, 99, 1, 1, and 19, the mean is calculated as follows:

Total of all values in the set: (57+64+15+37+11+99+1+1+19) = 304

Number of values in the set: 9

Mean: 304/9 = 33.78

▶ *Median*—The *median* is derived by putting a set of data in numeric order, from lowest to highest, and identifying the value that is in the middle.

EXAMPLE: For the set: 57, 64, 15, 37, 11, 99, 1, 1, and 19, the median is determined as follows:

Values in numeric order, lowest to highest:

1, 1, 11, 15, 19, 37, 57, 64, 99

Median (middle value): 19

▶ *Mode*—The *mode* is the value that appears most frequently in a set.

EXAMPLE: For the set: 57, 64, 15, 37, 11, 99, 1, 1, and 19, the mode is "1" because that is the value that appears most frequently.

▶ *Weighted Average*—Sometimes, not all factors or pieces of data that are being quantitatively analyzed are equally important. Weighted averages allow certain pieces of data to be multiplied by a particular factor to give them greater weight, or importance.

Qualitative Analysis

Qualitative analysis does not involve mathematical modeling or calculations. It is based more on judgments that are subjective in nature.

Two examples of qualitative analysis are the Delphi Technique and the nominal group technique, both of which are discussion in the section "Workforce Planning: What Will We Need to Get There?" in Chapter 4.

An Added Value of Analysis

There is a place in HR for both qualitative and quantitative analysis. Rely too heavily on qualitative analysis and you may be accused of not having facts to back up your assumptions. Rely exclusively on quantitative analysis and you may be undervaluing the knowledge and expertise of your seasoned colleagues (or, for that matter, your own). Both of these approaches, when used exclusively, can damage relationships with your clients and can also damage your professional credibility within the organization.

Each chapter in this book will identify ways in which the ability to conduct accurate and meaningful quantitative and qualitative analyses will strengthen your effectiveness as an HR professional. Again, this is representative of the ways in which HR has evolved into a true profession, and it supports the important reality that it's simply not enough to be a people person.

Core Area of Knowledge: Change Management Methods

Change is inevitable—for individuals, for organizations, and for society. Change is multifaceted, complex, and often unpredictable. Its fluid nature precludes the possibility of preparing for all possible contingencies. It impatiently demands our immediate attention and focus when it happens. Sometimes change occurs because of initiatives created within the organization, and sometimes it is foisted upon us. Change is universal and omnipresent. Change is here to stay.

There is no dimension of the six HR functional areas that can remain untouched by change, just as there is no area of the business that is immune from change. Although change cannot be prevented, it can be managed—and HR plays a key role in that process. This role will be more fully developed and explored in Chapter 5.

The Winds of Change Can Also Be the Wind Beneath Your Wings

Change is neither inherently good nor inherently bad. The way in which an organization handles change will, however, produce outcomes that *will* ultimately be viewed as positive or negative.

HR must seek out opportunities to play a proactive and integral role before, during, and after times of abundant change. Such an approach will require HR professionals to muster all the skills in their repertoire—particularly employee relations skills, analytical skills, and communication skills. The demands of such a response represent a valuable long-term investment: In addition to playing a significant role during the change that is currently evolving, HR professionals can also use this experience to bolster relationships throughout the organization. Demonstrate your ability to interact in a manner that is consultative, rather than directive. In short, times of change afford you the opportunity to make a choice: Will you function in a manner that is transactional? Or more strategic? Ideally, you will be able to navigate yourself to a carefully balanced combination of both. The choice is yours—so choose wisely, and consciously.

Core Area of Knowledge: Job Analysis and Job Description Methods

Like every other core area of knowledge, conducting a job analysis and creating job descriptions are functions that impact every dimension of the six functional areas of HR. Job analysis, for instance, generates job specifications, which relate directly to the skills, knowledge, and behavioral characteristics that are required for successful performance of the position. This contributes directly to determining the qualifications that must be assessed for each candidate during the recruiting process (see Chapter 4). Job analysis also provides information that will be used to determine appropriate compensation for each position and for each employee (see Chapter 6). On a different note, job analysis may also identify chemicals to which the employee will be exposed at work, which in turn triggers the need for Material Data Safety Sheets (MSDS), discussed in Chapter 8, "Risk Management." Similar links could be made to the three other functional areas of HR, as well.

Job Analysis

Job analysis is the process through which an inventory of data about a position is collected. The elements that compose each job in the organization are identified through this process. These elements often include

- Responsibilities, duties, and tasks performed by the position incumbent.

- How those responsibilities, duties, and tasks relate to each other and to other jobs within the organization. This includes how frequently each of those activities is performed, as well as how activities relate to each other in terms of importance.

Job analysis also identifies the KSAs required for successful performance of the position:

- *Knowledge*—What you need to know to perform in a position; the body of information with which the incumbent must be familiar with or fluent to successfully perform a position.

- *Skills*—The ability to perform certain tasks or functions that are required for successful performance of the position.

- *Abilities*—Personal characteristics or capabilities that are required by the incumbent to perform the job successfully.

Although someone within HR usually leads job analysis initiatives within HR, "leadership" must not become confused with "ownership." HR professionals perform job analysis on behalf of clients. The clients are the ones, however, who own the initiatives, and who must live with the results. HR must function in a consultative manner to ensure support and buy-in from our internal clients.

Job analysis is not about completing a form. It is also not just about the job description that will be produced as a byproduct of the job analysis. Rather, it is a building block as you continue to form relationships with your internal clients. It will either enhance or diminish how others within your organization perceive you.

> **CAUTION**
>
> There is a temptation to define a job according to the skills, abilities, or behavioral characteristics that the current—or former—incumbent brings to it. Job analysis must focus, however, on the *job, not on the individual* who holds, or held, that particular position. It must also not be unduly influenced by the current labor market—real or perceived.

How to Conduct Job Analysis

There are many ways to collect information that will be used in conducting a job analysis. Depending on what is appropriate in your organization, consider the following:

- Interviewing the incumbent, or the prior incumbent, if that person is available.

- Interviewing the person who supervises the position.

- ▶ Interviewing the supervisor's supervisor.

- ▶ Interviewing co-workers.

- ▶ Interviewing direct reports, if applicable.

- ▶ Interviewing clients or customers with whom the position interacts.

- ▶ Interviewing vendors with whom the position interacts.

- ▶ Observing the incumbent performing the position, if possible and appropriate.

- ▶ Reviewing work product.

- ▶ Reviewing any documentation, reports, and/or performance-related statistics or records generated by—or about—the position.

TIP

Take a 360 degree/multi-rater approach to the position. Consider collecting input from everyone with whom the position interacts.

Conducting Job Analysis Interviews

Interviews can be conducted in person, through written or emailed surveys, or by a combination of both. Either way, be sensitive to the amount of time you ask people to invest in this process. Work to ensure that this process remains as streamlined and efficient as possible, while still ensuring that you collect the information you need.

Interviews/questionnaires may vary in length and content, depending on the nature and amount of involvement and contact that the interviewee has with the position. Also be certain that you explain the purpose of the interview/questionnaires and the way in which participating in this process will ultimately benefit the interviewee.

Job Descriptions

One of the primary results generated by a job analysis is a *job description*. A job description is an inventory of important information gathered about the position during the job analysis process.

EXAM ALERT

It's important to understand the differences between job analysis, job descriptions, and job evaluation—as well as the relationships and connections that exist between them.

Different organizations structure their job descriptions differently. In large part, this is a function of the job evaluation system that will be used (see Chapter 6). Job descriptions, however, incorporate stylistic as well as substantive considerations. They reflect, to a degree, the culture of the organization.

How to Create a Job Description

However the job description is designed, certain elements should be included:

- ▶ Job title
- ▶ Date on which the description was completed
- ▶ Name of person preparing the description
- ▶ Department, unit, and/or division
- ▶ Supervisory reporting relationship(s)
- ▶ Direct reporting relationships, if applicable
- ▶ Essential functions
- ▶ Nonessential functions
- ▶ Working conditions and environment
- ▶ Physical requirements of the position
- ▶ Degree of financial accountability
- ▶ Qualifications required to perform the position

Though there is no one definitive, or master, list of what should be included in a job description, selecting and including appropriate elements (such as those listed above) in the job description ensures that the job description is accurate, thorough, and on target to serve (ultimately) as a valuable resource for other projects and initiatives.

Core Area of Knowledge: Employee Records Management (For Example, Electronic/Paper, Retention, Disposal)

With respect to record keeping, HR is responsible for maintaining much of the information and documentation required to ensure compliance with federal, state, and local laws. A few examples of some of these record-keeping requirements include, but are in no way limited to, tax information, applicant flow data, veteran status, and I9 reporting. As appropriate, we'll take a closer look at record-keeping requirements within the context of each functional area.

Maintaining documentation is, in a sense, a "Catch-22" for HR professionals. By definition, the actions associated with maintaining documentation are transactional. They are not strategic in nature. They are also driven, in large part, by compliance requirements. But if we don't perform this portion of our job well, it is unlikely that we will be given the opportunity to perform functions that are more strategic in nature. Why? One reason is fairly self-evident: If we cannot demonstrate the ability to successfully execute tasks of a more mundane and administrative nature, it is unlikely that we will be entrusted with initiatives that are more strategic or visible. The second reason can become painfully obvious: documentation, when mishandled, can lead to very real and tangible costs (human, as well as monetary) to the organization.

Documentation Strategies for HR Professionals

So what can you do to attain both of these objectives and ensure that they don't become mutually exclusive? Here are some ideas:

▶ Set up streamlined processes and procedures for handling routine and repetitive documentation requirements.

▶ Incorporate fail-safe mechanisms into those processes. Even in the best-designed systems, it's inevitable that things will go wrong. Make sure there is a way to identify and resolve insufficient and/or noncompliant documentation.

▶ Look for ways to use existing documentation more strategically. Ascertain how you can turn data into information, and how you can use that information as you work to earn, or maintain, a seat at the table.

Core Area of Knowledge: The Interrelationships Among HR Activities and Programs Across Functional Areas

The six functional areas of HR are clearly delineated for purposes of the PHR exam. In reality, however, these aren't very clear, and they aren't very delineated, either. The lines between them are blurred, as evidenced by these 23 core areas of knowledge. They overlap, entwine, and weave themselves into unique workplace tapestries, as do the six HR functional areas. This is part of what makes HR such an interesting and challenging profession, and part of what mandates our commitment to continuous professional development. For just when we think we have seen it all, we are presented with a new—and until that point unpredictable—set of circumstances.

Core Area of Knowledge: Types of Organizational Structures

HR professionals also need to be familiar with a variety of organizational structures (see Chapter 3, "Strategic Management," for a list of these structures).

Of those included in this list, three that warrant particular attention are functional, divisional, and matrix organizational structures.

Functional Organizational Structure

As the name implies, functional organizations are composed of departments, each of which is dedicated to a different function. This approach, the most common organizational structure, often consists of highly centralized departments, such as HR, operations, sales/marketing, accounting, and so on.

The functional organizational structure is generally hierarchical in nature—with each employee reporting to one, and only one, individual, as shown in Figure 2.4.

FIGURE 2.4 Functional organizational structure.

Divisional Organizational Structure

A more decentralized approach to organizational structure, divisional structures are segmented on the basis of some shared characteristic—for instance, geographic region, customer base, product line, and so on. Each division would encompass all the people and functions needed to attain its objectives (objectives pertaining to its designated geographic region, customer base, product line, and so on).

While still primarily hierarchical in nature, it is also possible for dotted-line reporting relationships to exist within a divisional organizational structure. By *dotted line*, we mean that while a straight-line reporting relationship exists to the division head, another, dotted-line relationship can also exist to traditional functional leaders (in the case of HR, for instance, this might mean a dotted-line reporting relationship to the VP of HR). An example of divisional organization structure is shown in Figure 2.5.

Matrix Organizational Structure

A matrix organizational structure is, in one sense, a combination of functional and divisional structures, as shown in Figure 2.6. It attempts to draw on the strengths of each, while minimizing the potential downside of "silos" that can emerge in a traditional hierarchical organization.

Unlike in a functional or divisional organizational structure, employees who work within a matrix structure may report to two managers, rather than to just one manager. Although each manager may be primarily accountable for different dimensions of the employee's work, neither is superior to the other; there are literally two chains of command.

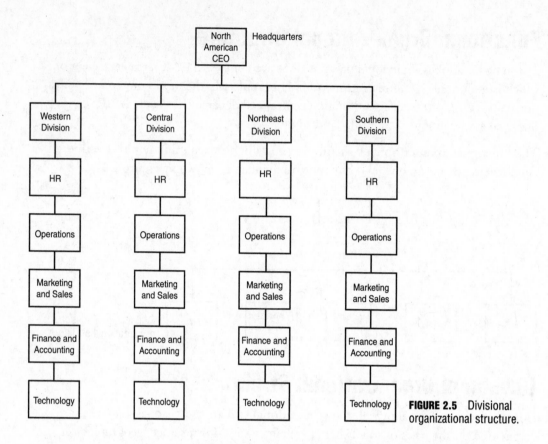

FIGURE 2.5 Divisional organizational structure.

While affording their own unique challenges, matrix organizational structures tend to be particularly effective in project-driven environments (for instance, consulting, construction, and so on).

Example of Matrix Organizational Structure

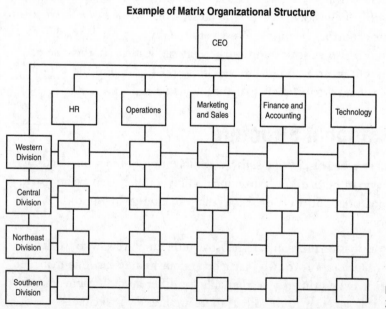

FIGURE 2.6 Matrix organizational structure.

EXAM ALERT

Familiarize yourself with the advantages and disadvantages of each of these—and other—types of organizational structures.

Core Area of Knowledge: Environmental Scanning Concepts and Applications

HRCI has reclassified *environmental scanning* into its newly expanded core areas of knowledge. Be sure to review this section in Chapter 3, as well as through your other study sources.

Core Area of Knowledge: Methods for Assessing Employee Attitudes, Opinions, and Satisfaction

As HR professionals, we have an obligation—as well as an opportunity—to keep our finger on the pulse of employees' attitudes and opinions. Though employee surveys are not new, what is perhaps somewhat new is the appreciation and recognition of exactly how important it is to monitor employees' perspectives and feelings. It's not enough for organizations, or for leaders within those organizations, to say that "people are our most important asset"; that statement must be brought to life through a commitment to the people who bring the organization to life—its employees. *Listening* to employees— whether through surveys, focus groups, and so on, is an important first step. (See Chapter 7, "Employee and Labor Relations," for more information on "Employee Involvement Strategies.")

NOTE

Although information about employee attitude and opinion surveys is included in Chapter 7, such surveys could potentially be used to collect information from employees pertaining to any functional area within HR.

Core Area of Knowledge: Basic Budgeting and Accounting Concepts

HRCI has reclassified basic budgeting and accounting concepts into its newly expanded core areas of knowledge. Be sure to review this section in Chapter 3, as well as through your other study sources.

Core Area of Knowledge: Risk Management Techniques

Proactively identifying and making choices relative to the potential consequences of various levels of risk is a practice known as *risk management*. Although it's a key focus—and the title—of Chapter 8, let's begin to explore this topic here. Specifically, let's establish a foundation from which we can develop an appreciation of the unique role that HR professionals can play with respect to risk management.

Organizations face potential exposure in many employment-related areas—allegations can be made relative to sexual harassment, wrongful discharge, unlawful discrimination, or negligent hiring and retention, to name just a few.

Legal actions stemming from employment-related issues cost organizations untold dollars in attorneys' fees, court fees, settlements, and judgments. These monetary costs do not even begin to recognize other costs that are far more difficult to calculate—costs resulting from diminished employee morale, decreased productivity, allocation (or misallocation) of internal resources, and perhaps even the organizations' reputation as a labor market competitor, vendor, or community member.

HR professionals are uniquely positioned to anticipate, identify, and intervene before problems become "cases." Look for areas of potential exposure. In our roles, we see more, hear more, and know more about situations that have the potential to escalate. Deescalation of potentially litigious situations constitutes one of the most valuable contributions that HR professionals can make to their organizations.

> **TIP**
>
> When it comes to litigation, even if you win, you lose.

Look for areas of potential exposure. Use all your skills and knowledge to identify them. Then, build on the collaborative relationships you have developed with managers to work through these challenges.

> **NOTE**
>
> Although there may be situations in which it's a good idea to "just say no," advisory discussions with managers usually don't fall into that category. Employment-related decisions are business decisions. This holds true even for those decisions that could potentially have legal ramifications. Depending on the culture of your organization, decisions are frequently "owned" by the individuals who make them—so you may want to think twice before declaring yourself (or HR) the owner. In addition, saying no may undermine your effectiveness, and even your credibility, if your no is ultimately overruled. Treat this situation as you would any other business decision, and utilize your best consultative skills.

Chapter Summary

This chapter provided an overview of each of the 23 core areas of knowledge identified by HRCI as required by HR professionals, as listed in the "Key Terms List" that follows this summary.

Perhaps even more important, it begins to provide you with the tools you will need to look for ways to integrate and link these core areas of knowledge to each other, and to each functional area, as you proceed through the rest of your test preparation.

In addition to addressing concepts and defining terms that you'll need to know for the PHR test, this chapter helped you practice another key skill that will be required for success on the PHR exam—the ability to think, look, and analyze across functional and disciplinary lines.

Key Terms List

- Needs assessment and analysis

- Third-party contract negotiation and management, including development of requests for proposals (RFPs)

- Communication skills and strategies (for example, presentation, collaboration, influencing, diplomacy, sensitivity)

- Documentation requirements to meet federal and state requirements

- Adult learning processes

- Motivation concepts and applications

- Training methods (for example, computer based, classroom, on the job)

- Leadership concepts and applications

- Project management concepts and applications

- Diversity concepts and applications

- Human relations concepts and applications (for example, interpersonal and organizational behavior)

- HR ethics and professional standards

- Technology to support HR activities (for example, HRIS, employee self-service, e-learning, ATS)

- Qualitative and quantitative methods and tools for analysis, interpretation, and decision-making purposes (for example, metrics and measurements, cost/benefit analysis, financial statement analysis)

- Change management methods

- ▶ Job analysis and job description methods

- ▶ Employee records management (for example, electronic/paper, retention, disposal)

- ▶ The interrelationships among HR activities and programs across functional areas

- ▶ Types of organizational structures (for example, matrix, hierarchy)

- ▶ Environmental scanning concepts and applications

- ▶ Methods for assessing employee attitudes, opinions, and satisfaction (for example, opinion surveys, attitude surveys, focus groups/panels)

- ▶ Basic budgeting and accounting concepts

- ▶ Risk management techniques

Apply Your Knowledge

Exercises

The following exercises present some scenarios you might encounter in your duties as an HR professional. Give each of these a try and later in the chapter you will find the correct answer and its explanation.

1. A competitor has recently hired three of your company's employees. An email is sent to all remaining employees reminding them of their obligation to protect proprietary information to which they are exposed during the performance of their jobs, and that disciplinary action up to and including termination could result as a result of violating this policy. Shortly thereafter, a fourth employee interviews with a different competitor. The employee knows that he or she could present him or herself better by discussing current research and development projects on which he is working. The employee decides, however, to discuss only projects that are unrelated to current (and proprietary) research and development.

   This represents an example of:

   A. Negative reinforcement

   B. Positive reinforcement

   C. Punishment

   D. Extinction

2. An organization conducts an employee survey and finds that many employees are bored with their jobs, unhappy with their pay, and feel as though they don't get enough vacation time. If the organization's primary goal is to motivate employees, what is the first step that should be taken?

- A. Conduct a survey to determine pay rates and vacation allotments among labor market competitors.

- B. Identify ways in which employees' jobs can be enriched, and implement them.

- C. Give everyone an across-the-board raise, and let employees know that you will be conducting a salary survey to see if further adjustments are needed.

- D. Conduct another employee survey to see if the results of this survey are consistent with the results of the first survey.

3. A manager with whom you have not previously worked comes to you for help with implementing two different solutions she has come up with to fix a turnover problem in her department. This manager is highly regarded—and highly visible—in the organization. You are eager to perform well on this project because you are confident it will help you strengthen your relationship with her. You are also certain that the manager will tell her peers about her experience with you, which makes it particularly critical that you handle yourself well. Your first response should be to

- A. Communicate your commitment to implementing the manager's solutions.

- B. Offer alternative solutions based on experience you have had with similar situations.

- C. Ask questions to obtain more information about the problems the manager is experiencing.

- D. Ask questions to obtain information that will help you implement the manager's solution more effectively.

4. You've been asked to make a recommendation relative to a new HRIS for your organization, and you need to collect information to assist you in formulating that recommendation. During the HRIS needs assessment, it would be important for you to ask all the following questions except

- A. To what degree are current employees familiar with the new system?

- B. What financial resources can you commit to purchasing and implementing the system?

- C. What human and capital resources will be required to support implementation of the system?

- D. What financial, human, and capital resources will be required to support and maintain the system?

Review Questions

1. Would transactional leaders be best described as coaches, directors, enforcers, or captains? Why?

2. What are some important considerations to keep in mind about confidentiality?

3. How do affinity groups relate to Maslow's hierarchy of needs?

4. According to Fred Fiedler's Contingency theory, what three factors contribute to determining a situation's level of favorableness for a particular leadership style?

5. What sources of information should be considered when conducting a job analysis?

Exam Questions

1. Which of the following is not a key element of the ADDIE model?

   A. Needs Assessment/Analysis

   B. Evaluation

   C. Data collection

   D. Design

2. Which of the following functions is least likely to be outsourced?

   A. Learning and development

   B. Recruiting

   C. Employee relations

   D. Retirement benefits

3. Which of the following does Maslow identify as each person's most fundamental need?

   A. Basic physical needs

   B. Esteem

   C. Recognition

   D. A living wage

4. Which of the following statements about RFPs is true?

   A. RFPs should be written in a broad and open-ended manner.

   B. RFPs should not initially request information relative to the vendor's estimated costs.

   C. Only government contractors or subcontractors need to use RFPs.

   D. RFPs can be used relative to a variety of organizational problems.

5. Which of the following statements about motivation-hygiene theory is accurate?

   A. Victor Vroom developed it.

   B. Motivation factors refer to non-work related factors such as pay, benefits, and relationships with co-workers.

   C. Unacceptable motivation factors won't cause an employee to be unhappy at work, but unacceptable hygiene factors will.

   D. Acceptable or positive motivation factors won't cause an employee to be happy at work, but acceptable or positive hygiene factors will.

6. Blake-Mouton's situational leadership theory

   A. Measures and assesses concern for the needs of direct reports and concern for the accomplishment of tasks.

   B. Identifies "impoverished managers" as ones who have not been given the opportunity to engage in training designed to enhance essential supervisory skills.

   C. Uses a 10-point scale along each axis.

   D. Builds on Hersey and Blanchard's model.

7. In the selling quadrant of Hersey and Blanchard's situational leadership model, employees

   A. Have mastered the technical aspects of a particular task and can perform it independently.

   B. Have shifted their focus from learning a specific task to instructing and/or mentoring others in the organization on how to perform that function.

   C. Have developed basic skills related to the task and can benefit from additional background and information about the task.

   D. Need to focus on developing self-confidence in their abilities—selling themselves, in a sense, on their own ability to perform a particular task.

8. Which of the following is not one of the six key elements of the HR Code of Ethics?

   A. Professional Development

   B. Commitment to Workplace Diversity

   C. Fairness and Justice

   D. Use of Information

9. Trait theories of leadership

   A. Support the belief that leaders are born, not made.

   B. Support the belief that individuals can be trained to be effective leaders.

   C. Support the belief that different situations require different leadership styles.

   D. Support the belief that relationship dimensions of leadership style are more important than task dimensions of leadership style.

10. The transformational leadership style

   A. Places greater emphasis on relationships than on tasks.

   B. Places greater emphasis on tasks than on relationships.

   C. Is characterized by the possibility of rewards, and by the threat of punishment.

   D. Encourages a coaching style of leadership.

Answers to Exercises

1. Answer A is the best answer. This employee is trying to avoid negative consequences that could result from revealing proprietary information, and thus makes a choice that is consistent with avoiding these negative consequences. The other answers refer to the three other possible consequences identified through Skinner's operant-conditioning theory.

2. Answer A is the best answer. According to Herzberg's Motivation-Hygiene theory, motivation factors will have a positive impact on an employee's motivation level *if, and only if*, hygiene factors are acceptable. In this situation, it appears as though neither motivation nor hygiene factors are fully acceptable. It's important to deal first with addressing hygiene factors to ensure that concerns relating to motivation factors—when addressed and resolved—will have a positive impact. Answer B is not the best answer; it jumps straight to motivation factors without dealing first with hygiene factors. Answer C is not the best answer; it takes a "ready, fire, aim" approach—although employees appear to be unhappy with their pay, that does not necessarily mean that pay levels are inappropriate, that they need to be increased, or that 5% is the right number to use. Answer D is not the best answer; although it will probably be necessary to collect more information (perhaps through follow-up meetings), it would not be effective to ask employees to give you the same information in the same way.

3. Answer C is the best answer. HR adds value to this process by asking questions that help to ascertain the underlying problems—and that help distinguish problems from symptoms. Answer A is not the best answer; although a manager may be convinced of the true nature of a problem, and/or of what the solution should be, the manager's assessment is not necessarily correct, so you shouldn't unthinkingly

commit to implementing it. Answer B is not the best answer for a related reason; you don't really know what the problem is, so it is not possible to suggest a solution. Additionally, if you use this approach, you are dismissing the manager's opinions and experience—and you risk damaging your relationship with the manager. Answer D is not the best answer; it assumes that the manager's assessment of the problem is correct and that the proposed solution is the best possible intervention.

4. Answer A is the best answer. The degree to which current employees are familiar with the new system is relatively unimportant during the needs assessment process, as long as communication is effective, training is provided, and support is available. Answers B, C, and D are not the best answers; each represents important questions to ask during the needs assessment process, and before selecting an HRIS.

Answers to Review Questions

1. Of these four choices, the term "enforcer" would best characterize transactional leaders. Transactional leaders use a system built on "the carrot and the stick" approach—and mainly the stick. Coaching doesn't reflect this approach, and instead is more characteristic of the transformational leadership style. The image of a captain might more closely reflect the role a leader plays in the selling quadrant of Hersey and Blanchard's situational leadership model. A director could imply a wider variety of leadership approaches under transactional as well as transformational styles.

2. Confidential information should be communicated in a manner consistent with the law, and on a strict need-to-know basis. Using that standard, it's important to remember that not all HR professionals within an organization should be granted access to all confidential work-related information. Communication that might occur outside the physical workplace (or in a less formal setting) does not negate the fact that the information you are communicating is confidential.

3. Organizational affinity groups bring together people who share common interests, goals, or backgrounds. As such, they primarily address the need that Maslow identified as "belonging and love." It is possible, however, that members of affinity groups might also derive benefits that impact their esteem (self, or as derived from others) or that enable them to self-actualize.

4. Fred Fiedler identified three factors of favorableness. He asserted that the relative strength or weakness of these factors would impact a leader's effectiveness. The three factors are

   ▶ *Leader-members relations*—This factor looks at how strong, and how significant, relationships between the leader and the team members are. It considers the degree to which those relationships make the leader more, or less, effective and influential.

   ▶ *Task structure*—This factor ascertains the degree to which the work that the team members perform is structured.

> ▸ *Position power*—This factor looks at the degree to which the leader's position holds, or can exert, power or influence. It also looks at the degree to which the leader can ensure accountability for team members' performance and the degree to which the leader has the authority to delegate.

5. Depending on what is appropriate in your organization, consider using the following sources of information when conducting a job analysis:

   > ▸ The incumbent, or the prior incumbent, if that person is available

   > ▸ The person who supervises the position incumbent

   > ▸ The supervisor's supervisor

   > ▸ Co-workers

   > ▸ Direct reports, if applicable

   > ▸ Clients or customers with whom the position's incumbent interacts

   > ▸ Vendors with whom the position's incumbent interacts

   > ▸ Work product

   > ▸ Documentation, reports, and/or performance-related statistics or records generated by—or about—the position

Answers to Exam Questions

1. **Answer C is the best answer.** The five key elements of ADDIE are Needs Assessment/Analysis, Design, Development, Implementation, and Evaluation. Although data collection would be a part of needs assessment and analysis, it does not constitute one of the five key elements (and, therefore, doesn't stand for either of the "Ds" in the acronym ADDIE).

2. **Answer C is the best answer.** Currently within HR, transactional functions are more likely to be outsourced than nontransactional functions. In part, this is because nontransactional (including tactical and strategic) functions provide HR professionals with the greatest opportunities to add value to the organization. Of these four choices, employee relations (when performed well) is the least transactional function. This information also highlights the need for HR professionals to recognize opportunities for performing seemingly transactional functions in a more strategic manner. Among the choices offered here, recruiting is the function that—while most likely to be performed in a transactional manner—offers the most untapped opportunity for strategic contribution.

3. **Answer A is the best answer.** Maslow identifies basic physical needs as a person's most fundamental, and foundational, need. Answer B is not the best answer; esteem is the second highest need on Maslow's hierarchy. Esteem encompasses both self and other components, recognition (answer C) falling into the category of other. Answer D is not the best answer; although it could be argued that a living wage falls under the category of basic physical needs, it is not—by definition—the

same as basic physical needs. In part, this is because the concept of a living wage (as we discuss and understand it today) did not exist when Maslow originally developed his hierarchy. Additionally, earning a living wage does not ensure that *all* of the dimensions of a person's basic physical needs will be met.

4. **Answer D is the best answer.** RFPs can be used relative to almost any function, task, or project that the organization is considering outsourcing. Answer A is not the best answer; writing RFPs in a highly structured manner increases the likelihood that the proposed solutions are responsive to the organization's specific needs. A structured approach also facilitates the process of comparing RFPs that are submitted from multiple vendors. Answer B is not the best answer; seeking information about pricing ensures that a company will not waste time by entertaining solutions that are cost-prohibitive. Answer C is not the best answer; RFPs should be used by most—if not all—organizations that are considering any kind of outsourcing; the process is unrelated to whether the organization is a government contractor or subcontractor.

5. **Answer C is the best answer.** According to this theory, unacceptable motivation factors won't cause an employee to be unhappy at work, but unacceptable hygiene factors will. Answer A is not the best answer; Vroom developed the expectancy theory, and Herzberg developed the motivation-hygiene theory. Answer B is not the best response; motivation factors refer to work-related factors (such as the nature of the work, and the challenge inherent to the work), while hygiene factors refer to the non-work–related factors identified in answer B. Answer D is not the best response; acceptable or positive motivation factors will cause an employee to be happy at work, but acceptable hygiene factors won't.

6. **Answer D is the best answer.** Blake-Mouton's situational leadership theory does build on Hersey and Blanchard's situational leadership model. Answer A is not the best answer; Blake-Mouton's situational leadership theory measures and assesses concern for people and concern for task/production, not the needs of direct reports and concern for the accomplishment of tasks. Answer B is not the best answer; Blake-Mouton's situational leadership theory identifies "impoverished managers" as those who delegate responsibility, then demonstrate no real concern for either people or task/production (rather than as ones who have not been given the opportunity to engage in training designed to enhance essential supervisory skills). Answer C is not the best answer; this model uses a nine-point scale along each axis.

7. **Answer C is the best answer.** An employee who performs a particular task in the selling quadrant of Hersey and Blanchard's situational leadership model has developed basic skills relating to that task and can still benefit from additional background and information about the task. Answer A is not the best answer; an employee who falls into the selling quadrant with respect to one particular task has not fully mastered the technical aspects of that particular task and cannot yet function in a fully independent manner. Answer B is not the best answer; none of the four quadrants in this model addresses the function of employees instructing or mentoring others. Answer D is not the best answer; an employee who performs a

particular task in this quadrant has not yet developed his or her skills or knowledge relative to a particular skill to the point where he or she should focus effort on developing others; he or she needs to continue working on practicing and honing their own skill level.

8. **Answer B is the best answer.** Although workplace diversity is one of the core areas of knowledge for HR professionals, it is not one of the six specific dimensions identified in the HR Code of Ethics. It is, however, one expression of the ethical mandate for fairness and justice.

9. **Answer A is the best answer.** Trait theories of leadership are predicated on the belief that leaders are born, not made. Answer B is not the best answer; the concept of training people to be leaders was introduced as part of behavior theories, introduced in the 1940s. Answer C is not the best answer; the idea that different situations require different leadership styles emerged under situational leadership theories. Answer D is not the best answer; none of the leadership theories specifically asserts that relationship dimensions of leadership style are universally more important than task dimensions of leadership style.

10. **Answer D is the best answer.** The transformational leadership style places greater emphasis on relationships than on tasks. Answer A is not the best answer; transformational leaders concern themselves with relationship as well as task dimensions—neither is emphasized to the exclusion of the other. Answer B is not the best answer; the transactional leadership style is characterized by the possibility of rewards and the threat of punishment, whereas the transformational leadership style focuses on coaching rather than enforcement (or threats of enforcement).

Suggested Readings and Resources

Society for Human Resource Management (SHRM). www.shrm.org, 2007.

Human Resource Planning Society. www.hrps.org, 2007.

Workforce Management. www.worforce.com, 2007.

Bohlander, George W. and Snell, Scott. *Managing Human Resources, 13th Edition*. Winfield, KS: Southwestern College Pub, 2003.

Pell, Arthur R. *The Complete Idiot's Guide to Human Resource Management*. New York: Alpha, 2001.

Smith, Shawn A., and Rebecca A. Mazin. *HR Answer Book, The: An Indispensable Guide for Managers and Human Resources Professionals*. New York: AMACOM/American Management Association, 2004.

Strategic Management

Study Strategies

Although the PHR exam is multiple choice, try writing and answering your own essay-based questions. Specifically, create a few open-ended questions that require a response of at least a full paragraph, and try writing your initial responses without looking back at your study materials. The process of actually writing down those answers will reinforce what you already know and will highlight what you need to study more. It will also likely help you as you work to recall this same information when you answer related multiple-choice questions on the actual PHR exam. Remember, if you can answer an essay-based question that incorporates content knowledge, the chances are good that you'll be able to answer a less-complex multiple-choice question that covers the same material.

Introduction

There is a familiar saying that goes something like this: "Some people make things happen, some people watch things happen, and some people wonder what happened." In our profession, we are fortunate to have the opportunity to choose which of those paths we will follow. Although this choice holds true for every functional area within HR (and for every chapter of this book), it is particularly true of strategic management.

In each of the following sections, we will look a bit more closely at some key underlying concepts and how we can leverage them to support our efforts to function more strategically in our roles as HR professionals. Some of the areas will include a step-by-step approach to the concepts being presented. Other sections will identify, define, and/or offer a brief explanation about items that HR professionals need to know but that are beyond the scope of this chapter.

EXAM ALERT

Perhaps more than for any of the six functional areas, PHR candidates are strongly urged to supplement the material presented in this chapter with other sources. Although the wisdom of seeking ancillary materials holds true for all of the functional areas, doing so for strategic management is particularly important for a number of reasons:

▶ The concepts covered in this area are prone to a variety of interpretations, which may differ slightly from each other.

▶ A number of different models relate to these topics. Familiarizing yourself with as many of them as possible will enable you to be better prepared for the test—*even if those specific models aren't referenced on the test.*

▶ A lot of information is covered in the strategic management functional area, which means that there's a lot of information that could be covered on the PHR exam. Although the functional area of strategic management represents a relatively small percentage of the PHR exam (12%), it covers a significant volume of information and spans a wide array of theories, disciplines, and practices. The SPHR exam, in fact, devotes 29% of its questions to this functional area—*more than twice the percentage found on the PHR exam.*

With such a large amount of territory to cover, it's impossible to predict what will be on the exam—so don't try. Give yourself plenty of time, curl up with a good periodical or two, and then prepare to learn a lot. This approach will increase the likelihood that you will perform better on the PHR exam. Perhaps even more important, it will help you function more effectively in your role as an HR professional.

The bottom line is to prepare as thoroughly as you can. Don't limit yourself to what is in the pages of this (or any other single) resource.

The Evolving Role of HR

As explored in Chapter 1, "The HR Profession and the PHR Exam," HR has been on a long and sometimes challenging journey through which it has redefined itself as a profession and redefined itself with respect to its role in the organization. Before we focus more explicitly on HR's current role and impact, let's briefly review the earlier legs of this evolutionary journey.

A Brief Historical Scan of HR

Much has changed about our profession in the past 50+ years, during which an ongoing discussion around professionalism and certification has continued to evolve. Perhaps the most outwardly recognizable sign of the journey in which we have been engaging is how we refer to our profession.

Originally, it was known as "Industrial Relations" (the "I" and the "R" in Cornell's "ILR" come from "industrial relations"; the "L" comes from "labor"). Sometime back in the 1950s, it started to be called "Personnel." Today, for the most part, we know it as "Human Resources." Tomorrow, who knows what it will be called; in some organizations, a "Chief People Officer" or a "VP of People" already leads our function.

One thing is certain: Our name hasn't changed just to keep up with the times. Rather, these changes reflect the transformation of our role from a "job" or a "support function" to a bona fide profession—from administrative support roles to strategic organizational partners.

Of course, just as the name of our department has not changed in all organizations, so, too, our role has not evolved at an even pace in all organizations, either. Let's take a closer look at what this means and at what its true impact is on how we carry out our roles.

HR as It Was, and HR as It Is (or Can Be)

As mentioned previously, the way in which HR professionals carry out their functions has changed and evolved over the years. Table 3.1 highlights some indicators of this shift:

TABLE 3.1 HR: Then and Now

Then	Now
Reactive	Proactive
Gatekeeper (or gate closer)	Facilitator
Policy enforcer	Policy strategy consultant
Authoritarian	Consultative
Focused on HR and its goals	Focused on the organization and its mission
Employee advocate (from managers' perspective)	"Truth advocate" ® (Mary Rudder, Rx Management)
Management advocate (from employees' perspective)	

The distinctions between then and now, however, aren't always quite as absolute and clear as this chart may indicate.

- ▶ Many organizations fall somewhere along the spectrum between then and now in terms of how their HR departments function in an overall sense.

- ▶ Other organizations might more closely resemble then with respect to some areas of responsibility and more closely resemble now with respect to others.

- ▶ So, too, each of us might function in some ways closer to the then end of the spectrum and function in other ways closer to the now end of the spectrum.

This can be true on an organizational, functional, or even on an individual level.

Larger, overarching questions can and should emerge through contemplation of where we fall (individually and/or collectively) along the then and now spectrum. These questions include the following:

▶ How does the organization perceive HR?

▶ How does HR perceive itself?

We can begin to explore and address these questions by developing a broader, more holistic understanding of the myriad required roles of HR within the organization. The HR Impact Model provides one road map within which to begin to develop this understanding.

The HR Impact Model

The HR Impact Model in Figure 3.1, developed by this author and Dr. Robert K. Prescott, SPHR, of Rollins College Crummer Graduate School of Business, uses four categories to explore the functional responsibilities of HR professionals:

FIGURE 3.1   HR Impact Model.
© 2005, Gibson and Prescott.

Traditionally, many HR professionals operate only within the policies and programs categories. For many of us, these categories represent our anchors—the zones within which we are most comfortable, and the ones within which many of our organizations traditionally (and sometimes currently) expected us to function.

We must now, however, migrate away from the familiar comfort offered by those two sectors we have inhabited for so long. This impact model illustrates and explains the other roles required of today's—and tomorrow's—HR professionals.

Policies and Procedures

Policies and procedures represent the dimension of the HR impact model with which many of us, as HR professionals, are most familiar. It is, in essence, our comfort zone. And although we must be prepared to expand beyond it, we also must ensure that we master our performance within it.

- ▶ *Organizational role*—Creating and implementing HR policies and procedures. There is no doubt that this is an important role for the HR function. However, although perceived as policy experts, HR professionals who focus only on policies and procedures tend not to be integrally involved in their organization's strategic planning or change efforts.

- ▶ *Organizational impact*—Influence the creation, appropriate interpretation, and implementation of organizational policy; ensure fair treatment of employees; and provide a decision-making framework.

In the next section, you learn about the importance—and potential impact—of programs and procedures.

Programs and Processes

Traditionally, HR professionals have been regarded as "people experts" who can help build and maintain effective work relationships, motivate performance, and develop employees. Those focused on programs and processes tend to work in functional-oriented teams (for example, employee relations, compensation, or training) to support the effective execution of those processes.

- ▶ *Organizational role*—Overseeing programs and processes to attract, motivate, develop, and retain employees.

- ▶ *Organizational impact*—Promote employee satisfaction and enhance performance. Provide effective process guidelines for the organization to follow in implementing people-management practices.

Next, let's take a look at the consultative dimensions of the HR impact model.

Consultation

In this client-oriented role, HR professionals help define the overall organizational strategy, structure, and culture as well as enhance the effectiveness of individuals within the organization. HR professionals who assume these roles within the organization improve their working relationships with their constituents and increase their credibility throughout the organization.

- ▶ *Organizational role*—Responding to or identifying the needs of management and working in partnership to enhance the management team's effectiveness, both individually and collectively.

- ▶ *Organizational impact*—Support, coach, develop, and challenge clients to take appropriate action on identified problems, issues, challenges, initiatives, or programs.

Last, let's take a closer look at the tremendous impact that HR can wield as true catalysts for change.

Catalyst

In this role, the HR professional stays abreast of market demographics, business needs, and employee attitudes and values as well as of state-of-the-art approaches to human resource management. The HR professional points out emerging HR issues and trends both within the company and in the external market and identifies their impact on the organization and how management might best respond to them.

In this context, it is also important to note that HR professionals do not work within any one dimension in isolation. It is the unique, customized mix of services for a given organization that yields the greatest impact. HR professionals have to assess their proper mix requirement for their respective organization.

- ▶ *Organizational role*—Focusing on the long-term, strategic needs of the organization to identify relevant trends and ensure that management is prepared to act appropriately in guiding the organization for the long term.

- ▶ *Organizational impact*—Help position the organization for the future, especially by designing a working environment and organizational culture that meet the changing needs, preferences, and demographics of current and future employees and by helping the organization address changes in its business and operating environments.

Next up, the administrative, strategic, and operational/tactical dimensions of HR.

Dimensions of HR—Three Legs of a Stool

With the HR Impact Model as one backdrop, another way to consider our evolving roles as HR professionals is to think of our function as a three-legged stool, where administrative, strategic, and operational/tactical elements are the legs.

Leg #1: Administrative

These are the transactions—the things that need to be done. Over the years, some of the transactions we used to perform have gone away. More often, however, those functions manifest themselves dramatically differently today than they did yesterday, or are being handled in different (and often more streamlined and/or more technologically sophisticated) ways (such as self-serve kiosks, intranets, HRIS applications, outsourcing, and so on).

Leg #2: Strategic

The difference between the administrative functions in HR and the strategic functions in HR is like the difference between being a person who designs automobiles and being a passenger. Both are important and, ultimately, each needs the other. Were there no automobile designers, the current generation of cars would become the future generation of cars, leaving certain safety and efficiency needs unmet (not to mention ever-changing stylistic trends). Were there no passengers, there would be little need for cars in the first place, and certainly no need for anyone to invest time and energy in looking toward the future.

Strategic HR takes a long-term, future-focused approach to the ways in which it will partner with the organization to attain its organizational mission. Strategic HR looks at business and organizational issues, rather than HR issues —because all meaningful HR issues are, in fact, business issues. Rather than endeavoring to maintain the status quo, strategic HR cultivates, nurtures, and embraces change. It is dynamic, effective, consultative, and ever-evolving—just like our profession itself.

Leg #3: Operational/Tactical

Somewhere in between the administrative functions that must be performed and the inventive and creative life force that is part of strategic management lies the operational—or tactical—dimension of the HR function.

One definition of the word "tactical" offers a militaristic reference, which might help to explain its particular relevance to the HR profession. *The American Heritage Dictionary of the English Language* defines "tactical" as follows:

▶ (a) Of, relating to, used in, or involving military or naval operations that are smaller, closer to base, and of less long-term significance than strategic operations.

▶ (b) Carried out in support of military or naval operations: *tactical bombing*.

This definition aligns well with the application of this term in the HR profession. The operational, tactical, or day-to-day performance and execution of the HR role can be accomplished in many ways—some of which place us more closely toward the administrative end of the spectrum, whereas others demonstrate more vividly how, and whether, the overarching strategic objectives of HR (and, therefore, of the organization) are being brought to life. In the automotive metaphor used previously, the tactical area might be depicted by the role of the driver. Passengers wouldn't get anywhere without drivers— even if a car had the most evolved designs and finest appointments imaginable. Also, the performance and safety features that were woven into the design will come to life only in the hands and feet of the driver—the person who plays a more active, involved, and immediately impactful role than any passenger.

The HR Professional as Internal Consultant

Throughout all the sectors of the HR impact model, and all three legs of the stool, HR professionals must make choices relative to how they will portray and conduct themselves within the organization. Within any of those sectors and any of those legs, one of the most critical choices that must be made is the degree to which an HR professional will function in a *truly consultative* manner.

So what is consulting? According to Peter Block, in the first edition of his must-have book *Flawless Consulting*:

> "You are consulting any time you are trying to change or improve a situation but have no direct control over the implementation. If you have direct control you are managing, not consulting. The consultant's lack of direct control and authority is what makes our task difficult and, at times, drives us crazy."

The HR profession is difficult and may even feel a little bit crazy at moments, as well as challenging, meaningful, and highly impactful. Through the role of internal consultants, each HR professional can magnify and leverage his or her contributions at the transformational, tactical, and even the transactional level. One way to do this is by applying a consistent, well-thought-out consulting process. The seven stages of internal consulting represent one such model.

> **EXAM ALERT**
>
> There are many sound consulting models and myriad ways to interpret and apply those models. Use this section as a starting point from which to review some of these other models before taking the PHR exam—and before choosing how to bring *your* consultative role to life within your organization.

The Seven Stages of Internal Consulting

The Seven Stages of the Internal Consulting model (Prescott, 2005) include Exploring the Situation; Gaining Agreement to the Project Plan; Gathering Data, Analyzing, and Identifying Findings; Developing Recommendations; Presenting the Findings and Recommendations; Implementing; and Reviewing, Transitioning, and Evaluating the Project .

Stage 1. Exploring the Situation

Step 1: Seek to gain a better understanding of the situation. Meet with the client to discuss the situation and to determine whether the project should go forward.

Stage 2. Gaining Agreement to the Project Plan

Step 1: Develop a draft project plan that defines the project and its goals. The plan should also include roles and responsibilities, information and resources needed, tasks required, data collection methods, measurements, and a project timeline.

Step 2: Meet with the client to gain agreement to move forward with the project based on the project plan. This plan is a dynamic document and it should be adjusted, as needed and appropriate, throughout the project.

Stage 3. Gathering Data, Analyzing, and Identifying Findings

Step 1: Collect, aggregate, and analyze information related to the project goals.

Stage 4. Developing Recommendations

Step 1: Formulate realistic and measurable recommendations based on the findings and goals of the project.

Stage 5. Presenting the Findings and Recommendations

Step 1: Present the findings and recommendations to the client. Gain the client's agreement to implement the recommendations, and explore ways to approach the implementation process.

Stage 6. Implementing

Step 1: Work collaboratively with the client to plan and implement the recommendations. Project management, communication, and monitoring are key components of this stage.

Stage 7. Reviewing, Transitioning, and Evaluating the Project

Step 1: Review the project and transition it to the client. Assess (and self-assess) what was accomplished, what worked well, and what may be done differently in the future.

Understanding Your Clients' Management Functions

To be an effective strategic business partner, it's also critical to have an understanding of some of the foundational underpinnings of management.

Principles of Management

Perhaps an unlikely guru, Henri Fayol was hired at the age of 19 to work as an engineer for a French mining company. He worked there for many years, ultimately serving as its managing director from 1888 to 1918. Based on the experience he gained at the mining company, Fayol, known as the Father of Modern Management, identified five functions of a manager, which he referred to as the following:

- Prevoyance
- To organize
- To command
- To coordinate
- To control

In modern parlance, these five functions are often referred to as *planning*, *organizing*, *coordinating*, *directing*, and *controlling*. Let's take a closer look at each of these so as to better understand organizational structure and the context within which our clients carry out their roles.

Planning

Planning lays the groundwork for how managers will work toward accomplishing the organization's goals. Through planning, managers decide what needs to get done, when it needs to get done, who will do it, how it will get done, and where it will be done. In the absence of planning, the organization—and the people in it—will lack direction, and perhaps even just coast along. In other words, to quote the immortal words of the great philosopher (and baseball Hall of Famer) Yogi Berra, "If you don't know where you are going, you will end up somewhere else."

Organizing

Organizing speaks to the ways in which the manager obtains and arranges the resources that he or she needs to implement the plans (the output of the planning function). Those resources could include people, facilities, materials, and so on. During the organizing function, the manager must also designate reporting relationships within the organization. In short, the linkages between people, places, and things must be established.

Coordinating

Through the coordinating function, the manager brings together all the resources that he or she has organized to accomplish the stated plan. The manager must also ensure that the pieces fit.

Directing

During the directing phase, the "rubber hits the road." The actual work is performed—goods are produced or services are provided. In addition to ensuring that things go smoothly from a technical perspective, in the directing phase, the manager must also focus attention on leading and motivating the human resources who are actually performing the work.

Controlling

Controlling assumes more of an oversight role, and in some senses an evaluative role (in an ongoing, iterative sense). In this phase, the manager ascertains the degree to which the planning he or she engaged in actually produced the desired results. If the manager determines that there is a gap between the targeted goals and the actual results, the manager must then focus on ways to bridge that gap.

Fayol subsequently broke these five functions further down into 14 principles of management:

1. Division of work

2. Authority and responsibility

3. Discipline

4. Unity of command

5. Unity of direction

6. Subordination of individual interests to general interests

7. Remuneration of personnel

8. Centralization

9. Scalar chain

10. Order

11. Equity

12. Stability of tenure of personnel

13. Initiative

14. Esprit de corps (union is strength)

Project Management—A Valuable Tool

More and more, work is project based. For many of us, and for many of our clients, project management is a critical skill needed to perform our own work and to support the work that our clients are performing.

A common difficulty of project-based work is the inherent challenge of balancing the day-to-day workload with efforts to complete high-priority special projects. Projects are frequently delegated with nothing more than a deadline—and with no additional resources for the individuals to whom those projects are delegated. Understandably, the person to whom the project has been delegated will seek additional resources—perhaps human and perhaps capital. Usually, however, such resources are often already being utilized to carry out the day-to-day responsibilities of the operation. As such, in addition to slowing down productivity with respect to the day-to-day ongoing workload, it is also possible that the project may not be accomplished within its stated time frame because of the impact of limited and/or insufficient resources.

Enter project management.

Project Management: Definition and Processes

Project management is interesting and somewhat unique in that it is both a means to an end as well as an end (and a profession) unto itself. (Sounds a bit like human resources, doesn't it?)

The Project Management Institute (PMI) defines project management as "the application of knowledge, skills, tools, and techniques to a broad range of activities in order to meet the requirements of a particular project." Project managers seek to accomplish their objectives by gaining control over five factors: *time*, *cost*, *quality*, *scope*, and *risk*. To do this, those who undertake a project must clarify the needs and scope of the project, work out a plan for meeting those needs, and manage the project according to that plan. These steps, however, are sometimes easier to talk about than they are to execute.

PMI goes on to identify five distinct (yet overlapping) processes within project management:

▶ *Initiation Processes*—Initiation processes are those processes that secure approval and/or authorization to undertake the project.

▶ *Planning Processes*—Through planning processes, objectives are established, as are the best alternatives that will support the attainment of those objectives.

▶ *Executing Processes*—Everything comes together through the executing processes—the scope, the objectives, and the deliverables all fall into place. To attain this level of successful execution, the right resources need to be in the right place at the right time.

▶ *Controlling Processes*—Controlling processes include managing the scope of the project and making sure the project stays in line with the original objectives. A significant degree of follow-up is required to carry out controlling processes.

▶ *Closing Processes*—Closing processes involve "sign-off" processes and mark the end of the project. As part of closing processes, stakeholders must determine whether, and to what degree, the project met its obligations.

These processes, although separate, are interrelated. The output from one set of processes contributes significantly to the inputs of subsequent processes. Although the processes are not wholly finite and discrete, they are more or less sequential, following the order presented here. Perhaps the best way to describe these processes is that they are interdependent, yet separate and somewhat sequential, though not linear.

> **EXAM ALERT**
>
> Be familiar with important project-planning terms and concepts, including the following:
> - ▶ Project manager
> - ▶ Project sponsor
> - ▶ Project charter
> - ▶ Project team
> - ▶ Project plan
> - ▶ Project schedule
> - ▶ Work breakdown structure (WBS)
> - ▶ Gantt chart
> - ▶ Program evaluation and review technique (PERT) charts

HR's Role in Change Management

It has been said that the only constant is change. That is particularly—and at times poignantly—evident in the workplace.

Organizationally, change is all around us and can manifest itself in many ways: downsizings, redeployments, introductions of new processes, reassignment among staff, mergers and acquisitions—the list goes on and on. Without a doubt, HR plays a major role with respect to managing that change positively and productively (in those organizations where HR has truly earned a "seat at the table," HR will ideally have an important role with respect to initiating, driving, and shaping change, as well).

HR's role, in this regard, is inextricably linked to the attainment of organizational objectives and the furtherance of the organization's mission. During times of change, HR is called on to lead people-management processes. HR professionals—individually and collectively within the organization—must align their people-management efforts with the strategic goals of the organization. HR must also be prepared to measure the degree of success that has been attained (see the section "Measuring HR Effectiveness" later in this chapter).

To meet the ever-accelerating pace of change, HR professionals must understand change as well as the environments that cause change. This understanding will be particularly important when HR is called on to adapt the organization's people-management practices to evolving workplace-based realities while maintaining and improving on current levels of organizational performance. As such, successfully designing, aligning, and implementing adaptive people-management practices is an essential component of being a strategic HR partner.

> **EXAM ALERT**
>
> Although these areas extend beyond the scope of this book, they don't extend beyond the scope of your potential responsibilities as an HR professional. Let this book serve as a starting point for your PHR exam prep, as well as for your continued growth and development as an HR professional.

Change theory and process is addressed more thoroughly in Chapter 5, "Human Resource Development."

Outsourcing

Outsourcing—otherwise known as the use of third-party contractors—is a growing trend that has directly impacted, and that will continue to directly impact, HR's role. That impact has two distinct dimensions: First, HR is an area that has, in many organizations, experienced partial or significant outsourcing of its components. Second, HR facilitates—and sometimes oversees or orchestrates—outsourcing that takes place within other parts of the organization.

Outsourcing Defined

Let's take a step back, however, and take a closer look at the concept of outsourcing. Outsourcing can be described as the reassignment of responsibilities, functions, or jobs that had been performed *within the organization* to resources that are based *outside the organization*.

> **NOTE**
>
> *Offshoring* is a specific type of outsourcing that seeks vendors that are way outside the organization—specifically, such third-party providers are located overseas.

How to Outsource: An Outline

Outsourcing is a complex process that can have a significant impact on the organization, on the people who work within the organization, on the attainment of organizational goals, and even on the organization's reputation in the marketplace. The decision to outsource should not be made lightly, and the three-step process outlined here is in no way intended to oversimplify the complexity inherent in outsourcing. Conversely, like so many other components of this book, this three-step process is intended to provide you with a starting point—an overarching framework on which you can continue to develop and expand.

Question #1: Is outsourcing appropriate?

In addressing this question, a number of factors need to be taken into consideration, a few of which are the following:

- ▶ Internal costs versus the costs associated with outsourcing

- ▶ Internal abilities and talents versus abilities and talents available through outsourcing

- ▶ The importance and complexity of the function that is being considered for outsourcing

- ▶ The degree of variability in the volume of transactions for the function that is being considered for outsourcing

Question #2: If outsourcing is appropriate, how will we select a vendor?

There are many factors to take into consideration, and questions to ask, when choosing a vendor. Here are a few that are particularly important to consider:

- ▶ *Technological strength*—Do the vendor's technological resources and capabilities meet or exceed your project requirements? If so, by how much? Are there appropriate backup systems and redundancies in place?

- ▶ *Scale*—How much growth do you anticipate? Is the vendor prepared to meet your growth expectations and requirements?

- ▶ *Experience*—Does the vendor have related experience? If so, how closely does that experience resemble the current project in terms of scope, complexity, and the like? Last, how *recent* is that experience?

- ▶ *Costs*—What are the up-front costs that would be incurred with this vendor? Up-front costs could include training, program design, IT setup, and many others. Additionally, what hidden costs might you incur, perhaps as a function of attrition, telecommunications charges, and the like?

▶ *Quality*—What is the vendor's commitment to quality? How does this commitment manifest itself, and how can it be measured? On average, how much time does it take for the vendor to resolve concerns that originate from customers and/or clients? What are current client/customer satisfaction rates with those resolutions?

▶ *Communications*—What is the nature and frequency of the communication that the organization can expect to engage in with the vendor? If appropriate, will someone (an individual with appropriate authority) be available 24/7 throughout the life of the project?

▶ *Success Record*—What is the vendor's track record with *recent* clients? To find out, talk with recent clients *of your choosing*. Ask them what went well in their experiences with the vendor and what didn't. Ask about lessons that the vendor learned and how well (and quickly) the vendor was able to incorporate and apply those lessons. Also ask about communication—as the relationship went on, did the nature and frequency of communication deviate from what the vendor had initially committed to at the beginning of the relationship (or project)?

Question #3: After we select a vendor, how will we manage the vendor and our relationship with the vendor?

There is sometimes a mistaken belief that relationships with vendors do not need to be managed as closely as one might manage a relationship with an employee. In truth, however, the relationship with a vendor *does* have to be managed closely—just in a different way.

▶ If possible, start out with a pilot program and see how it unfolds before devoting all necessary resources to the endeavor.

▶ Set clear and reasonable expectations (SMART performance management objectives—specific, measurable, action-oriented, realistic, and timebound—work well with vendors, as well. See Chapter 5).

▶ Observe, monitor, measure, and evaluate the vendor's actual performance.

▶ Give the vendor constructive and positive feedback (BASIC—behavioral, as soon as possible, specific, interactive, and consistent—see Chapter 5).

▶ As appropriate and possible, coach the vendor.

▶ As appropriate and possible, incorporate upside potential and downside risk into your negotiated agreements with vendors.

EXAM ALERT

Other outsourcing-related terms you should familiarize yourself with before taking the PHR exam are the following:

▶ Request for proposal (RFP) (see Chapter 2, "HR: A Body of Underlying Knowledge and Principles")

▶ Third-party vendor

HR Technology Concerns/Opportunities

Technology touches indirectly (or at times directly) all dimensions of the human resource function and profession. The speed with which this transformational impact has taken place has increased exponentially and will likely continue to do so into the foreseeable future.

Many organizations, small as well as large, use a human resource information system (HRIS) to better manage HR-related data. An HRIS is an integrated computer-based system that collects, processes, analyzes, stores, maintains, and retrieves information relating to all dimensions of the HR function.

EXAM ALERT

Before taking the PHR exam, familiarize yourself with the various ways in which an HRIS can support each of the various functional areas of HR.

HRISes have redefined, in many ways, how HR professionals perform their jobs. When utilized to its fullest extent, an HRIS can—and should—help HR professionals move from the then end of the spectrum to the now end of the spectrum—see this chapter's section titled "HR As It Was, and HR As It Is (or Can Be)." This is possible because an HRIS can help to free us from some of HR's required, albeit mundane, administrative responsibilities, and thus can afford us time that we may be able to redeploy toward addressing more strategic issues.

It is not enough, however, for an HRIS to make our lives easier. Instead, we must ensure that the HRIS we choose will truly address business needs, not just HR-specific concerns. By this, for example, we mean that an HRIS must be a tool that can be used to support initiatives that contribute to attainment of overall organizational objectives. For instance, an HRIS should provide us with information that will ultimately facilitate and support the following:

- ▶ Increasing overall employee productivity

- ▶ Identifying and rewarding top performers

- ▶ Investing in ongoing employee development

- ▶ Placing the right people in the right jobs at the right times

- ▶ Ensuring readiness to identify and appropriately respond to changing business strategies

In addition to this, however, HR professionals who are acting in a truly strategic manner must also look for ways to leverage an HRIS to address business issues (strategic or transformational), not just to expedite paperwork or enhance processes (transactional or tactical). Here, too, there is a choice to be made: whether to *look for opportunities* to function as true strategic organizational partners.

Changes on the Horizon—How They May Impact HR

In many ways, HR trends are best identified by looking first at business/organizational, industry, and societal trends. As a microcosm of the outside world, organizations are directly impacted by what happens in the external environment. It logically follows that because HR exists to support the attainment of organizational objectives, it is impossible—or at least extremely ill-advised—for us to isolate ourselves—from the organization, or from the world.

NOTE

Keep your finger on the pulse of the world around you and the world at large. Workplaces can change almost instantaneously, and trends can develop almost as quickly.

One devastatingly illustrative example of this can be found in the aftermath of Hurricane Katrina. In 2004, many of us gathered for the national SHRM conference at the New Orleans conference center to learn, to network, to groove to the music of the Doobie Brothers, and to be moved and inspired by the now stilled—but never silenced—voice of Christopher Reeve. Slightly more than one year later, that same building in which we congregated was literally overflowing with individuals displaced from their jobs, their homes, their loved ones, and nearly every other recognizable dimension of their lives. Years later, many are still experiencing this displacement and disconnection. Hurricane Katrina and its aftermath thrust many concerns to the forefront—issues that may not have been on everyone's radar screen just a few weeks earlier. As HR professionals, we cannot forget the lessons of Katrina; rather, we must use it as a reminder to vigilantly prepare for the unexpected, the unimagined, and the hard-hitting impact of events that take place in our ever-shrinking world.

Here are just a few of the trends that all HR professionals should monitor and revisit on a regular basis:

- ▶ Globalization

- ▶ Technology

- ▶ Safety and security

- ▶ Terrorism

- ▶ Aging workforce

- ▶ Polygenerational workplaces

- ▶ Work/life balance

- ▶ Changing technology

- ▶ Contingent workforce

- ▶ Climate changes

- ▶ Political shifts (global, national, and local)

- ▶ Remote teams/workplaces (telecommuting)

Strategic Planning

Strategic planning is a step-by-step process through which organizations engage in two types of activities. Specifically, the organization

1. Identifies where it wants to be and what it wants to accomplish long-term (often 3–5 years).

2. Begins to map out how its vision and mission for those years will be attained.

In an oversimplified sense, strategic planning is the process of looking into the future, painting a picture of where we want to be and what we want to achieve in that future, and ascertaining how we will get there. It is a type of extreme proactivity rather than reactivity, of planning for the future rather than simply responding to it as it unfolds.

There are a number of compelling reasons for organizations to engage in a strategic planning process, just a few of which are

- By methodically looking toward the future, the organization creates an opportunity to proactively shape and influence its own future.

- The organization will develop a clearer awareness of how it is positioned externally and how it measures up internally.

- It creates (or reaffirms) the overall vision, mission, and values of the organization and refocuses attention on how to bring these potentially ambiguous tenets to life in a meaningful, tangible way.

- It engages individuals throughout the organization in a meaningful and impactful initiative.

Strategic Planning—A Four-Phase Process

Many theorists describe and define the strategic planning process in different ways, and as containing different steps and components. The following is one way of looking at the strategic planning process.

Phase 1: Establish a Foundation for the Strategy

To be effective, the strategic planning process must be grounded in the organization's mission, vision, and values.

- *Vision*—An organization's vision is a brief yet comprehensive descriptive and inspirational statement that articulates where the organization wants to be and what it wants to become in the future. The vision should resonate in the hearts, minds, and day-to-day endeavors of the organization's employees. It should give those employees an awareness that they have a meaningful opportunity to be part of something bigger than themselves. It must motivate them to aspire to the legacy that the vision can create and that it ultimately can leave behind.

▶ *Mission*—An organization's mission statement articulates, in essence, its reason for being. It may speak to the nature of the organization's business or purpose, its customers, and sometimes even its employees and its role in the community. A mission statement should be broad (but not overly generalized), brief, clear, unambiguous, and designed to last for the long haul. The goals of an organization should cascade from its mission, so the mission is therefore far bigger than any goal—and thus must be able to withstand the test of time.

▶ *Values*—Values are the beliefs on which the organization has been built. They are the tenets that shape and guide strategic, tactical, and day-to-day decision making (the three legs of that stool again). These same tenets impact the behaviors that employees within the organization demonstrate as they carry out their responsibilities. Organizations identify values, in part, as a way to clearly guide those decisions and behaviors. Values are often represented in terms and principles such as integrity, honesty, respect, and so on.

Phase 2: Develop the Strategic Plan

Formulating a strategy on the basis of deliberately crafted statements that articulate the mission, vision, and values of the organization is critical, but it's only the first step. The next step is to actually develop the strategic plan.

There are several key components to the development phase of the strategic plan.

SWOT Analysis (Strengths, Weaknesses, Opportunities, and Threats)

A SWOT analysis is conducted to ascertain the strengths and weaknesses that are inherent to an organization, as well as the opportunities and threats that it faces from external forces. Though it sounds relatively simple and straightforward, the process of conducting a SWOT analysis can become challenging, in part because it is often difficult for organizations—as it is for people—to see themselves objectively.

When examining strengths and weaknesses, it is necessary for analysis to be directed inward. This clear and objective assessment would ascertain the resources of the organization, including the following:

▶ Human

▶ Financial

▶ Technological

▶ Capital

▶ Brand image

Opportunities and threats, conversely, look outward at factors such as competition, economic trends, customer needs and wants, and legislative or regulatory activity. This process, known as environmental scanning, is explored more thoroughly in "Environmental Scanning—An External Perspective," later in this chapter.

EXAM ALERT

Familiarize yourself with SWOT—what it stands for and what it consists of. Being able to conduct an effective SWOT analysis is one particularly critical way in which we can serve as strategic organizational partners, and thus it is likely to appear on the PHR exam.

Generate Strategic Objectives

After the SWOT analysis is completed, the outputs of that analysis can and should be scrutinized and, to the degree possible, addressed. After that process has been completed—or at least begun—it's time to begin generating ideas that will eventually grow, develop, and be cultivated into overarching organizational initiatives.

These overarching organizational initiatives must then cascade into specific strategies that enable each department, division, or other organizational unit to contribute directly to the attainment of the organization's overall objectives and mission. For this to happen, a top-down/bottom-up approach similar to that described in the performance management process must be implemented throughout the organization (see Chapter 5). To oversimplify the process, like any pyramidal structure—and even like Maslow's hierarchy of needs (see Chapter 2)—goals at the lower, more functional levels of the organization must ultimately support the more overarching objectives of the organization. Keep this process building and you'll be well on your way to bringing the vision, mission, and values of the organization to life in a highly tangible and visible manner.

Phase 3: Implement the Strategic Plan

Similar to Fayol's directing stage, the implementation phase is, again, where "the rubber meets the road." Strategies become tactics and tactics become operationalized. Management functions—from planning through controlling—are used to make the strategies a part of the day-to-day fabric and functioning of the organization. Because, at this level, we have also reached the point at which individuals will have a very real, albeit somewhat indirect, impact on whether the organization's objectives are attained, performance management principles become critical, as well (see Chapter 5).

Three factors that are critical to successfully implementing any strategic plan are commitment, credibility, and communication.

Commitment

It is absolutely critical to secure the support and commitment of leaders at all levels of the organization—particularly the upper levels—before even entertaining the idea of creating (let alone implementing) a strategic plan. This commitment can and should encompass everything from seeing the strategic process through to its conclusion, to striving to achieve the goals and implementing the changes that are generated through this process.

In short, strategic plans that sit on a shelf are useless. Talking the talk is not enough. Walking the walk is mandatory. Without commitment, a strategic plan is not only useless—it might even do more harm than good, in that it may serve to heighten awareness of needs, as well as of potential, that will subsequently remain unaddressed.

Credibility

Credibility is created and sustained through the following:

- Representative participation from all levels of the organization
- A commitment to follow through on every step of the process (rather than short cutting the process)
- Clear, complete, and appropriate documentation of the process.

Phase 4: Evaluate the Plan, Process, and Performance

Evaluating how well a strategic plan was envisioned, designed, and implemented is an involved process, as is any evaluative process. In Chapter 5, we provide a more in-depth discussion of evaluative processes (in a more general sense) as explored through ADDIE. Revisit the "E" in ADDIE, and also seek other sources and ideas for evaluating a plan, the process for developing that plan, and the overall performance against that plan.

Perhaps most important, be prepared to incorporate changes, insights, and revisions. Holding on to a flawed design or an ineffective implementation process is like "spending good money after bad." In an organization, the currency in question may be your own reputation and credibility, so be prepared to flex.

REVIEW BREAK

Strategic planning helps the organization to look toward the future and to begin to shape how it will position itself for that future.

One element of strategic planning that was mentioned in the previous section was external scanning. Let's take a closer look at that particular component.

Environmental Scanning—An External Perspective

Environmental scanning is the process through which organizations maintain awareness of the opportunities and threats presented by the surroundings—both macro and micro—within which they operate.

For information that is obtained through an environmental scan to be truly valuable, leaders within the organization must use the data that is collected to modify, as appropriate, organizational objectives or strategies. The *ability* to demonstrate organizational agility in response to environmental information is essential; the *willingness* to act on that information is perhaps even more important.

Some organizations conduct environmental scans on an ad hoc basis, often in response to crises or other unexpected events. Other organizations plan to conduct environmental scans on a more regular basis. Still other organizations choose to conduct scanning on a continuous basis—always collecting, processing, and analyzing data. Although there is no one right approach, in today's highly turbulent (and sometimes even volatile) business and organizational environments, it may be prudent to consider conducting environmental scanning more frequently, rather than less frequently.

External Trends—Things to Keep an Eye On

Organizations need to monitor trends of a wide and varying nature, including the following:

- Economic trends
- Competitive trends
- Political trends
- Global trends
- Business trends
- Industry trends
- Employment trends
- Technological trends
- Demographic trends

EXAM ALERT

In addition to being able to identify the areas that warrant external scanning, be prepared to recognize and/or identify specific sources through which you could obtain information relative to each of these categories of trends.

Organizations: Structure, Design, and Partnership

As we've stated numerous times, to be effective in our profession, we have to be savvy businesspeople. It's not enough to be skilled in our craft as HR professionals. Although our profession is our craft, we also need to be prepared to knowledgeably practice that craft within our organizations and our industries. To do so, one of the many things we need to understand is how organizations are structured.

As we begin to take a look at how organizations are functionally organized, let's go back and revisit Henri Fayol. Fayol identified six functional groups within organizations and suggested that all organizational activities can fit into one of those six functional areas:

- Technical activities

- Commercial activities: sales and marketing

- Financial activities

- Security activities

- Accounting activities

- Managerial activities

Despite the ongoing validity of Fayol's theories, a few things have changed since Fayol's time. One is the role of human resources in the organization, which at first glance is not well reflected in these six areas. Another is information technology, nonexistent in the early twentieth century when Fayol set forth his ideas. Something that can be said to hold true for both of these areas is that while each constitutes its own independent function, each also supports and reinforces the efforts of and impacts the success of every other area within the organization. This is important in and of itself because it reinforces the idea that these areas—although illustrative—are not necessarily as clearly dichotomized as they were when Fayol originally set forth his ideas.

What HR Professionals Need to Know About the Organizations They Support

As HR professionals, there is specific business-related information we need to know about the various structural elements of organizations. Although any of these items could conceivably be on the PHR exam, discussing them goes beyond the scope of this book. What we will do, then, is to set forth the concepts that are important for you to know and encourage you (in the strongest possible terms) to seek out, familiarize yourself with, learn, and (when appropriate) memorize facts, information, and formulas relating to the following:

- Technical activities/operations:

    - Capacity

    - Standards

    - Scheduling

    - Inventory

    - Control

- Commercial activities—sales and marketing

    - The 4 Ps:

        - Product

        - Place

        - Price

- ▶ Promotion
- ▶ Customer-centric marketing
▶ Finance and accounting activities
  ▶ Budgeting:
    - ▶ Incremental budgeting
    - ▶ Formula budgeting
    - ▶ Zero-based budgeting
    - ▶ Activity based budgeting
    - ▶ Assets
    - ▶ Liability
    - ▶ Equity
    - ▶ Accounts payable
    - ▶ Accounts receivable
    - ▶ Balance sheet
    - ▶ Income statement
    - ▶ Gross profit margin
    - ▶ Statement of cash flows
  ▶ Financial ratios:
    - ▶ Business activity ratios
    - ▶ Profitability ratios
    - ▶ Debt ratios
    - ▶ Liquidity
    - ▶ Current ratio
    - ▶ Acid test

Balanced Scorecard

In the early 1990s, a new approach to strategic management was developed by Dr. Robert Kaplan and Dr. David Norton. Called the "balanced scorecard," this new approach sought increased clarity and specificity by offering a clear and unequivocal prescription of what companies should measure to appropriately balance financial measures of success with (rather than against) *nonfinancial* measures of success.

In addition to being a *measurement* system, the balanced scorecard is also a *management* system. It transforms strategic planning into a hands-on, reality-based, functionally practical tool. It is important to note, however, that in creating and describing the balanced scorecard, Kaplan and Norton do not denounce the value of traditional financial measures. They do, however, operationalize their premise that financial measures by themselves are not enough. Other perspectives must be incorporated to obtain a more accurate assessment of organizational performance.

The balanced scorecard embodies the following four perspectives:

▶ *Learning and Growth Perspective*—This perspective looks at employee training, as well as attitudes toward individual and corporate growth. It emphasizes the criticality of the knowledge worker, of people as the organization's primary resource, and of the need for employees to continually grow and learn so as to be able to perform in a manner that will truly support the attainment of organizational goals.

▶ *Business Process Perspective*—This perspective scrutinizes key internal business processes so as to measure and ascertain how well those processes generate business results (such as products and services) that meet customer expectations. The business process perspective ascertains performance levels through specific measures that are unique to each particular organization.

▶ *The Customer Perspective*—This perspective focuses on the criticality of customer focus and customer satisfaction—for *every* business and organization. Dissatisfied customers will eventually look to others who will meet their needs and expectations (often without ever sharing their reasons for doing so), which, if the numbers are large enough, can ultimately lead to organizational decline.

▶ *The Financial Perspective*—The financial perspective is the most traditional of Kaplan's and Norton's four perspectives. As previously indicated, financial considerations cannot be overlooked—they simply have to be supplemented with other meaningful organizational measures.

Organizational Life Cycle

It's particularly important for HR professionals to be familiar with organizational life cycles because each phase will warrant different interventions. These phases or stages roughly approximate the phases of life experienced by humans—thereby further bolstering the perspective of the organization as a living, breathing entity.

The four stages of the lifecycle—though referred to slightly differently by different experts—are as follows:

▶ *Stage 1: Introduction (or "birth")*—Excitement and energy are high and cash flow may be low. Struggling start-ups often find themselves searching for solid footing, financially as well operationally. The core group of highly talented employees may focus fixedly on the founder as a source of direction, wisdom, and inspiration.

In the introduction phase, employees may find themselves paid above market rates as a reflection of the founder's desire to lure them onboard. Alternatively—and somewhat conversely—if money is in short supply, employees in the introduction phase may earn less cash compensation and have those diminished earnings offset by other noncash rewards (equity, intrinsic rewards, and so on).

Depending on the organization, HR may or may not have a presence in this phase of the organizational life cycle.

▶ *Stage 2: Development (or growth)*—The organization grows in so many ways during the development phase—market share, facilities, equipment, revenues, and the number of employees are all likely to expand, to varying degrees. Along with that growth, the organization is likely to experience some growing pains.

Though it may be a challenging process for some organizations—and one that might be met with resistance—it is important that policies and procedures are formalized as a way of fostering equity, compliance, and consistency.

▶ *Stage 3: Maturity*—The growing pains have passed, and the culture is well established. In fact, it's important to ensure that certain elements of the culture do not become a bit *too* well established. If this were to happen, an entitlement mentality could begin to emerge relative to pay, benefits, performance standards/expectations and the like. The organizational structure could evolve in a somewhat rigid manner, and resistance to change initiatives could be high.

As is the case with us humans, organizations must resist the onset of inertia during these years of maturity lest they begin to atrophy. In close partnership with senior leadership, HR must play a key role in ensuring that this doesn't happen.

▶ *Stage 4: Decline*—If that inertia does set in, and if the organization or its employees begin to atrophy, decline is likely not far behind. There are many examples of the demise of long-standing organizations—retailers, in particular—anchors in local and national communities that just weren't able to keep up with the changing times. This can happen for any number of reasons, such as salaries that are beyond what the organization can truly afford to pay, inflexible management, disengaged workers—the list goes on and on. In the wake of such decline, downsizing is likely to occur, either in pockets or across the organization as a whole.

Organizational Structure

Organizational structure refers to the various ways in which organizations can be designed to attain maximum levels of effectiveness and efficiency.

EXAM ALERT

As you prepare for the PHR exam, familiarize yourself with terms and concepts relating to organizational structure, including the following:

▶ Formalization, or formal authority
▶ Departmentalization ("departmentation")
▶ Functional structure
▶ Division structure
▶ Matrix structure
▶ Chain of command
▶ Span of control
▶ Centralization
▶ Decentralization
▶ Simple structure organization model
▶ Bureaucratic organization model
▶ Virtual organization model
▶ Boundaryless organization model
▶ Mechanistic organizations
▶ Organic organizations
▶ Concentrated structures

In addition to representing information that is likely to show up somewhere on the PHR exam, this list also reflects information that you need to know and understand to be a more effective HR professional.

Measuring HR Effectiveness

HR's effectiveness can no longer be measured according to nonspecific, nonquantifiable, "soft" assessments. Instead, HR must be able to unequivocally demonstrate the effectiveness with which it is executing its various roles and the degree to which it is meeting the needs of its clients.

This discussion leads us to a critical—and foundational—distinction between effectiveness and efficiency. *Effectiveness* is the degree to which carefully established (and, in our case, strategically aligned) goals are met. *Efficiency*, however, is a ratio of outputs to inputs. Another way of putting it is that efficiency is "doing things right," and effectiveness is "doing the right things."

Within this context, it's quite possible that HR professionals can be effective without being efficient, or that they can be efficient without being effective. Holding ourselves accountable to well-chosen, mission-driven HR metrics can help to ensure that we will achieve efficiency as well as effectiveness.

There are a variety of HR measurement tools with which HR professionals need to be familiar.

HR Audits

The HR audit is the primary tool that many HR departments use in an effort to assess their own effectiveness and efficiency. Whether conducted in-house or by an outside consultant, HR audits serve a number of purposes and produce a variety of results. Ultimately, however, the overall purpose is to ascertain how well the HR department—through all of its various functional areas—has aligned itself with the organization's strategic objectives (effectiveness), and how well it is contributing to the attainment of those objectives (efficiency).

More specifically, HR audits will scrutinize and draw conclusions relative to

- ▶ The degree to which the organization complies with legal requirements and appropriately operationalizes its risk management philosophy with respect to potential legal exposure.

- ▶ The degree to which HR services are user friendly.

- ▶ Grievances—their causes, and their impact.

- ▶ The degree to which the organization complies with I-9 and other documentation requirements.

- ▶ The degree to which success has been defined for each position, and to which corresponding core competencies have been identified and defined for each position, and for the organization as a whole.

- ▶ The degree to which recruiting, selection, and retention processes reflect the organization's core competencies.

- ▶ The degree to which the organization achieves the ways it has chosen to position itself in the marketplace with respect to compensation and benefits (lead, lag, or match).

- ▶ The usefulness, appropriateness, and effectiveness of the employee handbook.

- ▶ The degree to which existing OD initiatives, including training programs, meet the company's current and emerging human capital needs.

- ▶ The degree to which the organization's performance management system reflects, reinforces, cascades from, and contributes to attaining the organization's mission.

- ▶ The degree to which the organization's safety program complies with federal, state, and local guidelines, and the degree to which it supports the company's objectives.

- ▶ The degree to which the organization's policies, practices, and procedures reflect the organization's overarching risk-management philosophies.

Other HR Measurement Techniques

A variety of other measurement techniques exist with which HR professionals need to be familiar.

▶ Return on investment (ROI)

▶ Cost-benefit analysis

▶ Break-even analysis

EXAM ALERT

Be familiar with how these techniques can be used to generate meaningful HR measurement tools, standards, and metrics.

Research

Often, ascertaining the effectiveness and efficiency of HR practices is best accomplished through research. Research, in simple and decidedly unacademic terms, refers to finding answers to questions. In practice, research is a bit more involved.

Research can be either primary or secondary. *Primary research* involves collecting data firsthand, from the original source from which it emanates. *Secondary research*, conversely, involves collecting information second-hand—meaning not directly from the original source of the data. Secondary research references and assimilates data that has already been collected by others, and thus allows those secondary researchers to "stand on the shoulders" of those who already conducted the primary research.

One type of primary research with which HR professionals need to be familiar is the scientific method. The scientific method is a systematic approach of testing hypotheses and using the information that is subsequently gathered through the testing of those hypotheses to strengthen the degree to which HR can support the overall objectives of the organization.

The five steps in the scientific method are as follows:

1. Question, and observe. Formulate a question that addresses the problem you want to study and to solve.

2. Develop a hypothesis. A hypothesis is an educated guess about the outcomes that you think the research will produce.

3. Design a method. This is the step where you'll outline the specific steps that you'll take while conducting the experiment (your research).

4. Collect data, which are the unexamined results of your research.

5. Analyze your data and reach a conclusion. State why you think the experiment (your research) turned out the way it did and ascertain whether the results supported your initial hypothesis.

Ethical Considerations for HR Professionals

All too frequently, headlines broadcast the latest local and national corporate scandals. Whether it's cover-ups, money laundering, insider trading, outright theft, corrupt practices, or conflicts of interest, there is no shortage of highly public and highly publicized documentation of ethical lapses within this nation's corporations.

This phenomenon, however, is not limited to the private sector. The words just look a little different when we talk about ethical lapses in the public sector, where we might find ourselves reading headlines that talk about, for instance, misappropriation of public funds. In both school and governmental settings, there have been far too many examples of employees engaging in lavish and unauthorized spending, illegally financed personal trips, and corruption.

Ironically, approximately 90% of business schools offer ethics courses. In many curricula, those programs are not only offered—they are required. Yet, the headlines are still being printed, and in some cases, the violators are still going to trial (and sometimes to jail). And in many of the organizations from which these headlines emanate, it is often HR professionals who find themselves in the middle of the fray.

What Is Ethics?

Ethics has been defined in a number of ways. One way to look at ethics is as a shared values-based system that serves to guide, channel, shape, and direct the behavior of individuals in organizations in an appropriate and productive direction.

Taking this definition one step further, business ethics could be defined as a shared values-based system designed to inculcate within the organization's population a sense of how to conduct business properly.

HR's Role in Ethics

HR must play a leadership role in establishing, encouraging, and ensuring ongoing ethical behavior within organizations. HR cannot, however, "own" ethics, or even own the organization's ethical initiative. Like other programs that are viewed as HR's responsibility (for instance, performance management, interviewing, and the like), ethics must be operationalized so that ownership and responsibility are truly shared by all.

In her article "The Ethical Enabler: Empowering Employees to Become Chief Ethics Officers," Susan F. Alevas, President, Alevas Consulting Group, Inc., speaks of the process of promulgating and inculcating ethical values in the organization as follows:

> When it comes to combating ethical complacency, governing board members, chief executive officers and senior management need to become "ethical enablers," the folks who encourage, support, and champion their employees to become "Chief Ethics Officers." Moreover, there's nothing stopping organizations from also bestowing their vendors and customers with the "Chief Ethics Officer" role.

Why Ethics?

Maintaining an ethical organization isn't about being nice or being good. Instead, a number of business-driven reasons exist for cultivating an ethical organization. In short, an erosion of ethics can lead to an erosion of the organization. Just a few of the reasons why it is critical to ensure that our organizations remain ethical are discussed in the following sections.

To Prevent Erosion of Trust

Successful organizations are based on a network of trust—trust that their members will do the right thing. When that doesn't happen, or when negative actions are tolerated (or worse, encouraged), employees stop trusting. They may then begin to rationalize inappropriate and unethical behaviors. As the results of this erosion become more visible, employees with a strong sense of personal integrity may leave, and potential employees who do uphold high ethical standards might be difficult to attract.

To Prevent Cynicism

Some people describe skepticism as healthy, and perhaps some small measure of it is—unless it begins to degenerate into cynicism. The negativity that comes along with cynicism can poison the culture of an organization. Those who cannot tolerate that atmosphere will likely leave, which can make the atmosphere of the organization even more toxic.

To Prevent Dysfunctional Manifestations of Politics

Politics, to some degree, is inevitable within organizations. In unethical organizations, however, politics will likely become increasingly dysfunctional and perhaps even destructive.

To Prevent Aggression/Violence

The anger that can fester when employees perceive that the leaders of their organization have acted in an unjust or inequitable manner will usually find an outlet somewhere. Sadly, even tragically, that outlet is not always productive and can even be highly destructive, as we have all witnessed in well-publicized cases of workplace violence, such as the 1992 Royal Oak Post Office shooting. According to a letter written 10 years later by Charlie Withers, chief steward of the Royal Oak Post Office:

> This tragedy was the result of a hostile work environment, created by postal management and condoned by those in higher positions within the postal service. This militaristic autocratic management style was allowed to go unchecked, even though the Royal Oak District was feeling the backlash in service to its patrons... The workforce throughout the Royal Oak District was under attack by overzealous managers who used whatever tactics needed to disrupt their lives... This same group of managers had been investigated in a GAO (Government Accounting Office) investigation done in Indianapolis for the same problems 3 years prior...and nothing was done!!

Aggression can also manifest itself in less violent—and thus perhaps less easily identifiable—ways, such as theft, lying, tampering or vandalism—all in an effort to "get even" with those in power who are treating them unfairly. Aggressive acts such as these have financial as well as nonfinancial costs to the organization that could exponentially increase if the organization permits or perpetuates an unethical culture.

Cultivating an Ethical Organization

One important element of creating an ethical culture comes from establishing an organizational code of ethics. That code, which ideally should have an introduction from the CEO, must reaffirm the organization's commitment to the code. The code itself needs to start with the mission, vision, and values of the organization. Together, these three go a long way toward establishing a foundation and framework for ethics. From there, an organization's code of ethics needs to address myriad issues from the perspectives of employees, customers, shareholders, suppliers, and the community at large.

The Code of Ethics: A Living Document

The process of writing a code of ethics is only the beginning, as it cannot simply be written and forgotten. Instead, the code of ethics needs to have life, and it needs to have teeth—clear statements relative to how the code—along with the policies that emanate from the code—will be implemented and upheld.

After the code is established, individuals at *all* levels of the organization must be held to its standards. A single standard must apply to all within the organization. Nothing will erode a code of ethics faster than the revelation that it has been applied or enforced inconsistently. It is simply not possible to overlook ethical violations from one or more individuals while making an example of the ethical violations of others.

> **EXAM ALERT**
>
> SHRM has established its own code of ethics specifically for HR professionals. This is a likely topic for inclusion on the PHR exam, so be sure to review it beforehand.

Legislative Framework, Considerations, and Opportunities

At the introduction of this chapter, we referenced a familiar saying: "Some people make things happen, some people watch things happen, and some people wonder what happened." This is perhaps no more apparent than in our legislative process, created hundreds of years ago, yet perhaps more vibrant and vital now more than ever before.

As HR professionals, understanding the legislative process helps us to more effectively impact that process. It is both our right and our responsibility to do this. Why? Because the employment-related laws that are passed in our nation directly impact our profession, the organizations for which we work, and the way we perform our jobs (hint: think HIPAA, FMLA, and so forth).

How a Bill Becomes a Law

Some readers may recall the *Schoolhouse Rock* series from the 1970s and 1980s that explained—quite entertainingly (at the time, it seemed)—how a bill becomes a law. Although "I'm Just a Bill" may not grace our televisions anymore, the following 13-step process still accurately describes how laws are passed. It's a process that is worth revisiting now, as we reaffirm our commitment to being strategic and effective business and organizational partners.

Although anyone can draft a bill, only a member of Congress can actually introduce legislation. In so doing, that member of Congress becomes the sponsor of the bill.

There are four basic types of legislation: bills, joint resolutions, concurrent resolutions, and simple resolutions.

EXAM ALERT

Familiarize yourself with the definitions of these four types of legislation and the similarities and differences between them.

The legislative process officially begins when a bill or resolution is given a number (the number is preceded by "H.R." if it is a House bill, and "S." if it is a Senate bill). After a number is assigned, the following steps will ensue:

1. *Referral to Committee*—Bills are usually referred to standing committees in the House or Senate according to carefully delineated rules of procedure.

2. *Committee Action*—One of three things can happen to a bill after it reaches a committee: It can be sent to a subcommittee; it can be considered by the committee as a whole; or it can be ignored (at which point the bill dies, or is killed, depending upon one's point of view).

3. *Subcommittee Review*—Bills are often referred to subcommittee for study and hearings. Hearings provide the opportunity to put views of the executive branch, experts, other public officials, supporters, and opponents officially on the record. Testimony can be in person or submitted in writing.

4. *Mark Up*—When the hearings are completed, the subcommittee may meet to *mark up* the bill; that is, make changes and amendments prior to recommending the bill to the full committee. If a subcommittee votes not to report legislation to the full committee, the bill dies.

5. *Committee Action to Report a Bill*—After receiving a subcommittee's report on a bill, the full committee has two choices: It can conduct further study and hearings, or it can vote on the subcommittee's recommendations and any proposed amendments. The full committee then votes on its recommendation to the House or Senate. This procedure is called "ordering a bill reported."

6. *Publication of a Written Report*—After a committee votes to have a bill reported, the chairman instructs staff to prepare a report on the bill. This report describes the intent and scope of the legislation, impact on existing laws and programs, position of the executive branch, and views of dissenting members.

7. *Scheduling Floor Action*—After a bill is reported back to the chamber where it originated, it is placed in chronological order on the calendar. The House has several different legislative calendars, and the speaker and majority leader largely determine if, when, and in what order bills come up. In the Senate, only one legislative calendar exists.

8. *Debate*—When a bill reaches the floor of the House or Senate, there are rules or procedures governing the debate. These rules determine the conditions and amount of time that will be allocated for debate.

9. *Voting*—After the debate and the approval of any amendments, the bill is passed or defeated by the members voting.

10. *Referral to Other Chamber*—When the House or the Senate passes a bill, it is referred to the other chamber, where it usually follows the same process through committee and floor action. This chamber can choose from four courses of action: approve the bill as is, reject the bill, ignore the bill, or change the bill.

11. *Conference Committee Action*—If only minor changes are made to a bill by the other chamber, it is common for the legislation to go back to the first chamber for concurrence. However, when the actions of the other chamber significantly alter the bill, a conference committee is formed to reconcile the differences. If the conferees cannot reach agreement, the legislation dies. If agreement is reached, a conference report describing the committee members' recommendations for changes is prepared. Both the House and the Senate must approve the conference report.

12. *Final Actions*—After the House and Senate have approved a bill in identical form, it is sent to the president. At this point, there are two ways in which the legislation can become law:

    ▶ If the president approves of the legislation, he or she signs it and it becomes the law of the land.

    ▶ If the president takes no action for 10 days while Congress is in session, the legislation automatically becomes law.

    Alternatively, if the president opposes the bill, he or she can veto it; or, if he or she takes no action after the Congress has adjourned its second session, it is considered a *pocket veto* and the legislation dies.

13. *Overriding a Veto*—If the president vetoes a bill, Congress may attempt to override the veto. This requires a two-thirds roll-call vote of the members who are present in sufficient numbers for a quorum.

Be Heard—Reach Out to Your Elected Officials

There are a variety of ways to reach out to the members of Congress and other elected officials who represent you.

Write (Early, But Not Too Often)

Morris K. Udall (1922–1998), a congressman from Arizona, composed "The Right to Write—Some Suggestions on Writing to Your Representative in Congress." Although Udall retired from Congress in 1991 before the advent of the Internet as a popular method of day-to-day communication, his suggestions are as valid today as they were years ago:

▶ Address your correspondence properly (for instance, when writing to a member of Congress, address it to "The Honorable ____ ____").

▶ Use the correct physical address.

▶ Identify the bill or issue you're writing about, ideally using the bill number as well as the name by which it is popularly known.

▶ Send letters in a timely manner while there is still time for your member of Congress to consider your input.

▶ Communicate with those members of Congress who represent you.

▶ Be brief, and be legible. Our elected officials are busy and receive a great deal of communication to sort through.

▶ Personal letters may have greater impact than form letters or petitions.

▶ Be specific about why you hold your opinion, and about how the legislation would impact you.

▶ When possible, offer suggestions.

▶ If you have expertise in a particular area, say so—and then share it.

▶ Provide your elected officials with positive, as well as constructive, feedback.

Udall offers some basic "don'ts" as well:

▶ Don't threaten.

▶ Don't promise.

▶ Don't engage in name-calling.

▶ Speak for others you claim to represent (unless you actually do).

▶ Don't become a "pen pal."

▶ Don't demand commitment—especially before all the facts are in.

Lobbying

Lobbying is the process of reaching out to your elected officials to express your beliefs and opinions with the hope of influencing a governmental body.

> **NOTE**
>
> Before you begin lobbying, do your homework. Know the subject matter and draft your message clearly and concisely. Be firm, be knowledgeable, and be confident. Know the issue, explain your concerns relative to the consequences of the issue, and suggest a specific course of action. In addition, consider coordinating your efforts with others who share a similar viewpoint.

Personal Visits

Consider meeting with your elected official, or perhaps with one of his or her staff members.

Stay Informed

Perhaps most important, stay up-to-date on the issues that can potentially impact the HR profession, the organization in which you work, or the ways in which you will carry out the role of HR. Affiliate with organizations—such as SHRM—that are committed to shaping the laws that impact our profession and our workplaces. Sign up to receive "e-lerts"—legislative updates from organizations. Seek such e-lerts from organizations toward whose beliefs you feel inclined, as well as from organizations whose beliefs may not align as closely with your own predispositions. And don't stop paying attention after a law is passed—court interpretations can also have a big impact on how you execute your role.

Chapter Summary

Functioning effectively requires a number of areas of knowledge and expertise, all of which could be grouped into three critical categories: knowing our business (organization), knowing our profession (craft), and knowing our customers. Though simply stated, much goes into mastering these three areas, if they are to be performed at a highly efficient and effective level. In fact, that mastery should never end, as our organizations—and our roles—will never stop evolving.

This chapter addressed some of the specific areas of knowledge with which HR professionals need to become fluent. It is intended as a starting point, not an ending point. Strategic management is also an area within which many HR professionals will gain greater understanding and appreciation as they gain experience and expertise within their careers—so be patient with yourself.

Key Terms

- Strategic management
- Industrial relations
- Personnel
- Human resources
- Administrative HR functions
- Strategic HR functions
- Operational/tactical HR functions
- Henri Fayol
- Planning function
- Organizing function
- Coordinating function
- Directing function
- Controlling function
- Project management
- Initiating processes
- Planning processes
- Executing processes
- Controlling processes
- Closing processes
- Project manager
- Project sponsor
- Project charter
- Project team
- Project plan
- Project schedule
- Work breakdown structure (WBS)
- Gantt chart
- Program evaluation and review technique (PERT) charts
- Change management
- Outsourcing
- Offshoring
- Request for proposal (RFP) (see Chapter 2)
- Third-party vendor
- HRIS
- Globalization
- Technology
- Safety and security
- Terrorism
- Aging workforce
- Multigenerational workplaces

- Work/life balance
- Changing technology—and not losing relations
- Contingent workforce
- Strategic planning
- Vision
- Mission
- Values
- SWOT analysis (strengths, weaknesses, opportunities, threats)
- Environmental scanning
- Capacity
- Standards
- Scheduling
- Inventory
- Control
- The 4 Ps:
  - Product
  - Place
  - Price
  - Promotion
- Budgeting:
  - Incremental budgeting
  - Formula budgeting
  - Zero-based budgeting
  - Activity based budgeting
- Assets
- Liability
- Equity
- Accounts payable
- Accounts receivable
- Balance sheet
- Income statement

- Gross profit margin
- Statement of cash flows
- Financial ratios:
  - Business activity ratios
  - Profitability ratios
  - Debt ratios
- Liquidity
- Current ratio
- Acid test
- Gross profit margin
- Balanced scorecard
- Learning and growth perspective
- Business process perspective
- Customer perspective
- Financial perspective
- Organizational life cycle
- Introduction/birth
- Development/growth
- Maturity
- Decline
- Organizational structure
- Formalization, or formal authority
- Departmentalization ("departmentation")
- Functional structure
- Division structure
- Matrix structure
- Chain of command
- Span of control
- Centralization
- Decentralization
- Simple structure organization model

- ▶ Bureaucratic organization model
- ▶ Virtual organization model
- ▶ Boundaryless organization model
- ▶ Mechanistic organizations
- ▶ Organic organizations
- ▶ Concentrated structures
- ▶ HR audits
- ▶ Return on investment (ROI)
- ▶ Cost-benefit analysis
- ▶ Break-even analysis
- ▶ Research

- ▶ Primary research
- ▶ Scientific method
- ▶ Secondary research
- ▶ Ethics
- ▶ Business ethics
- ▶ Bills
- ▶ Joint resolutions
- ▶ Concurrent resolutions
- ▶ Simple resolutions
- ▶ Lobbying

Apply Your Knowledge

This chapter focuses on issues relating to strategic management. Complete the
following review questions and exam questions as a way of reviewing and reinforcing
the knowledge and skills you'll need to perform your responsibilities as an HR professional and to increase the likelihood that you will pass the PHR examination.

Review Questions

1. Describe the managerial function "planning."

2. Describe what the mission of an organization means.

3. What is a code of ethics, and why is it important to an organization?

4. Describe the introduction phase of the organizational life cycle.

5. Describe the controlling processes of project management.

Exam Questions

1. Which of the following is *not* a category of processes within project management?

   A. Planning

   B. Executing

   C. Coordinating

   D. Controlling

2. Which of the following statements about change is most true?

   A. HR professionals must proactively seek to understand change and what causes change.

   B. HR must serve as an employee advocate during times of change.

   C. HR must ensure that the pace of change does not exceed the organization's ability to adapt to it.

   D. HR must serve as a management advocate during times of change.

3. Which of the following statements about values is not true?

   A. Values are often expressed through terms such as "communication" and "decision making."

   B. Values impact behaviors that are exhibited on a day-to-day basis in the workplace.

   C. Values are the beliefs on which an organization is built.

   D. Values shape and guide strategic as well as day-to-day decision making.

4. The first step in the scientific method is

   A. Develop a hypothesis.

   B. Question and observe.

   C. Scan existing secondary research.

   D. Conduct a needs analysis.

5. One overarching purpose of an HR audit is

   A. To ascertain how well the HR department—through all its various functional areas—has aligned itself with the organization's strategic objectives.

   B. To ascertain the degree to which the HR department has complied with all legal requirements and the potential financial exposure associated with existing levels of noncompliance.

   C. To ascertain the performance of the HR department with respect to the nature and quality of the consultative services it provides to its internal clients.

   D. To ascertain the degree to which the HR department is poised to meet the current, future, and emerging human capital and talent needs of the organization.

6. Which of the following is not one of the four perspectives of the balanced score-card?

    A. The financial perspective

    B. The external perspective

    C. The learning and growth perspective

    D. The business process perspective

7. Effectiveness can be defined as:

    A. A ratio of inputs to outputs

    B. The degree to which goals are met

    C. The degree to which goals reflect desired outputs

    D. A ratio of outputs to inputs

8. Which of the following is not specifically recognized as being critically important to successfully implementing any strategic plan?

    A. Commitment

    B. Credibility

    C. Collaboration

    D. Communication

9. Project managers seek to accomplish their objectives by gaining control over five factors, one of which is:

    A. Regulatory compliance

    B. Risk

    C. Reward structures

    D. Staffing

10. All of the following are compelling reasons for organizations to engage in a strategic planning process except:

    A. Developing a clearer awareness of how the organization measures up, internally and externally

    B. Engaging individuals throughout the organization in a meaningful organizational effort

    C. Enabling employees to prepare themselves to react positively and constructively to future events

    D. Creating—or reaffirming—the vision, mission, and values of the organization

Answers to Review Questions

1. Planning, the first of five managerial functions, lays the groundwork for how managers will work toward accomplishing the organization's goals. Through planning, managers decide what needs to get done, when it needs to get done, who will do it, how it will get done, and where it will be done. In the absence of planning, the organization—and the people in it—will lack direction, and perhaps even just coast along.

2. An organization's mission statement articulates, in essence, its reason for being. It may speak to the nature of the organization's business or purpose, its customers, and sometimes even its employees and its role in the community. A mission statement should be broad (but not overly generalized), brief, clear, unambiguous, and designed to last for "the long haul." Because the goals of an organization must be based on the mission, the mission is far bigger than any goal—and thus must be able to withstand the test of time.

3. Establishing an organizational code of ethics is one important part of creating an ethical culture. The ethics code should begin with an introduction from the CEO that reaffirms the organization's commitment to the code. The code itself needs to start with the mission, vision, and values of the organization. From there, an organization's code of ethics needs to address myriad issues from the varying perspectives of employees, customers, shareholders, suppliers, and the community at large.

4. Introduction (or "birth") is the first step in the organizational life cycle. During this phase, excitement and energy run high, and cash flow may be quite tight. Struggling start-ups often find themselves searching for solid footing—financially as well operationally. The core group of highly talented employees who are part of a start-up operation may focus fixedly on the founder as a source of direction, wisdom, and inspiration.

   In the introduction phase, employees may find themselves paid above market rates as a reflection of the founder's desire to entice them to come on board. Alternatively, if money is in short supply, during the introduction phase of the life cycle employees may earn less cash compensation and have those diminished earnings offset by other noncash rewards (equity, intrinsic rewards, and so on).

   Depending on the organization, HR may or may not have a formal presence in this phase of the organizational life cycle.

5. Controlling processes include managing the scope of the project and making sure the project stays in line with the original objectives. A significant degree of follow-up is required to carry out controlling processes.

Answers to Exam Questions

1. **Answer C is the best answer.** Coordinating is a management function, not a project management process. Answers A, B, and D are not the best answers, because they each identify a project management process (those processes include initiation, planning, executing, controlling, and closing).

2. **Answer A is the best answer.** HR professionals must seek to understand change and what causes change—ideally before change descends upon the organization. Change, itself, brings considerable challenges of its own—and often does not afford HR professionals with the luxury of time to study change theory or process. (Those are lessons that HR professionals need to undertake in advance.) Answer C is not the best answer, because HR's role is not to regulate the pace of change. At times, the pace of change may not be controllable. At other times, the pace of change may, in fact, be controllable, but the organization's leaders may decide that it is not appropriate or advisable to slow the pace of change. Answers B and D are not the best answers; HR must serve as a "truth advocate" during times of change (in fact, at all times), not as dedicated advocates of management *or* employees.

3. **Answer A is the best answer.** Words like "communication" and "decision making" are terms that are often used to describe competencies (also called *success factors*), not values. Answers B, C, and D are not the best answers, because each makes a true statement about values.

4. **Answer B is the best answer.** Question and observe is, in fact, the first step in the scientific method. Answer A is not the best answer, because developing a hypothesis is the second step in the scientific method. Answer C is not the best answer, because the scientific method is a form of primary research and is therefore separate and distinct from secondary research. Answer D is not the best answer, because conducting a needs analysis and assessment is the first step in the ADDIE process, not the scientific method.

5. **Answer A is the best answer.** The primary and overarching purpose of an HR audit is to ascertain how well the HR department has aligned itself with the organization's strategic objectives. Answers B, C, and D are not the best answers; while each identifies a possible component of an HR audit, none of these is broad enough to encompass the overarching purpose of an HR audit.

6. **Answer B is the best answer.** Though various elements of the balanced scorecard take external factors into consideration, the external perspective is not one of the four specific perspectives. Answers A, C, and D are not the best answers, because they each identify one of the perspectives of the balanced scorecard.

7. **Answer B is the best answer.** Effectiveness is a measure of the degree to which goals—carefully established goals—are met.

8. **Answer C is the best answer.** While collaboration is an important element of the strategic planning process, it is not recognized as one of the three Cs—the most important keys to successful strategic planning. Those three Cs are commitment (answer A), credibility (answer B), and communication (answer D).

9. **Answer B is the best answer.** The five factors over which project managers seek to establish control are time, cost, quality, scope, and risk (answer B is "risk"). Project managers do not specifically seek to establish control over regulatory compliance (answer A), reward structures (answer C), or staffing (answer D), although all of those elements will be considerations as they work to attain their objectives.

10. **Answer D is the best answer.** The focus of strategic planning is on proactivity, not reactivity. Therefore, through strategic planning, the organization creates an opportunity for individuals at all levels of the organization to proactively shape and influence the future, rather than just react to it. Answers A, B, and C are not the best answers, because each one articulates a compelling reason to engage in strategic planning.

Suggested Readings and Resources

Bacharach, Samuel B. *Get Them On Your Side.* Avon, MA: Platinum Press Inc., 2006.

Bacharach, Samuel B. *Keep Them On Your Side: Leading And Managing for Momentum,* Avon, MA: Platinum Press Inc., 2006.

Becker, Brian E., Mark A. Huselid, and Dave Ulrich. *The HR Scorecard: Linking People, Strategy, and Performance* (hardcover). Cambridge, MA: Harvard Business School Press, 2001.

Block, Peter. *Flawless Consulting.* San Francisco: Pfeiffer, 2000.

Galbraith, Jay, Diane Downey, and Amy Kates. *Designing Dynamic Organizations: A Hands-On Guide for Leaders at All Levels* (paperback). New York: AMACOM/American Management Association, 2001.

Nadler, David A., Marc S. Gerstein, and Robert B. Shaw. *Organizational Architecture: Designs for Changing Organizations.* (Jossey Bass Business and Management Series) (hardcover). San Francisco: Jossey-Bass, 1992.

Rothwell, William J., Robert K. Prescott, and Maria W. Taylor. *Human Resources Transformation: Demonstrating Leadership in the Face of Future Trends.* Palo Alto, CA: Davies-Black Publishing, 2008.

Rothwell, William J., Robert K. Prescott, and Maria W. Taylor. *Strategic Human Resource Leader, How to Prepare Your Organization for the Six Key Trends Shaping the Future.* Washington, D.C.: Davies-Black Publishing, 1998.

Ulrich, David. *Human Resource Champions* (hardcover). Cambridge, MA: Harvard Business School Press, 1997.

Ulrich, David, and Wayne Brockbank. *The HR Value Proposition* (hardcover). Cambridge, MA: Harvard Business School Press, 2005.

Williams, Anne H. *Know Your Responsibilities: Ethics & Fiduciary Duties for HR* (HR Executive Special Reports) (hardcover). Brentwood, TN: M. Lee Smith Publisher, 2004.

"HR as a strategic partner: What does it take to make it happen?" An article from *HR. Human Resource Planning,* by Edward E. Lawler, III, Susan A Mohrman. Sept. 2003.

"The Ethical Enabler: Empowering Employees To Become Chief Ethics Officers." An article by Susan F. Alevas, Esq., President, Alevas Consulting Group, Inc., 2005.

Workforce Planning and Employment

Study Strategies

▶ On large index cards, write down the names of each of the laws, topics, and key concepts covered in this chapter. Then, on smaller, separate index cards (ideally ones that are a different color), make notes on important facts and details relating to each of these laws, topics, and key concepts (put the name of the law or the topic on the back of the card, not on the front). Then test your memory and understanding by matching the specific facts and details (each of which you wrote on a separate index card) with the laws, topics, and key concepts that you labeled on the larger business cards. After you match them up, you can assess how well you did by checking your matches.

▶ Try writing out your own multiple-choice test questions. Writing out the questions—along with detailed answers—can go a long way toward reinforcing what you are studying. If you've got a study partner, trade questions with that person.

▶ Although the PHR exam is multiple choice, try writing and answering your own essay-based questions, as well. Create open-ended questions that require a response of at least a full paragraph—and write your answers without looking back at your study materials. The process of actually writing down your answers will reinforce what you already know, and will highlight what you need to study more. It will also likely help you as you work to recall this same information when you answer similar multiple choice questions on the actual PHR exam.

▶ Although many HR professionals have experience in the areas of employment, that experience may more closely reflect their organization's practices rather than genuine "best practices." It's possible, therefore, that—while you're going through this chapter (and your other related study materials) and trying to match your experience to the materials—you may find some areas in which there is a disconnect between your personal experience and what you're reading. For purposes of the PHR exam, stick with the recommended practices that are written here and in your other prep materials. When you are actually on the job, look for ways to reconcile these best practices with "the way I've always done it" or "the way it's always been done around here." Seek to incorporate ideas that can revitalize the ways in which you carry out your role.

▶ As with each of the six functional areas of HR, determine what you already know and what you don't know. Then work to prepare yourself. Conduct research. Use the Internet to find relevant articles and whitepapers. Peruse textbooks that provide guidance relative to those particular areas. Be sure to find several real-life examples to ensure that you gain a variety of perspectives and insights. This is particularly important for the skill-based, rather than fact-based, components of this functional area.

Introduction

An organization's overall success will be determined to a significant degree by its ability to have the right people, with the right skills, in the right places, at the right times. Although this statement sounds somewhat straightforward, let's take a closer look at what it actually means.

"*Having*" in this context can refer to hiring employees to work a traditional work arrangement, hiring employees to work some sort of nontraditional work arrangement, or retaining nonemployees to perform services on an as-needed basis (consultants). Although most organizations secure most of their "people resources" through traditional employment relationships, many organizations are also augmenting this approach with nontraditional arrangements, such as consulting services.

"*The right people, with the right skills*" refers to employing or contracting with individuals who possess and demonstrate the knowledge, skills, abilities, and behavioral characteristics needed to support the organization's mission and to attain the organization's objectives. Employing individuals who don't have the necessary knowledge, skills, abilities, and behavioral characteristics can be problematic (or, at the very least, challenging). Employing—and retaining—individuals who possess skills that they want to put to use but that aren't needed can be equally—and sometimes even more—problematic.

"*In the right places, at the right times*" speaks to the importance of analyzing short-term and long-term organizational needs to ensure that the organization is neither overstaffed nor understaffed at any given moment. In this context, the terms "overstaffing" and "understaffing" can refer to the number of people employed, as well as the skills that those individuals bring to the organization.

Achieving this delicate balance requires a considerable amount of planning. It also requires that HR professionals continually maintain awareness of the organization's mission, as well as of its short-term, long-term, and emerging goals. In this way, HR professionals—in close collaboration with the leaders and managers of the organization—can determine how to strategically support the organization's goals.

To formulate and execute these plans, HR professionals must be well versed in those laws that impact our profession and that affect the ways in which we source, hire, promote, and terminate employees. Equal employment opportunity is the foundation on which these laws have been built and therefore constitutes one critical element of every HR professional's knowledge base. Laws are not static, however, for they are continually interpreted and reinterpreted by the courts. As such, HR professionals also have a mandate to familiarize themselves with important cases from the past and to monitor new cases. In this way, we will be better equipped to so as to understand and appreciate new interpretations of these laws and thus maintain currency with respect to how they will affect the workplace, and the ways in which we will carry out our strategic, tactical, and transactional roles.

Equal Employment Opportunity: The Basics

As mentioned previously, a commitment to ensure equal opportunities throughout all dimensions of the employment relationship serves as the backdrop to employment-related legislation. To be effective in their roles, therefore, HR professionals need to have an understanding of certain fundamental Equal Employment Opportunity (EEO)-related concepts.

Protected Class

A group of people who share a common characteristic and who are protected from discrimination and harassment on the basis of that shared characteristic are said to belong to a *protected class*.

Discrimination

Discrimination, in the truest sense of the word, is not necessarily illegal. To discriminate is to make a distinction, or to discern. When distinctions or discernments are made on the basis of factors, traits, or characteristics that are protected by law, however, discrimination becomes unlawful.

Types of Unlawful Discrimination

HR professionals must be knowledgeable about the following types of discrimination:

- Disparate (or "adverse") treatment
- Disparate (or "adverse") impact
- Perpetuating past discrimination

Disparate (or "Adverse") Treatment

Disparate (or "adverse") treatment is a type of unlawful discrimination that occurs when an employer *intentionally* treats applicants or employees differently on the basis of their race, color, sex, religion, national origin, age, disability, military or veteran status, or any other characteristic protected by law. The following would constitute examples of disparate treatment:

- Candidates who indicate on their employment application that they speak Spanish are interviewed (in part or in whole) in Spanish, whereas all other candidates are interviewed in English.
- Female members of a team or department are asked to take meeting minutes or provide refreshments, whereas male members are not.
- The quality or quantity or work that is performed by employees who request a modified work schedule so as to be able to attend religious services is more closely scrutinized than the quality or quantity of work performed by employees who do not make such a request.

Disparate (or "Adverse") Impact

Disparate (or adverse) impact occurs when a seemingly neutral policy or practice has a disproportionately negative effect upon one or more members of a protected class. In this context, policies or practices that do not reflect legitimate job requirements but which have a statistically significant impact on members of a protected class may constitute unlawful discrimination. For instance:

▶ An organization requires that all newly hired employees have a college degree, even though a degree is not required to perform some of the jobs that exist within the organization. If members of protected classes are "screened out" at a statistically higher rate, an allegation of disparate impact might be upheld.

▶ An organization requires that all newly promoted managers must spend the first six months on the job working at six different—and geographically dispersed—locations throughout the country. If members of a protected class are eliminated from consideration for employment at a statistically higher rate because of this policy, and if this policy is found to be unrelated to successful performance of the position, an allegation of disparate impact might be upheld.

How the Uniform Guidelines Determine Adverse Impact

It's important to know how to mathematically determine whether adverse impact exists within a selection process. The Uniform Guidelines on Employee Selection Procedures (1978), which will be discussed in the "Uniform Guidelines on Employee Selection Procedures (1978)" section in this chapter, discusses and defines adverse impact in two separate—but interrelated—ways. First, let's take a look at the "bottom-line" concept": according to www.dol.gov:

> If the information called for by sections 4A and B of this section shows that the total selection process for a job has an adverse impact, the individual components of the selection process should be evaluated for adverse impact. If this information shows that the total selection process does not have an adverse impact, the Federal enforcement agencies, in the exercise of their administrative and prosecutorial discretion, in usual circumstances, will not expect a user to evaluate the individual components for adverse impact, or to validate such individual components, and will not take enforcement action based upon adverse impact of any component of that process, including the separate parts of a multipart selection procedure or any separate procedure that is used as an alternative method of selection. However, in the following circumstances the Federal enforcement agencies will expect a user to evaluate the individual components for adverse impact and may, where appropriate, take enforcement action with respect to the individual components: (1) where the selection procedure is a significant factor in the continuation of patterns of assignments of incumbent employees caused by prior discriminatory employment practices, (2) where the weight of court decisions or administrative interpretations hold that a specific procedure (such as height or weight requirements or no-arrest records) is not job related in the same or similar circumstances. In unusual circumstances, other than those listed in paragraphs (1) and (2) of this section, the Federal enforcement agencies may request a user to evaluate the individual components for adverse impact and may, where appropriate, take enforcement action with respect to the individual component. (Source: www.dol.gov)

Next, let's take a look at the "four-fifths" rule:

> A selection rate for any race, sex, or ethnic group which is less than four-fifths (4/5) (or eighty percent) of the rate for the group with the highest rate will generally be regarded by the Federal

(continues)

(continued)

enforcement agencies as evidence of adverse impact, while a greater than four-fifths rate will generally not be regarded by Federal enforcement agencies as evidence of adverse impact. Smaller differences in selection rate may nevertheless constitute adverse impact, where they are significant in both statistical and practical terms or where a user's actions have discouraged applicants disproportionately on grounds of race, sex, or ethnic group. Greater differences in selection rate may not constitute adverse impact where the differences are based on small numbers and are not statistically significant, or where special recruiting or other programs cause the pool of minority or female candidates to be atypical of the normal pool of applicants from that group. Where the user's evidence concerning the impact of a selection procedure indicates adverse impact but is based upon numbers which are too small to be reliable, evidence concerning the impact of the procedure over a longer period of time and/or evidence concerning the impact which the selection procedure had when used in the same manner in similar circumstances elsewhere may be considered in determining adverse impact. Where the user has not maintained data on adverse impact as required by the documentation section of applicable guidelines, the Federal enforcement agencies may draw an inference of adverse impact of the selection process from the failure of the user to maintain such data, if the user has an underutilization of a group in the job category, as compared to the group's representation in the relevant labor market or, in the case of jobs filled from within, the applicable work force. (Source: www.dol.gov)

EXAM ALERT

Know what options and choices exist in the event that adverse impact is found to exist.

Whereas disparate treatment is an intentional form of discrimination, disparate impact may be either intentional *or* unintentional. Ultimately, however, the question of intent has limited importance, in that *lack* of intent does not alter or excuse the fact that unlawful discrimination has occurred.

Perpetuating Past Discrimination

Unlawful discrimination also occurs when an employer's *past* discriminatory practices are perpetuated through *current* policies or practices—even those that appear to be nondiscriminatory. When linked in some way with past discrimination, seemingly nondiscriminatory practices can have a discriminatory effect.

One of the most commonly recognized examples of how past discrimination can be perpetuated through current policy or practice can be found in the use of employee referral programs. For instance, if discriminatory hiring decisions have been made in the past, an employer's workforce may now be primarily composed of people who are not members of protected classes—perhaps people who are white, or male, or young. If that same employer uses referrals from current employees as the primary means of recruiting new employees, it is likely that the individuals who will subsequently be brought into the workforce may also be primarily white, or male, or young—thus perpetuating the potentially discriminatory (albeit unintentional) staffing decisions that were made in the past.

Harassment—Another Type of Unlawful Discrimination

Unlawful workplace discrimination can also manifest itself as harassment of a person on the basis of his or her membership in a protected class. Although most of the landmark court cases and media coverage on this topic focus on sexual harassment, HR professionals must be cognizant of the fact that harassment on the basis of *any* protected class—not just sex—may constitute unlawful discrimination.

Sexual Harassment

Sexual harassment is a form of sex discrimination, which was rendered illegal by Title VII of the Civil Rights Act of 1964 (see Title VII of the Civil Rights Act [1964] in this chapter). The EEOC defines sexual harassment as follows:

> Unwelcome sexual advances, requests for sexual favors, and other verbal or physical conduct of a sexual nature constitute sexual harassment when:
>
> 1. Submission to such conduct is made either explicitly or implicitly a term or condition of an individual's employment.
>
> 2. Submission to or rejection of such conduct by an individual is used as the basis for employment decisions affecting such individual.
>
> 3. Such conduct has the purpose or effect of unreasonably interfering with an individual's work performance or creating an intimidating, hostile, or offensive working environment.

There are two categories of sexual harassment:

▸ *Quid Pro Quo*—As previously articulated in point 2, quid pro quo harassment occurs when an individual's submission to or rejection of sexual advances or conduct of a sexual nature is used as the basis for employment-related decisions. Quid pro quo harassment, therefore, originates from a supervisor or from others who have the authority to influence or make decisions about the employee's terms and conditions of employment.

▸ *Hostile Work Environment*—Hostile work environment harassment occurs when unwelcome sexual conduct unreasonably interferes with an individual's job performance or creates a hostile, intimidating, or offensive work environment. Hostile work environment harassment can be found to exist whether or not the employee experiences (or runs the risk of experiencing) tangible or economic work-related consequences. By definition, a hostile work environment can be created by virtually anyone with whom an employee might come in contact in the workplace (or "workspace," in the event of remote harassment through electronic means such as emails, faxes, instant messages (IMs), and so on).

EEO Reporting Requirements

As described at www.eeoc.gov, the EEOC has established the following reporting requirements:

▶ *EEO-1 Report*—Otherwise known as The Employer Information Report, the EEO-1 is submitted to the EEOC and the Department of Labor's Office of Federal Contract Compliance Programs.

▶ *EEO-3 Report*—Formally known as the Local Union Report, the EEO-3 is a biennial survey conducted every other year in the even calendar years.

▶ *EEO-4 Report*—Formally known as the State and Local Government Report, the EEO-4 is collected on odd-numbered years from state and local governments.

▶ *EEO-5 Report*—Formally known as the Elementary-Secondary Staff Information Report, the EEO-5 report is a joint requirement of the EEOC and the Office for Civil Rights (OCR) and the National Center for Education Statistics (NCES) of the Department of Education. It is conducted biennially, in the even numbered years, and covers all public elementary and secondary school districts with 100 or more employees in the United States.

EXAM ALERT

Don't limit your knowledge of EEO compliance to requirements that apply to your current organization. Familiarize yourself with all EEO reporting requirements. Specifically, be sure to familiarize yourself with the nine job categories listed in the EEO reporting forms and with the different EEO reporting requirements for different industries.

According to the EEOC, the most commonly known and filed of these reports is the EEO-1.

EEO-1

The EEO-1 report must be filed by September 30 of each year by all employers with 100 or more employees. Additionally, federal contractors with at least 50 employees and federal contracts of at least $50,000 per year must also file an EEO-1 report.

EEOC Revised EEO-1 Report

In November of 2005, the EEOC approved a revised EEO-1 report, which employers were required to begin using for the reporting period beginning September 30, 2007. The EEOC provides the following information about the revised EEO-1 at www.eeoc.gov:

Questions and Answers: Revisions to the EEO-1 Report

Background and Basic Requirements

1. Q: What is the EEO-1 Report?

    A: The EEO-1 Report—formally known as the "Employer Information Report"—is a government form requiring many employers to provide a count of their employees by job category and then by ethnicity, race, and gender. The EEO-1 report is submitted to both the EEOC and the Department of Labor, Office of Federal Contract Compliance Programs (OFCCP).

(continues)

(continued)

2. Q: Who must file the EEO-1 report?

   A: The EEO-1 report must be filed by:

   ▶ Employers with federal government contracts of $50,000 or more and 50 or more employees; and

   ▶ Employers who do not have a federal government contract but have 100 or more employees

3. Q: When must the EEO-1 report be filed?

   A: The EEO-1 report must be filed annually with the EEOC by September 30. It must use employment numbers from any pay period in July through September of that year.

4. Q: When must employers begin using the revised EEO-1 report?

   A: The revised EEO-1 report must be used beginning with the survey due by September 30, 2007. For the surveys due by September 2006, employers should continue to use the EEO-1 report format from previous years. This report is still available on the EEOC's website at https://apps.eeoc.gov/eeo1/eeo1.jsp.

5. Q: How do employers file EEO-1 reports?

   A: We strongly recommend that EEO-1 reports be submitted through the EEO-1 Online Filing System or as an electronically transmitted data file. Paper EEO-1 forms will be generated on request only, and only in extreme cases where Internet access is not available to the employer. Instructions on how to file are available on the EEOC's website at http://www.eeoc.gov/eeo1survey/howtofile.html.

6. Q: Is EEO-1 data confidential?

   A: Yes. The Commission is required by law to keep individual employer EEO1 reports strictly confidential. 42 U.S.C. 2000e-8(e).

7. Q: Where can employers find more information about the EEO-1?

   A: General information about the EEO-1 can be found at the EEOC's website at http://www.eeoc.gov/eeo1survey/index.html.

Description of the Changes to the New EEO-1 Report

8. Q: What changes are being made to the ethnic and racial categories on the EEO-1 report?

   A: A number of changes are being made to the race and ethnic categories. The revised EEO-1 report:

   ▶ adds a new category titled "Two or more races"

   ▶ divides "Asian or Pacific Islander" into two separate categories: "Asian" and "Native Hawaiian or other Pacific Islander"

   ▶ renames "Black" as "Black or African American"

   ▶ renames "Hispanic" as "Hispanic or Latino"

   ▶ strongly endorses self-identification of race and ethnic categories, as opposed to visual identification by employers

9. Q: What changes are being made to the job categories on the EEO-1 report?

   A: First, the current category of "Officials and Managers" will be divided into two levels based on responsibility and influence within the organization.

(continues)

(continued)

These two levels will be:

1. Executive/Senior Level Officials and Managers (plan, direct and formulate policy, set strategy and provide overall direction; in larger organizations, within two reporting levels of CEO)

2. First/Mid-Level Officials and Managers (direct implementation or operations within specific parameters set by Executive/Senior Level Officials and Managers; oversee day-to-day operations)

The revised EEO-1 also will move business and financial occupations from the Officials and Managers category to the Professionals category (to improve data for analyzing trends in mobility of minorities and women within Officials and Managers).

You can find additional Q&A information about the EEO-1 at www.eeoc.gov.

Applicant Flow Data

Employers also need to be cognizant of the need to maintain applicant flow data. *Applicant flow data* refers to information tracked by the employer relative to those individuals who are considered to have officially applied for a position.

CAUTION

The EEOC's definition of an applicant can differ, in some ways from the OFCCP's definition of an applicant. Employers—and HR professionals—need to know which definition to use, and when.

Employers who are covered by EO 11246 have particular obligations with respect to maintaining applicant flow data (and, for that matter, with appropriately defining the term "applicant").

CAUTION

The actual employment application *cannot* seek information relative to gender, race, or any other information related to protected-class membership. Removable pull-out sheets, however, that contain information needed for applicant flow data are generally considered acceptable, when handled in an appropriate and legal manner. Such sheets request voluntary disclosure of such information from candidates; however, it must also be clear to the candidate that whether to reveal this information is a wholly voluntary choice.

Internet Applicants: A Tale of Two Definitions

On March 3, 2004, the EEOC—along with the Departments of Labor and Justice and the Office of Personnel Management (OPM)—published recordkeeping guidance to clarify the definition of a "job applicant" for Internet and related technologies. As published at www.eeoc.gov:

"In order for an individual to be an applicant in the context of the Internet and related electronic data processing technologies, the following must have occurred:

▶ the employer has acted to fill a particular position;

(continues)

(continued)

> ▶ the individual has followed the employer's standard procedures for submitting applications; and

> ▶ the individual has indicated an interest in the particular position."

On October 7, 2005, the OFCCP published a similar—but distinct—definition of an "Internet Applicant" as an individual who:

> ▶ "submits an expression of interest in employment through the Internet or related electronic data technologies;

> ▶ the contractor considers for employment in a particular position;

> ▶ whose expression of interest indicates the individual possesses the basic qualifications for the position; and

> ▶ at no point in the contractor's selection process prior to receiving an offer of employment from the contractor, removes himself or herself from further consideration or otherwise indicates that he or she is no longer interested in the position."

EXAM ALERT

In addition to these definitions, be certain to review and familiarize yourself with record retention requirements for applicants—Internet and otherwise—as stipulated by the EEOC, OFCCP, and other federal or state agencies.

With this foundational understanding of EEO and employment law, HR professionals are then better prepared to engage in the workforce planning and employment process in a more knowledgeable—and therefore a more responsible and effective—manner.

Equal Opportunity for Whom?

Ensuring equal employment opportunity (EEO) is an ever-evolving concept. As such, it might be more accurate to say that, as of today, these laws ensure equal opportunities for "most," rather than for "all."

There are still individuals who—at a federal level—can be excluded from consideration for employment on the basis of shared characteristics or traits—even though those characteristics or traits are not job-related. For instance, as of the time when this book was published, no federal law exists prohibiting employment discrimination on the basis of sexual orientation or on the basis of marital status, even though certain states do offer those additional protections.

This chapter is based under the assumption that all workforce planning and employment decisions should be based on job-related factors. Doing so will help ensure that we do not run afoul of the law. Additionally—and perhaps just as important—this will also ensure that we do not eliminate qualified individuals on the basis of factors that have nothing to do with whether they can perform the jobs for which they are applying.

Legal Dimensions of Workforce Planning and Employment

Congress has passed numerous pieces of federal legislation specifically designed to eradicate discrimination on the basis of a variety of factors. This legislation—while diverse with respect to the areas that are spanned—shares one thing in common: none of the characteristics or traits addressed by these laws has any impact on a person's ability to do the job. Each piece of legislation has brought the workplace one step closer to ensuring that hiring, promotional, and all other employment-related decisions are based solely on job-related factors.

> **EXAM ALERT**
>
> On a somewhat related note, because EEO-related matters are often of a private or personal nature, be familiar with laws designed to protect employee privacy, including the Privacy Act of 1974.

> **EXAM ALERT**
>
> When responding to questions on the PHR exam, be certain to answer on the basis of federal laws, not state or local laws that might govern your particular state or region (and with which you might be more familiar).

> **CAUTION**
>
> When it comes to employment law, HR professionals must tread carefully. To function effectively, we need a solid understanding of the laws that affect our profession, our clients, and our organizations. We must maintain currency with respect to how the courts interpret—and reinterpret—existing laws, and we must understand the impact of new laws and cases. There is, however, a line over which we cannot cross—under penalty of law. Ultimately, a person who is not an attorney cannot practice law or dispense legal advice. We must be cautious that our efforts do not unintentionally overstep this fine—but clearly defined—line.

Title VII of the Civil Rights Act, 1964

Though not the first antidiscrimination law, Title VII of the Civil Rights Act of 1964 was a landmark piece of legislation prohibiting employment discrimination on the basis of race, color, religion, sex, or national origin. The most inclusive piece of antidiscrimination legislation up to that time (and perhaps even up through this time), Title VII radically changed the workplace.

The Civil Rights Act of 1964 established the first "protected classes," and created the Equal Employment Opportunity Commission (EEOC). As published on its website (www.eeoc.gov), the EEOC's mission is "to promote equal opportunity in employment through administrative and judicial enforcement of the federal civil rights laws and through education and technical assistance."

Title VII of the Civil Rights Act of 1964 prohibits discrimination in all aspects of the employment relationship, including

- ▶ Hiring and firing
- ▶ Compensation, assignment, or classification of employees
- ▶ Transfer, promotion, layoff, or recall
- ▶ Job advertisements
- ▶ Recruitment
- ▶ Testing
- ▶ Use of company facilities
- ▶ Training and apprenticeship programs
- ▶ Fringe benefits
- ▶ Pay, retirement plans, and disability leave
- ▶ Other terms and conditions of employment

Title VII also prohibits retaliating against an employee who files a charge of discrimination, who participates in an investigation, or who opposes discriminatory practices.

Title VII covers

- ▶ All private employers
- ▶ Federal, state, and local governments
- ▶ Education institutions that employ 15 or more individuals
- ▶ Private and public employment agencies
- ▶ Labor organizations
- ▶ Joint labor management committees controlling apprenticeship and training

Under rare circumstances, exceptions can be made to Title VII requirements. Table 4.1 includes some of these exceptions.

TABLE 4.1   Exceptions to Title VII

Type of Exception	Definition	Example
Bona fide occupational qualification (BFOQ)	Certain job requirements that are mandated by business necessity may have an unintended discriminatory (disparate) impact upon applicants or employees on the basis of gender, religion, or national origin.	Hiring females to be bathroom attendants in a women's restroom. Hiring a person of a particular religious denomination to be a minister to members of that faith.

TABLE 4.1 *Continued*

Type of Exception	Definition	Example
Professionally developed test of abilities	Job-related tests that ascertain skill or ability may have an unintended discriminatory (disparate) impact upon people on the basis of gender, religion, or national origin.	Strength or physical skills or agility tests if those tests assess skills that have been shown to be necessary for successful performance of a particular position—as determined by the actual performance of current or former employees.
Seniority systems	Bona fide seniority or merit-based systems that are not intended or designed to descriminate unlawfully.	Bona fide collective bargaining agreements.
Piece-rate systems	Compensation programs under which individuals are paid according to their production volume.	Certain assembly line or factory assignments.

Executive Order 11246, 1965

Unlike laws, which are passed by Congress, executive orders (EOs) are enacted by the president. They do carry, however, the same weight as law. EOs provide guidance and assistance to federal agencies relative to the execution of their duties and to employers relative to what they must do to be in compliance with the executive order.

HR professionals need to be familiar with EOs pertaining to employment issues. These EOs are administered by the Department of Labor—specifically, the OFCCP.

EO 11246, the first employment-related EO, established two key requirements for federal contractors and subcontractors that have contracts in excess of $10,000 during any one-year period:

▶ These employers are prohibited from discriminating in employment decisions on the basis of race, creed, color, or national origin. This requirement reconfirmed the nondiscrimination requirements established by Title VII of the Civil Rights Act of 1964.

▶ These employers must take affirmative steps—or actions—in advertising open positions, recruiting, employment, training, promotion, compensation, and termination of employees to ensure the elimination of employment barriers for women and minorities (individuals who we might refer to today as "people of color").

According to the Department of Labor (www.dol.gov), in addition, any and all nonconstruction federal contractors and subcontractors who employ at least 50 employees are required to design and maintain formal affirmative action plans (AAPs) for each of its establishments if it has 50 or more employees and:

- ▶ (i) Has a subcontract of $50,000 or more; or

- ▶ (ii) Has Government bills of lading which in any 12-month period, total or can reasonably be expected to total $50,000 or more; or

- ▶ (iii) Serves as a depository of Government funds in any amount; or

- ▶ (iv) Is a financial institution which is an issuing and paying agent for U.S. savings bonds and savings notes in any amount.

NOTE

In 1967, EO 11375 was enacted, adding sex to the list of protected classes. In 1969, EO 11478 was enacted, adding age and people with a "handicap" to the list of protected classes. In 1998, EO 13087 was enacted, adding sexual orientation to the list of protected classes. Parental status was added as a protected class in 2000 through EO 13152.

Fact Sheet—Executive Order 11246

Familiarize yourself with the following text excerpted from a DOL Fact sheet on Executive Order 11246:

A. OFCCP Mission Description

The Department of Labor's Employment Standards Administration's Office of Federal Contract Compliance Programs (OFCCP) enforces the Executive Order 11246, as amended; Section 503 of the Rehabilitation Act of 1973, as amended and the affirmative action provisions (Section 4212) of the Vietnam Era Veterans' Readjustment Assistance Act, as amended. Taken together, these laws ban discrimination and require Federal contractors and subcontractors to take affirmative action to ensure that all individuals have an equal opportunity for employment, without regard to race, color, religion, sex, national origin, disability or status as a Vietnam era or special disabled veteran.

OFCCP's jurisdiction covers approximately 26 million or nearly 22% of the total civilian workforce (92,500 non-construction establishments and 100,000 construction establishments). The Federal Government awarded more than $179 billion tax-payer dollars in prime contracts in Fiscal Year 1995.

OFCCP requires a contractor, as a condition of having a federal contract, to engage in a self-analysis for the purpose of discovering any barriers to equal employment opportunity. No other Government agency conducts comparable systemic reviews of employers' employment practices to ferret out discrimination. OFCCP also investigates complaints of discrimination. In Fiscal Year 1999, OFCCP conducted 3,833 compliance reviews. Moreover, OFCCP programs prevent discrimination. Further information about the OFCCP programs may be obtained from the Internet.

B. Operation of the Executive Order Program.

Each contracting agency in the Executive Branch of government must include the equal opportunity clause in each of its nonexempt government contracts. The equal opportunity clause requires that the contractor will take affirmative action to ensure that applicants are employed, and that employees are treated during employment, without regard to their race, color, religion, sex, or national origin. American Indian or Alaskan Native, Asian or Pacific Islander, Black, and Hispanic individuals are considered minorities for purposes of the Executive Order. This clause makes equal employment opportunity and affirmative action integral elements of a contractor's agreement with the government. Failure to comply with the non-discrimination or affirmative action provisions is a violation of the contract.

(continues)

(continued)

A contractor in violation of E.O. 11246 may have its contracts canceled, terminated, or suspended in whole or in part, and the contractor may be debarred, i.e., declared ineligible for future government contracts. However, a contractor cannot be debarred without being afforded the opportunity for a full evidentiary hearing. Debarments may be for an indefinite term or for a fixed term. When an indefinite term debarment is imposed, the contractor may be reinstated as soon as it has demonstrated that the violations have been remedied. A fixed-term debarment establishes a trial period during which a contractor can demonstrate its commitment and ability to establish personnel practices that are in compliance with the Executive Order.

If a matter is not resolved through conciliation, OFCCP may refer the matter to the Office of the Solicitor of Labor, which is authorized to institute administrative enforcement proceedings. After a full evidentiary hearing, a Department of Labor Administrative Law Judges issues recommended findings of fact, conclusions of law, and a recommended order. On the basis of the entire record, the Secretary of Labor issues a final Administrative Order. Cases also may be referred to the Department of Justice for judicial enforcement of E.O. 11246, primarily when use of the sanctions authorized by the Order is impracticable, such as a case involving a sole source supplier.

The regulations implementing the Executive Order establish different affirmative action provision for non-construction (i.e., service and supply) contractors and for construction contractors.

C. Executive Order Affirmative Action Requirements

i. For Supply and Service Contractors

Non-construction (service and supply) contractors with 50 or more employees and government contracts of $50,000 or more are required, under Executive Order 11246, to develop and implement a written affirmative action program (AAP) for each establishment. The regulations define an AAP as a set of specific and result-oriented procedures to which a contractor commits itself to apply every good faith effort. The AAP is developed by the contractor (with technical assistance from OFCCP if requested) to assist the contractor in a self-audit of its workforce. The AAP is kept on file and carried out by the contractor; it is submitted to OFCCP only if the agency requests it for the purpose of conducting a compliance review.

The AAP identifies those areas, if any, in the contractor's workforce that reflect utilization of women and minorities. The regulations at 41 CFR 60-2.11 (b) define under-utilization as having fewer minorities or women in a particular job group than would reasonably be expected by their availability. When determining availability of women and minorities, contractors consider, among other factors, the presence of minorities and women having requisite skills in an area in which the contractor can reasonable recruit.

Based on the utilization analyses under Executive Order 11246 and the availability of qualified individuals, the contractors establish goals to reduce or overcome the under-utilization. Good faith efforts may include expanded efforts in outreach, recruitment, training, and other activities to increase the pool of qualified minorities and females. The actual selection decision is to be made on a non-discriminatory basis.

ii. For Construction Contractors

OFCCP has established a distinct approach to affirmative action for the construction industry due to the fluid and temporary nature of the construction workforce. In contrast to the service and supply affirmative action program, OFCCP, rather than the contractor, establishes goals and specifies affirmative action which must be undertaken by Federal and federally assisted construction contractors. OFCCP issued specific national goals for women. The female goal of 6.9 percent was extended indefinitely in 1980 and remains in effect today. Construction contractors are not required to develop written affirmative action programs. The regulations enumerate the good faith steps construction contractors must take in order to increase the utilization of minorities and women in the skilled trades.

(continues)

(continued)

D. Goals, Timetables, and Good Faith Efforts

The numerical goals are established based on the availability of qualified applicants in the job market or qualified candidates in the employer's work force. Executive Order numerical goals do not create set-asides for specific groups, nor are they designed to achieve proportional representation or equal results. Rather, the goal-setting process in affirmative action planning is used to target and measure the effectiveness of affirmative action efforts to eradicate and prevent discrimination. The Executive Order and its supporting regulations do not authorize OFCCP to penalize contractors for not meeting goals. The regulations at 41 CFR 60-2.12(e), 60-2.30, and 60-2.15, specifically prohibit quota and preferential hiring and promotions under the guise of affirmative action numerical goals. In other words, discrimination in the selection decision is prohibited.

Affirmative Action Plans (AAPs)

On November 13, 2000, 41 CFR Part 60-2 (the portion of the Federal Register that addresses affirmative action) was significantly revised, with the overall intention of reducing the size and complexity of written Affirmative Action Plans (AAPs). Some of the key AAP-related changes resulted in the following:

- ▶ Replaced the workforce analysis with a one-page organizational profile.

- ▶ Reduced the eight-factor availability analysis to two factors (those with requisite skills within a "reasonable recruitment area"; and those in the contractor workforce who are "promotable," "transferable," or "trainable").

- ▶ Reduced the number of "additional required elements" of the written AAP from 10 to 4.

- ▶ Reaffirmed that AAPs don't establish quotas; rather, they establish goals that are pursued through good faith efforts.

- ▶ Established an Equal Opportunity survey, designed to collect information on a contractor's federal government contracts and affirmative action programs, personnel activity, and compensation data. This survey is sent annually to certain contractors, who must then complete it.

- ▶ Granted employers with fewer than 150 employees permission to prepare a job group analysis that uses EEO-1 categories as job groups.

EXAM ALERT

Be familiar with the different AAP requirements for construction and nonconstruction employers.

It's important to familiarize yourself with all of the elements of an AAP and, specifically, with how to prepare each of them. Some of the elements that are required to be in an AAP are as follows:

▶ *Designation of Responsibility*—This person—identified by name—is often an HR professional. He or she must have the necessary authority and resources to implement the AAP successfully. This must include the support of, and access to, top management. This is particularly important because the DOL is quite direct in its position that commitment to affirmative action should be an integral part of the organization's functioning, rather than an administrative "add-on."

▶ *Organizational Display or Workforce Analysis*—Nonconstruction contractors must prepare an organizational profile, which can be presented as either the new "organizational display" or the older workforce analysis. The proposed organizational profile is a shorter, simpler format, which in most cases would be based on the contractor's existing organizational chart(s) to provide a depiction of the contractor's workforce. This profile is essentially an organizational chart that includes summary information about incumbents' race, gender, and wages.

▶ *Job Group Analysis*—Nonconstruction contractors must also prepare a "job group analysis" intended to begin the process of comparing the employer's representation of women and minorities to the estimated availability of qualified women and minorities who are available to be employed.

▶ *Availability Analysis*—The new regulations still require contractors to determine the availability of minorities and women for jobs in their establishments, compare incumbency to availability, declare underutilization, and establish goals to eliminate the underutilization.

▶ *Utilization Analysis*—Availability is then compared to incumbency, and if the percentage of minorities or women is lower than the availability—"less than would reasonably be expected given their availability percentage in that particular job group"—the contractor must establish a "placement goal" (41 C.F.R. §60-2.15); that is, the contractor must set goals to correct the underutilization.

▶ *Placement Goals*—Placement goals are established for areas in which underutilization exists. Placement goals must be pursued through good faith efforts—not through the establishment of quotas. The "bottom line" is that, when underutilization exists, the placement goal must be set at an annual percentage rate equal to the availability figure for women or minorities (it may be necessary, at times, to set goals for particular minority groups where significant underutilization exists).

▶ *Action-Oriented Programs*—The employer must develop and execute action-oriented programs that are specifically designed to correct any problem areas and to attain established placement goals. These action-oriented programs cannot just be "more of the same" less than fully effective procedures that resulted in these problem areas in the first place. Instead, the employer must demonstrate good faith efforts to remove identified barriers, expand employment opportunities, and produce measurable results.

▶ *Identification of Problem Areas*—The contractor must perform in-depth analyses of its total employment process to determine whether and where impediments to equal employment opportunity exist.

> *Internal Audit and Reporting System*—The contractor must develop and implement an auditing system that periodically measures the effectiveness of its total affirmative action program. The following actions are identified by the DOL as key to a successful affirmative action program:

1. Monitor records of all personnel activity—including referrals, placements, transfers, promotions, terminations, and compensation—at all levels to ensure the nondiscriminatory policy is carried out.

2. Require internal reporting on a scheduled basis as to the degree to which equal employment opportunity and organizational objectives are attained.

3. Review report results with all levels of management.

4. Advise top management of program effectiveness and submit recommendations to improve unsatisfactory performance.

EXAM ALERT

It's important to familiarize yourself with all of the elements of an AAP and with how to prepare each of them.

Affirmative Action Planning—Put It in Practice

EEO and Affirmative Action Guidelines for Federal Contractors Regarding Race, Color, Gender, Religion, and National Origin

BASIC PROVISIONS

Since 1965, the U.S. Department of Labor's Office of Federal Contract Compliance Programs (OFCCP) has been committed to ensuring that Government contractors comply with the equal employment opportunity (EEO) and the affirmative action provisions of their contracts.

OFCCP administers and enforces Executive Order 11246, as amended, which prohibits federal contractors and federally assisted construction contractors and subcontractors, who do over $10,000 in Government business in one year from discriminating in employment decisions on the basis of race, color, religion, sex, or national origin.

The Executive Order also requires Government contractors to take affirmative action to insure that equal opportunity is provided in all aspects of their employment.

AFFIRMATIVE ACTION REQUIREMENTS

Each Government contractor with 50 or more employees and $50,000 or more in government contracts is required to develop a written affirmative action program (AAP) for each of its establishments.

A written affirmative action program helps the contractor identify and analyze potential problems in the participation and utilization of women and minorities in the contractor's workforce.

If there are problems, the contractor will specify in its AAP the specific procedures it will follow and the good faith efforts it will make to provide equal employment opportunity.

Expanded efforts in outreach, recruitment, training and other areas are some of the affirmative steps contractors can take to help members of the protected groups compete for jobs on equal footing with other applicants and employees.

(continues)

(continued)

ENFORCEMENT AND COMPLIANCE

Compliance Reviews

OFCCP conducts compliance reviews to investigate the employment practices of Government contractors. During a compliance review, a compliance officer examines the contractor's affirmative action program; checks personnel, payroll, and other employment records; interviews employees and company officials; and investigates virtually all aspects of employment in the company.

The investigator also checks to see whether the contractor is making special efforts to achieve equal opportunity through affirmative action. If problems are discovered, OFCCP will recommend corrective action and suggest ways to achieve equal employment opportunity.

Complaint Investigations

Individuals may file complaints if they believe they have been discriminated against by federal contractors or subcontractors. Complaints also may be filed by organizations on behalf of the person or persons affected.

Complaints must be filed within 180 days from the date of the alleged discrimination, although filing time can be extended for a good reason.

If a complaint filed under Executive Order 11246 involves discrimination against only one person, OFCCP will normally refer it to the EEOC. Cases involving groups of people or indicating patterns of discrimination are generally investigated and resolved by OFCCP. Complaints may be filed directly with any of OFCCP's regional or district offices throughout the country, or with OFCCP in Washington, D.C.

Compliance Assistance

To help contractors understand their contractual obligations for EEO and affirmative action, OFCCP provides technical assistance. District office staff offers guidance to contractors on how to develop an affirmative program through company seminars, training programs held in conjunction with industry liaison groups, and one-on-one consultations on affirmative action practices and procedures.

Enforcing Contract Compliance

When a compliance review discloses problems, OFCCP attempts to work with the contractor, often entering into a conciliation agreement. A conciliation agreement may include back pay, job offers, seniority credit, promotions, or other forms of relief for victims of discrimination. It may also involve new training programs, special recruitment efforts, or other affirmative action measures.

When conciliation efforts are unsuccessful, OFCCP refers the case to the Office of the Solicitor for enforcement through administrative enforcement proceedings. A contractor cited for violating EEO and affirmative action requirements may have a formal hearing before an administrative law judge.

If conciliation is not reached before or after the hearing, sanctions may be imposed. For example, a contractor could lose its government contracts or subcontracts or be debarred, i.e., declared ineligible for any future government contracts.

Further Information

For more information about contact compliance, filing complaints, or compliance assistance, contact any of OFCCP's regional or district offices. All offices are listed in telephone directories under U.S. Department of Labor, Employment Standards Administration, Office of Federal Contract Compliance Programs.

(Source: www.dol.gov)

EXAM ALERT

It's also important to become familiar with compliance reviews: who is most likely to be audited and what happens before, during, and after audits. Be particularly cognizant that audits can—and do—vary significantly depending on a variety of factors, so it's important not to draw conclusions based only on your personal experiences with the OFCCP.

Age Discrimination in Employment Act (ADEA), 1967

The Age Discrimination in Employment Act (ADEA) prohibits discrimination on the basis of age for employees and job applicants who are age 40 and above. There is no upper cap on age limit (although there initially was). Under the ADEA, it is unlawful to discriminate against a person because of his/her age with respect to any term, condition, or privilege of employment, including hiring, firing, promotion, layoff, compensation, benefits, job assignments, and training.

The ADEA also makes it unlawful to retaliate against an individual for opposing employment practices that discriminate based on age or for filing an age discrimination charge, testifying, or participating in any way in an investigation, proceeding, or litigation under the ADEA.

ADEA covers private employers with 20 or more employees, state and local governments (including school districts), employment agencies, and labor organizations.

EXAM ALERT

Be familiar with the exceptions and requirements under ADEA, particularly as they apply to benefits such as early retirement incentives. In addition, be familiar with waivers of ADEA rights and ADEA rights as they pertain to employee benefits (see http://www.eeoc.gov/ for information on both of these topics).

Rehabilitation Act, 1973

The Rehabilitation Act of 1973 prohibits discrimination on the basis of physical and mental disabilities.

Section 503 of the Act requires affirmative action and prohibits employment discrimination by federal government contractors and subcontractors with contracts of more than $10,000.

Section 504 of the Act states that "no otherwise qualified individual with a disability in the United States…shall…be excluded from the participation in, denied the benefits of, or be subjected to discrimination under any program or activity receiving Federal financial assistance or activity conducted by any Executive agency or by the United States Postal Service."

Section 508 requires that federal agencies' electronic and information technology is accessible to people with disabilities, including employees and members of the public.

Vietnam Era Veterans' Readjustment Assistance Act (VEVRAA), 1974

VEVRAA requires employers with federal contracts or subcontracts of $25,000 or more to provide equal opportunity and affirmative action for Vietnam-era veterans, special disabled veterans, and veterans who served on active duty during a war or in a campaign or expedition for which a campaign badge has been authorized.

> **CAUTION**
>
> Don't let the acronym mislead you—VEVRAA affords protection to veterans in addition to those who served during the Vietnam era. Be familiar with the definitions of "special disabled veteran," Vietnam era veterans, and all other veterans covered by VEVRAA.

For purposes of VEVRAA, a Vietnam era veteran is a person who (1) served on active duty for a period of more than 180 days, any part of which occurred between August 5, 1964 and May 7, 1975, and was discharged or released with other than a dishonorable discharge; (2) was discharged or released from active duty for a service connected disability if any part of such active duty was performed between August 5, 1964 and May 7, 1975; or (3) served on active duty for more than 180 days and served in the Republic of Vietnam between February 28, 1961 and May 7, 1975.

VEVRAA requires employees with federal contracts or subcontracts of $100,000 or more must file a VETS-100 report by September 30 each year. This form must indicate the following:

▶ The number of employees in the work force of such contractor, by job category and hiring location, who are special disabled veterans, veterans of the Vietnam era, or other veterans who served on active duty during a war or in a campaign or expedition for which a campaign badge has been authorized.

▶ The total number of new employees hired by the contractor during the period covered by the report and the number of such employees who are special disabled veterans, veterans of the Vietnam era, or other veterans who served on active duty during a war or in a campaign or expedition for which a campaign badge has been authorized.

▶ The maximum number and the minimum number of employees of such contractor during the period covered by the report

The VETS-100 is shown in Figure 4.1:

FEDERAL CONTRACTOR VETERANS' EMPLOYMENT REPORT VETS-100

OMB NO: 1293-0005
Expires: 12-31-2002

Persons are not required to respond to this collection
of information unless it displays a valid OMB number

RETURN COMPLETED REPORT TO:
U.S. DEPARTMENT OF LABOR
VETERANS' EMPLOYMENT AND TRAINING SERVICE
VETS-100 REPORTING OFFICE
6101 STEVENSON AVENUE
ALEXANDRIA, VA 22304

TYPE OF CONTRACTOR (Check one as applicable)	TYPE OF FORM (Check only one)
☐ Prime Contractor ☐ Subcontractor	☐ Single Establishment ☐ Multiple Establishment-Headquarters ☐ Multiple Establishment-Hiring Location ☐ Multiple Establishment-State Consolidated (specify number of locations) _____ (MSC)

COMPANY IDENTIFICATION INFORMATION (Omit if items preprinted above)

COMPANY No:	TWELVE MONTH PERIOD ENDING		2 0 0 1
		M M D D Y Y Y Y	
NAME OF PARENT COMPANY:	ADDRESS (NUMBER AND STREET):		
CITY:	COUNTY:	STATE:	ZIP CODE:

NAME OF HIRING LOCATION:	ADDRESS (NUMBER AND STREET):		
CITY:	COUNTY:	STATE:	ZIP CODE:

SIC:	DUNS: __ __ __	Employer I.D. No. (IRS TAX No.) __

INFORMATION ON VETERANS

REPORT ALL PERMANENT FULL-TIME OR PART-TIME EMPLOYEES AND NEW HIRES WHO ARE VETERANS, AS DEFINED ON REVERSE. DATA ON NUMBER OF EMPLOYEES ARE TO BE ENTERED IN COLUMN L, M, AND N. DATA ON NEW HIRES ARE TO BE ENTERED IN COLUMNS O, P, Q, AND R. ENTRIES IN COLUMNS O THROUGH R, LINES 1 THROUGH 9, AND COLUMNS L, M, AND N, LINE 10 (GRAY SHADED AREAS) ARE OPTIONAL. **ENTRIES IN COLUMN N, LINES 1-9; COLUMN Q, LINE 10 AND THE MAXIMUM AND MINIMUM NUMBER OF EMPLOYEES (AREAS SHADED LIGHT GRAY) ARE OPTIONAL FOR 2001 ONLY AND WILL BE REQUIRED FOR THE 2002 REPORTING CYCLE.** DETAILED INSTRUCTIONS ARE FOUND ON THE REVERSE OF THIS FORM.

JOB CATEGORIES	NUMBER OF EMPLOYEES			NEW HIRES (PREVIOUS 12 MONTHS)			
	SPECIAL DISABLED VETERANS (L)	VIETNAM ERA VETERANS (M)	OTHER ELIGIBLE VETERANS (N)	SPECIAL DISABLED VETERANS (O)	VIETNAM ERA VETERANS (P)	OTHER ELIGIBLE VETERANS (Q)	TOTAL NEW HIRES, BOTH VETERANS AND NON-VETERANS (R)
OFFICIALS AND MANAGERS 1							
PROFESSIONALS 2							
TECHNICIANS 3							
SALES WORKERS 4							
OFFICE AND CLERICAL 5							
CRAFT WORKERS (SKILLED) 6							
OPERATIVE (SEMI-SKILLED) 7							
LABORERS (UNSKILLED) 8							
SERVICE WORKERS 9							
TOTAL 10							

Report the total maximum and minimum number of permanent employees on board during the period covered by this report.

Maximum Number   Minimum Number

FIGURE 4.1 The VETS-100 form.

NOTE

The threshold for filing a VETS-100 report was raised from $25,000 to $100,000 for contracts awarded on or after December 1, 2003, through the Jobs for Veterans Act (JVA). JVA also modified the report categories of veterans to: disabled veterans, other protected veterans, Armed Forces service medal veterans, and recently separated veterans (41 CFR 61.300 in clearance). Additionally, JVA requires Federal contractors and subcontractors to report the total number of all current employees in each job category and at each hiring location.

FEDERAL CONTRACTOR VETERANS' EMPLOYMENT REPORT (VETS-100)

WHO MUST FILE

The Vets-100 report is to be completed by all nonexempt federal contractors and subcontractors with contracts or subcontracts for the procurement of personal property and non personal services for $25,000 or more. Services include but are not limited to the following services: Utility, construction, transportation, research, insurance, and fund depository, irrespective of whether the government is the purchaser or seller. The existence of $25,000 or more in federal contracts or subcontracts during a given calendar year establishes the requirement to file a VETS-100 Report during the following calendar year.

WHEN TO FILE

This annual report must be filed no later than September 30. Mail to the address pre-printed on the front of the form.

LEGAL BASIS FOR REPORTING REQUIREMENTS

Title 38, United States Code, Section 4212(d) and PL 105-339, require that federal contractors report at least annually the numbers of: 1) special disabled veterans, and 2) veterans of the Vietnam era. The following requirement for reporting annually are optional until Final Rule is published. 1) other eligible veterans who served on active duty during a war or in a campaign or expedition for which a campaign badge has been authorized who are in their workforce, and 2) maximum and minimum number of employees. Reporting is required by hiring location and includes both the number employed and the number of new hires, within the two categories listed above. The number of veterans employed within these categories is to be broken out by job category.

HOW TO SUBMIT THE VETS-100 REPORTS

Single-establishment employers must file one completed form. All multi-establishment employers, i.e., those doing business at more than one hiring location, must file (A) one form covering the principal or headquarters office: (B) a separate form for each hiring location employing 50 or more persons: and (C) EITHER, (I) a separate form for each hiring location employing fewer than 50 persons, OR (ii) consolidated reports that cover hiring locations within one State that have fewer than 50 employees. Each state consolidated report must also list the name and address of the hiring locations covered by the report. Company consolidated reports such as those required by EEO-1 reporting procedures are NOT required for the VETS-100 report. Completed reports for the headquarters location and all other hiring locations for each company should be mailed in one package to the address indicated on the front of the form.

RECORD KEEPING

Employers must keep copies of the completed annual VETS-100 report submitted to DOL for a period of two years.

HOW TO PREPARE THE FORMS

As VETS only sends one copy of the VETS-100 Reporting form to each headquarters location, multi-establishment employers submitting hard copy reports should produce facsimile copies of the headquarters form for reporting data on each location.

Type of Contractor Indicate the type of contractual relationship (prime contractor or subcontractor) that the organization has with the Federal Government. If the organization serves as both a prime contractor and a subcontractor on various federal contracts, check both boxes.

Type of Form If a reporting organization submits only one VETS-100 Report form for a single location, check the Single Establishment box. If the reporting organization submits more than one form, only one form should be checked as Multiple Establishment-Headquarters. The remaining forms should be checked as either Multiple Establishment-Hiring Location or Multiple Establishment-State Consolidated. For state consolidated forms, the number of hiring locations included in that report should be entered in the space provided. For each form, only one box should be checked within this block.

COMPANY IDENTIFICATION INFORMATION

Company Number Do not change the Company Number that is printed on the form. If there are any questions regarding your Company Number, please call the VETS-100 staff at (703) 461-2460 or e-mail HELPDESK@VETS100.COM.

Twelve Month Period Ending Enter the end date for the twelve month reporting period used as the basis for filing the VETS-100 Report. To determine this period, select a date in the current year between July 1 and August 31 that represents the end of a payroll period. That payroll period will be the basis for reporting Number of Employees, as described below. Then the twelve month period preceding the end date of that payroll period will be your twelve month period covered. This period is the basis for reporting New Hires, as described below. Any federal contractor or subcontractor who has written approval from the Equal Employment Opportunity Commission to use December 31 as the ending date for the EEO-1 Report may also use that date as the ending date for the payroll period selected for the VETS-100 Report.

Name and Address for Single Establishment Employers COMPLETE the identifying information under the Parent Company name and address section. LEAVE BLANK all of the identifying information for the Hiring Location.

Name and Address for Multi Establishment Employers For parent company headquarters location, COMPLETE the name and address for the parent company headquarters, LEAVE BLANK the name and address of the Hiring Location. For hiring locations of a parent company, COMPLETE the name and address for the Parent Company location, COMPLETE the name and address for the Hiring Location.

SIC Code, DUNS Number, and Employer ID Number Single Establishment and Multi Establishment Employers should COMPLETE the SIC Code, DUNS Number, and Employer ID Number as described below.

SIC Code Enter the four (4) digit SIC Code applicable to the hiring location for which the report is filed. If there is not a separate SIC Code for the hiring location, enter the SIC Code for the parent company.

Dun and Bradstreet I.D. Number (DUNS) If the company or any of its establishments has a Dun and Bradstreet Identification Number, please enter the nine (9) digit number in the space provided. If there is a specific DUNS Number applicable to the hiring location for which the report is filed, enter that DUNS Number. Otherwise, enter the DUNS number for the parent company.

Employer I.D. Number (EIN) Enter the nine (9) digit numbers assigned by the I.R.S. to the contractor. If there is a specific EIN applicable to the hiring location for which the report is filed, enter that EIN. Otherwise, enter the EIN for the parent company.

INFORMATION ON VETERANS

Number of Employees Select any payroll period ending between July 1 and August 31 of the current year. Provide all data for permanent full-time and part-time employees who were special disabled veterans, Vietnam-era veterans, or other eligible veterans employed as of the ending date of the selected payroll period. Do not include employees specifically excluded as indicated in 41 CFR 61-250.2(b)(2). Employees must be counted by veteran status for each of the nine occupational categories (Lines 1-9) in columns L and M. The information in column N, lines 1-9 will be required for the 2002 reporting cycle but this information is optional for 2001. Blank spaces will be considered zeros.

New Hires. Report the number of permanent full-time and part-time employees by veteran status who were hired (both veterans and non-veterans) and who were included in the payroll for the first time during the 12-month period ending between July 1 through August 31 of the current year. The totals in columns O, P and R (Line 10) are required. The information in column Q, line 10 also will be required for the 2002 reporting cycle but this information is optional for 2001. Enter all applicable numbers, including zeros.

Maximum/Minimum Employees Report the maximum and minimum number of permanent employees on board during the period covered as indicated by PL 105-339.

DEFINITIONS:

'Hiring location' means an establishment as defined at 41 CFR 61 250.2(b).

'Special Disabled Veteran' means (A) a veteran who is entitled to compensation (or who but for the receipt of military retired pay would be entitled to compensation) under laws administered by the Department of Veterans' Affairs for a disability (I) rated at 30 percent or more, or (ii) rated at 10 or 20 percent in the case of a veteran who has been determined under Section 3106 of Title 38, U.S.C. to have a serious employment handicap or (B) a person who was discharged or released from active duty because of a service-connected disability.

'Veteran of the Vietnam-era' means a person who: (A) served in the military, ground, naval or air service of the United States on active duty for a period of more than 180 days, and was discharged or released therefrom with other than a dishonorable discharge, if any part of such active duty occurred: (I) in the Republic of Vietnam between February 28, 1961, and May 7, 1975; or (ii) between August 5, 1964, and May 7, 1975, in all other cases: or (B) was discharged or released from active duty for a service-connected disability if any part of such active duty was performed (I) in the Republic of Vietnam between February 28, 1961, and May 7, 1975; or (ii) between August 5, 1964, and May 7, 1975, in all other cases.

Other Eligible Veterans means veterans who served in the military, ground, naval or air service of the United States on active duty during a war or in a campaign or expedition for which a campaign badge has been authorized. To identify the campaigns or expeditions that meet this criterion, contact the Office of Personnel Management (OPM) and ask for the OPM VETS Guide, Appendix A. A local OPM telephone number may be found in the telephone book under Federal Government or consult Directory Assistance for your area code for the nearest OPM location. For those with Internet access, the information required to make this determination also is available at http://www.opm.gov/veterans/html/vgmedal2.htm.

Public reporting burden for this collection is estimated to average 30 minutes per response, including the time for reviewing instructions, searching existing data source, gathering and maintaining the data needed, and completing and reviewing the collection of information. Send comments regarding this burden estimate or any other aspect of this collection of information, including suggestions for reducing the burden to the Department of Labor, Office of Information Management, Room N-1301, 200 Constitution Avenue, NW, Washington D.C. 20210. All completed VETS-100 Reports should be sent to the address indicated on the front of the form.

Federal contractors and subcontractors are also required to meet certain obligations relative to mandatory job postings, with the general intention of giving preference to qualified targeted veterans:

According to the DOL, generally, *qualified targeted veterans* are entitled to priority for referral to Federal contractor job openings. Any contractor or subcontractor with a contract with the Federal Government meeting the criteria must take affirmative action to hire and promote qualified targeted veterans. The JVA states specifically that each contractor (and subcontract) shall list job openings with the appropriate employment service delivery system and may also post listings under the Workforce Investment Act or other appropriate delivery points or the America's Job Bank. This requirement is fulfilled by listing job openings with the nearest State Job Service (also known as State Workforce Agency locations, previously State Employment Service Agency) or One Stop Office. This requirement applies to vacancies at all contractor and subcontractor locations not otherwise exempt under Federal contractor provisions. Exemptions include positions which are to be filled in top management or executive staff and/or positions which are to be filled from within the contractor's organization, and positions lasting three days or less. (Source: www.dol.gov)

Pregnancy Discrimination Act, 1978

The Pregnancy Discrimination Act of 1978 amended Title VII of the Civil Rights Act of 1964. Specifically, this act prohibits discrimination on the basis of pregnancy, childbirth, or related medical conditions. In short, it requires that employers treat applicants or employees who are pregnant or otherwise affected by related conditions in the same manner as other applicants or employees with other short-term conditions. This act (also known as the PDA) covers employers with 15 or more employees, including state and local governments. It applies to employment agencies and to labor organizations, as well as to the federal government.

According to Title VII, pregnancy-related protections include:

► *Hiring*—An employer cannot refuse to hire a pregnant woman because of her pregnancy, because of a pregnancy-related condition, or because of the prejudices of co-workers, clients, or customers.

► *Pregnancy and Maternity Leave*—An employer may not single out pregnancy-related conditions for special procedures to determine an employee's ability to work. However, if an employer requires its employees to submit a doctor's statement concerning their inability to work before granting leave or paying sick benefits, the employer may require employees affected by pregnancy-related conditions to submit such statements.

If an employee is temporarily unable to perform her job due to pregnancy, the employer must treat her the same as any other temporarily disabled employee. For example, if the employer allows temporarily disabled employees to modify tasks, perform alternative assignments, or take disability leave or leave without pay, the employer also must allow an employee who is temporarily disabled due to pregnancy to do the same.

Pregnant employees must be permitted to work as long as they are able to perform their jobs. If an employee has been absent from work as a result of a pregnancy-related condition and recovers, her employer may not require her to remain on leave until the baby's birth. An employer also may not have a rule that prohibits an employee from returning to work for a predetermined length of time after child-birth.

Employers must hold open a job for a pregnancy-related absence the same length of time jobs are held open for employees on sick or disability leave.

▶ *Health Insurance*—Any health insurance provided by an employer must cover expenses for pregnancy-related conditions on the same basis as costs for other medical conditions. Health insurance for expenses arising from abortion is not required, except where the life of the mother is endangered.

Pregnancy-related expenses should be reimbursed exactly as those incurred for other medical conditions, whether payment is on a fixed basis or a percentage of reasonable-and-customary-charge basis.

The amounts payable by the insurance provider can be limited only to the same extent as amounts payable for other conditions. No additional, increased, or larger deductible can be imposed.

Employers must provide the same level of health benefits for spouses of male employees as they do for spouses of female employees.

▶ *Fringe Benefits*—Pregnancy-related benefits cannot be limited to married employees. In an all-female workforce or job classification, benefits must be provided for pregnancy-related conditions if benefits are provided for other medical conditions.

If an employer provides any benefits to workers on leave, the employer must provide the same benefits for those on leave for pregnancy-related conditions.

Employees with pregnancy-related disabilities must be treated the same as other temporarily disabled employees for accrual and crediting of seniority, vacation calculation, pay increases, and temporary disability benefits.

It is also unlawful to retaliate against an individual for opposing employment practices that discriminate based on pregnancy or for filing a discrimination charge, testifying, or participating in any way in an investigation, proceeding, or litigation under Title VII. (Source: www.eeoc.gov)

Uniform Guidelines on Employee Selection Procedures, 1978

The Uniform Guidelines on Employee Selection Procedures was intended to address the need to establish a uniform set of principles relative to all elements of the selection process—including interviewing, preemployment testing, and performance appraisal.

The purpose of these guidelines was defined as follows:

> These guidelines incorporate a single set of principles which are designed to assist employers, labor organizations, employment agencies, and licensing and certification boards to comply with requirements of Federal law prohibiting employment practices which discriminate on grounds of race, color, religion, sex, and national origin. They are designed to provide a framework for determining the proper use of tests and other selection procedures.

> These guidelines do not require a user to conduct validity studies of selection procedures where no adverse impact results. However, all users are encouraged to use selection procedures which are valid, especially users operating under merit principles. (Source: www.dol.gov)

> A key purpose of the Uniform Guidelines is to deal with the concept of "adverse impact" (also known as "disparate impact") as this concept pertains to the employment process, and to ensure that interview and selection processes are reliable (consistent) and valid. For more information on this concept, see the section entitled "Disparate (or "Adverse") Impact.

CAUTION

Maintain careful and consistent records of your organization's employment selection procedures.

Reliability

The degree to which a selection process or instrument is consistent will determine the degree to which that instrument is reliable.

All interviews for a position should generate consistent information for decision making—even if several interviewers are involved, and even when all interviewers don't meet every candidate.

In this context, one important function of a well-defined and well-documented interviewing process is to ensure the most consistent and reliable results possible, even given the inevitable differences among interviewers. This is one reason why it is critical that interviewers prepare and consistently use a list of job-related questions that will be asked of all candidates for a particular position.

Validity

Employment interviews measure applicants' skills. Valid interviews ensure that those skills relate meaningfully and clearly to the skills that are required to perform a particular job.

Validity establishes and demonstrates a clear relationship between performance on the selection procedure and performance on the job. Although it is very difficult to establish good measures of validity, it is possible to make a case for validity if the interview has the following characteristics:

- ▶ It is based on job analysis.

- ▶ It contains questions that provide evidence about important job-related skills.

- ▶ Interview information is systematically related to a specific job.

HR professionals need to be familiar with at least four types of validity:

- ▶ *Content Validity*—A selection procedure has content validity if it assesses a candidate's ability to perform representatively sampled significant parts of the job.

  Example: A typing test for an administrative assistant's position would demonstrate content validity.

- ▶ *Criterion-Related Validity*—A selection procedure has criterion-related validity if scores achieved by incumbents correlate highly with their respective job performance.

  Example: A requirement that candidates have fluency in a particular foreign language would have criterion-related validity if it were shown that people who demonstrate fluency in that language actually perform better on the job than those who do not demonstrate fluency.

- ▶ *Construct Validity*—A selection procedure has construct validity if it measures the degree to which the test taker possesses a particular psychological trait (if, of course, it can be shown that the trait is required for successful performance of the position). More specifically, according to the EEOC Uniform Employee Selection Guidelines, "Evidence of the validity of a test or other selection procedure through a construct validity study should consist of data showing that the procedure measures the degree to which candidates have identifiable characteristics which have been determined to be important in successful performance in the job for which the candidates are to be evaluated."

  Example: An instrument that assesses the degree to which candidates for a car salesperson's position are persistent would demonstrate construct validity.

- ▶ *Predictive Validity*—A selection procedure has predictive validity if the predictions that it makes actually manifest themselves in the test takers' subsequent performance.

  Example: An instrument that is designed to assess the degree to which candidates for a position possess and demonstrate empathy would have predictive validity if individuals who scored well on this test demonstrated, after being hired, that they actually did possess and demonstrate this characteristic.

A Second Look at Resting

The Uniform Guidelines set forth—quite literally—*uniform guidelines* to help ensure that the selection process remains focused on job-related criteria. It may also, however, serve as an opportunity to look more closely at our selection processes—even if we have not found that adverse impact exists—so as to ensure that it truly is focused on the job and not on other extraneous factors. This does not, by itself, necessarily include nor exclude the use of instruments that we commonly refer to as "tests." It does, however, challenge HR professionals and hiring managers to ensure that the use of any such tests remains fixedly (and statistically) focused on job-related qualifications and requirements.

It might also challenge us to revisit tests that we have already incorporated into the selection process, perhaps applying a closer degree of scrutiny, or a greater degree of rigor, to our design or selection of each particular test. Testing is often seen as a panacea, of sorts, in the selection process—a black-or-white, make-or-break decision point. (Unless or until, of course, we aren't comfortable with a particular set of test results.)

In addition to challenging us to look closer at the validity and reliability of the tests we use, consider allowing the Uniform Guidelines to also serve as a challenge to rethink testing in general, because, in the most literal sense, every step in the selection process constitutes a test of one sort or another, and could be interpreted/analyzed/scrutinized as such by the EEOC. This applies even to the interview itself—even though this step in the selection process is often perceived as a semistructured (or even unstructured) opportunity to just "get a feel" for the candidate. Try to keep this perspective in mind as you take a closer look at "Interviews and the Interview Process" section later in this chapter.

Immigration Reform and Control Act (IRCA), 1986

IRCA accomplishes a number of objectives. Specifically, IRCA

- ▶ Prohibits discrimination against job applicants on the basis of national origin. IRCA also, however, specifically prohibits giving employment preference to U.S. citizens.

- ▶ Creates penalties for knowingly hiring illegal aliens (people who are referred to by some individuals and organizations as "undocumented workers," rather than "illegal aliens").

IRCA accomplishes these objectives through several means. The most visible process requires employers to review and record information/documentation submitted by employees that establish that employee's identity and eligibility to work in the United States. The form used to record this information is known as the I-9 form. The I-9 form must be completed within three business days of the employee's date of hire (but not before the employer starts). Certain portions of the I-9 must be completed by the employee and certain portions must be completed by the employer.

CAUTION

The I-9 lists acceptable documents for establishing identity and eligibility to work in the United States. Employees must provide either one document from Column A or one document each from Column B and Column C. Under no circumstances can an employer express preference for any particular document.

The Department of Justice provides the following information sheet on IRCA, as shown in Figure 4.2:

The Immigration Reform and Control Act (IRCA) Prohibits Employment Discrimination

What You Should Know

Under IRCA, when hiring, discharging, or recruiting or referring for a fee, employers with four or more employees may not:

- Discriminate because of **national origin** against U.S. citizens, U.S. nationals, and authorized aliens. (Employers of 15 or more employees should note that the ban on national origin discrimination against any individual under Title VII of the Civil Rights Act of 1964 continues to apply.)

- Discriminate because of **citizenship status** against U.S. citizens, U.S. nationals, and the following classes of aliens with work authorization: permanent residents, temporary residents (that is, individuals who have gone through the legalization program), refugees, and asylees.

Employers can demonstrate compliance with the law by following the verification (I-9 Form) requirements and treating all new hires the same. This includes the following steps:

- **Establish a policy of hiring only individuals who are authorized to work.** A U.S. citizens only" policy in hiring is illegal. An employer may require U.S. citizenship for a particular job *only* if it is required by federal, state, or local law, or by government contract.

- **Complete the I-9 Form for all new hires.** This form gives employers a way to establish that the individuals they hire are authorized to work in the United States.

- **Permit employees to present any document or combination of documents acceptable by law.** Employers *cannot* prefer one document over others for purposes of completing the I-9 Form. Authorized aliens do not carry the same documents. For example, not all aliens who are authorized to work are issued "green cards." As long as the documents are allowed by law and appear to be genuine on their face and to relate to the person, they should be accepted. Not to do so is illegal. Acceptable documents are listed on the reverse side.

IRCA established the Office of Special Counsel for Immigration-Related Unfair Employment Practices to enforce the IRCA antidiscrimination provision. Discrimination charges are filed with this Office. Charges or written inquiries should be sent to: Civil Rights Divison, The Office of Special Counsel for Immigration-Related Unfair Employment Practices, 950 Pennsylvania Ave., N. W., Washington, DC 20530. For more information, call the OSC Employer Hotline at 1-800-255-8155 (toll free); 1-800-362-2735 (TDD device for the hearing impaired). For questions about Title VII, please contact the Equal Employment Opportunity Commission at 1-800-669-4000 (toll free) or 202-275-7518 (TDD).

FIGURE 4.2 IRCA fact sheet.

List of Acceptable Documents

List A	List B	List C
Documents that Establish Both Identity and Employment Eligibility	**Documents that Establish Identity**	**Documents that Establish Employment Eligibility**

OR ... AND

List A — Documents that Establish Both Identity and Employment Eligibility

1. U.S. Passport (unexpired or expired)

2. Certificate of U.S. Citizenship (*INS Form N-560 or N-561*)

3. Certificate of Naturalization (*INS Form N-550 or N-570*)

4. Unexpired foreign passport, with I-551 stamp or attached INS Form I-94 indicating unexpired employment authorization

5. Alien Registration Receipt Card with photograph (*INS Form I-151 OR I-551*)

6. Unexpired Temporary Resident Card (*INS Form I-688*)

7. Unexpired Employment Authorization Card (*INS Form I-688A*)

8. Unexpired Reentry Permit (INS Form I-327)

9. Unexpired Refugee Travel Document (*INS FORM I-571*)

10. Unexpired Employment Authorization Document issued by the INS which contains a photograph (*INS Form I-688B*)

List B — Documents that Establish Identity

1. Driver's License or ID card issued by a state or outlying possession of the United States provided it contains a photograph or information such as name, date of birth, sex, height, eye color, and address

2. ID card issued by federal, state or local government agencies or entities provided it contains a photograph or information such as name, date of birth, sex, height, eye color, and address

3. School ID card with a photograph

4. Voter's registration card

5. U.S. Military card or draft record

6. Military dependent's ID card

7. U.S. Coast Guard Merchant Mariner Card

8. Native American tribal document

9. Driver's license issued by a Canadian government authority

For persons under age 18 who are unable to present a document listed above:

10. School record or report card

11. Clinic, doctor, or hospital record

12. Day-care or nursery school record

List C — Documents that Establish Employment Eligibility

1. U.S. social security card issued by the Social Security Administration (*other than a card stating it is not valid for employment*)

2. Certification of Birth Abroad issued by the Department of State (*Form FS-545 or Form DS-1350*)

3. Original or certified copy of a birth certificate issued by a state, county, municipal authority or outlying possession of the United States bearing an official seal

4. Native American tribal document

5. U.S. Citizen ID Card (*INS Form I-197*)

6. ID Card for use of Resident Citizen in the United States (*INS Form I-179*)

1. Unexpired employment authorization document issued by the INS (*other than those listed under List A*)

CAUTION

Employer penalties for nonadherence to hiring and record-keeping requirements—even wholly unintentional ones—are steep. Ensure that you are in compliance with both the letter and the spirit of the law.

Worker Adjustment and Retraining Notification Act (WARNA), 1988

As its name implies, the Worker Adjustment and Retraining Notification Act (WARN) is designed to give displaced workers time to make arrangements for other employment. "Arrangements," in this sense, span a spectrum of possibilities ranging from transferring to another worksite to participating in retraining programs, or anything in between.

WARN covers employers with 100 or more full-time employees (or the equivalent—100 or more full-time and part-time employees who work a combined total of 4,000 or more hours per week).

> **CAUTION**
>
> Exceptions and clarifications abound when it comes to determining whether an employer is covered by WARN. Review www.dol.gov for more information about how to make this determination.

WARN requires these employers to give employees at least 60 days' written notice before either a "mass layoff" or "plant closing."

According to WARN (www.dol.gov), a "mass layoff" occurs under the following sets of circumstances:

> Mass Layoff: A covered employer must give notice if there is to be a mass layoff which does not result from a plant closing, but which will result in an employment loss at the employment site during any 30-day period for 500 or more employees, or for 50–499 employees if they make up at least 33% of the employer's active workforce. Again, this does not count employees who have worked less than 6 months in the last 12 months or employees who work an average of less than 20 hours a week for that employer. These latter groups, however, are entitled to notice.

> An employer also must give notice if the number of employment losses which occur during a 30-day period fails to meet the threshold requirements of a plant closing or mass layoff, but the number of employment losses for 2 or more groups of workers, each of which is less than the minimum number needed to trigger notice, reaches the threshold level, during any 90-day period, of either a plant closing or mass layoff. Job losses within any 90-day period will count together toward WARN threshold levels, unless the employer demonstrates that the employment losses during the 90-day period are the result of separate and distinct actions and causes.

WARN Act is also triggered in the event of a "plant closing":

> Plant Closing: A covered employer must give notice if an employment site (or one or more facilities or operating units within an employment site) will be shut down, and the shutdown will result in an employment loss (as defined later) for 50 or more employees during any 30-day period. This does not count employees who

have worked less than 6 months in the last 12 months or employees who work an average of less than 20 hours a week for that employer. These latter groups, however, are entitled to notice.

Within the context of WARN Act, the DOL defines an employment loss as:

(1) An employment termination, other than a discharge for cause, voluntary departure, or retirement;

(2) a layoff exceeding 6 months; or

(3) a reduction in an employee's hours of work of more than 50% in each month of any 6-month period.

The DOL also cites certain exceptions to WARN Act:

"An employee who refuses a transfer to a different employment site within reasonable commuting distance does not experience an employment loss. An employee who accepts a transfer outside this distance within 30 days after it is offered or within 30 days after the plant closing or mass layoff, whichever is later, does not experience an employment loss. In both cases, the transfer offer must be made before the closing or layoff, there must be no more than a 6 month break in employment, and the new job must not be deemed a constructive discharge. These transfer exceptions from the "employment loss" definition apply only if the closing or layoff results from the relocation or consolidation of part or all of the employer's business."

Under WARN, notice must be given to

"…the chief elected officer of the exclusive representative(s) or bargaining agency(s) of affected employees and to unrepresented individual workers who may reasonably be expected to experience an employment loss. This includes employees who may lose their employment due to "bumping," or displacement by other workers, to the extent that the employer can identify those employees when notice is given. If an employer cannot identify employees who may lose their jobs through bumping procedures, the employer must provide notice to the incumbents in the jobs which are being eliminated. Employees who have worked less than 6 months in the last 12 months and employees who work an average of less than 20 hours a week are due notice, even though they are not counted when determining the trigger levels.

The employer must also provide notice to the State dislocated worker unit and to the chief elected official of the unit of local government in which the employment site is located."

The DOL provides the following guidance with respect to required notification periods under WARN Act:

"With three exceptions, notice must be timed to reach the required parties at least 60 days before a closing or layoff. When the individual employment separations for a closing or layoff occur on more than one day, the notices are due to the representative(s), State dislocated worker unit and local government at least 60 days before each separation. If the workers are not represented, each worker's notice is due at least 60 days before that worker's separation.

The exceptions to 60-day notice are:

(1) Faltering company. This exception, to be narrowly construed, covers situations where a company has sought new capital or business in order to stay open and where giving notice would ruin the opportunity to get the new capital or business, and applies only to plant closings;

(2) Unforeseeable business circumstances. This exception applies to closings and layoffs that are caused by business circumstances that were not reasonably foreseeable at the time notice would otherwise have been required; and

(3) Natural disaster. This applies where a closing or layoff is the direct result of a natural disaster, such as a flood, earthquake, drought or storm.

If an employer provides less than 60 days advance notice of a closing or layoff and relies on one of these three exceptions, the employer bears the burden of proof that the conditions for the exception have been met. The employer also must give as much notice as is practicable. When the notices are given, they must include a brief statement of the reason for reducing the notice period in addition to the items required in notices."

CAUTION

Exceptions to this and other portions of WARN have been built into the act (relating, for instance, to job retraining programs, bankruptcies, and so on). In addition, be aware that some states such as California have "baby WARN" laws in effect, which may have different notification thresholds and/or requirements. So, as always, be sure to check for—and ensure you are in adherence with—any relevant state laws.

Americans with Disabilities Act (ADA), 1990

The EEOC proudly describes the ADA as "the world's first comprehensive civil rights law for people with disabilities" and likens it to the Emancipation Proclamation for people with disabilities.

The ADA covers employers with 15 or more employees, including state and local governments. It also applies to employment agencies and to labor organizations. The ADA's nondiscrimination standards also apply to federal sector employees under section 501 of the Rehabilitation Act, as amended, and its implementing rules. According to the EEOC, Title I of the ADA prohibits private employers, state and local governments, employment agencies and labor unions from discriminating against qualified individuals with disabilities in job application procedures, hiring, firing, advancement, compensation, job training, and other terms, conditions, and privileges of employment. Title I also covers medical examinations and inquiries, as well as drug and alcohol abuse:

▶ *Medical Examinations and Inquiries*—Employers may not ask job applicants about the existence, nature, or severity of a disability. Applicants may be asked about their ability to perform specific job functions. A job offer may be conditioned on the results of a medical examination, but only if the examination is required for all entering employees in similar jobs. Medical examinations of employees must be job related and consistent with the employer's business needs.

▶ *Drug and Alcohol Abuse*—Employees and applicants currently engaging in the illegal use of drugs are not covered by the ADA when an employer acts on the basis of such use. Tests for illegal drugs are not subject to the ADA's restrictions on medical examinations. Employers may hold illegal drug users and alcoholics to the same performance standards as other employees.

(Source: www.eeoc.gov)

Title V of the ADA provides additional instructions with respect to its enforcement of the ADA by the EEOC, the federal agency charged with enforcing the employment provisions of the ADA.

The ADA also renders it unlawful to retaliate against an individual for opposing employment practices that discriminate based on disability or for filing a discrimination charge, testifying, or participating in any way in an investigation, proceeding, or litigation under the ADA.

At a minimum, HR professionals need to develop a solid understanding of the basic terminology used throughout the ADA to be able to effectively implement its provisions—and in order to move beyond simple compliance ("transactional") toward a more strategic application of the ADA ("tactical", or perhaps even "transformational").

Individual with a Disability

According to the EEOC, an "individual with a disability" is a person who

▶ Has a physical or mental impairment that substantially limits one or more major life activities;

▶ Has a record of such an impairment; or

▶ Is regarded as having such an impairment.

Qualified Person

To be a considered a "qualified person," a candidate must meet minimum job requirements (education, experience, licenses, and so forth) and must be able to perform the essential functions of the position with or without reasonable accommodation.

Reasonable Accommodation

A *reasonable accommodation* represents a change in the way that one (or more) responsibilities relating to the execution of a position is performed, so as to enable a person with a disability to perform the essential functions of the position. Accommodations, however, do not have to be adopted if they cause undue hardship to the organization.

Undue Hardship

An *undue hardship* is one that creates significant difficulty (enough to disrupt business operations); results in a significant financial outlay; or changes something about the essential nature of the business. If this language seems unclear, it is. Even the language drawn directly from the EEOC website relative to undue hardship is somewhat ambiguous: "Undue hardship is defined as an action requiring significant difficulty or expense when considered in light of factors such as an employer's size, financial resources, and the nature and structure of its operation." Perhaps this could be rephrased to say "it depends"—because it does.

> **CAUTION**
>
> Things are not always what they appear to be, so don't unilaterally make a determination about what constitutes undue hardship. Confer with legal counsel, client managers, and/or senior HR colleagues, as appropriate.

Disability

The ADA defines a current "disability" as a medical condition or disorder (called an "impairment") that substantially limits a person's ability to perform basic activities (called "major life activities").

Major Life Activities

According to the EEOC, "major life activities" include—but are not necessarily limited—to walking, seeing, hearing, breathing, caring for oneself, performing manual tasks, sitting, standing, lifting, learning, and thinking.

> **EXAM ALERT**
>
> The ADA is a multifaceted, multilayered law. In addition to those items discussed here, ensure that you understand related concepts including direct threat, current and past drug and alcohol use, and so on.

Civil Rights Act (CRA), 1991

The Civil Rights Act of 1991 significantly expanded upon employees' rights and remedies under Title VII of the Civil Rights Act of 1964. First, it established the right for plaintiffs to enjoy jury trials when bringing charges of discrimination. Second, it allowed for the awarding of compensatory and punitive damages. Total damages cannot exceed $300,000 per employee and could be capped as low as $50,000 per employee depending upon the number of people employed by the employer. In short, the larger the workforce, the higher the cap on damages.

Compensatory damages are designed to "make the employee whole" with respect to lost wages, benefits, and other expenses and losses. Punitive damages, as the name implies, are intended to punish employers who violate the act.

Congressional Accountability Act (CAA), 1995

Touted on the informational poster as "advancing safety, health, and workplace rights in the legislative branch," the Congressional Accountability Act expanded coverage of the following 12 laws to Congressional employees:

- ▸ Fair Labor Standards Act (FLSA), 1938

- ▸ Title VII of the Civil Rights Act of 1964, as amended

- ▸ Age Discrimination in Employment Act of 1967

- ▸ Occupational Safety and Health Act of 1970

- ▸ Rehabilitation Act of 1973

- ▸ Civil Service Reform Act of 1978

- ▸ Employee Polygraph Protection Act of 1988

- ▸ Worker Adjustment and Retraining Notification Act of 1988

- ▸ Americans with Disabilities Act of 1990

- ▸ Family and Medical Leave Act of 1993

- ▸ Veterans Reemployment Act of 1994

- ▸ Uniformed Services Employment and Reemployment Rights Act of 1994

Relevant Cases

HR professionals need to be familiar with key precedent-setting cases relating to EEO, workforce planning, and employment. The following summaries (presented in chronological order) describe the significance of some of those landmark cases.

Griggs v. Duke Power, 1971

Key Issue: Adverse impact

Significance: Discrimination need not be deliberate or observable to be real. Rather, it can exist if a particular policy or practice has a statistically significant adverse impact on members of a protected class. This is true even when the same requirement applies to all employees or applicants, as was the situation in this case. When a particular requirement does have an impact on members of a protected class, the burden of proof rests with the employer to demonstrate that the requirement is, in fact, job-related and consistent with business necessity.

McDonnell Douglas Corp v. Green, 1973

Key Issue: Disparate treatment/prima facie

Significance: The initial burden of proof for establishing a prima facie (Latin for "at first view") case of discrimination against an employer (or potential employer) under Title VII of the Civil Rights Act of 1964 rests with the employee (or applicant), who must be able to establish four key elements:

▸ The person is a member of a protected class.

▸ The person applied for a job for which the employer was seeking applicants.

▸ The person was rejected, despite being qualified for the position.

▸ After this rejection, the employer continued to seek other applicants with similar qualifications.

After the employee establishes a prima facie case for disparate treatment, the burden of proof then shifts to the employer, who must then provide a nondiscriminatory reason for its decision.

Albemarle Paper v. Moody, 1975

Key Issue: Employment tests—job relatedness and validity

Significance: Any tests that are used as part of the hiring or promotional decision-making process must be job related. This applies to any instrument that is used as a "test," even if that was not its original purpose. This case also established that employment tests must demonstrate predictive validity, consistent with the Uniform Guidelines for Employee Selection Procedures.

Washington v. Davis, 1976

Key Issue: Employment tests—disparate impact

Significance: A test that has an adverse impact on a protected class is still lawful, as long as the test can be shown to be valid and job related.

Regents of California v. Bakke, 1978

Key Issue: Affirmative action

Significance: The Supreme Court ruled that although race could be a factor in college admission decisions, quotas could not be established.

Although this case was based on a college admissions program, its significance extended to workplace affirmative action programs.

This case falls under the category of "reverse discrimination" because it alleged race discrimination and was brought by someone who was not a minority/person of color.

United Steelworkers v. Weber, 1979

Key issue: Affirmative action

Significance: Affirmative action plans that establish voluntary quotas that have been jointly agreed to by an organization as well as its collective bargaining unit do not constitute race discrimination under Title VII of the Civil Rights Act of 1964 if they are designed to remedy past discrimination that has resulted in current underutilization.

This case falls under the category of "reverse discrimination" because it alleged race discrimination and was brought by someone who was not a minority/person of color.

Meritor Savings Bank v. Vinson, 1986

Key Issue: Sexual harassment

Significance: This was the first ruling to establish that sexual harassment (whether quid pro quo or hostile environment) constitutes a violation of Title VII of the Civil Rights Act of 1964. In addition, the court ruled that it isn't enough for an organization to have a policy prohibiting discrimination. Instead, the ruling stated that "Reasonable care requires effective communication of policies and training. The employer has the burden of proof."

Johnson v. Santa Clara County Transportation Agency, 1987

Key Issue: Affirmative action

Significance: Gender can be used as a factor in the selection process if there is under-representation in a particular job classification, as long as the AAP does not set forth a quota.

This case falls under the category of "reverse discrimination" because it alleged sex discrimination and was brought by a man.

Martin v. Wilks, 1988

Key Issue: Affirmative action

Significance: Current employees who are negatively affected by consent decrees that were established in an earlier time and that sought to resolve discrimination that was present in an earlier time may challenge the validity of such decrees.

This case falls under the category of "reverse discrimination" because it alleged race discrimination and was brought by individuals who were not minorities/people of color.

Harris v. Forklift Systems, 1993

Key Issue: Sexual harassment

Significance: The court clarified the standard relative to what constitutes a sexually hostile work environment: "This standard, which we reaffirm today, takes a middle path between making actionable any conduct that is merely offensive and requiring the conduct to cause a tangible psychological injury. Conduct that is not severe or pervasive enough to create an objectively hostile or abusive work environment—an environment that a reasonable person would find hostile or abusive—is beyond Title VII's purview. Likewise, if the victim does not subjectively perceive the environment to be abusive, the conduct has not actually altered the conditions of the victim's employment, and there is no Title VII violation."

Taxman v. Board of Education of Piscataway, 1993

Key Issue: Affirmative action

Significance: The U.S. Court of Appeals for the Third Circuit ruled that—in the absence of underrepresentation as demonstrated and documented through an affirmative action plan—organizations cannot take race into account when making decisions relative to who will be laid off and who will be retained. Doing so would constitute a violation of Title VII of the Civil Rights Act of 1964.

This case falls under the category of "reverse discrimination" because it alleged race discrimination and was brought by a person who was not a minority/person of color.

St. Mary's Honor Center v. Hicks, 1993

Key Issue: Burden of proof

Significance: To ultimately prevail in an allegation of discrimination under Title VII of the Civil Rights Act of 1964, the charging party (meaning, the employee who filed the charge) must go beyond a prima facie case and *actually prove* that the employer's actual reasons for an employment action are, in fact, discriminatory.

McKennon v. Nashville Banner Publishing Co., 1995

Key Issue: After-acquired evidence

Significance: An employer will be held accountable for discriminatory employment actions even if it discovers evidence after taking the discriminatory employment action that would have led the employer to that same employment action for legitimate, nondiscriminatory reasons.

Faragher v. City of Boca Raton, 1998, and Ellerth v. Burlington Northern Industries, 1998

Key Issue: Sexual harassment

Significance: If an employee is subjected to a tangible adverse employment action because of a supervisor's sexually harassing behavior, the employer is liable. The employer is also vicariously liable when its supervisors create a sexually hostile work environment, even if the employee is not subjected to an adverse employment action. This is true whether or not the employer itself was negligent or otherwise at fault. However, if the employee *is not* subjected to tangible adverse employment action, the employer may be able to raise as a defense that he acted reasonably to prevent and/or promptly correct any sexually harassing behavior and that the plaintiff unreasonably failed to take advantage of the employer's preventive or corrective opportunities.

Kolstad v. American Dental Association, 1999

Key Issue: Punitive damages under the Civil Rights Act of 1991

Significance: Punitive damages can be awarded only when the employer has acted with malice and reckless indifference to the employee's federally protected rights. This subjective standard was considered to be easier to establish than the more objective standard that would be required if employees had to prove that the nature of the actual behavior to which they had been subjected reached a level where it would be considered "egregious."

Grutter v. Bollinger and Gratz v. Bollinger, 2003

Barbara Grutter was applying for admission to the University of Michigan Law School, and Jennifer Gratz was applying for the University of Michigan as an undergraduate student. Lee Bollinger was the president of the University of Michigan.

Key Issue: Affirmative action

Significance: Race can be taken into account as an admissions factor because it furthers the establishment of diversity—a "compelling state interest"—as long as the admissions process is "narrowly tailored" to achieve the objective of achieving a diverse student body.

Interestingly, Supreme Court Justice Sandra Day O'Connor indicated that cases of this sort will likely be ruled differently in the future: "Race-conscious admissions policies must be limited in time. The Court takes the Law School at its word that it would like nothing better than to find a race-neutral admissions formula and will terminate its use of racial preferences as soon as practicable. The Court expects that 25 years from now, the use of racial preferences will no longer be necessary to further the interest approved today."

These cases fall under the category of "reverse discrimination" because they alleged race discrimination and were brought by people who were not minorities/people of color.

167

Workforce Planning: Where Are We Going, and What Do We Need to Get There?

General Dynamics Land Systems v. Cline, 2004

Key Issue: Age discrimination (relative)

Significance: Younger employees (even if they are over the age of 40) cannot allege age discrimination because of the establishment of programs or decisions that favor older employees. As Justice David Souter wrote in the opening of his opinion, "The Age Discrimination in Employment Act of 1967 (ADEA or Act), 81 Stat. 602, 29 U.S.C. § 621 *et seq.*, forbids discriminatory preference for the young over the old. The question in this case is whether it also prohibits favoring the old over the young. We hold it does not."

REVIEW BREAK

At this point, we've scanned the legislative environment surrounding the functional area known as "workforce planning and employment." We've also taken a closer look at relevant cases pertaining to these laws. And although this is critical, by itself this knowledge isn't enough. Let's now take the insights we've gleaned from this legal perspective and bring them with us as we take a more hands-on approach to leveraging this functional area so as to have a positive impact—transactionally, tactically, and strategically—within the overall organization.

Workforce Planning: Where Are We?

Effective workforce planning ensures that the organization has the "people resources" in place that will enable it—through those very same people—to fulfill its mission and achieve its objectives. Workforce planning encompasses myriad activities relating to how employees enter into—and exit from—the organization. It looks at these functions primarily from the perspective of meeting the organization's needs and ideally takes a long-term (more tactical, or perhaps transformational, in nature)—as well as a short-term (more transactional in nature)—approach.

By effectively performing responsibilities relating to workforce planning and development, HR professionals can seize another opportunity to forge a business partnership with their internal clients. For this to happen, HR professionals must take a deliberate and consistent approach to workforce planning that starts with the organization's strategic plan and with how HR can align its efforts and work product with that plan.

Workforce Planning: Where Are We Going, and What Do We Need to Get There?

Determining "what" and "who" the organization needs to achieve its goals is more involved than it might appear. Accurate forecasting requires selecting from among numerous nonmathematical (qualitative) as well as mathematical (quantitative) analyses.

Nonmathematical Forecasting Techniques

In most organizations, qualitative judgments are made all the time. These judgments can relate to a whole host of issues—marketing, product development, philanthropy, staffing, or any other business-related issues. These judgments can be structured or unstructured, informal or formal.

Management Forecasts

Sometimes, individuals who perform qualitative analysis draw on the knowledge and experience of the organization's managers—and the institutional knowledge that those managers have acquired in their roles. Savvy managers—especially those who couple their awareness of the organization with knowledge of the industry and of the economy in general—can provide HR with a wealth of information. As a caution, however, it's also important to remember that the information derived from this somewhat unstructured approach may not always be accurate. Relying too heavily on managerial predictions can result in significant errors in judgment, and therefore should ideally be coupled with other, more structured mathematical and nonmathematical approaches.

The Delphi Technique

The Delphi technique is an example of a structured nonmathematical technique in which expert opinions from a variety of individuals are sought, distilled, and distilled again. An objective, neutral, uninvolved leader recaps what the experts submit, summarizes that information, and condenses it into a more concise format. (The leader is not one of the "experts" and does not inject his or her opinions or interpretations into the process.) This happens several times until a final position is identified—one that incorporates the evolving and iterative input of many individuals, but that does not unduly reflect any one position or viewpoint.

A distinguishing—and critical—element of the Delphi technique is that the "experts" from whom opinions are sought, and whose ideas are culled down, never meet in person and never discuss their submissions—all of which are made in writing. Rather, their submissions are collected and processed by an objective third party. In this way, the Delphi technique ensures that factors such as group dynamics, overpowering personalities, or just plain politics do not taint the assessment process. The anonymity of the process further encourages individuals to "take a risk" and submit their ideas without fear of reprisal, retribution, or judgment. The sanitized nature of this process puts expert contributors on a more even footing, further ensuring the integrity of this process.

Nominal Group Technique

Like the Delphi technique, the nominal group technique takes a nonmathematical approach to forecasting. The nominal group technique is also similar to the Delphi technique in that it calls upon the expertise and predictive ability of experts. Most of the similarities between these two techniques, however, end there. With the nominal group technique, experts meet in person and process their ideas as a group. Led by a facilitator,

169

Workforce Planning: Where Are We Going, and What Do We Need to Get There?

the meeting begins with each expert writing down and presenting his or her ideas to the group. Neither discussion nor assessment of ideas, however, is permitted at this point—only *presentation* is acceptable. The group then comes together to discuss each others' ideas, after which each individual group member is called on to independently rank the ideas. The meeting facilitator will then combine all the individual rankings to determine which are the most important and valued to the group. Through this process, the forecast is made.

Mathematical Forecasting Techniques

Mathematical—or quantitative—forecasting techniques are predicated on the belief that the best predictor of future performance is past performance (think "behavior-based interviewing," which we'll explore later in this chapter in the section entitled "Behavior-Based Interviews").

Trend Analysis

Trend analysis looks at and measures how one particular factor changes over a period of time. Trend analysis, for instance, can provide information—albeit unrefined—that can be helpful in developing a better understanding of business cycles, which in turn will affect staffing needs.

Ratio Analysis

Ratio analysis is similar to trend analysis, in that it examines changes, movements, and trends over a period of time. Instead of looking at just one variable alone, however, it looks at two variables (one of which, for instance, could relate to staffing levels) and how the relationship between those two variables has evolved over time. This becomes the basis for a number of applications, which could include forecasting staffing needs.

For example, a rental car company might look at how the number of cars rented per day, or per shift, compares to the number of employees assigned to work per day or per shift. This might help the car rental company predict future staffing requirements.

NOTE

Ratio analysis assumes that the relationship between the two factors being looked at will hold constant. In this example it also assumes that there will not be any turnover (which, of course, is not usually a reasonable assumption). Other assumptions may be operating, as well—consciously, or unconsciously. Because the degree to which those assumptions are identified—and are sound—will significantly affect the overall quality of the ratio analysis, these underlying assumptions must be surfaced and factored into the analysis. Also, ratio analysis—like any other analysis—usually should not be the only type of analysis that you use. A combination of analyses will generally yield a more reliable result.

Turnover Analysis

Turnover measures the percentage of the workforce that has left the organization during a specified period of time. Most often expressed on an annual basis, turnover is calculated as follows:

$$\frac{\text{\# of terminations during a specified period of time}}{\text{the average \# of employees in the workforce during that same period of time}}$$

This information can be used in a number of ways—one of which is to help predict future turnover rates, which can affect staffing needs. Turnover can be voluntary (for instance, an employee accepts employment at another organization) or involuntary (for instance, an employee is laid off). Turnover can be broken down in any number of ways:

- ▶ Total for the entire organization

- ▶ Total for one—or more—particular departments

- ▶ FLSA (exempt or non-exempt) status

- ▶ Length of service

> **NOTE**
>
> Despite popular opinion, turnover is not inherently bad. Just like cholesterol, there is "good turnover" and "bad turnover." An example of good turnover might be an individual who accepts a more challenging or appropriate position in a different unit or division within the organization. An example of "bad turnover" might be a relatively new employee who quits after two weeks because he or she did not accurately understand the requirements of the position for which he or she was hired.

> **NOTE**
>
> Whether turnover is deemed "good" or "bad," of course, involves making value judgments, which will vary from organization to organization. In one organization, for instance, an employee resigning to pursue higher education on a full-time basis or to serve the nation (through military service or the Peace Corps, for instance) might be counted as "good" turnover. In other organizations, these same reasons might be counted as "bad" turnover. Some organizations use the terms "acceptable" and "unacceptable" rather than "good" or "bad," so as to downplay the value judgments inherent to these labels. It's also possible to look at turnover in terms of controllability. Controllable turnover might include voluntary terminations, and noncontrollable turnover might include death or retirement.

Simple Linear Regression

Simple linear regression provides a different way of looking at statistical relationships. It examines the past relationship between two factors (in this case, one of which is staffing), determines the statistical strength of that relationship, and—on the basis of that analysis—projects future conditions. In the previous example of the rental car company, the relationship between car rentals and staffing levels would be measured, and—on the basis of the strength of that relationship—would be extrapolated into the future.

Multiple Linear Regression

Multiple linear regression is similar to simple linear regression, except that several factors are taken into consideration. In the rental car example, for instance, other factors that could be looked at in addition to staffing levels might be the number of vehicles that were actually available to be rented, the number of customers that "no-showed," or the number of potential customers who were turned away.

Simulations

Simulations create scenarios through which different "realities" can be tested out mathematically to see what could happen under a variety of changing conditions.

Workforce Planning: What Jobs Will Need to Be Performed?

After you have made an estimate relative to the number of employees it will take to accomplish the organization's short-term, long-term, and emerging staffing needs, the next step is to determine functionally—and on a job-by-job basis—what these employees will need to do to move the organization to where it needs to go. It is in this context that we will look at jobs.

> **NOTE**
>
> Not all organizations conduct this process in exactly the same order. It's more important to ensure that all these steps are taken in a logical way that will yield solid results than it is to mandate a particular process.

Job Analysis

As stated in Chapter 2, "HR: A Body of Knowledge and Principles," a job analysis is the process by which information about a specific position is collected (refer back to Chapter 2 for additional information). Job analysis produces three important outputs that are critical to the workforce planning process:

- Job description
- Job specifications
- Job competencies

Job Description

Job descriptions are a key tool for many of the functions that HR professionals perform. Though they can take many different formats, most job descriptions have several elements in common:

- *Identifying information*—Such as job title, department and/or division name, reporting relationship, FLSA status, the date on which the description was written, the name of the person who wrote it, and so on.

▸ *Scope information*—The area of responsibility for, over, or within which this position has authority and/or responsibility.

▸ *Responsibility for supervision, if applicable*—Any positions whom the position incumbent supervises.

▸ *Physical work conditions and/or physical demands*—Though easy to overlook, it's critical to include this information in the job description.

▸ *Minimum requirements*—Often, this refers to experience, education, and or other mandatory credentials required to perform the position successfully. These are often the factors that will be initially used to screen candidates in or out during the résumé review process, and to determine who will be interviewed.

▸ *Knowledge, skills, and abilities required*—Acceptable levels of knowledge, skills, and abilities (also known as KSAs). These go beyond the minimum requirements noted previously and may include items that organizations or interviewers sometimes mistakenly take for granted and do not explore enough with candidates during the selection process.

▸ *Knowledge*—Simply stated, what the incumbent needs to know about a specific body of information to be able to perform the position successfully. For instance, an instructor who conducts training onsite at a particular organization may need to have knowledge of organizational dynamics. An automotive mechanic may need to have knowledge of mechanical, electronic, and computer technology.

▸ *Skills*—A skill refers to the ability to perform a particular task. For instance, the instructor may need to possess the ability to engage participants in facilitated discussions about the workshop topics. The automotive mechanic may needs to possess the ability to drive a standard (or "stick") shift.

▸ *Abilities*—Abilities refer to specific traits or behavioral characteristics required to perform successfully in a position. For instance, the instructor may need to demonstrate a willingness and comfort engaging quickly with people with whom he or she is not previously acquainted (which could perhaps be referred to as "outgoing"). The automotive mechanic might need to be mechanically inclined.

▸ *Overall purpose of the position*—A short (usually less than a paragraph, and maybe even as short as a sentence) statement summarizing why the position exists and what it is intended to accomplish.

NOTE

> Some organizations also choose to include the mission of the organization on each job description, as a way of ensuring that the mission of the position is—and remains—meaningfully linked to and aligned with the mission of the organization.

▸ *Duties and responsibilities*—Tasks and functions that the incumbent is expected to perform. Sometimes, job descriptions also indicate the percentage of time that is spent on each major responsibility or group of responsibilities (which may or may not correlate to the importance of the responsibility).

Essential and Nonessential Job Functions

For ADA and other purposes, duties and responsibilities must be divided into two categories: essential and nonessential job functions.

CAUTION

The ADA states that "consideration shall be given to the employer's judgment as to what functions of a job are essential, and if an employer has prepared a written description before advertising or interviewing applicants for the job, this description shall be considered evidence of the essential functions of the job." Failure to have a job description in place, therefore, could diminish the strength of the employer's position in defending an allegation that an employee or applicant has been discriminated against on the basis of disability. In short, employers can't make up (or look like they are making up) requirements after the fact.

Essential functions are those that are inherently fundamental and necessary to a position. Together—and perhaps even on their own—they constitute part or all of the reasons the job exists. Often, an essential function cannot be performed by many—or perhaps even any—other employees in the organization.

Conversely, nonessential functions are more peripheral to the position. They generally constitute a smaller and relatively unimportant part of the position and could fairly easily be performed by other employees.

CAUTION

Confer with managers, senior HR staff, and counsel—as appropriate—relative to delineating essential from nonessential functions.

Job Specifications (or "Specs")

Job specifications refer to the qualifications that a successful candidate must possess and/or demonstrate to perform effectively in a position. They do not refer to the qualifications that the best-qualified candidate might possess; instead, they refer to what it will take to get the job done in a manner that fully meets expectations of the position.

Job specs can be expressed as

- KSAs
- Credentials (years of experience, educational requirements, and so on)
- Physical and/or mental requirements

CAUTION

Credentials, although important to establish and consider, can in reality be misleading. Specifically, a person who possesses or has earned a particular credential doesn't necessarily have the knowledge or skills that one might assume go along with that credential. Earning a four-year degree in accounting, for instance, doesn't necessarily mean that a candidate can perform certain accounting functions. Alternatively, the greatest accomplishment of a candidate who has five years of related professional-level experience may, in fact, be that he or she was not terminated during those five years. Or, he or she might have one year's worth of professional level experience that he or she has repeated five times. The bottom line—don't make assumptions. Credentials should be a starting point, not an ending point.

Job Competencies

Job competencies speak to broad categories of skills, abilities, behavioral characteristics, or even values that are required to perform successfully in a particular position, department, or organization. They are often embraced by organizations with terms such as "key success factors," "competencies for success," or "performance factors." They could include things such as "communication skills," "teamwork," and/or "initiative." The same competencies may manifest themselves differently in different positions or departments throughout the organization.

Preemployment, Phase 1: Recruiting Candidates

"Recruiting and selection" are often thought of as a single process. In fact, however, they are two separate components of the staffing process and need to be approached, and carried out, separately. *Recruiting* is the process of attracting and creating a pool of qualified candidates. *Selection* is the process of identifying the candidate(s) to whom the position will be offered.

Employer Branding

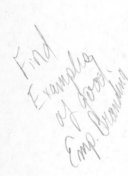

Before an employer goes out in search of new employees, it needs to consider how potential candidates in the labor market will perceive the organization. Organizations create a "brand" as an employer in much the same way they create a brand for the product or service that they market to their customers. So, just as an organization markets its products or services deliberately and intentionally, it must deliberately and intentionally decide on a marketing strategy that will be used to promote the employer brand within the labor market.

Selection Criteria

The first step that must be taken to begin the process of creating a pool of qualified candidates is to identify and develop selection criteria for the position. Selection criteria can be likened to a shopping list of what you're looking for in the individuals who will populate your candidate pool (and, ultimately, the employee(s) who will join the organization). This could—and often will—include KSAs, job specifications, and specific requirements stemming from the job competencies.

Never Go Shopping—or Recruiting—Without a List

If you go grocery shopping without a list, you can lose your focus, forget items you need, get things that are on sale (even if you don't really need them), or be attracted to items that are marketed well but that might lack substance. If this happens when you're going grocery shopping, it's no big deal—you can just go back to the store again to get what you missed the first time around. If you begin the recruitment and selection process, however, without a clear idea of the qualifications that your successful candidate must ultimately possess, the stakes can be a bit higher.

(continues)

(continued)

> Sometimes, our ideas about the requirements for a particular position could unintentionally be tainted by other factors—for instance, the qualifications that the prior incumbent possessed, or the qualifications of the individuals in the broader labor pool or who are actually applying for an open position. The best, most objective, and most legally defensible way to establish selection criteria is to do so objectively, within the context of the job-related information that has been generated through the job description, job specs, and the like. It's also critical to do this up front before you look at a single résumé.

Internal and External Recruiting

After you've determined (in collaboration with your internal client—most likely the hiring manager, in this case) the selection criteria for a particular position, the next step is to decide whether to seek to create a candidate pool internally, externally, or through a combination of both approaches.

Recruiting Internal Candidates

Many—in fact, most—organizations embrace the idea of promoting current employees from within the organization. There are two primary mechanisms for seeking internal candidates for positions within the organization—job posting and job bidding.

Job Posting

Job posting systems announce position openings to current employees within the organization. Candidates who believe that they meet the minimum requirements of the position (as posted) are invited to apply for positions—sometimes even before external candidates are sought.

Job Bidding

Although the job posting process isn't triggered until a job opens, job bidding systems invite employees to express interest in positions at any time, even if a position is not currently available. Candidates who are determined to be qualified for a position in which they express interest will automatically be put into consideration when that position becomes available.

Skill Inventories

Organizations can and often do maintain a central database that captures the many KSAs possessed by its employees, even when those KSAs are not being used by an employee in his or her current position. When a position opens up, the organization can then generate a list of current employees who meet the minimum qualifications for the position

> **TIP**
>
> Skill inventory systems may identify employees who meet the minimum qualifications for other positions, but who are not interested in applying for them. As long as an employee has not been specifically hired into a particular position as a "feeder pool" for a higher level position, it's important to ensure that there are no subtle or overt negative consequences for employees who decide not to pursue higher-level positions for which they have been identified as qualified through the skill inventory process. Every organization needs "Steady Eddies" and "Steady Bettys"—employees who are solid contributors in their current roles, who are happy and fulfilled in those roles, and who are not interested in climbing the corporate ladder. Creating a culture in which promotion is the only acceptable career track devalues the contributions of these solid contributors and can subsequently increase the likelihood that these underappreciated employees may eventually leave the organization. It can also increase the likelihood of turnover because of unrealistic expectations that are not fulfilled. The bottom line is that not everyone in an organization can or even wants to be promoted—so it doesn't serve an organization well to imply that "moving up" is the only option available to its employees.

Replacement Charts

Replacement charts identify names of individuals who could potentially fill a particular position in the event that an opening becomes available.

Internal Candidates: Advantages and Disadvantages

Recruiting internal candidates can benefit employees as well as employers. Through internal recruitment, employees can grow and develop without leaving the organization. Employers can select from a pool of internal candidates about whom they have more job-related knowledge than they would normally have about an external candidate. Both employees and employers can build on the investments they have already made in each other, and may even experience an enhanced sense of loyalty and dedication to each other.

Recruiting internal candidates, however, also presents certain risks, such as

▶ Relying too heavily on performance appraisals that, for a variety of reasons, may not be reflective of actual past performance (see Chapter 5, "Human Resource Development").

▶ Relying too heavily on performance appraisals that, even when accurate, may reflect KSAs that are not wholly relevant to the position for which the candidate is applying.

Particular "danger" exists when a position is posted for which a strong internal candidate has already been identified. If it is fully expected (in other words, predetermined) that a particular individual will be selected for an open position, the integrity of the job posting or bidding system could be seriously—and perhaps irreparably—compromised.

Policy Considerations

The organizational policies surrounding internal recruiting systems must be thought through carefully and administered consistently. For instance

▶ Is an employee who posts or bids for a position required to notify his or her current supervisor? Is the supervisor required to grant "permission" for the employee to post for another position?

▶ If an employee is selected for a position, how long must that employee wait before being allowed to start his or her new job? Must a replacement for the employee's former position be found before the employee can move on to his or her new position?

▶ Must an employee be performing satisfactorily in his or her current position to be considered for another position within the organization? Would certain areas of unsatisfactory performance be acceptable, such as those that are unrelated to the new position?

▶ Must an employee work for a particular period of time in one position before posting for a different position within the organization?

▶ Are employees who currently hold exempt-level positions subject to different requirements than employees who hold non-exempt–level positions?

Any of these considerations, depending on how they are handled, can either strengthen or diminish the ultimate effectiveness of the job posting or bidding system.

> **CAUTION**
>
> Be familiar with other advantages and disadvantages of techniques used to source internal candidates.

Recruiting External Candidates

There are a wide variety of options available for recruiting external candidates. A few of these options include

▶ Internet job listing websites

▶ Newspaper advertisements

▶ Radio advertisements

▶ ".jobs" websites

▶ College and university career development/placement offices

▶ Job fairs

▶ Open houses

▶ Alumni networks (alumni of colleges/universities, as well as alumni of companies)

▶ Former employees

▶ Walks-ins

▸ Professional organizations

▸ Referrals from current employees or industry network colleagues

▸ State unemployment offices

▸ Organizational websites

▸ Prior applicants

CAUTION

Considering prior candidates for openings for which they did not specifically apply can have repercussions relative to who is considered an applicant, particularly with respect to EO 11246. This can pertain, for instance, to "walk in" candidates who are filling out applications for "any" position, rather than for one particular job opening. It can also impact the way in which you phrase rejection letters; you may want to become familiar with possible ramifications before committing to candidates in their "rejection letters" that you will "consider them for any future job openings for which they may be qualified," or before digging through files to find a "great candidate" you remember interviewing for a different position.

▸ Employment agencies

▸ *Employment Agencies—State*—Each state has a service through which unemployed individuals who are currently looking for work are often required to register, thus providing a potentially rich pool of candidates to employers. These public agencies will also provide preliminary screening and candidate referral services to employers.

▸ *Employment Agencies—Temporary*—Many organizations utilize temporary employment agencies to secure services that are needed on a short-term basis. This allows organizations the flexibility to meet temporary, short-term, or unexpected needs. Some organizations also use a "temp to hire" model through which the organization tries out the employee before extending an offer of regular employment. This gives the employee the opportunity to try out the organization, as well, before deciding whether to make a commitment to a particular organization or position.

NOTE

This process was often referred to as "temp to perm." It is no longer advisable to use this language because there is no such thing as permanent employment. Employers should be careful not to say anything that could potentially imply otherwise, or that could unintentionally create an implied contract.

▸ *Private Employment Agencies (also known as private search firms)*—Employers may also enlist the services of private employment agencies to assist them in finding regular employees. There are two primary options:

▸ *Contingency employment agencies/search firms*—The employer pays a fee to the firm only when a candidate is hired through its efforts. This type of agency would be selected more often for entry-level professional or supervisory recruiting efforts.

▶ *Retained employment agencies/search firms*—The employer pays a fee to the firm whether or not a candidate is hired. This type of agency would be selected more often for executive-level recruiting efforts.

CAUTION

Different terms, conditions, and "guarantees" apply to different types of agencies. Terms can differ from employer to employer, or even position to position. It's important to negotiate knowledgeably, to finalize terms before beginning a search, and to review any agreements carefully before signing.

CAUTION

Be aware of less-traditional and non-traditional sources for recruiting external candidates—such as prisons, houses of worship, displaced homemaker services, and so on.

A Hybrid Approach: Employee Referral

Many organizations embrace employee referral systems—a recruiting technique whereby current employees are used as a source for recruiting external candidates into the applicant pool.

This approach offers distinct advantages—and potential disadvantages, as well. Some potential advantages include

▶ Candidates who are referred by current employees may have a better understanding of the culture and values of the organization and thus have more realistic expectations about the job and about the organization.

▶ Current employees are more likely to refer individuals who they believe (rightly or wrongly) have a high likelihood of succeeding. This happens because current employees often believe that the performance of the person whom they refer will have an impact on how they are perceived by the organization.

▶ Employee referral programs—even those that offer rich rewards—are significantly more cost-effective than most other forms of recruiting.

Employee referral programs also have the potential for significant disadvantages:

▶ If the current organization is not particularly diverse (with respect to gender, age, race, education background, or a host of other factors), employee referral programs might perpetuate that lack of diversity.

▶ If an affirmative action plan is in place, and if there are areas of underutilization, an employee referral program is not likely to demonstrate "good faith efforts" to recruit candidates who are women or minorities.

▶ In organizations where there are prior patterns of hiring discrimination, employee referral programs are likely to reinforce those patterns.

In many cases, organizations will not rely exclusively on employee referral programs for creating pools of candidates. Instead, employee referral programs are often one of several techniques used to create a pool of qualified and, ideally, diverse candidates.

Other Nontraditional Staffing Alternatives

HR professionals also need to be familiar with other, more flexible, less-traditional staffing arrangements. These arrangements do not necessarily fall within "internal" or "external" sources, because these options could be offered to existing employees within the organization, or could be used as a way to attract external candidates, or could even result in the outsourcing of functions that were formerly performed within the organization.

Some of the nontraditional staffing arrangements that an employer might choose to implement involve securing the services of individuals who are *not* employees of the organization. Examples of this could include the use of temporary help, temp-to-hire arrangements, or consultants, as described previously. Current or newly hired employees can also participate in flexible programs through part-time employment, telecommuting, job sharing arrangements, or seasonal employment.

> **CAUTION**
>
> Be familiar with the advantages and disadvantages of flexible staffing arrangements, as well as HR's role in implementing and executing these arrangements. Make sure you look at—and can assess and measure—these arrangements from a business perspective.

Measuring Recruiting Costs and Effectiveness

There are numerous ways to calculate the costs associated with recruiting as well as the overall effectiveness of the recruiting process. Some of those measures focus on the actual recruiting process (for instance, cost-per-hire, or time-to-hire), while others take a more forward-looking approach (for instance, voluntary and/or involuntary turnover percentage for new hires within the first 3, 6, or 12 months).

The most critical point to keep in mind about measuring recruiting costs and effectiveness is this:

Do it. And do it consistently.

In situations such as this, HR professionals can become their own worst enemies by settling for subjective answers to the question, "How am I doing?" The good news, however, is that herein lies yet another opportunity to be more strategic. So, in conjunction with your clients, and with HR leadership, determine which measures will be most relevant and valuable. Ask questions such as

- ▶ Which recruiting sources yield the most applicants?

- ▶ Which recruiting sources yield the best qualified applicants?

- ▶ On that note, how will you define a "good applicant"? Is it one who meets the minimum qualifications of the position? One to whom an offer of employment is extended? One who accepts an offer of employment? Or, one who is still with the organization 3, 6, or 12 months after being hired?

- ▶ Which recruiting sources are the least expensive, on a cost-per-hire basis?

- ▶ How much time, effort, and attention does each recruiting source require from HR, or from the manager, during the recruiting process?

To calculate many of these measures, you'll need to calculate yield ratios. A yield ratio calculates the percentage of applicants from a particular recruiting source who advance to a particular stage in the recruiting process. For instance, one pertinent yield ratio might refer to the number of résumés from minimally (at least) qualified candidates as a percentage of the number of total résumés received (from particular recruiting sources). It might also be helpful to compare this yield ratio for different recruiting sources.

Preemployment, Phase 2: The Selection Process

After you've put together a pool of candidates who—at the very least—meet the minimum qualifications for the position, the recruiting process is essentially complete. At this point, the selection process can begin.

The Employment Application

In most cases, candidates submit résumés during the recruiting process (this may not be true for all positions, such as for certain entry-level positions). From the candidate's perspective, résumés are essentially advertisements that are designed to get the candidate's foot in the door. This statement is actually quite literal, because the candidate's goal at this point is to be invited for an interview.

Résumés: Fact or Fiction?

A résumé is often written by someone other than the candidate who is submitting it; someone who may have great skill at presenting the candidate in the best possible light; someone who can perhaps make the candidate look stronger than he or she actually is. Résumés can also be created as the product of highly structured and preformatted software programs. These programs provide a host of possible qualifications, accomplishments, and responsibilities for hundreds of different positions that a candidate can choose to include in his or her résumé . Although software such as this can be very helpful in

(continues)

(continued)

constructing a résumé, it can also enable candidates to craft résumés that are not wholly reflective of reality. In other words, candidates can end up appearing much better on paper than they actually are in person.

HR professionals and hiring managers must recognize that although résumés are intended to provide a record of candidates' employment, education, skills, and job-related experiences, they are sometimes more "story" than "history." In addition, there is nothing on the résumé *itself* that requires the candidate to formally attest to the truthfulness of its contents—so relying on it to make employment-related assessments (beyond selecting whom to interview) may be ill-advised.

In addition to requesting a résumé, most organizations require candidates to complete an application form, usually before being interviewed.

CAUTION

Some organizations may require some, but not all, candidates to complete an evaluation form before being interviewed. When this happens, individuals applying for "lower-level" positions are often more likely to be required to complete the application before the first face-to-face interview, whereas applicants for "higher-level" positions are sometimes more likely to be permitted to postpone that requirement until it is determined that they will move forward in the selection process. Although commonplace, this practice is potentially problematic, on a number of levels. First, it is unfair and inconsistent. Second, if more women and people of color apply for lower-level positions (and are therefore required to complete an application form), there could potentially be adverse impact against women or people of color.

Like all other recruiting and selection tools, the application must seek information that is job-related and that is valid with respect to its ability to predict the applicant's ability to successfully perform the position.

NOTE

The EEOC considers the employment application to be a test—so be sure to scrutinize and assess it the same way you would scrutinize or assess any other test.

Types of Employment Applications

Employment applications provide a means for ensuring that all candidates present information about their work history, education, and experience—*in a consistent format*. Be careful on this point, however, especially if the same organization operates in different states in which different laws might be in effect. In addition, different types of applications are sometimes used for different types of positions within the same organization. This practice is generally considered to be permissible, as long as similarly situated applicants are required to complete the same type of application at the same point in the selection process.

Short-Form Employment Applications

Short-form employment applications are shorter versions of an organization's standard employment application. In this sense, the word "short" is used in a relative sense; even the short-form application could still be several pages in length.

Short-form employment applications may be used as a prescreening tool, or for certain "lower-level" positions within the organization that require fewer, less complex, or less technical skills. Short-form employment applications could also be used at an early phase in the selection process. In this case, candidates who progress to a later stage of the selection process might be required to complete a longer application at that time.

Long-Form Employment Applications

Long-form employment applications require candidates to provide more detailed and comprehensive information.

Job-Specific Employment Applications

Job-specific employment applications are sometimes used when an organization does high-volume recruiting for a particular position, or for particular types of positions. In such cases, the application would be tailored to seek highly specific and relevant information pertaining to the specific position or job category for which the candidate is seeking employment.

Weighted Employment Applications

Weighted employment applications are intended to facilitate the process of evaluating candidates' qualifications in a consistent and objective manner by assigning relative weights to different portions of the application. These different weights will vary depending on the relative importance of each section, as determined by the requirements of the position.

> **CAUTION**
>
> Weighted employment applications are difficult and time consuming to create and maintain because positions are almost constantly evolving and changing in some way. They can also run afoul of EEO guidelines (for instance, if extra credit is granted for factors that are not truly related to the job or that are not as important/unimportant as the weighting might imply).

Critical Parts of the Employment Application

Whatever type of employment application an organization chooses, many applications share a variety of elements.

The application will often require the candidate to provide information relative to the following areas:

- Personal data (name, address, contact information)
- Education

> ▶ Training
>
> ▶ Credentials/certificates/job-related skills
>
> ▶ Employment history (including organizations, dates of employment, titles, supervisors' names, and reasons for leaving prior positions)
>
> ▶ Names of professional references
>
> ▶ The candidate's ability to provide proof during the first three days of employment of his or her identity and eligibility to work in the United States (in the event that he or she is hired)

The application also serves as a vehicle to formally secure permission from and/or communicate information to the candidate—and to require the candidate to acknowledge the granting of that permission and/or the receipt of that information by signing the application. Examples of this might include

> ▶ Permission to verify information provided on the application.
>
> ▶ Permission to check references (former employers, supervisors, and/or professional references).
>
> ▶ Employment-at-will statement. This statement articulates and reaffirms that in almost every state the organization can terminate the individual's employment at any time, with or without cause. Most employment applications also confirm and articulate that the employee also has the right to leave the organization at any time, with or without notice.
>
> ▶ EEO statement (and, if applicable, affirmative action statement).
>
> ▶ Acknowledgement that the organization reserves the right not to hire the candidate if it is determined that he or she has provided any information that is not truthful.
>
> ▶ Acknowledgement that the organization may, or will, terminate the candidate if it is determined (after the candidate has been hired) that he or she provided any information on the application that was not truthful at the time the application was completed.

CAUTION

Whoever accepts applications from the candidate (whether electronically or face-to-face) must ensure that the application is fully completed before it is accepted. What this means in practice is that the candidate may not write the words "see résumé" on any portion of the application. It also means that all questions have been answered completely (sometimes candidates will leave a question blank that they do not want to answer so that they can still attest to the truthfulness of the information they have provided on the application and can thus attempt to avoid the sanctions that can stem from lying on an application).

Interviews and the Interview Process

As stated previously, from the perspective of the candidate, the purpose of a résumé is to get a job interview. From the perspective of the organization, the purpose of a résumé is to decide whom to interview. Taking this a step further, the purpose of an interview is to collect information that will enable the interviewer and the organization to determine the degree to which each candidate possesses and demonstrates the knowledge, skills, abilities, and other job specifications required to successfully perform the position.

Interviewing is one of those skills that most people learn by observation or through practice. Unfortunately, however, this skill is too critical to be learned through osmosis—in other words, the "sink or swim" approach doesn't always work. Sometimes, what happens instead is that interviewers will learn to swim, but will swim poorly (and perhaps even risk drowning). In addition, sometimes the people who new interviewers observe (and emulate) may not be skilled in the process.

Increased knowledge about and skill in interviewing can have a significant impact on the quality of the selection process.

Styles of Selection Interviews

Interviews fall into two primary types of styles—directive and nondirective.

▶ *Directive Interviews*—Directive interviews take a more structured approach by asking consistent questions of all candidates. The interviewer maintains control of the interview—despite the fact that candidates sometimes make significant attempts to seize that control away from them.

▶ *Nondirective Interviews*—Nondirective interviews are relatively unstructured. The candidate, not the interviewer, ends up guiding the interview, and therefore ends up controlling the flow and content of information.

To Direct, or Not To Direct

Which style is better to use in selection interviews—directive or nondirective? Generally speaking, a directive style is more effective and appropriate than a nondirective style, for a number of reasons:

▶ If a résumé is equivalent to a candidate's advertisement, giving a candidate control of the interview is like letting her or him broadcast an infomercial. Candidates will unfailingly present and highlight information that is most flattering to them—but that information won't necessarily coincide with the information that the interviewer needs to collect and assess relative to each candidate's ability to perform the job. It also isn't likely to be consistent with information provided by other candidates, which can lead to unfair and even flawed comparisons between candidates—comparisons that would be difficult to defend in the event of a legal challenge.

▶ To conduct a fair, reliable, and legally defensible interview, interviewers must ask candidates consistent questions. This is exceedingly difficult, if not impossible, to accomplish during a nondirective interview.

Perhaps the most effective approach is a combination of *both* of these approaches—a combination that, in a sense, reflects the reality that selection interviewing is an art as well as a science. Developing a style that reflects a structured conversation ensures that all candidates are asked consistent questions, yet allows for related follow-up questions that keep the interaction lively, dynamic, revealing, and informative (all within a consistent and job-related context).

Types of Selection Interviews

There are a variety of selection interviews. In this section, we'll look at some of the better-known types of preemployment interviews:

- ▶ Phone interviews
- ▶ Prescreen interviews
- ▶ Behavior-based interviews
- ▶ Stress interviews
- ▶ One-on-one versus panel/team interviews

Phone Interviews

Sometimes, organizations choose to conduct a short phone interview before deciding whether to bring a candidate in for a face-to-face interview. This can be particularly helpful in surfacing legitimate job-related "knock-out" factors that could either cause the employer to decide to eliminate a candidate from consideration, or that could cause a candidate to self-select out of the selection process. Factors that might be discussed could involve job requirements (such as overtime or work conditions), salary requirements, or basic technical knowledge or skill, just to name a few possibilities.

TIP

Phone interviews can be an efficient and effective way of showing respect for your candidates, your internal clients, and yourself. Just be certain to be consistent in the questions you ask each candidate—even at this point in the process.

Prescreen Interviews

In many organizations, HR conducts initial prescreening interviews with candidates. The purpose of prescreen interviews is to determine which candidates meet specific job requirements—the same ones that were identified in advance. This can include the process of verifying that the candidate actually meets the minimum requirements for the position, as well as establishing whether the candidate meets other specific fundamental requirements. (We have used the word "actually" in light of the recognition, once again, that a résumé might be more "history" than "story.")

TIP

Here, too, the HR professional has an opportunity to partner with line managers. Don't make assumptions about what qualifications you should try to assess during a prescreen interview; instead, work collaboratively with your clients to develop an effective, streamlined, cohesive strategy.

Behavior-Based Interviews

Behavior-based interviews require the candidate to describe past experiences that demonstrate the degree to which he or she possesses the knowledge, skills, and behavioral characteristics that are required to successfully perform the position for which the candidate is applying.

Behavior-based questions ask the candidate to describe a specific situation in which he or she demonstrated a particular job requirement. In their responses, candidates should describe the situation, the specific way in which the candidate behaved in the situation, and the outcome that resulted from his or her actions.

TIP

Behavior-based questions are effective only if the candidate provides a thorough and complete answer. Candidates, however, often are not conditioned to respond in this way, so it's incumbent upon the interviewer to ask probing follow-up questions. Probing follow-up questions must focus on the original question and not allow the candidate to stray into a different area about which the candidate might prefer to speak. Probing questions must also be asked with the intention of getting the information the interviewer needs (the information that the original question sought to obtain), even if the interviewer doesn't get the information he or she wants.

Stress Interviews

During stress interviews, the interviewer (or interviewers) deliberately creates a high-stress environment in an effort to ascertain how the candidate would respond in a high-stress work situation.

CAUTION

There are two primary concerns with respect to stress interviews. First, interviewers run the risk of jeopardizing the degree to which they can ascertain all of the other KSAs required for the position. In some jobs, where the ability to handle extreme levels of stress is absolutely essential and foundational (such as homeland security), this may be wholly appropriate. In other situations where extreme stress is a factor—but is not a constant, immutable, or defining element of a position—stress interviews may not be the most effective choice.

A second area of potential concern with respect to stress interviews is that the interviewer must be certain that a consistent level of stress is created in each employment interview, that the stress that is created in different interviews is of a consistent nature, and that it is created in a consistent manner. Otherwise, the "stress test" element of the interview could be found to be inconsistent and, therefore, unreliable. This could, in turn, increase the possibility of a legal challenge or allegations of unlawful discrimination.

One-on-One Versus Panel/Team Interviews

Sometimes, for a variety of reasons, organizations choose to conduct *panel* or *team* interviews—interviews in which more than one interviewer interviews a candidate at the same time. Panel interviews can save time and money. They can also backfire. To help ensure that panel interviews are successful and productive, keep the following ideas in mind:

▶ Let the candidate know ahead of time that he or she will be participating in a panel interview. Eliminating the element of surprise will help prevent additional unnecessary anxiety.

▶ Plan—even choreograph—the interview in advance. Make sure all participants know their respective responsibilities. Plan who will ask which questions and how probing follow-up questions will be handled. Arrange for "hand offs" from one interviewer to another, much the same way as is done during a team-based television newscast.

▶ Consider the seating arrangements. If possible, interview in a room that has a round table. If you must interview in a room with an oval or rectangular table, position the chairs in a way that creates the feeling of a round table. At all costs, avoid placing all of the interviewers on one side of the table and the candidate on the other side of the table. It is also best to avoid placing the candidate at the head of the table when there are multiple interviewers, as this can lead to a "tennis match" need to continually look from one side of the table to the other.

Key Components of the Selection Interview

An interview is part science, part art, and part architecture. The interview process must be carefully structured to support its overall purpose: to provide the interviewer *and* the candidate with information that can be used to make accurate assessments and, ultimately, sound decisions. The interviewer needs to assess the degree to which the candidate possesses the qualifications for the position. The candidate needs information to make an informed decision about whether to join the organization, in the event that an offer of employment is extended. And, throughout all of this, interviewers have to be careful not to give away the answers before they even ask the questions (this becomes particularly important when an organization uses a sequential interview process).

Though there is no single best way to structure an interview, the following presents one effective approach:

1. *Establish Rapport*—It's important to help the candidate feel welcome at the beginning of the interview. Establishing rapport through a warm greeting, an offer of a glass of water, or brief "chit chat" about the weather can help the candidate to relax—and, in turn, hopefully provide more candid, honest responses.

> **CAUTION**
>
> Rapport-building is a way of breaking the ice—just be careful that you don't fall though. Don't let your chit chat stray into areas about which you should not be conversing with candidates. Avoid, for instance, discussions about children, hobbies, mode of transportation, world events, or political happenings. Don't allow the conversation to stray into small talk that would reveal information that is unrelated to the position.
>
> In addition, recognize and remember that you will (hopefully) be interviewing a diverse pool of candidates and may encounter individuals who dress, speak, behave, or interact in ways that are different from your own. A candidate, for instance, may choose not to shake your hand, or may choose not to make eye contact with you. Don't inappropriately read into these or any other potentially unexpected behaviors. Be open and inclusive of these differences, and make sure you base your assessments solely on job-related factors.

2. *Ask Primary and Probing Questions*—Primary questions are asked of all candidates for a particular position during a particular interview process. They are designed to elicit relevant information about how well the candidate possesses and can demonstrate the skills, knowledge, and behavioral characteristics required to perform the position successfully.

   Probing questions are the follow-up questions to those primary questions. Because they are asked in response to each candidate's initial response to a primary question, probing questions will vary from interview to interview. Interviews can still ensure consistency, however, by only asking probing questions that relate to the original primary question. Don't get derailed by an evasive candidate, an interesting tangent, or a candidate's inability to answer the original primary question.

> **CAUTION**
>
> Probing is a double-edged sword! We need to probe until we get what we need, not until we get what we want. Make sure that your probing stays focused on the original primary question, and don't get distracted or derailed. And after you get the answer to your primary question—***stop probing***. Be particularly careful not to let your curiosity get you to probe too deeply.

3. *Invite the Candidate to Ask Questions*—After you have finished asking your primary and probing questions, invite the candidate to ask you any questions he or she might have. It is important to provide this opportunity only *after* you have asked your questions, so as to ensure that the candidate does not obtain information from you that will enable him or her to better answer your questions. In other words, as already mentioned, interviewers need to be careful not to give away the answers before they even ask the questions.

> **TIP**
>
> A candidate's questions can also provide insight into his or her motivations, professional interests, or the seriousness with which he or she is approaching the job search. Pay careful attention to what you hear. Be equally careful not to be overly impressed by well-developed questions; many candidates understand that one of the rules of interviewing is to have good questions prepared in advance. It is particularly important to remember that there can be a vast difference between a candidate's ability to interview well for a job and a candidate's ability to perform the job for which he or she is interviewing.

4. *Realistically Describe the Position and the Organization*—Provide each candidate with complete, honest, realistic, and consistent information about the position and the organization. Ensure that you share information in a consistent manner with all candidates—those in whom you preliminarily think you might be more interested, as well as those in whom you think you might be less interested. "Pitching" the position more positively or enthusiastically to one candidate over another could potentially raise questions later about why you did not share information in a consistent manner, and why you chose to encourage or discourage particular candidates.

> **TIP**
>
> The interview is a time to collect information—assessment comes later. Maintain an open mind about all candidates at this point, and focus on what is taking place in the actual interview. Evaluate the information you collect during the interview after it's over. During the interview, make a conscious effort not to be distracted by anything that might cause you to make a snap judgment about the candidate or about his or her qualifications for the position. Recognize any such items/distractions and set them aside to think about later—*after* the interview is over. Remaining nonjudgmental and remaining "in the moment," are two of the most important keys to being an effective interviewer.

5. *Close the Interview*—In that same spirit, end all your interviews in a consistent and nonjudgmental manner. Let the candidate know what will happen next in the process, and provide the candidate with a reasonable time frame during which he or she can expect to hear back from you. Make no promises, offer no assessments, and provide no "feedback" relative to how the candidate performed during the interview. An interviewer's role is one of information gatherer, not career counselor (at least with respect to external candidates. And any career counseling for internal candidates should take place after the interview/selection process is completed—not during the actual process).

Essential Intra/Inter Personal Skills Required to Conduct an Effective Interview

Within this structure, interviewers must bring the interview to life. They must use their skills—interpersonal and otherwise—to attain a variety of goals, including ensuring that

- ▶ All needed information is obtained.

- ▶ All interviews are conducted in a consistent manner and yield consistent information.

- ▶ The interview is positive, upbeat, and affirming, and does not assume a robotic tone.

- ▶ The rapport that was established at the beginning of the interview is maintained—or, as necessary, rebuilt—throughout the interview.

- ▶ They do not allow personal feelings or biases that are unrelated to the position to enter into the interview process.

- ▶ They remain within both the letter and the spirit of the law.

The following section highlights some of the skills essential for conducting an effective interview.

Intra/Inter Personal Skills

Listen carefully, attentively, and effectively. Paraphrase what you hear the candidate saying. When you do, preface your statements with phrases like

- ▶ "What I think I hear you saying, and please feel free to correct me if I am mistaken, is…"

▶ "So what I'm getting from you on this point, and please let me know if I've heard this correctly, is…"

In this way, you actually give the candidate permission to correct your understanding (something that most candidates are probably reluctant to do). You invite them, essentially, to tell you if you're wrong. This approach—and any clarifying information that you elicit from candidates—will help you attain your objective of ensuring that you leave the interview with an accurate understanding of each candidate's qualifications for the position.

Nonverbals

Observe each candidate's nonverbal behavior. When you notice a significant change in that behavior, pay attention, and consider probing for more information around whatever question the candidate was answering when that change occurred. Be careful not to assign specific meaning to any specific gesture. For instance, folding one's arms across one's chest may not necessarily mean that a candidate is distant, aloof, or hiding something. It may mean that the candidate is cold (literally, not figuratively). And be careful that any probing questions you ask remain strictly job-related. In addition to killing the cat, curiosity also has the potential to land an employment interview in hot water.

It's also important to be aware of the messages that you may be transmitting to candidates through your own nonverbal behavior. Try to convey openness through your posture and movements. Deliberately use your nonverbal communication cues to encourage the candidate's engagement. Make sure you do not unintentionally communicate any sort of judgment—either positive (for example, through nodding) or negative (for example, through a frown or furrowed brow).

Take Notes

During the interview, jot down keywords or phrases that the candidate offers in response to your primary and probing questions. If you leave whitespace in between your list of questions, you'll have a convenient place where you can jot down keywords that pertain to the specific questions you are asking. Be careful not to take too many notes—this could detract from your connection with the candidate. You can—and should—go back after the interview is complete to fill in any gaps and details that will provide a more complete picture around the key words that you already wrote down.

> **TIP**
>
> It's important to let the candidate know at the *beginning* of the interview that you will be taking notes. Otherwise, the minute you jot something down, the candidate may assume that he or she said something "wrong," and may spend time and energy trying to determine what that was, and how they can back their way out of whatever they shouldn't have said. When you let the candidate know you will be taking notes, you can use it as a rapport building opportunity. Let them know, in your own words, that what they'll be telling you during the interview is important, and that you want to be sure that you accurately capture, and remember, what they say.

> **CAUTION**
>
> All notes must be strictly job related. Do not use any sort of code that will help you recognize individual candidates. In addition, do not take any notes on the résumé; instead, use the whitespace that you have left between each of the primary questions you prepared (including two or three questions on each 8-1/2 by 11 sheet of paper serves as a good starting point).

Manage Your Biases—Individual, Organizational, and Societal

Although we all have the right to think or feel however we choose, we don't always have the right to act on those feelings. This is particularly true in an employment context, and with respect to interviewing. Interviewers are human beings, and, like all human beings, we have biases. However, we should not make—and are often barred by law from making—assessments or decisions that are based on those biases rather than on predetermined job-related factors.

As interviewers, it is incumbent upon us to vigilantly recognize how our individual biases could taint our assessments and decisions. Biases at the organizational level—and even at the societal level—could also affect our assessments and must also be recognized, managed, and set aside.

Interviewers must develop the ability to—recognize and eliminate from consideration—factors that are not job related when making employment-related recommendations and decisions. These factors can relate to legally protected classes, such as a person's race or religion, or could relate to things that are (for the most part) generally unrelated to the law, such as a candidate's appearance, personal mannerisms, name, or even cologne.

Manage Your Biases—Interviewer Errors

Another category of interviewer bias also warrants attention. These biases essentially constitute "errors"—meaning "errors in judgment"—that are sometimes made by interviewers. Interestingly, these errors are similar to those that are sometimes made by HR professionals or managers during the performance management and appraisal process, as well. Learning to address and prevent these errors up front, therefore, can yield benefits throughout the entire employment life cycle. Table 4.2 describes some types of interviewing bias.

TABLE 4.2   Interviewing Bias or Errors

Type of Interviewing Bias or Errors	How It Manifests Itself in the Interviewing Process
Contrast	The interviewer compares candidates to each other instead of comparing them to the requirements of the position.
	Although it is essential to eventually compare candidates to each other, this comparison—by itself—can be misleading. Even the "best qualified candidate" won't necessarily meet the requirements of the position. Becoming professionally enamored with a candidate because he or she is "the best of the bunch" could result in a substandard hire, and, ultimately, an unsatisfactory hiring decision. Before comparing candidates to each other, therefore, interviewers should compare each individual candidate's qualifications to the requirements of the position.

TABLE 4.2   *Continued*

Type of Interviewing Bias or Errors	How It Manifests Itself in the Interviewing Process
First impression	The interviewer places an inordinate level of emphasis on the impression that the candidate makes on him or her during the first few minutes or even seconds of the interview.
	It has been said that "first impressions last." While the impression may last, that impression may be incorrect. At best, it is incomplete. Interviewers need to remind themselves that good candidates, at times, get off to a slow start during the interview. So, too, poor candidates may initially appear quite polished and impressive.
Halo	The interviewer evaluates the candidate disproportionately positively on the basis of one outstanding and impressive qualification or characteristic.
	This evaluation, however, is often incomplete and inaccurate. One positive quality or qualification—no matter how impressive it may be—is not reflective of all of the KSAs required to perform a position successfully.
Horns	The interviewer evaluates the candidate disproportionately negatively on the basis of one poor qualification or characteristic.
	This evaluation, however, is often incomplete and inaccurate. One negative quality or qualification—no matter how unimpressive it may be—is not necessarily reflective of all of the KSAs required to perform a position successfully.
Leniency	The interviewer applies an inappropriately lenient standard to one or more candidates, resulting in a higher overall assessment of the candidate.
	Being "nice" to one or more candidates doesn't help the organization and is unfair to the candidate, as well.
	Instead, an organization needs to hire qualified candidates to fulfill its mission and attain its overarching objectives. Extending offers to unqualified or less-qualified candidates as a way of being "nice" undermines those efforts.
	In addition, it's important to keep in mind that a candidate who is invited to accept a position for which he or she is not truly qualified is, in one sense, being "set up to fail."
Strictness	The interviewer applies an inappropriately harsh and demanding standard to one or more candidates, resulting in a lower overall assessment of the candidate.
	Being "strict" with one or more candidates doesn't help the organization and is unfair to the candidate, as well.
	An organization needs to hire qualified candidates to fulfill its mission and attain its overarching objectives. Eliminating qualified candidates from consideration because of unrealistically high standards undermines those efforts.
	A candidate who is denied the opportunity to join the organization and perform a position for which he or she is truly qualified can end up with a negative impression of the organization. If enough candidates have an experience such as this, and share it with enough individuals, the organization's reputation in the labor market could ultimately end up being damaged.
Recency	The interviewer recalls the most recently interviewed candidates more vividly than candidates who were interviewed earlier in the process.
	Again, this error allows unfairness to enter into the process. The random scheduling of candidate interviews should not result in any candidate being unduly favored or discounted.

(continues)

TABLE 4.2 *Continued*

Type of Interviewing Bias or Errors	How It Manifests Itself in the Interviewing Process
Similar-to-me	The interviewer evaluates a candidate on the basis of how much that candidate is similar to, or different from, the interviewer.
	If interviewers recognize characteristics or attributes in candidates that they dislike about themselves, this recognition—whether conscious or unconscious—can have a negative impact on how the interviewer evaluates the candidate. Conversely, if interviewers recognize characteristics or attributes in candidates that they like about themselves, this recognition—whether conscious or unconscious—can have a positive impact upon how the interviewer evaluates the candidate. Either way, the impression is personal in nature, unrelated to the candidate's qualifications, and is therefore inappropriate.

Showing Respect Throughout the Recruiting and Selection Processes

Sometimes, in the heat of the recruiting and selection process, HR professionals overlook the reality that candidates are not the only ones being assessed or interviewed. At every stage of the recruitment and selection processes, candidates are paying careful attention to how they are treated by the employees with whom they come into contact. As such, professionalism is essential—as is discretion and respect. It might be helpful to remember the "golden rule" when it comes to how you treat a candidate. So, throughout the recruiting and selection processes, try to empathize with the candidate. For instance, ask yourself—if you were a candidate, what kind of voice-mail message would you like a potential employer to leave for you? Would you want a telephone interviewer to just jump into his or her questions, or would you prefer him or her to set up a time that is mutually convenient? And always remember that when you participate in the recruiting and selection process, you are representing more than just yourself individually. To candidates, you represent and define—to a significant degree—the entire organization.

Legal Considerations for Interviewing and Selection

Interviewers need to be cautious not to wander intentionally or unintentionally into areas that present potential legal pitfalls.

The following tables provide some examples of questions that should not be asked during an interview, why they should not be asked, and questions (if any) that you might want to ask instead. You'll start with Table 4.3, which covers inappropriate questions regarding sex discrimination, and then you'll cover Table 4.4, which discusses inappropriate questioning in regard to race and national origin discrimination. Next is Table 4.5, which covers religious discrimination; Table 4.6 covering age discrimination; Table 4.7 covering disability discrimination; and we wrap up with Table 4.8, which covers inappropriate questioning regarding disability and worker's compensation discrimination.

TABLE 4.3   Inadvisable Questions Regarding Sex Discrimination

Don't Ask	Why	Ask This Job-Related Question Instead
Are you married? What is your marital status?	Sex discrimination	This is an illegal question. There is no way to reformulate it.
Do you wish to be addressed as Miss? Mrs.? Ms.? What is your spouse's name?	Sex discrimination	This is an illegal question. There is no way to reformulate it. Address the candidate either by his or her first name, or the prefix "Ms." or "Mr.", followed by the candidate's last name. Do not, however, address men by their first names and women by "Ms.", as this inconsistency could be interpreted as an effort to seek information relative to marital status from female candidates.
Are you planning on starting a family?	Sex discrimination	This is an illegal question. There is no way to reformulate it.
How will your husband feel about your traveling overnight 30% of the time?	Sex discrimination	*This position requires 30% overnight travel. Can you meet this requirement of the position?*
How many children do you have?	Sex discrimination	This is an illegal question. There is no way to reformulate it.
What childcare arrangements have you made?	Sex discrimination	*Our hours are 10 AM to 6 PM. Can you meet this requirement of the position?*
		This position requires approximately 10 hours of overtime per week, often with little or no notice. Can you meet this requirement of the position?
		This position requires you to work shifts that can rotate on a monthly or even a weekly basis with little or no notice. Can you meet this requirement of the position?

TABLE 4.4   Inadvisable Questions Regarding Race and National Origin Discrimination

Don't Ask	Why	Ask This Job-Related Question Instead
Where are you from?	May get national origin information in response.	This is an illegal question. There is no way to reformulate it.
What languages do you speak?	Response may give national origin information.	Ask about specific language skills only if they are required for the position for which you are interviewing the candidate. *Can you speak _____ fluently?*
Do you own your home, or rent? How long have you lived at your current address?	Possible race or national origin discrimination	*What is your address?* (This question is often included as part of the application.)
What type of military discharge did you receive?	May be acceptable if U.S. military-related project. Otherwise, potential race discrimination.	*What job did you have in the military? Can you qualify for the security clearance?*

(continues)

TABLE 4.4 Inadvisable Questions Regarding Race and National Origin Discrimination *(continued)*

Don't Ask	Why	Ask This Job-Related Question Instead
Have you ever been arrested?	Potential race discrimination. (disparate impact)	*Have you ever been convicted of a crime?* (This question is often included as part of the application.)
What is your maiden name?	Sex or national origin discrimination.	*Have you ever worked for this company under a different name? Is additional information relative to change of name, use of a nickname, or assumed name necessary to enable a check on your work record? If so, please provide this information.*

TABLE 4.5 Inadvisable Questions Regarding Religious Discrimination

Don't Ask	Why	Ask This Job-Related Question Instead
What holidays do you require for religious observance?	Religious discrimination	*The required schedule for this position is Monday to Friday, from 9 AM to 5:30 PM. Can you meet this requirement of the position?* Please note, however, that a candidate does not need to reveal the need for reasonable accommodation on the basis of religion during the interview. As such, a candidate could answer this question "yes" and still request a reasonable accommodation on the basis of his or her religious beliefs as soon as he or she is hired. If so, seek advice from senior HR colleagues, and/or from legal counsel, as appropriate.

TABLE 4.6 Inadvisable Questions Regarding Age Discrimination

Don't Ask	Why	Ask This Job-Related Question Instead
How old are you? What is your date of birth?	Age discrimination	This is an illegal question. There is no way to reformulate it.

TABLE 4.7 Inadvisable Questions Regarding Disability Discrimination

Don't Ask	Why	Ask This Job-Related Question Instead
Is there any health-related reason why you may not be able to perform the job for which you are applying?	Disability discrimination	These are illegal questions. There is no way to reformulate them.
Have you ever been treated for a mental condition by a psychiatrist or psychologist?		
Are you taking prescription drugs?		
I see that you're a veteran; is that how you lost your arm?		
Will you always be confined to a wheelchair?		
How many days were you absent from work because of illness last year?		

TABLE 4.7   Inadvisable Questions Regarding Disability Discrimination

Don't Ask	Why	Ask This Job-Related Question Instead
Will you need a leave for medical treatment or for other reasons related to a disability?		
Will you need reasonable accommodation to get to the cafeteria?		
Tell me about any restriction you have that would prevent you from lifting 30-pound metal sheets onto a conveyor belt for about four hours each day.	Disability discrimination	*This job requires lifting 30-pound metal sheets onto a conveyor belt for about four hours each workday. Can you meet this requirement of the position?*
The job requires visiting different company locations every week to on-site compliance audits. If you need that cane to get around, you must be suffering from some sort of disability that would interfere with doing that much travel. What is your disability, and how bad is it?	Disability discrimination	*The job requires visiting different company locations throughout the country every week to conduct on-site compliance audits. Can you travel by airplane about six times a month?*

TABLE 4.8   Inadvisable Questions Regarding Disability and Worker's Compensation Discrimination

Don't Ask	Why	Ask This Job-Related Question Instead
Have you ever had an on-the-job injury or filed a Workers' Compensation claim?	Likely to elicit information about disability discrimination, and is a violation of Workers' Compensation law	This is an illegal question. There is no way to reformulate it.
Have you ever had any job-related injuries?	Family and medical leave, worker's compensation, and disability discrimination	This is an illegal question. There is no way to reformulate it.
Do you or anyone in your family have a serious illness that may require you to take time off from work?	Family and medical leave discrimination	This is an illegal question. There is no way to reformulate it.

Source: © Susan W. Brecher and Cornell University-ILR, 2007.

CAUTION

Any preemployment conversations that candidates have must adhere to all legal guidelines—regardless of whether the conversations were held with HR professionals, managers, or potential colleagues. This includes any casual conversations that take place over meals.

Realistic Job Previews (RJP)

At some point in the interview process, it is critical that candidates be given—and, perhaps more important, process and understand—a realistic picture of the position and the organization. This, in turn, will help the candidate make a realistic and accurate assessment of whether he or she will be willing and/or able to function effectively within the day-to-day realities of the position, the department or unit, and the organization (in other words, it will help the candidate determine whether he or she is likely to "fit").

Realistic job previews can be conveyed and communicated in a number of ways, including through

- ▶ Verbal descriptions of the work, the work environment, and/or the work conditions

- ▶ Facility tours

- ▶ The opportunity to read the employee handbook

- ▶ Opportunities to speak with current employees, particularly those who would be the incumbent's peers and/or colleagues

Different methods of communicating a realistic job preview can be used at different phases of the interview process. Whatever techniques are used, however, must be used at a consistent point in the interview process, and in a consistent manner.

Preemployment Testing

Preemployment testing is another way of ascertaining the degree to which a candidate possesses and can demonstrate the knowledge, skills, and abilities/behavioral characteristics required to successfully perform the position. Any tests that are used must be job-related and valid (see the section "Uniform Guidelines on Employee Selection Procedures" earlier in this chapter).

Some of the most commonly used types of preemployment exams are shown in Table 4.9:

TABLE 4.9 Preemployment Exams

Type of Test	Test Is Designed to Ascertain
Agility Tests	Whether the candidate can perform the physical requirements of the position.
Aptitude Tests	The candidate's ability to learn new skills and/or acquire knowledge.
Cognitive Ability Tests	A candidate's intelligence and/or current skill level with respect to a job-related function. Cognitive tests could be administered to assess skills such as typing, problem solving, mathematical skill, or numeric ability.
Integrity, or Honesty, Tests	The degree to which a candidate would be likely to engage in behavior that is dishonest or that lacks integrity.
Personality Tests	Candidates' personality traits, motivation, discipline, and other characteristics.

Drug tests are another significant category of preemployment testing conducted by many employers. Designed to detect the presence of illegal drugs in the candidate's system, drug tests are not considered to be medical exams.

Medical Exams

Medical tests, or exams, can be conducted only if the exam is job related and consistent with business necessity, and after an offer (or a conditional offer) of employment has been extended to the candidate.

An offer of employment cannot be rescinded simply because a medical test reveals that a candidate has a disability. Instead, in this situation, the employer would then determine the feasibility of extending a reasonable accommodation that does not cause undue hardship.

Employment: Background Checks

After the interview process is complete and any appropriate and relevant tests have been successfully completed, the final candidate(s) should then be subjected to a rigorous background-checking process.

In a sense, conducting a background check is almost like starting the interviewing process all over again. This is sometimes easier said than done, especially because managers (and HR professionals) have invested a great deal of time, energy, and interest in the final candidate by this point in the process.

The person conducting a reference check must maintain—or regain, if necessary—a wholly objective perspective on the candidate. This person must be completely open to the fact that a reference check can yield a variety of possible outcomes. It could confirm, for instance, that the information that was collected through the interview (and testing processes, if relevant) was accurate. This is, of course, a good thing. Alternatively, the background check may reveal previously unidentified problems or concerns with the candidate's past performance or credentials. Because past performance is, in many ways, the best predictor of future performance, obtaining such information at any point before an offer of employment is extended is also a good thing.

Background checks can explore any or all of the following areas:

▶ *Work history*—Employers, dates of employment, titles, salaries, and performance records.

▶ *Academic records*—Degrees, diplomas, certificates, certifications, and the dates when they were earned.

▶ *Criminal background checks*—Many employers seek information relative to whether the final candidate(s) has been convicted of, pled guilty to, or pled no contest to a crime. In addition to identifying potentially serious performance issues, the organization may also discover convictions related to prior instances of workplace violence.

> **TIP**
>
> In the event that you learn of a conviction at any point in the selection process, consult with senior HR leadership and counsel, as appropriate, before making any assessments, judgments, or decisions.

> **CAUTION**
>
> An arrest is not a conviction and cannot be treated as such. In our justice system, individuals are innocent until proven guilty. Discriminating on the basis of arrest record could lead to adverse impact on the basis of race. From a nonlegal perspective, it could also lead to losing a really good candidate.

- *Driving history*—Employers may—and should—choose to review the motor vehicle reports for candidates who are applying for positions for which driving is an essential job function.

- *Credit history*—Employees who will have access to financial resources or who are entrusted with certain types of financial responsibility may be required to permit the potential employer to review their credit report.

> **CAUTION**
>
> Some organizations assert that there is a connection between a candidate's integrity and the candidate's credit rating. Other organizations assert that a candidate's individual financial habits provide insight into how that person would handle the organization's financial resources. Before implementing credit-checking procedures, consult with senior HR leadership and counsel, as appropriate, to ensure that these assumptions—along with all other reasons for requiring candidates to submit to a review of their credit report— are accurate and defensible in the event of a challenge. It is also critical to ensure that all activities relating to credit checks are conduced in a manner consistent with the Fair Credit Reporting Act.

Employment: Extending the Offer

The story doesn't end when you decide whom you want to hire—you still need to extend the offer. And then, of course, the candidate needs to decide whether to accept it. The way you extend the offer will say a lot to the candidate about the organization—not just about you. (One of the exciting and challenging things about interviewing allows us to be a part of something that is bigger than any of us individually. "You" represent more than just "you.") The way you extend an offer will also have a big impact on whether the candidate accepts the offer.

Tips for Extending an Employment Offer

Many organizations extend a verbal offer of employment over the phone and then follow that up with a formal written offer of employment. Other organizations meet with candidates personally and hand them an offer letter immediately upon extending an offer of employment.

Whichever method your organization uses, the manner in which an offer of employment is extended is important and must be approached with the same degree of care that has been infused into the rest of the preemployment process. The following are some particular considerations to keep in mind:

- Avoid expressing earnings in annual terms. Some organizations choose to indicate what the candidate would earn each pay period, whereas others choose to express earnings in monthly, daily, weekly, or even hourly rates.

CAUTION

Be sure to take any potential FLSA-status ramifications into consideration when calculating "breakdowns" that are shorter than one week in duration.

- Avoid language that alludes to guarantees of earnings or employment, or dates through which the employee will be paid.

- Avoid language that hints of any sort of a long-term employment relationship, or that speaks of the employer as a "family" (while not impossible, it's a lot harder to fire a family member than it should be to fire a noncontracted, "at will" employee. Don't make things more challenging by mixing metaphors).

- Use the offer letter as an opportunity to reaffirm that the employment relationship is "at-will," and—if counsel agrees—define what that means.

- State that the only agreements or promises that are valid are those that are included in the offer letter.

- State the date by which the candidate must either accept or decline the offer of employment. Ensure that you permit a reasonable period of time—not too much time and not too little.

In short, an overly exuberant offer of employment can cause more harm that good. Such letters must be carefully crafted, and the template for such letters should be approved by counsel before implementation.

Employment Contracts

Some organizations use employment contracts for individuals in certain (often "higher-level") positions. The contract addresses and outlines different aspects of the employment relationship and is binding on the organization as well as the employee.

Some of the boilerplate items that are likely to appear in an employment contract could be:

- Identifying information and contact information for the employer and the employee.

- Position title, as well as the duties and responsibilities of the position.

▶ Duration of the contract, or a specific statement that the contract is indefinite.

▶ Type of compensation (salary, commission, and so on), frequency of compensation, and formulas for calculating compensation (if appropriate).

▶ Benefits, including vacation allotment.

▶ Clauses covering terms of noncompete agreements, confidentiality, and nonsolicitation of clients or customers, and so on.

▶ Termination clause, which could include conditions under which the employee could be terminated, as well as any mandatory notice requirements that would apply.

> **CAUTION**
>
> Familiarize yourself with oral, written, implied, and express contracts as they pertain to the employment relationship. More information on these topics can be found in Chapter 7, "Employee and Labor Relations."

Relocation

From time to time, an organization may choose to relocate employees. Some organizations relocate employees on an ongoing basis.

Relocation is one of the functions in HR that an organization may decide to outsource.

> **CAUTION**
>
> Familiarize yourself with the advantages and disadvantages of outsourcing the relocation function.

Employment: Onboarding

Onboarding, formerly referred to as "employee orientation," refers to the process by which an employee is supported as he or she transitions into the organization. This support can—and should—be provided by HR as well as by the hiring manager, and can encompass a number of different components including the following:

▶ Introduction (or, assuming the interview process was conducted effectively, "reintroduction") to the mission and overarching objectives of the organization, as well as how this position contributes to the fulfillment of that mission and the attainment of those objectives.

▶ Introduction (or, ideally, reintroduction) of the values of the organization.

▶ Discussion of the performance management system, in a macro as well as a micro sense. *Macro* would refer, for instance, to the structure and design of the performance management system, as well as expectations relative to how the employee will actively engage in the system. *Micro* might refer to each employee's specific goals and/or the competencies against which he or she will be evaluated.

203

Termination: The End of the Employment Life Cycle...or Is It?

- Personal introductions to co-workers and peers.

- A tour of the facilities. Be sure not to forget the rest room, copy machine, printers, and fax machine—the little things can make a big difference, especially at the beginning of the employment relationship.

- Review of safety guidelines.

- Review of "rules and regulations."

- Completion of required paperwork.

Unfortunately, many organizations still focus primarily or even exclusively on the completion of required paperwork, rather than on critical nonadministrative elements, such as those inventoried above. This is not to imply that paperwork is not important. It is. But it's not enough. Work with managers to build an onboarding program that will capture and channel the nervous excitement that new employees often experience during their first days and weeks in a new job. Get the employee started on the "right foot." Make sure the employee's first days, weeks, and months on the job are positive, memorable, and meaningful.

Termination: The End of the Employment Life Cycle...or Is It?

Terminations reside at the other end of the spectrum of the employment life cycle. Terminations are often not given the degree of attention they deserve and require. Knowing how to effectively facilitate the process of employee terminations—whether voluntary or involuntary—is just as critical as knowing how to effectively facilitate the process of bringing employees into the organization. Whatever the reason or cause, an employee's exit from the organization should be just as positive and respectful as the onboarding process for that employee's replacement will be.

Involuntary Terminations

Involuntary terminations—regardless of the specific reasons for the terminations—are challenging. There are several types of involuntary terminations.

Layoffs

Most HR professionals—at one time or another in their careers—will participate in the process of laying off employees. No matter what you call it—downsizing, rightsizing, reduction in force (RIF), or any of the other monikers in use these days—layoffs are never easy. The decision to lay off one or more employees should not be made lightly, and the manner in which the layoff is conducted is absolutely critical.

Determining Who Will Be Laid Off

Layoffs are handled differently in different organizations, and under different conditions. When the employment relationship is governed by a collective bargaining agreement, the terms and conditions governing who will be selected for layoff will likely be clearly spelled out and are usually heavily weighted toward seniority ("last in, first out", or LIFO). In the absence of a collective bargaining agreement, decisions relative to who will stay and who will go may be based less on seniority and more on skills, past performance, job function, or perceived potential.

CAUTION

Before choosing to rely on performance appraisal information or ratings when making employment decisions, it is critical to ensure the integrity and accuracy of the performance system. Any number of rater or process errors could significantly skew performance ratings and could therefore diminish the legitimacy and defensibility of layoff decisions made under these assumptions. Don't assume that performance rating are meaningfully and accurately calibrated across the organization—or even within a particular department. Instead, take a closer—and open-minded—look.

The Role of HR in the Layoff Process

HR's role in the layoff process can vary greatly from organization to organization. Often, HR professionals help prepare for the layoff in an administrative (transactional or "paperwork") capacity. This may include calculating severance pay, vacation entitlements, or preparing COBRA paperwork. In addition, HR is often a primary source within the organization for information about outplacement services, in the event those services are being provided to assist employees as they transition out of the organization, and as they begin the process of seeking new employment.

HR's role often extends beyond administrative responsibilities such as these. Sometimes, HR professionals participate in meetings that are held with employees who will be terminated as part of the layoff. These meetings must be conducted with respect, consideration, empathy, integrity, and alacrity. This is a difficult situation for the employees who are leaving the organization, as well as for the employees who are staying. It is also a difficult process for the managers and HR professionals who are involved in the process.

NOTE

As difficult as it may be, HR professionals cannot allow themselves to become lost in the emotional dimensions of the layoff process. Ultimately, all layoffs should occur because of business necessity, and only after all other viable options have been considered. As strategic business partners, however, HR professionals are called upon to participate in even the most difficult parts of carrying out that business strategy. We can, however, commit ourselves to performing this role in a compassionate and professional manner.

205

Termination: The End of the Employment Life Cycle...or Is It?

Those Who Remain

It's critical not to overlook those employees who are still employed after the layoff. Although these individuals have not been laid off, they did witness the layoff and are therefore significantly affected by it. The impact on these individuals can be tangible as well as intangible. In a tangible sense, employees who are left behind may now face heavier workloads. They may also be concerned about their former colleagues, as well as about what the future—both short term and long term—holds in store for them. "Waiting for the other shoe to drop" can be distracting and can significantly diminish morale. Also, employees who remain after a layoff may feel some degree of uncertainty, and may even begin looking for employment elsewhere. If decisions relative to whom to lay off and whom to retain were made in part or in whole on the basis of performance, the organization risks losing its most valuable talent.

There is no single roadmap for handling this situation. Two tenets, however, should always be observed:

- ▶ Communicate clearly, frequently, and in a truthful manner. Credible communication about the layoff and the impact of the layoff on the organization is essential to rebuilding some sense of comfort and/or security.

- ▶ No matter how much you might want to, and no matter how much you believe it, do not offer any assurances or make any promises to the effect that the layoffs are over, or that no one else will be laid off. The reality of an employment-at-will relationship—particularly one that is not governed by a contract or other agreement—is that anyone can be let go at any time for any lawful reason. Make no promises that you cannot keep—and make no statements that could unintentionally create an implied contract.

You also might want to consider eliminating the term "survivor" when referring to "employees who remain." The term "survivor" implies that some did not "survive." Such language can serve to unintentionally escalate an already negative situation by overlaying unnecessarily dramatic language.

CAUTION

There aren't too many "nevers" or "no brainers" when it comes to HR, but here's one: Never, under any circumstances, reveal the names of individuals who are on a layoff list unless and until you are explicitly directed to do so within the context of the overall communication strategy that has been developed. First and foremost, HR professionals cannot, under any circumstances, break the commitment to confidentiality with which they have been entrusted. Second, on a more practical note, such lists often change multiple times before the actual layoffs occur.

Other Involuntary Terminations

Many, if not most, employers have the legal right to terminate an employee at any time, for any lawful reason—or for no reason at all. In reality, however, using employment-at-will principles in a "willy-nilly" manner can seriously damage morale, diminish loyalty, increase turnover, and damage the employer's reputation in the labor market. It could also increase the likelihood of litigation.

Most of the time, the decision to terminate an employee is well thought out, carefully scrutinized, and based on legitimate performance-related issues. It should also be made only after whatever progressive discipline process is in place within the organization has been followed—and followed with the expectation, hope, and intention of empowering employees to bring about a positive outcome, rather than with the sole intention of creating a paper trail that will let you terminate an employee with a greater degree of comfort (although that is one possible outcome, it shouldn't be the initial objective).

Managers—HR's clients—make termination decisions. Sometimes (and ideally), they make these decisions in conjunction with HR. At other times, they make these decisions independently and bring HR into the process only when it comes time to execute the decision. In either scenario, HR can add value to this process. Sometimes, when it appropriate to do so, HR can suggest alternative approaches. HR can also ensure that the termination has been made in accordance with the organization's policies and practices and that it is nondiscriminatory. At times, HR can also point out information that has been unintentionally overlooked, such as consistently positive performance appraisals in the file of a person who is being terminated for poor performance. In short, HR can provide a "second set of eyes," and can help managers think through this all-important business decision.

Voluntary Terminations

There are a number of reasons why an employee might decide to voluntarily terminate his or her employment with the organization. Among these could be

- Accepting employment elsewhere ("other" or "different" employment, not necessarily "better" employment)

- Returning to school

- Retirement

- Avoiding an anticipated involuntary termination

- Dissatisfaction with the current employer, manager, or job

- Health- or disability-related reasons

- Enrollment in the military

- Personal reasons (birth or adoption of a child, illness of a family member)

- Early retirement

relocation

> **CAUTION**
>
> Early retirement can present a positive alternative to involuntary layoffs. Early retirement, however, presents multiple risks—in particular, the possibility of allegations of age discrimination. Consult with counsel before implementing any retirement program to ensure that the program is lawful and defensible in the event of a challenge.

> **EXAM ALERT**
>
> Be familiar with how to conduct early retirements in a lawful manner that is consistent with the provisions outlined in the Age Discrimination in Employment Act.

Constructive Discharge

Constructive discharge does not fit neatly into either "voluntary" or "involuntary" terminations. It may, however, constitute a wrongful discharge. An employee who alleges constructive discharge asserts that he or she was subjected to such intolerable working conditions that remaining employed with the organization had become an impossibility. Essentially, the employee is saying that he or she was forced to quit. Claiming constructive discharge, however, does not make it so—instead, this must be proven.

Exit Interviews

HR's responsibility extends beyond replacing an employee who has been terminated, whether voluntarily or involuntary.

> **TIP**
>
> Replacing an employee should not be a "knee jerk" reaction in the wake of a termination. HR professionals are not order takers, or order fillers, and should not behave as such. Partner with your clients to explore creative options. Determine whether a position truly needs to be replaced. If it does, explore whether it should be replaced in its current form. Use terminations as an opportunity to revisit old assumptions and to support your clients by exploring new and creative approaches.

HR professionals are often called on to participate in the exit interview process. Exit interviews provide employers with an invaluable opportunity. If departing employees are assured—and if they believe—that their comments will not be attributed personally to them in any way, they will be more likely to provide candid and valuable feedback relative to their employment experiences with your organization.

Exit interviews should focus on job-related factors rather than feelings. An exit interviewer may want to ask for feedback relative to myriad topics, just a few of which could be

- ▶ The interview and selection process, and whether it provided a realistic and accurate depiction of the job

- ▶ The degree to which the employee felt as though he or she was making a valuable contribution that ultimately furthered, in some way, the mission of the organization

- ▶ The nature of the supervision received, and the employee's relationship with his or her supervisor

- ▶ Training opportunities, and the degree to which the employee was truly encouraged (and permitted) to take advantage of those opportunities

Although some organizations conduct exit interviews using forms that the employee is asked to complete, many organizations find that in-person exit interviews yield more valuable results. The quality and the information provided will also be enhanced if the exit interviewer maintains a neutral and nonjudgmental demeanor during the interview—regardless of what the departing employee might say. In fact, many of the same intra- and interpersonal skills that enhance the preemployment interview process can also enhance the exit interview process.

Chapter Summary

Responsibilities relating to workforce planning and employment provide HR professionals with the opportunity to have a lasting impact on the organization. Whether this impact is positive, however, depends in large part on the way in which HR professionals execute these responsibilities.

To function successfully with respect to the functional area of workforce planning and employment, HR professionals must develop an understanding of, and an appreciation for, equal employment opportunity (EEO).

It's also critical for HR professionals to understand the many laws and cases that shape this functional area, and to commit to maintaining currency with respect to emerging cases that offer additional interpretation, and reinterpretation, of these laws. In addition, HR professionals must be prepared to contribute meaningfully to ensuring that the organization will be able to meet its future goals by making sure the right people, with the right skills, are in the right places, at the right times.

The ability to execute this functional area effectively is also predicated on knowing and understanding the organization's strategic plan. HR professionals who have already earned a "seat at the table" in their organization are likely to have a good grasp of where the organization is going. HR professionals must proactively seek opportunities for learning about the organization's long-term objectives. Unless we do, our efforts may be less productive, less relevant, less valued, and less impactful.

Ultimately, the choice of how we will perform in this area rests with us. The choices that we make will go a long way toward defining how we are perceived by the organization, our overall effectiveness in the organization, and the degree to which we will participate in a transformational manner within the organization.

> **EXAM ALERT**
> Be sure to familiarize yourself with international dimensions of workforce planning and employment.

> **EXAM ALERT**
> Be sure to familiarize yourself with record-keeping requirements.

Key Terms

- EEO (Equal Employment Opportunity)
- Protected class
- Discrimination
- Disparate treatment
- Disparate (or "adverse") impact
- Perpetuating past discrimination
- Harassment
- Sexual harassment
- Quid pro quo

- Hostile work environment
- Applicant
- Title VII of the Civil Rights Act, 1964
- Affirmative Action Plans (AAPs)
- Age Discrimination in Employment Act (ADEA), 1967
- Rehabilitation Act, 1973
- Vietnam Era Veterans' Readjustment Assistance Act (VEVRAA), 1974
- Pregnancy Discrimination Act, 1978
- Uniform Guidelines on Employee Selection Procedures, 1978
- Reliability
- Validity
- Content validity
- Criterion-related validity
- Construct validity
- Predictive validity
- Immigration Reform and Control Act (IRCA), 1986
- I-9
- Worker Adjustment and Retraining Notification Act (WARN), 1988
- Mass layoff
- Plant closing
- Americans with Disabilities Act (ADA), 1990
- Qualified person
- Reasonable accommodation
- Undue hardship
- Disability
- Major life activities
- Civil Rights Act, 1991

- Congressional Accountability Act (CAA), 1995
- The Delphi Technique
- Nominal Group Technique
- Trend analysis
- Ratio analysis
- Turnover analysis
- Simple linear regression
- Multiple linear regression
- Simulations
- Job analysis
- Job description
- Job specifications
- Job competencies
- KSAs
- Recruiting
- Selection
- Employer branding
- Selection criteria
- Internal recruiting
- External recruiting
- Job posting
- Job bidding
- Skill inventories
- Replacement charts
- Contingency employment agencies
- Retained employment agencies
- Employee referral
- Non-traditional staffing alternatives
- Employment application
- Short-form employment applications
- Long-form employment applications

▶ Job-specific employment applications

▶ Weighted employment applications

▶ Directive interviews

▶ Nondirective interviews

▶ Phone interviews

▶ Prescreen interviews

▶ Behavior-based interviews

▶ Stress interviews

▶ Panel interviews

▶ Rapport

▶ Primary questions

▶ Probing questions

▶ Nonverbals

▶ Interviewing bias

▶ Contrast

▶ First impression

▶ Halo

▶ Horns

▶ Leniency

▶ Strictness

▶ Leniency

▶ Similar-to-me

▶ Realistic job previews

▶ Pre-employment testing

▶ Agility tests

▶ Aptitude tests

▶ Cognitive ability tests

▶ Integrity, or honesty, tests

▶ Personality tests

▶ Drug tests

▶ Medical tests

▶ Background checks

▶ Employment contracts

▶ Relocation

▶ Orientation

▶ Involuntary terminations

▶ Voluntary terminations

▶ Constructive discharge

▶ Exit interviews

▶ *Griggs v. Duke Power, 1971*

▶ *McDonnell Douglas Corp v. Green, 1973*

▶ *Albemarle Paper v. Moody, 1975*

▶ *Washington v. Davis, 1976*

▶ *Regents of California v. Bakke, 1978*

▶ *United Steelworkers v. Weber, 1979*

▶ *Meritor Savings Bank v. Vinson, 1986*

▶ *Johnson v. Santa Clara County Transportation Agency, 1987*

▶ *Martin v. Wilks, 1988*

▶ *Kolstad v. American Dental Association, 1999*

▶ *Harris v. Forklift Systems, 1993*

▶ *Taxman v. Board of Education of Piscataway, 1993*

▶ *St. Mary's Honor Center v. Hicks, 1993*

▶ *McKennon v. Nashville Banner Publishing Co., 1995*

▶ *Faragher v. City of Boca Raton, 1998, and Ellerth v. Burlington Northern Industries, 1998*

▶ *Grutter v. Bollinger and Gratz v. Bollinger, 2003*

▶ *General Dynamics Land Systems v. Cline, 2004*

Apply Your Knowledge

This chapter focuses on issues relating to workforce planning and employment. Complete the following exercises, review questions, and exam questions as a way of reviewing and reinforcing the knowledge and skills you'll need to perform your responsibilities as an HR professional, and to increase the likelihood that you will pass the PHR examination.

Exercises

1. For some time, you've wanted to implement an exit interview process at your organization. You feel strongly that there's a lot of valuable information that can be gleaned from departing employees, and you want to convince "the powers that be" of this, as well. You're ready to put together a proposal and want to present the best possible arguments for establishing an exit interview program. Which of the following would be the strongest reason that you could include in your proposal to senior HR and line leadership?

    A. If managers know that departing employees will have the opportunity to provide feedback as they are leaving the organization, they may be less likely to intentionally behave in ways that are problematic, or to treat employees in an unprofessional manner.

    B. Because managers will be able to attribute comments made during exit interviews to specific employees, they will be better able to assess the validity of the feedback that departing employees provide.

    C. Exit interviews provide an excellent opportunity to learn about how employees truly feel. Although employees may have been hesitant to express their thoughts while employed with the organization, this same level of anxiety will not exist during the exit interview process—so departing employees can articulate their feelings more comfortably.

    D. Exit interviews provide a unique opportunity to capture useful and relevant feedback from employees about a number of factors, such as the nature of the supervision that the employee experienced and the employee's relationship with his or her supervisor. This is information that in the absence of an exit interview process might not otherwise be obtained.

2. When you conduct employment interviews, you sometimes notice that candidates appear extremely nervous throughout most of the interview. To try to combat this, you've decided to rethink the way you begin your interviews and do more rapport building. Which of the following would be the best way to build rapport with your candidates?

    A. Look at the candidate's résumé to see if you have anything in common with the candidate—such as hobbies, interests, former employers, place of residence, or any other shared commonality.

    B. Place personal pictures—for instance, of your family members—within easy view of the candidate. This way, the candidate can ask you about something that they know you'd be interested in talking about.

    C. Talk about the weather. It's something that you know the two of you are certain to share in common, it's often changing, and it's neutral. If a blizzard or heat wave comes your way, you're certain to have rapport building for at least a week.

    D. Choose a prominent current event—one that you are confident the candidate would know about—and refer to it in a somewhat general manner. This way, even if you and the employee are not in full agreement on the topic, the conversation will be superficial enough that no one will be offended, and you've still found something interesting to talk about (certainly more interesting than the weather).

3. In reviewing your organization's most recent affirmative action plan, you notice that there is underutilization of women in a particular job group. Which of the following actions would be most appropriate to take?

    A. Try to convince women in other job groups to accept transfers into the job group in which there is underutilization.

    B. If both male and female candidates apply for position openings in the underutilized job group, hire the women.

    C. Hire the best qualified candidate for the position, whether that person is male or female.

    D. Reach out to related professional organizations that are likely to have women as members.

4. You've recently been given feedback that the onboarding process is too cumbersome, time consuming, and overly focused on administrative paperwork. You're focusing on a number of areas where you can streamline and improve this process, including how verification of employees' identity and employment is handled. Which of the following would be an appropriate step to consider?

   A. When you send out offer letters, send new hires a list of acceptable documents that they can bring with them on their first day of work to establish identity and eligibility to work.

   B. Instead of having new hires prepare their I-9s on their first day of employment, ask them to submit all required paperwork in advance.

   C. Have the newly hired employees complete the entire I-9 form, except for the signature section, to minimize the number of times that the I-9 needs to be passed back and forth between HR and the employee.

   D. Allow employees a full week to present their I-9 documents. In that way, the administrative responsibilities associated with onboarding can be spread out over a longer period of time.

5. You strongly prefer to conduct directive interviews because in your experience you end up with better information and can make better hiring recommendations to your client managers. At the beginning of one particular interview, the candidate pulls out a list of questions that she wants to ask you before she decides whether to proceed with the balance of the interview. Which of the following responses would be most appropriate?

   A. Explain to the candidate that you use a directive approach to interviewing and that it helps you make better hiring recommendations. As such, you'll be happy to answer her questions at the end of the interview.

   B. Explain to the candidate that you will be happy to answer her questions at the end of the interview, after she has had an opportunity to answer the questions that you will be asking her.

   C. Because there is nothing to be gained by getting into a confrontation with a candidate, you decide to answer her questions. Besides, in light of her approach, you've already decided to eliminate her from consideration for the position.

   D. Because there is nothing to be gained by getting into a confrontation with a candidate, you decide to answer her questions. Besides, in light of her approach, you think she might have just the kind of spunk and tenacity that your organization needs.

Review Questions

1. Describe directive and nondirective interviews. In general, which is the preferred approach?

2. What are some of the factors that need to be taken into consideration when using performance as a criterion for determining who will be let go in a layoff situation?

3. What are some best practices with respect to taking notes during an interview?

4. Describe sexual harassment that takes the form of a hostile work environment.

5. Define and describe the differences between a mass layoff and a plant closing (according to WARNA).

Exam Questions

1. Which of the following forms of discrimination is not covered by Title VII of the Civil Rights Act of 1964?

    A. Age

    B. Color

    C. Race

    D. National Origin

2. Which of the following statements is true about quid pro quo sexual harassment?

    A. It can be exacted by any employee on any other employee.

    B. It creates a hostile work environment that can ultimately lead to constructive discharge.

    C. It creates a situation in which an employee's terms and conditions of employment are affected by acceptance or rejection of sexual advances.

    D. It cannot occur during the preemployment selection process, because it refers to tangible or economic work-related consequences that, by definition, can be experienced only by current employees.

3. Which of the following employers would be required to prepare formal affirmative action plans?

    A. Federal contractors who receive federal grants of any amount

    B. Federal contractors with $50,000 or more in federal contracts

    C. Federal contractors with at least 50 employees who have federal contracts of at least $50,000 per year

    D. All federal contractors, regardless of the size or scope of the contract

4. In the event of a mass layoff or plant closing, WARN requires employers to notify all of the following individuals or entities except

    A. Affected employees or their representatives (such as a collective bargaining unit)

    B. The State Dislocated Worker Unit

    C. The appropriate local government unit

    D. The EEOC, which will conduct an adverse impact analysis before layoffs are implemented

5. A defining Supreme Court case for interpreting the Civil Rights Act of 1991 was

    A. Kolstad v. American Dental Association, 1991

    B. Grutter v. Bollinger and Gratz v. Bollinger, 2003

    C. St. Mary's Honor Center v. Hicks, 1993

    D. United Steelworkers c. Weber, 1979

6. Which of the following statements is true about the Delphi technique?

    A. It looks at one particular factor, over a period of time, to track changes.

    B. It requires all individual experts to present their own ideas to each other, without immediate discussion or assessment.

    C. It utilizes a neutral facilitator who compiles and condenses input.

    D. It is a structured, mathematical approach to forecasting.

7. A properly conducted job analysis will produce all of the following except

    A. Job competencies

    B. Job postings

    C. Job specifications

    D. Job description

8. Which of the following is not one of the main elements in a job description?

    A. Scope information

    B. Physical work conditions and physical demands

    C. Compensation rates

    D. Minimum requirements

9. Which of the following would be least likely to be considered a job competency?

    A. Communication skills

    B. Facilitation skills

    C. Teamwork skills

    D. Interpersonal skills

10. All of the following represent benefits of employee referral programs except

    A. Highly cost-effective recruiting

    B. Employees who are more likely to succeed

    C. Demonstration of good faith efforts to remedy underutilization

    D. Increased candidate familiarity with the organization

Answers to Exercises

1. **Answer D is the best answer.** Employees are not likely to provide candid information about many dimensions of their employment experience—especially their relationship with their manager—while they are still employed with the organization. A well-structured exit interview process, therefore, can provide a one-time opportunity to glean information that might otherwise remain unspoken (at least to anyone within the organization who can actually use it in a productive manner). Answer A is not the best answer; the exit interview process will fail if it is used as a deterrent for management misbehavior, or in a threatening manner. Answer B is not the best answer; comments that an employee makes during exit interviews should be "sanitized" and should not be attributable to him or her. Answer C is not the best answer; to be truly informative and effective, exit interviews should focus primarily on facts, not feelings.

2. **Answer C is the best answer.** Weather is a safe topic of discussion, and you can be relatively certain that the candidate has some awareness of it. If you work in a windowless workspace, or if you haven't had a chance to go outside for a while, asking about the weather affords the candidate the opportunity to "update" you on something that is relevant to both of you. Also, when spoken about in an animated manner, even the weather can help to "break the ice" with a candidate. Answer A is not the best answer; interviewers should not discuss any factors that are not job related (the weather, of course, is an exception to this)—including hobbies and interests. You never know what information candidates might reveal about themselves as they speak about their hobbies or interests, and it's much easier to avoid this discussion than to have to deal with unwanted information that the candidate has disclosed. Such discussions can also get the interview off track. Answer B is not the best answer; positioning photos of family members in visible locations is equivalent to discussing your own family, which is akin to nonverbally inviting the

candidate to self-discuss about his or her own family. Answer D is not the best answer; discussing any prominent current event is likely to lead to issues that relate to politics, religion, personal beliefs, or a host of other topics that should not be discussed during an interview. Additionally, there is no way to be certain that a candidate is aware of the event that you bring up—no matter how prominent you think it is. And, even if the candidate is aware of the event, he or she may have no interest in or knowledge of it. This can result in increasing—rather than decreasing—the candidate's anxiety level.

3. **Answer D is the best answer.** Reaching out to professional organizations that are likely to include women as members would likely constitute a good-faith effort at addressing underutilization by creating a more diverse pool of candidates. Answer A is not the best answer; trying to convince women or minorities to change job groups is not an appropriate way to address underutilization. Answer B is not the best answer; that approach as described would constitute sex discrimination. It could also result in hiring less qualified (or unqualified individuals), simply because those individuals happen to be women. Answer C is not the best answer; underutilization cannot simply be ignored. Additionally, although it is appropriate (and advisable) to hire qualified—and ideally the best qualified—candidates, an organization does have the obligation to make good-faith efforts to create a pool of qualified candidates that includes women or minorities for those job groups in which there is current underutilization.

4. **Answer A is the best answer.** Although anyone who has started a new job since 1986 should be familiar with the requirement to present documents proving identity and eligibility to legally work in the United States, sending new hires a list of acceptable documents along with their offer letter gives them ample time to pull together the required materials. It also reaffirms that a wide range of documents is acceptable, and that none is preferred over any other. Answer B is not the best answer; the I-9 form specifically states that the form is to be "completed and signed by employee at the time employment begins." Answer C is not the best answer; certain portions of the I-9 must be completed by the employer. Answer D is not the best answer; the I-9 form must be completed within the first three business days of the new hire's employment.

5. **Answer B is the best answer.** As the interviewer, *you—not* the candidate—are in control of the interview. There is no need to cede that control simply because a candidate asks you to. Answer B also responds to the candidate's request in a positive manner: You are not telling her "no"; instead, you are telling her "not now" (and you are managing to do so without even alluding to the word "no"). Answer A is not the best answer; it is not necessary to explain to the candidate why you have chosen to structure the interview in a particular way. Additionally, using technical terms (such as "directive interviews") adds no value to this discussion and might even create distance between you and the candidate (distance that *no* amount of discussion about the weather will be able to bridge). Neither answer C nor answer D is the best answer, for a couple of reasons. First, in both instances, you have ceded control of the interview to the candidate simply because she asked you to do

so. In addition, in both scenarios, you made assumptions (one could even say "sweeping judgments") about this candidate based on a single behavior that is not necessarily accurate or reflective of how that candidate would behave in the workplace. An interview is a unique situation governed by unique "norms and mores." There are also a lot of people who make a living giving other people advice about how they "should" behave during an interview. Sometimes, that advice just isn't good. At other times, it encourages a candidate to behave in a markedly different manner from how he or she would act outside the interview, but it can be difficult to argue with so-called experts sometimes (especially when you need or want to find a new job). Give candidates an opportunity to understand and comply with the expectations that you have of them for *your* interview process, and don't jump to conclusions too quickly.

Answers to Review Questions

1. Directive interviews take a more structured approach. The interviewer(s) asks the same questions of all candidates and maintains control of the interview. Conversely, nondirective interviews are more conversational and relatively unstructured. In a nondirective interview, the candidate—not the interviewer—ends up controlling the interview and primarily determines what will be discussed.

   Generally speaking, a directive style is more effective and appropriate than a nondirective style because it yields more consistent results, facilitates the process of comparing candidates to the job requirements and to each other, and generally provides greater defensibility in the event of a legal challenge. Although the directive approach is the better approach, the interview must still remain dynamic and interactive.

2. Before choosing to rely solely on employees' prior performance ratings to determine who should be laid off and who should be retained, the organization needs to carefully examine its performance appraisal system and assess its validity and overall worth. The system itself could be flawed, or—even if it is sound—there could be problems with the way in which individual raters have applied it over time. Either factor could result in misguided assessments, which could consequently diminish the legitimacy (and defensibility) of layoff decisions made on the basis of employees' past performance.

3. At the beginning of the interview—perhaps at the end of the formal "rapport building" process—let the candidate know that you will be taking notes. The candidate may otherwise assume that he or she has said something wrong the minute your pen hits the paper. Letting the candidate know you will be taking notes can actually constitute another element of rapport building: You are interested in and care about what the candidate is going to tell you, and want to be certain that you remember it correctly.

   Note taking should not interfere in any way with the interview process. It also should not harm the personal connectedness that the interviewer establishes with the candidate during the initial rapport building portion of the interview. Jotting down key words and phrases that the candidate offers in response to the interviewer's questions will help the interviewer to remember the candidate's responses after the interview is over. Interviewers can then go back after the interview is done and "flesh out" more details around each of the candidate's answers.

4. Sexual harassment that manifests itself as a hostile work environment exists when unwelcome sexual conduct unreasonably interferes with an employee's job performance or creates a hostile, intimidating, or offensive work environment. A hostile work environment can be found to exist whether or not the employee experiences (or runs the risk of experiencing) tangible or economic work-related consequences.

   Hostile work environment harassment is unrelated to any decisions that are made relative to the employee's employment. As such, hostile work environments can be created by virtually anyone with whom an employee might come in contact in the workplace or "workspace."

5. According to WARN, a "mass layoff" occurs under the following sets of circumstances:

   Mass Layoff: A covered employer must give notice if there is to be a mass layoff which does not result from a plant closing, but which will result in an employment loss at the employment site during any 30-day period for 500 or more employees, or for 50–499 employees if they make up at least 33% of the employer's active workforce. Again, this does not count employees who have worked less than 6 months in the last 12 months or employees who work an average of less than 20 hours a week for that employer. These latter groups, however, are entitled to notice.

   An employer also must give notice if the number of employment losses which occur during a 30-day period fails to meet the threshold requirements of a plant closing or mass layoff, but the number of employment losses for 2 or more groups of workers, each of which is less than the minimum number needed to trigger notice, reaches the threshold level, during any 90-day period, of either a plant closing or mass layoff. Job losses within any 90-day period will count together toward **WARN** threshold levels, unless the employer demonstrates that the employment losses during the 90-day period are the result of separate and distinct actions and causes.

   WARN Act defines a "plant closing" as follows:

   Plant Closing: A covered employer must give notice if an employment site (or one or more facilities or operating units within an employment site) will be shut down, and the shutdown will result in an employment loss (as defined later) for 50 or more employees during any 30-day period. This does not count employees who have worked less than 6 months in the last 12 months or employees who work an average of less than 20 hours a week for that employer. These latter groups, however, are entitled to notice.

Answers to Exam Questions

1. **Answer A is the best answer.** Title VII of the Civil Rights Act of 1964 established five protected classes: color (answer B), race (answer C), national origin (answer D), religion, and sex. Age did not become a protected class until 1967, with the passage of the Age Discrimination in Employment Act (ADEA).

2. **Answer C is the best answer.** Quid pro quo harassment occurs when an individual's submission to or rejection of sexual advances or conduct of a sexual nature is used as the basis for employment-related decisions. Because this sort of impact can usually only be brought about by a supervisor or someone else in a position of authority in the organization, answer A is not the best answer. Answer B is not the best answer; quid pro quo harassment is a separate concept from hostile work environment harassment (although both types of harassment could potentially lead to constructive discharge). Answer D is not the best answer; either quid pro quo or hostile work environment harassment could occur during the recruiting or selection processes.

3. **Answer B is the best answer.** Federal contractors with $50,000 or more in federal contracts would be required to prepare formal affirmative action plans. Answer A is not the best answer; Executive Order 11246 does not use the awarding of federal grants as a factor that determines whether an organization needs to prepare a formal affirmative action plan. Answer C is not the best answer; this threshold refers to an organization's obligation to file annual EEO reports, not to the organization's obligation to prepare a formal affirmative action plan. Answer D is not the best answer; not all contractors are required to prepare formal affirmative action plans.

4. **Answer D is the best answer.** There is no WARN requirement to notify the EEOC of impending mass layoffs or plant closings. The organization should, however, conduct an adverse impact analysis before making any layoff decisions. Answers A, B, and C are not the best answers; each one indicates individuals or entities who are required to be notified in the event that WARN is triggered.

5. **Answer A is the best answer.** In Kolstad v. American Dental Association, 1991, the court ruled that punitive damages can be awarded only when the employer has acted with malice and reckless indifference to "the employee's federally protected rights." Answers B, C, and D each address different legal principles.

6. **Answer C is the best answer.** This neutral facilitator does not serve as an expert in this process, but does condense the submissions of the designated experts. Answer A is not the best answer; looking at one particular factor over time to track changes is trend analysis. Answer B is not the best answer; this is a description of a technique used in the nominal group technique. Answer D is not the best answer; the Delphi technique is a structured, *nonmathematical* approach to forecasting.

7. **Answer B is the best answer.** A properly conducted job analysis will produce job competencies (answer A), job specifications (answer C), and a job description (answer D). Although information generated through the job analysis should be used to write a job posting, this is not one of the specific outputs of the job analysis process.

8. **Answer C is the best answer.** Compensation rates are generally not included in a job description. Scope information (answer A), physical work conditions and physical demands (answer B), and minimum requirements (answer C) do constitute important parts of the job description for each position.

9. **Answer B is the best answer.** Job competencies speak to broad categories of skills that are required to perform successfully in a particular position, department, or organization. Of the four answers, "facilitation skills" is least likely to be defined in this way, since it is more of a discrete, observable, and perhaps even measurable skill. Communication skills (answer A), teamwork skills (answer B), and interpersonal skills (answer D) are all more likely to be considered "key success factors" or "performance factors."

10. **Answer C is the best answer.** If underutilization exists within an organization, employee referral programs are not likely to remedy that problem. Answers A and D are not the best possible answers; "highly cost-effective recruiting" and "increased candidate familiarity with the organization" both represent benefits of employee referral programs. Answer B is not the best answer; although the employee who makes the referral may believe that the candidate whom they refer will succeed, that assessment is not necessarily accurate.

Suggested Readings and Resources

Department of Justice. www.usdoj.gov, 2007.

Department of Labor. www.dol.gov, 2007.

Equal Employment Opportunity Commission (EEOC). www.eeoc.gov, 2007.

Other Internet Resources: Search the Web for any of the words listed in the Key Terms section of this chapter.

Society for Human Resource Management (SHRM). www.shrm.org, 2007.

www.amazon.com: Search any of the words listed in the Key Terms section of this chapter, 2007.

Gibson, Cathy Lee. *Mission-Driven Interviewing: Moving Beyond Behavior-Based Questions.* Huntington, CT: PTI Publishing, 2006.

Human Resource Development

Study Strategies

▶ On large index cards, write down the names of each of the laws, topics, and key concepts covered in this chapter. Then, on smaller, separate index cards (ideally, ones that are a different color), make notes on important facts and details relating to each of these laws, topics, and key concepts (put the name of the law or the topic on the back of the card, not on the front). Then, test your memory and understanding by matching the specific facts and details (each of which you wrote on a separate index card) with the laws, topics, and key concepts that you labeled on the larger business cards. After you match them up, you can check how well you did by comparing your matches to the names of the laws and topics that you wrote on the back of the smaller index cards.

▶ Try writing out your own multiple-choice test questions. Writing out the questions—along with detailed answers—can go a long way toward reinforcing what you are studying. If you've got a study partner, trade questions with that person.

▶ Although the PHR exam is multiple choice, try writing and answering your own essay-based questions. Write open-ended questions that require a response of at least a full paragraph—and write your answers without looking back at your study materials. The process of actually writing down your answers will reinforce what you already know and will highlight what you need to study more. It will also likely help you as you work to recall this same information when you answer related multiple-choice questions on the actual PHR exam.

▶ As with each of the six functional areas of HR, determine what you already know and what you don't know. Then, work to prepare yourself. Conduct research. Use the Internet to find articles and whitepapers that highlight HR development. Peruse textbooks that provide guidance relative to those particular areas. Be sure to find several real-life examples of each concept, topic, and responsibility to ensure that you gain a variety of perspectives and insights. This is particularly important for the skill-based, rather than fact-based, components of this functional area.

Introduction

Human resource development (HRD) can be defined, in its simplest terms—well...it actually isn't all that easy to define. A review of the research describes HRD in myriad and sometimes ambiguous ways. If you have had a chance to study and review HRD-related books, articles, and documents as part of your preparation for the PHR exam and still aren't 100% clear in your understanding of where and how it fits within the broader field of HR, you are not alone. And, when you throw organization development (OD) into the mix, things can seem even a bit more unclear.

In an effort to lend as much clarity as possible to this critically important HR functional area, let's approach HR development with this working definition:

> HRD consists of processes and initiatives that improve current—and prepare for future—organizational effectiveness by ensuring that those who work within the organization will be prepared to demonstrate levels of performance consistent with organizational needs. To bridge the gap between where employees are at any one point in time with where they need to be at a targeted, subsequent point in time, myriad interventions could be used, including training, career development, and organization development initiatives. These interventions are the stuff of which HRD consists.

To understand, appreciate, and begin to perform HRD more effectively, HR professionals need to be familiar with key foundational concepts as well as relevant legal dimensions of human resource development. HR professionals also need to be able to knowledgeably navigate the three primary areas of HRD:

- *Organization development (OD)*—The development of effective and productive organizations that simultaneously develop, empower, and support their employees.

- *Training (also known as "learning and development")*—The learning and transfer of skills and knowledge that will enable an employee to perform his or her current job more effectively, thus contributing to the overall effectiveness of the organization.

- *Career development*—The deliberate preparation for, and unfolding of, the professional pathway along which each individual travels during his or her adult working life.

It is worthwhile to note that although OD has more of an organizational focus, and training and career development are more individualized in nature, all three areas contribute significantly to the overall implementation of effective HRD.

Two other areas that also contribute to the overall effectiveness of HRD are leadership development and performance management. Although both areas are inextricably woven into the tapestry of HRD, each also maintains its own presence and uniqueness—even in those organizations that do not openly espouse HRD initiatives. As such, these two areas will be explored separately, but still as part of this chapter.

Legal Dimensions of Human Resource Development

In addition to the HR-related laws that are explored in the other HR functional areas, there are several other laws—ones that are not exclusively HR-related—that need to be considered carefully because of the impact they can have on the way we perform our jobs. Here, we will look at:

▶ Copyright Act of 1976

▶ Public domain

▶ Fair use

▶ U.S. Patent Act

Copyright Act of 1976

The idea of protecting the work of authors, artists, and others who create original materials dates back all the way to the Constitution. Article I, Section 8 of the United States Constitution states: "The Congress shall have Power…to promote the Progress of Science and useful Arts, by securing for limited Times to Authors and Inventors the exclusive Right to their respective Writings and Discoveries." Fast forward 189 years to the Copyright Act of 1976.

What's Covered, and What Rights Are Granted

A copyright grants certain rights to authors and others who create original works. According to Section 102 of the Act, this protection extends to "original works of authorship fixed in any tangible medium of expression, now known or later developed, from which they can be perceived, reproduced, or otherwise communicated, either directly or with the aid of a machine or device." Works of authorship that are protected include the following:

▶ Literary works

▶ Musical works, including any accompanying words

▶ Dramatic works, including any accompanying music

▶ Pantomimes and choreographic works

▶ Pictorial, graphic, and sculptural works

▶ Motion pictures and other audiovisual works

▶ Sound recordings

▶ Architectural works (this category was added in 1990)

The Act grants copyright holders exclusive rights to the following six specific categories of activities:

- ▶ The right to duplicate/reproduce/copy the work
- ▶ The right to create derivative works that are based on the original work
- ▶ The right to sell, lease, rent, or otherwise distribute copies of the work to the public
- ▶ The right to perform the work publicly
- ▶ The right to display the work publicly
- ▶ The right to digital performance in sound recordings

    In so doing, the Act also prohibits those who do not hold the copyright from engaging in those activities without permission of the copyright holder.

Copyright Holders

Most of the time, the author, artist, or individual who created the work owns the copyright to the work. The Copyright Act, however, does establish two important "work-for-hire" exceptions to this rule. These exceptions pertain specifically to work product created by

- ▶ *Employees*—The work product that an employee generates in the normal course of his or her employment is automatically owned by the employer.
- ▶ *Consultants/independent contractors*—The work product generated by a consultant or independent contractor is usually automatically owned by the organization with whom the consultant contracts. From the perspective of the organization that has contracted with the consultant, it is important to have a signed written agreement that states that a work-for-hire arrangement has been established, and that the organization owns all work product that is produced.

EXAM ALERT

Be familiar with these two important work-for-hire exceptions to the Copyright Act.

Copyright law covers only the particular form or manner in which ideas or information were first fixed. Copyrights do not, however, cover the actual ideas, concepts, or facts that are included in the fixed work.

Copyrights last for the lifetime of the author, plus 70 years. After that, the work passes into the public domain. Anonymous works and works that were created under work-for-hire agreements enter the public domain 95 years after the first year of publication or 120 years after the year in which they were created, whichever comes first.

Public Domain

As previously indicated, copyrights—and the protections afforded by copyrights—eventually expire. After a copyright for a particular work expires, that work enters the public domain. This means that the copyright holder no longer enjoys the six areas of protection cited previously, and that the works are available, and free, for all to use.

TIP

> Work created by the federal government is, by definition, considered to be in the public domain. This provision of the Act can be very helpful to HR professionals, especially with respect to work product that is generated relative to legal and/or compliance-related issues.

EXAM ALERT

> Familiarize yourself with the criteria that exist for determining whether a particular work is in the public domain.

CAUTION

> Just because a work is publicly accessible does not mean that it is in the public domain. With access to countless numbers of websites, combined with the ability to copy, paste, and save text and images on almost any topic, the temptation may exist to incorporate existing materials into HRD/training presentations, handouts, or other work-related documents. For legal, professional, and ethical reasons, resist the temptation. Don't do it.

Fair Use

In addition to works that are in the public domain, HR professionals (and anyone else, of course) can use copyrighted works under certain circumstances. This is known as *fair use*. According to the Copyright Act, portions of copyrighted works can be used without the permission of the author for purposes of "criticism, comment, news reporting, teaching (including multiple copies for classroom use), scholarship, or research." Even then, however, what constitutes fair use is contingent upon a number of factors:

▶ Whether the work will be used for commercial purposes or for not-for-profit or educational purposes.

▶ The nature of the way in which the work will be used.

▶ How much of the work is used, both in terms of the overall size of the portion of the work that is being used, as well as the percentage of the total work that is being used.

▶ Whether the use could impact the potential market and/or the market value of the work.

EXAM ALERT

> Be familiar with the considerations that contribute to determining what constitutes fair use.

U.S. Patent Act

In addition to being familiar with copyrights, HR professionals also need to have a working understanding of patents.

Patents confer certain rights upon the individual to whom the patent is granted. Specifically, a patent holder has "the right to exclude others from making, using, offering for sale, or selling" the invention in the United States or "importing" the invention into the United States. Interestingly, a patent does not grant the patent holder the right to take any specific action relative to the patent that he or she has been granted, or relative to the invention for which the individual was granted the patent. Instead, it prohibits others from taking the preceding actions. The responsibility for enforcing those rights, however, falls squarely upon the individual to whom the patent has been granted (with no assistance from the U.S. Patent Office).

There are three types of U.S. patents:

Type of Patent	Patent Issued to Individuals Who	Duration of Patent (from Date of Filing)
Utility	Invent or discover any new and useful process, machine, article of manufacture, or composition of matter, or any new and useful improvement thereof	20 years
Design	Invent a new, original, and ornamental design for an article of manufacture	14 years
Plant	Invent or discover and asexually reproduce any distinct and new variety of plant	20 years

HR professionals and the organizations for which they work need to understand and consider patent issues, particularly if employees might (or do) create inventions in the course of their work. To avoid costly and time-consuming litigation—which could even potentially impact the marketability of the invention—organizations should consult with counsel, in advance, relative to drafting and implementing written agreements governing patent-related issues.

REVIEW BREAK

Although HRD isn't directly impacted by as many laws as the other functional areas of HR, it's still important to have a solid understanding of relevant laws—specifically, The Copyright Act of 1976 and the U.S. Patent Act. It's also important to always remain cognizant of the fact that other HR-related laws (such as the Civil Rights Act of 1964) have far-reaching impact and must be carefully considered with respect to potential HRD implications.

Now that we've paused to consider possible legal considerations, let's begin to look at some key HRD concepts, as well as their applications.

HRD: The Importance of ADDIE

Although the ADDIE model can be applied in any of the functional areas within HR, it is perhaps most frequently referenced with respect to HRD (specifically, training and instructional design). Therefore, much of the information in this chapter (and, perhaps, on the PHR exam) relating to ADDIE uses training-specific examples. As you move through the chapter, however, keep in mind the broader applications of ADDIE.

ADDIE: An Overview

As mentioned in Chapter 2, "HR: A Body of Underlying Knowledge and Principles," in the "Needs Assessment and Analysis" section, the acronym ADDIE represents the following five steps:

- ► A: Analysis/assessment (of needs)
- ► D: Design
- ► D: Development
- ► I: Implementation
- ► E: Evaluation

Because the ADDIE model is so integral to HRD—specifically in terms of instructional design—let's take a look at each of these steps more closely.

ADDIE: "A" Is for Analysis/Assessment

As we begin to explore needs analysis/assessment—the first step in the ADDIE model—it's helpful to keep in mind that HR professionals have the greatest impact and add the greatest value when they seek to carry out their responsibilities—whatever those responsibilities might involve—in a consultative manner. As such, it's helpful to proactively think about the kinds of questions you might encounter as you prepare for and work your way through this phase. In this way, you'll be better able to recognize and be prepared to respond to these questions when you hear them, and—more important—you can look for opportunities to ask them yourself. Some representative questions that might come up in the needs analysis/assessment phase might include the following:

- ► Why is an HRD/training initiative being considered?
- ► Why is one particular type of HRD/training initiative being considered? (If applicable.)
- ► If the HRD/training initiative under consideration is being motivated by a perceived performance problem, what is the nature of the substandard performance? (We need to recognize that reason before we can begin to determine whether an HRD/training initiative might constitute an appropriate intervention.)
- ► What level of subject-matter knowledge and skill do employees possess?

▸ What level of subject-matter knowledge and skill do employees need?

▸ What is the gap between current performance levels and desired or expected performance levels?

▸ What are the learning objectives that the HRD/training initiative would need to attain to bridge that gap?

▸ What level of organizational/leadership support exists to bridge that gap? (This may be a function of how closely the skills or knowledge that is missing relates to the mission and goals of the organization.)

▸ By what date must the organization begin to address the gap?

▸ By what date must the organization bridge the gap?

▸ What are the costs of various HRD/training options, and what would be the benefits?

▸ What resources are available to address this gap? (Resources can include people, money, and time.)

Analysis/Assessment: Theoretical/Scholarly Foundation

Before getting into the nuts-and-bolts of needs analysis/assessment, it's helpful and important to understand what's behind it.

EXAM ALERT

In addition to helping you perform your job better, it's important for you to be familiar with HR-related theories (such as this, for instance), because they are likely to appear on the PHR exam.

In 1961, McGehee and Thayer identified three levels of HRD/training needs analysis and assessment. More than four decades later, their theory still constitutes an important tool for HRD/training needs analysis/assessment (although some of the terminology has evolved a bit over time, as indicated in the following table):

Level of Needs Analysis (1961 Verbiage)	Level of Needs Analysis (Contemporary Verbiage)	Definition/Description of the Level of Analysis	Examples of What the Analysis Looks At
Organizational analysis	N/A	Determine where HRD/training can and should be used within the overall organization	What is the organization's mission? What are its objectives? In the future, what KSAs will the organization's employees need to possess and demonstrate?
			What is the pool of skills currently available within the organization?

Level of Needs Analysis (1961 Verbiage)	Level of Needs Analysis (Contemporary Verbiage)	Definition/Description of the Level of Analysis	Examples of What the Analysis Looks At
			What is the gap between those two?
			What is the organization's culture like?
Operations analysis	Task or work analysis	Collect data about a particular job or group of jobs	What are the perform-ance standards for a particular job?
			What KSAs and behavior characteristics must an incumbent possess and demonstrate in order to achieve those standards?
Man analysis	Individual or person analysis	Assess performance of a particular individual	How well is a particular employee performing? Where does the employee's performance fall below the expected standards of the posi-tion? Is that lag attribut-able to skills or knowl-edge the employee needs to attain or develop? How might training or other HRD initiatives address any performance issues (areas in which actual performance does not match the level of performance required to attain established job standards)?

EXAM ALERT

Be familiar with how internal and external factors can impact a needs analysis/assessment and how they can impact the recommendations that are generated through that needs analysis/assessment. Know what those environmental considerations could be as well as how to conduct an effective scan using strengths, weaknesses, opportunities, and threats (SWOT) analysis.

Needs Analysis/Assessment—Why Do It?

There are a number of reasons to conduct a needs analysis/assessment before embarking on an HRD/training initiative. Some of those reasons are

▸ To identify—objectively and factually—performance-related problems within the organization. (Engaging in this process with internal clients constitutes another concrete example of how HR can truly function as strategic and consultative busi-ness partners, even on seemingly transactional or tactical related matters.)

- ▶ To collect facts with which to establish a baseline level of performance. This baseline will then provide a valid basis of comparison for pretraining/posttraining (or, more broadly, pre-HRD initiative/post-HRD initiative) assessments.

- ▶ To generate increased involvement with and, therefore, buy-in for the HRD/training solution that is ultimately implemented. Securing buy-in at all levels of the organization (especially at the senior leadership level) is critical.

- ▶ To ensure that your decisions and recommendations are based on facts, rather than on assumptions. This is another way to help to dispel the "fuzzy-wuzzy, touchy-feely, party-planning, people-people" stereotype, which many HR professionals are still wrestling to redefine. This process provides HR professionals with an opportunity to enhance their reputation in the organization as legitimate business partners—not as people who rely solely on their ability to intuitively read a situation.

- ▶ To increase the likelihood of identifying a solution that will truly bridge the performance gap.

- ▶ To ensure that a legitimate cost-benefit analysis is conducted before a commitment is made to any particular HRD/training solution. The costs associated with implementing the HRD/training initiative must also be compared to the costs that would accrue if the current situation were allowed to persist without implementing the HRD/training intervention.

An unintended, but potentially significant, benefit of conducting a needs analysis/assessment is that you may also identify other organizational issues that had previously gone unnoticed. Even if these concerns are not best addressed by an HRD/training-based initiative—and even if they do not fall within the purview of HR—you still will have made a meaningful contribution to the overall effectiveness of your organization.

Needs Analysis/Assessment—What Are the Risks of *Not* Doing It?

Having looked at the benefits of conducting a needs analysis/assessment, it's also important to look at the situation from a different perspective—specifically, the risks associated with *not* conducting a needs analysis/assessment. A few of these risks might be the following:

- ▶ Misidentifying problems

- ▶ Overlooking problems

- ▶ Eliminating the only means of establishing a basis from which to make meaningful assessments of the impact of an HRD/training initiative

- ▶ Possibly increasing skepticism relative to the value of—and necessity for—the HRD/training initiative

- ▶ Damaging HR's reputation, either collectively or relative to specific individuals, by contributing to the impression that HR folks just try to "get a feel for things" instead of making rigorous, fact-based business decisions

Needs Analysis/Assessment—How Do You Do It?

Though experts may differ on the specifics, and different models might include different steps, a well-constructed needs analysis should include the following four steps:

1. Gather data that will enable you to identify specific needs.

2. Determine which of those needs can be addressed through HRD/training interventions.

3. Propose/select a solution (depending upon HR's role in the organization and in this process) for those needs that are best addressed through HRD/training interventions.

4. Compare the costs of implementing an HRD/training initiative to the benefits that will accrue from delivering the HRD/training initiative.

> **NOTE**
>
> From time to time, HRCI may prescribe steps that differ slightly from research and recommendations that are available elsewhere. Essentially, however, "good practice is good practice," and most minor differences generally will not impact your ability to effectively carry out the function or process that is being described. It could, however, impact the ultimate determination of what the best possible choice is on any particular PHR question.

Step 1 of Needs Analysis/Assessment: Gathering Data

Data Collection Techniques	Sample Strengths	Sample Weaknesses
General surveys (closed-ended questions)	Easier to tabulate (especially if done electronically). Confidentiality can be ensured, which may lead to greater candor of response.	Information may be overly general in nature, in part because of the nature of closed-ended questions.
"Felt-needs" employee surveys (asking people to identify the areas in which they feel they need training	Can reach a large number of employees in a short time frame.	Employees may identify "wants" instead of "needs." The training that the employees are requesting, therefore, may not directly translate into enhanced work performance that supports attainment of organizational objectives.
"Organizational challenges" employee surveys (asking employees to identify individual, group, or organizational performance issues)	Can reach a large number of employees in a short time frame. Ensures a focus on performance issues, which can then be translated by those who administer the survey into HRD/training solutions.	Since these questions are more open-ended in nature, results may take longer to tabulate.

(continues)

Data Collection Techniques	Sample Strengths	Sample Weaknesses
Review of published business documents	Provides factual, objective data with which many decision makers should already be familiar (and in which they likely already have confidence).	Reflects past situations, which may not be reflective of more recent trends.
Interviews	Obtain in-depth information from individuals at all levels of the organization (thus providing a variety of valuable perspectives).	Time consuming. Labor intensive. Requires a skilled interviewer (who also can establish trust).
Focus groups	Provides a qualitative approach. A skilled facilitator may be able to extract particularly valuable information. The synergy present in a well-functioning group may generate more valuable and insightful data than would have been generated by the same members individually.	Labor intensive and time consuming. More difficult to reach large numbers of people, within a relative short time frame. Direction of discussion may be swayed by group dynamics, or by the presence and/or contributions of one or more influential individuals. It may be challenging to replicate identical conditions across various focus groups, which could theoretically taint/impact the consistency of the data that is collected. May be prohibitive because of limited resources (time, cost, or facilitator availability).
Observation	Provides a realistic viewpoint, rather than one that might be "sanitized," obsequious, or self-serving.	Labor intensive and time consuming. Requires a trained observer (trained in making observations, as well as in the work that is being observed).
Performance appraisals	If done well, the performance management and appraisal process can establish criteria.	Performance appraisals—for myriad reasons—do not always provide an accurate reflection of actual performance (or of that performance as it compares to standards) (see "Performance Appraisal (and Management)—Pitfalls to Avoid").
Skills assessment	Results are easily quantified.	Does not measure whether the skills that are being assessed are actually being used on the job.

As indicated, each data-gathering method has advantages and disadvantages. For this reason, a combination of two or more methods might be more effective.

Data gathering can be performed by someone within the organization, or with some level of support and assistance from external experts (for instance, consultants).

Regardless of who gathers the data, however, establishing trust is absolutely essential. Otherwise, the overall objective of enhancing organizational performance and attaining overarching organizational objectives could be undermined by mistrust or morale problems engendered by flawed data-gathering processes.

It's also essential to make a commitment to following through on the information you collect through the data-gathering phase, even if the organization ultimately decides not to launch an HRD/training initiative. In short, the first time that employees tell you about their concerns cannot be the last time that you communicate with them about those concerns. The very process of gathering data, especially through survey or focus group techniques, raises awareness, and thus raises expectations. Don't let those expectations be ignored—even if the answer ends up being that they will not be addressed through an HRD initiative at this time.

Step 2 of Needs Analysis: Identify Needs That Can Be Addressed Through Specific HRD/Training Initiatives

Organizations implement different HRD/training initiatives for a variety of reasons. Ultimately, however, these reasons fall into two primary categories: to gain knowledge, and to develop skills. Both of these, ultimately, are intended to change behavior, to enhance performance, and to achieve the organization's stated goals.

Knowledge

HRD/training initiatives that are implemented for the purpose of expanding upon employees' knowledge base will expose participants to a body of information they must know, or with which they must be familiar, to perform their jobs effectively. Sometimes, knowledge training is even mandated by law (for instance, sexual harassment training in California). Knowledge-based training generally focuses more on what a person knows, rather than on how he or she applies that knowledge. Knowledge-based training can also be implemented to educate employees about organization-specific topics that are unrelated to specific skills or to general areas of knowledge. Either way, this acquisition of knowledge is directly intended to manifest as specific desired behaviors (that employees now know more *about*), which in turn will produce desired results (that employees now know *how* to deliver).

Skills

As the name implies, skills training is designed to teach participants how to *do* something related to their job. That something, however, can span a wide range of possibilities.

Skills training can address certain specific, discrete functions that are important to the individual's ability to perform his or her job and that contribute to the organization's ability to attain its overall objectives. Skills training can also, however, address and cultivate behaviors that are reflective of the values of the organization, or that support demonstration of organizational competencies (see "Performance Management," later in this chapter).

Attitude Versus Behavior

Attitude is important to consider—particularly with respect to training and performance management. It's also exceedingly difficult, however, to get one's hands around the concept of "attitude" in any sort of concrete, consistent, objective manner. Attitude, in short, is subjective and personal. By defining attitude behaviorally, however, an organization can accomplish two objectives: It can create a basis for designing HRD/training interventions that will cultivate *behaviors that manifest desired attitudes*, and it can provide a framework within which to evaluate employees in a more objective and more defensible manner (for performance management purposes, or should any other need arise).

For instance, consider the attitudinal characteristic "flexibility." This word can, of course, mean different things to different people—particularly to managers and their direct reports. By identifying flexibility behaviorally, however, within the context of the results that the employee is expected to produce, it's easier to discuss, address, and resolve attitude problems relating to flexibility. In this case, some behavioral definitions of flexibility might be

- ▶ Displays agility, openness, and responsiveness in the face of rapidly changing conditions.

- ▶ Performs a wide range of assignments accurately, efficiently, and willingly.

- ▶ Handles multiple projects simultaneously without experiencing a decline in quality or quantity of performance.

By framing and defining them in terms of behaviors, therefore, attitudes become easier to address, discuss, and resolve.

Step 3 of Needs Analysis: Propose/Select a Solution (Depending upon HR's Role in the Organization, and in This Process)

In proposing/selecting a solution, it is essential to use a logical, fact-based approach. One dimension of that approach will include comparing the resources that are *available*, to the resources that are *required* to deliver each specific HRD/training initiative. Resources, in this context, could mean financial, human, temporal, and technological, to name a few.

For instance, if the resources required to implement a particular solution would be impossible to secure, it would be counterproductive to continue considering a particular solution. And that's the kind of information that you're better off knowing up front, before making a commitment to any particular course of action.

It is also critical to prepare a cost-benefit analysis as part of the process of proposing/selecting a solution. As with other dimensions of needs analysis, there is no one right way to conduct a cost-benefit analysis. Calculating return on investment (ROI), however, is essential. ROI can be calculated by considering the following:

1. Calculate the costs associated with the current situation, as is, if no HRD/training intervention were implemented (in other words, the cost of *not* implementing the HRD/training initiative).

2. Calculate the costs associated with implementing the HRD/training intervention. Be sure to consider all direct and indirect costs, including (but not limited to):

   - ▶ The trainer's/facilitator's salary (prep time, delivery, and follow-up) and/or fees associated with an external trainer/consultant

- Wages and salaries paid to participants during the HRD/training session
- Lost revenue from nonproduction of goods or nondelivery of services during the HRD/training session
- Any overtime expenses that might result because of work that was not completed during the HRD/training session
- Food and beverages
- Materials
- Facility fees
- Travel

3. Calculate the financial gains that will accrue from implementing the HRD/training initiative. Financial gains could accrue from a variety of sources, such as

- The value of the skills that employees develop and the knowledge that employees gain through the HRD/training intervention (after those skills and that knowledge is applied in the workplace).
- Costs (or potential costs) that will not be incurred (or that will no longer be incurred) after the HRD/training initiative is delivered.
- Benefits that are less tangible (but no less real). Please note that some of these benefits might be more difficult to attribute directly to the HRD/training initiative (for instance, increased morale, retention, and customer satisfaction, to name a few).

4. Compare the costs of implementing the HRD/training initiative to the benefits that will accrue from conducting the HRD/training initiative.

In doing this, it's important to keep in mind that the objective is not to sell anyone on a particular initiative—*including ourselves*. The objective is to make a well-informed decision that focuses on meeting the needs of the organization.

In addition to conducting this analysis, many organizations use a measure referred to as "cost per trainee" or "cost per participant," which is calculated as follows:

$$\frac{\text{Total of all costs associated with the HRD/training initiative}}{\text{Number of individuals who participate in the HRD/training initiative}}$$

This formula can provide valuable information that can be used to make a wide variety of HRD/training-related decisions. For instance, just a few of the decisions that this analysis could help you make might be the following:

- Whether to sponsor an in-house HRD/training initiative or send participants to publicly offered training programs
- Whether to develop an HRD/training initiative internally or purchase/license it externally

▶ If the HRD/training initiative will be secured through a source that is external to the organization:

▶ Whether to purchase or license the product

▶ Whether to have the vendor supply trainers, or to implement a "train the trainer" program

▶ Whether to use the external product "as is" or pay for customization

▶ The length of the HRD/training initiative

▶ Who will attend the HRD/training initiative

▶ The frequency with which HRD/training initiatives—on any single topic, and across the board—will be delivered

▶ Whether to hold the HRD/training initiative onsite at the organization's facility or secure conference space at an offsite location, such as a hotel or conference center

By changing one or more than one variable, HR professionals will generate a variety of different scenarios for comparison. This will enable you to do a more effective job of making rigorous, fact-based recommendations that will truly help bolster your role as a business partner.

> **EXAM ALERT**
>
> Be familiar with the specific strengths and weaknesses associated with developing and delivering an HRD/training initiative internally versus externally, and the factors that should be taken into consideration when making this decision.

REVIEW BREAK

The deliverable that is most commonly associated with the needs analysis/assessment is just that—an actual HRD/training needs analysis/assessment. The balance of the ADDIE process will focus on designing, developing, implementing, and evaluating HRD/training initiative(s) that will grow out of that needs analysis/assessment.

ADDIE: "D" Is for Design

In the design phase (the first "D" in ADDIE), you will plan—and prepare to build—the HRD/training initiative that will address the specific needs that were identified through the needs analysis/assessment phase. More specifically, the design phase of the ADDIE process will generate a design plan. Looking at this phase of the process within the framework of the 5 Ws and an H, some of the questions that are likely to be addressed during the design phase might include:

- Who:

    - Who is the target population?

    - Who will develop the HRD/training initiative?

    - Who will deliver the HRD/training initiative?

    - Who will evaluate the HRD/training initiative?

- What:

    - What will the HRD/training initiative accomplish? In other words, what are the HRD/training objectives?

    - What content will be included to meet those HRD/training objectives?

    - What methodologies will be incorporated into the HRD/training initiative?

    - In what order will the various components of the HRD/training initiative be delivered?

    - What delivery method(s) will be used?

    - By what means and measures will the attainment (or nonattainment) of objectives be evaluated?

- When:

    - When will the HRD/training initiative be delivered?

    - When must the delivery of the HRD/training be completed (by what date, and/or before what organizational milestone)?

    - When will the HRD/training initiative be announced?

- Where:

    - Where will the HRD/training program be delivered?

    - What logistical considerations/requirements are associated with each specific location?

- How:

    - Within each method, how will content specifically be addressed?

    - How will the learning objectives be attained through the HRD/training initiative?

Design—The Theoretical/Scholarly Foundation

What is design? Like so much of the information that can be found about ADDIE, the definition of the design component differs from expert to expert. In 1992, Gagne described instructional design (ISD) as a systematic process with a strong planning component. He also identified three commonalities that exist. He found that most instructional design models:

▸ Identify what the outcomes of the HRD/training will be

▸ Develop the actual instructional methods and materials

▸ Create a component that will serve to evaluate the effectiveness of a program/initiative

In 1998, Hannafin and Peck put forth the idea that the instructional design process consists of a series of interrelated steps based on principles derived from educational research and theory. The three phases that they identify in their model (needs assessment, design, and development/implementation) each involve a process of continual evaluation, reevaluation, and revision, *as the program is being developed.*

Design: The Steps

Combining the wisdom of these and other experts, let's look at the design process as consisting of four distinct steps:

1. Identify outcome objectives.

2. Identify learning methodologies.

3. Establish a time frame.

4. Gain agreement and sign-off.

Next, let's take a closer look at each of these individual steps.

Design—Identify Outcome Objectives

Similar to performance management applications, learning objectives should follow the acronym SMART. Although numerous definitions of this acronym exist, one particularly effective one is

▸ *S—Specific*

The HRD/training objectives must be clearly articulated, unambiguous, and understood in the same way by everyone involved in the HRD/training process (the instructional designer, the manager, the facilitator, the participant, and so forth).

▸ *M—Measurable*

If an HRD/training intervention is to be considered a valid solution that will truly support the overall performance objectives of the organization—and of the individuals in the organization—then the outcomes of that HRD/training initiative must be measurable and must be able to withstand the rigor to which those measures will ultimately be subjected through the assessment phase.

▶ *A—Action-oriented*

Objectives should be written so that the behaviors/actions that the learner is expected to demonstrate at the conclusion of the HRD/training initiative are described using strong, robust, action verbs (for instance: generate, produce, resolve, demonstrate, complete, apply, and so on). Don't write objectives with verbs that are not as effective at articulating observable or measurable behaviors (for instance, understand, appreciate, value, and so forth).

▶ *R—Realistic*

Writing realistic training objectives means avoiding *both* ends of the difficulty spectrum. At one end of the spectrum, HRD/training objectives that are too easy to attain aren't challenging enough and may not hold the attention and interest of participants. In addition, overly easy objectives also might not generate desired results (it may also be helpful to keep in mind that if the results could be attained that easily, there would have likely been a less-formal solution than a full-blown HRD/training initiative). At the other end of the spectrum, HRD/training objectives that are virtually impossible to attain will serve only to discourage participants. Despite the belief that some individuals have that setting unrealistically high expectations results in an overall higher level of attainment than would have been achieved if goals were set lower, the reality is often quite different. Setting objectives that are consistently unrealistically high will create a cycle of failure. Over time, this could result in employees feeling frustrated, resentful, and even manipulated or exploited. No matter what results have been attained through overly aggressive goal setting, they won't be worth the long-term negative repercussions of this approach—including morale issues, disengagement, and even high turnover (probably of your better employees, which is often the bad kind of turnover).

▶ *T—Time-bound*

Time is a valuable resource—often, more valuable than money. Ensure that the HRD/training objectives identify goals that can be attained and applied to the actual performance of the position within a period of time that is acknowledged and agreed to in advance. This time frame should be determined collaboratively, taking the input of all stakeholders into consideration.

Design—Identify and Select Learning Methodologies

Identifying and selecting appropriate learning methodologies means deliberately choosing specific techniques and activities that will be most effective at giving participants the opportunity to learn and practice their enhanced skills and apply their expanded knowledge. There are many methodologies from which you might choose, some of which are the following:

▶ Lecture/lecturette

▶ Demonstration

▶ Reading

- ▶ Small group discussions/instructor-facilitated large group discussions

- ▶ Individual, small-group, or large-group activities/applications

- ▶ Case study

- ▶ Role play

Let's take a closer look at each of these methodologies.

Lecture/"Lecturette"

Lectures or lecturettes (very short lectures) are primarily one-way delivery mechanisms through which instructors/speakers present information *to* participants. Often, this information is detailed and/or technical in nature. It often consists of material that is substantially new to most of the learners, so they'll probably need some time to absorb it.

Lectures/lecturettes afford the opportunity to take detailed notes, which can be particularly helpful for those learners for whom note taking is an effective means of reinforcing and retaining content. These notes can be taken freely, without the expectation that learners will contribute conversationally to a topic about which they may not be very knowledgeable (yet). Lectures and lecturettes might also be particularly valuable for auditory learners.

When lectures/lecturettes are overused, participants may lose interest. Boredom (or even fatigue) can set in, in significant part because of the minimal degree of interaction permitted by the didactic format inherent to most lectures/lecturettes.

So, how long is too long for a classroom-based training lecture? As is so often the case, that depends. Some experts say—especially for online applications—that any lecture longer than 5 minutes is too long. Others assert that, in a classroom setting, lectures can last as long as 20 minutes without becoming excessive. Before deciding on a particular length of time for a lecture/lecturette, however, it's important to weigh a variety of factors, a few of which are:

- ▶ The nature and complexity of the topic

- ▶ The time of day

- ▶ How much time has passed since the last break

- ▶ What learning methodology preceded the lecture

- ▶ The overall effectiveness of the lecturer

- ▶ How the participants normally spend their day when they are actually performing their jobs (rather than participating in a training session)

- ▶ The overall percentage of lecture in the training program

Demonstration

Lectures are to demonstrations as *tell me* is to *show me*. During a demonstration, the instructor/facilitator literally shows the participants how to perform a particular function, duty, or role.

Demonstrations are more engaging in nature than lectures because something is actually happening. The skill is not just being referenced—it is being exhibited. Visual learners, in particular, might benefit greatly from this aspect of demonstrations.

> **TIP**
>
> Demonstrations might be of even greater value if participants are also invited to try out—through an exercise or case study—what they are being shown. This multiple-step approach literally moves the activity from passive to active, and thus appeals to visual as well as tactile/kinesthetic learners.

Reading

In recent years, reading hasn't been used much during most training programs. In fact, it has often been given a "bad rap." Perhaps this is because some working adults still recall unpleasant experiences from grade school during which they were directed by a teacher to spend long periods of class time reading. Or, perhaps some participants think of reading as a waste of time because they feel that they could read on their own time.

Dedicating short periods of time during a training session to reading, however, can actually reap numerous benefits. First, it appeals to visual learners who effectively process and retain printed information. Reading can also provide a welcome change of pace during a training session. For instance, if participants have completed some sort of self-analytical instrument, they may appreciate having a few minutes to review information that will help them begin to process and interpret what their results mean (particularly when compared to the option of sharing those results aloud, and having them interpreted in front of the rest of the group). Reading printed material can also be extremely helpful when such material contains details that participants must refer to repeatedly, such as instructions for a case study or role play.

Small Group Discussions/Instructor-Facilitated Large-Group Discussions

When considering discussions as a learning methodology, it may be helpful to think back to one of Knowles's tenets about adult learning: the role of a learner's experience. This is the principle that says that adult learners believe that they have a significant amount of valuable experience on which they can draw to enhance their own learning—and from which others can benefit, as well. Skillfully facilitated discussions will allow participants to do exactly that, and to feel more engaged in the learning experience. What's even better is that these feelings are legitimate. Participants can learn a great deal from each other during small- and large-group discussions.

Individual, Small-Group, or Large-Group Activities/Applications

Hearing information is one thing; seeing it demonstrated is another—and following up one or both of those techniques with an activity that requires hands-on involvement can be an extremely effective way of reinforcing learning. Giving participants the chance to immediately apply the knowledge or skills about which they have just learned can also lead to significantly higher retention rates than lecture or demonstration alone.

Case Studies

Case studies draw on two of Knowles' other theories:

▶ *Learner's self-concept*—"I'm an adult, and I can direct myself. That includes in a classroom setting, so please treat me accordingly."

▶ *Orientation to learning*—"What I learn today needs to be able to help me solve problems in the workplace tomorrow—not at some unspecified time in the future."

Case studies present participants with real-life situations that allow them to apply the knowledge they have learned and practice the skills they have developed during the training session. In the safe environment of the classroom, learners can try out their newly acquired knowledge and newly expanded skills before they must return to the workplace (where it might not be quite as safe to make mistakes). Participants will benefit from receiving feedback from the instructor/facilitator relative to those aspects of the case study that were handled well. Participants will also benefit (perhaps even more) from receiving feedback from the instructor/facilitator relative to those aspects of the case study that could have been handled differently, or better. In both cases, the participant will be able to incorporate this feedback before bringing the knowledge and skills learned during the training back to the workplace. This can, potentially, increase the value of the training experience even more.

Role Plays

Role plays are similar to case studies and can even be used as a natural culmination of a case study. Role plays, in one sense, take case studies one step further, in that participants actually act out the ways in which they would apply their knowledge and practice their skills in particular situations.

One of the advantages of role playing is that—when well executed—they can provide one of the most realistic re-creations of workplace conditions that is possible in a training situation. It also presents participants with the opportunity to practice skills and apply knowledge—opportunities that they otherwise might not be afforded for quite some time. This is particularly important because, as reviewed earlier, retention levels are higher if training is followed closely by opportunities to put that training into practice.

CAUTION

Role plays, however, can backfire if not handled delicately by the trainer. For instance, although feedback must be candid and honest, it also must be delivered in a way that does not diminish the self-esteem of the role-play participants or negatively impact the way in which others will perceive participants after the training ends. Role playing is risky—for the participant, for the instructor, and ultimately for the HR or training professional who designed and pitched the training. Role plays should be led by skilled instructors/facilitators who are adept at providing positive, constructive, and productive feedback in classroom settings, and who have the ability to defuse a variety of (potentially sensitive) situations.

Design—Establish a Time Frame

As explored previously, it's critical to make sure that HRD/training objectives are time bound. At this point in the process, timing continues to be just as important. Establishing and agreeing on a time frame for the development, implementation, and evaluation of the learning processes is critical. Establishing a time frame for implementing the entire project—as well as for reaching important milestones along the way—helps to ensure accountability, increase management support, and treat HRD/training with the same level of rigor as any other organizational (meaning, business) initiative.

Design—Gain Agreement and Sign-off

Often, this step of the design process may be minimized or even overlooked. Without a signed agreement that specifies all the elements and terms of the HRD/training initiative, however, you are more likely to experience misunderstandings (and all the problems that go along with misunderstandings). There may be perceptions that you didn't deliver what you promised, when you promised it, and how you promised it. One incident like this can significantly damage your credibility (or the credibility of HRD/training initiatives, or even the credibility of HR in general). Don't allow room for misunderstandings; even if it may at first feel a bit formal, secure formal written agreement of the design plan before you begin the development phase of ADDIE.

ADDIE: "D" Is for Development

In this phase, you will develop (or oversee/participate in the development of) the design plan that was created in the previous phase. This will include the development of the actual materials. Alternatively, you may decide that the best way to execute the design plan is to purchase or license materials from a source outside the organization. Either way, during this phase, every exercise, resource, handout, activity, and/or training element is created, built, or otherwise secured. The outputs from this phase, therefore, will include program materials (for participants and instructors/facilitators) as well as instructional guides (for instructors/facilitators).

ADDIE: "I" Is for Implementation

By now, the HRD/training program has been designed and developed. You've made sure that it is practical rather than overly theoretical, in a balance that is consistent with the culture and expectations of your organization. It has been designed and built to deliver knowledge and skills that participants will be able to use in the workplace, *not just in the classroom*. Now it's time to prepare for the actual launch—in the classroom, online, or through some blended combination of both.

Pilot Programs

By the time an HRD/training program is ready to be implemented (or delivered), a great deal of time, talent, and financial resources have probably been invested in the successful launch of the program. As such, it may be difficult (or even painful, at moments), to entertain the possibility that some dimension of the program, as conceived and/or designed, may need to be refined, overhauled, or even scrapped. Yet it is precisely this possibility to which we must be open—and that we must even consciously invite.

It is for this reason that—assuming a program will be delivered more than one time—it is critical to run a pilot program before launching a full-fledged HRD/training initiative.

Options for Running Pilot Programs

A pilot program is generally delivered to a subsection of the population of individuals who would ultimately be expected to participate in the HRD/training initiative, as well as to decision makers, senior managers (from whom you want to resecure buy-in), and other key stakeholders.

Pilot sessions can be run in a number of different ways, two of which are

▶ *Identical Program Format*—The pilot program is identical to the actual training program that you have designed and developed. In this way, the attendees of the pilot program will be able to experience and assess the same program that subsequent attendees will attend.

▶ *Abbreviated Program Format*—The pilot program enables participants to experience some, but not all, of the program elements. Some portions might be described, and others might be introduced, but not executed. Other portions of the program might be skipped entirely.

Ideally, an HRD/training pilot should be identical to the actual training program that subsequent participants will experience (the first option). Realistically, however, this will not always be possible, nor will your clients always be open to this option. So, as an alternative, be prepared to deliver an abbreviated format.

Collecting and Using Feedback from Pilot Programs

With either pilot program format, a critical component of the pilot involves receiving feedback from those who attend the pilot program. This feedback should be far more extensive than the single page workshop evaluation forms (sometimes called "smile sheets") that participants are often asked to complete at the end of training sessions. Ideally, pilot evaluation will afford the opportunity for a candid exchange of ideas with all stakeholders. Encourage your pilot participants to share their feedback during a post-training feedback session, at which time they could present questions, comments, and thoughts about which they have made notes during and after the session. Be prepared, however, that your client may not be open to scheduling a formal follow-up session after the pilot. Instead, you may be asked to move in and out of role (instructor versus training designer/developer), as appropriate, during the actual pilot program.

After pilot program participants have provided you with their feedback and insights, the next step is to review, assess, and incorporate (as appropriate) that feedback into the next iteration of the training program. This feedback—and even your own observations—may help you address issues relating to any number of potential concerns, including content, exercises, use of specific methodologies, pace, complexity, clarity, the order in which the content is delivered, and so forth.

> **NOTE**
>
> Yes, you've invested a lot of time and effort into the HRD/training initiative by this point. It can even be said that you have invested a lot of yourself. And yes, this process of scrutiny and review may feel a bit frustrating. But know that you are not wasting your time. Instead, think of it this way—you are being provided with insights and reactions that will make the time you have already invested pay off even more, because it will enable you to produce an even better training program.

> **CAUTION**
>
> Demonstrating defensiveness at this point in the process can harm you in two ways—it can keep you from delivering the best training product possible, and it can diminish your credibility as an HR professional—something that goes well beyond the scope of even the broadest HRD/training initiative. So, as you are being provided with feedback, be sure to practice your active listening skills—even if it hurts. The end result, for all involved (including you), will be of a higher quality because of your efforts, your willingness to listen, your flexibility, and your commitment to the outcome and to your clients.

Facilitator/Instructor

Now that we've taken a close look at content, let's take a close look at delivery. Another important dimension of effective implementation focuses on the facilitator/instructor. Effective facilitation is an artful science, and a scientific art. There are myriad factors that can be taken into consideration when selecting a trainer. Different factors might be more relevant or important in different situations. The following list represents a partial inventory of skills that are crucial to effective facilitation/instruction (and also provides a basis from which to evaluate afterward):

Clarity of Presentation

The clarity of an instructor/facilitator's presentation refers to the effective use of practices that foster better understanding of the subject matter and prevent confusion. An instructor or facilitator who has strong clarity of communication would likely do the following:

- ▶ Provide a written outline of the key points that will be addressed during the workshop.
- ▶ Regularly define new terms, concepts, and principles when they are introduced (rather than assuming a certain level of audience knowledge, or putting participants on the spot relative to who does or does not understand a particular concept).
- ▶ Explain why particular processes, techniques, or formulas are incorporated into the program (rather than just throwing information at participants).
- ▶ Use real-world examples to bring workshop concepts to life.
- ▶ Relate new ideas and concepts covered in the program to more familiar ones, and/or to participants' own experiences.

- Provide occasional summaries and restatements of important ideas and ensure smooth transitions to new, yet related, topics.

- Adjust the pace of delivery when introducing complex and difficult material.

- Avoid excessive digressions from the outline and/or key topics.

- Use materials and visual aids to support and clarify concepts.

- Use well-organized and well-written handouts, workbooks, computerized presentations, and the like.

EXAM ALERT

Be familiar with what does and does not constitute effective facilitation practices.

Presentation Effectiveness

Some of the behaviors that might be indicative of presentation effectiveness could include:

- Clearly stating the objectives of the workshop

- Presenting subjects in a logical order

- Allowing ample time for participants to grasp, explore, and practice concepts

- Periodically confirming with participants that they are "with you" (of course, paraphrasing and asking discussion questions represent far more effective ways of accomplishing this than literally asking participants if they are with you)

- Designing and using exercises that are practical and helpful to participants and that support concepts and objectives

- Referring to and utilizing training materials (including the participant manual) throughout the program

- Using videos, music, or other special audio/visual aids to enhance the learning experience and to appeal to auditory and/or visual learners

- Ensuring that writing on boards/easel pads is organized, legible, and captures important points of the subject matter

- Summarizing major points throughout, and at the conclusion of, the workshop (in an interactive manner, whenever possible)

EXAM ALERT

Be familiar with what does and does not constitute presentation effectiveness.

Participant Dynamics

Effective presentations maintain participants' interest and strive for a high level of involvement. Instructors who are skilled with respect to engaging participants might do the following:

- Periodically modify the pace of the program to maintain—or recapture—participants' interest and engagement.

- Use instructional techniques that promote interactivity.

- Address participants by name (using table tents can help facilitate this).

- Encourage participant feedback.

- Provide constructive feedback in a nonthreatening and affirming manner.

- Utilize activities and exercises that are challenging, and that encourage participants to reach above their previous level of skill or knowledge.

- Utilize techniques, methods, and logic that can be applied back at the workplace.

EXAM ALERT

Be familiar with what does and does not constitute effective practices for engaging participants.

Question/Answer Technique

Effective presentations incorporate questions that challenge participants to analyze information and to apply their newly acquired (or enhanced) skills and/or knowledge. Effective question/answer facilitation techniques might include

- Ask factual questions to provide participants with the opportunity to demonstrate their knowledge—existing, as well as expanding.

- Ask open-ended, thought-provoking questions that engage participants.

- Ask questions that afford participants the opportunity to apply information or principles addressed during the workshop.

- Ask questions that challenge participants to exercise analysis or judgment relative to the instructional materials.

- Ask follow-up questions to clarify and interpret instructional materials, as well as participants' responses and comments.

- Allow ample opportunity (silence) for participants to think through their responses before answering a question.

- Rephrase and repeat difficult questions, as appropriate.

- Respond to unclear (or wrong) participant responses in an honest, yet affirming, manner.

- Repeat participants' questions and answers when they have not been heard by all participants (it's usually important to acknowledge the reason for this, acoustic or otherwise, at an appropriate time).

- Redirect participant questions to other program participants, as appropriate.

- Defer difficult, irrelevant, or time-consuming questions or comments from participants for discussion outside the workshop (in other words, know when to take a discussion offline).

EXAM ALERT

Be familiar with what does and does not constitute effective question/answer facilitation techniques.

Verbal and Nonverbal Communication

Communicating effectively verbally and nonverbally (and combining those two expressions of communication in an effective manner) would require behaviors such as the following:

▶ Speaking audibly

▶ Modulating voice level to ensure variety of emphasis

▶ Not using an excessive amount of "minimal encourages" as speech fillers (okay, ah, uh-huh, um)

▶ Speaking at a pace of that is neither too fast nor too slow

▶ Projecting excitement and enthusiasm about the program and the materials

▶ Establishing and maintaining eye contact with workshop participants, as appropriate

▶ Moving throughout the room/area in an engaging (rather than distracting) way

▶ Using facial expressions and hand gestures to reinforce and emphasize verbal messages

▶ Listening carefully to participants' comments and questions

EXAM ALERT

Be familiar with what does and does not constitute effective verbal and nonverbal communication techniques.

ADDIE: "E" Is for Evaluation

The evaluation phase allows for—and in fact mandates—a comparison of the results or outputs of the HRD/training to the learning objectives that were established during the needs analysis/assessment phase. In this way, the degree to which the specific HRD/training objectives were met can be ascertained through measurement, not guesswork. There will be no question, either way, whether the gap between actual performance (pre-training) and desired performance (post-training) has been bridged.

The Theoretical/Scholarly Foundation

The works of two experts—Donald L. Kirkpatrick and Robert Brinkerhoff—are particularly relevant to evaluation of training (and—through transferability—of other HRD) initiatives.

Kirkpatrick: Four Levels of Evaluation

Kirkpatrick's theory—most recently revisited in the third edition of *Evaluating Training Programs: The Four Levels,* by Donald L Kirkpatrick and James D Kirkpatrick, takes a "summative" approach to evaluation, in that it is predicated on the interpretation of data that is collected *after* the initiative has been implemented. Kirkpatrick's approach allows for a complete analysis of the entire initiative on four levels.

Kirkpatrick's Level 1: Reaction

Reaction-level evaluation measures participants' responses and reactions to the program immediately after the program has been delivered. This level of evaluation often takes the form of a short survey that participants are asked to complete at the end of a training session.

Reaction level evaluation is fast, relatively easy, and frequently utilized. Its value lies in its ability to provide insights into participants' immediate reactions to instructor delivery, training environment, refreshments, and other immediately apparent factors of the HRD/training experience.

CAUTION

Although post-evaluation training forms may ask participants to speculate relative to the degree to which they will be able to transfer content learned during the training program back to the job, this process of speculation is not factual, nor is it necessarily accurate. As such, don't be tempted to assess the ultimate success of a training program on the results of those initial "smile sheets." Instead, remember that true success can only be determined by the long-term attainment of the learning objectives, the transfer of learning to the workplace, ROI, and the like.

Kirkpatrick's Level 2: Learning

Learning-level evaluation measures whether—and to what degree—participants have mastered skills or acquired knowledge that were identified in the learning objectives. Pre-tests and post-tests——frequently seen in e-learning applications—are one means of assessing the development of skills and the acquisition of knowledge.

Kirkpatrick's Level 3: Behavior

Behavior-level evaluation measures whether participants' on-the-job behaviors have changed in a manner consistent with training objectives. In short, it measures *transfer of training*—the degree to which participants apply the skills and knowledge covered in the training session back to the workplace.

In conducting behavior-level assessment, it is important to recognize that individuals can choose to change their workplace behavior for a variety of reasons—some of which are completely unrelated to the training in which they participated. A few of these reasons might relate to:

▶ Receiving positive reinforcement for demonstrating desired behaviors in the workplace

▶ Experiencing progressive disciplinary actions as a result of demonstrating substandard behavior in the workplace

▶ Receiving explicit feedback as part of a performance management and/or appraisal process—feedback that described the performance problem in explicit terms: terms that, to the employee, might ultimately motivate change

Kirkpatrick's Level 4: Results

Results-level evaluation looks specifically at whether the business or organizational results that were expected to occur as a result of the HRD/training initiative did, in fact, occur. This level of results-based evaluation is measurable, concrete, and usually of keen interest to the leaders of the organization because results speak volumes.

As with Kirkpatrick's level 3 analysis, however, it is important to recognize the degree to which other factors (such as a direct competitor going out of business, for instance) could have affected the results. It's important that ROI calculations made as part of results-level analysis truly reflect the implementation of HRD/training initiatives and not other unrelated factors.

EXAM ALERT

Be familiar with ways in which each of the four levels of evaluation in Kirkpatrick's model can be conducted.

Brinkerhoff: Formative Evaluation Model

As discussed previously, Kirkpatrick's model takes a summative evaluation approach that is implemented only after training has been delivered. Brinkerhoff's approach is different. Published in *Achieving Results Through Training*, Brinkerhoff's model incorporates formative evaluation. Within a formative evaluation model, evaluative feedback and input is sought *throughout* the development and implementation phases in an effort to strengthen the ultimate training initiative through real-time incorporation of evaluative feedback. Brinkerhoff's formative evaluation model mandates an iterative process in which feedback, analysis, and assessment conducted at one phase of the process will be used to make enhancements throughout the current and subsequent phases.

Brinkerhoff's model identifies six stages of evaluation:

1. Goals—What is really needed?

2. HRD design—What will work?

3. Program implementation—How is the training working?

4. Immediate outcomes—Did participants learn, what did they learn, and how well did they learn it?

5. Intermediate or usage outcomes—Are participants continuing to retain what they learned and continuing to transfer that learning to the workplace?

6. Impacts and worth—Ultimately, did the training initiative make a difference to the organization? If so, did it make *enough* of a difference to be truly worthwhile?

REVIEW BREAK

ADDIE—A catchy acronym that delineates a critical process. Regardless of what kind of HRD intervention or HR program you are considering implementing, ADDIE can help you approach it in a more structured manner that, ideally, will lead to more predictable and productive results.

With this understanding of ADDIE as a backdrop, let's begin to take a look at some of the key elements within HRD: organization development, training, career development, leadership development, and performance management.

Organization Development

Organization development (OD) refers to the process through which the overall performance, growth, and effectiveness of an organization is enhanced through strategic, deliberate, and integrated initiatives. The interesting and complex area of OD incorporates four academic disciplines: psychology, sociology, anthropology, and management.

OD does not happen haphazardly. Instead, it represents a systematic, planned, and usually multifaceted approach to organizational enhancement. OD interventions are intended to identify an organization's competitive advantages and to ensure the organization's success.

OD helps maintain the organization's focus on this one truth: that it is the people within organizations—literally, its human resources—who accomplish the work of the organization. This, in turn, significantly impacts the overall success of the organization. In that sense, a big part of OD is human development, or in this case, employee development, and is thus inextricably related to the HR function.

> **EXAM ALERT**
>
> Familiarize yourself with international issues (for example, culture, local management approaches/practices, societal norms) that might impact the ways in which you implement and conduct OD (and, for that matter, any HRD and HR) initiatives.

Elements of OD

Acknowledging that OD is a values-driven approach, R. T. Golembiewski identified and articulated important characteristics related to OD, some of which are

▶ Trust, openness, and collaboration are valued and emphasized.

▶ The needs of individuals as well as the needs of the organization and smaller units of the organization are important and relevant.

▶ Feelings, emotions, ideas, and concepts are important.

▶ Group interaction is emphasized and important with respect to change, as well as choice and problem identification and resolution.

Purposes of OD

OD serves a variety of purposes within an organization—purposes that have been defined differently by different individuals and organizations. Some of these purposes are the following:

▶ Enhancing the overall effectiveness of organizations

▶ Promoting openness toward differences, and to resolving the problems that can sometimes arise from those differences (diversity initiatives, in particular, would deal with matters related to this)

▶ Aligning employee goals with unit and organizational goals

▶ Clarifying individual and organizational goals and objectives

▶ Encouraging, supporting, and facilitating collaborative working relationships between and among managers/leaders, individuals, and teams

▶ Improving decision making, individually as well as organizationally

▶ Improving employees' work performance and promotability

▶ Supporting the development of new or replacement knowledge and skills

▶ Dealing more effectively with problems of a human, as well as of a technical, nature

▶ Managing change more effectively

EXAM ALERT

Familiarize yourself well with specific human resource and OD theories and applications, as well as how they interrelate. Specifically, be familiar with how to develop, implement, and evaluate programs to address the unique needs of particular employees (for example, work/family programs, diversity programs, outplacement programs, repatriation programs, and fast-track programs).

Role of the HR Professional in OD

Sometimes, HR professionals are asked to consult with OD professionals. OD professionals may be employed within the organization or may be brought in from outside the organization to work on a particular assignment. Alternatively, HR professionals may be assigned to work on a specific OD project without the assistance of specialized OD professionals (or, for that matter, specialized OD training). Either way, HR's role in the OD process is critical.

OD and Organizational Culture

An important factor to take into consideration when contemplating any OD intervention is the culture of the organization. Organizational culture can be, and has been, defined in myriad ways. Sometimes, it is referred to as "the way things are done around here." This seemingly flippant statement actually incorporates a number of important factors, such as the following:

▶ The shared values of the organization

▶ The external environment in which the organization functions

▶ The way the organization responds to specific individual, group, and organization-level behaviors (punishment, rewards, tolerance, and so on)

> **EXAM ALERT**
>
> Be prepared to answer a question on organizational culture on the PHR exam.

Organizational culture helps establish organizational identity—one to which employees can relate, to which they can belong, and against which they can measure themselves as one way of ascertaining the degree to which they fit within the organization. The culture of an organization can entice candidates to join an organization and can have a seemingly disproportionate impact on an employee's decision to leave an organization. The culture of the organization is also a unifying force for those who work within it, and it helps provide guidance with respect to the norms and behavioral expectations of the organization—in short, it helps employees figure out how they are supposed to act. Organizational culture also contributes to shaping the goals of an organization and is passed on from one generation of employees to the next through stories, publications, and the like.

Organization culture is powerful. It can be productive as well as counterproductive. It needs to be recognized, acknowledged, and understood by HR professionals—in general and as part of efforts to increase the likelihood that OD interventions will be appropriate and effective.

Change Management

Successful OD initiatives will, by definition, bring about change within the organization. As such, it's important for HR professionals to have some basic understanding of *change management*, the process by which that change is managed.

There are two types of change management theory with which HR professionals need to be familiar: change process theory and implementation theory.

Change Process Theory

Change process theory looks at the dynamics behind how change happens within organizations. Kurt Lewin took a close look at the change process, and is an important contributor in the area of change process theory. He identified two primary motivational sources of change:

1. Change that is driven within an individual, arising out or his or her own needs

2. Change that is imposed upon an individual from the environment

In this discussion of change management, we will focus on the second motivational source of change—environmental (meaning, external).

Lewin first described the change process as one that involves three stages: unfreezing, moving, and refreezing:

► *Unfreezing*—"The bus is leaving, so get on board." During the unfreezing stage, everyone who is involved with and impacted by the change must be brought to the point where he or she can understand and accept that a particular change *will* happen. (Understanding and accepting the change, however, does not necessarily mean agreeing with the change—nor does it have to.) An important part of that acceptance involves letting go of behaviors that reflect resistance to change or that can actually impede the change process.

► *Moving*—"You're on the bus; now, let's get moving." Moving, in this context, represents the process through which people are brought to accept the change, and the process through which they are brought to the point where they actually experience the new state that the change was designed to bring about.

► *Refreezing*—"You know, I almost can't remember a time when we **didn't** take this bus." In this phase, what once represented a change has now become, in simplest terms, the norm.

Implementation Theory

The other change-related theory with which HR professionals need to be familiar is *implementation theory*. Implementation theory focuses on carrying out specific strategies—in this case, OD interventions—that are designed to bring about the unfreezing, moving, and refreezing described previously.

Let's take a look at four categories of OD interventions that might be executed as part of that implementation process:

▶ *Human processual interventions*—Seek to effect change and impact relationships within (and between) groups and individuals.

▶ *Technostructural interventions*—Focus on improving what work gets done, as well as the ways and processes through which the work gets done. It looks at job design, job redesign, job restructuring, work content, workflow, work processes, and the like.

▶ *Sociotechnical interventions*—Focus on groups in the workplace and the ways in which those groups can become more (or, at least, semi-) autonomous with respect to the performance and execution of work. Examples of this might include job enrichment, work rescheduling, and participative management.

▶ *Organization transformation change*—The organization is a complex human system that must be continually examined and reexamined. Leaders in organizations must, as such, be able to take the vision of the organization and translate it into goals, which in turn should become the foundation for managing the organization, for assessing performance, and for distributing rewards.

Specific OD Interventions

Although there are a wide variety of possible OD interventions, two specific ones that HR professionals need to be familiar with are team building and total quality management (TQM).

Team Building

Team-building exercises can take many forms, all of which share a common objective: helping the team learn to function more effectively so that it can attain its overall objectives (which must link, of course, to the overall organizational objectives). Team-building exercises will give teams the opportunity to explore topics such as trust, communication, problem solving, the role of the individual within the team, and the impact that the team has on the customer. Team-building exercises often provide scenarios through which participants can hone the same skills and learn about the same principles that are required for the team to function effectively at the workplace.

Total Quality Management

Total Quality Management (TQM) is an OD intervention that is ultimately aimed at meeting or exceeding customer expectations through the commitment of everyone in an organization (often through a team-based approach) to continuous improvement of the production of products and/or the delivery of services.

Total Quality Pioneers

Several individuals figure prominently in the history of quality management:

- ▶ W. Edwards Deming, a true quality pioneer, began his focus on and study of quality in the 1940s, but, like most prophets, was not fully appreciated in his homeland (in Deming's case, that homeland was America). Deming subsequently brought his expertise to Japan in the 1950s, where he has been revered ever since. Deming reemerged as a strong business presence in America in 1980 after an NBC documentary featured him prominently. From that time until his death in 1993, Deming consulted extensively with American organizations, finally disseminating his 14-point quality management program in the nation of his birth—and finally earning the recognition and respect that had previously eluded him.

- ▶ Joseph M. Juran was another giant in the area of quality. Like Deming, Juran centered his attention on the perspectives and needs of customers. His quality management ideas focused on three key areas: quality planning, quality improvement, and quality control. Juran's commitment to quality is still present today through the Juran Institute, whose stated mission is to "enable our clients to attain quality leadership by achieving sustainable breakthrough results. We focus on improving the 'customer experience' of our clients' clients!"

- ▶ Philip B. Crosby, a third quality guru, is well-known for his "zero defects" standard, in contrast to "acceptable quality levels" (AQLs). This management philosophy asserted that employees would perform at whatever level management sets for them. Settling for "goodness"—rather than the full attainment of objectives—would, therefore, effectively preclude the possibility of attaining those objectives.

  Crosby, however, raised the bar even higher. He established four *absolutes of quality management*:

  - ▶ Quality means conformance to requirements, not goodness.

  - ▶ Quality is achieved by prevention, not appraisal.

  - ▶ Quality has a performance standard of zero defects, not acceptable quality levels.

  - ▶ Quality is measured by the price of nonconformance, not indexes.

- ▶ Kaoru Ishikawa believed in the idea of continued customer service—even *after* the customer purchases the product. He saw quality as a never-ending process, in that it can always be taken one step further. Ishikawa also believed strongly in the criticality of securing top-level management support, and dramatically increased worldwide awareness and acceptance of the idea of quality circles, originally a Japanese philosophy.

EXAM ALERT

Be familiar with these change gurus, their guiding principles, and their philosophical legacies.

Quality Tools

As part of developing a basic understanding and knowledge of TQM, HR professionals need to be familiar with several important quality tools:

▶ **Cause-and-effect, Ishikawa, or Fishbone diagram**

Ishikawa developed an important quality tool called the cause-and-effect diagram, which is also known as an Ishikawa diagram, or the fishbone diagram. This tool presents a visual representation of factors that affect whether a desired outcome will be obtained. Ishikawa believed that by presenting all of the possible factors that contribute to a particular result, any potential process imperfections can be identified in advance and eliminated. Figure 5.1 shows an example of an Ishikawa diagram.

FIGURE 5.1 An Ishikawa diagram.

▶ **Histogram**

Histograms are graphs that depict information about a single factor. In addition to being used to graphically communicate information, they also sometimes can help identify patterns or explanations. See Figure 5.2 for an example.

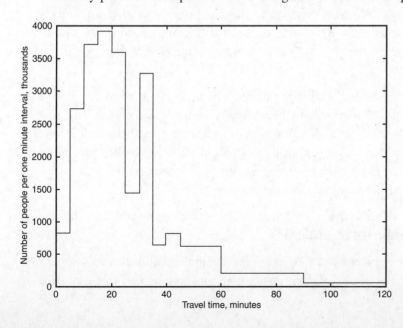

FIGURE 5.2 A histogram.

▶ **Pareto Chart**

The Pareto principle, also referred to as the "80-20 rule," asserts that 80% of effects result from 20% of causes. The Pareto principle and the chart that visually depicts it are intended to help individuals focus efforts where there is the greatest likelihood of maximizing the payoff—that is, where there is greatest likelihood of bringing about positive change. A Pareto chart is shown in Figure 5.3.

Courtesy of Professor Sid Sytsma, Ferris State University   **FIGURE 5.3**   A Pareto chart.

EXAM ALERT

Familiarize yourself with other quality tools (for instance, scattergrams, run charts, process control charts) and approaches (for instance, the Theory of Constraints and Six Sigma).

Training

After an overall strategy has been established for developing the organization and the individuals within the organization, training is one possible intervention that can be considered. Training is one way, but not the only way, to cultivate learning within an organization.

Learning organizations are ones in which individuals at all levels strive to acquire knowledge and develop skills that will enable them, individually and collectively, to attain higher levels of performance. The concept of a "learning organization" is fundamental to HRD, and is often supported through training initiatives. In his pivotal work *The Fifth Discipline*, Peter Senge identifies five disciplines, or overarching principles, that synergistically foster learning within learning organizations:

▶ *Systems thinking*—The ability to identify patterns and to recognize how those patterns can be impacted or changed.

▶ *Personal mastery*—Subject matter expertise that an individual possesses and demonstrates in a particular area, along with a commitment to maintain that expertise through lifelong learning.

- *Mental models*—Deeply-rooted, firmly-held beliefs and assumptions that impact how we perceive the world around us, as well as the actions we choose to take.

- *Shared vision*—A forward-looking perspective that inspires and secures a commitment to working toward a common vision.

- *Team learning*—The ability of a team to work wholeheartedly toward creating and attaining its stated objectives and desired results.

To Train, or Not to Train

Training—or, as it is often called, *learning and development*—is a solution that can be easily overused or underused by organizations.

Training may be overused when it is used as a cure-all for problems that may be unrelated to skills and/or areas of knowledge that are required to perform a particular task or function, or achieve a particular level of performance. It is not the act of sponsoring, providing, or attending a training program that improves individual or organizational performance; rather, it is the experience of participating in a program that will develop specific skills or impart specific areas of knowledge that are needed, at that moment, to support organizational success. Implementing a training solution when it is not appropriate to do so could diminish the likelihood that a more appropriate training initiative might be accepted at a later time, when it might be more successful.

Training may be underused if an organization chooses not to avail itself of training options that could remedy performance issues relating to gaps between current and needed levels of skill or knowledge. There are also circumstances in which training may not be effective or helpful that reach beyond the question of whether individuals have specific skills or knowledge. A few of those might be:

- When there are systemic issues that would exist even if all employees were fully proficient with the proposed content

- When there are underlying cultural issues or problems that the training would not address

- When there are leadership issues, such as lack of trust

- When organizational mission, vision, or values are either not clearly defined or are incongruous with each other, or with reality

- When training has been used before as a "flavor of the month" approach to problem solving

- When training is viewed as or has been used as a symbolic gesture rather than a means of creating real organizational change

In short, training is not a panacea. It is, however, an effective way of addressing issues involving skills development and transference of knowledge.

The Adult Learner

Even when training is an appropriate intervention, it can be effective only when it is learner centered, and when the learners/participants are treated as adults.

Andragogy, the study and science of adult learning, is significantly different from pedagogy, the study and science of how children learn. One of the key contributors to andragogy was Malcolm Knowles. In 1978, Knowles stated:

"Andragogy assumes that the point at which an individual achieves a self-concept of essential self-direction is the point at which he psychologically becomes adult. A very critical thing happens when this occurs: The individual develops a deep psychological need to be perceived by others as being self-directing. Thus, when he finds himself in a situation in which he is not allowed to be self-directing, he experiences a tension between that situation and his self-concept. His reaction is bound to be tainted with resentment and resistance."

Based upon this observation, Knowles identified five key assumptions about how adults learn:

▶ *Learner's need to know*—"I understand why I need to learn this. It makes sense to me."

▶ *Learner's self-concept*—"I'm an adult, and I can direct myself. That includes in a classroom setting, so please treat me that way."

▶ *Role of learner's experience*—"I've got lots of valuable experience that I want to draw upon to help me as I learn. Maybe I can help others learn through that experience, as well."

▶ *Readiness to learn*—"I'm ready to learn this because what I learn will help me function better in some way."

▶ *Orientation to learning*—"What I learn today will help me solve problems at my workplace tomorrow—not at some unspecified time in the future."

> **EXAM ALERT**
>
> Be familiar with the distinctions between andragogy and pedagogy.

Learning Styles—How We Learn

It's also important for HR professionals to have an understanding of learning styles. Learning styles refer to different ways in which people learn and process ideas and information. There are three different learning styles:

▶ *Visual learners*—Visual learners learn most effectively through what they see. Visual learners might best benefit from videos or DVDs, the use of presentation software, easel pad notes, printed binders that include significant amounts of printed information, extensive note taking, and the like.

PHR Exam Prep application: Reading this book, highlighting this book (perhaps with color coded highlighters), preparing study cards, and using self-sticking color-coded flags.

▶ *Auditory learners*—Auditory learners learn most effectively through what they hear. Auditory learners might best benefit from lectures, facilitated discussions, "ask the expert" style lecturettes on e-learning platforms, and the like.

PHR Exam Prep application: Audio recordings (self-made or otherwise) of materials from study guides.

▶ *Tactile/kinesthetic learners*—Tactile/kinesthetic learners learn best when they can be hands on, in the most literal sense of the word. They like to touch, to feel, to explore, and to experience the world around them. Kinesthetic learners are most likely to enjoy—and learn best from—role plays that reinforce and synthesize key learning points. They like to move around during training sessions and to be physically involved in the learning process.

PHR Exam Prep application: In studying for the PHR exam, tactile learners might be most likely to use note cards as a study tool (especially if they created the cards).

Learning Curves

Learning curves refer to the patterns through which individuals learn new material. There are four types of learning curves with which HR professionals need to be familiar.

Negatively Accelerating Learning Curve

Initially, learners process and absorb information quickly. Subsequently, the pace of learning tapers off as the learner becomes more skilled and comfortable. Negatively accelerating learning curves, as shown in Figure 5.4, are commonly associated with training for repetitive or routine tasks.

Negatively accelerating learning curve

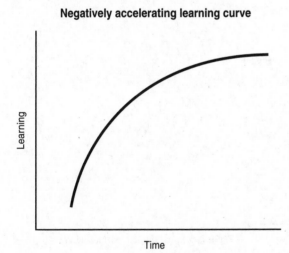

FIGURE 5.4 Negatively accelerating learning curve.

Positively Accelerating Learning Curve

Initially, learners process and absorb information relatively slowly. Ultimately, the pace of learning picks up as the learner masters the complexities of whatever it is about which he or she is learning. Positively accelerating learning curves, as shown in Figure 5.5, are more commonly associated with training for material or content that is more complex.

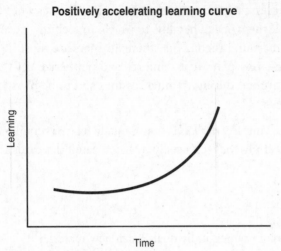

FIGURE 5.5 Positively accelerating learning curve.

S-Shaped Learning Curve

S-shaped learning curves, as shown in Figure 5.6, combine elements of negatively *and* positively accelerating learning curves. With s-shaped learning curves, the pace of learning ebbs and flows as learners attain greater levels of competence through training, as well as through hands-on experience.

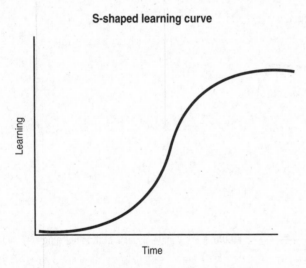

FIGURE 5.6 S-shaped learning curve.

Plateau Learning Curve

Plateau learning curves, as shown in Figure 5.7, are similar to positively accelerating learning curves in that learners process and absorb information quickly at first, but then the pace of learning slows significantly, or even stops—at least temporarily.

EXAM ALERT

Be familiar with key learning curve patterns.

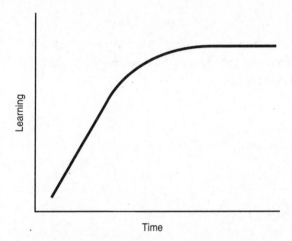

FIGURE 5.7 Plateau learning curve.

Retaining What Is Learned

Effective trainers will incorporate experiences and methodologies that appeal to a variety of learning styles into their programs, so as to increase participant involvement and improve the degree to which participants will retain what they experience. Although this may vary from person to person, the following statement generally holds true: the greater the level of learner participation, the greater the level of retention.

Learning Experience	Level of Retention
Lecture	5%
Reading	10%
A/V	20%
Demonstration	30%
Discussion	50%
Practical/application	70%
Teaching others	90%

Environmental Factors/Elements to Consider

There are some nuts-and-bolts considerations relative to training programs that, even though they may initially appear to be somewhat mundane in nature, can have a big impact on the ultimate success of a training program.

Seating Configurations

One of the factors that must be considered is how the training space will be physically arranged. There are a variety of seating arrangements from which to choose. Figure 5.8 illustrates the symbols used in the models that follow.

FIGURE 5.8 Instructor/participant legend.

Classroom/Theater

Classroom/theater style works well if there are a large number of participants in the training session (see Figure 5.9). By design, however, this style reduces the opportunity for participation by, and instructor interaction with, attendees. In some cases, especially when the size of the training group is particularly large and/or when the training is conducted in a room that has particularly bad acoustics, the instructor (who will likely become more of a lecturer in a setting like this) may require a microphone.

FIGURE 5.9 The classroom/theater seating style.

Chevron

Chevron style works well for narrower rooms (see Figure 5.10). It allows for more participation and interaction and facilitates the process of participants working in small groups.

Modified Restaurant

A modified restaurant style works well when participants will be engaging in a number of small group activities during the training session. This arrangement will provide the instructor with easy access to groups as well as individual participants during individual and small group activities.

FIGURE 5.10 The chevron seating style.

U-Shaped

The U-shaped style encourages interaction and participation through increased visual contact among participants and with the instructor (see Figure 5.11). Participants sit in chairs that are placed by tables (usually rectangular and narrow) that are set up in the shape of a letter "U."

FIGURE 5.11 The U-shaped seating style.

By moving forward and backward through the U, an instructor may be able to move physically closer to individuals from whom he would be farther away in a classroom or chevron style. This movement and proximity may encourage engagement and interaction. Although this style works particularly well with small groups, it may also provide a viable alternative (sometimes the *only* viable alternative) for long, narrow training spaces where there is no large center table.

Boardroom

The boardroom setup is similar to the U-shaped setup, except that there is a large table in the center of the room around which participants sit (see Figure 5.12). Sometimes, the boardroom setup may not be a choice at all, but rather may be the only option if training is to be held in a room that has one large table.

FIGURE 5.12 The boardroom seating style.

TIP

Most trainers have a preferred room setup, which may vary from program to program depending on the nature, content, and level of interaction needed in each program. When possible, know what your preferred style is for a particular program and request it. Recognize, however, that you may not have a choice relative to room configuration—sometimes, "it is what it is." Be prepared to train in a variety of settings. Also, be flexible—the training setup you expect may not be the training setup in which you must deliver the program.

Room Temperature

Room temperature may or may not be within your control. It's important to know this in advance. Also, as the instructor, you may be so involved in leading the training experience that you may not be aware of changes in room temperature. Be sensitive to cues that a temperature adjustment might be needed (participants putting on sweaters, or even jackets). If you have any degree of control over the temperature in the room, invite participants to tell you when the temperature needs to be adjusted. Just remember that you can't please everyone when it comes to room temperature; the best that you can do is to try to maintain the room temperature within a reasonable range that is acceptable to most people in the room. If you have no control over the temperature in the room, be up-front with participants about this as well, as soon as possible (ideally, before the start of the session, so that they can wear appropriate clothing—which usually means dressing in layers). In this way, participants won't mistakenly think that you are being insensitive or unresponsive to their needs.

Air Flow/Movement/Freshness

Know whether there are windows in the training room and whether those windows can safely be opened. If there are no windows, determine whether the room has sufficient airflow. If not, determine whether you can bring a fan (a quiet fan) into the room to increase air movement.

Noise

Distracting noises can emanate from inside or outside the building in which you are conducting training. Unwanted noise can come from factors that are controllable, uncontrollable, or semicontrollable, depending upon the situation. Do what you can to anticipate possible noise distractions, and try to eliminate them in advance.

Breaks

Short breaks should be scheduled, ideally, once every 90 minutes. However, it's also important to create an environment where participants are free to leave the room if they need to (adults don't like to have to ask permission to use the bathroom or to get a drink of water). Allow enough time during breaks to use the restroom, chat with a colleague, and perhaps check voicemail or handheld email devices. Generally, 10 to 15 minutes is sufficient and appropriate. Allowing longer breaks might tempt participants to "steal away" to their desks or laptops—in which case, it may be difficult to get them back on time. Allowing shorter or fewer breaks might unintentionally encourage participants to engage in these activities anyway (perhaps even while you are trying to deliver the program).

Telephones, Personal Technology, and Training Expectations

As communication technology has evolved, etiquette hasn't always evolved along with it. More and more, instructors are encountering situations in which beepers, cell phones, handheld email devices, text messaging, pagers, laptop computers, and the like are being used during instructional portions of training sessions.

Communicate your expectations about electronic communication devices up front, at the beginning of the training program. Encourage participants to give themselves as well as those around them the gift of an uninterrupted training experience. Gently remind them that their organization wants them to be there, and that is where they should focus their attention. Also, however, let participants know that you recognize that life goes on outside of the training room, that emergencies do occur, and that you understand participants might need to be reachable during a session. Encourage participants to find the least disruptive way in which to do this—ideally, they will choose to turn off their electronic devices and ensure that someone knows where to find them in the event of an emergency. If participants decide that they must keep their devices turned on, encourage them to set them to vibrate or silent, and to leave the room in the event that they must take a call or respond to an electronic communication.

Food

Another decision that must be made is whether to provide meals, snacks, or beverages to participants. Different organizations have different philosophies on this topic. Some organizations feel that they should not have to "bribe" individuals to attend a program that will benefit them and the organization. Other organizations take a more hospitable approach, seeing training as an opportunity for them to demonstrate their appreciation while adding a bit of celebration and festivity (or, as some organizations say, "if you feed them, they will come").

To varying degrees, food-related decisions will be a function of organizational culture as well as of budgetary considerations. Whatever choice you make, try to make it one that the organization feels comfortable committing to for the foreseeable future (otherwise, you'll never stop hearing about how "we used to have such great meals at training sessions, but now they expect us to buy our own food in the cafeteria"). Additionally, be aware that some people have dietary preferences and restrictions that relate to religion, health conditions, or other factors.

Career Development

One way of looking at OD is that it takes a macro, overarching approach to the growth and development of the organization. Career development, on the other hand, takes a more micro approach in that it looks at the development of individuals *within* the organization. Those two ends of the spectrum are inextricably linked in that they both share the objective of developing the organization: Essentially, the growth and development of individuals within the organization contributes to the overall development and advancement of the organization as a whole.

Responsibility for an employee's career development is shared. Managers can support employees in their career development through coaching, counseling, and offering honest and candid performance feedback and appraisals. The organization can also support and encourage employees who actively seek to grow and enhance their skills through activities such as establishing a skills database or encouraging cross-training, transfers, and other opportunities for employees to expand their skills and knowledge.

Organizations can also ensure that resources are allocated to employee career development. In addition to financial resources, employees will also need time to develop new skills or attain new knowledge through cross-training or workshops. Organizations also need to ensure that psychological and/or emotional resources are not withheld—employees may be less likely to avail themselves of development opportunities if they feel that their current supervisors will want to hold them back, out of fear of losing them (in which case, of course, employees would already likely be halfway out the door so as to look for employers who will treat them less like property and more like people).

Ultimately, however, each employee must take responsibility for his or her own growth and development. An organization cannot force an employee to grow. Learning can't be mandated, either. Each employee must determine whether—and how—he or she wants to grow, and follow through on the opportunities that exist to do so.

EXAM ALERT

Be familiar with the stages of career development, as well as specific ways in which organizations, managers, and employees can contribute to that development.

Leadership Development

To understand leadership development, it's first necessary to grasp the concepts of *leadership* and *management*. Let's start by looking at how these two concepts are different, and how they can and should be intertwined and related.

EXAM ALERT

Chapter 2 of this book addressed various leadership models designed to provide a conceptual framework for understanding management and leadership. Though those two concepts were addressed within the framework of the 23 core competencies, revisit those theories and concepts. First, as an HR professional, you will be called on to understand the how management and leadership differ and how those differences impact how you might apply these theories. Second, it is likely that you will be presented with questions relating to these theories and concepts when you take the PHR exam.

Management and Leadership: Bridging the Gap

Managers are seen as those individuals who manage the process or the activities of a department or organization. Leaders are those who provide the vision and direction that leads to a motivating force of accomplishment. To be an effective manager, you need to bridge both.

As described in a leadership-management model developed by Tony Panos (President, Performance Training, Inc.), "*Success is an anesthetic that dulls the drive for change.*" We see evidence of this phrase in many organizations and more specifically in many managers and potential leaders. As with employees, some managers feel that if things are going well, there is no need for change. Leaders who allow themselves to fall into the same trap, however, are destined to a fate of mediocrity or failure.

According to Panos's model, there are five components to building the bridge between management and leadership:

- Commit to achieve.
- "It's not about you."
- Establish credibility.
- Align people.
- Impact people significantly.

Commit to Achieve

The first component to building the bridge between management and leadership is developing and embracing a commitment to achieve. This can be accomplished by understanding the organization's goals and striving with your staff to attain them, while being aware of and incorporating the personal goals and aspirations of your staff members. Furthermore, and possibly more importantly, be honest with yourself about what kind of organization you want to create. There needs to be honesty of purpose and intent. Ensuring consistency between intent and reality will eliminate the confusion that occurs often between what employees thought they signed up for and what is really going on.

"It's Not About You"

Next, it's important to remember that "it's not about you." Your focus must remain on the success of the employees who report to you, not on your success. That will come later. For now, spotlighting your *employees* is key. Leave the headlining for someone else, and give recognition to those who are excelling. When you allow your employees to do their jobs and do them well, they become responsible and empowered. And you, in turn, attain success.

Establish Credibility

To continue in this process you must establish credibility. This does not occur by the application of your authority; rather it comes from consistency, competence, dedication, and commitment. For you to lead, you must have the permission of the people whom you lead. You get that permission by the establishment of your credibility.

Align People

The next step is the alignment of people. Often, after the strategic planning is done, we put (hopefully) the right people in the right jobs to accomplish the plan. To properly align people, you first must align them with the vision, mission, and values of the organization. Build a team of staff members that share common values. Align their professional needs with the organization's needs. Cascade the organization's strategic plan so that it manifests itself in some way into every employee's individual objectives.

Impact People Significantly

Last, impact people significantly. How can you do that? Everyone is different, but through communication and understanding, you know what triggers people have. Without being manipulative, push those buttons. Be sensitive and responsive to their needs and tie them to the needs of the organization. Make connections between how their interests, skills, talents, and developmental needs tie to the organization and vice versa.

According to Panos, managers must provide direct reports with feedback, development, a sounding board. In short, managers help clear the path to their direct reports' success. Those who can bridge the gap between leader and manager do all of the above *and* look out over the horizon to see where the next bump or opportunity is coming from. Leadership development, and the specific interventions that will accomplish it, should be aimed at attaining these end results.

One important tool that can be used to support the accomplishment of many of these objectives is effective performance management.

Performance Management

Though not always thought of as an HRD intervention, well-executed performance management is wholly consistent with the mission of HRD. Why? Individual performance directly impacts team, unit, and organizational performance. So, performance management is a critical element of an organization's ultimate overall success.

Performance management is the process by which managers and their direct reports communicate about, plan for, and—as the name implies—manage the individual performance of each direct report.

> **NOTE**
>
> Performance management is sometimes confused with performance appraisal. Though the two are related, there are important, definitional differences. Most important, *performance appraisal* is, essentially, an event. It is the form that is reviewed during the meeting that takes place at the end of the performance measurement period. During this meeting, the manager and the employee review the employee's performance during the prior year and look ahead to the next year.

> **NOTE**
>
> *Performance management*, conversely, consists of a continuous flow of collaborative feedback, coaching, and opportunities for communication during in which the manager and the employee engage throughout the entire performance measurement period.

Performance Management—Its Organizational Roots

Effective performance management and appraisal can't take place in a vacuum. Instead, every step of the ongoing performance management process *must* be rooted in the organization's mission, vision, and values.

Performance Management and Organizational Mission

An organization's mission represents the reason why it exists: its ultimate purpose—the focus that drives (or should drive) every initiative, every employee, and within the context of performance management, every goal. In short, goals cascade throughout the organization, beginning with the mission statement and moving down, and throughout, the hierarchy of the organization. Eventually, that mission statement should impact every goal for every employee in every position within the organization.

In turn, each employee's performance will ultimately contribute to the successful attainment of objectives at every level of the organization, up through and including the mission. This combination of top-down/bottom-up goal setting and achievement helps ensure that time, effort, energy, and all other organizational resources are focused upon the ultimate objective—furthering the mission of the organization.

This is the practical, performance-focused definition of mission-driven performance management, within a mission-driven organization, illustrated in Figure 5.13.

Performance Management and Organizational Values

An organization's statement of values reflects its underlying philosophies, its guiding tenets, what it, quite literally, values most closely.

This concept can be difficult to define and even more difficult to link to business objectives. The organization's values, however, must be explicitly clear for several reasons. First, the organization's values contribute significantly to defining the organization's culture. Culture, in turn, has a huge impact on how the organization—and the individuals within the organization—functions on a day-to-day basis.

In thinking about this day-to-day functioning, a link can be made back to performance management. Values, if simply listed as catchy-sounding phrases, can be ambiguous. For instance, what does "integrity" look like? "Professionalism" is no easier to define, nor is "customer service" or "loyalty." From a performance management perspective, organizational values take on their true value when they are defined in behavioral terms. This can be done by providing specific behavioral examples of how each value might manifest itself behaviorally in a particular organization.

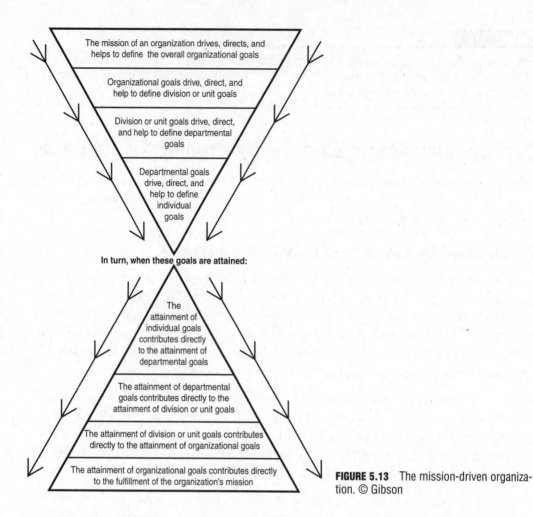

FIGURE 5.13 The mission-driven organization. © Gibson

In addition to ensuring that an organization's values are truly lived out on a day-to-day basis, the process of defining values behaviorally also provides a more objective, productive, and defensible basis from which to incorporate values-related considerations throughout the performance management and appraisal process. This is a critical consideration because values-based performance management is one important way of addressing and appraising *how* work should be accomplished, instead of just *what* needs to be accomplished.

The Performance Management Process/System

With this foundation of mission and values, let's take a look at a typical performance management process.

Step 1: Setting and Communicating Performance Standards

Performance standards can be expressed in different ways and through different measures:

- *Goals/objectives*—Using the top-down/bottom-up model described previously, performance goals or performance objectives express and communicate expectations in terms of what should be produced. Just like any other OD initiative, performance management goals and objectives must be SMART (see "ADDIE: 'D' Is for Design"). The "M" in SMART—measurable—is particularly important with respect to setting and communicating performance goals and objectives.

▶ *Competencies*—Like values, competencies also describe how employees are expected to perform as they deliver the performance goals/objectives. Unlike values, however, competencies are more frequently rooted in skills. Competencies (also sometimes referred to as success factors, performance factors, or the like) are often the same for all employees who work in a particular organization. Some organizations also establish additional competencies that managers are expected to demonstrate. Examples of competencies for all employees (managers as well as nonmanagers) might be communication, customer focus, or dependability. Examples of additional managerial competencies might be staffing and development or (even better) performance management.

As with values, competencies must be expressed in terms of specific behaviors, rather than in terms of attitudes or personality traits. This is the best and perhaps the only way to ensure clarity and mutual understanding with respect to competency-based performance expectations. Failure to define competencies in behavioral terms can result in employee (and, sometimes, even managerial) frustration, confusion, resentment, and/or suspicion.

As an example, let's look at the competency "customer focus." An attitudinal or personality-based approach to customer focus might say that an employee needs to be friendly and helpful. A behavioral approach to customer focus would look more like this:

▶ Demonstrates understanding of customers, as well as knowledge of their goals, needs, and wants.

▶ Accurately anticipates—and communicates an understanding of—the spoken and unspoken needs of customers.

▶ Seeks out, obtains, and processes information that enables the employee to meet the needs of the customer.

▶ Responds to customer concerns in a timely, accurate, and thorough manner, and confirms that his or her response meets with the customer's satisfaction.

Sometimes, the ways in which competencies manifest themselves behaviorally are fairly easy to measure. At other times, however, competencies might manifest themselves through behaviors that are observable, but that do not lend themselves as easily to measurement. It is, in part, an organizational decision (that may, to a significant degree, be affected by organizational culture) whether documented observation is an acceptable way of measuring some of these harder-to-quantify competencies.

Step 2: Feedback and Documentation

Employees need feedback. So do managers (this would be the purpose of a 360-degree appraisal). Feedback about how each employee performed relative to performance expectations that were set with/for him or her at the beginning of the performance measurement period should be provided *throughout the performance measurement period*, not just at the end when it's time to complete the performance appraisal form.

Performance feedback serves a number of important purposes, including the following:

- Recognizing (and thereby reinforcing) good performance

- Making the employee aware of performance problems

- Focusing attention on performance standards, not on nebulous, potentially subjective personality or attitude traits

- Furthering the employee's development

- Supporting the larger performance culture

It's important for employees to understand (ideally, from the time they are initially interviewed as candidates), that they will be given feedback—positive as well as constructive—and that they are expected to actively participate in the process of discussing and implementing that feedback.

To be effective, feedback needs to be BASIC (© Gibson):

- *B: Behavioral*—Measurable and/or observable, rather than attitudinal.

- *A: As Soon as Possible*—Do not provide feedback when you are angry or upset, and in most cases, wait until you are alone to have a feedback discussion with employees. This always holds true for constructive feedback, and can hold true for positive feedback, as well.

- *S: Specific and Single Subject*—The performance expectations you established with and communicated to your employees were specific; the feedback you provide about the employee's performance as compared to those expectations should be specific, as well (remember the "S" in SMART). Also, don't let things build up. Communicating about the employee's performance on a regular basis—*one behavior at a time*—helps increase the likelihood that feedback will be accepted and implemented and that the employee will make the desired behavioral change.

- *I: Interactive*—Feedback is a two-way, dynamic interaction, not just a one-way monologue. Use feedback discussions (whether positive or constructive in nature) as an opportunity to collaboratively discuss and explore the employee's performance.

- *C: Consistent*—Be consistent in the way you provide feedback to different employees. Consistency, however, does not mean sameness. Also try to behave and manage in a consistent manner, in general. Working for "Dr. Jekyll" and "Mr. Hyde" (and trying to figure out who will show up on any given day) can waste a lot of your direct reports' energy that could be better invested in working toward achieving performance expectations, demonstrating desired competencies, and living out the values of the organization.

When you put all this feedback into writing (assuming you do it well, and in accordance with the feedback principles listed previously), you've got documentation. Without documentation, feedback is merely opinion (Ron Katz, 2005). *With* appropriate documentation, feedback can provide the basis for a shared understanding of how performance compares to expectations. It also might be just what it takes to make your feedback real enough to motivate the employee to act on it appropriately. It also creates a paper trail in the event that a performance-related decision is ever challenged.

> **NOTE**
>
> Don't let the previous paragraph fool you—documenting performance isn't always easy. Be sure to familiarize yourself with your organization's practices and policies on documentation (and progressive discipline).

Step 3: Performance Appraisal

Performance appraisals are often completed to evaluate and document the performance of one individual employee during a specific period of time (the performance-measurement period). They can also be completed, however, to evaluate the performance of a group of employees. Either way, the performance appraisal should be, in one sense, a nonclimactic conclusion to an ongoing and continuous performance management cycle.

Performance appraisals look backward at the employees' performance over the performance-measurement period. They also look forward to short-term and long-term goals, as well as to development opportunities.

In some organizations, completed performance appraisals may contribute in part—or in whole—to decisions about salary or wage increases. Systems such as this are called *pay-for-performance* programs. Although many benefits exist to implementing pay-for-performance programs, it's critical that the discussion of performance does not get lost in the discussion of pay when a pay-for-performance program is in place.

Types of Performance Appraisals

There are three primary categories of performance appraisals.

> **EXAM ALERT**
>
> Be familiar with each of the three primary categories of performance appraisals.

Rating Methods

Appraisers use rating scales and checklists to appraise employee performance.

> ▶ *Rating scales*—Appraisers who use rating scales to appraise employee performance rate the employee on a variety of different categories using a three-, four-, or five-point scale. Those categories can consist of individual goals, individual competencies, multiple goals, groups of competencies, and the like. Each point on the scale corresponds to a different level of performance against standards. On a five-point scale, for instance, the numbers might correspond to the following words:

Rating	Description
5	Far Exceeds Expectations
4	Exceeds Expectations
3	Successfully Meets Expectations
2	Meets Some, Does Not Fully Meet Expectations
1	Unacceptable

Generally considered to be the least complex and most frequently used type of performance appraisal tool, rating scales can vary significantly in terms of reliability, objectivity, accuracy, and defensibility. This can depend on a number of factors, including the skill level of the person who developed the appraisal, as well as the skill level of the individual completing and delivering the appraisal. *Skill*, in this case, does not refer to the goal or competency that is being evaluated; rather, it refers to the individual's ability to effectively appraise performance.

▶ *Checklist*—Appraisers who use checklist appraisals review a series of statements that could describe an employee's performance and literally check off those statements that are reflective of the employee's performance during the performance-measurement period. Sometimes, checklists are weighted (called *weighted checklists*), in which case the weightings are used to generate a mathematically calculated score.

As with other performance appraisal methods, the value of a checklist appraisal is, in part, a function of the skill level of the person completing the appraisal, as well as that person's ability to recognize and manage any rater biases that he or she might have (see "Performance Appraisal (and Management)—Pitfalls to Avoid").

Comparative Methods

Comparative performance appraisal methods require the appraiser to compare employees to each other.

▶ *Ranking method*—Appraisers who use the ranking method literally rank their direct reports, in terms of overall performance, from best to worst. While fairly simple to use, this method has several shortcomings. First, although it compares employees to each other, ranking does not compare employees' performance to the objective performance standards that were set for the position. So, although it might be nice to be able to know who your best-performing employees are, it's much more important to know which of them meets or exceeds the requirements of the position. Conversely, with the ranking method it's also possible (though perhaps unlikely in larger groups) that even the lowest-ranked employees might still be meeting the performance requirements of the position; they may just not be as stellar as those employees who were ranked higher.

▶ *Paired-comparison method*—Appraisers who use the paired-comparison method compare each employee in the group, one at a time, to every other employee in the group. Although this method provides more information than simple ranking, it still leaves out the all-important comparison of individual performance to performance standards.

▶ *Forced distribution*—Appraisers who use the forced-distribution method (also known as *forced ranking*) are required to rank or evaluate their employees according to a bell-shaped curve. Most employees, therefore, will be ranked or evaluated toward the middle of the curve, and a few will be ranked at the high and low ends of the performance spectrum. Although this technique might be useful in helping to avoid (or at least identify) appraiser errors (see "Performance Appraisal (and Management)—Pitfalls to Avoid"), it is possible that the mandated ranking levels may not, in fact, reflect employees' actual performance levels. As such, evaluations are literally (and admittedly) being forced into categories that may not be accurate, which can lead to all sorts of complications (for instance, with respect to layoff decisions that are based on performance levels). This is more likely to happen when such distributions must occur within a relatively small group of employees, rather than in larger groups of employees where it would be more reasonable to expect a normal distribution to occur.

Narrative

Appraisers who use narrative methods write down their observations and assessments of each employee's performance.

▶ *Essay*—Appraisers who use the essay method write short essays describing and documenting each employee's performance during the performance-measurement period. Some managers may prefer this method because it gives them ample freedom to accurately and fully evaluate an employee's performance. The method, however, is highly time consuming and requires considerable writing ability—perhaps in a different style than what the manager might be required to use in the normal course of performing his or her job. Better writers, therefore, might prepare more powerful or convincing performance appraisals than those managers who are not as skilled at expressing themselves in an essay format. This, of course, does not necessarily make those appraisals more accurate. Also, because of the largely unstructured nature of an essay appraisal, it also might be easier for rater bias to emerge. Short essays can also become long (and thus time-consuming) essays.

▶ *Critical incident*—Appraisers who use the critical incident method create and maintain documentation throughout the year relative to specific situations in which the employee met and did not meet the performance expectations of the position. The effectiveness of this method (which may or may not be combined with rating scales) will vary widely depending on how the appraiser defines "critical incidents." For instance, if an appraiser documents only extreme examples of behavior (ones that either far exceed or fall well below expected performance standards), those performers who are solid (but not outstanding) may receive little attention, and thus be provided with insufficient documentation. This method also requires that managers consistently and contemporaneously document critical incidents, which may not always be a realistic expectation. And, again, this method relies on the writing skill—as well as the objectivity—of the appraiser.

▶ *Field review*—Field-review appraisals are prepared by someone other than the employee's supervisor—for instance, someone from HR. One serious concern with field-review appraisals is that they may unintentionally send a message that performance management and appraisal is an extra part of a supervisor's job, rather than an integral part of his or her day-to-day responsibilities. Instead of being valued as a way of getting work done more productively and in a manner that is consistent with performance expectations, the appraisal process may be perceived as separate, distinct, and therefore less relevant and valuable.

Behavioral Anchored Rating Scales

An appraisal method known as *behavioral* (or *behaviorally*) *anchored rating scales* (BARS) starts by identifying the most critical responsibilities or requirements of a position. Then, for each responsibility or requirement, anchor statements offering a specific description of a particular type of behavior (which corresponds to a particular level of performance) are written.

For instance, for a programmer analyst, a three-level BARS for responsibilities relating to organizing and planning might look like this:

Description of Behaviors

3. This person normally generates effective plans requiring at least a year of development and a budget of around $750,000. He almost always includes time for unseen emergencies in project timeliness and activities. On most projects, he can schedule the team's activities to coincide with the activities of other teams, users, computer operations personnel, and so on. He normally makes long-term plans to use in effectively making schedule adjustments as a project progresses.

2. This person generally establishes her own goals and the steps to achieve them. He can generally organize a project or task into smaller tasks and time frames. He can generally plan her own and others' efforts on a project but may have difficulty organizing efforts on several concurrent projects. He may sometimes omit lesser elements from a plan that results in underutilization of resources or delays in project completion.

1. Generally, this person can handle one project, but not multiple projects. He has trouble breaking down a large project into smaller tasks and establishing time frames. He delegates tasks to others but not according to who is best qualified and may not properly coordinate activities with other teams or team members.

Results Based

Though several types of performance appraisals incorporate, to a greater or lesser degree, results as part of the measure of success, management by objectives is driven almost exclusively by this measure.

▶ *Management by Objectives*: Management by Objectives (MBO) is a goal-centered OD intervention that focuses primarily on collaboratively generating individual employee objectives that align with organizational objectives. Measurement is an absolutely essential element of an MBO program. As follows logically, MBO is often used as a method of appraising performance, as well, because of its strong orientation toward goal establishment and attainment.

An MBO-based performance appraisal process will certainly ensure that individual objectives are aligned with organizational objectives. There are, however, some potential disadvantages. Because MBO focuses exclusively on results (*what* is produced or delivered), *how* goals are accomplished is not given any attention. This could potentially result in an employee choosing to engage in problematic behaviors to achieve goals, including behaviors that are inconsistent with the values of the organization. In addition, an MBO system is time consuming to develop and maintain because it must be continually updated to reflect the current expectations associated with each position. Because jobs change so quickly, this can become a daunting task.

Guidelines for Conducting Effective Performance Appraisals

Knowing the mechanics of performance appraisals is important. But even the best-designed performance appraisal will be rendered ineffective (and perhaps even harmful) if a performance appraisal meeting is executed poorly.

The following chart outlines some of the basic "DO's" and "DON'Ts" of conducting an effective performance appraisal meeting:

DOs	DON'Ts
Listen actively	Talk too much
Maintain a professional tone	Behave in an overly "chummy" manner
Remain calm	Lose your composure, show anger, or behave emotionally—even if the employee does
Show empathy	Show sympathy
Treat employee with respect	Demean the employee
Listen for understanding	Psychoanalyze (even when you paraphrase)
Empower the employee	Don't make decisions for the employee, or try to solve his or her problems
Seek solutions	Argue
Stay focused on job-related issues	Pry into employee's personal life
Share appropriate information	Disclose confidential information
Be straightforward	Play games
Respect each employee's privacy	Discuss the performance of other employees
Be prepared	"Wing it"
Treat employees like adults	Infantilize employees

Performance Appraisal "Do's" and "Don'ts," © Gibson, Katz, and Cornell University-ILR, used with permission.

Performance Appraisal and Management—Pitfalls to Avoid

In addition to these performance appraisal "DOs" and "DON'Ts," there are other potential pitfalls to be aware of, as well. These other pitfalls relate more to the fact that we are all human and, as such, have biases, beliefs, and reactions that could potentially compromise our ability to manage and appraise performance effectively—that is, if we allow that to happen.

You may recall that we addressed these same concerns in Chapter 4, "Workforce Planning and Employment," during our exploration of interviewing and employment. In this chapter, we'll now look at them in terms of how they could potentially taint the performance management and appraisal process:

Type of Performance Management and Appraisal	How It Manifests in the Performance Management Bias or Errors and Appraisal Process
Contrast	The appraiser compares the performance of each employee to the performance of other employees instead of comparing it to the performance standards that were established for the position at the beginning of the performance-measurement period. Please note: This bias is, to a degree, inherent to ranking systems if not combined with other appraisal techniques linked specifically to performance expectations.
First Impression	The appraiser forms an impression of the employee's performance early in the performance measurement period (or even worse, early in the individual's employment) and places an inordinate level of emphasis on that impression. Please note: An employee's performance during each performance measurement period should be assessed separately from that employee's performance during any prior performance measurement period(s). In addition, although it's important to recognize performance trends that an employee might demonstrate during a single performance-measurement period, it's also critical to ensure that the performance appraisal reflects the employee's performance during the entire performance-measurement period—not just their level of performance at the end of the performance-measurement period.
Halo	The appraiser evaluates the employee positively on the basis of one outstanding qualification or characteristic that is inherently incomplete and inaccurate. One particularly impressive skill, or one hard-fought goal, does not reflect the employee's overall performance.
Horns	The appraiser evaluates the employee negatively on the basis of one poor qualification or characteristic that is inherently incomplete and inaccurate, in that it will not reflect the employee's overall performance.

Type of Performance Management and Appraisal	How It Manifests in the Performance Management Bias or Errors and Appraisal Process
Leniency	The appraiser applies an inappropriately lenient standard to one or more employees, resulting in a higher overall assessment of the employee's (or employees') performance. Being "nice" to one or more employees by "giving" inflated performance evaluations doesn't help the organization, and doesn't help the employee, either. An organization needs to ensure that its employees are provided with honest feedback about performance if the organization is to fulfill its mission and attain its overarching objectives. Evaluating employees in an overly lenient (and thus dishonest) manner undermines those efforts. Employees who are, in fact, performing at or above expectations may be confused and/or demotivated if (we should actually say "when," to be realistic) they learn that other employees who perform at a level below them are given similar ratings. Those employees who are given inaccurate and overinflated ratings may cease any efforts to improve their performance—after all, they got a good rating. Because other appraisers in the organization will not apply this same degree of leniency, rating consistency across the organization is compromised. In addition to employee (de)motivation and morale issues, this can also create problems with respect to internal transfers, promotions, salary and wage increases, disciplinary actions, and layoff decisions.
	Please also note: generally speaking, when speaking of performance ratings, it is more accurate and effective to say that an employee "earned" a rating rather than saying that an employee was "given" a rating. After all, performance management is intended to empower employees. When ratings are inflated, however, they then have (unfortunately) been given, not earned.
Strictness	The appraiser applies an inappropriately harsh and demanding standard when evaluating the performance of one or more employees, resulting in a lower overall assessment of the employee(s). Being overly (and inaccurately) strict in one's assessment of the performance of one or more employees doesn't help the organization and is unfair to employees, as well, for a number of reasons: An organization needs to ensure that its employees are provided with honest feedback about performance if the organization is to fulfill its mission and attain its overarching objectives. Evaluating employees in an overly strict (and thus dishonest) manner undermines those efforts because it disconnects the employee's performance with any meaningful linkage to the organization's performance. In addition, employees who are, in fact, performing at or above expectations may be confused and/or demotivated by such unrealistically harsh ratings, in that inaccurate (and manipulative) ratings will inevitably create a "cycle of failure"—a history of never being quite good enough. Because other appraisers in the organization will not apply this same degree of harshness, rating consistency across the organization is compromised. In addition to employee (de)motivation and morale issues, this can also create problems with respect to internal transfers, promotions, salary and wage increases, disciplinary actions, and layoff decisions. Please note: Generally speaking, when speaking of performance ratings, it is more accurate and effective to say that an employee "earned" a rating rather than saying that an employee was "given" a rating. After all, performance management is intended to empower employees. When ratings are diminished, however, then they have (unfortunately) been given, not earned.

(continues)

Type of Performance Management and Appraisal	How It Manifests in the Performance Management Bias or Errors and Appraisal Process
Recency	The appraisal places undue emphasis on the employee's most recent performance, rather than considering performance demonstrated throughout the entire performance measurement period. Appraisers who find themselves "under the gun" with a looming performance appraisal deadline might be more likely to fall prey to this error—especially if they have not maintained consistent documentation throughout the performance measurement period. But make no mistake: Just like children who are anticipating a holiday replete with presents brought by a magical judge (let's face it—those naughty and nice lists have to be based on something), many employees recognize that outstanding performance near the end of the performance measurement period might help to make up for less-than-stellar performance during the earlier portions of the performance measurement period. Don't fall prey to the "Santa Claus" effect.
Similar-to-me	The manager evaluates an employee's performance on the basis of how much a direct report is similar to, or different from, him or her. If appraisers recognize characteristics, attributes, or performance patterns in an employee that they dislike about themselves, this recognition—whether conscious or unconscious—could cause the appraiser to evaluate the employee inappropriately negatively. Conversely, if appraisers recognize characteristics or attributes in an employee that they like about themselves, this recognition—again, whether conscious or unconscious—could cause the appraiser to evaluate the employee inappropriately positively. Either way, the impression is wholly unrelated to the employee's actual performance, and must be compartmentalized from the appraisal process.

Chapter Summary

Responsibilities relating to human resource development afford HR professionals with the opportunity to have a significant impact on the growth and development of the organization and on the people within the organization.

To function successfully with respect to the functional area of human resource development, HR professionals must develop a working knowledge of related legislation. They also must develop facility with the key areas within HRD, specifically the following:

- OD
- Training
- Career development
- Leadership development
- Performance management

As with every other functional area, the ability to execute HRD-related responsibilities effectively is predicated on knowing and understanding the organization's strategic plan, as well as its mission, vision, and values. Taking those big picture considerations and translating them into practical HRD applications will enhance the degree to which an HR professional can be effective within the organization.

Key Terms

- Human resource development (HRD)
- Copyright Act of 1976
- Public domain
- Fair use
- U.S. Patent Act
- Utility, design, and plant patents
- ADDIE (analysis/assessment [of needs], design, development, implementation, evaluation)
- McGehee and Thayer
- Organizational level analysis
- Operations (task or work) level analysis
- Man (person) level analysis
- Cost per trainee/cost per participant
- SMART (specific, measurable, action-oriented, realistic, time-bound)
- Lecture/lecturette

- ▸ Demonstration
- ▸ Reading
- ▸ Small group discussions/instructor-facilitated large group discussions
- ▸ Individual, small group, or large group activities/applications
- ▸ Case study
- ▸ Role play
- ▸ Pilot programs
- ▸ Donald L. Kirkpatrick
- ▸ Summative evaluation
- ▸ Reaction level evaluation
- ▸ Learning level evaluation
- ▸ Behavior level evaluation
- ▸ Results level evaluation
- ▸ Robert Brinkerhoff
- ▸ Formative evaluation
- ▸ Organization development (OD)
- ▸ R. T. Golembiewski
- ▸ Organizational culture
- ▸ Change management
- ▸ Kurt Lewin
- ▸ Change process theory
- ▸ Unfreezing
- ▸ Moving
- ▸ Refreezing
- ▸ Implementation theory
- ▸ Human processual interventions
- ▸ Technostructural interventions
- ▸ Sociotechnical interventions
- ▸ Organization transformation change
- ▸ Team building
- ▸ Total quality management (TQM)
- ▸ W. Edwards Deming

- ▶ Joseph M. Juran
- ▶ Philip B. Crosby
- ▶ Zero defects
- ▶ Acceptable quality levels (AQLs)
- ▶ Four absolutes of quality management
- ▶ Kaoru Ishikawa
- ▶ Cause-and-effect, Ishikawa, or Fishbone diagram
- ▶ Histogram
- ▶ Pareto chart
- ▶ Learning organization
- ▶ Adult learner
- ▶ Andragogy
- ▶ Pedagogy
- ▶ Malcolm Knowles
- ▶ Learning styles
- ▶ Visual learners
- ▶ Auditory learners
- ▶ Tactile/kinesthetic learners
- ▶ Learning curves
- ▶ Classroom/theatre style
- ▶ Chevron style
- ▶ U-shaped style
- ▶ Boardroom style
- ▶ Career development
- ▶ Leadership development
- ▶ Performance management
- ▶ Performance appraisal
- ▶ Performance standards/expectations
- ▶ Goals/objectives
- ▶ Competencies
- ▶ Feedback
- ▶ Documentation

- BASIC (behavioral, as soon as possible, specific, interactive, consistent)
- Rating methods
- Rating scales
- Checklist
- Comparative methods
- Ranking method
- Paired comparison method
- Forced distribution method
- Narrative method
- Essay method
- Critical incident
- Field review
- Behavioral anchored ranking scales (BARS)
- Management by Objectives (MBO)
- Contrast error
- First impression error
- Halo effect
- Horns effect
- Leniency error
- Strictness error
- Recency effect
- Similar-to-me effect

Apply Your Knowledge

This chapter focuses on issues relating to human resource development (HRD). Complete the following exercises, review questions, and exam questions as a way of reviewing and reinforcing the knowledge and skills you'll need to perform your responsibilities as an HR professional and to increase the likelihood that you will pass the PHR examination.

Exercises

1. You've recently been hired as the HR manager within a unit of your organization that hasn't met its production goals (or, for that matter, hasn't even come *close* to meeting its production goals) in about eight months. Turnover is high and getting higher, morale is low, revenues are plummeting, and stress is rising. You know you're facing a significant challenge, but you are up for it. Shortly after you assume your new role, your managing director advises you that the situation is getting even worse, and something has to be done to change the situation—fast. She wants your input relative to what direction to take overall, and she's already made one decision: No training programs will be conducted "until the numbers improve." You understand that the situation is serious, and you're concerned about the decision to halt all training. Which of the following statements would summarize how you would respond to your managing director.

   A. Training is an important way for employees to position themselves for promotional opportunities, and the employees in this unit may need a ticket out of this underperforming unit.

   B. You'd like to have the opportunity to determine where the gap is between actual and desired performance, to see whether training might be an effective way of addressing the bottom-line performance issues in this unit.

   C. You accepted the position of HR Manager in this unit with the understanding that you'd be able to engage in training initiatives. You believe strongly that you should at least be given the opportunity to do so, until or unless those efforts prove to be ineffective.

   D. Historically, the employees in this unit have taken full advantage of the training opportunities with which they have been presented. Removing training opportunities now could damage morale even more than it already is, which would be the last thing this unit needs.

2. You've designed and developed a one-day training program on effective interviewing, and you're ready to deliver the pilot program. Your manager has told you
that the senior leaders of your organization are interested in and supportive of
what you've done and will commit to give you two hours at their next meeting so
you can deliver a pilot program to them. They're not, however, willing to participate in any role plays during the pilot. Which of the following statements would
summarize how you would respond to your manager?

   A. You're glad that the organization's senior leaders are interested and are
   confident that you can condense the training program pilot down to two
   hours for purposes of providing a high-level review.

   B. It's essential that the senior leaders of your organization experience the
   program in the same way in which the program participants will experience
   it, in order for the roll-out of the program to be successful.

   C. You'd like to present the senior leaders with a brief written comparison of
   the benefits of a two-hour pilot and the benefits of a full-length pilot, and
   will support the leaders' decision.

   D. You think it might be more valuable to carve out and deliver a two-hour
   portion of the training so that the leaders get a feel for it, rather than trying
   to condense the program down to two hours.

3. One of the new managers in your unit has had great success during the past year
or so with motivating and inspiring employees in his unit. (The unit had been
experiencing significant production and quality issues prior to this manager's
arrival.) His use of positive reinforcement, for instance, has been particularly well
received by his direct and indirect reports. Employee satisfaction results are
soaring, as well. This morning, you reviewed the final draft of the performance
appraisals that he prepared for the employees in his unit, and noticed that all 100+
employees have been rated as meeting or exceeding performance expectations.
Which rating error is this manager likely experiencing?

   A. Halo effect

   B. Leniency effect

   C. Inflationary effect

   D. Contrast effect

4. You're delivering a training program on supervising and managing people. It's highly interactive and very well received. You've arranged for a U-shaped setup, which you've consistently found to be the most effective room setup for this program. You show up to deliver the program at an offsite location and find that the room is set up with classroom-style seating. You try to get someone to rearrange the room for you, but you've been told that the tables are secured to the floor, and no other rooms are available. What would be the best step to take next?

A. Postpone the training. You know that it won't be effective with a rigid, classroom-style room setup, and you'd rather not deliver the training at all than deliver training that you know is likely to be unsuccessful.

B. Deliver the training and hope for the best. You've made a commitment and will fulfill that commitment because you don't want to earn a reputation as someone who doesn't keep promises.

C. Speak to your client contact, if he or she is available, and describe the challenge you're facing. Ensure that he or she understands that you didn't get the setup that you had requested and been promised, and therefore cannot be held 100 percent responsible for attaining the training objectives.

D. Speak to your client content, if he or she is available, and describe the challenge you're facing. Tell the client the backup plan that you have in place for the situation, and see if he or she has any additional comments, suggestions, or ideas.

Review Questions

1. Describe some of the key differences between *performance management* and *performance appraisal*.

2. What does it mean when a document or work is in the public domain?

3. Why is it important that HRD/training objectives remain realistic (the "R" in the acronym SMART)?

4. What are some of the benefits of the case-study methodology?

5. Describe Brinkerhoff's formative evaluation approach.

Exam Questions

1. Which of the following rights is not granted to copyright holders by the Copyright Act of 1976?

   A. The right to duplicate/reproduce/copy the work

   B. The right to exclude others from making, using, offering for sale, or selling the invention in the United States

   C. The right to display the work publicly

   D. The right to sell, lease, rent, or otherwise distribute copies of the work to the public

2. All of the following are reasons for conducting needs analysis/assessment *except*

   A. To identify performance related problems within the organization.

   B. To increase the likelihood of identifying a solution that will truly bridge the performance gap.

   C. To begin the initial creation of the HRD/training program before meeting with any organizational resistance that could slow progress.

   D. To ensure that a legitimate cost-benefit analysis is conducted before a commitment is made to any particular HRD/training solution.

3. Which of the following statements about using reading as a training methodology is true?

   A. It should be included at least once, whenever possible, in training programs, because ideally all training methodologies should be included in every training program.

   B. It should be avoided in training programs unless truly necessary, because participants generally do not find it engaging or stimulating.

   C. It represents a particularly effective methodology for auditory learners.

   D. It should be included in training programs when participants would benefit from time to absorb and process detailed materials.

4. Which of the following statements does not reflect a statement by which the presentation effectiveness of instructors/potential instructors could be assessed/evaluated?

   A. Summarizes major points throughout and at the conclusion of the workshop.

   B. Refers to and utilizes training materials (including the participant manual) throughout the program.

   C. Allows ample time for participants to develop concepts.

   D. Scores consistently well on post-training evaluation forms.

5. Taking a summative approach to evaluation means that

   A. The designer/instructor/HRD professional collects, summarizes, and incorporates feedback throughout the program development and implementation phases.

   B. The designer/instructor/HRD professional collects, summarizes, and incorporates feedback at the conclusion of the program design and development phases.

   C. The designer/instructor/HRD professional collects, summarizes, and incorporates feedback after implementing the HRD/training program.

   D. The designer/instructor/HRD professional does not collect, summarize, and or incorporate feedback until summary data from a representative number of participants has been collected and analyzed.

6. All of the following statements about Kirkpatrick's behavior-level evaluation are true *except*

   A. It measures transfer of training—the degree to which participants apply the skills and knowledge covered in the training sessions in the workplace.

   B. It measures whether and to what degree participants have mastered the skills or acquired the knowledge explored through the learning objectives.

   C. It measures changes in behavior that might be the result of factors unrelated to the HRD/training initiative.

   D. It measures whether participants' on-the-job behaviors have changed in a manner consistent with training objectives.

7. Which of the following would *not* be considered to be a major purpose of OD?

   A. Identifying and implementing more cost-effective ways of increasing employee retention.

   B. Enhancing the overall effectiveness of organizations.

   C. Promoting openness toward differences.

   D. Aligning employee goals with unit and organizational goals.

8. "Unfreezing" refers to

   A. The process by which an instructor establishes rapport with a reticent group of participants.

   B. The process by which resistance to change is addressed and worked through.

   C. The process by which managers are convinced to provide their employees with career development opportunities that could result in them leaving their current positions.

   D. The process by which budgetary funds are released for allocation to HRD/training initiatives.

9. The Pareto principle says that

   A. An organization's commitment to customer service must extend even beyond the point of purchase.

   B. Quality is achieved by prevention, not appraisal.

   C. In organizations, individuals tend to be promoted up to their "level of incompetence."

   D. 80% of consequences can be attributed to 20% of causes.

10. Of the following learning methodologies, which is likely to yield the highest level of participant retention?

    A. Discussion

    B. Demonstration

    C. Application

    D. Association

Answers to Exercises

1. **Answer B is the best answer.** Communicate in terms of organizational results and guide your suggestions and approaches accordingly. Answer A is not the best answer, because giving employees "a ticket out" is not an appropriate focus for your attention at this point in time. Answer C is not the best answer, because this is not about you. It is about addressing and resolving individual and collective performance issues in a struggling unit, and that is where you must focus your efforts. Answer D is not the best answer; your recommendations should not be motivated by avoiding difficult decisions that might upset employees. It must remain on attaining organizational and unit objectives and carrying out appropriate interventions (even difficult ones) in the most productive and positive way possible. In other words, don't just run away from tough situations and decisions.

2. **Answer C is the best answer.** It's advisable at this point to help the managers understand the advantages and disadvantages of each approach, and to make their own decisions on how they would like to proceed. Answer A is not the best answer; part of taking a consultative approach means outlining choices and challenging the status quo, and then allowing others to make decisions based on the information you share. Answer B is not the best answer; it represents a condescending, didactic, and closed-minded answer. Answer D is not the best answer; give the managers the choice of whether to carve out a portion of the program, condense it, or take some other approach—but don't make that decision for them.

3. **Answer B is the best answer.** Although it is possible that all of the 100+ employees in this manager's unit performed at or above performance expectations during the performance measurement period, this is unlikely (particularly since the unit had been experiencing substandard performance levels with respect to productivity and quality before the manager came onboard). More likely, the manager is rating his direct and indirect reports in an overly lenient—and thus inaccurate—manner, in an attempt to avoid the possibility of demotivating them. Ultimately, however, this inherently dishonest (albeit well-intentioned) approach is counterproductive and problematic. Answer A is not the best answer; the halo effect occurs when an appraiser evaluates a single employee (not necessarily a group of employees) on the basis of one outstanding dimension of performance. Answer C is not the best answer, because there is no performance management rater error known as the inflationary effect. Answer D is not the best answer; the contrast effect occurs when an appraiser compares the performance of each employee to the performance of other employees instead of comparing it to the performance standards that were established at the beginning of the performance measurement period.

4. **Answer D is the best answer.** Communicating with the client is essential, as is being open to the client's ideas and suggestions. Maintain responsibility for the training program, and don't go to the client expecting him or her to solve your problems. Answer A is not the best answer; although it is appropriate to know what setup is likely to be most effective, and to request that setup, trainers must also have the flexibility and wherewithal to "roll with the punches" and deliver a program in less-than optimal conditions (also, taking what could be considered a "high maintenance" approach generally won't help to strengthen your reputation within the organization). Answer B is not the best answer, because it implies that you are leaving too much up to chance. "Hoping for the best" isn't enough—you need to actively prepare to excel even in conditions that are different from what you would have preferred or expected. Answer C is not the best answer; while communicating with the client is essential, communicating in a manner that seeks to shed responsibility or assign blame is unprofessional and counterproductive. Respond to the situation in a responsible manner, demonstrate resilience, and move forward.

Answers to Review Questions

1. Performance appraisal is, essentially, an event or form. It refers to the document that is completed and the meeting during which that document is delivered/presented to the employee (usually at the end of the performance measurement period). During this meeting, the manager and the employee review the employee's performance during the prior year and look ahead to the next year. Performance management, on the other hand, consists of a continuous flow of collaborative feedback, coaching, and communication opportunities in which the manager and the employee engage throughout the entire performance measurement period.

2. Copyrights—and the protections afforded by copyrights—eventually expire. After a copyright for a particular work expires, that work enters the public domain. This means that the copyright holder no longer enjoys the six rights cited earlier in this chapter, and that the works are available and free for all to use. Work created by the federal government is also, by definition, considered to be in the public domain.

3. Writing realistic training objectives helps to ensure that those objectives are neither too easy to achieve, nor too difficult (or even impossible) to achieve. HRD/training objectives that are too easy to attain aren't challenging and may not hold the attention and interest of participants. Ultimately, overly easy goals also might not generate desired results (if the results could be attained that easily, there would have likely been a less-formal solution than a full-blown HRD/training initiative). At the other end of the spectrum, HRD/training objectives that are impossible to attain will only serve to create a cycle of failure and will, in turn, discourage participants.

4. Case studies present participants with real-life situations that challenge them to apply the knowledge they have learned and practice the skills they have developed during the HRD/training initiative. In the safe environment of the classroom/workshop, learners can try out their newly acquired knowledge and newly developed skills before they must return to the workplace (where it might not be quite as safe to make mistakes). Participants will benefit from receiving feedback from the instructor/facilitator relative to those aspects of the case study that were handled well. Participants will also benefit (perhaps even more) from receiving feedback from the instructor/facilitator relative to those aspects of the case study that could have been handled differently or better. In both cases, the participant will be able to incorporate this feedback before transferring the knowledge and skills learned during the training back to the workplace. This can potentially increase the value of the training experience even more.

5. Published in *Achieving Results Through Training*, Brinkerhoff's formative evaluation model espouses seeking evaluative feedback and input *throughout* the development and implementation phases in an effort to strengthen the ultimate training initiative through real-time incorporation of that evaluative feedback. Brinkerhoff's

formative evaluation model mandates an iterative process, in which feedback, analysis, and assessment conducted at one phase of the process will be used to make enhancements in other stages, as well.

Answers to Exam Questions

1. **Answer B is the best answer.** The right to exclude others from making, using, offering for sale, or selling the invention in the United States is granted to patent holders under the U.S. Patent Act. Answer A is not the best answer, because the Copyright Act of 1976 does grant copyright holders the right to duplicate/reproduce/copy the work. Answer C is not the best answer, because the Copyright Act of 1976 does grant copyright holders the right to display the work publicly. Answer D is not the best answer, because the Copyright Act of 1976 does grant copyright holders the right to sell, lease, rent, or otherwise distribute copies of the work to the public.

2. **Answer C is the best answer.** The HRD/training initiative should not be created/developed until the needs analysis/assessment and design phases have been completed (and agreed to in writing). Answers A, B, and D are not the best answers, because each one articulates a legitimate reason for conducting a needs analysis/assessment.

3. **Answer D is the best answer.** Although reading is not always valued as a learning methodology, it does serve a number of valuable purposes, one of which is allowing participants the opportunity to absorb and process detailed information. Answer A is not the best answer; although it is important to use a variety of training methodologies, it is not necessary—and would not always be appropriate—to include all training methodologies in all training programs. Answer B is not the best answer, because reading can serve a variety of valuable purposes in training programs. Answer C is not the best answer, because reading can be a particularly effective methodology for visual learners, more so than for auditory learners.

4. **Answer D is the best answer.** Scoring consistently well on post-training evaluation forms is not necessarily a valid measure of training effectiveness. That evaluation technique provides more insight into how well participants liked the trainer than to how effective the trainer was of ensuring that participants leave the program with the skills and knowledge they will need to bridge the performance gap. Answer A is not the best answer, because summarizing major points throughout and at the conclusion of the workshop is one valid measure of presentation effectiveness. Answer B is not the best answer, because referring to and utilizing training materials (including the participant manual) throughout the program is one valid measure of presentation effectiveness. Answer C is not the best answer, because allowing ample time for participants to develop concepts is one valid measure of presentation effectiveness.

5. **Answer C is the best answer.** Summative evaluation takes place at the end of the implementation phase. Answer A is not the best answer, because it more closely

describes the formative evaluation technique. Neither answer B nor answer D is the best answer, because both describe evaluation techniques that are not espoused by recognized ISD or HRD experts.

6. **Answer B is the best answer.** The degree to which participants have mastered the skills or acquired the knowledge explored through the learning objectives is a function of Kirkpatrick's learning-level of evaluation (level 2). Answer A is not the best answer, because behavior level evaluation does measure transfer of training—the degree to which participants apply the skills and knowledge covered in the training sessions in the workplace. Answer C is not the best answer, because behavior-level evaluation could potentially measure changes in behavior that might be the result of factors unrelated to the HRD/training initiative (these changes would taint the evaluation, and must somehow be accounted for). Answer D is not the best answer, because behavior-level evaluation does measure whether participants' on-the-job behaviors have changed in a manner consistent with training objectives.

7. **Answer A is the best answer.** Although effective OD interventions might, in fact, result in increased retention of employees, it would not constitute a major purpose of OD. Answer B is not the best answer, since enhancing the overall effectiveness of organizations is a major purpose of OD. Answer C is not the best answer, because promoting openness toward differences is a major purpose of OD. Answer D is not the best answer, because aligning employee goals with unit and organizational goals is a major purpose of OD.

8. **Answer B is the best answer.** In Kurt Lewin's change process theory, *unfreezing* refers to the process by which everyone who is involved with and impacted by the impending change is brought to the point where they can understand and accept that a particular change *will* happen. An important part of that acceptance involves letting go of behaviors that reflect resistance to change, or that actually can impede the change process. Thus, answers A, C, and D are not the best answers.

9. **Answer D is the best answer.** The Pareto principle does assert that 80% of consequences can be attributed to 20% of causes. Answer A is not the best answer, because the belief that an organization's commitment to customer service must extend even beyond the point of purchase is part of Kaoru Ishikawa's TQM philosophy and is unrelated to causes and effects. Answer B is not the best answer, because the statement that quality is achieved by prevention, not appraisal, is one of Philip B. Crosby's four absolutes of quality management. Answer C is not the best answer, because the belief that individuals tend to be promoted up to their "level of incompetence" within organizations is the "Peter Principle" (Laurence J. Peter), not the Pareto principle.

10. **Answer C is the best answer.** Application is likely to result in a 70% retention level. Answer A is not the best answer, because discussion is likely to result in only a 50% retention level. Answer B is not the best answer, because demonstration is likely to result in only a 30% retention level. Answer D is not the best answer, because association is not a recognized instructional methodology.

Suggested Readings and Resources

Gagne, Robert M., Leslie J. Briggs, and Walter W. Wager. *Principles of Instructional Design*, 3rd edition. Austin, TX: Holt, Rinehart and Winston, 1988.

Gibson, Cathy Lee, and Ronald M.Katz, and Cornell University-ILR School, Extension Division, Management Programs. *Performance Appraisal "Do's" and "Don'ts."* New York: Cornell University, 2003.

Kirkpatrick, Donald L., and James D. Kirkpatrick. Evaluating Training Programs: The Four Levels, 3rd edition. San Francisco: Berrett-Koehler Publishers, 2006.

McGehee W., and P.W. Thayer. *Training in Business and Industry*. New York: John Wiley & Sons, 1961.

Senge, Peter M. *The Fifth Discipline: The Art & Practice of The Learning Organization*. New York: Currency, 2006.

Total Rewards

Study Strategies

▶ On large index cards, write down the names of each of the laws, topics, and key concepts covered in this chapter. On smaller, separate index cards (ideally ones that are a different color), makes notes on important facts and details relating to each of these laws, topics, and key concepts (put the name of the law or the topic on the back of the card, not on the front). Then test your memory and understanding by matching the specific facts and details (each of which you wrote on a separate index card) with the laws, topics, and key concepts that you labeled on the larger business cards. After you match them up, you can check how well you did by comparing your matches to the names of the laws and topics that you wrote on the back of the smaller index cards.

▶ Try writing out your own multiple choice test questions. Writing out the questions along with detailed answers can go a long way toward reinforcing what you are studying. If you've got a study partner, trade questions with that person.

▶ Although the PHR exam is multiple choice, try writing and answering your own essay-based questions. Write open-ended questions that require a response of at least a full paragraph—and write your answers without looking back at your study materials. The process of actually writing down your answers will reinforce what you already know and will highlight what you need to study more. It will also likely help you as you work to recall this same information when you answer related multiple-choice questions on the actual PHR exam.

▶ As with each of the six functional areas of HR, determine what you already know and what you don't know. Then work to prepare yourself. Conduct research. Use the Internet to find relevant articles and whitepapers. Peruse textbooks that provide guidance relative to those particular areas. Be sure to find several real-life examples of each responsibility to ensure that you gain a variety of perspectives and insights. This is particularly important for the skill-based, rather than fact-based, components of this functional area.

Introduction

In the first edition of PHR Exam Prep, we introduced this chapter with the following words:

> It could be argued that the functional area titled compensation and benefits has been, in one sense, misnamed. This is because these separate areas, when joined together, represent an exponentially larger and more dynamic discipline that is often referred to as 'total compensation.'

It appears as though our words had a fair amount of merit, for this functional area is now being referred to by HRCI as *total rewards*.

Total rewards encompasses all the rewards that an organization gives, grants, or otherwise bestows on its employees in exchange for the services those employees have rendered through their employment. It includes more obvious items—such as wages and salaries—that would fall under the subheading "compensation," as well as mandatory and optional benefits such as social security contributions, health and welfare programs, and the like. It also includes items that some, but not all, employees enjoy, such as incentives, bonuses, stock options, and so on.

In this chapter, we'll look at foundational questions relating to total rewards, starting with one of the most basic (and often overlooked) question: who *is* an employee? We'll then look at the concept of total rewards before looking at its separate, more frequently recognized components—first compensation, and then benefits. In an effort to make this fact-rich chapter easier to digest, we will separate our scan of compensation-related legislation (which appears at the beginning of this chapter) from our scan of benefits-related legislation (which appears after we have completed our discussion of compensation-related items and before we begin our discussion of benefits-related items). In addition to looking at legislation, we will examine each major component of total rewards.

Total Rewards Footing #1: Employee or Independent Contractor?

As indicated previously, one of the first steps that an organization needs to take is to ensure that individuals who contribute to the attainment of organizational objectives are accurately designated as either "employees" or "independent contractors."

As with most areas of HR, this question is not as simple as it might initially appear. There is no immediate answer—no single test to resolve the question of whether an individual is an employee or an independent contractor. To assist in this effort, the Department of Labor (DOL) has published a fact sheet citing U.S. Supreme Court rulings that offer the following seven factors, which help to appropriately resolve the seemingly perpetual employee/independent contractor conundrum (see www.dol.gov):

1. The extent to which the services rendered are an integral part of the principal's business.

2. The permanency of the relationship.

3. The amount of the alleged contractor's investment in facilities and equipment.

4. The nature and degree of control by the principal.

5. The alleged contractor's opportunities for profit and loss.

6. The amount of initiative, judgment, or foresight in open market competition with others required for the success of the claimed independent contractor.

7. The degree of independent business organization and operation.

The IRS also offers guidance at its website (www.irs.gov) with respect to properly classifying employees and independent contractors. According to the IRS, it is critical to examine the nature of the relationship between the worker and the organization. Specifically, all evidence of "control" and "independence" must be carefully considered. The IRS identifies three categories of control into which facts and evidence can be divided: behavioral control, financial control, and the type of relationship.

▸ *Behavioral Control*—Who controls and directs how the work is done? For instance, it could be argued that the business maintains behavioral control if it provides the individual with training, instructions, and so forth.

▸ *Financial Control*—Does the business have a right to control the financial and business aspects of the worker's job? More specifically

  ▸ To what extent does the worker have unreimbursed business expenses?

  ▸ What is the extent of the worker's investment in the facilities used in performing services?

  ▸ To what extent does the worker make his or her services available to the relevant market?

  ▸ How does the business pay the worker?

  ▸ To what extent can the worker realize a profit or incur a loss?

▸ *Type of Relationship*—Is there a written contract in place? If so, to what extent does it describe

  ▸ The relationship the parties intended to create?

  ▸ The extent to which the worker is available to perform services for other, similar businesses?

  ▸ Whether the business provides the worker with employee-type benefits, such as insurance, a pension plan, vacation pay, or sick pay?

  ▸ The permanency of the relationship?

  ▸ The extent to which services performed by the worker are a key aspect of the regular business of the company?

> **CAUTION**
>
> Exercise care in determining whether an individual is classified as an employee or as an independent contractor. Don't make this decision alone. There are many ramifications of misclassification, including the possibility of settlements that have cost some employers millions of dollars.

Total Rewards Footing #2: Exempt or Non-exempt?

As mentioned earlier, Federal Labor Standards Act (FLSA) addresses four areas: minimum wage, record keeping, child labor, and overtime. In this "Footing #2" section, we will focus on the minimum wage and overtime provisions because ascertaining exempt and non-exempt status is foundational to a discussion of total compensation.

On August 23, 2004, new minimum wage and overtime regulations to the FLSA were enacted.

> **NOTE**
>
> Interestingly, the DOL website specifically states that these revisions pertain to the overtime *and* minimum wage provisions of the FLSA. However, the $455 weekly threshold is more than twice the minimum wage that was in effect at the time these regulations passed, and no increase in the minimum wage was included with these revisions (a new federal minimum wage took effect as of July 24, 2007). The focus of the 2004 revisions, therefore, seems to be more on the overtime provisions of the FLSA, which is where we will maintain our focus in this section.

> **TIP**
>
> These provisions were hotly debated and widely discussed before implementation. Be alert to any changes that might be implemented.

Exemptions: The Basics

Known as FairPay, the 2004 revisions marked some significant changes relative to determining whether an employee is exempt or non-exempt from the overtime provisions of the FLSA. According to these regulations, employees would be classified as exempt if they

- Meet certain tests regarding their job duties
- Are paid on a salary basis
- Earn no less than $455 per week

Salary Basis

HR professionals need to have a solid understanding of what it means when an employee works on a *salary basis*. According to the DOL, being paid on a salary basis means that

> "An employee regularly receives a predetermined amount of compensation each pay period on a weekly, or less frequent, basis. The predetermined amount cannot be reduced because of variations in the quality or quantity of the employee's work. Subject to exceptions listed below, an exempt employee must receive the full salary for any week in which the employee performs any work, regardless of the number of days or hours worked. Exempt employees do not need to be paid for any work-week in which they perform no work. If the employer makes deductions from an employee's predetermined salary, i.e., because of the operating requirements of the business, that employee is not paid on a 'salary basis.' If the employee is ready, willing and able to work, deductions may not be made for time when work is not available."

> **CAUTION**
>
> Job duties—*not* job titles—must be used to determine an employee's FLSA status. (In other words, don't use an employee's title to determine whether the employee is eligible to earn overtime; go by the work that an employee actually performs.)

It's important to be aware of a number of notable changes that were enacted with the FairPay provisions (see www.dol.gov/esa for more information). These changes included

- The elimination of separate "short" and "long" tests (based on what an employee earned each week).

- Any employees earning less than $455 per week (equivalent to $23,660 per year) are automatically covered by the overtime provisions of the FLSA ("non-exempt")—regardless of the duties that they perform in their jobs. In other words, any employee who earns less than $23,660 is automatically eligible to earn over-time pay.

- The elimination of the long test resulted in the elimination of the well-known requirement that exempt employees cannot spend more than 20% of their time each week on non-exempt–level activities.

Types of Exemptions: Non-computer Employees, Non-highly Compensated Employees, and Outside Sales Employees

> **NOTE**
>
> One concept that is integral to a discussion of FLSA exemptions is *primary duty*, which refers to the principal, main, major, or most important duty that the employee performs.

NOTE

> Determination of an employee's primary duty must be based on all the facts in a particular case, with the major emphasis being on the character of the employee's job as a whole.

Consistent with the 2004 FairPay revisions, employers must now apply one of the following four standard tests to employees (except those who do computer work) who are paid on a salaried basis and whose salaries are between $23,660 and $99,999 per year.

Please note that in order to qualify for any particular exemption, an employee must meet all of the tests listed in that exemption.

Executive Exemption

- The employee's primary duty must be managing the enterprise or managing a customarily recognized department or subdivision of the enterprise.

- The employee must customarily and regularly direct the work of at least two or more other full-time employees or their equivalent.

- The employee must have the authority to hire or fire other employees, or the employee's suggestions and recommendations as to the hiring, firing, advancement, promotion, or any other change of status of other employees must be given particular weight.

Administrative Exemption

- The employee's primary duty must be the performance of office or nonmanual work directly related to the management or general business operations of the employer or the employer's customers.

- The employee's primary duty includes the exercise of discretion and independent judgment with respect to matters of significance.

Learned Professional Exemption

- The employee's primary duty must be the performance of work requiring advanced knowledge, defined as work which is predominantly intellectual in character and which includes work requiring the consistent exercise of discretion and judgment.

- The advanced knowledge must be in a field of science or learning.

- The advanced knowledge must be customarily acquired by a prolonged course of specialized intellectual instruction.

Creative Professional Exemption

▶ The employee's primary duty must be the performance of work requiring invention, imagination, originality, or talent in a recognized field of artistic or creative endeavor.

Types of Exemptions: Computer Employees

The Computer Employee exemption is slightly different with respect to pay. To qualify for the computer employee exemption, the following tests must be met:

▶ The employee must be compensated either on a salary or fee basis (as defined in the regulations) at a rate not less than $455 per week or, if compensated on an hourly basis, at a rate not less than $27.63 an hour.

▶ The employee must be employed as a computer systems analyst, computer programmer, software engineer, or other similarly skilled worker in the computer field performing the duties described next:

1. The application of systems analysis techniques and procedures, including consulting with users to determine hardware, software, or system functional specifications.

2. The design, development, documentation, analysis, creation, testing, or modification of computer systems or programs, including prototypes, based on and related to user or system design specifications.

3. The design, documentation, testing, creation, or modification of computer programs related to machine operating systems.

4. A combination of the aforementioned duties, the performance of which requires the same level of skills.

Types of Exemptions: Outside Sales

Unlike the other types of exemptions, a minimum salary is not required to establish an exemption on the basis of outside sales. The following criteria, however, must be met:

▶ The employee's primary duty must be making sales (as defined in the FLSA), or obtaining orders or contracts for services or for the use of facilities for which a consideration will be paid by the client or customer.

▶ The employee must be customarily and regularly engaged away from the employer's place or places of business.

Types of Exemptions: Highly Compensated Employees

FairPay defines highly compensated employees as those who

▶ Earn $100,000 or more annually (of which at least $455 per week must be paid on a salary or fee basis).

▶ Perform office or nonmanual work.

▶ Customarily and regularly perform at least one of the duties of an exempt executive, administrative, or professional employee identified in the standard tests for exemption.

Other Key FairPay Items

HR professionals also need to be familiar with several important considerations relative to the overtime provisions of the FLSA that were clarified in the 2004 revisions.

Specific Non-exempt Designations

Non-exempt: Manual laborers and other "blue collar" workers who perform work involving repetitive operations with their hands, physical skill, and energy cannot be exempted from the overtime provisions of FLSA, no matter how much they earn. This would include nonmanagement employees who work in maintenance or who are carpenters, electricians, mechanics, plumbers, iron workers, and so on.

Police, Firefighters, Paramedics, and Other First Responders

The act also specifically identifies other positions that are likely to be non-exempt (in other words, positions that are likely to be eligible for overtime pay), although a case-by-case review is still needed. These positions include the following:

Police officers, detectives, deputy sheriffs, state troopers, highway patrol officers, investigators, inspectors, correctional officers, parole or probation officers, park rangers, firefighters, paramedics, emergency medical technicians, ambulance personnel, rescue workers, hazardous materials workers, and similar employees, regardless of rank or pay level, who perform work such as preventing, controlling, or extinguishing fires of any type; rescuing fire, crime, or accident victims; preventing or detecting crimes; conducting investigations or inspections for violations of law; performing surveillance; pursuing, restraining, and apprehending suspects; detaining or supervising suspected and convicted criminals, including those on probation or parole; interviewing witnesses; interrogating and fingerprinting suspects; preparing investigative reports; or other similar work.

Safe Harbor Provisions (from Improper Deductions from Salary)

Improper salary deductions can cause an employer to lose the FLSA exemption—and not just for the employee from whom the deduction was improperly made.

EXAM ALERT

Familiarize yourself with circumstances under which employers *can* make deductions from an employee's salary.

If it is found that an employer has "actual practice" of making improper salary deductions, *the employer will lose the exemption* during the time period of the deductions for employees in the same job classification working for the same managers responsible for the improper deductions.

Under the new safe harbor provision, however, an employer can protect itself from losing the exemption if the employer

1. Has a clearly communicated policy prohibiting improper deductions and including a complaint mechanism.

2. Reimburses employees for any improper deductions.

3. Makes a good faith commitment to comply in the future.

C&B Footing #3: Compensation + Benefits = Total Rewards

An organization's total rewards philosophy represents far more than just the amount of cash it pays to employees, or even the "fringe benefits" that it provides. Instead, an organization's total rewards philosophy speaks volumes about what the leaders of that organization value, the results they want to attain, the behavior they want to encourage, and their commitment to their employees. It will also have a significant impact on the organization's efforts to attract, motivate, and retain talent.

In many ways, an organization's total compensation philosophy is a clear and direct expression of the organization's mission, vision, and values—*whether or not the organization intends it to be so*. Even the absence of a clearly defined compensation system or philosophy says something—and nothing can stop those messages from being received, loud and clear, by employees. Just as it is impossible for a person *not* to communicate, so too it is impossible for an organization's total rewards program (or absence thereof) not to send a clear message to employees and potential employees about what is important to the organization.

Objectives of a Total Rewards Program

Because an organization's total rewards program says so much, it's imperative that it be designed deliberately, intentionally, and with overarching as well as specific objectives in mind.

Those specific objectives will vary from organization to organization, and during different phases of the organization's life cycle, and to some degree from position to position. Certain overarching objectives, however, should be kept in mind when crafting a total compensation program—objectives that can be addressed, at least initially, by asking the following questions:

How can—and will—we design a total rewards system that

▸ Supports and reinforces the mission, vision, and values of the organization?

▸ Is consistent with the culture of the organization?

▸ Attracts, motivates, and retains targeted/appropriate employees?

▸ Ensures internal equity between positions within the organization?

▸ Supports our philosophy toward the external labor market?

▸ Is affordable, sustainable, and cost effective?

▸ Is legally defensible in the event of a challenge?

▸ Is appropriate for the organization's current position in its life cycle?

▸ Is flexible and easily adaptable?

In an effort to better appreciate the nuances that need to be considered when crafting a total rewards philosophy, let's take a closer look at two of these questions.

Attracting, Motivating, and Retaining Targeted/Appropriate Employees

For some organizations, there may be great value in attracting, motivating, and retaining high-performing employees who (hopefully) are "in it for the long haul." In these situations, important considerations may need to be factored in, such as long learning curves, maintaining sensitive and critical client relationships, and so on. For these organizations, there may be a strong focus on designing a total compensation system that would be perceived as very competitive in the relevant labor market and that would encourage high-performing employees to stay with the organization for the long term.

Conversely, some organizations are perfectly comfortable with relatively high (or just plain high) levels of turnover. Although these organizations might be interested in developing a total rewards program that will attract employees, motivating and retaining their employees might be of far less importance. Alternatively, those organizations whose employees do not require much training and/or whose employees form only transient relationships with customers might develop a total rewards philosophy that positions them less competitively in the relevant labor market. By itself, neither approach is right nor wrong. However, if you were to switch the two total rewards systems for these two types of organizations, the mismatch could create a significant disconnect—rendering both philosophies ineffective and even counterproductive.

Supporting the Philosophy Toward the Relevant Labor Market

There are three primary approaches from which organizations choose when deciding how they want to position themselves relative to the external labor market with respect to total rewards. We'll look at those three approaches in a moment. First, however, it's necessary to understand the meaning of the term *relevant labor market*.

The relevant labor market relates to the size and scope of the geographic area within which an organization would seek to attract qualified candidates. Even within the same organization, the relevant labor market for different positions can vary widely depending on the knowledge, skills, abilities, and behavioral characteristics required to perform each position successfully. Other factors that impact how an organization defines the relevant labor market might be the degree of competition that exists among employers for particular skills and/or knowledge and the degree to which certain skills and/or knowledge requirements are industry specific.

> **NOTE**
>
> Depending on the size and scope of the relevant labor market, you may need to take geographic differentials in pay into consideration. For instance, the same position could be compensated significantly differently in different parts of the nation, particularly if the relevant labor market for that position is relatively small. Conversely, if a relevant labor market for a particular position is truly nationwide in scope, it is possible there may be relatively little difference in pay rates regardless of where the position is geographically based.

After the relevant labor market has been defined for a particular position, the organization must choose between the three approaches alluded to earlier—leading, lagging, or matching the market.

> **NOTE**
>
> It's critical to note that any of these three approaches could be adopted across an entire organization or just for certain positions within an organization. It's important, however, to ensure that internal equity is consistently maintained if different approaches (lead, lag, or match) are applied to different positions within the same organization.

Lead the Market

Organizations may choose to offer total compensation packages that are "better" than packages being offered by their labor market competitors. Organizations that lead the market may believe that higher compensation packages will attract higher-performing employees who will, in turn, "pay for themselves," and then some. In short, these organizations want the "best of the best" and are willing to pay for it.

Lag the Market

Organizations may choose—by design, or simply because of budgetary constraints—to offer total rewards packages that are "less attractive" than the total rewards packages that are being offered by their labor market competitors. Organizations that lag the market might offset this potential disadvantage by reinforcing and maximizing the intrinsic rewards that it offers—long-term potential growth opportunities, the ability to contribute to a particularly significant organizational mission, and so on.

Match the Market

Organizations may choose to offer total rewards packages that are comparable to the total rewards packages being offered by their labor market competitors. Organizations that match the market make a conscious choice to be "externally competitive" with respect to total compensation.

> **NOTE**
>
> It's important to keep in mind that how an organization addresses even the most overarching questions can vary considerably, depending on the organization itself, the phase of the business life cycle in which the organization finds itself, and even the positions under consideration. As with all other areas of HR, therefore, there are no simple answers. (If you're tempted to say that *any* situation in which you find yourself as an HR professional is a "no brainer," look again—you may have overlooked something.)

Elements of a Total Rewards Program

Total rewards consists of a variety of elements, all of which can be divided into *direct compensation* and *indirect compensation*.

Direct compensation refers to components that are presented to employees in the form of cash, and indirect compensation refers to components that are presented to employees in forms other than cash (noncash).

Some examples of direct compensation are

- Hourly wages/base salary
- Shift differentials
- Overtime pay
- Commissions
- Sign-on bonuses
- Variable pay (such as short-term and long-term incentives)

Some examples of indirect compensation are

- Legally mandated benefits (such as social security)
- Medical insurance
- Dental insurance
- Long-term disability insurance
- Vision coverage
- Vacation time
- Holiday time

▶ Recognition programs (such as peer recognition programs, noncash spot awards, achievement awards, "pizza parties," desirable parking, and so on)

▶ Perquisites (also known as "perks," such as a company car, club memberships, financial planning, and so on)

NOTE

In addressing problems and questions that might come up, it's important to keep in mind that what may initially appear to be a compensation problem may in fact not be one. It is very possible that the problem under consideration is unrelated to compensation, or that it is related to compensation as well as other issues. Although it is also possible that the problem under consideration might truly be a compensation problem, even then, it's important to think in terms of "total rewards" instead of just automatically "throwing money" at a problem. Without a doubt, your internal consulting skills will really come in handy here as you work to identify the true root causes of your clients' challenges with them.

Communicating the Total Rewards Program

It's not enough to "walk the walk"—you've also got to "talk the talk."

Often, when we look around our organizations, our country, or even our world, we see people who "talk the talk" but don't "walk the walk." Or, to put it differently, people don't always "put their money where their mouths are." Interestingly, when it comes to total rewards programs, the opposite tends to be true. Organizations often don't communicate enough with employees about the total compensation/benefits programs that they have in place, the benefits of these programs, or about what those programs really cost.

For a number of reasons, it's important to change this practice, and to communicate with employees. Most employees simply do not know the real costs—let alone the actual value—of the benefits they receive. Also, in a very real sense, employees earn benefits, just like they earn cash compensation—and it's important to ensure that employees understand and recognize that. This holds true for benefits that are voluntarily provided by employers, as well as for benefits programs that are mandated by the government. Otherwise, even those benefits that are *not* entitlements may ultimately begin to *feel like* entitlements to employees.

There are myriad ways to communicate with employees about the benefits they receive, just a few of which are

▶ Employee meetings

▶ Newsletters

▶ DVDs

▶ Employee handbooks

▶ Annual total rewards statements

▶ Personal letters/emails

▶ Internet/intranet

Communicate early, and communicate often. Perhaps most important, don't rely on any single method of communication to get your message across. Just as people learn differently in training programs (see Chapter 5, "Human Resource Development"), people also process and absorb information differently. Finally, *always* make sure that at least one of your methods of communication is in writing—something that employees can refer to after-the-fact.

REVIEW BREAK

At this point, we've established a strategic and theoretical foundation that will provide us with a context within which to consider some of the fact-based and practical elements of total rewards. Next, let's review some key compensation-related legislation.

Related Legislation: Compensation

Although many laws have some relevance to compensation, the following are some of the most important ones with which HR professionals need to be familiar.

Davis-Bacon Act, 1931

The Davis-Bacon Act was the first piece of legislation to consider the topic of—and actually establish—a minimum wage. Davis-Bacon, however, was and still is limited to the construction industry, specifically those contractors and subcontractors on

- ▶ Any and all federal government construction contracts
- ▶ Nonfederal government construction projects in excess of $2,000 that receive federal funding

Contractors and subcontractors who meet either of these criteria are required to provide laborers and mechanics who are employed at the actual worksite with wages and benefits that are equal to (or better than) what workers on similar local projects receive.

Walsh-Healey Public Contracts Act (PCA), 1936

The next significant piece of compensation-related legislation was the Walsh-Healey Public Contracts Act (PCA), enacted in 1936.

The Walsh-Healey PCA requires contractors who have contracts with the federal government that exceed $10,000 to pay an established minimum wage to workers employed through that contract. In addition to minimum wage, Walsh-Healey PCA also addressed issues including overtime pay and safe and sanitary working conditions.

Fair Labor Standards Act (FLSA),1938

NOTE

In the section titled "Total Rewards Footing #2: Exempt or Non-exempt?," we explored the overtime provisions of the FLSA, particularly with respect to the 2004 FairPay revisions. Here we'll focus on the other three provisions of the law, as well as some of the more technical aspects of the overtime provision.

Although it was initially enacted in 1938, the Fair Labor Standards Act (FLSA) still has a profound impact on employees today because of its wide scope and the degree to which it directly impacts the lives of nearly every American worker.

The FLSA covers full-time and part-time workers in the private sector and in federal, state, and local governments. It addresses minimum wage, overtime, equal pay, record keeping, and child labor standards (referred to by the government now as "youth employment standards"). For private enterprise employees, it is administered by the Wage and Hour Division of the DOL. For federal employees, the FLSA is administered either by the Wage and Hour Division or the U.S. Office of Personnel Management (which, interestingly, refers to itself as "The Federal Government's Human Resources Agency" on its website).

In looking at the FLSA, let's take a look at each of the areas it covers, in the following order:

▶ Minimum wage

▶ Overtime pay

▶ Child labor standards (youth employment standards)

▶ Record keeping

Minimum Wage

The FLSA established a federal minimum wage for private sector employees and for all other employees covered by the act. From time to time, minimum wage has become a hotly debated issue in Congress, because Congress has the responsibility for introducing legislation that will change the federal minimum wage. In our nation's system of checks and balances, however, that hotly debated congressional issue quickly becomes a hotly debated presidential issue, because it is the president who must either sign or veto legislation to increase the minimum wage.

In May of 2007, the federal minimum wage was increased for the first time in 10 years from $5.15 to $7.25 per hour in stages over two years, as shown in Figure 6.1.

EXAM ALERT

Be familiar with government-sponsored programs that enable employers to pay certain employees (full-time students, certain people with disabilities, and so on) at an hourly rate of pay that is less than the federal minimum wage.

NOTE

Many states have established a minimum wage that is higher than the federally established minimum wage. In these circumstances, employees would be entitled to the state minimum wage (because in this case, the state law is more generous than the federal law, and thus supersedes the federal law).

EMPLOYEE RIGHTS
UNDER THE FAIR LABOR STANDARDS ACT
THE UNITED STATES DEPARTMENT OF LABOR WAGE AND HOUR DIVISION

FEDERAL MINIMUM WAGE

$5.85 PER HOUR	$6.55 PER HOUR	$7.25 PER HOUR
BEGINNING JULY 24, 2007	BEGINNING JULY 24, 2008	BEGINNING JULY 24, 2009

OVERTIME PAY

At least $1\frac{1}{2}$ times your regular rate of pay for all hours worked over 40 in a workweek.

YOUTH EMPLOYMENT

An employee must be at least **16** years old to work in most non-farm jobs and at least **18** to work in non-farm jobs declared hazardous by the Secretary of Labor.

Youths **14** and **15** years old may work outside school hours in various non-manufacturing, non-mining, non-hazardous jobs under the following conditions:

No more than
- **3** hours on a school day or **18** hours in a school week;
- **8** hours on a non-school day or **40** hours in a non-school week.

Also, work may not begin before **7 a.m.** or end after **7 p.m.**, except from June 1 through Labor Day, when evening hours are extended to **9 p.m.** Different rules apply in agricultural employment. For more information, visit the YouthRules! Web site at **www.youthrules.dol.gov**.

TIP CREDIT

Employers of "tipped employees" must pay a cash wage of at least $2.13 per hour if they claim a tip credit against their minimum wage obligation. If an employee's tips combined with the employer's cash wage of at least $2.13 per hour do not equal the minimum hourly wage, the employer must make up the difference. Certain other conditions must also be met.

ENFORCEMENT

The Department of Labor may recover back wages either administratively or through court action, for the employees that have been underpaid in violation of the law. Violations may result in civil or criminal action.

Civil money penalties of up to $11,000 per violation may be assessed against employers who violate the youth employment provisions of the law and up to $1,100 per violation against employers who willfully or repeatedly violate the minimum wage or overtime pay provisions. This law prohibits discriminating against or discharging workers who file a complaint or participate in any proceedings under the Act.

ADDITIONAL INFORMATION

- Certain occupations and establishments are exempt from the minimum wage and/or overtime pay provisions.
- Special provisions apply to workers in American Samoa and the Commonwealth of the Northern Mariana Islands.
- Some state laws provide greater employee protections; employers must comply with both.
- The law requires employers to display this poster where employees can readily see it.
- Employees under 20 years of age may be paid $4.25 per hour during their first 90 consecutive calendar days of employment with an employer.
- Certain full-time students, student learners, apprentices, and workers with disabilities may be paid less than the minimum wage under special certificates issued by the Department of Labor.

For additional information:

 # 1-866-4-USWAGE

U.S. Wage and Hour Division

(1-866-487-9243)   TTY: 1-877-889-5627

WWW.WAGEHOUR.DOL.GOV

U.S. Department of Labor | Employment Standards Administration | Wage and Hour Division

WHD Publication 1088 (Revised June 2007)

FIGURE 6.1 2007-2008-2009 Minimum Wage Updates poster.

Want a Good Tip?

Here's one—be sure your tipped employees earn at least the minimum wage.

The FLSA specifically addresses the question of employees who receive tips. According to the act, an employer of "tipped employees" must pay those employees for every hour worked, even if the employees' tips alone would result in them earning more than the minimum wage. The minimum rate of pay that can be paid to tipped employees (available at www.dol.gov/esa), however, is substantially less ($2.13 as of the date this book was printed) than the minimum wage that must be paid to employees who do not receive tips. To be eligible to pay tipped employees this lower hourly rate, the employer must meet certain conditions, including (but not limited to) the following:

- ▶ The employer must claim a tip credit against its minimum wage obligation.

- ▶ Each employee's tips combined with the hourly rate that the employer is paying must meet or exceed the federal minimum hourly wage. Otherwise, the employer must make up the difference.

Overtime Pay

According to the FLSA, non-exempt employees must be paid at least the minimum wage for the first 40 hours worked during the workweek. If an employee works more than 40 hours during the workweek (commonly referred to as "overtime"), he or she must be paid those overtime hours at a rate that is at least 150% (commonly referred to as "time and a half") of his or her regular rate of pay per hour—which may be different from the employee's stated hourly wage rate.

In addition to the all-important questions of who is (and isn't) exempt from the overtime provisions of the FLSA, at least two additional pivotal questions related to overtime must be addressed:

1. How is the number of hours worked calculated?

2. What rate of pay must be used to determine the regular rate of pay per hour (which will, in turn, be used to calculate the overtime pay rate)?

Calculating the Number of Hours Worked During the Workweek

To calculate the number of hours worked during the workweek, it's first necessary to understand the government's definition of and rules regarding workweeks (as published at www.dol.gov):

- ▶ A workweek is any fixed and regularly recurring period of 168 hours (24 hours in a day, seven days a week).

- ▶ The employer can select any day (and any hour) of the "calendar week" on which to begin the "workweek." Once chosen, however, that day (and hour) must remain constant (hence the "fixed" and "recurring" requirement).

- ▶ The employer can establish different workweeks for different employees or groups of employees.

- ▶ The hours that an employee works during different workweeks cannot be "averaged" (to avoid overtime payments, or for any other reason).

After you've got a handle on what a workweek is, the next step is to understand how to determine what "hours worked" really means.

First of all, "hours worked" means "hours worked"—*not* "hours paid." In other words, according to the FLSA, hours that have been paid but not worked (vacation time, sick time, holiday time, jury duty time, and the like) do *not* count toward the 40-hour threshold (although some organizations may voluntarily *choose* to count these hours toward the 40-hour threshold).

> **CAUTION**
>
> "Hours worked" also doesn't mean "hours approved to work." If an employer "suffers or permits" a non-exempt employee to work, that employee must be compensated for time worked. So, whether the employer *requires* the employee to work or simply *allows* the employee to work, the time counts as "hours worked" and must be compensated accordingly.

Calculating the Regular Rate of Pay

An employee's regular rate of pay includes more than just his or her hourly rate of pay; it would also include any incentives and commissions. It would not, however, include bonuses (which, unlike incentive programs, are discretionary), pay for time not worked, premium pay for weekend or holiday work, and the like.

> **CAUTION**
>
> It is critical that employers calculate overtime payments on the basis of each employee's *regular* rate of pay, not on each employee's *hourly* rate of pay.

> **NOTE**
>
> As with minimum wage, some states have established more generous overtime laws—for instance, laws that require overtime pay after an employee has worked eight hours in any one day, regardless of how many hours the employee works during the entire workweek. As is also the case with minimum wage, a more generous state law would supersede the federal law.

Child Labor Standards

The child labor provisions of the FLSA restrict the number of hours (and the times of the day) that children under the age of 16 can work, as well as the types of work that children under the age of 18 can perform.

Under the Fair Labor Standards Act (FLSA)

▸ Children under the age of 14 years cannot be employed (different guidelines exist for certain jobs, such as for farm work or work performed for the child's parent).

▸ Hours worked by 14- and 15-year-olds are limited to

> ▸ Nonschool hours
>
> ▸ 3 hours in a school day

- ▸ 18 hours in a school week

- ▸ 8 hours in a nonschool day

- ▸ 40 hours in a nonschool week

- ▸ Hours between 7 a.m. and 7 p.m. (except from June 1 through Labor Day, when evening hours are extended to 9 p.m.)

▸ Youth who are under 18 years of age may perform nonhazardous jobs. Youth who are 14 and 15 years of age are also restricted from performing manufacturing, mining, and hazardous jobs.

▸ Youth who are 16 years of age and older (and adults) may work an unlimited number of hours per day.

▸ The FLSA does not require work permits or working papers, but certain states do.

Record Keeping

Employers must maintain accurate and complete records for each non-exempt employee of hours worked and wages earned. Certain identifying information (such as social security number, address, and so on) is also required. No specific method of timekeeping is required. See the act for more specific information about these record-keeping (and retention) requirements.

> **NOTE**
>
> Employers are required to post the provisions of the FLSA.

Portal-to-Portal Act, 1947

In May of 1947, the FLSA was amended by the Portal-to-Portal Act. Section 254(a) of the Portal-to-Portal Act offered clearer definitions of "hours worked" for purposes of minimum wage and overtime payments. According to the act, employers are required to compensate workers only for working time that they spend on activities that relate to the performance of their job.

> **EXAM ALERT**
>
> This statement, while accurate, is also incomplete, in that it does not even begin to address the nuances of the Portal-to-Portal Act. The act, for instance, addresses travel time (on public transportation, on private transportation, during work hours, outside work hours), pre-shift work, post-shift work, idle waiting time, overnight travel, training time, and many other considerations. Familiarize yourself with this act before paying your employees and before taking the PHR exam.

Equal Pay Act (EPA), 1963

The EPA prohibits discrimination on the basis of sex in the payment of wages or benefits to men and women who perform substantially equal (but not identical) work, for the same employer, in the same establishment, and under similar working conditions. (An "establishment" generally refers to one specific physical location.) Similar to the way in which FLSA status is determined, "substantial equality" is determined by job content, not job titles. More specifically, the substantial equality of job content is assessed on the basis of the following four factors:

▶ *Skill*—The amount or degree of experience, ability, education, and training required to perform the job. Comparisons must be made on the basis of the skills that are required to perform the job—not on the skills that the incumbents happen to possess.

▶ *Effort*—The amount of physical or mental exertion required to perform the job.

▶ *Responsibility*—The degree of responsibility and accountability that an employer entrusts to and expects from a particular person in a specific position.

▶ *Working Conditions*—The physical surroundings of the position, as well as any hazards associated with a particular position.

Employers can, however, set forth "affirmative defenses" to explain inequities in pay between men and women. These arguments can be based on—and must be proven to be—a function of

▶ Seniority

▶ Merit

▶ Quantity or quality of production

▶ Any factors other than sex

REVIEW BREAK

This section has provided an overview of some of the laws that are most relevant to compensation-related topics. Now let's take a look at the actual building blocks that you can use to bring compensation principles to life within your organization.

Compensation: Job Evaluation

Job evaluation is the process through which every job in an organization is assessed and compared to other jobs in the organization. At the conclusion of the job evaluation process, you will be able to ascertain the relative worth of each job within the organization. When this is done, you will have generated an overall job-worth hierarchy.

Job evaluation techniques fall into two categories: nonquantitative and quantitative.

Nonquantitative Job Evaluation Techniques

Nonquantitative job evaluation techniques, as the name implies, determine the relative value of jobs within the organization without using mathematical techniques. Instead, these methods focus on the "whole job" (which is why these techniques are also referred to as *whole job* methods).

Whole Job Ranking

In whole job ranking techniques, jobs are ranked from lowest to highest, according to the importance that each job holds (or, stated differently, the value that each job brings) to the organization. In essence, a list is generated that reflects which jobs are more important to the organization, and which jobs are less important to the organization, in ranked order.

Whole job ranking is easy to perform and is also relatively inexpensive to maintain. It fails, however, to establish specific factors about each job that would need to be taken into consideration when comparing jobs to each other, and it can be prone to rater subjectivity. It is also limited to a job-to-job comparison, rather than to any specific competencies or responsibilities that are universally valued throughout the organization. Also, if more than just a few positions need to be ranked, this system may prove to be unwieldy within the organization. Finally, although the list that is generated through whole job ranking will show which jobs are most and least important, it will not demonstrate the *relative* worth of one job to another.

Job Classification

Job classification is a nonquantitative job evaluation technique that categorizes jobs into broad categories, or *levels*, based on the level—and, ultimately, value to the organization—of the work that is performed by jobs within each level. Each level incorporates specific responsibilities and "benchmark statements" that describe the nature, complexity, autonomy, and so on of the work that is performed by positions in that level.

In addition to being inexpensive, job classification is relatively simple to implement and administer. One potential disadvantage, however, is that jobs may not match perfectly with the benchmark statements listed in each category. In such cases, the evaluator would use his or her judgment (which can, of course, be imperfect and/or subjective at times) to choose the best possible classification. Another potential weakness of the job classification method is that raters are also more likely to evaluate jobs on the basis of the current incumbent, rather than on the basis of the jobs themselves, thus violating a key principle of sound job evaluation.

Job Slotting

Job slotting incorporates (or "slots") newly created or revised positions into an existing job hierarchy. This process of slotting is accomplished by comparing the new or revised job descriptions to jobs (and job descriptions) that have already been evaluated and slotted within the hierarchy.

Like the other nonquantitative job evaluation methods, job slotting is relatively inexpensive and simple to administer and implement. Job slotting can be used, however, only when a job structure is already in place. As with the other nonquantitative job evaluation methods, there is an increased possibility that rater error and subjectivity can taint the job evaluation process. It is also more likely that jobs will be evaluated on the basis of the current incumbent, rather than on the basis of the jobs themselves, thus violating a key principle of sound job evaluation.

Quantitative Job Evaluation Techniques

Quantitative (or *factor based*) job evaluation methods identify the degree to which each position is responsible for or requires specific compensable factors. *Compensable factors* are those skills, abilities, characteristics, or areas of responsibility that an organization values, and for which it is willing to pay. Some sample compensable factors include education, experience, financial responsibility, responsibility for contacts, and so on.

Factor-based methods generate a mathematical score that reflects each position's relative worth to the organization.

Point Factor

Point factor systems first identify specific compensable factors and then establish levels of performance *within* each of those compensable factors. The relative importance of each compensable factor to the organization is then weighted. A different point value is then assigned to each level within each compensable factor.

After a point factor system has been established, each job is evaluated according to this system by determining which level within each compensable factor is most reflective of the position being evaluated, thus generating a point value for each compensable factor. The evaluator then adds up the points associated with each compensable factor to calculate a total point value. When the point values associated with each job are compared to each other, a mathematical depiction of the relative and absolute value of the jobs will emerge, thus indicating where the job falls within the established job worth hierarchy.

The point factor system affords greater reliability between different raters and minimizes the potential impact of evaluator error or subjectivity. Developing a point factor system, however, can be time consuming and difficult—and purchasing one can be expensive. In addition, using it properly requires some measure of training.

Factor Comparison

Factor comparison is a quantitative job evaluation technique that involves the ranking of each compensable factor of each job. A corresponding monetary value for each level with each factor is subsequently identified. Similar to the point factor method, each job is evaluated with respect to each compensable factor. The appropriate level is selected. Unlike the point factor method, however, a "dollar value" is associated with each level with each compensable factor. When all the levels that have been selected are added together, a pay rate will emerge for each job.

Although this system affords a degree of objectivity and reliability across raters, it is difficult and expensive to develop. It also requires a great deal of monitoring and updating to ensure that the dollar value associated with each level remains appropriate, in a relative as well as in an absolute sense.

Compensation: Market Pricing

Market pricing involves looking at the relevant labor market to ascertain what the "going rate" or "market rate" is for a particular position. Market pricing can yield valuable pay data about "benchmark" jobs—jobs for which close matches can be identified in the relevant labor market.

Data collected through market pricing can be used in a number of ways. For example, market data can be obtained about a number of benchmark positions as part of a larger initiative. Market data can also help in the building of a job-worth hierarchy, around which other positions can be placed using a whole job slotting technique. Market data can also be used to obtain information for one particular job, in combination with other job evaluation techniques that might be used.

Market Data Considerations

In preparing to collect market data, there are a number of considerations that need to be taken into account and a number of decisions that need to be made. Let's take a look at some of the questions that might be relevant.

What Is the Relevant Labor Market?

We first looked at the topic of relevant labor markets when we started considering the importance of the organization's total rewards philosophy. Within the context of collecting market data, determining an appropriate relevant labor market for each position is foundational to ensuring that the market data we collect—and about which we will be making decisions—is truly relevant.

Who Are Our Labor Market Competitors in General, and for Specific Jobs?

Determining who your labor market competitors are within the relevant labor market is also critical. One important consideration is whether you are competing only within your industry for talent, or whether you are also competing for talent with organizations in different industries or sectors.

What Sources of Market Data Are Currently Available to You, and What Sources Could You Secure?

Pay surveys provide one important source of market data. Pay surveys can be developed internally or secured externally (either by purchasing existing survey data or by contracting with an outside organization to develop a customized survey).

Market data can also be obtained through

- ▶ Government resources (the Bureau of Labor Statistics—www.bls.gov—is one excellent resource)

- ▶ Websites designed for this purpose (for example, go to your favorite search engine and type in `"competitive salaries"`, or similar language)

- ▶ Local economic development councils

- ▶ Professional associations

- ▶ Career development offices at college, universities, and/or tech training schools

- ▶ Employees (including departing employees) and managers

- ▶ Search firms and employment agencies

EXAM ALERT

Be familiar with the advantages and disadvantages associated with each of the different methods of securing market data—in particular, the advantages and disadvantages of survey-based methods.

Which Matches Are Appropriate?

As mentioned earlier, matching benchmark positions to available market data provides valuable information. Note that the positions within any organization, however, are benchmark positions. It simply won't be possible to find market data for some positions, in which case you may want to consider other options (for instance, internal job evaluation or a combination of job slotting with benchmark market data).

CAUTION

Match jobs on the basis of the duties and responsibilities that are performed—not on job titles. Job titles can be misleading or even inaccurate, which could in turn corrupt your analysis and recommendations.

Does the Data Need to Be Adjusted in Any Way?

There are a number of ways to adjust market data, including

- ▶ *Aging*—Ideally, market data should be collected from multiple sources. It is likely that the dates on which these salaries were "effective" will be different for each source of data, so it's necessary to adjust all the data to a common date (usually the date on which the market analysis is being conducted).

- ▶ *Quality of job match*—Sometimes (perhaps even "often"), it's impossible to make a perfect job match, especially for positions that are not benchmark jobs. This can occur because of differences in scope, work conditions, financial responsibility, or a variety of other factors. In situations like this, the best choice you can make is to find the best possible match, even if it is not ideal. After you've made the best possible match, you can then "weight" different market data differently as a way of reflecting each source's relative value. "Weighting" market data means putting greater importance on certain data you've collected, and less importance on other data you've collected, when you use that data to perform calculations or formulate recommendations. This can help account for the inevitable imperfections that you'll come across during the process of job matching.

After the market data has been collected and appropriately adjusted, the recommendations that you'll make on the basis of that data can support sound decision making. Those recommendations may pertain to one particular position, or they may make a broader contribution toward developing a job-worth hierarchy. It's also important to recognize that market data does not stand alone as the only factor that should be taken into consideration—ideally, it should be used in conjunction with existing job evaluation methods, pay structures, and so on. It is also quite possible that externally generated data may present a different perspective than internally generated data, and it is important to consider and reconcile the two.

Compensation: Base Pay and Variable Pay

After the overall compensation strategy is established, the next step is to determine how that strategy will come to life within the organization. As we discussed earlier, total compensation (rewards) can be divided into direct (cash) and indirect (noncash) elements. In this section, we'll consider two critical elements of direct compensation: base pay and variable pay.

Base Pay

Base pay refers to the fixed rate of pay that an employee receives for performing his or her job. Base pay does not, however, include earnings obtained through shift differentials, benefits, overtime, incentive premiums, or any pay element other than the employee's fixed rate of pay.

A number of factors go into setting base pay rates, including the relative worth of the job to the organization, the market rate for a particular position, and other special circumstances (for instance, unique skills that are in great demand—also sometimes referred to as "hot skills").

Variable Pay

Sometimes, organizations choose to compensate employees through variable pay programs in addition to base pay programs. Variable pay is also known as "at risk" pay (but is not often referred to in those terms when such pay programs are being discussed directly with employees, in that "risk" is not universally embraced).

There are a variety of variable pay programs, each of which can be used on a standalone basis, combined with other variable pay programs, or customized to meet the needs and objectives of an organization's own unique compensation and total rewards philosophy.

Incentive Plans

Incentive plans establish specific financial and nonfinancial goals and targets for individuals, groups, and organizations. For incentive programs to be effective, employees need to believe that they can attain the goals that have been set as part of the incentive program, and that the reward that they would earn by attaining those goals is "worth it" (see "Vroom's Expectancy Theory," in Chapter 2, "HR: A Body of Underlying Knowledge and Principles").

Incentive plans also need to be designed with an awareness of how much downside risk—as well as upside potential—exists for incentive plan participants. It's also critical to look at the design of the incentive program and the accompanying message that it sends to employees. For instance

▶ Are there "thresholds" in place, so that a partial incentive will be paid even if the goal is not fully attained? Or will employees/teams be paid only for meeting or exceeding objectives?

▶ Is the incentive program an "add on" to a current base pay program, or does it truly constitute earnings that are "at risk"? For instance, will participants' base pay be reduced, now or at some point in the future, as a result of participating in the incentive program?

▶ What is the overall degree of upside potential, and what is the overall degree of downside risk?

Regardless of the answers to these and many other questions, one thing is certain—any incentive program will speak volumes to employees about what the organization values.

There are many types of incentive programs, a few of which are described here.

Short-term Incentives—Individual

Short-term individual incentive programs are used to financially motivate individual employees to attain specific financial or nonfinancial objectives. Short-term incentive programs are usually one year or less in duration.

Short-term Incentives—Team/Group

Short-term team/group incentive programs are similar to short-term individual incentive programs, except that targets are set for groups of people instead of for individual employees. These incentive programs are intended to foster collaborative efforts and synergies among employees who are pursuing a common goal.

Gainsharing

Gainsharing incentive plans are designed to motivate (or, you could say, to "incent" or "incentivize") employees to reach specific goals relating to cost cutting or revenue generation, by offering to share a portion of that savings (or that increased revenue) with the employees who helped to generate it. Gainsharing plans are based on team/group performance, rather than on individual performance.

Profit Sharing

Profit-sharing plans are organizationwide plans that establish an organizationwide profit goal. If the goal is reached, the profits are shared with employees. Profits can either be shared immediately (cash profit sharing plans) or at a later time (deferred profit sharing plans).

Compensation: Building and Using Pay Structures

After an organization has identified a total rewards philosophy, it can productively turn its attention to building a compensation system to support that philosophy.

The overarching and specific objectives that the organization has established relative to total are brought to life through the organization's pay structures. Pay structures provide direction relative to wage and salary rates, pay increases, and incentive programs. They operationalize the organization's philosophies relative to internal equity and external competitiveness. In a very real sense, the pay structures that an organization puts in place make the organization's total rewards strategy tangible.

EXAM ALERT

Pay structures provide a reminder about the criticality of effectively communicating with employees about the organization's total rewards philosophy and programs. Familiarize yourself with ways to engage in meaningful and effective communication with employees around these all-important topics.

Elements of Pay Structures

Two important elements of pay structures are grades and salaries, both of which are often referred to as elements of a "salary administration" system.

Grades

Grades (also referred to as "job grades") represent a hierarchy of levels into which jobs of similar internal worth can be categorized. It may be helpful to liken job grades to school grades—just as students within a particular grade demonstrate similar levels of academic accomplishment, jobs within the same grade share a similar level of value or worth to the organization.

Different organizations will have different numbers of pay grades, with differing degrees of distinction between each of those grades.

Ranges

If grades provide the framework for clustering positions in accordance with their relative value to the organization, ranges provide corresponding compensation levels for each of those clusters.

Ranges specify the lowest (minimum) and the highest (maximum) compensation rates for which positions within each grade are generally paid. The halfway point between those two figures is known as the *midpoint* and is calculated as follows:

$$\frac{Maximum + Minimum}{2}$$

NOTE

As is often the case, exceptions can exist, for a variety of reasons. Employees who are paid above the maximum of the range are considered to be "red-circled"; employees who are paid below the minimum of the range are considered to be "green-circled."

The *range spread* is a percentage that is calculated by subtracting the minimum of the range from the maximum of the range and dividing that number by the minimum of the range. For instance:

Range Minimum:	$40,000
Range Maximum:	$60,000
Range Spread:	$60,000
	− $40,000
	$20,000

$$\frac{\$20,000}{\$40,000} = 50\%$$

Range spreads allow organizations to recognize and compensate employees within the same job and within jobs that are in the same grade, for different levels of skill, experience, tenure (if appropriate and consistent with organizational culture) or performance. Of course, how an organization compensates employees within each range will, to a degree, depend on the total rewards philosophy of the organization.

There is no one "right" percentage for range spreads. Range spreads do, however, tend to grow wider at higher grade levels. Traditionally, range spreads are approximately

- ▸ 35% for non-exempt positions

- ▸ 50% for exempt positions

- ▸ 60% + for senior leadership positions

A series of ranges, along with their accompanying minimums, maximums, and midpoints, is known as a *range table*. For identification purposes, numbers or letters are often assigned to each grade in a range table.

Broadbanding

Sometimes, organizations choose to use a relatively small number of grades, an approach known as *broadbanding*. Organizations might choose to use broadbands to bring about a cultural change (for instance, to support the implementation of a "flatter" organization), or to shift employees' focus away from traditional promotions and place it instead on professional growth. Broadbands typically have range spreads of 100% or more.

Using Pay Structures for Decision Making

Although it's important to build pay structures, building them—by itself—isn't enough. Organizations also need to develop the policies that will guide day-to-day decisions regarding pay. As alluded to earlier, these policies are a reflection of the overarching total rewards philosophies of the organization.

Pay guidelines can be based on performance, experience, seniority, effort, and a variety of other factors. One important consideration to keep in mind is that whatever factor(s) is used to determine how day-to-day pay-related decisions are made will be viewed as having great importance—and will likely become a key driver of employee efforts.

Pay guidelines also need to be developed to guide other types of increases (promotions, adjustments, general increases, cost-of-living increases, and so on) as well as the amount and timing of those increases.

Compa-ratio

Another important tool that can provide valuable information for decision making is the *compa-ratio*.

The compa-ratio for each employee is calculated by dividing the employee's pay rate by the range midpoint for his or her position. For example, if an employee earns $40,000 per year, and the midpoint of his or her range is $50,000, the compa-ratio is calculated as follows:

$$\frac{\$40,000}{\$50,000} = 80\%$$

Compa-ratios can be a particularly valuable measure for organizations that seek to match the market, because in such systems midpoints are often considered to be a close approximation of the "market rate" for a position. By calculating the compa-ratio, therefore, it is possible to compare the employee's rate of pay with the market rate for his or her position. If you take this percentage in combination with length of service, time in job, performance level, and other employees' earnings, you'll end up with a significant amount of information to help you manage employee compensation.

EXAM ALERT

In this section, we covered many areas related to the discipline of compensation—areas that are highly likely to show up on the PHR exam. There are other areas, however, that we have not touched on directly, which are also included in the repertoire of responsibilities you need to perform and the cache of knowledge you need to possess as an HR professional. This (in a practical sense) means they also could appear on the exam. So, in addition to what's discussed here, be sure to review other sources in an effort to familiarize yourself with

HR-related responsibilities:

▶ Develop/select and implement a payroll system.

▶ Administer payroll functions.

HR-related knowledge:

▶ Executive compensation methods.

REVIEW BREAK

At this point, we've covered a lot of ground, including the question of who is (and who is not) an employee; FLSA status; total rewards; and a host of issues relating to compensation. Now let's move into the other part of the total rewards equation—benefits.

As mentioned at the beginning of the chapter, we're going to take a slightly different approach to the way we look at benefits-related legislation. Instead of looking at it all together, we're going to divide benefits-related laws into two categories:

▶ Laws that exist for the purpose of regulating, governing, or guiding optional benefits programs

▶ Laws that actually created specific mandatory and optional benefits programs

In this way, we hope to make it easier for you to navigate the (relatively) heavily legislated discipline of benefits.

Related Legislation: Benefits—Laws That Regulate, Govern, and Guide Optional Benefits Programs

Many laws have an impact on the benefits that employers offer to their employees. Let's take a look at some of the most significant ones.

Employee Retirement Income Security Act (ERISA), 1974

The Employee Retirement Income Security Act is perhaps better known by its acronym, ERISA. ERISA's overall purpose is to protect the interests of those who participate—and the beneficiaries of those who participate—in employee benefit plans. ERISA applies only to programs established by private industry employers.

ERISA established minimum participation and vesting standards for retirement programs (ERISA covers defined benefit plans and defined contribution plans; see "Defined Benefit Plan"). ERISA also established minimum standards for welfare benefit (including health) plans.

> **NOTE**
>
> It is important to note that the private industry plans that ERISA is designed to regulate are _voluntary_. ERISA does not require private industry employers to establish any pension or health plans. It does, however, impose minimum standards on those employers who choose to do so—all in the interest of protecting plan participants and their beneficiaries.

If you have must follow ERISA

A Few Words About Vesting: Cliff and Graded

Vesting is the process by which an employee earns a nonforfeitable right to the employer's contribution of his or her defined benefit/defined contribution plan. Organizations can choose between two vesting options for defined benefits and defined contribution plans: cliff vesting or graded vesting.

In 2002, separate vesting rules were enacted for plans that provided for matching employer contributions, such as 401(k) plans, as shown in Table 6.1.

TABLE 6.1   Vesting Schedule for Defined Benefit/Defined Contribution Plans as of 2002

	401(k) Plans*	All Other DB and DC Plans**
Cliff Vesting	100% after 3 years	100% after 5 years
Graded Vesting	20% after 2 years	20% after 3 years
	40% after 3 years	40% after 4 years
	60% after 4 years	60% after 5 years
	80% after 5 years	80% after 6 years
	100% after 6 years	100% after 7 years

Participants are always 100% vested in their own contributions.
*Includes other plans with matching contributions.
**Includes plans without employer matching contributions, such as profit-sharing arrangements.

The Protective Nature of ERISA

The safeguards established by ERISA have a strong, but not exclusive, focus on protecting participants with respect to the financial dimensions of plans. Here are two examples of requirements established by ERISA that demonstrate this effort to protect participants:

> ▶ _Under ERISA, participants must be provided with plan information, specifically about the features and funding of the plan_—For instance, when an employee (or beneficiary) becomes a participant in a retirement plan that is covered under ERISA, he or she is entitled to receive a summary plan description (SPD), at no cost, from the plan administrator. The SPD describes what the plan provides and how it operates. It also provides information relative to when an employee can begin to participate in the plan, how service and benefits are calculated, when benefits becomes vested,

when and in what form benefits are paid, and how to file a claim for benefits. In addition to the SPD, the plan administrator must automatically provide participants with a copy of the plan's summary annual financial report, which includes the same information that employers are required to file with the government on Form 5500.

EXAM ALERT

Be aware of ERISA participation rules for defined benefit and defined contribution plans. In general, an employee must be allowed to participate in a qualified plan after meeting the following requirements:

▶ *The employee is at least 21 years old*—Note that an employee can be excluded for not having reached a minimum age (which cannot exceed age 21) but cannot be excluded for having reached a maximum age. In other words, no matter how old an employee is, he or she can still—and always—participate in the plan.

▶ *The employee has at least one year of service*—For qualified plans, a year of service is generally 1,000 hours of service performed during the plan year. Employees who do not perform 1,000 hours of service are not considered to have performed one year of service, even if services were performed for a 12-month period. (Note: For plans other than 401(k), this requirement is two years, as long as the plan has fully vested after not more than two years of service.)

An employer may, however, choose to implement less-restrictive eligibility requirements, such as a minimum age requirement that is younger than 21 or a service requirement of less than one year.

▶ *ERISA provides fiduciary responsibilities for those who manage and control plan assets*— ERISA establishes fiduciary responsibility for "persons or entities who exercise discretionary control or authority over plan management or plan assets, have discretionary authority or responsibility for the administration of a plan, or provide investment advice to a plan for compensation or have any authority or responsibility to do so are subject to fiduciary responsibilities" (www.dol.gov). Plan fiduciaries could include, for example, plan trustees, plan administrators, and members of a plan's investment committee.

Fiduciaries are charged with running the plan(s) for which they are responsible solely in the interest of participants and beneficiaries. They must ensure that the sole purpose of the plan is—and remains—providing benefits to participants and beneficiaries and paying plan expenses.

Fiduciaries must also act with "skill, care, prudence, and diligence." For instance, they must protect plan participants by diversifying plan investments (in other words, just like any of us, they can't keep all of their financial "eggs in one basket"). In addition, they must follow the terms of plan documents to the extent that those terms are consistent with ERISA. They also must avoid conflicts of interest—and, many would argue, even the possibility of an appearance of a conflict of interest (the same standard to which HR professionals should hold themselves, as well).

All of this may sound simple—perhaps as though it should be common sense. Common sense, however, is often somewhat uncommon. All it takes is a quick scan of recent headlines trumpeting the news of unethical behavior and defunct pension plans to appreciate the fact that fiduciary responsibility is not something to be taken for granted. According to the Employment Benefits Security Administration (EBSA), ERISA enforcement yielded the following results, as shown in Table 6.2.

TABLE 6.2   ERISA Enforcement

Latest Enforcement Statistics	FY 2002	FY 2003	FY 2004
Prohibited Transactions Corrected	$398M	$460M	$2388.3M
Plan Assets Restored	$189.7M	$169.8M	$199.7M
Participant Benefits Restored	$125.3M	$105.4M	$47.8M
Plan Assets Protected	$168.2M	$662.1M	$141.6M
Voluntary Fiduciary Correction Program	$1.9M	$8.7M	$264.6M
Total Monetary Results	$883M	$1.4B	$3042M
Individuals Indicted	134	137	121

A sample of civil violations included

▶ Failing to operate the plan prudently and for the exclusive benefit of participants.

▶ Using plan assets to benefit certain related parties to the plan, including the plan administrator, the plan sponsor, and parties related to these individuals.

▶ Failing to properly value plan assets at their current fair market value, or to hold plan assets in trust.

▶ Failing to follow the terms of the plan (unless inconsistent with ERISA).

▶ Failing to properly select and monitor service providers.

▶ Taking adverse action against an individual for exercising his or her rights under the plan (for example, being fired, fined, or otherwise being discriminated against).

CAUTION

Plan administrators can be held personally liable for losses that result from breaching their fiduciary responsibility.

NOTE

ERISA also requires plans to establish a grievance and appeals process for participants and gives participants the right to sue for benefits and for breaches of fiduciary duty.

Administrative Responsibility for ERISA

Administrative responsibility for enforcement of ERISA is divided among three government agencies:

▶ *IRS*—The IRS focuses on tax-related dimensions of ERISA.

▶ *DOL*—Within the DOL, ESBA focuses on fiduciary responsibility and transactions that are prohibited by ERISA. Within the DOL, Employee Benefits Security

Administration is responsible for administering and enforcing the fiduciary, reporting, and disclosure provisions of ERISA.

▶ *Pension Benefit Guaranty Corporation (PBGC)*—The PBGC—a government corporation created by ERISA—functions as an insurer that provides a minimum guaranteed benefit for certain pension plans. PBGC protects participants in most defined benefit plans and cash balance plans (within certain limitations). So, for instance, if a covered plan is terminated, PBGC ensures that participants will receive payment of certain benefits.

PBGC is funded by insurance premiums that are paid by plan sponsors—not by general tax dollars. Funding also comes from investment income, assets from underfunded pension plans it has taken over, and recoveries from companies formerly responsible for those plans.

> **EXAM ALERT**
>
> ERISA is highly detailed and complex. If you do not have recent, in-depth, and first-hand experience with the application of ERISA, be sure to dig deeper. Be familiar with the rules under ERISA, the enforcement of ERISA, administrative requirements placed on employers by ERISA, the role of the PBGC, vesting guidelines, and so on.

Retirement Equity Act (REA), 1984

The Retirement Equity Act (REA), an amendment to ERISA, incorporated a number of key revisions, many of which addressed the concerns of former (in the event of divorce) and surviving (in the event of death) spouses. Specifically, REA enacted a number of important provisions, seven of which are that the REA

1. Lowered the minimum age requirement for pension plan participation.

2. Increased the years of service that "count" for vesting purposes.

3. Allowed for longer breaks in service (with respect to vesting rules).

4. Prohibited plans from counting maternity and paternity leaves as breaks in service for participation and vesting purposes.

5. Required qualified pension plans to provide automatic survivor benefits and allow for waiver of survivor benefits only with the consent of the participant and the spouse.

6. Clarified that pension plans may obey certain qualified domestic relations (court) orders (QDROs) requiring them to make benefit payments to a participant's former spouse (or another alternative payee) without violating ERISA's prohibitions against assignment or alienation of benefits.

7. Expanded the definition of accrued benefits that are protected against reduction.

Consolidated Omnibus Budget Reconciliation Act (COBRA), 1985

The Consolidated Omnibus Budget Reconciliation Act (COBRA) is technically an amendment to Title I of ERISA and is thus administered by EBSA. COBRA requires employers who employed 20 or more people during the prior year to offer continuation of group health care coverage to employees and their family members who experience certain "qualifying events"—events that would have otherwise resulted in the discontinuation of their health insurance benefits.

COBRA places certain requirements on plan participants who want to extend coverage, and it places certain requirements on the plan provider—in particular with respect to notification requirements.

COBRA Qualifying Events

Employees, their spouses, and their dependent children can experience qualifying events that would immediately entitle them to continue group health insurance coverage under COBRA.

> **NOTE**
>
> Those who choose to extend coverage are responsible for paying the full cost of the health premium, plus a 2% administrative fee (if the plan sponsor chooses to charge one).

COBRA Qualifying "Life Events" for Employees

The following table describes the different type of life events that would trigger COBRA coverage, as well as the corresponding length of time that COBRA can be continued *for the employee*.

COBRA qualifying events for employees are shown in Table 6.3.

TABLE 6.3   COBRA Qualifying Events for Employees

COBRA Qualifying Event	Length of Continuation Coverage Eligibility
Voluntary or involuntary termination of the covered employee's employment for any reason other than gross misconduct	18 months
Reduction in the hours worked by the covered employee	18 months

COBRA Qualifying "Life Events" for Employees' Spouses

The following table describes the different type of life events that would trigger COBRA coverage, as well as the corresponding length of time that COBRA can be continued *for the employee's spouse*.

COBRA qualifying events for employees' spouses are shown in Table 6.4.

TABLE 6.4   COBRA Qualifying Events for Employees' Spouses

COBRA Qualifying Event	Length of Continuation Coverage Eligibility
Voluntary or involuntary termination of the covered employee's employment for any reason other than gross misconduct	18 months
Reduction in the hours worked by the covered employee	18 months
Covered employee's becoming entitled to Medicare	29 months
Divorce or legal separation of the covered employee	36 months
Death of the covered employee	36 months

COBRA Qualifying Events for Employees' Dependent Children

The following table describes the different type of life events that would trigger COBRA coverage, as well as the corresponding length of time that COBRA can be continued *for the employee's dependent children*.

COBRA qualifying events for employees' dependent children are shown in Table 6.5.

TABLE 6.5   COBRA Qualifying Events for Employees' Dependent Children

COBRA Qualifying Event	Length of Continuation Coverage Eligibility
Loss of dependent child status under the plan rules	18 months
Voluntary or involuntary termination of the covered employee's employment for any reason other than gross misconduct	18 months
Reduction in the hours worked by the covered employee	18 months
Covered employee's becoming entitled to Medicare	29 months
Divorce or legal separation of the covered employee	36 months
Death of the covered employee	36 months

NOTE

Extensions of the length of continuation coverage may be available under certain circumstances, such as when a second qualifying event occurs.

CAUTION

COBRA is *not* available to employees, their spouses, or their dependent children when an employee is terminated for gross misconduct.

Older Worker's Benefit Protection Act (OWBPA), 1990

The Older Worker's Benefit Protection Act (OWBPA), passed in 1990, is an amendment to the ADEA that makes it illegal to discriminate against older workers with respect to benefits or to target older workers for layoffs.

Title 2 of OWBPA prohibits individuals from waiving rights or claims under ADEA unless such a waiver is "knowing and voluntary." OWBPA established nine specific criteria for ensuring that such waivers are knowing and voluntary. One particularly important criterion states that employers must allow employees at least 21 days to consider any right-to-sue waivers that the employer offers in exchange for early retirement benefits.

Health Insurance Portability and Accountability Act (HIPAA), 1996

The Health Insurance Portability and Accountability Act (HIPAA) was a more recent amendment to ERISA. HIPAA has two main areas of focus: the security and portability of health care coverage, and privacy considerations.

Security and Portability of Health Care Coverage

One of HIPAA's two key purposes was to help workers experience greater security and portability with respect to health care coverage—even when an employee changes jobs. HIPAA also afforded significantly greater protections for employees who have or who have a family member with a preexisting medical condition.

NOTE

Under HIPAA, a preexisting condition is defined as one for which medical advice, diagnosis, care, or treatment was recommended or received during the 6-month period prior to an individual's enrollment date.

Under HIPAA, in the worst-case scenario, employees (or their family members) with preexisting health conditions can have those conditions excluded from coverage for no more than 12 months (18 months for late enrollees). If an employee maintains health coverage continuously, he or she can reduce or even eliminate this period of exclusion.

HIPAA also prohibited employers from denying certain employees coverage—or from charging them higher premiums—because of preexisting health conditions. HIPAA affords protection to employers, as well, by mandating that health insurance providers must renew coverage for employers (as long as premium payments are made).

HIPAA Privacy Rule

HIPAA also addresses the issue of privacy for patients and health-care consumers. Although this rule is not specifically directed at employers, employers who offer group health insurance to employees may be considered a "covered entity" and thus be required to comply with HIPAA's privacy rule.

The primary purpose of the HIPAA privacy rule is to protect patients and other consumers of health care services from the unauthorized disclosure of any personally identifiable health information (also referred to as *protected health information*, or *PHI*).

Health information is considered to be personally identifiable if it relates to a specifically identifiable individual. The following items would generally be considered PHI (whether communicated electronically, on paper, or verbally):

- ▶ Health care claims or health care encounter information, such as documentation of doctor's visits and notes made by physicians and other provider staff

- ▶ Health care payment and remittance advice

- ▶ Coordination of health care benefits

- ▶ Health care claim status

- ▶ Enrollment and disenrollment in a health plan

- ▶ Eligibility for a health plan

- ▶ Health plan premium payments

- ▶ Referral certifications and authorization

- ▶ First report of injury

- ▶ Health claims attachments

If it is determined that an employer is a "covered entity" under the HIPPA privacy rule, the employer would need to take specific actions, some of which would include

- ▶ Enact written PHI privacy procedures.

- ▶ Designate a privacy officer.

- ▶ Require business associates to sign agreements stating that they will respect the confidentiality of PHI.

- ▶ Train all employees in HIPAA privacy rule requirements.

- ▶ Establish a complaint handling and resolution process for issues related to the HIPAA privacy rule.

- ▶ Ensure that PHI is not used for making any employment-related decisions.

EXAM ALERT

Like ERISA and COBRA, HIPAA is a highly complex and involved law. Don't let the apparent simplicity of the information presented here mislead you; it's necessary to dig much deeper to truly understand the nuances and subtleties of this law.

CAUTION

Employers should consult with counsel relative to compliance with the HIPAA privacy rule.

Mental Health Parity Act (MHPA), 1996

The Mental Health Parity Act (MHPA) prohibits group health plans providers, insurance companies, and HMOs that offer mental health benefits from setting annual or lifetime dollar limits on mental health benefits that are lower than any such dollar limits for medical and surgical benefits. This means that plans that don't impose annual or lifetime monetary caps on medical and surgical benefits *cannot* impose annual or lifetime caps on mental health benefits, either (benefits for substance abuse or chemical dependency are exempted). MHPA is under the jurisdiction of the Departments of Labor, Treasury, and Health and Human Services.

> **NOTE**
>
> MHPA *does not require* health plans to offer mental health benefits. It only applies to plans that voluntarily choose to offer mental health benefits.

Under MHPA, plans can still dictate/define the terms and conditions of benefits provided under mental health plans (for instance, cost sharing, limits on the number of visits or days of coverage, and so forth).

There are certain circumstances under which plan providers that offer mental health benefits are exempt from MHPA, including

- ▶ Small employers who have fewer than 51 employees

- ▶ Any group health plan whose costs increase 1% or more because of the application of MHPA's requirements (the increased cost exemption must be based on actual claims data, not on an increase in insurance premiums)

Sarbanes-Oxley Act (SOX), 2002

The Sarbanes-Oxley Act (SOX) was created in the wake of huge corporate accounting scandals, including Enron and Tyco, to name just two. Designed to protect investors, SOX enacted reforms designed to enhance corporate responsibility and financial disclosures and to combat corporate and accounting fraud. For more information on the Sarbanes-Oxley Act, see Chapter 8, "Risk Management." There are a number of SOX provisions that HR professionals needs to be particularly concerned with, four of which are

- ▶ Prohibition against insider trading during certain pension plan blackout periods—section 306(a).

- ▶ Requirement that plan administrators must provide 30-day written notice in advance of blackout periods to individual account plan participants and beneficiaries—section 306(b).

▸ Requirement to disclose whether the company has adopted a code of ethics that applies to the company's key officers (at a minimum, this code must apply to the company's principal executive officer, principal financial officer, principal accounting officer or controller, or persons performing similar functions)—section 406.

▸ Establishment of whistleblower protection in a wide variety of situations for employees who report fraud against shareholders—section 806(a).

REVIEW BREAK

At this point, we've completed a review of the major benefits-related laws that govern—rather than created—voluntary benefits programs. As you continue your review and test preparation, be sure to review other benefits-related laws that are less prominent than these (COBRA, Tax Reform Act, and so on).

Now let's turn our attention to laws that actually created benefits programs—optional benefits programs, as well as mandatory benefits programs.

Related Legislation: Benefits—Laws That Created Mandatory and Optional Benefits Programs

Some of the laws that we'll look at created benefits programs that are optional, whereas others created benefits programs that are mandatory.

Worker's Compensation—*Mandatory Benefit Program*

Worker's compensation (also known as "worker's comp") laws were adopted at the state level between 1911 and 1940. These laws were designed to provide medical care to injured employees and death benefits to families of those who lost their lives in the performance of their jobs. Worker's comp is a "no fault" system—injured workers receive medical and/or compensation benefits regardless of who caused the injury or death.

Social Security Act (SSA), 1935—*Mandatory Benefit Program*

In August of 1935, President Franklin D. Roosevelt signed the Social Security Act into law. Social security is a social insurance program (although some would define it differently) that is funded through payroll taxes. Approximately 96% of all workers are covered under the Social Security Act.

> **NOTE**
>
> Since the program's inception, social security has been designed so that employers and the workers they employ contribute equal dollar amounts each pay period (originally 2% of the first $3,000 of the employee's earnings. That cap, along with that percentage, has been raised significantly over the decades). Independent contractors and self-employed individuals are required to pay both the employer and the employee portions.

Social security is also known as the Old Age, Survivors, and Disability Insurance program (OASDI), in reference to its three primary components, which are now referred to as retirement income, disability benefits, and survivor's benefits.

Retirement Income

Workers earn credits toward social security benefits. As of 2005, workers earned one credit for each $920 in earnings—up to a maximum of four credits per year. (The amount of money that a worker must make to earn one credit generally increases each year, but the four-credit-per-year maximum remains the same.) Workers born in 1929 or later need 40 credits to earn retirement benefits. Younger people need fewer credits to be eligible for disability benefits or for their family members to be eligible for survivors' benefits.

Social security tracks each worker's earnings throughout his or her lifetime. It is the employee's record of earnings—combined with the age at which he or she retires—that will determine the monetary amount of each worker's monthly benefit.

> **NOTE**
>
> The earliest age at which a worker can retire and still receive benefits is 62. These benefits, however, are reduced from what they would have been if the worker had worked until his or her full retirement age. Full retirement age ranges between age 65 (for those who were born in 1937 or earlier) and age 67 (for those who were born in 1960 or later). Workers who work beyond their full retirement age will increase their monthly retirement—the longer they work past their full retirement age, the higher their monthly retirement income will be (everyone, however, must start receiving retirement benefits at the age of 70—including individuals who continue to work).

Disability Benefits

Disability benefits were added to the social security program in 1956. Under social security, workers who become "totally disabled" can receive benefits under social security. Total disability, however, can be a fairly strict standard to meet. Total disability cannot begin until after five full calendar months of continuous disability. Even then, to be considered totally disabled, the worker must be unable to continue in his or her previous job and unable to adjust to other work; in addition, the disability must be expected to last for at least one year or to result in the worker's death.

In addition to being deemed to have a total disability, the disability eligibility formula requires that the worker has earned a certain number of credits (during his or her entire working life), and that the worker must have earned a certain number of credits within the 10 years preceding the disability (younger workers who haven't had a chance to earn as many credits are held to more lenient requirements than older workers). Similar to the way in which retirement benefits are calculated, the actual disability benefit that the worker would receive depends on the worker's age and how many credits the worker has earned.

Survivors' Benefits

When a person who has worked and paid social security taxes dies, his or her family members may be eligible to receive survivors' benefits. Depending on the person's age at the time of death, up to 10 years of work is needed for survivors to be eligible for benefits.

As described at www.ssa.gov/pubs, social security survivors' benefits can be paid under the following conditions:

► Your widow or widower may be able to receive full benefits at age 65 if born before January 1, 1940. (The age to receive full benefits is gradually increasing to age 67 for widows and widowers born January 2, 1940, or later.) Reduced widow or widower benefits can be received as early as age 60. If your surviving spouse is disabled, benefits can begin as early as age 50.

► Your widow or widower can receive benefits at any age if she or he takes care of your child who is entitled to a child's benefit and is age 16 or younger or who is disabled.

► Your unmarried children who are under age 18 (or up to age 19 if they are attending elementary or secondary school full-time) also can receive benefits. Your children can get benefits at any age if they were disabled before age 22 and remain disabled. Under certain circumstances, benefits also can be paid to your stepchildren, grandchildren, or adopted children.

► Your dependent parents can receive benefits if they are age 62 or older. (For your parents to qualify as dependents, you would have had to provide at least one-half of their support.)

Medicare

Passed in 1965 as an amendment to the Social Security Act, Medicare provides hospital and medical insurance for the elderly and people with disabilities.

There are four parts to Medicare: hospital insurance (sometimes called Part A), medical insurance (sometimes called Part B), Medicare offered through private health insurance companies (Part C), and prescription benefits (sometimes called Part D).

> **NOTE**
>
> Neither Part A nor Part B pays for all of a covered person's medical costs. In addition, the program contains deductibles and copays (payments due from the covered individual).

Medicare—Part A: Hospital Insurance

Part A helps pay for inpatient hospital care, skilled nursing care, and other services.

People age 65 or older are eligible for benefits under Part A of Medicare if they meet *any* of the following criteria:

- ▸ Receive social security or railroad retirement benefits
- ▸ Are not getting social security or railroad retirement benefits, but have worked long enough to be eligible for them
- ▸ Would be entitled to social security benefits based on a spouse's (or divorced spouse's) work record
- ▸ Worked long enough in a federal, state, or local government job to be insured for Medicare

People under age 65 are eligible for Part A Medicare benefits if they experience certain disabilities (for instance, Lou Gehrig's disease, permanent kidney failure, and so on) and meet other specified criteria (for instance, having worked long enough to receive disability benefits under social security).

Medicare Medical Insurance (Also Known as Part B)

Part B helps pay items such as doctor's fees, outpatient hospital visits, and other medical services and supplies.

Almost anyone who is 65 or older *or* who is under 65 but eligible for hospital insurance can enroll for Medicare medical insurance by paying a monthly premium. People over age 65 don't need any social security or government work credits for this part of Medicare.

Medicare Part C: Medicare Offered Through Private Health Insurance Companies

Part C of Medicare is available to persons who are eligible for Part A and enrolled in Part B. It is a program through which private health insurance companies can contract with the federal government to offer Medicare benefits through their own policies.

Medicare Prescription Benefits (Also Known as Part D)

In December of 2003, the Medicare Prescription Drug, Improvement, and Modernization Act (also known as the Medicare Modernization Act, or MMA) was signed into law. This law, which became effective on January 1, 2006, added prescription drug benefits for all individuals eligible for Medicare Part A and enrolled in Medicare Part B.

Although additional information about this plan is available at www.medicare.gov, be certain to familiarize yourself with (at least) basic information about this important new protection (as provided at www.medicare.gov):

What is Medicare prescription drug coverage?

Medicare prescription drug coverage is insurance that covers both brand-name and generic prescription drugs at participating pharmacies in your area. Medicare prescription drug coverage provides protection for people who have very high drug costs or from unexpected prescription drug bills in the future.

Who can get Medicare prescription drug coverage?

Everyone with Medicare is eligible for this coverage, regardless of income and resources, health status, or current prescription expenses.

When can I get Medicare prescription drug coverage?

You may sign up when you first become eligible for Medicare (three months before the month you turn age 65 until three months after you turn age 65). If you get Medicare due to a disability, you can join from three months before to three months after your 25th month of cash disability payments. If you don't sign up when you are first eligible, you may pay a penalty. If you didn't join when you were first eligible, your next opportunity to enroll will be from November 15, 2007 to December 31, 2007.

How does Medicare prescription drug coverage work?

Your decision about Medicare prescription drug coverage depends on the kind of health care coverage you have now. There are two ways to get Medicare prescription drug coverage. You can join a Medicare prescription drug plan or you can join a Medicare Advantage Plan or other Medicare Health Plan that offers drug coverage.

Whatever plan you choose, Medicare drug coverage will help you by covering brand-name and generic drugs at pharmacies that are convenient for you.

Like other insurance, if you join, generally you will pay a monthly premium, which varies by plan, and a yearly deductible (between $0–$265 in 2007). You will also pay a part of the cost of your prescriptions, including a payment or coinsurance. Costs will vary depending on which drug plan you choose. Some plans may offer more coverage and additional drugs for a higher monthly premium. If you have limited income and resources, and you qualify for extra help, you may not have to pay a premium or deductible. You can apply or get more information about the extra help by calling Social Security at 1-800-772-1213 (TTY 1–800–325–0778) or visiting www.socialsecurity.gov.

Unemployment Insurance—*Mandatory Benefit Program*

The Federal-State Unemployment Insurance Program was established as part of the federal Social Security Act of 1935 and is administered at the state level. Federal rules are developed by the DOL.

In general, the maximum period for receiving benefits is 26 weeks, although the federal government may (and sometimes does) choose to extend the benefit period during difficult economic times.

Unemployment insurance is funded through employer taxes (except in three states, where employees contribute as well). Unemployment insurance is intended to help employees financially "bridge" the time between positions, when a position has been lost through no fault of their own.

Unemployment Insurance—Eligibility

There are a number of requirements for establishing eligibility, two of which are

- ▶ You must meet the state requirements for wages earned or time worked during an established (one year) period of time referred to as a *base period*. (In most states, this is usually the first four out of the last five completed calendar quarters prior to the time when your claim is filed.)

- ▶ It must be determined that you were unemployed through no fault of your own (as determined under state law) and meet other eligibility requirements of state law.

Unemployment benefits are subject to federal income taxes.

Revenue Act, 1978—*Optional Benefit Program*

The Revenue Act brought with it many changes, including a reduction in individual income taxes, a reduction in corporate taxes, and so on. It also added two sections to the tax code that essentially resulted in the creation of two new—and ultimately very important—employee benefits.

Section 125

Section 125 created flexible benefits plans (often referred to as "cafeteria" plans). Section 125 plans can help employers as well as employees save money by reducing payroll taxes.

Before looking at the three types of Section 125 plans, let's consider some of the reasons that an organization might have for implementing a section 125 plan.

Reasons for Considering Section 125 Plans

Thinking back to where we started in this chapter, recall that each organization's total compensation program communicates a great deal to employees—and to potential employees—about what the organization values. As such, Section 125 plans might be one way of communicating some of the following messages (to the degree they are appropriate) to employees:

- ▶ "*We recognize that not everyone's life is the same, and that everyone has different needs. Because of that, different employees may want to allocate—or spend—the money they earn in different ways.*" (Section 125 plans are one way to acknowledge and support these different and changing employee needs.)

- ▶ "*When it comes to benefits, we may not always know what's best for you, but you do. In this sense, our goal becomes to give you tools and information with which* you *can make benefits-related decisions that are right for* you.*"

> ▶ *"We know you have a choice regarding the company for which you will work. Every day that you choose to remain employed with us, you are casting a vote. We know this, and we appreciate it. Giving you some choice regarding the benefits you select is one way we can say 'thanks'."*

Types of Cafeteria Plans

There are three types of cafeteria plans:

▶ *Premium Only Plans (POPs)*—With POPs, the simplest and most transparent (from employees' perspectives) of the three Section 125 plans, employees pay for their portion of certain insurance premiums (health, dental, and so on) on a pretax basis. The net effect is that each employee's taxable income is reduced, which is how employers and employees can reduce taxes—and save money.

▶ *Flexible Spending Accounts (FSAs)*—FSAs take POPs one step further. With FSAs, employees can set aside pretax dollars to pay for medical expenses that are not covered by insurance. FSAs can also be set up for dependent care. Employees decide how much money to set aside for the following year, and that amount is automatically deducted from the employee's pay on a pretax basis. After incurring and paying for eligible expenses, employees apply for reimbursement from the FSA.

> **EXAM ALERT**
>
> FSAs offer distinct advantages as well as potentially distinct disadvantages for employers as well as for employees. Look into the rules governing FSAs before instituting this plan at your organization—and before taking the PHR exam.

▶ *Full Cafeteria Plans*—Employers who offer full cafeteria plans provide their employees with a specific amount of money they can use to pick and choose from a variety of benefits.

Although they offer distinct advantages, especially for employees, full cafeteria plans are the most administratively burdensome of the three Section 125 options.

Section 401(k)

The second employee benefit that was created by the Revenue Act is the 401(k) plan. A type of defined contribution plan, 401(k) plans allow employees to set aside pretax dollars to save for their retirement. This can be done through salary deduction, which may or may not be matched in part or (less frequently) in whole by employer contributions. 401(k) dollars can also be set aside through deferral of profit-sharing income.

CAUTION

Like most benefits plans, 401(k)s are more complex than they might initially appear. This is particularly true because of the tax implications associated with 401(k)s. Be sure that your plan is in full compliance with government regulations, because lack of compliance can result in significant consequences, financial and otherwise.

EXAM ALERT

The IRS regulates 401(k) tax-related issues, such as maximum deduction amounts, nondiscrimination tests, and distribution rules. Be familiar with these rules and regulations because questions about them may appear on the PHR exam.

Family and Medical Leave Act (FMLA), 1993—*Mandatory Benefit Program*

The Family and Medical Leave Act (FMLA) (see www.dol.gov) entitles eligible employees (who work for covered employers) up to 12 weeks of unpaid, job-protected leave during any 12-month period for one or more of the following reasons:

- ▶ For the birth and care of the newborn child of the employee

- ▶ For placement with the employee of a son or daughter for adoption or foster care

- ▶ To care for an immediate family member (spouse, child, or parent) with a serious health condition

- ▶ To take medical leave when the employee is unable to work because of a serious health condition

Under some circumstances, leave can be taken intermittently.

The FMLA is administered and enforced by the DOL.

Employee Eligibility for FMLA

To be eligible to take FMLA leave, an employee must

- ▶ Work for a covered employer (public agencies, state, local, and federal employers, local education agencies [schools], and private-sector employers with 50 or more employees)

- ▶ Have worked for the employer for a total of at least 12 months (this time does not have to have been uninterrupted)

- ▶ Have worked at least 1,250 hours over the previous 12 months

- ▶ Work at a location in the United States or in any territory or possession of the United States where at least 50 employees are employed by the employer within 75 miles

FMLA—Employer Requirements

As described at www.dol.gov, the FMLA places specific requirements upon employers before and during FMLA leaves. Specific requirements pertain to

- Posting requirements
- Notifying employees of their rights under FMLA
- Designating use of leave as FMLA leave
- Maintaining group health benefits
- Restoring an employee to his or her original job, or to an equivalent job with equivalent pay, benefits, and other terms and conditions of employment

According to the DOL, all covered employers are required to display and keep displayed a poster summarizing the major provisions of the FMLA and telling employees how to file a complaint. The poster must be displayed in a conspicuous place where employees and applicants for employment can see it—even if there are no FMLA-eligible employees at a particular location. The following is the DOL-approved poster, as shown in Figure 6.2.

FMLA—Employee Requirements

Employees are also subject to certain requirements under the FMLA:

- 30-day advance notice (when foreseeable and practicable).
- Employers may also require employees to provide the following:
    - Medical certification.
    - Second or third medical opinions (at the employer's expense) and periodic recertification.
    - Periodic reports during FMLA leave regarding the employee's status and intent to return to work.
    - For intermittent leaves, employees must try to "work around" the needs of the workplace.

FMLA Specific Terms

There are many terms used in FMLA, the definitions of which need to be carefully reviewed to ensure compliance with the law (and solid preparation for the PHR exam). For instance, be certain that you are familiar with the following terms:

- Job-protected leave
- 12-month period
- Health care provider
- Key employee
- In loco parentis

Your Rights
under the
Family and Medical Leave Act of 1993

FMLA requires covered employers to provide up to 12 weeks of unpaid, job-protected leave to "eligible" employees for certain family and medical reasons. Employees are eligible if they have worked for their employer for at least one year, and for 1,250 hours over the previous 12 months, and if there are at least 50 employees within 75 miles. The FMLA permits employees to take leave on an intermittent basis or to work a reduced schedule under certain circumstances.

Reasons for Taking Leave:

Unpaid leave must be granted for *any* of the following reasons:

- to care for the employee's child after birth, or placement for adoption or foster care;
- to care for the employee's spouse, son or daughter, or parent who has a serious health condition; or
- for a serious health condition that makes the employee unable to perform the employee's job.

At the employee's or employer's option, certain kinds of *paid* leave may be substituted for unpaid leave.

Advance Notice and Medical Certification:

The employee may be required to provide advance leave notice and medical certification. Taking of leave may be denied if requirements are not met.

- The employee ordinarily must provide 30 days advance notice when the leave is "foreseeable."
- An employer may require medical certification to support a request for leave because of a serious health condition, and may require second or third opinions (at the employer's expense) and a fitness for duty report to return to work.

Job Benefits and Protection:

- For the duration of FMLA leave, the employer must maintain the employee's health coverage under any "group health plan."

- Upon return from FMLA leave, most employees must be restored to their original or equivalent positions with equivalent pay, benefits, and other employment terms.
- The use of FMLA leave cannot result in the loss of any employment benefit that accrued prior to the start of an employee's leave.

Unlawful Acts by Employers:

FMLA makes it unlawful for any employer to:
- interfere with, restrain, or deny the exercise of any right provided under FMLA:
- discharge or discriminate against any person for opposing any practice made unlawful by FMLA or for involvement in any proceeding under or relating to FMLA.

Enforcement:

- The U.S. Department of Labor is authorized to investigate and resolve complaints of violations.
- An eligible employee may bring a civil action against an employer for violations.

FMLA does not affect any Federal or State law prohibiting discrimination, or supersede any State or local law or collective bargaining agreement which provides greater family or medical leave rights.

For Additional Information:

If you have access to the Internet visit our FMLA website: **http://www.dol.gov/esa/whd/fmla.** To locate your nearest Wage-Hour Office, telephone our Wage-Hour toll-free information and help line at 1-866-4USWAGE (1-866-487-9243): a customer service representative is available to assist you with referral information from 8am to 5pm **in your time zone;** or log onto our Home Page at **http://www.wagehour.dol.gov.**

U.S. Department of Labor
Employment Standards Administration
Wage and Hour Division
Washington, D.C. 20210

WH Publication 1420
Revised August 2001

*U.S. GOVERNMENT PRINTING OFFICE 2001-476-344/49051

FIGURE 6.2 Family Leave Act of 1993 poster.

As an example of the complexity and the criticality of understanding the language of the FMLA, let's look at one particular term, "serious health condition."

Serious Health Conditions

FMLA defines a serious health condition as

An illness, injury, impairment, or physical or mental condition that involves either:

▶ Any period of incapacity or treatment connected with inpatient care (that is, an overnight stay) in a hospital, hospice, or residential medical-care facility, and any period of incapacity or subsequent treatment in connection with such inpatient care

or

▶ Continuing treatment by a health care provider, which includes any period of incapacity (that is, inability to work, attend school, or perform other regular daily activities) because of any of the following:

1. A health condition (including treatment therefore, or recovery therefrom) lasting more than three consecutive days, and any subsequent treatment or period of incapacity relating to the same condition, that also includes either of the following:

   ▶ Treatment two or more times by or under the supervision of a health care provider

   ▶ One treatment by a health care provider with a continuing regimen of treatment

2. Pregnancy or prenatal care. A visit to the health care provider is not necessary for each absence.

3. A chronic serious health condition that continues over an extended period of time, requires periodic visits to a health care provider, and may involve occasional episodes of incapacity (for example, asthma, diabetes). A visit to a health care provider is not necessary for each absence.

4. A permanent or long-term condition for which treatment may not be effective (for example, Alzheimer's, a severe stroke, terminal cancer). Only supervision by a health care provider is required, rather than active treatment.

5. Any absences to receive multiple treatments for restorative surgery or for a condition that would likely result in a period of incapacity of more than three days if not treated (for example, chemotherapy or radiation treatments for cancer).

The paradox of the term "serious health condition" (and so many other FMLA terms) is that, despite the large amount of effort and large number of words dedicated to defining it, in practice its meaning remains somewhat ambiguous. As with all other aspects of the FMLA, HR-related law, and the HR profession in general, a significant amount of analysis (coupled with sound judgment and careful monitoring of relevant court interpretations) is essential.

NOTE

You may also want to consider reviewing the DOL's Report on the Request for Information relative to the FMLA, published in mid-2007. As stated in the executive summary of this report:

"After nearly fourteen years of experience implementing and administering the new law, the Department's Employment Standards Administration/Wage and Hour Division undertook a review of the FMLA regulations, culminating in the publication of a Request for Information ("RFI") on December 1, 2006. The RFI asked the public to assist the Department by furnishing information about their experiences with FMLA and comments on the effectiveness of the current FMLA regulations."

The RFI generated a very heavy public response from employers as well as from employees. The final report can be viewed at http://www.dol.gov/esa/whd/FMLA2007Report/2007FinalReport.pdf.

Uniformed Services Employment and Reemployment Rights Act (USERRA), 1994—*Mandatory Benefit Program*

The Uniformed Services Employment and Reemployment Rights Act (USERRA) provides reinforcement rights for individuals who miss work because of "service in the uniformed services," which is defined as voluntary or involuntary uniformed service.

Employers are required to inform their employees of their rights under USERRA. This requirement can be met by displaying the following poster, as shown in Figure 6.3, that clearly outlines employees' rights and obligations under USERRA.

NOTE

Be aware of special USERRA rules that apply for returning reservists. Specifically, according to a 2002 DOL News Release:

National Guard and reservists returning to civilian occupations after serving in support of President Bush's post-Sept. 11 national emergency declaration should have their active duty time counted toward their eligibility to take time off from work under the Family and Medical Leave Act (FMLA). The Department of Labor has issued a memorandum that clarifies its position on the rights of returning uniformed service members to family and medical leave under the Uniformed Services Employment and Reemployment Rights Act. USERRA entitles returning service members to all the benefits of employment that they would have obtained if they had been continuously employed. Under ordinary circumstances, a worker becomes eligible for leave under the FMLA after working for a covered employer for at least 12 months, during which he or she completed at least 1,250 hours of work. The memorandum says that employers should count the months and hours that reservists or National Guards would have worked if they had not been called up for military service toward FMLA eligibility.

REVIEW BREAK

We've looked at laws—those that guide and regulate as well as those that create certain benefits. Now let's take a look at specific types of optional, or voluntary, benefits (which therefore, by definition, are not government mandated).

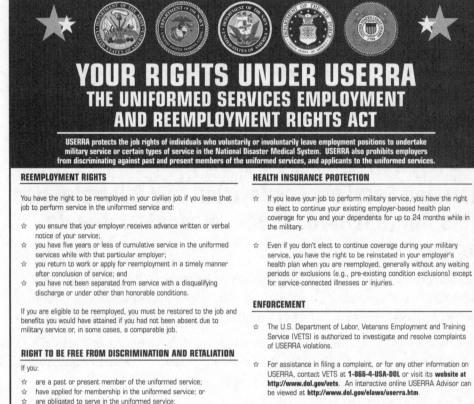

FIGURE 6.3 Employees' rights and obligations under USERRA poster.

Optional Benefits Programs

Let's now take a look at some of the different types of benefits programs organizations offer that are voluntary.

CAUTION

Voluntary benefits are ones that the organization freely chooses to offer, perhaps because those benefits are consistent with designing a total rewards package that is consistent with the organization's total rewards philosophy.

Retirement Plans

By definition, retirement plans "defer" income—and therefore defer the tax that must be paid on that money until it actually becomes income, which occurs at the time of distribution. Following are some examples of specific retirement plans.

Defined Benefit Plan

Defined benefit plans represent a more traditional type of pension plan, in which the employer shoulders the balance of the risk. This risk stems from the non-negotiable fact that defined benefit plans promise to pay the employee a specified monthly benefit at retirement. This "specified monthly benefit" could be expressed as an actual dollar amount, or it could be calculated through some sort of formula (this is the more common method). Either way, the PBGC protects participants in defined benefit plans by ensuring that, within certain limitations, the promised benefits will be paid.

NOTE

Defined benefit plans tend to be more advantageous to longer-term employees.

EXAM ALERT

Be familiar with some of the formulas that can be used to calculate defined benefit plan benefits. Examples could include

▶ Flat benefit times years of service

▶ Career average

▶ Final average earnings

One interesting, and slightly different, type of defined benefit plan is the *cash balance plan*. A cash balance plan is a defined benefit plan that expresses the promised benefit in terms of a stated account balance (similar to the way a defined contribution plan works). Most of the time, each participant's cash balance plan account is credited annually with a *pay credit* (the percentage of compensation that his or her employer contributes) and an *interest credit* (either a fixed or variable rate of interest).

Defined Contribution Plan

Unlike defined benefit plans, defined contribution plans do not "promise" a specific monthly benefit (or total benefit) at retirement. Instead, the employer and/or the employee contribute to the employee's individual retirement savings account. Those contributions are then invested—investments that can either make money or lose money. In this way, defined contribution plans shift the risk away from the employer (which is where it rests for defined benefit plans) and back to the employee.

> **NOTE**
>
> This "shift" may account for part of the reason why defined contribution plans are increasing in popularity, while defined benefit plans are decreasing in popularity (keep in mind that neither of these is legally mandated).

At the "end of the day" (meaning, at the time of retirement), what's there is there. No promises have been made, therefore no promises about total payouts can be broken. (This does not, of course, mean that the ERISA guidelines of fiduciary responsibility are waived—they absolutely apply to defined benefit plans as well as to defined contribution plans.)

> **NOTE**
>
> Defined contribution plans tend to be more advantageous to shorter-term employees.

Examples of defined contribution plans include 401(k) plans, employee stock ownership plans, and profit-sharing plans.

Employee Stock Ownership Plan (ESOP)

An employee stock ownership plan (ESOP) is a type of defined contribution plan in which investments to individual accounts are made primarily in the form of employer stock. ESOPs offer certain tax advantages to employers, as well as to employees.

Profit Sharing Plan

A profit sharing plan is a type of defined contribution plan under which the organization makes contributions to its employees' accounts. These contributions often come from profits, and thus also serve as an incentive to performance.

Simplified Employee Pension Plan (SEP)

A simplified employee pension plan (SEP) allows employers to make contributions on a tax-favored basis to individual retirement accounts (IRAs) that employees set up for this purpose.

Health and Welfare Benefits

Organizations can choose from a wide array of health and welfare benefits, a few of which are explored here.

Medical Insurance

Employers and employees can choose from several types of medical insurance plans.

Indemnity Insurance

The most traditional type of medical insurance plan, indemnity plans provide participants with (virtually) unrestricted choices relative to their doctors, hospitals, and other health care providers. Health care providers are paid a fee for the services they actually provide and perform. Hence, the more services that are provided, the greater the fees that will be paid. This is one reason why indemnity plans are usually one of the most expensive type of medical insurance programs from which employers and employees can choose.

Health Maintenance Organizations (HMOs)

Health maintenance organizations, or HMOs, offer a very different model of health care—one that is referred to as "managed care." One significant difference between HMOs and indemnity plans centers around "choice." While participant "choices" are nearly unlimited in indemnity plans, participant choices are more closely managed (and many would argue more limited) with HMOs.

For instance, with indemnity plans, participants make choices relative to which doctors they will go to and how often they will go. In an HMO, each participant chooses a primary care physician, or PCP, who serves as a "gatekeeper." Participants must see their PCPs first, and the PCP then decides whether to refer the patient to a specialist or for additional tests.

In this sense, HMOs truly do "manage" participants' health care experiences. There are advantages and disadvantages to this approach. Some would argue that HMOs are beneficial in that they emphasize preventive care and control health care costs. And because participants can change their PCP, there is still a critical element of choice inherent to the plan. In addition, HMOs provide a full range of health care, including doctor's visits, specialist services, hospitalization, surgical services, and so on.

Others would argue that HMOs are overly restrictive. With an HMO, a referral from a primary care physician is required before a participant can see a specialist or get any tests done. In addition to being administratively burdensome (and, at times, inconvenient), some would argue that this disempowers participants relative to their own personal health care choices.

Another concern relative to HMOs centers around *capitation*, the basis on which doctors are paid. What this means, essentially, is that each PCP is paid each month for every person who chooses that doctor to be his or her PCP—*not* for the actual amount of care that is provided. In short, providing more care won't generate more revenue—in fact, it dilutes the physician's earnings (not in terms of actual dollars, but in the sense that the physician gets paid the same amount of money for doing "more work"). Some individuals do not feel this is problematic, whereas others believe it incents physicians to provide patients with fewer services, or to spend less time with each patient.

Preferred Provider Organizations (PPOs)

A preferred provider organization (PPO) is a managed care health insurance plan that offers a network of health care providers who band together to offer services at a discounted rate to plan participants. PPOs resemble indemnity plans, in that network providers are paid when they render services and plan participants can choose which doctors they want to visit and when they want to visit them. Plan participants can also choose to avail themselves of doctors or other health care providers who are outside the network; however, the costs to the member will be higher than they would have been if the member had chosen a doctor within the network.

Point of Service (POS)

Point of service (POS) plans are a combination of the HMO and PPO managed care models. Like the PPO model, there is a network of physicians and health care providers who have agreed to provide services at a discounted rate. Like the HMO model, there is a gatekeeper—a primary care physician who must provide plan members with referrals to specialists and for other services. Unlike the HMO model, however, referrals can be made to physicians who are either inside or outside the network. Although out-of-network referrals will cost participants more, they are permissible.

Dental Insurance

Like medical insurance, dental insurance can be offered through an indemnity program, an HMO network, or a PPO network. There are also some specific categories of coverage within dental plans, each of which is likely to offer a different level of reimbursement.

Preventive Care

"*An ounce of prevention is worth a pound of cure*"—that adage is perhaps no more apparent than in dental care (with, of course, the possible exception of performance management—see Chapter 5). Preventive care includes such things as regular dental checkups, exams, cleanings, and sometimes X-rays. It is often reimbursed at 100% of cost (or at 100% of reasonable and customary (R&C) expenses), so as to encourage plan members to take advantage of measures that encourage good oral health and that potentially decrease long-term costs.

Restorative Care

Restorative care, as its name implies, refers to oral "repairs" that are usually of a relatively minor nature, such as cavities or root canals. The reimbursement for restorative care is generally less than the reimbursement rate for preventive care (perhaps 80% instead of 100%).

Major Restorative Care

For those readers who are thinking, "You think a root canal is *minor*?" please understand that "minor" is a relative term that is used to describe the degree of restoration that is required, not necessarily the degree of discomfort that is experienced. By comparison, major restorative care—which would be reimbursed at an even lower rate (perhaps 50%)—refers to things such as bridgework and crowns.

Orthodonture

Orthodonture—braces, headgear, retainers, and the like—is a benefit that is often reimbursed at 50%. Unlike the other types of dental insurance discussed previously, orthodonture is often subject to a lifetime cap—perhaps in the vicinity of $1,000–$1,500. Plan members who have multiple children (dependents under the age of 19) with multiple orthodontic challenges might find that they can burn through this benefit relatively quickly. It still, however, represents a significant savings over full-cost orthodonture and may be highly valued by that segment of your employee population with children to raise, palates to spread, and teeth to straighten.

Vision Coverage

Vision coverage is a little different from the other health and welfare benefits we've looked at so far. Unlike those other plans, an employer will typically offer vision coverage as a discount program (generally around 10%). Vision coverage generally includes items such as exams, contact lenses, and glasses.

Prescription Drug Coverage

As the cost of prescription drugs rises, prescription drug coverage is becoming an even more highly valued employee benefit. Some employers provide prescription drug coverage as part of their medical plan, whereas others provide this coverage under a separate plan. Plan members may be required to pay a copay, to purchase their prescriptions at certain pharmacies, to use generic drugs (when available), or to use mail-order services for maintenance drugs (prescriptions that are prescribed for chronic, or longer-term conditions, and that are taken on a regular, recurring basis). Even with these restrictions, prescription drug coverage can be a huge benefit to employees.

Life Insurance

Term life insurance is also considered to be a valuable benefit by many employees, as a way of ensuring that they can provide their beneficiaries and loved ones with income in the event of their deaths. Many employers offer a certain amount of life insurance at no cost to employees and offer optional supplemental life insurance, as well.

Long Term Disability Insurance

Long term disability (LTD) insurance replaces a designated percentage of an employee's income that is lost through illness or injury.

EXAM ALERT

In addition to being familiar with different types of health and welfare plans, be sure to familiarize yourself with various funding options for those plans. such as fully insured plans, partially insured plans, administrative services only (ASO) plans, third-party administrator (TPA) plans, and self-insured plans. It's equally important to be familiar with cost-shifting and cost-containment strategies and options.

Pay for Time Not Worked

As its name implies, *pay for time not worked* refers to situations in which employees receive compensation for sick days, vacation days, jury duty, personal time, designated holidays, floating holidays, bereavement leave, and the like.

> **NOTE**
>
> Pay for time not worked is a benefit that is highly valued by many employees, overused by some, and underused by others. "Free time" for employees, however, isn't free of charge to the organization. From the organization's perspective, pay for time not worked needs to be costed out just like any other benefit.

Work-Life Programs

The same can be said for work-life ("balance") programs. Programs such as flexible schedules, job sharing, telecommuting, and compressed work weeks can be a great advantage for employees, and a great way for employers to market themselves in the relevant labor market, as well. Still, don't institute any program without first conducting careful analysis and assessment (see "ADDIE: An Overview," in Chapter 5). Initiatives have to make business sense, and—ideally—should be sustainable for the foreseeable future. For although there are never any guarantees, it's not advisable to implement a program that might need to be revoked in the near time. When this happens, legitimate efforts at enhancing the workplace experience for employees can really backfire.

Chapter Summary

Compensation, benefits, and the synergies created by the combination of those two disciplines are both technically challenging and strategically impactful. Knowledge and insight in both of those areas is critical.

The specific areas we've looked at are

- Total Rewards Footing #1: Employee or independent contractor?

- Total Rewards Footing #2: Exempt or non-exempt?

- Total Rewards Footing #3: Compensation + Benefits = Total Compensation

- Related Legislation: Compensation

- Compensation: Job evaluation

- Compensation: Market pricing

- Compensation: Base pay and variable pay

- Compensation: Building and using pay structures

- Related Legislation—Benefits: Laws that regulate, govern, and guide optional benefits programs

- Related Legislation—Benefits: Laws that created mandatory and optional benefits programs

- Optional benefits programs

HR professionals can increase their value to the organization by enhancing their knowledge and skills in these areas—even if such knowledge and skills do not immediately appear to be relevant to our current "primary functions." In addition, this constitutes a crucial portion of the PHR exam. For that reason, start by learning what is included in this chapter, and then go beyond. The value that will accrue to you, and to your organization, is unquestionably worthwhile.

Key Terms

- Total rewards
- Total compensation
- Compensation
- Benefits
- Employee
- Independent contractor
- Exempt
- Non-exempt
- Fair Labor Standards Act (FLSA)

- Minimum wage
- Overtime
- FairPay
- Salary
- Primary duty
- Executive exemption
- Administrative exemption
- Learned professional exemption
- Creative professional exemption

- Computer employee exemption
- Outside sales exemption
- Highly compensated employee
- Safe harbor provisions
- Total compensation
- Relevant labor market
- Lead the market
- Lag the market
- Match the market
- Direct compensation
- Indirect compensation
- Davis-Bacon Act, 1931
- Walsh-Healey Public Contracts Act, 1936
- Fair Labor Standards Act, 1938
- Workweek
- Hours worked
- Regular rate of pay
- Child Labor
- Portal to Portal Act, 1947
- Equal Pay Act, 1963
- Skill
- Effort
- Responsibility
- Working conditions
- Affirmative defenses
- Job evaluation
- Nonquantitative job evaluation techniques
- Whole job ranking
- Job classification
- Job slotting
- Quantitative job evaluation techniques
- Point factor

- Factor comparison
- Market pricing
- Market data
- Labor market competitors
- Job match
- Aging
- Base pay
- Variable pay
- Incentive plans
- Short-term incentives—individual
- Short-term incentives—team/group
- Gainsharing
- Profit sharing
- Pay structures
- Grades
- Ranges
- Range spread
- Broadbanding
- Compa-ratio
- Employee Retirement Income Security Act (ERISA), 1974
- Vesting
- Cliff vesting
- Graded vesting
- Plan administrator
- Summary plan description
- Fiduciary
- Fiduciary responsibility
- Pension Benefit Guaranty Corporation (PBGC)
- Retirement Equity Act, 1984
- Qualified Domestic Relations Order (QDRO)
- Consolidated Omnibus Budget Reconciliation Act (COBRA), 1985

- COBRA qualifying event
- Older Worker's Benefit Protection Act (OWBPA), 1990
- Health Insurance Portability and Accountability Act (HIPAA), 1996
- Preexisting condition
- HIPAA privacy rule
- HIPAA covered entity
- Mental Health Parity Act (MHPA), 1996
- Sarbanes-Oxley Act (SOX), 2002
- Worker's Compensation
- Social Security Act (SSA), 1935
- Old Age, Survivors, and Disability Insurance (OASDI)
- Retirement benefits
- Disability benefits
- Survivor's benefits
- Medicare
- Medicare—Part A
- Medicare—Part B
- Medicare—Part C
- Medicare—Part D
- Unemployment insurance
- Revenue Act, 1978
- Section 125
- Flexible benefits
- Cafeteria plans
- Premium-only plans (POPs)
- Flexible spending accounts (FSAs)
- Full cafeteria plan
- Section 401(k)
- Family and Medical Leave Act (FMLA), 1993
- Job protected leave

- 12-month period
- Health care provider
- Key employee
- In loco parentis
- Serious health condition
- Uniformed Services Employment and Reemployment Rights Act (USERRA), 1994
- Defined benefit plan
- Cash balance plan
- Defined contribution plan
- Employee stock ownership plans (ESOPs)
- Profit sharing plans
- Simplified employee pension plan (SEP)
- Health and welfare benefits
- Medical insurance
- Indemnity insurance
- Health maintenance organization (HMO)
- Primary care physician (PCP)
- Preferred provider organization (PPO)
- Point of service (POS)
- Dental insurance
- Preventive care
- Restorative care
- Major restorative care
- Orthodonture
- Vision coverage
- Prescription drug coverage
- Life insurance
- Long term disability insurance (LTD)
- Pay for time not worked
- Work life programs

Apply Your Knowledge

This chapter focuses on issues relating to total rewards. Complete the following exercises, review questions, and exam questions as a way of reviewing and reinforcing the knowledge and skills you'll need to perform your responsibilities as an HR professional, and to increase the likelihood that you will pass the PHR examination.

Exercises

1. You've recently been promoted to a position as an HR generalist, and you're anxious to get to work. One day, a manager who you haven't worked with before comes to you to talk about a problem he's having with one of his direct reports. This direct report happens to be an executive assistant and is a highly trusted and valued member of the department. He handles sensitive information and is always looking to grow and to learn new things. The employee feels, however, that he has been "held back" because he's classified as non-exempt, and therefore can't join in with the team on special projects that require overtime or weekend work (there is no money in the budget for overtime hours). This employee ends up feeling excluded and less important. The manager wants you to help him find a way to reclassify the position as exempt. Which of the following answers would be the least appropriate?

    A. Coach the manager on how to help the employee understand that he truly is a valued member of the team.

    B. Change the employee's title to "Assistant Manager" and then upgrade the position to exempt.

    C. Evaluate the position to see how it has changed since the last review, and determine whether it should be upgraded.

    D. Coach the manager on how to have a conversation with the employee about his career objectives.

2. You work as the sole HR professional in a relatively small organization. Recently, the company conducted its first employee survey, and the results indicated that employees don't understand how the company sets its pay rates—in other words, they don't know *why* they are paid what they are paid. The company president, who happened to recently read an article during a cross-country flight about "total rewards philosophy," has asked you to draft one. He wants it "fast, good, and cheap." You know that no one source of information alone will give you everything that you need, but you've got to start somewhere. Which of the following do you think would be of greatest initial value to you as you put together this document?

   A. A sample "total rewards philosophy" statement from a reputable HR-related website.

   B. A "total rewards philosophy" statement from a local company that is well-known for being an employer of choice.

   C. Your organization's mission, vision, and values statement, along with your organization's employee handbook.

   D. A brochure from a consulting firm that specializes in communicating with employees about compensation-related issues.

3. A manager who you know fairly well, and with whom you have a good working relationship, leaves a voice mail message for you, asking you to please call her back about a benefits question. You return her call, and she comes down to your office to speak with you in person. She explains that her former assistant, who left nearly a year and a half ago to go back to college, is about to run out of COBRA. She explains to you that he still is one semester away from earning his degree and can't get decent health insurance through the college plan. She asks if you could leave him on COBRA, just for a few more months. As part of your overall response to this manager, which of the following would be the most appropriate to share?

   A. Under COBRA, former employees who are full-time students at the time that COBRA runs out are entitled to an extension for up to 18 additional months if he or she remains a full-time student.

   B. Although COBRA requires an employer to continue benefits coverage for only 18 months, the employer has the option to extend COBRA benefits for an additional 18 months.

   C. COBRA can be continued for another 18 months, as long as the employee pays the company 110% of the monthly premium costs.

   D. COBRA cannot be continued beyond 18 months in this particular situation, but other situations would warrant an extension, and you would be happy to share that information with her.

4. You're the HR manager at your organization and report directly to the president. (You happen to know that his sister died of cancer about six months ago.) One afternoon, an employee comes to you with a problem. Her sister (who lives out of state) has been diagnosed with a very aggressive form of cancer and has less than six months to live. The employee wants to spend the last few months of her sister's life with her. The employee has already requested a leave of absence, but was advised by an HR representative and her manager that this sort of leave isn't covered under FMLA. Your department is going into its "busy season," so her manager is unwilling to grant any other type of leave. She is concerned about how she will support herself while she is staying with her sister. She asks you whether it would be possible for the company to call this a layoff and let her get unemployment insurance. Sadly, she knows that her sister won't live longer than six months, so unemployment insurance benefits would carry her through. After you express your sincere concern for her sister's condition, which of the following answers would be best?

A. Tell the employee that it's up to the state, not the company, whether unemployment insurance will be granted, and that, although you do sympathize with her situation on a personal level, it's not possible for you to code the termination as a layoff.

B. Tell the employee that it's up to the state, not the company, whether unemployment insurance will be granted. However, as long as the president approves (and you're pretty sure he will), you're willing to code the termination as a layoff.

C. As HR, your role is that of employee advocate, and you are willing to advocate on her behalf to the president. You are fairly confident that he will approve this request, and will get back to the employee either way as soon as possible.

D. You remind the employee, as gently as possible, that, as HR, your role is to ensure that all of the company's policies and procedures are followed, and falsifying the termination code would be a violation of policy. As such, you can't code the termination as a layoff.

5. As the HR manager, you've been looking for creative ways to provide employees with greater benefits without incurring significant additional costs. Your company already has a POP in place. Which of the following would you be most likely to recommend?

A. FSAs

B. PCAs

C. ESOPs

D. PNGs

Review Questions

1. Describe the similarities and differences between defined benefit plans and defined contribution plans.

2. Why is it important to communicate with employees about their compensation and benefits ("total rewards") programs?

3. Define what is meant by "total rewards" and "total rewards philosophy."

4. What is meant by the term "internal equity"?

5. What is meant by the term "relevant labor market"?

Exam Questions

1. Which of the following statements about workweeks is not true?

    A. A workweek is any fixed and regularly recurring period of 168 hours.

    B. The employer can select any day (and any hour) of the calendar week on which to begin the workweek.

    C. The employer can establish different workweeks for different employees or groups of employees.

    D. The hours that an employee works during different workweeks within the same pay period can be "averaged."

2. Which of the following would not be considered an affirmative defense under the Equal Pay Act?

    A. Seniority

    B. Diversity

    C. Quality of production

    D. Merit

3. Which of the following statements about the point factor method of job evaluation is true?

    A. Point factor systems do not establish levels of performance within each compensable factor, because that would constitute making the error of evaluating the person instead of the position.

    B. There is a greater likelihood of rater subjectivity with point factor methods of job evaluation than with whole job methods because point factor systems require the evaluator to make more judgments.

    C. The product of a completed job evaluation will generate information that will be helpful to establishing a job worth hierarchy.

    D. Although point factor systems address evaluative information about different compensable factors, they do not address the relative importance of each compensable factor.

4. Which of the following could generate a calculation that represents "range spread"?

A. $\dfrac{\$55,000}{\$61,000} = 90.1\%$

B. $\dfrac{\$80,000 - \$50,000}{\$50,000} = \dfrac{\$30,000}{\$50,000} = 60\%$

C. $\$100,000 - \$40,000 = \$60,000$

D. None of the above

5. Which of the following was established by ERISA?

A. Enhanced protection for plan members with preexisting medical condition.

B. A clearer definition of "hours worked" for purposes of minimum wage and overtime payments.

C. Whistleblower protection for employees who report fraud against share-holders.

D. Minimum participation and vesting standards for retirement programs.

6. Fiduciaries must do all of the follow *except*

A. Protect plan participants by diversifying plan investments.

B. Act with skill, care, prudence, and diligence.

C. Avoid conflicts of interest.

D. Follow the terms of plan documents without deviation.

7. Which of the following did the REA not accomplish?

A. Lowered the minimum age requirement for pension plan participation and increased the years of service that count for vesting purposes

B. Prohibited plans from counting maternity and paternity leaves as breaks in service for participation and vesting purposes

C. Required qualified pension plans to provide automatic survivor benefits that could be waived only with the written consent of the plan participant

D. Clarified that pension plans may obey certain qualified domestic relations (court) orders (QDROs) without violating ERISA

8. PHI refers to

    A. Health information that relates to a specific individual

    B. A managed care health option offered to federal and state government employees

    C. Information that was used as part of the "long form" test under the old provisions of the FLSA

    D. Information that must be maintained in according with the record-keeping requirements of the FLSA

9. Which of the following is not one of the three main provisions of the Social Security Act?

    A. Retirement income

    B. Pension protection

    C. Survivor's benefits

    D. Disability benefits

10. Which of the following is not required of covered entities by the HIPAA privacy rule?

    A. Designation of a privacy officer

    B. Creation of a code of ethics that applies to all employees who have access to health-related information

    C. Establishment of a complaint-handling and resolution process for issues related to the HIPAA privacy rule

    D. Agreements signed by business associates stating that they will respect the confidentiality of patient information

Answers to Exercises

1. **Answer B is the best answer.** First, reclassifying a position from "non-exempt" to "exempt" is a decision that must be made after much analysis—analysis that is grounded in actual job responsibilities, rather than because of a particular incumbent (or a particular incumbent's feelings). Also, FLSA status is determined on the basis of the responsibilities that are performed, not on the basis of job title. Finally, it is best to refer to this process as "reclassifying," not "upgrading," in that the word "upgrading" seems to reinforce the fallacy that it is better or more desirable to be exempt than it is to be non-exempt. Answer A is not the best answer; it would be appropriate for the manager to help the employee understand how he contributes to, and is valued by, the team. Answer C is not the best answer; it is possible that the position might have changed enough to warrant a reclassification, and a job evaluation would provide information that is necessary for making that assessment. Answer D is not the best answer; this might be an appropriate opportunity for a manager to have a discussion with the employee about his career objectives.

2. **Answer C is the best answer.** The first, and best, source of information that you can have when communicating with employees about total rewards is any resource (written, or otherwise) that expresses, reflects, and articulates the mission, vision and/or values of your own organization. This is the best way to be sure that your total rewards philosophy truly aligns with, and will therefore help fulfill, your organization's "reason for being." Although other items are important, if you don't capture the true essence of your own organization (and why it exists in the first place), any statement of total rewards philosophy that you draft will likely ring hollow, and have limited effectiveness. Answer A is not the best answer; although it may be useful to review (and perhaps even be inspired by) a sample total rewards statement from a reputable HR-related website, "vanilla" statements aren't as valuable to you in this process as information about your own organization. Answer B is not the best answer; a total rewards philosophy that works brilliantly for one organization (no matter how successful that organization might be) may be completely inappropriate and/or ineffective for a different organization. Answer D is not the best answer; outside consultants may be able to develop a "good" statement "fast," but "cheap" might be a bit unrealistic. Give this a try on your own first—your organization will appreciate your efforts as well as your budget-sensitive approach.

3. **Answer D is the best answer.** It is true that, according to the facts you have been given, COBRA can't be extended; however, it's also true that there may be other facts of which you're not aware. Be helpful, and also be factual and accurate. Answer A is not the best answer; there is no provision under COBRA that states that an extension beyond 18 months is available for former employees who are full-time students. Answer B is not the best answer; COBRA does not allow employers to continue benefits coverage beyond legally specified time frames. Answer C is not the best answer; COBRA allows for participation to continue for up to another 18 months only under specific circumstances (and those circumstances cannot be "bought" with a 10% surcharge).

4. **Answer A is the best answer.** First, it is important for the employee to understand how the process works, so it is appropriate to share that information with her. No matter how much empathy you feel for her, however, and regardless of any other personal circumstances that might be "pulling at your heart strings," there are many reasons (ethical, legal, procedural, financial, and so on) why you would not falsify a termination code. You don't, however, need to go into all those reasons with the employee (although you might want to consider following up with the manager to see if you can come up with any creative solutions). Answer B is not the best answer; although the factual information at the beginning of this answer is correct, there are many reasons (ethical, legal, procedural, financial, and so on) why you should not falsify the termination code. Answer C is not the best answer; as HR, your role is to be a "truth advocate," not just an employee advocate (and the truth, in this case, is that the employee wasn't laid off). Answer D is not the best answer; prattling on about policies and procedures at this moment (and at most moments) isn't the best approach and might only serve to reinforce the notion of HR as the "personnel police."

5. **Answer A is the best answer.** Like a POP (Premium Only Plan), an FSA (flexible spending account) falls under Section 125. An FSA goes one step further than a POP by allowing employees to set aside pretax dollars to pay for medical expenses that are not covered by insurance. This lowers the employee's taxable income, which benefits the employer as well as the employee. Answer B is not the best answer; PCA refers to the Walsh-Healey Public Contracts Act (PCA), which was passed in 1936. Answer C is not the best answer; an ESOP (employee stock ownership plan) involves the distribution of stock and is much more complex than establishing FSAs. Creating an ESOP has many implications and would not constitute an appropriate solution for a problem such as this. Answer D is not the best answer; PNG is not a commonly known acronym in HR.

Answers to Review Questions

1. Some of the differences and similarities between defined benefit and defined contribution plans are summarized in Table 6.6.

TABLE 6.6   Defined Benefit Plans and Defined Contribution Plans Comparison

	DB Plans	DC Plans
Nature of the plan	More traditional type of pension plan	Less traditional type of pension plan
More risk is shouldered by…	The employer	The employee
What will the plan pay out to the employee?	Promises to pay a specified monthly benefit at retirement	Makes no guarantees about the value of the plan as of the time of retirement

2. It is important for organizations to communicate with employees about their total rewards programs with respect to each element of each program and to the program as a whole. First, employees may not truly understand all the benefits that they enjoy as employees of an organization. This leads to a second reason why communicating with employees about total rewards is important—most employees do not know the real costs, let alone the actual value, of the benefits they receive (this holds true for mandatory as well as optional benefits). In a very real sense, employees earn benefits, just like they earn cash compensation, and they should know what they are earning. Without this measure of communication, it is more likely that even those benefits that are *not* entitlements may ultimately begin to *feel* like entitlements to employees, rather than something *of value* that they have earned in return for their services to the organization.

3. The term "total rewards" refers to all the compensation- and benefits-related elements that employees within an organization earn and enjoy in return for the services they have provided to their employer. An organization's total rewards philosophy, however, represents far more than just the amount of cash it pays to employees or even the "fringe benefits" that it provides. Instead, it speaks volumes

about what the leaders of that organization value, the results they want to attain, the behavior they want to encourage, and their commitment to their employees. It is a clear and direct expression of the organization's mission, vision, and values—*regardless of whether that was the organization's intention*. Even the absence of a clearly defined total rewards or compensation system or philosophy sends a very clear message, so be certain that it is the message that your organization truly intends to convey.

4. "Internal equity" refers to fairness (or "equity") within a department and/or organization with respect to the ways in which jobs are ranked and individuals are compensated.

5. The relevant labor market relates to the size and scope of the geographic area within which an organization would seek to attract qualified candidates. Even within the same organization, the relevant labor market for different positions can vary widely depending on the skills, knowledge, abilities, and behavioral characteristics required to perform each position successfully. Other factors that impact how an organization defines the relevant labor market might be the degree of competition that exists among employers for particular skills and/or knowledge, and/or the degree to which certain skills and/or knowledge requirements are industry specific.

Answers to Exam Questions

1. **Answer D is the best answer.** The hours that an employee works during different workweeks cannot be averaged, even when those weeks are during the same pay period. Answer A is not the best answer; a workweek is any fixed and regularly recurring period of 168 hours. Answer B is not the best answer; the employer can select any day (and any hour) of the calendar week on which to begin the workweek. Answer C is not the best answer; the employer can establish different workweeks for different employees or groups of employees.

2. **Answer B is the best answer.** Diversity has not designated as an affirmative defense under the Equal Pay Act. Answer A is not the best answer; seniority would be considered an affirmative defense under the Equal Pay Act. Answer C is not the best answer; quality of production would be considered an affirmative defense under the Equal Pay Act. Answer D is not the best answer; merit would be considered an affirmative defense under the Equal Pay Act.

3. **Answer C is the best answer.** The information that is generated through the job evaluation process *will* provide information that is helpful to establishing a job worth hierarchy. Answer A is not the best answer, because point factor systems *do* establish levels of performance within each compensable factor. (As long as evaluations are conducted relative to the performance expected of the position rather than on the basis of the incumbent's individual performance, the job evaluation will still be job-based rather than person-based.) Answer B is not the best answer, because the potential for rater subjectivity is *lower* with the point factor job evaluation method than it is with whole job method of job evaluation. Answer D is not the best answer, because point factor systems *do* address the relative importance of each compensable factor.

4. **Answer B is the best answer.** The formula to calculate range spread is

$$\frac{\text{Maximum} - \text{Minimum}}{\text{Minimum}} = \_\%$$

Answer A is not the best answer; it represents a calculation that could generate a compa-ratio, not range spread. Answer C is not the best answer; it represents a calculation that could generate the numerator of the range spread formula. Answer D is not the best answer, because A was correct.

5. **Answer D is the best answer.** ERISA did establish minimum participant and vesting standards for retirement programs. Answer A is not the best answer; enhanced protection for plan members with preexisting medical conditions was established by COBRA. Answer B is not the best answer; a clearer definition of "hours worked" for purposes and minimum wage and overtime payments was established by the Portal-to-Portal Act. Answer C is not the best answer; whistle-blower protection for employees who report fraud against shareholders was established by Sarbanes-Oxley.

6. **Answer D is the best answer.** Under ERISA, fiduciaries must follow the terms of plan documents *to the extent that those terms are consistent with ERISA, not* simply without deviation. Answer A is not the best answer; fiduciaries are required to protect plan participants by diversifying plan investments. Answer B is not the best answer; fiduciaries must act with skill, care, prudence, and diligence. Answer C is not the best answer; fiduciaries must avoid conflicts of interest

7. **Answer C is the best answer.** The Retirement Equity Act (REA) requires that the participant *and his or her spouse* must waive the provision that provides for automatic survivor benefits. (This provision cannot be waived independently by the plan participant, as answer C implies.) Answer A is not the best answer; REA did lower the minimum age requirement for pension plan participation and did increase the years of service that count for vesting purposes. Answer B is not the best answer; REA did prohibit plans from counting maternity and paternity leaves as breaks in service for participation and vesting purposes. Answer D is not the best answer; REA did clarify that pension plans may obey certain qualified domestic relations (court) orders (QDRIs) without violating ERISA.

8. **Answer A is the best answer.** PHI stands for "protected health information" that relates back to one individual. Answers B, C, and D are not the best answers, because each offers a fabricated definition that is wholly unrelated to the real meaning of PHI.

9. **Answer B is the best answer.** Pension protection is addressed through ERISA, not through the Social Security Act. Answers A, C, and D are not the best answers, because retirement income (answer A), survivor's benefits (answer C), and disability benefits (answer D) are the three major provisions of the Social Security Act.

10. **Answer B is the best answer.** The HIPAA privacy rule requires creation of a code of ethics that applies to the company's key officers (within a "covered entity"). At a minimum, this code must apply to the company's principal executive officer, principal financial officer, principal accounting officer or controller, or persons performing similar functions. It does not, however, have to apply more broadly within the organization. Answer A is not the best answer; the HIPAA privacy rule does require designation of a privacy officer. Answer C is not the best answer; the HIPAA privacy rule does require the establishment of a complaint-handling and resolution process for issues relating to the HIPAA privacy rule. Answer D is not the best answer; the HIPAA privacy rule does require business associates to sign agreements stating that they will respect the confidentiality of patient information. answer,

Suggested Readings and Resources

Bureau of Labor Statistics. www.bls.gov, 2007.

Department of Labor. www.dol.gov, 2007.

eCornell, offering online programs on total rewards. www.ecornell.com, 2007.

International Foundation of Employee Benefit Plans (IFEBC)—CEBS (Certified Employee Benefit Specialist) Designation. www.ifebp.org/cebs/usprogram.asp, 2007.

World at Work. www.worldatwork, 2007.

Beam Jr., Burton T., and John J. McFadden. *Employee Benefits*. Chicago: Dearborn Real Estate Education (Dearborn Financial Publishing, Inc.), 2004.

Berger, Lance A. and Dorothy R. Berger, *The Compensation Handbook*. New York: McGraw-Hill, 1999.

Martocchio, Joseph J. *Employee Benefits: A Primer for Human Resource Professionals*. New York: McGraw-Hill/Irwin, 2002.

Milkovich, George, and Jerry Newman. *Compensation*. New York: McGraw-Hill/Irwin, 2007.

7

Employee and Labor Relations

Study Strategies

Although the PHR exam is multiple choice, try writing and answering your own essay-based questions. Specifically, write open-ended questions that require a response of at least a full paragraph and try to write your answers without looking back at your study materials. The process of actually writing down your answers will reinforce what you already know and will highlight what you need to study more. It will also likely help you as you work to recall this same information when you answer related multiple-choice questions on the actual PHR exam.

As with each of the six functional areas of HR, it's important to determine what you already know and what you don't know with respect to Employee and Labor Relations. Then, work to bridge the gap. Conduct research. Use the Internet to find articles and whitepapers that highlight employee relations and labor relations (particularly if you don't have experience working in a unionized—organized—workplace). Peruse textbooks that provide guidance relative to those particular areas. Be sure to find several real-life examples of each responsibility to ensure that you gain a variety of perspectives and insights. This is particularly important for the skill-based, rather than fact-based, components of this functional area.

Introduction

Employee relations, labor relations—what are these topics all about, and why are they important to HR professionals? The answer to this question is sometimes presented in ways that are overly simple, and it is sometimes presented in ways that are exceedingly complex. In this chapter, we'll try to strike an appropriate balance between these two ends of the spectrum.

Let's first take a look at employee relations, because all employees, whether members of a union or not, *are*, in fact employees.

> **NOTE**
>
> Although this may seem like an axiomatic statement, it warrants mention. Why? Because sometimes, in the midst of the complexities, challenges, and opportunities of dealing with organized labor, organizations (and the people within those organizations, including HR professionals) wrongly perceive "labor" as an amorphous entity, perhaps even an opponent, without a specific identity. In fact, quite the opposite is true. Labor—or a labor organization/union—is a group of people (*employees*) who happen to be organized to speak with a collective voice.

In its most straightforward sense, the definition of *employee relations* can be found in the words "employee" and "relations." Within this context, employee relations can be described as

- The way in which an organization responds to, handles, and/or addresses any issue that has impact on employees, and their relationships

- To and with other employees

- To and with managers

- To and with those outside the employment in the organization with whom they come in contact as part of their employment experience

For many, this is a new and unfamiliar way of looking at employee relations, because many individuals, HR professionals and non-HR professionals alike are more accustomed to thinking of employee relations in functional terms. By this, we mean that employees may define employee relations in terms of what the Employee Relations Department does within their individual organization. All too often, this perspective can lead to a limited and/or a misguided definition of what employee relations is all about. Why? Because HR can end up being saddled with the reputation of being "party planners," "personnel police," "the terminators," and other unhelpful, incomplete, and inaccurate stereotypical roles.

In thinking about this broad, more encompassing definition of employee relations, you might be left to wonder whether there is anything that *isn't* part of employee relations. The answer to this question, as you might expect, is "that depends." In many ways, so much of what happens in our world, our nation, the states and localities in which we live, and the organizations in which we work has an impact, in one way or another, on our workplaces and on the people who work there.

Let's now shift for a moment to labor relations, which, in some ways, is a subset of employee relations. How? Because the term *labor relations* is most frequently used to refer to those individuals who are "organized"—or, in other words, who belong to and are represented by a union who will collectively bargain on their behalf.

When considering labor relations, it's particularly important to keep a historical perspective in mind, not only because the history of labor is so rich, but also because the history of labor has had such a significant impact on the lives of *all* workers—whether or not those workers happen to belong to a union.

EXAM ALERT

PHR test preparation warrants a review of some of the key people, events, and concepts that emerged in the historical timeline of labor history—a timeline that spans the history of our nation (and some would argue even prior to that). Some of the key people, events, and concepts with which you should familiarize yourself are

- ▶ Knights of Labor
- ▶ Great Uprising
- ▶ Samuel Gompers
- ▶ "Bread and butter unionism"
- ▶ Haymarket
- ▶ AFL
- ▶ Industrial Workers of the World (IWW)
- ▶ Mary Harris "Mother" Jones
- ▶ Triangle Shirtwaist Company
- ▶ Electric Auto-Lite Strike
- ▶ CIO
- ▶ UAW
- ▶ Walter Reuther
- ▶ AFL-CIO

Before you take the PHR exam, you may want to go to your favorite search engine, enter the topic, person, or event about which you want to learn more, and read, read, read—and learn about some really rich and valuable dimensions of labor history.

Let's start our journey into employee and labor relations by looking at those principles that unite these disciplines. We'll then move into the distinctions that apply separately to these two areas.

Employee Relations/Labor Relations (ER/LR) Unifying Principle #1: EEO

Beginning with the passage of the Civil Rights Act of 1964 (the first major civil rights legislation), a series of laws has been enacted in an effort to end unlawful discrimination in all terms and conditions of employment. These laws fall under the broad category often referred to as *equal employment opportunity*, or EEO.

Key EEO-Related Terms

In going through this section, and as you prepare for the PHR exam, there are some terms that you'll need to be familiar with:

- *Charge*—A formal complaint, submitted to an agency, that alleges unlawful discrimination.

- *Charging Party*—A person who alleges that he or she has experienced unlawful discrimination (also called the *complainant*).

- *Complainant*—A person who alleges that he or she has experienced unlawful discrimination (also called the *charging party*).

- *Plaintiff*—A party who files a lawsuit alleging unlawful discrimination.

- *Respondent*—The employer, person, or party against whom a charge of unlawful discrimination has been filed.

- *Fair Employment Practices Agencies (FEPAs)*—State or local agencies responsible for enforcing EEO laws that are specific to their respective jurisdiction.

> **NOTE**
>
> At the state level, 47 states (all except Alabama, Arkansas, and Mississippi) have agencies that respond to charges of EEO violations.

Federal, State, and Local Jurisdictions

On the federal level, the agency charged with enforcing many of the laws that are aimed at eliminating discrimination is the Equal Employment Opportunity Commission (EEOC).

> **NOTE**
>
> More information about EEO laws can be found in Chapter 4, "Workforce Planning and Employment."

The following information about filing a charge of discrimination is available at www.eeoc.gov:

Sometimes, charges can be filed under two or even three jurisdictions. For instance,

- If a charge is filed with a FEPA and is also covered by federal law, the FEPA "dual files" the charge with EEOC to protect federal rights. In this scenario, the FEPA will usually maintain responsibility for handling the charge.

▶ If a charge is filed with EEOC and is also is covered by state or local law, EEOC "dual files" the charge with the state or local FEPA. In this scenario, the EEOC will usually maintain responsibility for handling the charge.

At other times, when a state or local EEO law is more protective than the corresponding federal law (or when a corresponding federal law does not exist), a charge may be filed only with the FEPA whose laws offer greater protection to employees.

Filing Charges: Time Limits and Related Information

The EEOC offers the following guidelines relative to filing charges of discrimination (www.eeoc.gov):

Filing a Charge of Employment Discrimination

> **NOTE**
>
> Federal employees or applicants for Federal employment should see Federal Sector Equal Employment Opportunity Complaint Processing.

Who Can File a Charge of Discrimination?

▶ Any individual who believes that his or her employment rights have been violated may file a charge of discrimination with EEOC.

▶ In addition, an individual, organization, or agency may file a charge on behalf of another person in order to protect the aggrieved person's identity.

How Is a Charge of Discrimination Filed?

▶ A charge may be filed by mail or in person at the nearest EEOC office.

▶ Individuals who need an accommodation in order to file a charge (e.g., sign language interpreter, print materials in an accessible format) should inform the EEOC field office so appropriate arrangements can be made.

▶ Federal employees or applicants for employment should see Federal Sector Equal Employment Opportunity Complaint Processing.

What Information Must Be Provided to File a Charge?

▶ The complaining party's name, address, and telephone number;

▶ The name, address, and telephone number of the respondent employer, employment agency, or union that is alleged to have discriminated, and number of employees (or union members), if known;

▶ A short description of the alleged violation (the event that caused the complaining party to believe that his or her rights were violated); and

> ▸ The date(s) of the alleged violation(s).

> ▸ Federal employees or applicants for employment should see Federal Sector Equal Employment Opportunity Complaint Processing.

What Are the Time Limits for Filing a Charge of Discrimination?

All laws enforced by EEOC, except the Equal Pay Act, require filing a charge with EEOC before a private lawsuit may be filed in court. There are strict time limits within which charges must be filed:

> ▸ A charge must be filed with EEOC within 180 days from the date of the alleged violation, in order to protect the charging party's rights.

> ▸ This 180-day filing deadline is extended to 300 days if the charge also is covered by a state or local anti-discrimination law. For ADEA charges, only state laws extend the filing limit to 300 days.

> ▸ These time limits do not apply to claims under the Equal Pay Act, because under that Act persons do not have to first file a charge with EEOC in order to have the right to go to court. However, since many EPA claims also raise Title VII sex discrimination issues, it may be advisable to file charges under both laws within the time limits indicated.

> ▸ To protect legal rights, it is always best to contact EEOC promptly when discrimination is suspected.

> ▸ Federal employees or applicants for employment should see Federal Sector Equal Employment Opportunity Complaint Processing.

What Agency Handles a Charge that is also covered by State or Local Law?

Many states and localities have anti-discrimination laws and agencies responsible for enforcing those laws. EEOC refers to these agencies as "Fair Employment Practices Agencies (FEPAs)." Through the use of "work sharing agreements," EEOC and the FEPAs avoid duplication of effort while at the same time ensuring that a charging party's rights are protected under both federal and state law.

> ▸ If a charge is filed with a FEPA and is also covered by federal law, the FEPA "dual files" the charge with EEOC to protect federal rights. The charge usually will be retained by the FEPA for handling.

> ▸ If a charge is filed with EEOC and also is covered by state or local law, EEOC "dual files" the charge with the state or local FEPA, but ordinarily retains the charge for handling.

How Is a Charge Filed for Discrimination Outside the United States?

U.S.-based companies that employ U.S. citizens outside the United States or its territories are covered under EEO laws, with certain exceptions. An individual alleging an

EEO violation outside the U.S. should file a charge with the district office closest to his or her employer's headquarters. However, if you are unsure where to file, you may file a charge with any EEOC office.

EEOC—Handling Charges

After a charge of discrimination has been filed, the EEOC sends a letter to the employer notifying it that a complaint has been filed. At this point, some employers will decide to "settle." There are any number of reasons why an organization might decide to settle, just a few of which are

- ▸ To elude the requirement of providing information to the EEOC.

- ▸ To avoid allocating resources (financial, human, emotional, and otherwise) to the process of responding to a charge of discrimination, especially if it appears that the costs of fighting may outweigh the benefits of prevailing ("winning")—even if the organization believes that no unlawful discrimination has taken place.

- ▸ To prevent the possibility of bad press that can, at times, be generated even by the mere filing of a charge of discrimination.

- ▸ To seek a resolution to a situation where the employer believes that there may be exposure (in other words, where the charge of discrimination may be valid).

Alternatively, many employers choose *not* to seek a settlement agreement when a charge of discrimination is first filed. In such situations, there are four primary ways that the EEOC can handle the charge:

- ▸ *Investigate it*—Investigations can be designated as "high priority" or "non-high priority," depending upon the strength of the facts that have been presented in the charge. An EEOC investigation can take myriad forms, including written requests for information, in-person interviews, document reviews, and even a visit to the location where the discrimination allegedly occurred.

- ▸ *Settle it*—A charge can be settled at any stage of the investigation if the charging party and the employer are both interested in doing so. If no settlement is reached, the investigation resumes.

- ▸ *Mediate it*—The EEOC offers a confidential mediation program as an alternative to a lengthy investigative process. For a charge to be mediated, the charging party and the employer must both be willing to participate. If the mediation process is not successful, the charge will be investigated.

- ▸ *Dismiss it*—A charge can be dismissed at any point in the process if the agency determines that further investigation will not be able to establish that the alleged unlawful discrimination actually occurred. When a charge is dismissed, a notice is issued in accordance with the law that gives the charging party 90 days within which to file a lawsuit on his or her own behalf.

EEOC Determinations

The EEOC determines whether there is "reasonable cause" to believe that unlawful discrimination has occurred.

If the EEOC determines that there is *no reasonable cause*, the case is closed, the parties are notified, and the charging party is given a "right to sue" letter. The charging party then has 90 days to file a private lawsuit.

If the EEOC determines that there *is reasonable cause*, the EEOC will attempt conciliation with the employer in an effort to develop a remedy for the discrimination. If the EEOC cannot conciliate the case, the EEOC will decide whether to take the case to court (the EEOC chooses to litigate a very small percentage of cases). If the EEOC does not take the case to court, it will close the case and issue the charging party a "right to sue" letter.

The charging party can also request a right to sue letter from the EEOC 180 days after the charge was filed (60 days for ADEA). Under the EPA, however, the rules are a little different—lawsuits can be filed within two years of the alleged discriminatory act (three years if the act was "willful").

> **NOTE**
>
> A charging party may not bring a case to court if the charge has been successfully conciliated, mediated, or settled.

> **NOTE**
>
> Different processing guidelines are in effect for federal employees.

EEO—Going to Court

If a case *does* proceed to court, HR's role will vary significantly, depending on a host of factors. For instance, in some organizations, HR may be called on to assist in-house or outside counsel with responding to a complaint, or to collect data as part of the discovery process, and/or to be available to assist and facilitate the process. Depending on HR's role in the actual case, HR professionals may be deposed, testify, and/or represent the organization during the trial—in a sense, being the "face" of the organization to the judge and jury.

> **NOTE**
>
> It is important to keep in mind the critical and unique role of juries. A "jury of one's peers" might be more likely to identify with a plaintiff than with an organization. In short, from the perspective of the organization, the stakes are higher, and the turf is a bit less friendly, than they were before 1991.

Remedies

When a plaintiff prevails, he or she may be awarded the following forms of *relief* or remedies (whether the discrimination was intentional or unintentional):

- Back pay

- Hiring, or front pay (instead of hiring the individual)

- Promotion

- Reinstatement, or front pay (instead of rehiring the individual)

- Reasonable accommodation

- Other actions that will make an individual "whole" (in the condition that he or she would have been but for the discrimination)

- Attorneys' fees

- Expert witness fees

- Court costs

Compensatory and punitive damages may also be available when the discrimination is found to be intentional (and in rare cases, even when the discrimination is found to be unintentional).

Understanding Front Pay

The concept of *front pay* is one with which HR professionals should be familiar. According to the EEOC (www.eeoc.gov):

The remedy of front pay compensates a victim in situations where reinstatement or nondiscriminatory placement would be an available remedy, but is denied for reasons peculiar to the individual claim. The compensation of front pay makes the victim of discrimination whole generally until such nondiscriminatory placement can be accomplished. See *Romero v. Department of the Air Force*.

Numerous decisions of the Commission have recognized the Commission's authority to award front pay as a remedy, and have discussed the propriety of such an award under the particular facts of those cases. The Commission decisions discussed in this article were selected to illustrate the Commission's treatment of the front pay remedy.

Reinstatement or nondiscriminatory placement is preferred over the remedy of front pay. See Romero. However, front pay may be determined to be more appropriate in certain situations. The Court in *EEOC v. Prudential Federal Savings and Loan Association* stated that front pay should be awarded "when the employer has exhibited such extreme hostility that, as a practical matter, a productive and amicable working relationship would be impossible." The Commission in *Finlay v. United States Postal Service*, and in earlier cases cited in Finlay, set out three circumstances in which front pay may be awarded in lieu of reinstatement: (1) Where no position is available; (2) Where a subsequent working relationship between the parties would be antagonistic; or (3) Where the employer has a record of long-term resistance to discrimination efforts.

NOTE

This highlights the reality that any situation could potentially devolve into a lawsuit. Sometimes, there is nothing you can do to prevent that from happening. It's also not helpful to worry excessively about the possibility of litigation. The best that any of us can do is to ensure that we handle situations well (and consistently), that we seek to deescalate situations whenever possible, that we invite employees to raise concerns internally, and that we—along with the clients with whom we consult—conduct ourselves in a manner that will, if subjected to scrutiny, hold up.

CAUTION

HR professionals play various roles in the organization; one of the most important is the role of proactive observer. In short, if you believe that a situation has the possibility to produce a charge of discrimination or any other legal challenges, notify your senior HR colleagues and, as appropriate, counsel. Depending on the culture of your organization, you may want to consider seeking input from counsel along the way. Also remember the fine line that HR cannot cross—HR professionals cannot practice law. We must, however, recognize *when* we need to call in someone who can (such as in-house or outside counsel). This can, at times, be a fine line to walk.

REVIEW BREAK

Now that we've had an opportunity to look at employee relations principles and EEO guidelines laws and regulations that apply to all employees—whether or not employees are covered by a collective bargaining agreement—let's take a look at an equally fundamental premise that applies to employee relations as well as labor relations: the fact that "good employee relations is good employee relations."

Employee Relations/Labor Relations (ER/LR) Unifying Principle #2: "Good Employee Relations Is Good Employee Relations"

Good employee relations is good employee relations, *whether or not* the employees in question happen to belong to a union. In turn, good employee relations fosters enhanced morale, which in turn strengthens the organization's culture. A stronger culture impacts and shapes the kinds of employee relations initiatives that will be most effective. When well-handled, this circle of influence can evolve positively and productively.

Employee Relations: External Considerations

As mentioned earlier, it's hard to think of anything that *doesn't* have an impact on employee relations. This is just as true of external considerations as it is of internal considerations.

To demonstrate this, we chose a newspaper at random and scanned the headlines. Within minutes, we compiled a list of factors that can have a direct impact on employee relations (as defined earlier). Just a small portion of that list (in alphabetical order) included the following:

- Aging workforce

- Climate changes

- Crime (corporate and otherwise)

- Drug use in professional sports

- Drug use in schools

- Economic conditions—national, regional, and local

- Energy prices

- Energy supplies

- Ethical breaches

- Executive compensation

- Globalization: management/leadership

- Home prices

- Misappropriation of funds

- Mortgage crisis

- Organ donation

- Outsourcing/offshoring

- Same sex marriage

- Security/homeland security

- Social promotion (in schools)

- Sports

- Supreme Court

- Technology and technological developments

- Terrorism

- Unemployment

- War/international unrest

- Weather-related events and disasters

Even with a cursory review of these items, it's relatively easy to make legitimate, meaningful connections that demonstrate how each of these topics could, in one way or another, impact employee relations, as defined earlier.

Even if the organization decides not to respond to factors such as those already listed, make no mistake: the organization is still making a decision. As is mentioned throughout this book, "you can't not communicate." In that sense, employee relations is defined just as much by what an organization *doesn't* do as it is by what an organization *does* do.

Employee Relations: Internal Considerations

The considerations listed previously represent external elements that impact employee relations. Although these are critical, it's just as important to consider internal elements that can impact employee relations. Perhaps the most important internal consideration impacting employee relations is organizational culture.

Organizational Culture

Organizational culture casts an expansive, inclusive, and incredibly wide net. It encompasses historical events, current events, and future events (whether potential, likely, or simply rumored). More specifically, organizational culture reflects and embodies the norms, mores, values, beliefs, customs, and attitudes of the organization, and of those who work within the organization. It is thought of by some as the "personality" or even the "soul" of the organization.

Organizational Culture—What It Is

Sometimes, we don't fully recognize the importance that organizational culture has on the day-to-day functioning of the organization. There is also sometimes a tendency to think of organizational culture as something nebulous. In reality, the opposite is true.

To begin to get a grasp on this idea, let's consider the work of Terrence E. Deal and Allan A. Kennedy, who have studied culture extensively for decades. Deal and Kennedy's work spans several milestone works, including *Corporate Cultures*.

Deal and Kennedy identified four specific dimensions of culture:

- *Values*—The beliefs that lie at the heart of the corporate culture

- *Heroes*—The individuals who embody those values

- *Rites and rituals*—Routines relative to the way that people interact that have strong symbolic qualities

- *The culture network*—The information system of communication, or the "hidden hierarchy of power" within an organization

In this sense, Deal and Kennedy's definition of culture helps us recognize the tangible impact and manifestation of organizational culture. This hands-on expression of organizational culture is what employees see and experience every day. To employees, these four dimensions of culture provide a much more meaningful description of culture than any formal organizational communication strategy (by itself) ever could. It is for this reason, in part, that we as HR professionals do a disservice to our clients and ourselves if we limit our awareness of organizational culture solely to its "formal" definitions.

In addition to Deal and Kennedy, Edgard Schein of MIT's Sloan School of Management also sheds important insights into organization culture, which, when boiled down to its basics, is about shared assumptions, adapting, integrating, and assimilating new members. In short, Schein seems to be saying that organizational culture speaks to "the way we do things around here."

Like Deal and Kennedy, Schein reaches beyond the formal dimensions of culture to recognize the power and impact inherent in the more subtle dimensions of culture, which in turn begins to speak to the *importance* of organizational culture.

Organizational Culture—Its Importance

Schein was quite direct about the importance of organizational culture. In his 2004 book, *Organizational Culture and Leadership*, Schein wrote about the possibility that a group's very survival could be threatened by the emergence of problems relating to its culture, and the resulting need for leaders to rise to the occasion and address those cultural issues.

At this point, some readers may be wondering, "Threatened survival? Isn't that a bit overly dramatic?" The answer, however, is a clear and unequivocal "no." Deal and Kennedy also identify culture as the single most important factor contributing to an organization's success or failure. And Deal and Kennedy are not alone in their assertion:

▶ In *Ideas Are Free*, Robinson and Schroeder explore the ways in which organizational culture can impact the ideas generated by the organization.

▶ In *HR from the Heart*, Sartain and Finney stress the criticality of culture as a business issue.

▶ In *Reinventing Strategy*, Pietersen links organizational culture to employee performance, and ultimately to the overall success or failure of the organization.

▶ In *The Fast Forward MBA in Business*, O'Brien looks at culture in terms of productivity, profitability, and overall performance.

If we can agree to the premise that culture is a significant factor contributing to the overall success of an organization, the next step that we as HR professionals must take is to focus on how we can leverage effective employee relations initiatives as a way of strengthening an organization's culture and, therefore, moving the organization closer to the attainment of its objectives. Two important ways this can be accomplished are through employee communication programs and employee involvement strategies.

Employee Involvement and Employee Communication

Employee communication and employee involvement are two separate, albeit closely interrelated, types of programs. Both are important components to effective employee relations, and neither is as effective without the other. In addition, when well executed, each can strengthen the role of the other.

Let's take a look at each of these topics, and—more important—the tools and initiatives that can bring them to life.

Employee Communication Strategies

One cornerstone, perhaps *the* cornerstone, of effective employee relations is effective communication. We'll look at communication in terms of communicating *with*—not just communicating *to*—employees.

Handbooks

Employee handbooks are an important and frequently used method that organizations use to communicate information about policies, procedures, and rules. Handbooks provide, in a sense, the "rules of the road" in that they ensure that employees are fully informed (in writing) about the obligations, responsibilities, and benefits that are associated with being an employee.

Handbooks can vary widely in terms of the information they contain, their length, the topics they cover, and the tone in which they are written. The following topics represent a sampling of what employee handbooks can address:

▶ Introduction (for example, welcome, history, mission, vision, and values)

▶ Statement relating to collective bargaining unit (if applicable)

▶ EEO-related policies (for example, statements and/or policies pertaining to EEO and/or affirmative action (AA); diversity and inclusion; employees with disabilities; sexual harassment; religious accommodation; and employment eligibility and verification [I-9 form])

▶ Job performance (for example, probationary period for new employees/transferred employees, performance management and appraisal, progressive disciplinary process)

▶ Behavioral expectations (for example, conduct and work rules, work behavior, appropriate attire, workplace equipment and supplies, and absenteeism and tardiness)

▶ Positions (for example, job grading system, job regrading, and nonexempt and exempt FLSA status)

▶ Benefits programs (for example, health plans, prescription drug plans, dental plans, retirement plans, flexible spending accounts, life insurance, disability insurance, child care, and elder care)

▶ Pay (for example, compensation policy, overtime pay, comp pay, time reporting system, pay procedures, and direct deposit)

▶ Workplace as community (for example, transportation, parking, public transportation, carpooling, cafeteria, health and fitness center, ATM, company store, travel agency, bowling league, and softball league)

▶ Leave programs (for example, FMLA, jury duty, holiday/sick/vacation leave, and so on)

▶ Terminations (for example, voluntary [resignation, retirement]; involuntary [layoff, dismissal, job abandonment, and failure to successfully complete probationary period])

▶ Employee records

▶ Conflicts of interest

▶ Substance abuse policy

▶ Smoking policy

▶ Inclement weather and other emergency conditions

▶ New hire/new transfer orientation

▶ Company ID cards

▶ Hours of work (workweek, meal/break periods)

▶ Safety and security

▶ Development and training

▶ Employee assistance programs

▶ Retirement programs

▶ Educational and tuition reimbursement benefits

Although they do not necessarily have to be written in a legalistic manner (and may be even more valuable and effective if they are not), handbooks can have a significant legal impact. In the event that an employment-related decision (for instance, relating to discipline, termination, or other terms or conditions of employment) is questioned or challenged, the handbook will serve as one key piece of evidence that will be closely scrutinized by all parties.

One factor that will significantly impact whether the handbook will more closely support the *employer's* position or the *employee's* position is the presence or absence of an *employee acknowledgement*. From the perspective of the employer, every employee should acknowledge, either in writing or electronically, that he or she received, read, had the opportunity to ask, and in fact did ask any questions that he or she might have relative to the information contained within it. This, in effect, removes or greatly diminishes the effectiveness of the "I had no idea" defense. In addition, when policies are added or updated, organizations should strongly consider obtaining a written or electronic acknowledgement from each employee (that, again, confirms that the employee received, read, had the opportunity to ask, and in fact did ask any questions that he or she might have relative to the new or updated policy).

NOTE

Cultural as well as legal considerations need to be looked at carefully when deciding how to handle the distribution and updating of employee handbooks. As is so often the case with HR, *how* we handle and communicate relative to a situation is just as important as *what* we handle and communicate.

"But What I Meant by That Was..."

Because handbooks can have such far-reaching legal impact, it is critical that counsel review and approve handbooks, policies, and updates to either of these before they are distributed to employees. In this way, counsel can ensure that legal concerns/problems do not unintentionally arise from the language that is used.

For instance, handbooks sometimes are written using language that can unintentionally create an implied contract and thereby potentially jeopardize "employment-at-will." The term *permanent employee*, for example, can raise questions of this sort. For this reason, most attorneys advise that employees should be referred to as "regular" or "ongoing," rather than "permanent." Equal care must be taken when the progressive disciplinary and probationary policies are crafted, for similar reasons.

In addition to all the carefully crafted language that must be included throughout the handbook, organizations also often choose to have an attorney draft an overall statement that is included at the beginning of the handbook, on the signed acknowledgement sheet, or in both places. This statement reaffirms that the employment relationship is "at will," that the handbook does not create a contract, and that no other oral or written agreements or statements can override the employment-at-will relationship unless they are specifically designated as doing so.

Despite all this apparent legalese, handbooks must be user friendly. If the culture is the organization's "soul" then the handbook is (in one sense) its voice. It is the document to which employees will refer over and over again, and it must be written in a clear and readable manner. It may even be appropriate to publish the handbook in a variety of languages, depending on the demographics of the workforce.

Town Hall/Department/Staff Meetings

In short, hold them routinely. Share information, and be open to receiving and acting upon feedback.

Newsletters, Emails, and Intranet Communication

All of these methods represent potentially excellent ways of sharing information, and can be made even more effective if employees are encouraged to make these traditionally one-way communication methods more dynamic. Create mechanisms through which feedback is sought and collected, and develop ways to encourage employees to avail themselves of this information.

"Word of Mouth"

Don't waste your energy trying to deny that informal communications and methods exist. They do, and they can't be eliminated. Nor should they be, as long as they do not become destructive. Instead of trying to wish away the grapevine, consider shifting your perspective. In other words, to the degree that is possible and appropriate, consider how you might be able to use those informal communication channels to your advantage.

Employee Involvement Strategies

The line between *communication strategies* and *employee involvement strategies* is cloudy, as—in many ways—it should be.

For an organization to practice effective employee relations, the employment experience can't just happen *to* employees. Such an approach implies detachment and disempowerment. Instead, HR professionals must seek to actively and meaningfully involve employees in the experience of their own employment.

There are a variety of employee involvement strategies. In this section, we'll focus on the following:

▶ Employee surveys

▶ Focus groups

▶ Employee participation groups

▶ Open-door policies

▶ Suggestion programs

▶ Management by walking around (MBWA)

Employee Surveys

Employee surveys (also sometimes called *attitude surveys* or *climate surveys*) provide employees with the opportunity to express their opinions and to share their perspectives. Sometimes, employee surveys can even provide a vehicle through which employees can truly contribute in a meaningful and significant way to their organizations by having a voice in shaping the policies, practices, and direction of their organizations.

For employees to fully participate in the survey process and to make truly valuable contributions, employees must fully and clearly understand the purpose of the survey, be assured anonymity, and receive feedback relative to the survey results.

Four functional reasons for organizations to conduct surveys are

▶ To gauge and measure employees' perceptions, viewpoints, and attitudes.

▶ To take the pulse of specific current and/or potential issues which are of importance to employees.

▶ To collect information that can be used by the organization to help set priorities.

▶ To provide a benchmark—a snapshot, in a way—of employees' viewpoints and perspectives. This will enable you to establish a baseline from which you can later draw comparisons.

NOTE

Although they offer many advantages, surveys are not the only, nor are they necessarily the best, employee involvement tool for any particular situation. Before you choose whether to use a survey, be sure to consider the advantages and disadvantages of various employee involvement tools. If you work in an organization where a survey has been used in the past, be careful to look thoroughly into that process: what was done, how it was done, and what the outcomes were. This is particularly important because there is a great deal of disparity with respect to how employee surveys can be conducted, as well as the potential quality of the overall employee survey experience.

If you decide that you are going to conduct an employee survey, there are 10 general steps to follow:

1. Secure management buy-in, starting with the senior levels of management.

2. Determine the survey content.

3. Determine the survey methodology (for instance, online, hardcopy, in person, mail, open-ended, closed-ended, and so on).

4. Develop the survey.

5. "Market" the survey.

6. Conduct the survey.

7. Calculate the results.

8. Interpret the results.

9. Share the results.

10. Act upon the results.

How a survey is designed and conducted are two critically important factors that will contribute significantly to determining the overall success or failure of the survey process. Surveys can be designed and/or conducted either within the organization, or by consultants who reside outside the organization.

Either way, the process of simply conducting an employee survey isn't enough to make it a valuable involvement strategy. First, whether the survey is administered internally or through a consultant, it is absolutely essential to ensure that the survey is conducted in a confidential manner, and it is just as important that participants *believe* in the confidentiality of the process. Another critical element that will contribute significantly to determining the ultimate success of a survey is the degree of follow-up that occurs after the survey is administered. This does not mean that all requests expressed through surveys must be granted. It does, however, mean that the *summary* of survey results must be reported back—in a *sanitized* manner—to participants, and that specific requests and recommendations must be acknowledged and addressed.

Focus Groups

Focus groups provide another means of communicating with and involving employees in the organization. A focus group consists of a small but representative sample of individuals within an organization. Focus group discussions are led by a neutral facilitator who seeks to elicit feedback and input on a specific subject. Focus groups can range in size, with an ideal number of participants ranging from 10 to 15 people. In determining the size of the focus group, the objective is to ensure that you have enough people to generate a dynamic and synergistic discussion, but not so many people that there is insufficient time for participants to meaningfully contribute their ideas—to be, as well as to feel—heard. It's also essential to ensure "groupthink" does not emerge.

Focus groups can be used independently or as a follow-up tool to an employee survey because focus groups afford a degree of flexibility that a survey simply cannot provide. Successfully facilitating a focus group, however, does require a far greater level of interpersonal skill than is required for survey administration. In addition, whereas surveys require a significant level of trust if they are to be successful, focus groups require an even greater level of trust. This is true in part because anonymity is by definition impossible when people are participating face-to-face in a focus group setting.

If you decide to use a focus group, be sure to thoroughly address the five following steps for success:

1. Develop the right questions.

2. Involve/include all stakeholders.

3. Determine how many focus groups you need to conduct (this may be a function of the size of the population involved, the scope of the issues involved, the number of distinct stakeholder groups, the amount of time you have, the amount of money you have, and the number of skilled and consistent facilitators at your disposal).

4. Arrange the logistics (who, when, where, how, how long, and so on).

5. Conduct the meetings, select the moderator/facilitator, establish and agree upon ground rules, ensure consistent participation, ask probing questions, ensure continuity across focus groups, and so on.

> **EXAM ALERT**
>
> Be familiar with the techniques, advantages, and disadvantages of focus groups. In addition, based on the potential strengths and weaknesses of surveys and focus groups, be prepared to identify situations in which a focus group would be the preferred employee involvement approach, situations in which a survey would be the preferred employee involvement approach, and situations in which a combined approach might be most effective.

Employee Participation Groups

Employee participation groups invite employees to participate actively in the process of managing the organization. Through these groups, employees can contribute ideas and provide feedback. Employee participation groups can also provide an excellent way of encouraging creative involvement and enhancing commitment.

> **CAUTION**
>
> Under the National Labor Relations Act (NLRA), *it is possible* that employee participation groups could be found to be "company dominated" and therefore be rendered illegal.

> **CAUTION**
>
> Although employee participation groups are neither legal nor illegal by definition, the way in which they are managed/administrated can have a huge impact on whether any particular group is deemed to be legal or illegal.

Open-Door Policy

An *open-door policy* is just what its name implies—a standing invitation for employees to raise their concerns with managers and/or human resources, face to face. The use of an open door cannot result in penalties, formal or otherwise, against those employees who avail themselves of these resources.

"Betrayer? Me? I Was Only Doing My Job."

Open-door policies highlight another reason why we must not inappropriately promise confidentiality, lest we end up being perceived as betrayers of trust. There are times when *we are obligated* to reveal information that has been shared with us. Such situations can crop up unexpectedly, especially in organizations where an open-door policy is in effect.

Ensuring discretion and reassuring that you will reveal information only on a "need-to-know basis" is one thing. Promising blanket confidentiality is something entirely different.

Complaint handling and resolution is a skill, an art, and a discipline. Proceed with skill, knowledge, and caution to ensure that you do not unintentionally step into a situation that can damage your credibility, perhaps even beyond repair.

Suggestion Programs

Suggestion programs invite employees to submit their ideas, usually anonymously, unless they choose to reveal their identity. Ideas are usually welcomed relative to any work-related topic, such as improving work systems, identifying or eliminating safety concerns, or exposing unethical (or criminal) behavior.

Questions submitted through suggestion programs or "suggestion boxes" (physical or electronic) need to be responded to quickly, regardless of whether the suggestion is implemented. For any suggestion program to be successful, employees must *be* heard, and *feel* heard.

Management by Walking Around

Management by walking around (MBWA) is an acronym that has been around for decades and is just as relevant now as it was years ago. Neither HR professionals nor managers can hide in their offices. If we isolate ourselves, we may likely find that we end up being marginalized. It is up to each of us, individually and collectively, to make the choice to "get out there" and to keep our finger on the pulse of the workplace and the workforce.

Progressive Discipline as Employee Relations

Though not often thought of as an employee relations or employee involvement program, progressive discipline programs can be both. This is despite the fact that the word "discipline" evokes unpleasant associations for many of us. For some, it may elicit thoughts of a relationship where there is an imbalance of power, a sense of disempowerment or helplessness, or even a tendency to judge or to blame. For others, it may simply conjure up images of "being in trouble," and therefore represent one or more steps along the path to termination. A third possibility is that it may simply equate to punishment.

It is in this context that we must again ensure that we fix the true definition of employee relations in the forefront of our awareness: *anything that impacts relationships with*, *among*, *or for employees*. For even—perhaps even *especially*—through the disciplinary process, our focus on employee relations and relationship building must be maintained.

It is also in this context that we can benefit greatly from remembering Dick Grote's idea of "discipline without punishment" (published in his 1995 book of the same name). Discipline must be seen as a way to give employees the opportunity to help themselves. More specifically, discipline can be used as a tangible way of supporting employees in their efforts to address and resolve their own performance issues. It can, in short, serve as a wake-up call through which an employee will choose to turn around his or her performance so that it meets or even exceeds expectations.

> **TIP**
>
> This vision may be consistent with the culture of your organization and the mindset of the managers whom you support. It is also important to recognize, however, that it might contradict the ideas of managers who might view discipline as a way to "pave a paper trail" that will enable them to terminate an employee (without a whole lot of time-consuming pushback from HR). If you encounter that mindset, move cautiously. Remember your role—you are a consultant and a business partner. You are not there to "just say no," nor are you there to enable behaviors that might eventually prove to be problematic and/or counterproductive. Keep the ultimate objectives of the organization in mind as you work with your managers—you might be surprised to see just how far a collaborative problem-solving approach can take you.

It is in this spirit that the process of progressive discipline emerges as a truly untapped opportunity. *Progressive discipline* is a system that incorporates a series of steps, each more progressively involved, advanced, or serious, than the last.

The progressive discipline process is predicated on the belief that—assuming that an employee is at least minimally qualified for the position for which he or she was hired— each employee chooses whether to perform his or her job satisfactorily. There are, of course, other factors involved—for instance, the very assumption that the employee is *still* at least minimally qualified for the position for which he or she holds, especially if the minimum requirements for that position have evolved (meaning, increased) over time.

> **NOTE**
>
> Like most of the general concepts that we're exploring in this section, the concept of progressive discipline generally holds true for employees who belong to a union as well as for employees who do not. As always, however, specific progressive disciplinary steps that are outlined in a collective bargaining agreement could overrule the concepts explored here.

Principles of Progressive Discipline

There is no single best approach to the specific steps in progressive discipline; however, there are some important concepts to keep in mind.

Employees Choose to Discipline and Even Terminate Themselves

Technically speaking, it is true that either the employer or the employee can make a decision to terminate the employment relationship for any lawful reason (assuming, of course, the absence of an employment contract or collective bargaining agreement that stipulates otherwise). Within that range of possibilities, it's also true that an employer can choose to fire an employee who doesn't meet the performance standards of his or her position.

Another way of looking at this, however, is that, within the structure of progressive discipline, each employee makes choices relative to whether he or she will meet the expectations of his or her position. These choices can, ultimately, lead to a larger choice: whether to terminate him/her self.

What does this mean? Well, let's first say what it *doesn't* mean—we're not talking about employees who "see it coming" and quit before their employer terminates them.

Now, let's take a look at what it *does* mean. An employer's decision to terminate an employee is made, to a greater or lesser degree, because an employee will not, or cannot, bring his or her performance up to expected levels. Employees have some degree, perhaps even a large degree, of control over that decision. How? An employee may not perform at expected performance levels, for instance, because he or she chose

- ▶ Not to participate in training opportunities

- ▶ Not to turn to his or her manager for support or assistance

- ▶ Not to change specific counterproductive or problematic behaviors

- ▶ Not to cease certain counterproductive or problematic behaviors

- ▶ Not to "turn over a new leaf" and demonstrate certain positive or productive behaviors

Ultimately, progressive discipline provides multiple opportunities at multiple decision points for employees to make choices that will result in them maintaining their employment in a positive and productive manner. When applied appropriately, therefore, progressive discipline truly is an empowering process.

Fairness Isn't Sameness

When it comes to progressive discipline (and, for that matter, many other dimensions of the employment relationship), fairness doesn't mean sameness. Or, to use other words, just because you're treating everyone the same way doesn't mean that you're treating everyone fairly.

An idea that needs to be taken into consideration during the progressive discipline process, as at other times, is referred to as *similarly situated employees*. This term does have a legal meaning, and thus needs to be defined by lawyers. However, just for purposes of understanding the concept better, let's look at this concept in an admittedly nonlegal manner. With that caveat, similarly situated employees are employees who are, in one way or another, in "the same boat." In terms of the ADEA, for instance, this could mean employees who are all over 40 years of age, or who are all under 40 years of age. In the context of Title VII of the Civil Rights Act of 1964, similarly situated employees might share the same gender, race, or color. The concept of similarly situated employees, however, isn't limited to civil rights legislation. For example, employees who are being considered for a position and who possess similar credentials could, in one sense, be considered to be similarly situated.

It's also possible, and often advisable, to look at progressive discipline in terms of whether different employees are similarly situated. In this context, being similarly situated could be a function, in part, of each employee's level of performance—ideally, in comparison to the SMART goals that were established for and with the employee at the beginning of the performance measurement period (see Chapter 5, "Human Resource Development"). In addition to performance against goals, it might also be important to consider other factors such as the length of time the employee has been employed with the organization, how long it has been (if ever) since the employee demonstrated any performance that is below predetermined standards, whether there are extraordinary reasons for the substandard performance, and the like.

To reiterate, looking at whether employees are similarly situated doesn't mean that we, as employers and HR representatives, should treat all employees the same. It does mean that we should be, in one sense, "consistently inconsistent." This is part of what makes our profession an art as well as a science.

> **CAUTION**
>
> Nothing in this section changes the fact that many organizations (whether unionized or not) identify specific behaviors that can, do, and will result in immediate termination. Those behaviors might be listed in an employee handbook, a collective bargaining agreement, or the like. It is also important to remember that it is not possible to enumerate every behavior that could result in disciplinary action or immediate termination, so situations must also be looked at—in concert with management and with counsel—with an open mind.

Progressive Discipline Steps

Often, progressive discipline processes will include the following steps:

1. *Discussion of the substandard performance issue ("coaching," rather than "counseling")*—If progressive discipline is truly an employee relations initiative, it must be grounded in open communication, collaboration, and an effort to achieve a common objective: the attainment of the organization's objectives and the furtherance of its mission. And all of this can start with discussion. Sometimes (and there are those who would argue "often"), this step, when performed well, may be able to preclude

the need to engage in the balance of the progressive discipline process, thereby taking less of a toll on the organization itself and on the employees who work within it.

2. *Verbal warning*—The next step in the progressive discipline process is verbal warning. This step moves a step beyond discussion because the tone is closer to "counseling," rather than "coaching." In other words, when the process moves to a verbal warning, there is a problem, not just a situation. There are those, however, who say that a verbal warning is "not worth the paper it's not written on." These individuals might assert that the most important aspect of a verbal warning is the message that is conveyed by the tone of the communication, rather than the specific words that are used (though we must always be mindful of the words we use—as we never know when we may hear them again, and in what venue). Again, the idea or hope is that in response to the "escalation" from coaching to verbal warning, the employee will choose to bring his or her behavior up to predetermined performance standards.

3. *Written warning*—At this point, the counseling has escalated to a formal level. Sometimes, the reality of seeing a written warning is enough to help an employee recognize the gravity of a situation. In other words, sometimes messages do not truly seem real until they are written. In addition, a written warning can serve as a formal record of precisely what was communicated to the employee, and when, in the event that such documentation becomes relevant.

4. *Final written warning and/or suspension*—This is the final opportunity the employee has to change his or her behavior before that behavior, if continued, will result in termination. Some organizations will suspend employees with or without pay (FLSA considerations must be observed for exempt employees so as not to forfeit their exempt status). Others will present the employee with a date by which he or she must make a commitment to bring his or her behavior up to the expected standards.

> **NOTE**
>
> Depending on the organization, this step could actually be broken into one, two, or even three substeps.

Either way, the written documentation accompanying this step will likely include language to the effect that continuing substandard performance will lead to further disciplinary action, up to and including termination.

> **CAUTION**
>
> Here again, it is particularly important to consult with counsel relative to the language that is used in any warning letters, and particularly in final written warning letters. Care must be taken neither to create any sort of implied contract that the employee's employment will continue for any period of time, nor to use language that can limit the employer's response to continued substandard performance.

5. *Involuntary termination*—There comes a point at which it is no longer advisable or productive to continue the employment relationship. It is at this point that managers, with the assistance and support of HR, need to end the employment relationship. Even this, however, must be done with respect, empathy, and dignity.

> **EXAM ALERT**
>
> Review best practices relative to progressive discipline and be prepared to answer questions related to those practices.

> **NOTE**
>
> Carrying out a progressive discipline process isn't easy, or comfortable. However, tolerating substandard performance and/or inappropriate behaviors is unacceptable and ill-advised for a number of even more compelling reasons. First, those employees who *are* meeting standards will get a message—a troubling message—loud and clear: "Why should I work so hard, since nothing happens to those who aren't pulling their weight?" Those who are *not* meeting standards will get a message, as well: "I guess I can continue to act this way, or perform at this level, since no one seems to have a problem with it."

Employee Relations—What's the Bottom Line?

Often, HR professionals think that the purpose or "bottom line" of effective employee relations is making employees happy. It isn't. Even setting aside the fact that no one can "make" anyone else happy, there are problems with this premise. First, using the goal of making employees happy as our benchmark of success merely reaffirms the erroneous perception of HR professionals as people people rather than as business people. Second, it ignores the organization's measures of success. It is against these organizational measures of success that we must be prepared to measure our employee relations initiatives. So, to be considered successful, an employee relations initiative must bring the organization closer to achieving its objectives, furthering its mission, and attaining its vision—all while remaining consistent with the organization's values. In short, the bottom line is that employee relations must measurably support and reinforce the bottom line of the organization.

Measuring Employee Relations Initiatives

As with all other areas of HR, we need to be prepared to use measures when ascertaining the success of employee relations initiatives. Just a few of the measures that might be appropriate to determine the success of employee relations initiatives could be

▶ Turnover levels

▶ Absenteeism (particularly unplanned)

▶ Work-related accidents/injuries/"preventable" illnesses

▶ Productivity

▶ Quality

▶ Customer satisfaction

▶ Employee survey results

▶ Return on investment (ROI)

REVIEW BREAK

Up to this point, we've focused on the commonalities that unite employee relations and labor relations. Next, however, we'll begin to look at how these two areas begin to diverge, starting with laws and legal principles.

We'll start by looking at common law and the individual employee rights that accrue from common law. In the next major section of this chapter, we'll then focus specifically on labor law and the history of labor law.

Legal Dimensions: Common Law and Individual Employee Rights

Common law refers to a system of law in which traditions, customs, and precedents have the same force of law as existing laws or statutes that have been enacted as a result of the full legislative process. With a common law system, laws and statutes are quite literally interpreted and reinterpreted on a case-by-case basis. The way this works is that each interpretation and each case sets a precedent, but each can also be reinterpreted, thus setting a new precedent. As it evolves, this continual process of interpretation and reinterpretation results in rights being granted to employees on an individual basis.

NOTE

Although—in a technical sense—common law applies to all employees, common law is eclipsed by the presence of an individual employment contract or collective bargaining agreement. In other words, if there is an employment contract in place, or if an employee belongs to a union that has negotiated an agreement, the terms that are outlined in that contract or agreement will supersede the precedents created by common law.

We'll start by looking at common law and the individual employee rights that go along with it. We'll then take a closer look at the legal doctrines associated with common law—tort doctrines and contract doctrines. Last, we'll look at some of the legal agreements that employees are asked to make in exchange for securing employment with the organization (specifically, mandatory arbitration agreements, noncompete agreements, and confidentiality agreements).

> **NOTE**
>
> Unionized employees might also be asked to adhere to one or more of these three types of agreements, in which case corresponding articles would almost certainly be included as part of a larger collectively bargained agreement.

The common law system holds true at the federal and state levels (with the exception of Louisiana, which follows Napoleonic Law). It is composed of two subtypes of law: tort law and contract law.

Common Law—Tort Doctrines

Torts are wrongful acts committed against another individual's property or person. By definition, the commission of a tort infringes on another person's rights.

Torts can include anything from damage or injuries sustained in automobile accident, to malicious prosecution, to false imprisonment—the list could go on and on. This section, however, will specifically address some of the major tort doctrines that affect individual employee rights in the absence of an employment or labor contract. Specifically, we'll take a look at the following:

- ▶ Employment-at-will
- ▶ Wrongful termination
- ▶ Implied contracts
- ▶ Defamation
- ▶ Invasion of privacy
- ▶ Negligent hiring
- ▶ Negligent training
- ▶ Negligent retention
- ▶ Negligent referral

Employment-at-will

Under the employment-at-will doctrine, the employer and the employee are both granted broad rights, most of which focus around the right of either party to terminate the employment relationship at any time for any *lawful* reason. A number of important exceptions to the employment-at-will doctrine exist, some of which are discussed in the following sections.

Lawful Reasons

Although seemingly self-explanatory, *lawful reasons* deserves a second look. Employees cannot be fired, for instance, for engaging in protected concerted activity or because they belong to a particular protected class.

> **CAUTION**
>
> Although everyone involved in the hiring/employment/termination process shares in this responsibility, HR must be particularly diligent about ensuring that a lawful, legitimate, nondiscriminatory reason exists and can be articulated when a decision is made to terminate an employee.

Public Policy Exception

Most states have adopted the *public policy exception*, which holds that an employer may not terminate an employee if the termination would violate public policy. For instance, an employee cannot be fired for serving on jury duty, for engaging in protected whistle-blower activity, or for reporting safety violations to OSHA.

Wrongful Termination

In certain circumstances, employees who believe that they have been terminated wrongfully—in a legal sense, that is—may pursue a tort action. One possible basis for wrongful termination could exist if an employee was terminated in violation of an individual employment contract in which specific requirements were articulated. Others might apply as well, but would vary from state to state.

Implied Contracts

Just because a formal written employment contract isn't in existence doesn't mean that a contract—specifically, an *implied contract*—is not in force.

There are two primary ways that an implied contract can be created: through documents that the employer has "published," and through oral statements.

Written Documents or Publications

Sometimes, the language that is used within employer-published publications (electronic or hardcopy) can be sufficient to create a contract between the employer and the employees. As one example, this can happen because of language that is used in an employee handbook. For instance, language in a handbook stating that an employee will only be terminated for "good cause" or "just cause" could be problematic, in that a court could then interpret that an employer may terminate an employee only when that standard is met.

> **CAUTION**
>
> Don't dismiss the possibility of an implied contract just because your counsel has determined that your handbook doesn't create one. Any document—whether it is directed toward just one employee, all employees, or anything in between—can be submitted as evidence in an effort to support the existence of an implied contract.

"Just Cause" or "Good Cause"

"Just cause" or "good cause" refers to a particular legal standard or test that is used to ascertain whether a specific disciplinary action was appropriate. Factors that may be considered in determining whether this standard was met could include the following:

▶ Whether the employee was warned in advance

▶ Whether the rule or standard that was violated was reasonable

▶ Whether a legitimate investigation looking into the totality of the circumstances around the alleged violation was conducted

▶ Whether reasonable "proof" of the violation existed or was obtained through investigation

▶ Whether the rule has been applied consistently

▶ Whether the punishment is proportionate to the violation

Oral Contract

An oral contract can be created when an agent of the employer promises some benefit or right. The term *agent* is legal and involved, but the point is this—be careful what your supervisors, recruiters, and others say to current (and also to potential) employees. If you have your doubts as to the veracity of this statement, look back at the avalanche of oral contract claims that resulted from the boon of "dot coms"—many of which became "dot bombs." Even a cursory glance should dispel any doubts you might have.

CAUTION

Be particularly careful not to create implied contracts through your dealings with employees or candidates. This may hold particularly true if you find yourself trying to sell the company to a prospective employee, or convince a current employee not to leave for another employment opportunity (this process, by the way, which is sometimes accompanied by a counter offer, may not always be advisable, and should not be made lightly).

Good Faith and Fair Dealing

Good faith and fair dealing is a somewhat less frequently recognized exception to the employment-at-will doctrine.

The good faith and fair dealing exception to employment-at-will kicks in when a court decides that an employer has treated an employee unfairly or has failed to provide some benefit to that employee. Two examples of this might be an employer who terminates an employee to avoid paying stock options, or one who terminates an employee right before his or her retirement benefits vest.

NOTE

If you have an employment contract with an employee, you have an obligation to treat the employee fairly. In other words, *good faith and fair dealing* would likely apply.

Defamation

Defamation is a legal term that, in a general and practical sense, refers to making a false statement that damages someone's character or reputation. Defamation that is in written form is referred to as *libel*, and defamation that is made through the spoken word is referred to as *slander*. An employee could sue an employer for libel or slander for a variety of reasons. Just one example of this might be providing a false reference to potential employers.

> **NOTE**
>
> A key requirement for defamation is that the statement (whether oral or written) must be false.

Invasion of Privacy

The right to privacy is a highly complex doctrine relating to several amendments of the U.S. Constitution, in particular the Fourth Amendment:

> The right of the people to be secure in their persons, houses, papers, and effects, against unreasonable searches and seizures, shall not be violated, and no warrants shall issue, but upon probable cause, supported by oath or affirmation, and particularly describing the place to be searched, and the persons or things to be seized.

The Fourth Amendment, however, addresses and protects individuals only against searches and seizures that are conducted by the government. Invasions of privacy by individuals who are not *state actors* (a person who is acting on behalf of the government) must be addressed through private tort law, which is why we are discussing it here.

Modern tort law includes four categories of invasion of privacy:

- ▶ Intrusion of solitude
- ▶ Public disclosure of private and embarrassing facts
- ▶ False light
- ▶ Appropriation of identity

Negligent Hiring

Negligent hiring refers to the process of hiring an employee without engaging in appropriate due diligence into that candidate's credentials, prior work experience, and the like. Negligent hiring tort claims might be filed after an employee who was hired through a flawed hiring process inflicts some sort of harm on another person—harm that could have been predicted (and therefore prevented) if the employer had conducted a background check. A hiring process can be flawed for a number of reasons. For instance, a sound hiring process that is applied in an unsound manner would be flawed, as would a hiring process that is designed in a flawed manner. Flaws could relate to inadequate or poorly conducted reference checks, job requirements that do not reflect the skills or credentials that are truly required for a position, and the like.

Example: **Tallahassee Furniture Co. v. Harrison, 1991**

Tallahassee Furniture Company hired a delivery person without interviewing him, having him fill out an employment application, or conducting any sort of background check. After entering a customer's home to deliver furniture, the delivery person stabbed and raped her. It was subsequently found that this employee had a long history of psychiatric problems (which had been serious enough to result in his hospitalization) as well as a history of drug abuse. The court ruled that the company should have conducted a background check before giving him a job that afforded him access to customers' homes, and awarded $2.5 million.

Negligent Training

Negligent training refers to an employer's failure to provide proper training to an employee when that failure results in some sort of unfit performance by the employee. A negligent training tort claim might be filed, for instance, when an employee inflicts some sort of harm on another person, harm that might not have been inflicted by that employee if the employer had provided him or her with appropriate training.

Negligent training can emerge as an issue either when an employee who was hired for one position assumes another position for which he or she may not be fully qualified and/or appropriately trained, or when an employee's job duties and responsibilities change over time, thus requiring additional training if the employee is to continue performing the job in a fit manner.

Example: **Gamble v. Dollar General Corp., 2002**

Heather Gamble went to a Dollar General Store in Purvis, Mississippi, to buy a shirt. At some point, Gamble left the store, returned to her car, and realized that a Dollar General employee had followed her out of the store. The employee subsequently followed Gamble to a Family Dollar store and parked behind Gamble. Gamble stepped out of her car and asked the employee why she was following her. Words were exchanged, and the employee—who decided that Gamble had not (as she had suspected) shoplifted anything from Dollar General—left Gamble in the parking lot of Family Dollar. During the trial, it was shown that although Dollar General had a written shoplifting policy that prohibited employees from leaving the store to pursue suspected shoplifters and from touching shoplifters, Dollar General had not provided its employees with training on how to handle actual or suspected shoplifting situations. The jury awarded Gamble $75,000 in compensatory damages and $100,000 in punitive damages, in part on the basis of a finding of negligent training.

Negligent Retention

Negligent retention refers to the continued employment of an individual who is performing in an unfit manner and therefore should have been terminated. Negligent retention tort claims might be filed when an employee who should have been terminated, but was not, inflicts some sort of harm on another person.

Negligent retention claims are often filed in conjunction with other tort claims, such as negligent training, intentional infliction of emotional distress, and the like.

Negligent Referral

Negligent referral refers to the failure of an organization to reveal truthful, negative information about an employee (or former employee) to a potential employer.

> **NOTE**
>
> Negligent referral highlights the complexities of navigating the choppy waters of tort litigation. The irony in this situation lies in the reality that many organizations confine their remarks about current and former employees to the employee's name, title, and dates of employment—often in an effort to avoid defamation claims. Although this approach may limit the employer's liability for defamation claims, it could simultaneously increase the employer's liability with respect to negligent reference if the employer conceals truthful negative information about an employee.

Example: **Randi W. v. Muroc Joint Unified School Dist., 1997**

Officials at several school districts recommended a former employee, even though that employee had been the subject of several complaints relating to sexual misconduct with students. Two situations were so serious that the employee was forced to resign. Despite all of this, the employee moved from one school district to another, bolstered in large part by recommendations from the school districts for which he had worked. Letters from the former employers recommended the employee "for almost any administrative position he wishes to pursue," and commended his efforts to make "a safe, orderly and clean environment for students and staff." He was hired at another school district and ultimately molested a 13-year-old girl in his office. The court found that these misleading employment recommendations amounted to "an affirmative misrepresentation presenting a foreseeable and substantial risk of physical harm to a third person," and that the student who filed the complaint had successfully established a prima facie case of negligent misrepresentation.

Common Law—Contract Doctrines

Another way in which common law directly impacts the employment relationship is through *contract doctrines*. A contract is an agreement that is enforceable by law. Contracts can either be oral or written.

Employment contracts are made between an employer and an employee. They can include topics such as term or length of employment, compensation and benefits, job responsibilities, and termination.

> **NOTE**
>
> The terms and conditions under which an employee can be terminated constitute a critical element of any employment contract. Specifically, the contract should state whether the employee is employed under the employment-at-will doctrine, or—conversely—whether the employee can be terminated only for just cause.

Employees are often asked to sign specific agreements in exchange for the opportunity to work for the employer. Three agreements that we'll look at in this section include the following:

- ▸ Mandatory arbitration agreements
- ▸ Noncompete agreements
- ▸ Confidentiality agreements

Mandatory Arbitration Agreements

More and more, potential employees are being asked to agree in writing to mandatory arbitration. This means that, in return for the opportunity to be employed by the organization, the employee agrees to resolve employment-related issues through a neutral third party (the arbitrator/s) *instead of* filing a private lawsuit against the employer.

> **EXAM ALERT**
>
> Familiarize yourself with the advantages and disadvantages of mandatory arbitration agreements, from the perspectives of the employer *and* the employee.

The landmark U.S. Supreme Court case that confirmed the legality of mandatory arbitration agreements was *Circuit City Stores, Inc. v. Adams, 2001*, in which the court ruled that requiring employees to sign mandatory arbitration agreements as a condition of employment is legal, and that such agreements are enforceable under the Federal Arbitration Act (FAA).

Less than 10 months later, in *EEOC v. Waffle House, Inc., 2002*, the court ruled that although the existence of a signed mandatory arbitration agreement precluded the employee from being allowed to file a private lawsuit, it did *not* preclude the EEOC from seeking its own independent action against an employer, because the EEOC cannot be bound by a private arbitration agreement to which it was not a party. More specifically, the EEOC is not required to "relinquish its statutory authority if it has not agreed to do so," and that, as "the master of its own case," the EEOC can independently determine whether it will commit resources to specific cases.

Noncompete Agreements

Noncompete agreements prohibit current and (within stated limitations) former employees from competing against the employer. "Competing" can manifest itself in a number of different ways, and must be defined within the agreement, with language similar to this:

> The term "not compete" as used herein shall mean that the employee shall not own, manage, operate, consult, or be employed in a business substantially similar to or competitive with the present business of the company or such other business activity in which the company may substantially engage during the term of employment.

In return for signing the noncompete agreement, the employee is given the opportunity to work for the organization.

The strength, enforceability, and even legality of noncompete agreements depends on state and/or local laws, precedents that have been set by court cases, and a variety of other factors, such as

▶ Whether there is a time frame established in the agreement, and, if so, how long it is in effect

▶ The existence (and reasonableness) of any geographic limitation within which the employee cannot compete

▶ Whether there is anything in the agreement that would preclude the employee from earning a living in his or her chosen field

▶ Whether the employee is fairly compensated for signing the noncompete agreement, particularly if the employee was already employed at the time that he or she was asked to sign the agreement

Confidentiality Agreements

Confidentiality agreements prohibit employees from revealing any confidential information to which they might be exposed during the course of their employment. This could include trade secrets, patent information, and the like. It also prohibits employees from using confidential information in any way other than the purposes for which it was intended and is necessary within the context of the employee's job.

REVIEW BREAK

In this section, we looked at common law issues, including tort law and contract law, and the impact that they have on workplaces. As stated at the beginning of this section, however, these common law provisions are overridden by any situation where a labor or employment contract is in place. Let's take a look now at those laws that govern and have shaped labor and labor-management relations.

Related Legislation: Labor Relations (and a Historical Backdrop)

We will be looking at a number of laws that have impacted and continue to impact labor and employee relations, including the following:

- Sherman Antitrust Act, 1890

- Clayton Act, 1914

- Railway Labor Act, 1926

- Norris-LaGuardia Act, 1932

- National Industrial Recovery Act, 1933

- National Labor Relations Act or Wagner Act, 1935

- Labor Management Relations Act or Taft-Hartley Act, 1947

- Labor Management Reporting and Disclosure Act or Landrum-Griffin Act, 1959

> **NOTE**
>
> All these laws impact labor and labor relations. As specifically indicated in this section, however, some of them impact employees who do not belong to a union.

Sherman Antitrust Act, 1890

The Sherman Antitrust Act, named for its sponsor, John Sherman of Ohio, was passed in an effort to curb the growth of monopolies. Under the act, any business combination that sought to restrain trade or commerce would, from that time forward, be illegal. Specifically, the act stated

- Section 1: "Every contract, combination in the form of trust or otherwise, or conspiracy, in restraint of trade or commerce among the several States, or with foreign nations, is declared to be illegal."

- Section 2: "Every person who shall monopolize, or attempt to monopolize, or combine or conspire with any other person or persons, to monopolize any part of the trade or commerce among the several States, or with foreign nations, shall be deemed guilty of a felony."

If, after reading the two sections cited here, you're feeling a bit bemused and confused, you share something in common with those who wrestled to interpret this law more than a century ago. The vague language of the act, however, proved to be quite challenging—particularly terms such as "trust," "combination," "conspiracy," and "monopoly." This confusion opened the door for the Sherman Antitrust Act to be used against labor unions by those who chose to define those unions as monopolies. For instance, the act allowed the use of injunctions—court orders that could be issued to restrict certain activities, such as strikes. The first example of this was when an injunction was issued against the American Railway Union in 1894 to end its strike against the Pullman Palace Car Company. George Pullman, the president of this company, decided to reduce his workers' wages. The company refused to arbitrate, and the American Railway Union called a strike, which started in Chicago and spread across 27 states. The attorney general sought and was awarded an injunction against the union.

> **NOTE**
>
> The Sherman Antitrust Act also placed responsibility for pursuing and investigating trusts on government attorneys and district courts.

Clayton Act, 1914

Passed in 1914, the Clayton Act was enacted to build on and clarify the Sherman Antitrust Act.

The provision of the Clayton Act that is most relevant to labor—and therefore to HR professionals—is that Section 6 of the act specifically exempted labor unions and agricultural organizations from the Sherman Antitrust Act:

> The labor of a human being is not a commodity or article of commerce. Nothing contained in the antitrust laws shall be construed to forbid the existence and operation of labor, agricultural, or horticultural organizations, instituted for the purposes of mutual help, and not having capital stock or conducted for profit, or to forbid or restrain individual members of such organizations from lawfully carrying out the legitimate objects thereof; nor shall such organizations, or the members thereof, be held or construed to be illegal combinations or conspiracies in restraint of trade, under the antitrust laws.

This section rendered labor unions exempt from the Sherman Antitrust Act, and effectively legalized boycotts, peaceful strikes, and peaceful picketing—thus rendering illegal injunctions of the sort that was filed against the American Railway Union during the Pullman strike.

Railway Labor Act, 1926

In 1926, the Railway Labor Act (RLA) was passed. As its name implies, the Railway Labor Act applied only to interstate railroads and their related undertakings—at the time, the most critical element of the nation's transportation infrastructure. In 1936, it was amended to include airlines engaged in interstate commerce.

The Railway Labor Act was critical in that it provided what was perhaps the first win-win scenario for labor and management. Railroad management wanted to keep the trains moving, which meant they needed to end wildcat strikes. Railroad workers wanted to organize, to be recognized as the exclusive bargaining agent in dealing with the railroad, and to negotiate and enforce agreements.

The Railway Labor Act is also significant in that it is where the *work now, grieve later* rule originated. In an effort to keep the rails running, which Congress felt was in the public's interest, Congress mandated that when disputes arise in the workplace, transportation workers covered by the RLA must "work now and grieve later" (with a few exceptions, such as for safety).

Norris-LaGuardia Act, 1932

The Norris-LaGuardia Act strengthened unions even more. First, it established the rights of labor unions to organize and to strike. Second, it prohibited federal courts from enforcing "yellow dog" contracts or agreements.

> **NOTE**
>
> A *yellow dog* contract is a contract or an agreement between an employer and an employee, the terms of which are essentially that the employer will give the employee a job, as long as the employee agrees not to join or have any involvement with a labor union.

National Industrial Recovery Act, 1933

In 1933, Congress passed the National Industry Recovery Act (NRA). Title I of the act guaranteed laborers the right to organize and bargain collectively. The act also established that employees could not be required, as a condition of employment, to join or refrain from joining a labor organization.

In May of 1935, the National Industrial Recovery Act was held unconstitutional by the U.S. Supreme Court (*Schechter Poultry Corp. v. United States, 1935*). Although this decision was wholly unrelated to labor and collective bargaining, the Supreme Court decision rendered the labor-related provisions illegal, as well. The right to organize and bargain reverted, once again, back to railway workers—and no one else. This would not, however, be the case for long.

National Labor Relations Act (Wagner Act), 1935

Two months later, Congress passed the National Labor Relations Act (NLRA). Also known as the Wagner Act (named for Senator Robert R. Wagner of New York), the NLRA guaranteed "the right to self-organization; to form, join, or assist labor organizations; to bargain collectively through representatives of their own choosing; and to engage in concerted activities for the purpose of collective bargaining or other mutual aid and protection."

> **NOTE**
>
> Certain groups or categories of employees are excluded under the NLRA from membership in a bargaining unit. Examples would include managers, supervisors, confidential employees (essentially secretaries and administrative assistants to managers who can make labor relations decisions), and several others.

The NLRA also established procedures for selecting a labor organization to represent a unit of employees in collective bargaining and prohibited employers from interfering with that selection. In addition, under the NLRA, the employer would then be required to bargain with the appointed representative of its employees. Although bargaining does not require that either side agree to a proposal or to make concessions, it does require each side to bargain in good faith. The NLRA also established regulations relative to what tactics (such as strikes, lockouts, and picketing) could be employed during bargaining in an effort to bolster bargaining objectives.

The NLRA applied to all employers involved in interstate commerce, with the exception of agricultural employees, government employees, and employees covered by the Railway Labor Act.

The Act also established the National Labor Relations Board (NLRB), a then-new federal agency that would be (and still is) responsible for administering and enforcing the rights established by the NLRA. As stated on its website, the NLRB has two principle functions:

▶ To determine, through secret-ballot elections, the free democratic choice by employees whether they wish to be represented by a union in dealing with their employers and if so, by which union.

▶ To prevent and remedy unlawful acts, called unfair labor practices, by either employers or unions.

NOTE

Initially, unfair labor practices (ULPs) were identified only for employers. ULPs, as they pertained to unions, were subsequently added through the passage of the Labor-Management Relations Act (also known as the Taft-Hartley Act) in 1947.

The NLRA identified five categories of employer ULPs:

▶ To "interfere with, restrain, or coerce employees" in the exercise of their rights to engage in concerted or union activities or refrain from them

▶ To dominate or interfere with the formation or administration of a labor organization

▶ To discriminate against employees for engaging in concerted or union activities or refraining from them

▶ To discriminate against an employee for filing charges with the NLRB or taking part in any NLRB proceedings

▶ To refuse to bargain with the union that is the lawful representative of its employees

The terms of the NLRA originally permitted closed shops and union shops. A *closed shop* is one in which an employer agrees to hire only union members. A *union shop* is one in which an employer agrees to require anyone hired to join the union. These practices were subsequently prohibited, however, through the next major piece of labor-related legislation, the Labor Management Relations Act (also known as the Taft-Hartley Act). Read on:

Labor Management Relations Act (Taft-Hartley Act), 1947

The Labor Management Relations Act (LMRA), also known as the Taft-Hartley Act, was an amendment designed to remedy what the Republican Congress saw as two major omissions in the Wagner Act: first, the identification of behaviors and practices that would be considered ULPs on the part of unions, and second, a provision that would allow the government to issue an injunction against a strike that threatened national interests.

Taft-Hartley identified the following unfair labor practices that could be committed by unions:

- ▶ Restraining or coercing employees in the exercise of their rights or an employer in the choice of its bargaining representative

- ▶ Causing an employer to discriminate against an employee

- ▶ Refusing to bargain with the employer of the employees it represents

- ▶ Engaging in certain types of secondary boycotts

> **NOTE**
>
> *Secondary boycotts* are defined as efforts to convince others to stop doing business with a particular organization that is the subject of a primary boycott.

- ▶ Requiring excessive dues

- ▶ Engaging in featherbedding

> **NOTE**
>
> *Featherbedding* agreements require the employer to pay union members wages whether or not their work is needed.

- ▶ Picketing for recognition for more than 30 days without petitioning for an election

- ▶ Entering into hot cargo agreements

> **NOTE**
>
> An employer who makes a *hot cargo agreement* agrees to stop doing business with another entity. Hot cargo agreements can thus help to protect union work by allowing union members to refuse to handle or process work produced by nonunion entities.

▶ Striking or picketing a health care establishment without giving the required notice

In addition, the Taft-Hartley Act imposed these additional changes:

▶ Reaffirmed that employers have a constitutional right to express their opposition to unions, so long as employees are not threatened with reprisal for their union activities or promised benefits for refraining from such activities

▶ Expressly excluded supervisors from coverage under the act

▶ Permitted employers to fire supervisors who engaged in union activities or did not support the employer's position

▶ Outlawed closed shops, agreements that stated that employers could hire only individuals who were members of labor unions

▶ Expressly permitted union shops, in which nonunion workers must join the union within a certain amount of time after being hired

NOTE

In *right-to-work* states, union shops are illegal. In other words, no employee is required to join the union.

TIP

The list of right-to-work states can, and does, change. Be sure to do an online search to confirm the status for any particular state(s).

▶ Established a 60-day no-strike and no-lockout notice period requiring unions as well as employers to give each other 60 days' notice before strikes (on the part of the union) and lockouts (on the part of the employer) if either party wishes to change or cancel an existing collective bargaining agreement

▶ Prohibited jurisdictional strikes

NOTE

A *jurisdictional strike* is a strike through which a union seeks to pressure an employer to assign particular work to its members, rather than to members of other unions or to nonunion workers.

▶ Abolished the U.S. Conciliation Service and established the Federal Mediation and Conciliation Service (FMCS)

▶ Authorized the President to intervene in strikes or potential strikes that create a national emergency (a provision that President George W. Bush invoked in 2002 in connection with the employer lockout of the International Longshore and Warehouse Union during negotiations with west coast shipping and stevedoring companies)

Labor Management Reporting and Disclosure Act (Landrum-Griffin Act)—1959

By 1959, it became clear—painfully clear—that more guidelines were necessary. Senate committee hearings revealed improper activities by labor as well as by management, uncovered evidence of collusion between labor and management, exposed violent practices used by certain labor leaders, and uncovered the diversion and misuse of labor union funds by senior-level union leaders.

Enter the Labor Management Reporting and Disclosure Act (also known as Landrum-Griffin). Some of the protections instituted through this act are

► A requirement that unions submit annual financial reporting to the Department of Labor (DOL) to document how union members' dues were spent

► A bill of rights for union members, guaranteeing them freedom of speech and periodic secret elections

► The designation of every union official as a fiduciary

► Even stronger provisions relative to secondary boycotting and organizational and recognition picketing

Labor Relations: Understanding Unions and Union-Related Activities

HR professionals also need a solid understanding of unions, union structure, and union-related activities. To that end, this section will look at the following subjects:

► How unions are structured

► Union organizing (the organizing process)

► Union decertification and deauthorization

► Protected concerted activities

► Strikes

How Unions Are Structured

Unions are structured democratically, in that union officers are elected. They are also hierarchical.

HR professionals need to be familiar with the following four types of union entities:

Local Unions

Local unions are largely responsible for the day-to-day administration of the labor agreement and relationship with union members. "Locals" generally have an elected president and elected stewards who represent the workers in the workplace. Larger local unions might have a full-time paid business agent. Most locals belong to and are chartered by a larger national union.

National Unions

National unions bring together all the union locals who are scattered across the country. There are usually different hierarchical levels in between the local union and the national union. National unions have far more power with respect to bargaining and political influence than the union locals could have on their own. National unions also advise and guide local unions, and may also manage nationwide benefits programs (such as retirement programs and health insurance plans).

Federations

A federation is a group of national unions. Its many members speak with one voice, thus wielding even greater influence and lobbying power. Federations do not, however, get involved with bargaining or contract administration.

Until the summer of 2005, the AFL-CIO was, in many ways, a federation that was *the* voice of labor in America. In 2005, however, several major national unions quit the AFL-CIO, including the following:

▶ The Service Employees International Union (SEIU)

▶ The International Brotherhood of Teamsters

▶ The United Food and Commercial Workers (UFCW)

▶ UNITE HERE

▶ United Farm Workers

▶ Carpenters Union

Together, these departing unions—representing about 4.5 million workers—nearly 35% of the AFL-CIO's previous member of out of the previous total membership of 13 million workers—formed Change to Win (CTW).

International

International labor organizations operate on the international level in much the same manner as federations operate on the national level, only "bigger." For instance, the International Confederation of Free Trade Unions (ICFTU) is an international labor organization that has been in existence for more than 55 years and has a membership of 145 million people, across five continents and more than 150 countries. All member unions have a democratic structure. ICFTU consists of three major regional organizations:

▶ APRO for Asia and the Pacific

▶ AFRO for Africa

▶ ORIT for the Americas

The ICFTU is highly active. According to its website, IFCTU's five "priorities for action" include the following:

- Employment and international labor standards

- Tackling the multinationals

- Trade union rights

- Equality, women, race, and migrants

- Trade union organization and recruitment

Union Organizing (The Organizing Process)

Through the organizing process, a union seeks to become the recognized representative of a bargaining unit of individuals within an organization. Members of a bargaining unit share common interests with respect to items that are negotiated through a collective bargaining agreement. A bargaining unit can represent part or all of an organization's workforce (except supervisors, or others who are otherwise excluded from membership in unions).

There are five steps involved in this union organizing process:

1. *Make a Connection—Express Interest*—In this step, contact is established. Either the union initiates contact with employees in an effort to begin the process of exploring whether there is interest in forming a union, or one or more employees who have an interest in forming a union initiate contact with the union.

> **EXAM ALERT**
>
> Be familiar with reasons why unions might initiate contact with employees within an organization, and why employees within an organization might initiate contact with a union.

2. *Confirm Interest—Obtain Authorization Cards*—After contact has been established and cultivated, unions confirm and demonstrate employees' interest by obtaining *authorization cards* signed by employees. When 30% of the employees who would be in the collective bargaining unit have signed authorization cards, the union can petition NLRB to hold an election (the 30% threshold demonstrates a "showing of interest" to the NLRB). Often, however, unions may seek to obtain signed authorization cards from 50% or more employees before petitioning the NLRB, so as to ascertain the seriousness of employees' interest in joining a union.

    In general, petitions from the union will not be accepted if an election has been held within the prior year, if a union has been certified within the past year but has not successfully negotiated a contract, or if there is a valid contract (not to exceed three years) in effect.

3. *Obtaining Recognition*—The next step in the process is for the union to gain recognition. There are a number of ways this can happen, both voluntary and involuntary.

After the union has obtained recognition—regardless of the way in which that recognition has been obtained—the employer must provide the NLRB with a list of the names and addresses of all of the employees who are eligible to vote in the union certification election (the "Excelsior List"). The NLRB will, in turn, provide that list to the union. The nickname "Excelsior List" is derived from the NLRB decision *Excelsior Underwear, Inc.* v. *NLRB*, 1966, in which the NLRB considered whether "a fair and free election [can] be held when the union involved lacks the names and addresses of employees eligible to vote in that election, and the employer refuses to accede to the union's request." The NLRB ruled that it could not. As a result, the employer must provide the list of employees' names and addresses within seven days after the NLRB has scheduled an election.

4. *The Campaign*—The NLRB will carry out a secret ballot election 30–60 days after the NLRB determines that an election will be held. As always, unfair labor practices, by employers as well as by unions, are prohibited during the union organizing campaign. See "Collective Bargaining: The Process," to review specific information about ULPs.

The employer and the union are each permitted to engage in certain activities, and are each prohibited from engaging in other activities, during the organizing and campaign processes.

5. *The Election*—The NLRB conducts the secret ballot election, usually at the workplace, between 30 and 60 days after the NLRB issues its decision. Management and the union are both permitted to have observers present at the election. Observers may object to a vote if they feel that a vote is being cast illegally. The NLRB is responsible for resolving all voter eligibility issues prior to the final vote count.

If a majority of the individuals vote in favor of the proposed bargaining unit, the unit will be established. Even if there is more than one union competing to represent the proposed collective bargaining unit, a simple majority vote is *still* required in order for a union to be recognized. If there is no majority vote, the top two choices will have an election, so as to generate a majority vote.

The NLRB can order a new election under certain circumstances if it is determined that the "laboratory conditions" of the secret ballot were disturbed in a way that impacted the outcome of the election.

In rare circumstances, the NLRB can require the employer to recognize and bargain with the union in the event that the employer conducted itself in such a seriously egregious manner that the NLRB deems "the holding of a fair election unlikely." This rare situation is referred to as a *bargaining order*.

Permissible Union Activities

Some of the activities in which unions are permitted to engage are

- Inside organizing, where pro-union individuals can seek to influence others at the workplace (unless a no-solicitation rule in effect).

> **CAUTION**
>
> Employers must apply a no-solicitation rule 100% of the time for it to be upheld with respect to any form of inside organizing. Something as simple as selling cookie dough or wrapping paper can be enough to invalidate a no-solicitation rule.

- Mailing campaign literature to employees' homes.
- Leafleting—Distributing leaflets and flyers offsite or onsite.
- Local media, such as newspaper ads or radio spots.
- Dedicated websites.
- Salting—A *salt* is a union organizer who seeks employment with the organization for the express purpose of actively organizing and campaigning within the organization.
- Organizational picketing—Designed to generate interest on the part of employees to vote for union representation.

Permissible Employer Activities

Like unions, employers have the right to engage in certain activities during a union organizing effort or campaign. Some of those activities include the following:

- Voicing an opinion about unions and the unionization of its operation, as long as its communications carry no direct or implied threat toward employees, and as long as those communications are in no way coercive. This can be done in a number of ways:
    - Email
    - Hardcopy mail to home addresses
    - Payroll stuffers

> ▶ Captive audience meetings—In the workplace, during regular working hours, the employer can hold mandatory presentations during which the employer can share its opinions relative to unions and the unionization of its operations. Unions do not have this opportunity. Captive audience meetings may not be held within 24 hours of the actual election.

▶ Secure the services of a consultant in its efforts to remain union free.

Impermissible Union Activities

Like employers, unions are prohibited from engaging in unfair labor practices during a union organizing campaign. Some activities that would constitute an unfair labor practice on the part of a union would include the following:

▶ Coercing

▶ Threatening

▶ Retaliating, or threatening to retaliate

Impermissible Employer Activities

So, too, there are a number of activities in which employers cannot engage during a union campaign—activities that would constitute an unfair labor practice. Some of those activities include the following:

▶ Telling workers that the employer will fire or punish them if they engage in any union activity

▶ Laying off or discharging any worker for union activity

▶ Granting workers wage increases or special concessions in an effort to bribe people from joining a union

▶ Asking workers about confidential union matters, meetings, members, and so on

▶ Asking workers about the union or about union representatives

▶ Asking workers how they intend to vote in a union election

▶ Asking workers whether they belong to a union or have signed up for a union

▶ Threatening or coercing workers in an attempt to influence their vote

▶ Telling workers that existing benefits will be discontinued if the employer is unionized

▶ Saying unionization will force the employer to lay off workers

▶ Promising employees promotions, raises, or other benefits if they get out of the union or refrain from joining it

▶ Spying on union gatherings

Union Decertification and Deauthorization

From time to time, employees may engage in an election process, vote in a union, and ultimately find that things didn't turn out quite the way they expected. It is in situations like this when decertification or deauthorization elections may be held.

Union Decertification

If employees decide that they no longer wish to be represented by their union, they must prepare for and hold another election. The process of removing the union's rights to represent the employees is called *decertification*. This process is similar to certification, only in reverse. It starts with a petition requesting decertification that is signed by at least 30% of employees who belong to the bargaining union being sent to the NLRB. (Decertification cannot occur within the 12-month period following certification after a contract has been negotiated.) The NLRB will then conduct a decertification election if it decides that the petition is in order. If at least 50% of employees who vote (as opposed to 50% of the members of the collective bargaining unit, or CBU) cast a vote to remove the union, then the union will be officially decertified. The union will also be decertified if the vote is exactly even.

Union Deauthorization

Far less frequently, a deauthorization election may be held. Deauthorization revokes the security clause in the contract and effectively creates an "open shop" (see the section "Collective Bargaining: Agreements"). Deauthorization requires a majority vote of the entire bargaining union, not just the members of the unit who vote in the deauthorization election.

Protected Concerted Activities

Protected concerted activity refers to associational rights that are granted to employees through Section 7 of the NLRA:

> Employees shall have the right to self-organization, to form, join, or assist labor organization, to bargain collectively through representatives of their own choosing, and to engage in other concerted activities for the purpose of collective bargaining or other mutual aid or protection, and shall also have the right to refrain from any or all such activities.

CAUTION

Through this language, the NLRA protects associational rights for employees who do not belong to a union, as well as for employees who are unionized. This interpretation was confirmed by *NLRB v. Phoenix Mutual Life Insurance Co., 1948*. As such, it is for this reason that employers need to be careful not to interfere with protected concerted activities—even in nonunionized workplaces.

In order not to interfere with concerted activity, employers need to understand what concerted activity is.

Concerted Activity

Any activities undertaken by individual employees who are united in pursuit of a common goal are considered to be *concerted activity*. For an employee's activity to be concerted, the activity must be engaged in with or on the authority of other employees, rather than just on behalf of the individual employee (Meyers Industries, 281 NLRB 882, 1986).

Activity must be concerted before it can be protected by the NLRA.

Protected Concerted Activity

Section 8 of the NLRA specifically states that

> It shall be an unfair labor practice for an employer to interfere with, restrain, or coerce employees in the exercise of the rights guaranteed in [Section 7].

Protected concerted activity can include activity aimed at improving employees' terms and conditions of employment. If an employee is engaged in protected concerted activity, an employer might be considered to have violated the NLRA if

- ▶ The employer knew of the concerted nature of the employee's activity.

- ▶ The concerted activity was protected by the act.

- ▶ The adverse employment action in question (for instance, termination) was motivated by the employee's protected concerted activity.

Remedies for unfair labor practices include reinstatement with full back pay plus interest. Employers also are required to post a notice to all employees detailing the violation and the remedy.

Example of Protected Concerted Activity

The following are specific cases in which employers were found to have committed an unfair labor practice by interfering with protected concerted activities:

- ▶ An employer fired a salesman for being an "outspoken critic" against two-hour meetings that sales personnel were required to attend (without compensation) before regular work hours. The employee was awarded reinstatement with full back pay plus interest (*NLRB v. Henry Colder Co., 1990*).

- ▶ An employer fired two employees who composed a letter protesting a change to the compensation system. The employees were reinstated with full back pay plus interest (*NLRB v. Westmont Plaza, 1990*).

- ▶ An employer fired employees who mailed a letter to the employer's parent company complaining about working conditions and bonuses. (The employer's president was requiring employees to spend large amounts of time on the president's personal projects.) The employees were reinstated with full back pay plus interest (*NLRB v. Oakes Machine Corp., 1990*).

Labor Strikes

No dialogue about unions would be complete without some discussion of strikes.

There are two very different types of strikes (or work stoppages)—unfair labor practice strikes and economic strikes.

Unfair Labor Practice (ULP) Strikes

Unions sometimes allege, correctly or incorrectly, that the employer has committed an unfair labor practice during contract negotiations and call a strike in response to those alleged ULPs. Employers cannot hire permanent strike replacements during a ULP strike, and the striking workers must be returned to their original positions after the strike is over.

It is not enough to "assume" that a ULP strike is a ULP strike. The courts would need to determine that a strike was, in fact, a ULP strike, and not an economic strike in disguise.

Economic Strikes

Any strike that is not directly tied to the employer's commission of a ULP is considered, by law, to be an *economic strike*. Economic strikes are called in an effort to obtain some sort of economic concession from the employer during collective bargaining negotiations—concessions relating to higher wages, better working conditions, low health-insurance premiums, and the like.

NOTE

Economic strikers cannot be terminated except under highly limited situations, such as if they engage in serious misconduct during the strike. Economic strikers can, however, be permanently replaced by the employer.

TIP

Under the Mackay Doctrine, employers have the right to permanently replace workers who strike during an economic strike. This right and its nickname derived from the Supreme Court decision in *NLRB v. Mackay Radio and Telegraph Co., 1938.*

CAUTION

Although it is advisable to avoid using the word "permanent" when describing employment relationships, the term "permanent replacement" is used here, because it is the recognized vernacular with respect to strikes.

Perhaps the most renowned example of the use of permanent replacement workers occurred in 1981 when President Ronald Reagan replaced 12,000 striking air traffic controllers. This event had a chilling impact on economic strikes because of concerns relative to employees losing their jobs to permanent replacement workers.

> **NOTE**
>
> The historic impact of this type of strike is not diminished by the fact that workers who have been permanently replaced are entitled to priority status as the employer hires new employees.

Strike-Related Protected Concerted Activities

Economic strikes are considered to be a protected concerted activity under the NLRA. Other protected concerted strike-related activities include sympathy strikes and picketing.

Sympathy Strikes

Employees who are not directly involved in an economic dispute but who choose not to cross a picket line out of support for striking workers are engaging in a sympathy strike. Sympathy strikers do not need to be employed by the same employer as the employees who are actually on strike in order to engage in a sympathy strike.

> **EXAM ALERT**
>
> Familiarize yourself with how organizations can prepare for a strike and the rules that management must follow during a strike.

Picketing

Picketing is an expression of free speech that takes place when people congregate outside a workplace. In order to be considered protected concerted activity, picketing must remain nonviolent. Pickets can be used to inform the public, to discourage nonstriking workers from entering the workplace (also referred to as *crossing the picket line*), and to encourage people to boycott the products or services of the employer who is the subject of the picket.

Double Breasting Picketing

Double breasting picketing, which is actually a type of secondary boycott, takes place when a company that owns or operates union as well as nonunion operations shifts work to the nonunion operation in an effort to diminish the impact of the strike. In this situation, the nonunion operation to which the work has been shifted *can* be picketed.

Common Situs Picketing

Common situs picketing, which is actually a type of secondary boycott, occurs when members of a labor union picket a workplace in which multiple employers work—the employer with whom the labor union has the dispute, as well as one or more employers with whom the labor union does not have a dispute. Common situs picketing is legal as long as the picket signs indicate the name of the employer with whom the picketers have a dispute.

> **NOTE**
>
> Double breasting picketing and common situs picketing are both examples of secondary boycotts. Secondary boycotts are actions that are ultimately intended to impact a primary party by taking action against a secondary party. Depending on the circumstances, secondary boycotts may or may not be legal.

One specific situation that can clear the way for the union to engage in a secondary boycott is the ally doctrine.

> **EXAM ALERT**
>
> Familiarize yourself with the *ally doctrine*, which states that a union may expand upon its primary picketing activity to include employers who are allies of the primary employer.

Strike-Related Activity That Is Not Protected Concerted Activity

In addition to strike-related activity that is considered to be protected concerted activity, and which is therefore protected by law, there are certain strike-related activities that are not considered to be protected concerted activity.

Wildcat Strikes

If a collective bargaining agreement contains a no-strike clause prohibiting striking during the duration of the agreement, any strikes that occur are considered *wildcat strikes*. Wildcat strikes are no longer considered to be protected concerted activity.

Jurisdictional Strike

A *jurisdictional strike* is used to force an employer to assign work to bargaining-unit employees instead of nonbargaining-unit employees. Jurisdictional strikes constitute a ULP, and those who engage in a jurisdictional strike can experience discipline up to and including termination.

> **EXAM ALERT**
>
> Also familiarize yourself with other strike-related terms and conditions, such as work slowdowns, strike benefits, strike insurance, strike preparation, and so on.

> **EXAM ALERT**
>
> The area of striking, picketing, and boycotting is not as simple or direct as it appears (and, quite frankly, it doesn't appear all that simple to begin with). Be certain to familiarize yourself thoroughly with this area before sitting for the PHR exam.

Collective Bargaining: The Process

Collective bargaining is the process by which an employer and a labor union negotiate the terms of the collective bargaining agreement that will govern the employment relationship for those employees who are represented by the union.

This section will look at a number of specific dimensions of collective bargaining:

- Good faith bargaining

- Subjects of bargaining (mandatory, permissive, and illegal)

- Approaches to collective bargaining

Good Faith Bargaining

According to Section 8(d) of the NLRA, the employer and the union are both required to bargain in good faith. The failure of either the union or the employer to do so is considered to be a ULP. Determining what does and does not constitute good faith bargaining, however, isn't always clear or simple.

Bargaining in good faith *doesn't* mean that either side is *required* to reach an agreement or to make concessions. Instead, when ascertaining whether an employer has bargained in good faith, the NLRB will take a more comprehensive look at the activities in which each side has engaged, in their totality.

Sometimes, good faith bargaining is more easily defined by what it's not than by what it is. In other words, good faith bargaining can sometimes be defined by the absence of behaviors that are characteristic of "bad faith bargaining." The following behaviors, when demonstrated by either the union or the employer, could constitute bad faith bargaining:

- Failing to agree to meet at reasonable and convenient places and/or times

- Failing to show up at the agreed-upon places and/or times

- Repeatedly canceling meetings

- Failing to maintain an "open mind" during negotiations

- Surface bargaining—Going through the motions of bargaining, with no real intention of ultimately reaching agreement (in other words, keeping bargaining "at the surface," without moving toward true agreement)

- Repeatedly withdrawing previous positions/concessions

- Refusing to bargain on mandatory items, insisting on bargaining on permissive items, or attempting to bargain on illegal items (see "Illegal Subjects," later in this chapter)

- Committing any sort of ULP(s)

In addition to these items, all of which can be committed by either the employer or the union, there are other examples of bad faith bargaining that could be committed by the employer:

- Taking any action that is deliberately designed to weaken the union's status as the bargaining agent

▶ Presenting proposals directly to employees instead of the union bargaining team

▶ Instituting unilateral changes to wages, hours, and/or terms and conditions of employment while negotiations are in process

▶ Providing the union with insufficient information with which to make informed proposals and counterproposals

Subjects of Bargaining

The NLRB is empowered to categorize bargaining issues into three categories: mandatory, permissive, and illegal (derived from the Supreme Court decision *NLRB v. Wooster Division of Borg-Warner Corporation, 1958*).

Required Subjects

Required subjects are those that must be bargained in good faith if either the employer or the employees' representative requests it. It's important to keep in mind, however, that according to the NLRA, bargaining in good faith does not require "either party to agree to a proposal or require the making of a concession."

Examples of required subjects include pay, wages, hours of employment, pensions for present employees, bonuses, group insurance, grievance procedures, safety practices, seniority, procedures for discharge, layoff, recall, or discipline, and union security.

> **NOTE**
>
> Sometimes, although a certain item may not be considered to be a required subject, implementing that item might have an impact on a required subject. The bargaining that would take place as a result of these impacts is referred to as *effects bargaining*. For instance, an organization's decision to close a particular plant is not a required subject. The decisions that are made relative to how employees will be treated during and impacted by the closure *is* a required subject, and is therefore an example of effects bargaining.

Voluntary or Permissive Subjects

Voluntary or *permissive* subjects are topics that can be submitted to collective bargaining if and only if the employer and the employees' representative are willing to do so. Attempting to force bargaining on a voluntary or permissive subject constitutes a ULP.

For example, voluntary or permissive subjects could include closing plants, shutting down parts of the business, instituting preemployment testing, and/or modifying retiree benefits.

Illegal Subjects

Certain topics simply cannot be collectively bargained. These would include items that would constitute a violation of the NLRA, labor laws, or, for that matter, *any* law.

Examples of illegal subjects would include closed-shop agreements, hot cargo clauses, or featherbedding.

Approaches to Collective Bargaining

This section will discuss three primary approaches to collective bargaining: distributive, integrative, and interest-based.

> **EXAM ALERT**
>
> Be familiar with approaches to collective bargaining.

Distributive Bargaining

Distributive bargaining takes an approach to bargaining in which each side sets forth its position and does its best to "stick to it." By the end of the process, one side will have won some (or all) of what it wanted, and one side will have lost some (or all) of what it wanted.

Distributive bargaining is essentially adversarial in nature. It assumes that there's only so much to go around. When you divide up the pie, therefore, one side will end up with more of the pie, and one side will end up with less of the pie.

By its very nature, the distributive approach to bargaining tends to encourage stubbornness, and also has a greater likelihood of damaging the parties' relationship with each other.

Integrative Bargaining

The integrative approach to bargaining doesn't look at issues one at a time—instead, it looks at multiple issues as a whole (hence the term *integrative*). Integrative bargaining looks at the same pie, but in a different way: Instead of just splitting up the pie, it creatively considers how it might be able to make the pie bigger. It looks at how the needs of both sides can be better met when looked at in their entirety, and at how a win-win solution can be explored, rather than settling for the win-lose scenario that will almost invariably result from distributive bargaining.

In essence, advocates of integrative bargaining believe that an agreement that renders one side "better off" does not necessarily have to result in the other side being "worse off." Instead, through creativity and cooperation, trade-offs are sought that will ultimately benefit both sides.

Interest-Based Bargaining

Roger Fisher and William Ury, authors of *Getting to Yes: Negotiating Agreement Without Giving In*, assert that a "good" agreement is one that is wise and efficient and that ultimately results in everyone involved developing a stronger relationship with each other than they would have had if they had *not* gone through this negotiation process together.

Fisher and Ury set forth four principles of principled negotiation that can be used effectively in a variety of situations to resolve many types of disputes. Those four principles are

▶ Separate the people from the problem

▶ Focus on interests rather than positions

▶ Generate a variety of options before settling on one

▶ Resolve disagreements by focusing on objective criteria

Observing these principles throughout the entire negotiation process will enhance the process itself as well as the outcome that results from the process. Remaining aware of the other party's perspectives and perceptions throughout the entire process will also greatly strengthen the consensus-building process.

Collective Bargaining: Agreements

The output of successful collective bargaining is a collective bargaining agreement (CBA). The CBA contains provisions related to a variety of conditions of employment and also outlines the procedures to be used in settling disputes that may arise during the duration of the contract.

Typical Provisions of Collective Bargaining Agreements (Excluding Disciplinary and Grievance Procedures)

Most collective bargaining agreements will include specific guidelines around discipline and discharge, addressing topics such as the following:

▶ A statement that prohibits discipline or discharge without "cause" or "just cause"

▶ Establishment of a progressive discipline process (for instance, oral warning, written warning, suspension, discharge), as well as consideration of mitigating factors

▶ A list of acts that can result in immediate discharge

▶ A requirement to notify the union of disciplinary actions

▶ A statement that protects whistleblowers

▶ Limits on methods that employers may use to conduct investigations (for instance, polygraphs)

▶ A notification to the employee that he or she has the right to union representation during a potential disciplinary interview, and a guarantee that the interview will not be held until union representation is provided (Weingarten Rights)

NOTE

Weingarten Rights, derived from the Supreme Court decision in *NLRB v. Weingarten, 1975*, established the right of unionized employees to have union representation at an investigatory interview with management if the employee reasonably believes that discipline might result from that meeting. Although the NLRB reversed this decision in 2000 (*Epilepsy Foundation of Northeast Ohio, 331 NLRB 676, 2000*) and held that nonunion employees also have the right to have a representative present at a meeting of this sort, in 2004 the NLRB returned to its original determination and held that nonunion employees do not have the right to have a co-worker or other representative present in a meeting that the employee reasonably believes might result in discipline.

EXAM ALERT

Familiarize yourself with Weingarten Rights. Be sure that you verify whether the NLRB has issued any more opinions on Weingarten Rights (after the printing of this book) before you take the PHR exam.

The provisions that are contained within collective bargaining agreements will vary from employer to employer, from union to union, and from situation to situation. Some provisions of a collective bargaining agreement are relatively self-explanatory, and others are less self-evident.

NOTE

For those terms that are relatively self-explanatory, we have indicated either a description or a bullet-point list of the types of stipulations that the provision would seek to address. For those provisions that are somewhat less self-evident, we have also included a definition as well as a sample clause.

The specific provisions that we'll present in this section are the following:

- Preamble
- Duration of agreement
- Nondiscrimination clause
- Union dues deductions
- Management rights clause
- Probation
- Seniority
- Bumping rights
- Hours worked/schedules/rest periods/workdays/overtime
- No strike/no lockout (also referred to as *continuous performance*)
- Wage rates/wage increases
- Zipper clause

- Union security clauses:
    - Open shop
    - Closed shop
    - Union shop
    - Agency shop
    - Maintenance of membership
- Holidays
- Vacation and personal days
- Sick days
- Leaves of absence
- Performance evaluation
- Layoff and recall

Preamble

Definition: The introductory and first clause of the collective bargaining agreement. The preamble may articulate the purposes of the agreement, formally recognize the employees' representative, define terms that will be used in the agreement, and basically set the stage for the remaining provisions of the agreement.

Sample preamble clause:

This Agreement is between (the employer), hereinafter called the "Employer" and (the union), hereinafter called the "Union."

This Agreement has as its purpose the joint commitment to achieve the Employer's goals of (A, B, and C) between (the Employer) and the Union; the establishment of an equitable and peaceful procedure for the resolution of differences; and the expression of the full and complete understanding of the parties pertaining to all terms and conditions of employment.

The term "employee" when used hereinafter in this Agreement shall refer to employees represented by the Union in the bargaining unit unless otherwise stated. Any member of the Employer's management referenced in this Agreement may specify a designee.

Titles of articles, sections, and subsections of this Agreement are meant for ease of reading and may not be used to interpret or clarify the text of the language.

Duration of Agreement

Definition: Identifies the first date on which the contract is effective and the last date on which the contract is effective.

Sample duration of agreement clause:

> This Agreement shall be effective as of 12:00 a.m. July 1, 2007 and shall continue in full force and effect until midnight, June 30, 2010.

Nondiscrimination Clause

Definition: The contract expressly prohibits discrimination on various grounds such as sex, race, creed, color, religion, age, national origin, political affiliation or activity, disability, sexual orientation, or union activity. The nondiscrimination clause might also specifically prohibit sexual harassment.

Sample nondiscrimination clause:

> There shall be no discrimination or intimidation by (the Employer) or by (the employees' representative) against any unit member as a result of, or because of such Member's race, color, creed, sex, age, national origin, disability as qualified by law, or membership/nonmembership in the Union.

Union Dues Deductions

Definition: Employers agree to deduct and forward to the union dues amounts agreed to by workers. By law, employees must agree in writing to this deduction. There is some debate, litigious and otherwise, as to whether dues checkoff constitutes a union security clause.

Sample union dues deductions clause:

> (The Employer) agrees to deduct from the wages of any employee who is a member of the Union a deduction as provided for in written authorization. Such authorization must be executed by the employee and may be revoked by the employee at any time by giving written notice to both (the Employer) and the Union. (The Employer) agrees to remit any deductions made pursuant to this provision promptly to the Union together with an itemized statement showing the name of each employee from whose pay such deductions have been made and the amount deducted during the period covered by the remittance. Deductions shall be sent by the Board to the Union by separate check from membership dues and/or fair share fees.

Management Rights Clause

Definition: Management reserves the right, in terms that are either general or highly specific, to manage the organization as it sees fit, unless those rights have been specifically modified in the labor contract through a reserved rights doctrine.

Sample management rights clause:

> The parties agree that only the written specific, express terms of this Agreement bind (the Employer). Except as specifically and expressly provided in this written Agreement, (the Employer) has full and complete discretion to make decisions and implement changes in operations including those affecting wages, hours, terms, and conditions of employment of members of the bargaining unit, without prior negotiation with or the agreement of the (employees' representative) except as to the effects of such decisions. The (employees' representative) expressly waives any and all right that it may have to bargain about the decision to make any change in operations, practices, or policies which affect wages, hours, and terms and other conditions of employment of employees in the bargaining unit. Any arbitrators used by the parties under Article (XX) shall give full force and effect to this section.

Probation

Definition: The length of the probationary period, the purpose of probationary period, and employee status and rights during probationary period.

Sample probation clause:

> ▸ A new employee shall be appointed on probation for a period of three months and may be extended for a further three months if deemed necessary by (the Employer) to assess the employee's suitability or otherwise for confirmation in his or her appointment provided such extension shall be made at least one week prior to the completion of his or her probationary period.

> ▸ At any time during the probationary period, such employment may be terminated by either (the Employer) or the employee on one day's notice being given without any reason being assigned for such termination.

> ▸ On completion of an employee's probation, (the Employer) shall normally inform the employee in writing whether or not the employee is confirmed in his or her employment. But in the event that (the Employer) has omitted to do so, the appointment of the employee concerned shall be deemed to have been confirmed from the date of the completion of his or her probation and the period of probation shall be deemed as part of the employee's period of service.

Seniority

Definition: The length of time that an employee has been employed by the employer. Seniority can also be defined, however, as seniority within a position, seniority within a department, seniority within a location, and the like. In collective bargaining agreements, seniority can play an important role with respect to decisions such as promotions layoffs, shift bids, bumping rights, and so on.

Sample seniority clause:

> It shall be the policy of the department to recognize the seniority principle. Seniority time shall consist of the total calendar time elapsed since the date of

original employment with (the Employer); no time prior to a discharge for cause or a quit shall be included. Seniority shall not be diminished by temporary layoffs or leaves of absence or contingencies beyond the control of the parties to this Agreement.

Bumping Rights

Definition: The process by which a more senior employee whose position is being eliminated may, instead of losing employment with the organization, choose to replace a less senior employee (assuming that the more senior employee is qualified for the position into which he or she "wants to bump"). This can ultimately lead to a situation in which a person who was not originally slated for job elimination, in fact, loses his or her job.

Sample bumping rights clause:

A regular employee who is to be laid off may elect to displace an employee with less service seniority where the laid off employee has the necessary skills, abilities, experience, education, qualifications, and certifications to perform the other position. Where an employee elects to displace another employee with less service seniority, he or she shall notify (the Employer) within ten (10) days of his or her receipt of notice of layoff; or where an employee exercises his or her right to displace an employee with less service seniority, the (employees' representative) shall be notified in writing by copy of the acknowledgement letter to the employee.

Hours Worked/Schedules/Rest Periods/Workdays/Overtime

Definition: Clauses related to hours worked, rest period, workdays, and overtime help to further establish the tangible terms and conditions of employment. Topics including shifts worked and changes to scheduled shifts may also be addressed.

Sample hours worked/schedules/rest periods/workdays/overtime clause:

The standard workweek consists of seven consecutive days and shall begin at 12:01 a.m. Saturday. The standard work schedule for full-time employees shall be forty (40) hours per workweek, normally scheduled in shifts of eight (8) hours. Meal periods shall consist of thirty minutes and shall not count as time worked if the employee is completely relieved from duty. Employees who are completely relieved from duty shall not be required to be accessible during the meal period. Normal hours of work are from 7:00 a.m. to 3:30 p.m. Shifts are: Day, 7:00 a.m. to 3:30 p.m.; Swing, 3:00 p.m. to 11:00 p.m.; and Owl, 11:00 p.m. to 7:00 a.m. Rest periods not to exceed 15 minutes, once during each half of an eight-hour shift, will be granted to employees. The time shall not be taken at the beginning or end of a work period, and rest periods shall not be accumulated. Rest periods shall be taken unless operational necessity requires that they be denied.

No Strike/No Lockout (Also Referred to as "Continuous Performance")

No-strike—definition: The union agrees not to strike for the duration of the contract. Usually, a union will agree to a no-strike clause in exchange for a clause to engage in binding arbitration in the event that an impasse is reached relative to administration of the contract.

Sample no-strike clause:

> No strike of any kind shall be instigated, encouraged, condoned, or caused by (the employees' representative) during the term of this Agreement.

No lockout—definition: The employer agrees not to lock out employees for the duration of the contract. In this context, a lockout is defined as a situation in which the employer prevents some or all employees from working. Usually, an employer will agree to a no-lockout clause only in exchange for a no-strike clause.

Sample no-lockout clause:

> No lock out of employees shall be instituted by the Employer during the term of this Agreement.

Wages Rates/Wage Increases

Definition: How much, and when, employees will be paid for the various services they render. This clause can also address shift differentials, standby or on-call pay, reporting/call-back pay, and roll-call pay.

Sample wage rates clause:

- ► (The Employer) agrees to pay and the (employees' representative) agrees to accept the schedule of job classifications and wage rates attached hereto as Wage Schedule I and Wage Schedule II for the term of this Agreement.

- ► When an employee is temporarily assigned to a position having a lower rate of pay than his/her regular position, his/her rate of pay shall not be reduced during such temporary assignment. It is understood that this clause does not apply to any situation when the downward assignment has been as a result of a layoff within the Bargaining Unit.

- ► When an employee is temporarily assigned to a position having a higher rate of pay than his/her regular position, and such assignment is in excess of two (2) consecutive hours, he/she shall be paid at the higher rate of pay for the entire time served in such higher assignment.

Sample wage increases clause:

> Wages for bargaining unit members are set forth in the Wage Schedule attached as Appendix A. "Steps" set forth in the wage schedule generally reflect a member's years of continuous service with (the Employer) as a regular contract (employee in a particular position), unless placement in the wage schedule was modified upon

the employee's initial hiring in accordance with provisions of this Article. Step increases shall be effective on the first day of July following the completion of one (1) year.

Effective July 1, 2005, all members shall advance to the next step in the wage scale each year in accordance with the terms of this Agreement.

Unit members who have transferred from other positions in (the employer) may be placed at any step on the wage scale not to exceed their years of service in the district.

Each member shall receive written notice of the wage schedule step he or she is placed at effective within thirty (30) days of (Employer) approval of this Agreement, and thereafter shall receive written notice of the step he or she advances to each subsequent July.

Zipper Clause

Definition: Both parties agree that the agreement is an exclusive and complete "expression of consent"—in other words, the only items that can be collectively bargained until the expiration of the agreement are those contained within the agreement In other words, after the agreement is signed, new subjects cannot be added and existing subjects cannot be reopened for negotiation. The contract has been "zipped" closed.

Sample zipper clause:

All matters within the scope of bargaining have been negotiated and agreed upon. The terms and conditions set forth in this Agreement represent the full and complete understanding and commitment between (the Employer) and (the employees' representative). During the term of this Agreement, there shall be no change in (the Employer's) regulations or departmental policies on matters within the scope of negotiations without notice to the (employees' representative) and providing the (employees' representative) the opportunity to bargain the impacts and effects.

Union Security Clause

Definition: Union security clauses are included in some agreements in an effort to protect the interests, strength, and security of the union. Union security clauses regulate membership in the union and, consequently, relate to the payment of dues. Some of the more common types of union security clauses include

- *Open shop*—Employees are required neither to join the union nor to pay union dues. This is the *only* type of union security clause that is legal in right-to-work states (and for federal government employees).

- *Closed shop*—Employers can hire only employees who are already members of the union. Closed shops were ruled illegal by the Taft-Hartley Act; however, *hiring halls* do in one sense encourage a closed shop arrangement. A hiring hall is a union-operated placement office that refers registered applicants to jobs on the basis of a seniority or placement system.

- *Union shop*—Newly hired employees must join the union within a specified period of time, usually 30 days, and must remain a member of the union as a condition of employment. In a union shop, employers must terminate employees who are not union members.

   Union shops are illegal in right-to-work states.

- *Agency shop*—Employees are not required to join the union. They must, however, pay a monthly fee that is typically equivalent to union dues.

   Agency shops are illegal in right-to-work states.

- *Maintenance of membership*—Employees who voluntarily choose to join a union must maintain their individual memberships for the duration of the labor contract. Each employee then has a 30-day window at the beginning of the next contract period during which he or she may terminate membership. Maintenance of membership arrangements are illegal in right-to-work states.

> **NOTE**
>
> *Beck Rights* are the right for bargaining unit members to pay only that portion of union dues which is attributable to mainline union responsibilities (collective bargaining, organizing in the same industry, contract administration, and the like). It is up to the employee, however, to exercise his or her Beck Rights. These rights were established by the Supreme Court decision in *Communication Workers of America v. Beck, 1988*.

Holidays

Terms and conditions that could be delineated in the bargaining agreement clause might include the following:

- Number of holidays granted per year
- Designated holidays (with specific dates) versus "floating" holidays
- Terms of pay for working on a holiday
- Right to equivalent time off for time worked on a holiday
- Procedures for assigning holiday work
- Special circumstances—for example, "one-time" holidays

Vacation and Personal Days

Terms and conditions that could be delineated in the bargaining agreement clause might include the following:

- Number of vacation and personal days accrued per year and procedure for using
- Right to take accrued vacation
- Procedure and time of year for scheduling

- ▶ Role of seniority in scheduling vacations and personal days

- ▶ Right to carry over vacation to next year, and the amount that can be carried over

- ▶ Procedure for payment upon death, resignation, or retirement of employee

- ▶ Prorated vacation for part-time employees

Sick Days

Terms and conditions that could be delineated in the bargaining agreement clause might include the following:

- ▶ Days accrued per year and maximum accumulation

- ▶ Right to use for doctor's appointments

- ▶ Right to use for ill family members

- ▶ Provision for cash out of sick leave

- ▶ Provision for sick leave bank

- ▶ Prorated sick leave for part-time employees

- ▶ Interaction of sick leave policy with Family and Medical Leave Act (FMLA) and Americans with Disabilities Act (ADA)

- ▶ Documentation required for sick leave; protections of employee privacy rights

Leaves of Absence

Terms and conditions that could be delineated in the bargaining agreement clause might include the following:

- ▶ Right to take leave, administrative rules for requesting leave, duration of leave, pay during leave, continuation of benefits during leave, and reinstatement after leave

- ▶ Parental leave, including adoption leave

- ▶ Elder care leave

- ▶ Bereavement leave: relatives or household members covered, number of days, extra time when travel required

- ▶ Educational leave, leave to attend professional meetings, sabbaticals

- ▶ Leave for jury duty

- ▶ Military leave with responsibility of employer to hold open same job, shift, and other conditions

- ▶ Leave for union business

- ▶ Leave for voting

▶ Family and medical leave: benefits, if any, in addition to those in law (for example, longer period of paid leave than required by law), description of employee and employer rights and responsibilities under law

Performance Evaluation/Management

Terms and conditions that could be delineated in the bargaining agreement clause might include the following:

▶ Criteria for evaluations

▶ Frequency of evaluations

▶ Right of employee to receive copies of evaluations

▶ Right to rebut or grieve performance evaluations

▶ Limitations on use of performance evaluations (for example, not to determine pay, bidding rights, and so on)

Layoff and Recall

Terms and conditions that could be delineated in the bargaining agreement clause might include the following:

▶ Procedures for layoff based on seniority provisions

▶ Prior notification to union of layoffs, right of union to offer alternative proposals or plans

▶ Rights of employees to bump into positions of less-senior employees

▶ Procedures for recalling employees; duration of recall list

Discipline and Discharge, and Grievance Handling

Discipline and discharge and *grievance procedures* are two critical elements of the collective bargaining agreement that, in one sense, bring together all the other provisions in the agreement. Together with mediation and arbitration, they form the basis for contract administration.

Because of the unique impact of these two types of contract provisions, we will introduce them briefly here before exploring them in greater detail later, in the section, "Contract Administration."

Discipline and Discharge

Management reserves the right to discipline (a more positive approach than "punishing" or "penalizing") employees for subpar performance and/or nonperformance. Discharge (the termination of the employment relationship by the employer) is the culmination of unsuccessful discipline—meaning discipline that does not result in the employee bringing his or her performance up to an acceptable level.

Grievance Handling

Grievance handling is the formal process established by the collective bargaining agreement through which disagreements arising from the administration of the labor agreement are resolved. These difficulties could arise from a number of sources, including but not limited to interpretation of contract language or alleged unfair or inconsistent application of employment provisions. Grievances most often arise out of decisions relating to discipline and discharge.

Contract Administration

As indicated earlier, the collective bargaining process results in a collective bargaining agreement. In many ways, however, the collective bargaining agreement is more of a beginning than an ending. It is a living document that provides the structure and framework within which the daily happenings of the employment relationship are brought to life. It also provides the language that will govern the employment relationship—language that is at times subject to different interpretations, thereby presenting challenges that need to be resolved.

Grievance Procedure

Each collective bargaining agreement outlines a grievance procedure for resolving these sorts of differences. This procedure establishes the formal process through which problems and challenges associated with the interpretation or application of the collective bargaining agreement will be addressed and resolved. Sometimes, challenges arise out of differences in opinion relative to the interpretation of the language that was used to craft the agreement. Challenges can also emerge when there is a perception that the contract has been applied in an unfair or inconsistent manner, particularly with respect to decisions relating to discipline and discharge.

Although management and labor both have the right to use the grievance process, management does not often choose to do so. Instead, the process is usually initiated by an employee who is a member of the collective bargaining unit or by the union itself. Either way, the grievance alleges that the labor contract has been violated in some way, and seeks resolution.

Although the actual grievance procedure will vary widely from one collective bargaining agreement to another, they are similar in that they consist of a series of prescribed steps, each of which has an accompanying time limit for action. The process by which appeals can be filed is also clearly delineated in the agreement.

Many, though not all, agreements outline a four-step grievance procedure:

1. Initiate a complaint.

2. Escalate the complaint internally.

3. Reach the highest level of internal escalation.

4. Participate in binding arbitration.

Step One: Initiate a Complaint

Either the employee or the union must initiate a complaint within a specified time frame after the date on which the alleged contract violation took place (or, alternatively, the date on which the employee or union became aware of the alleged violation). In some contracts, this step must be formally filed (in writing), whereas other contracts permit this initial complaint to be informal (verbal). This initial complaint is usually filed with the supervisor of the person who experienced the alleged violation. This first-line supervisor then has a prescribed number of days within which to meet with the employee and the union steward to discuss the situation. In most cases, the supervisor will then have a prescribed number of days after that initial meeting to reach a decision relative to the situation. The supervisor can then choose to grant the requested relief in part, in whole, or not at all.

If the employee and/or the union decide to accept the resolution that the supervisor proposes, the grievance is considered to be settled. If the employee and/or the union decide not to accept the resolution, the union has a prescribed number of days within which to appeal the grievance to the next step.

> **NOTE**
>
> In many agreements, management's failure to abide by all prescribed time limits will result in the grievance being automatically appealed to the next level. On the other hand, the union's failure to abide by all prescribed time limits will often result in the immediate dismissal of the grievance and the termination of the grievance process.

Step Two: Escalate the Complaint Internally

Step two is similar to step one with respect to the actual process and the requirements to abide by prescribed time frames. An important difference at this step, however, is that the meetings occur between higher levels of union and management leadership. At step two, for instance, the president of the local union might meet with manager of the plant at which the employee works. If resolution is not reached at step two, an appeal can be made to move to step three.

Step Three: Reach the Highest Level of Internal Escalation

Step three is similar to step two, except that the level of the meetings that are being held have escalated even more. At this level, it is quite possible to find someone from the union's national office sitting across from someone from the organization's corporate headquarters.

If step three does not produce a resolution that is acceptable to the union, the union must decide (within a prescribed period of time, of course) whether to appeal to binding arbitration—the final step.

Step Four: Participate in Binding Arbitration

In this step, the disagreement is referred to an outside party—an arbitrator—who will render a decision that will be binding upon the union and management. Most of the time, the collective bargaining agreement will fully outline the arbitration process to which the parties will be held if the grievance is appealed to step four.

Arbitration that is used to resolve grievances during the administration of the contract (as is described here) is called *rights arbitration*.

EXAM ALERT

For the PHR exam, it's important to be familiar with arbitration-related terms and practices. In addition to the rights arbitration process described here, be prepared to respond to questions on

▶ *Interest arbitration*—Arbitration that is used to resolve conflicts around contract language during the collective bargaining process.

▶ *Arbitrator*—An individual selected to participate in the resolution of an agreement and the rendering of a binding decision.

▶ *Arbitrator panels*—Panels that are usually composed of three arbitrators, one of whom is selected by management, one of whom is selected by the union, and one of whom is selected jointly (this person is referred to as the *neutral arbitrator*).

▶ *Federal Mediation and Conciliation Service (FMCS)*—A source that maintains lists of qualified arbitrators.

▶ *American Arbitration Association (AAA)*—A source that maintains lists of qualified arbitrators.

▶ *Arbitration hearing*—A relatively formal process (not wholly unlike a court hearing) that can be conducted by an individual arbitrator or by a panel of arbitrators. The hearing includes the presentation of evidence, the testimony of witnesses, and opening and closing statements from both sides. Lawyers are often present, as well, which adds even more to the judicial "feel" of the hearing.

▶ *Permanent arbitrators*—An individual arbitration arrangement in which one arbitrator who is selected for a fixed period of time (often the duration of the contract) hears all arbitration cases that arise during that period of time. One advantage to this approach is that the arbitrator becomes very knowledgeable about the contract. One potential disadvantage could emerge if the union, management, or both are dissatisfied with the arbitrator for some reason.

▶ *Ad hoc arbitrators*—More frequently, each arbitration will result in the selection of an arbitrator. The arbitrator who is selected may specialize in the particular topic with which the arbitration deals, which can be a distinct advantage. Also, neither party will be "stuck" with an arbitrator with whom it is not happy.

▶ *Decisions*—Arbitrators must resolve grievances on the basis of an objective interpretation of the contract as it was written. In the event that the contract language is unclear, the arbitrator must then work to ascertain what the intent of the parties was at the time that the contract was written. Past practice is an extremely important element in this process, especially if the contract language is somewhat ambiguous.

Chapter Summary

Chapter Summary

Employee relations. Labor relations.

These are terms that encompass practices and responsibilities that are far reaching and of critical importance. They are also terms that can sometimes evoke strong feelings and reactions.

In the beginning of this chapter, we described employee relations as

> The way in which an organization responds to, handles, and/or addresses any issue that has impact on employees, and their relationships

> - To and with other employees
>
> - To and with managers
>
> - To and with those outside the organization with whom they come in contact as part of their employment experience

During this chapter, we attempted to explore the myriad ways in which these relationships can manifest themselves, as well as the many factors that need to be taken into consideration when it comes to relationships with employees. We also looked at the history, legality, processes, tools, and importance of labor relations.

It is our hope that, after having journeyed through this chapter, you will understand the true impact of your role more fully—and, therefore, be better equipped to perform it even more effectively. (We also hope that you perform exceedingly well in your role as PHR candidate, as well.)

> **EXAM ALERT**
>
> The PHR exam covers a wide range of information relating to employee and labor relations. Those topics have been explored in this chapter, with three exceptions:
>
> - Public sector labor relations issues and practices (this includes federal, state, and local government employees)
> - Expatriation and repatriation issues and practices
> - Employee and labor relations for local nationals (for example, labor relations in other countries)
>
> As part of your preparation for the PHR exam, be certain to review matters pertaining to each of these areas.

Key Terms

- Employee relations
- Labor relations
- Knights of Labor
- Great Uprising
- Samuel Gompers
- "Bread and butter unionism"
- Haymarket
- Industrial Workers of the World (IWW)

- Mary Harris "Mother" Jones
- Triangle Shirtwaist Company
- Electric Auto-Lite Strike
- Walter Reuther
- AFL-CIO
- Equal Employment Opportunity (EEO)
- Charge
- Charging party
- Complainant
- Plaintiff
- Respondent
- Fair Employment Practices Agencies (FEPAs)
- Reasonable cause
- Right to sue letter
- Relief
- Remedies
- Organizational culture
- Employee handbooks
- Employee communication strategies
- Employee involvement strategies
- Employee surveys
- Focus groups
- Employee participation groups
- Open door policy
- Suggestion programs
- Management by walking around (MBWA)
- Progressive discipline
- Common law
- Tort doctrines
- Employment-at-will

- Wrongful termination
- Implied contracts
- Defamation
- Invasion of privacy
- Negligent hiring
- Negligent training
- Negligent retention
- Negligent referral
- Contract doctrines
- Mandatory arbitration agreements
- Non-compete agreements
- Confidentiality agreements
- *Circuit City Stores, Inc. v. Adams, 2001*
- Sherman Antitrust Act, 1890
- Clayton Act, 1914
- Railway Labor Act, 1926
- Norris-LaGuardia Act, 1932
- "Yellow dog" contract
- National Industrial Recovery Act, 1933
- *Schechter Poultry Corp. v. United States, 1935*
- National Labor Relations Act or Wagner Act, 1935
- National Labor Relations Board
- Unfair Labor Practice (ULP)
- Labor Management Relations Act or Taft-Hartley Act, 1947
- Secondary boycott
- Featherbedding
- Hot cargo agreements
- Right-to-work states
- Jurisdictional strikes

- Federal Mediation and Conciliation Service (FMCS)
- Labor Management Reporting and Disclosure Act or Landrum-Griffin Act, 1959
- Local union
- National union
- Federations
- International labor organizations
- APRO for Asia and the Pacific
- AFRO for Africa
- ORIT for the Americas
- Authorization cards
- No-solicitation rule
- Leafleting
- Salting
- Organizational picketing
- Captive audience meetings
- Union decertification
- Union deauthorization
- Protected concerted activities
- ULP strikes
- Economic strikes
- Mackay doctrine
- *NLRB v. Mackay Radio and Telegraph Co., 1938*

- Sympathy strikes
- Wildcat strikes
- Picketing
- Double breasting
- Common situs picketing
- Ally doctrine
- Good faith bargaining
- Required subjects
- Voluntary subjects
- Permissive subjects
- Illegal subjects
- Distributive bargaining
- Integrative bargaining
- Interest based bargaining
- Collective bargaining agreement
- Weingarten rights
- *NLRB v. Weingarten, 1975*
- Zipper clause
- Union security clauses
- Open shop
- Closed shop
- Union shop
- Agency shop
- Maintenance of membership

Apply Your Knowledge

This chapter focuses on issues relating to employee and labor relations. Complete the following exercises, review questions, and exam questions as a way of reviewing and reinforcing the knowledge and skills you'll need to perform your responsibilities as an HR professional, and to increase the likelihood that you will pass the PHR examination.

Topics to Explore

In this chapter, we delved into many topics and highlighted certain others with which you will need more familiarity in order to be an effective HR professional (and in order to enhance your preparation for the PHR exam). As you continue your study and preparations, be sure to review the following terms, concepts, people, and events:

- Knights of Labor
- Great Uprising
- Samuel Gompers
- "Bread and butter unionism"
- Haymarket
- AFL
- Industrial Workers of the World (IWW)
- Mary Harris "Mother" Jones
- Triangle Shirtwaist Company
- Electric Auto-Lite Strike
- CIO
- UAW
- Walter Reuther
- AFL-CIO
- Voluntary recognition
- Involuntary recognition
- Strike preparation
- Work slowdowns
- Strike benefits
- Strike insurance
- Strike preparation
- Interest arbitration
- Arbitrators
- Arbitrator panels
- Federal Mediation and Conciliation Service (FMCS)
- American Arbitration Association (AAA)
- Arbitration Hearing
- Permanent arbitrators
- Ad hoc arbitrators

▶ Ally Doctrine

▶ Public sector labor relations issues and practices (this includes federal, state, and local government employees)

▶ Expatriation and repatriation issues and practices

▶ Employee and labor relations for local nationals (for example, labor relations in other countries)

Your research will pay off professionally as well as in terms of your preparation for the PHR exam.

Review Questions

1. Explore and discuss "progressive discipline" within the context of its role as an employee involvement program.

2. Describe and compare local unions and national unions.

3. Compare and contrast distributive and integrative approaches to collective bargaining.

4. Describe negligent hiring.

5. If an employee EEO charge is not settled, what are the four primary ways that the EEOC can handle the charge?

Exam Questions

1. All of the following represent measures that could be helpful in measuring the effectiveness of employee relations initiatives except

   A. Turnover

   B. Absenteeism

   C. Unionization

   D. Work-related accidents/injuries/"preventable" illnesses

2. FEPAs are

   A. State or local agencies that provide employers and unions with lists of qualified arbitrators

   B. State or local agencies that have antidiscrimination laws and agencies responsible for enforcing those laws

   C. State or local agencies that are responsible for administering and enforcing the rights established by the NLRA

   D. State or local agencies responsible for approving the recognition of union federations

3. The NLRA identified all of the following as unfair labor practices (for employers) except

   A. To dominate or interfere with the formation or administration of a labor organization

   B. To discriminate against employees for engaging in concerted or union activities or refraining from them

   C. To discriminate against an employee for filing charges with the FMCS or taking part in any FMCS proceedings

   D. To refuse to bargain with the union that is the lawful representative of its employees

4. Which of the following terms means the same as "charging party"?

   A. Complainant

   B. Plaintiff

   C. Respondent

   D. Defendant

5. Featherbedding refers to

   A. A requirement that anyone who is hired by the organization must join the union

   B. An agreement that requires the employer to pay wages to union members whether or not their work is needed

   C. A requirement to pay "prevailing wages" on federal government construction contracts and most contracts for federally assisted construction greater than $2,000

   D. An agreement that an employer will stop doing business with another entity (most frequently a nonunion entity)

6. Weingarten Rights, derived from the U.S. Supreme Court decision in *NLRB v. Weingarten*, 1975, established the right of unionized employees to

   A. Have union representative at meetings with supervisors/management if the employee chooses to do so

   B. Have union representation at investigatory meetings with management if the employee reasonably believes that discipline might result

   C. Have the EEOC take its own independent action even when a binding arbitration agreement is in place

   D. Pay only that portion of union dues that is attributable to mainline union responsibilities

7. Many, though not all, agreements outline a grievance procedure that includes all of the following steps except

   A. Initiating a formal complaint

   B. Notifying the NLRB of the complaint

   C. Escalating the complaint internally

   D. Participating in binding arbitration

8. Which of the following would be least relevant to determining the degree to which a noncompete agreement might be found to be valid:

   A. Whether the agreement specified a time frame established in the agreement, and, if so, how long it is in effect

   B. Whether the agreement specified any geographic limitations within which the employee cannot compete

   C. Whether there is anything in the agreement that would preclude the employee from earning a living in his or her chosen field

   D. Whether the employee was employed by the organization at the time that he or she was asked to sign the agreement

9. All of the following are important steps to take to ensure the success of a focus group except

   A. Develop effective questions

   B. Involve/include all stakeholders

   C. Arrange the logistics

   D. Conduct the survey

10. Which of the following would be least likely to be considered an employee involvement strategy?

    A. Open door policy

    B. Progressive discipline

    C. Suggestion programs

    D. Captive audience meetings

Answers to Review Questions

1. Progressive discipline programs can, in fact, function as a type of employee involvement (and employee relations) program, if we keep the true definition of employee relations in mind: anything that impacts a relationship with an employee. Even throughout the progressive discipline process, there should be a focus on building a relationship. Discipline can and should be seen as a way to give employees every opportunity to help themselves in their efforts to address their performance issues and, in short, "turn them around" so that they can meet or exceed performance expectations.

2. Local unions, which truly operate at the "local" level, are largely responsible for the day-to-day administration of the labor agreement and relationship with union members. Locals generally have an elected president and elected stewards who represent the workers in the workplace. Larger local unions might have a full-time paid business agent. Most locals belong to and are chartered by a larger national union.

   National unions, conversely, bring together all the union locals for a particular group that are scattered across the country. There are usually different hierarchical levels in between the local union and the national union. National unions have far more power with respect to bargaining, and with respect to political influence, than the union locals could have on their own. They also advise and guide local unions, and may also manage nationwide benefits programs (such as retirement programs and health insurance plans).

3. Distributive bargaining takes an approach to bargaining in which each side sets forth its position, and at the end of the process one side has "won" some (or all) of what it wanted, and the other has "lost" some (or all) of what it wanted. Distributive bargaining is adversarial in nature. It assumes that there's only so much to go around, so when you divide up the pie, one side will get more and one side will get less.

   Integrative bargaining doesn't look at bargaining issues one at a time—instead, it looks at multiple issues as a whole (hence the term *integrative*). Integrative bargaining looks at that same pie in a different way. Instead of just splitting up the pieces, it creatively considers how it might be able to make that pie bigger; how the needs of both sides can be better met when looked at in their entirety; and how a win-win solution can be explored, rather than settling for the win-lose scenario that will inevitably result from distributive bargaining.

   In essence, integrative bargaining is predicated on the idea that an agreement that renders one side better off does not necessarily have to result in the other side being worse off. Instead, through creativity and cooperation, trade-offs of some sort are sought that will ultimately benefit both parties to the agreement.

4. Negligent hiring refers to the process of hiring an employee without engaging in appropriate "due diligence" into that candidate's credentials, prior work experience, and the like. Negligent hiring tort claims might be filed when an employee who was hired through a flawed hiring process inflicts some sort of harm on another person—harm that could have been predicted and therefore prevented if the employer had conducted the background check. A hiring process can be flawed for a number of reasons, such as the application of a sound hiring process in an unsound manner, or the use of a hiring process that was originally designed in a flawed manner. Flaws could relate to inadequate or poorly conducted reference checks, job requirements that do not reflect the skills or credentials that are truly required for a position, and the like.

5. Assuming that it is not settled, there are four primary ways that a charge can be handled by the EEOC, which can:

   ▶ *Investigate it*—Investigate either on a priority or non–high priority basis, depending on the strength of the facts that have been presented in the charge. An EEOC investigation can take myriad forms, including written requests for information, in-person interviews, document reviews, and even a visit to the location where the alleged discrimination occurred.

   ▶ *Settle it*—This can happen at any stage of the investigation if the charging party and the employer are interested in reaching a settlement. If no settlement is reached, the investigation resumes.

   ▶ *Mediate it*—The EEOC offers a confidential mediation program as an alternative to a lengthy investigative process. For a charge to be mediated, both the charging party and the employer must be willing to participate. If the mediation process is not successful, the charge will be investigated.

   ▶ *Dismiss it*—A charge can be dismissed at any point in the process if the agency determines that further investigation will not establish that unlawful discrimination occurred. When a charge is dismissed, a notice is issued in accordance with the law, which gives the charging party 90 days in which to file a lawsuit on his or her own behalf.

Answers to Exam Questions

1. **Answer C is the best answer.** The presence or absence of a union should not be used as a way to measure the success or failure of employee relations initiatives. Unions provide a voice, and the right to join a union is afforded to most workers under the NLRA. The choice to exercise that right must not be used to draw unrelated conclusions. Answers A, B, and D are not the best answers; turnover, absenteeism (especially unplanned), and work-related accidents/injuries/"preventable" illnesses can all provide valid measures of the effectiveness of employee relations initiatives.

2. **Answer B is the best answer.** FEPAs (which stands for Fair Employment Practices Agencies) are state or local agencies responsible for enforcing antidiscrimination laws. Answer A is not the best answer; there are no state or local agencies that provide employers and unions with lists of qualified arbitrators (the Federal Mediation and Conciliation Service [FMCS] and the American Arbitration Association [AAA] do provide this service on a national scale, however). Answer C is not the best answer; there are no state or local agencies responsible for administering and enforcing the rights established by the NLRA (the NLRB, however, does do this on a national scale). Answer D is not the best answer; there are no state or local agencies responsible for approving the recognition of union federations

3. **Answer C is the best answer.** Discriminating against an employee for filing charges with the FCMS or taking part in any FCMS proceedings does not constitute an unfair labor charge. (FCMS stands for the Federal Mediation and Conciliation Service, and is a source that maintains lists of qualified arbitrators. Charges, therefore, cannot be filed with the FCMS.) Answers A, B, and D are not the best answers because each one has been specifically identified as an unfair labor practice (ULP) by the NLRA.

4. **Answer A is the best answer.** Complainant means the same as charging party. Answer B is not the best answer; a "plaintiff" in this context would refer to a charging party or complainant who has filed a lawsuit. Answer C is not the best answer; the organization against whom the charging party files a charge is the respondent. Answer D is not the best answer; a respondent against whom a lawsuit has been filed would be referred to as a defendant.

5. **Answer B is the best answer.** Featherbedding refers to an agreement that the employee will pay wages to union members whether or not their work is needed. Answer A is not the best answer; a requirement that anyone who is hired by the organization must join the union refers to a union shop. Answer C is not the best answer; the requirement to pay prevailing wages on federal government construction contracts and most contracts for federally assisted construction over $2,000 refers to the Davis-Bacon Act. Answer D is not the best answer; an agreement that an employer will stop doing business with another entity is a hot cargo agreement.

6. **Answer B is the best answer.** Weingarten Rights refer to the rights of unionized employees to have union representation at investigatory meetings with management if the union member reasonably believes that discipline might result. Answer A is not the best answer; unionized employees do not have the right to have a representative at a meeting with a supervisor/manager unless the employee reasonably believes that discipline might result from that meeting. Answer C is not the best answer; the EEOC's right to take its own independent action even when a binding arbitration agreement is in place refers to *EEOC v. Waffle House, Inc.*, not *NLRB v. Weingarten, 1975.* Answer D is not the best answer; the right of unionized employees to pay only that portion of union dues that is attributable to mainline union responsibility is known as Beck Rights, not Weingarten Rights.

7. **Answer B is the best answer.** A grievance procedure would not include a requirement to notify the NLRB. Answers A, C, and D are not the best answers; each represents a common step in many grievance processes.

8. **Answer D is the best answer.** Although the question of whether an individual was fairly compensated may be answered differently depending on whether the individual who was asked to signed the agreement was employed at the time that he or she was asked to do so, the issue in that situation would be fair compensation, not employment status. Answers A, B, and C are not the best answers; each represents an important consideration for determining the validity of a noncompete agreement.

9. **Answer D is the best answer.** Although focus groups can be used as follow-up to an employee survey, they can also be used independently from a survey. Answers A, B, and C are not the best answers; each represents an important step that must be taken to ensure the success of a focus group.

10. **Answer D is the best answer.** Although captive audience meetings involve employees (in that the "captive audience" consists of employees), such meetings are held in response to efforts to organize and are not considered to be a true employee involvement strategy. In addition, they are mandatory meetings, which undermines the element of choice that is inherent to authentic employee involvement strategies. Answers A, B, and D are all not the best answers; each represents a legitimate employee involvement strategy.

Suggested Readings and Resources

Department of Labor. www.dol.gov, 2007.

Equal Employment Opportunity Commission (EEOC). www.eeoc.gov, 2007.

An Eclectic List of Events in U.S. Labor History. www.lutins.org/labor.html, 2007.

"A Curriculum of United States Labor History for Teachers," sponsored by the Illinois Labor History Society: http://www.kentlaw.edu/ilhs/curricul.htm, 2007.

Fisher, Roger, William L. Ury, and Bruce Patton (Editor). *Getting to Yes: Negotiating Agreement Without Giving In*. United Kingdom: Arrow Business Books, 1997.

Grote, Dick. *Discipline Without Punishment/The Proven Strategy That Turns Problem Employees into Superior Performers* (Hardcover). New York: American Management Association, 1995.

Holley, William H., Kenneth M. Jennings, and Roger S. Wolters. *The Labor Relations Process*. Winfield, KS: Southwestern College Pub, 2007.

Kaufman, Bruce E. (Editor), Inc. Industrial Relations Counselors (Corporate Author), Richard A. Beaumont (Editor), Roy B. Helfgoff (Editor). *Industrial Relations to Human Resources and Beyond: The Evolving Process of Employee Relations Management (Issues in Work and Human Resources)* (Hardcover). Armonk, NY: M. E. Sharpe, 2003.

Kearney, Richard C., and David G. Carnevale. *Labor Relations in the Public Sector (Public Administration and Public Policy)*. New York: Marcel Dekker Inc., 1984.

Losey, Mike (Editor), Dave Ulrich (Editor), and Sue Meisinger (Editor). *The Future of Human Resource Management: 64 Thought Leaders Explore the Critical HR Issues of Today and Tomorrow*. New York: Wiley, 2005.

Phillips, Larry. *SPHR Exam Prep: Senior Professional in Human Resources*, Second Edition. Indianapolis: Pearson Education, 2007.

Sparrow, Paul, and Cary L. Cooper. *The Employment Relationship: Key Challenges for HR*. Burlington, MA: Butterworth-Heinemann, 2003.

St. Antoine (Editor), Theodore J. *The Common Law of the Workplace: The Views of Arbitrator*. Arlington, VA: Bureau of National Affairs, 2005.

Ury, William. *Getting Past No: Negotiating Your Way from Confrontation to Cooperation*. New York: Bantam, 1993.

"Effective Employee Discipline: A Case of the Internal Revenue Service." An article from *Public Personnel Management*, by Cynthia J. Guffey, and Marilyn M. Helms. March 2001.

Risk Management

Study Strategies

► On large index cards, write down the names of each of the laws, topics, and key concepts covered in this chapter. On smaller, separate index cards (ideally ones that are a different color), make notes on important facts and details relating to each of these laws, topics, and key concepts (put the name of the law or the topic on the back of the card, not on the front). Then, test your memory and understanding by matching the specific facts and details (each of which you wrote on a separate index card) with the laws, topics, and key concepts that you labeled on the larger business cards. After you match them up, you can check how well you did by comparing your matches to the names of the laws and topics that you wrote on the back of the smaller index cards.

► Although this functional area accounts for a relatively small percentage of the total questions asked on the PHR exam questions (7%), there is a tremendous amount of data from which those questions can be selected. Make lists of terms, definitions, dates, and other factual information—and review them frequently, and thoroughly. Also note that it would be impossible to include all the information that could be covered on this test in this chapter. So, as we've said all along, be sure to use multiple study resources as you prepare to take the PHR exam!

► For many HR professionals, risk management (formerly referred to by HRCI as "occupational health, safety, and security") risk management is the functional area in which we have the least amount of practical experience. As such, it's particularly important to carefully review the responsibilities and information relating to this functional area. Objectively assess your background and knowledge base. Identify specific areas in which you don't have a sufficient (or sufficiently valuable) amount of knowledge, experience, or depth of experience. After you've identified these areas, it's time to start doing your homework. Conduct research. Use the Internet to find articles and whitepapers that highlight risk management. Peruse textbooks that provide insight, knowledge, and guidance relative to those particular areas. Be sure to find several real-life examples of each responsibility to ensure that you gain a variety of perspectives and insights. This is particularly important for the skill-based, rather than fact-based, components of these functional areas.

Introduction

Evolving Role of Risk Management

We've said it before, and we'll say it again here—HR is an ever-evolving, ever-expanding profession. Perhaps nowhere is this more evident than in this area—formerly known as "Occupational Health, Safety and Security" and now renamed/reclassified as "Risk Management." This shift represents far more than just a change in title; rather, it reflects a shift in focus that recognizes HR's role in the proactive identification, anticipation, mitigation, and management of risks. It's also important to keep in mind that this shift in focus represents an expansion of HR's former role, rather than a replacement of it, because our prior more-transactional responsibilities still remain.

Like every other functional area in HR, risk management has a wide-ranging impact on the long-term—as well as the day-to-day—operations of the organization. This impact is real, direct, and significant—even for those HR professionals who don't have formal responsibility for risk management. Why? Because, ultimately, as HR professionals, we all share a degree of accountability for these critical, highly impactful dimensions of the workplace experience.

Risk management, and the results thereof, can impact the workplace (along with the organization's bottom line) in myriad ways—some of which are obvious, and others that are more subtle. On a somewhat mundane level, productivity and performance can be derailed by health-related concerns, security breaches, or noncompliance with mandatory OHSS-related government requirements. But risk management means much more than this.

As we've seen time and time again in recent years, risk can manifest itself in many forms—some of which seem unthinkable (and are therefore difficult, if not impossible, to predict) until they are either experienced or witnessed first-hand, as was the case with the tragedy of September 11, 2001. In cases such as this, although it is imperative to deal swiftly and competently with the immediate aftermath of the situation, we cannot stop there. We must also work with our business partners and clients to learn as many lessons and glean as much knowledge as possible—lessons and knowledge that will enable us to prepare to deal more effectively with other similar situations that we might encounter in the future.

In light of all of this, it becomes even clearer that risk management issues are business issues, which means they are HR issues. As HR professionals, we must consider these issues from a proactive perspective, as well as from a reactive perspective. We must also recognize the specific ways in which having a better understanding of risk management issues can bolster our efforts to advance the mission of our the organization and to contribute meaningfully to achieving its overarching organizational objectives.

So, starting from the beginning, what, specifically, is meant by *risk management*? According to the 2006 unabridged edition of the *Random House Dictionary*, risk management refers to, "the technique or profession of assessing, minimizing and preventing accidental loss to a business, as through the use of insurance, safety measures, etc."

There is, however, another dimension to risk management—and it incorporates the potential for a slightly more positive perspective: risk can also refer to choices and decisions that are made taking into account upside and well as downside potential. These are choices that—whether made with a great degree of caution or by throwing caution to the wind—can have, by their very nature, significant impact on the organization, on its operations, and on its employees.

> **NOTE**
>
> Let us be clear at this point. For clarity, in no way are we implying that risk is something that should be avoided at all costs, or in all circumstances. If that were the case, this functional area would be called "Risk Avoidance," rather than "Risk Management." In the words of Lorayne Fiorillo, author of *Financial Fitness in 45 Days*, "Risk is uncertainty, and in uncertainty lies opportunity. Without uncertainty, there's little chance to profit." This is true for individuals, and it's true for organizations. As HR professionals, we must not seek solely to avoid risk; rather, we must strive to wisely navigate the waters of risk—acting in a manner that is consistent with our organization's mission and overarching objectives.

> **EXAM ALERT**
>
> Familiarize yourself with specific categories of business risk. Learn more about those that are addressed in this chapter—and don't stop there! Dig more deeply deeper into the topics that are covered here, as well—particularly safety and security. Risk management is a wide and deep well, and test questions will emanate from a vast body of information. Be ready.

With this as our backdrop, let's look at some of the multiple kinds of risk that organizations face on an ongoing basis.

Risk Management: An Overview

Before we delve into some of the specific ways in which risk management impacts organizations (and the HR professionals who work within those organizations), let's try to gain a fuller understanding of what risk management is all about.

Risk Management: A Process Model

One way to begin to gain a better understanding of almost any topic, including risk management, is to look at models. Though many risk management models have been developed, one particularly thought-provoking model was developed by the Nonprofit Risk Management Center (www.nonprofitrisk.org).

> **EXAM ALERT**
>
> In addition to this model, be sure to familiarize yourself with other risk management models, particularly those highlighted by HRCI and SHRM.

Although designed specifically for nonprofit organizations, this model provides a valuable starting point for organizations within the for-profit (and perhaps even the municipal) sector, as well. Their model of the risk management process contains the following five steps:

1. Establish the context: It's important to begin a risk management program by setting goals and identifying any potential barriers or impediments to the implementation of the program. In the goal setting exercise, ask, "what are we trying to accomplish by integrating risk management into our operations?."

2. Acknowledge and identify risks: There are many ways to undertake risk identification; the key is using a framework or strategy that allows you to identify all major risks facing your nonprofit.

3. Evaluate and prioritize risks: The third step in the process helps you keep things in perspective and establish a list of action items in priority order. The risk of an asteroid crashing into your organization's annual Black Tie Event is remote, so it probably makes more sense to work on a more likely risk—that someone could slip and hurt themselves on a waxed dance floor.

4. Select appropriate risk management strategies and implement your plan: We'll discuss four risk management techniques that can be used individually or in combination to address virtually every risk.

5. Monitor and update the risk management program: Organizations constantly face new challenges and opportunities. Risk management techniques and plans should be reviewed periodically to make certain that they remain the most appropriate strategy given the organization's needs and circumstances.

Risk Management: Techniques

This model also identifies a variety of risk management techniques—each of which (or a combination of which) might be more appropriate under different circumstances:

▶ *Avoidance*—Whenever an organization cannot offer a service while ensuring a high degree of safety, it should choose avoidance as a risk management technique. Do not offer programs that pose too great a risk. In some cases avoidance is the most appropriate technique if an organization doesn't have the financial resources required to fund adequate training, supervision, equipment, or other safety measures. Always ask, "Is there something we could do to deliver this program/conduct this activity safely?" If you answer "yes," risk modification may be the more practical technique.

▶ *Modification*—Modification is changing an activity to make it safer for all involved. Policies and procedures are examples of risk modification. For instance, an organization concerned about the risk of using unsafe drivers may add DMV record checks to its screening process, or an annual road test for all drivers.

- *Retention*—There are two ways to retain risk. The first is by design. An organization may decide that other available techniques aren't suitable and it will therefore retain the risk of harm or loss. Organizations make conscious decisions to retain risk every day. For example, when an organization purchases liability insurance and elects a $1,000 deductible or self-insured retention, it's retaining risk. This can be a rational and appropriate approach to managing risk. Where organizations get into trouble is when risk is retained unintentionally. The unintentional retention of risk can be the result of failing to understand the exclusions of an insurance policy, insufficient understanding of the scope of risk an organization faces, or simply because no one has taken the time to consider the risk and how it can be addressed.

- *Sharing*—Risk sharing involves sharing risk with another organization through a contract. Two common examples are insurance contracts that require an insurer to pay for claims expenses and losses under certain circumstances, and service contracts whereby a provider (such as a transportation service or caterer) agrees to perform a service and assume liability for potential harm occurring in the delivery of the service.

As this model and these techniques begin to demonstrate, risk is part of the everyday fabric of organizational life. It spans every workplace responsibility from hiring a new employee, to serving a customer, to expanding into a new market, to launching an advertising campaign, to making a charitable contribution. In a broader sense, however, risk management also speaks to being prepared to weather the storms of unavoidable (or unavoided) risk, in part through emergency and business continuity planning.

Emergency/Business Continuity Planning

So, what's an emergency? In its "Emergency Management Guide for Business and Industry", the Federal Emergency Management Agency (FEMA) offers a relatively all-encompassing definition of *emergency*:

> An emergency is an unplanned event that can cause deaths or significant injuries to employees, customers or the public; or that can shut down your business, disrupt operations, cause physical or environmental damage, or threaten the facility's financial standing or public image.

Nearly limitless types of emergencies could fall within the broad scope of this definition—natural, chemical, biological, terrorist, technological. The list could go on and on.

Knowing what an emergency is, however, is only part of this equation. It's also critical to have a working knowledge of *emergency management*, which this same FEMA document describes as follows:

> Emergency management is the process of preparing for, mitigating, responding to and recovering from an emergency... Emergency planning is a dynamic process. Planning, though critical, is not the only component. Training, conducting drills, testing equipment, and coordinating activities with the community are other important functions.

Interestingly, this same document—although not written directly for HR professionals—goes on to address emergency planning in a way that speaks to the essence of our role as HR business partners—partners who must function tactically and strategically, as well as transactionally:

> To be successful, emergency management requires upper management support. The chief executive sets the tone by authorizing planning to take place and directing senior management to get involved.

> When presenting the 'case' for emergency management, avoid dwelling on the negative effects of an emergency (e.g., deaths, fines, criminal prosecution) and emphasize the positive aspects of preparedness. For example:

> ▶ It helps companies fulfill their moral responsibility to protect employees, the community, and the environment.

> ▶ It facilitates compliance with requirements of federal, state, and local agencies.

> ▶ It enhances a company's ability to recover from financial losses, regulatory fines, loss of market share, damage to equipment/products, or business interruption.

> ▶ It reduces exposure to civil or criminal liability in the event of an incident.

> ▶ It enhances a company's image and credibility with employees, customers, suppliers and the community.

> ▶ It may reduce your insurance premiums.

Continuity of HR-Related Operations

When looking at the areas of emergency management and business continuity, be careful not to unintentionally overlook the continuity of HR-related operations. On the transactional, tactical, and transformational levels, HR professionals must have a method in place to continue functioning and to continue meeting the fast-changing needs of the organization.

Many HR departments were unexpectedly faced with extreme situations of this nature in the wake of the terrorist attacks of September 11, 2001. In an instant, HR professionals had to think—and live—the unthinkable, and had to function effectively in unimaginable circumstances. Some literally gave their lives in service to their organizations, and to their colleagues. Now, in the wake of September 11, it is incumbent upon us to ensure that those sacrifices were not in vain. We must do all that we can to prepare for the unthinkable, in whatever form it could ultimately take.

Employment Practices Liability Insurance (ELPI)

Employment practices liability insurance (EPLI) can help employers be prepared for facing such situations, and for withstanding the costs associated with them.

As HR professionals, and as human beings, there are some things that are within our control and other things that are outside our control. One of the things that falls outside our control, to a significant degree, is the fact that U.S. organizations must operate within a culture that—whether right or wrong, whether good or bad, and whether justified or unjustified—is highly litigious.

In the words of Dennis Masino, Esq., anyone can sue anyone else for any reason—they don't have to be right, but they won't necessarily win. However, regardless of who wins or who loses, there are many costs—financial and otherwise—associated with employment litigation. Employment practices liability insurance (EPLI) can help employers be prepared for facing such situations and the costs associated with them.

As described by the Insurance Information (www.iii.org), EPLI covers businesses against claims by workers who allege that their legal rights as employees of the company have been violated. Some insurers provide this coverage as an endorsement to their Businessowners Policy (BOP), whereas others offer EPLI as a standalone coverage.

EPLI provides protection against many kinds of employee lawsuits, including claims of

- ▶ Sexual harassment

- ▶ Discrimination

- ▶ Wrongful termination

- ▶ Breach of employment contract

- ▶ Negligent evaluation

- ▶ Failure to employ or promote

- ▶ Wrongful discipline

- ▶ Deprivation of career opportunity

- ▶ Wrongful infliction of emotional distress

- ▶ Mismanagement of employee benefit plans

The cost of EPLI coverage depends on the type of business, the number of employees, and various risk factors such as whether the company has been sued over employment practices in the past. The policies will reimburse your company against the legal costs of defending a lawsuit in court and for judgments and settlements, regardless of whether your company wins or loses the suit. Policies typically do not pay for punitive damages or civil or criminal fines. Liabilities covered by other insurance policies such as workers compensation are excluded from EPLI policies.

EXAM ALERT

Familiarize yourself with other employment-related insurance products, such as errors and omissions (E&O) insurance and directors' and officers' (D&O) liability insurance.

REVIEW BREAK

The information discussed up to this point in this chapter is intended to provide a framework for approaching and understanding risk management. Now let's shift gears and take a look at some specifics—starting with the legislative environment (traditional as well as emerging) around risk management.

Related Legislation/Legal Dimensions: Risk Management

Each HR professional must have a solid understanding of—and familiarity with—key legislation relating to risk management, as well as of overarching legal dimensions, to be able to effectively handle routine and nonroutine health, safety, and security-related situations.

Some of the laws that impact risk management were crafted specifically around health and safety concerns, whereas others address these topics more tangentially (for instance, through worker's compensation laws). Congress passed three laws to encompass other dimensions of risk management, including privacy, security, and credit-related issues.

In this section of the chapter, we'll take a look (in chronological order) at some of the key legislation most traditionally associated with occupational health, safety, and security, as well as legislation that extends into the broader definition of risk management described previously:

- Occupational Safety and Health Act (OSH Act), 1970
- Mine Safety and Health Act (MSH Act), 1977
- Drug-Free Workplace Act, 1988
- USA Patriot Act, 2001
- Homeland Security Act, 2002
- Sarbanes-Oxley Act, 2002

NOTE

In addition to these six laws, there are other areas of legislation that (although they do have an impact on risk management) fall more directly within other functional areas:

- Labor-Management Relations Act—Employee and Labor Relations, 1947 (Chapter 7, "Employee and Labor Relations")
- Health Insurance Portability and Accountability Act—Total Rewards, 1996 (Chapter 6, "Total Rewards")

EXAM ALERT

There are other laws that, to a degree, relate to risk management, and—more specifically—to privacy. Although we won't be specifically covering them in-depth in this book, be sure to familiarize yourself with them:

- *Fair Credit Reporting Act (FCRA), 1970*—The FCRA, enforced by the Federal Trade Commission, is designed to promote accuracy and ensure the privacy of information used in consumer reports.
- *Employee Polygraph Protection Act (EPPA), 1988*—According to the U.S. Department of Labor, "The Employee Polygraph Protection Act of 1988 (EPPA) generally prevents employers from using lie detector tests, either for pre-employment screening or during the course of employment, (with certain exemptions).... In addition, employers are required to display the EPPA poster in the workplace for their employees." EPPA is enforced by the Employment Standards Administration's Wage and Hour Division (WHD), located within the U.S. Department of Labor.

(continues)

(continued)

> ▶ *Fair and Accurate Credit Transactions Act (FACTA), 2003*—FACTA added new sections to the already-existing Federal Fair Credit Reporting Act (FCRA). These additions were primarily intended to help consumers fight identity theft, a crime which had (and has been) increasing at an alarming pace. FACTA also established other protections including limits on information sharing, and new consumer rights relative to disclosure.
>
> ▶ *Privacy Act, 1974*—The Privacy Act of 1974 was enacted in response to concerns about how the creation and use of computerized databases might impact the privacy rights of federal employees. There are several exceptions to the Privacy Act. As just one example of such exceptions, government agencies that are engaged in law enforcement can excuse themselves from the Act's rules.

EXAM ALERT

Revisit other laws, such as the Americans with Disabilities Act (ADA) and the Fair Labor Standards Act (FLSA), to reacquaint yourself with portions of these laws that relate to health and safety issues.

Occupational Safety and Health Act (OSH Act), 1970

The OSH Act was the first law to establish consistent workplace health and safety standards. The act's opening words communicate the reason for its creation—which is, essentially, to protect workers by ensuring safe and healthful workplaces.

This purpose is also reflected in the mission statement of OSHA, which is "to assure the safety and health of America's workers by setting and enforcing standards; providing training, outreach, and education; establishing partnerships; and encouraging continual improvement in workplace safety and health."

According to various governmental reports, OSH Act has been successful. A 2003 Department of Labor (DOL) report, for example, states that: Since its passage, workplace deaths have decreased by 62% and occupational injury and illness rates have dropped 40% since the passage of OSH Act—all while the size of the workforce has doubled. Nonetheless, according to www.dol.gov, there is still much work to do, since each day nearly 16 workers die on the job and more than 14,000 experience an injury or illness. Using these results as a place from which to look forward—rather than solely as a place from which to review the past—OSHA established the following two objectives for the five-year period spanning 2003–2008:

▶ Reduce the rate of workplace fatalities by at least 15%

▶ Reduce the rate of workplace injuries and illnesses by at least 20%.

OSHA also sees its role, however, as extending beyond these two traditional areas, because it recognizes the degree to which the workplace has changed and expanded since its inception. As stated on its website, OSHA's responsibilities have gained depth as well as breadth in the past 35 or so years:

Specifically, OSHA covers more than 114 million workers at 7 million worksites, twice the number under the agency's jurisdiction when it began operations in 1971. These workplaces and the working population are becoming increasingly diverse.

New safety and health issues continually emerge. Workplace violence and work-related motor vehicle accidents now account for more than 40 percent of workplace fatalities. OSHA also must be ready to assist with emergency preparedness and national security concerns.

As described here, therefore, OSH Act falls squarely within the functional area now known as "risk management"—and not just within what we used to call "occupational health and safety."

With this in mind, let's take a closer look at OSH Act and its implications to HR professionals.

The act established three key mechanisms to ensure safe and healthful workplaces. Specifically, the act

▶ Established a means of enforcement

▶ Encouraged and assisted states to take steps to ensure safe and healthful workplaces

▶ Provided for relevant research, information, education, and training

Purpose of OSHA

Why was OSHA established? In short, because there was a need. Specifically, "The Congress finds that personal injuries and illnesses arising out of work situations impose a substantial burden upon, and are a hindrance to, interstate commerce in terms of lost production, wage loss, medical expenses, and disability compensation payments." (www.osha.gov)

Be sure to familiarize yourself with OSHA's 13 specific objectives, shown in Section 2 of the Act ("Congressional Findings and Purpose") as articulated at www.osha.gov:

SEC. 2. Congressional Findings and Purpose

(b) The Congress declares it to be its purpose and policy, through the exercise of its powers to regulate commerce among the several States and with foreign nations and to provide for the general welfare, to assure so far as possible every working man and woman in the Nation safe and healthful working conditions and to preserve our human resources—

(1) by encouraging employers and employees in their efforts to reduce the number of occupational safety and health hazards at their places of employment, and to stimulate employers and employees to institute new and to perfect existing programs for providing safe and healthful working conditions;

(2) by providing that employers and employees have separate but dependent responsibilities and rights with respect to achieving safe and healthful working conditions;

(3) by authorizing the Secretary of Labor to set mandatory occupational safety and health standards applicable to businesses affecting interstate commerce, and by creating an Occupational Safety and Health Review Commission for carrying out adjudicatory functions under the Act;

(4) by building upon advances already made through employer and employee initiative for providing safe and healthful working conditions;

(continues)

(continued)

(5) by providing for research in the field of occupational safety and health, including the psychological factors involved, and by developing innovative methods, techniques, and approaches for dealing with occupational safety and health problems;

(6) by exploring ways to discover latent diseases, establishing causal connections between diseases and work in environmental conditions, and conducting other research relating to health problems, in recognition of the fact that occupational health standards present problems often different from those involved in occupational safety;

(7) by providing medical criteria which will assure insofar as practicable that no employee will suffer diminished health, functional capacity, or life expectancy as a result of his work experience;

(8) by providing for training programs to increase the number and competence of personnel engaged in the field of occupational safety and health; affecting the OSH Act since its passage in 1970 through January 1, 2004.

(9) by providing for the development and promulgation of occupational safety and health standards;

(10) by providing an effective enforcement program which shall include a prohibition against giving advance notice of any inspection and sanctions for any individual violating this prohibition;

(11) by encouraging the States to assume the fullest responsibility for the administration and enforcement of their occupational safety and health laws by providing grants to the States to assist in identifying their needs and responsibilities in the area of occupational safety and health, to develop plans in accordance with the provisions of this Act, to improve the administration and enforcement of State occupational safety and health laws, and to conduct experimental and demonstration projects in connection therewith;

(12) by providing for appropriate reporting procedures with respect to occupational safety and health which procedures will help achieve the objectives of this Act and accurately describe the nature of the occupational safety and health problem;

(13) by encouraging joint labor-management efforts to reduce injuries and disease arising out of employment.

The OSH Act also called for the establishment of the Occupational Safety and Health Administration (also known as OSHA). Residing within the Department of Labor (DOL), OSHA administers and enforces OSH Act.

OSHA Coverage

OSH Act offers broad coverage. In a 1999 letter, OSHA defined its coverage as including "employees of an organization." Unlike most other employment laws, smaller employers are not exempt from OSHA. Exceptions do exist, however—for instance, family farms that do not employ anyone outside the family are not covered under OSHA. Also excluded from the act are self-employed individuals, state government employees, and local government employees. State and local government employees, however, are often covered by state-sponsored OHSS legislation. Employees who work in specific industries (such as mining) that are covered by their own industry-specific laws are also exempt from OSHA.

General Duty Clause—Section 5(a)

The General Duty Clause of the act identifies two primary duties for employers, and one for employees, on which all subsequent requirements (called *standards*) are ultimately built:

1. Employers must ensure a safe workplace. The act defines "safe workplace" as one which is "free from recognized hazards that are causing or are likely to cause death or serious physical harm to his employees."

2. Employers must comply with all current and future OSHA-related standards.

The General Duty Clause comes into play when there are no existing standards covering a particular job or industry. Standards will be discussed later in this chapter.

The General Duty Clause also identifies a duty for employees—that that they must follow all safety and health-related rules stemming from the act. This duty is defined broadly, as well, in that it would include

- Reporting hazardous conditions to their supervisor

- Immediately reporting any and all job-related injuries or illnesses to their employer

- Cooperating in the event of an OSHA inspection or investigation

Employee Rights Under OSHA

The OSHA 3165 poster—which must be displayed in a conspicuous place that is easily visible to employees and applicants for employment—lists each employee's rights:

- You have the right to notify your employer or OSHA about workplace hazards. You may ask OSHA to keep your name confidential.

- You have the right to request an OSHA inspection if you believe that there are unsafe and unhealthful conditions in your workplace. You or your representative may participate in the inspection.

- You can file a complaint with OSHA within 30 days of discrimination by your employer for making safety and health complaints or for exercising your rights under the OSH Act.

- You have a right to see OSHA citations issued to your employer. Your employer must post the citations at or near the place of the alleged violation.

- Your employer must correct workplace hazards by the date indicated on the citation and must certify that these hazards have been reduced or eliminated.

- You have the right to copies of your medical records or records of your exposure to toxic and harmful substances or conditions.

- Your employer must post this notice, as shown in Figure 8.1, in your workplace.

Job Safety and Health
IT'S THE LAW!
OSHA
Occupational Safety
and Health Administration
U.S. Department of Labor

FIGURE 8.1   Job Safety and Health notice.

EMPLOYEES:

▶ You have the right to notify your employer or OSHA about workplace hazards. You may ask OSHA to keep your name confidential.

▶ You have the right to request an OSHA inspection if you believe that there are unsafe and unhealthful conditions in your workplace. You or your representative may participate in that inspection.

▶ You can file a complaint with OSHA within 30 days of retaliation or discrimination by your employer for making safety and health complaints or for exercising your rights under the OSH Act.

▶ You have a right to see OSHA citations issued to your employer. Your employer must post the citations at or near the place of the alleged violation.

▶ Your employer must correct workplace hazards by the date indicated on the citation and must certify that these hazards have been reduced or eliminated.

▶ You have the right to copies of your medical records or records of your exposure to toxic and harmful substances or conditions.

▶ Your employer must post this notice in your workplace.

▶ You must comply with all occupational safety and health standards issued under the OSH Act that apply to your own actions and conduct on the job.

EMPLOYERS:

▶ You must furnish your employees a place of employment free from recognized hazards.

▶ You must comply with the occupational safety and health standards issued under the OSH Act.

Source: www.osha.gov—OSHA 3165 poster

Employer Requirements Under OSHA—Record Keeping, Reporting, and Posting

HR professionals must have a solid understanding of record keeping, reporting, and posting requirements under the OSH Act. The first step for any organization is to determine whether it needs to maintain such records.

Determining Whether an Employer Is Required to Maintain Records

Most organizations employing fewer than 11 employees are exempt from OSHA record-keeping requirements. In addition, OSHA also publishes a list of specific low-risk industries that are exempt from this requirement, even if they employ more than 10 people.

Distinguishing Injury from Illness

For OSHA reporting purposes, OSHA defines a work-related injury as "any wound or damage to the body resulting from an event in the work environment." Identifying and classifying a work-related illness is somewhat more complicated. Illnesses can fall into any one of the following categories: skin diseases or disorders, respiratory conditions, poisoning, hearing loss, or a very broad category called "all other illnesses."

Determining What Must Be Recorded

According to OSHA, an injury or illness must be recorded if it results in one or more of the following:

- ▶ Death

- ▶ Days away from work

- ▶ Restricted work or job transfer to another job

- ▶ Loss of consciousness

- ▶ Medical treatment beyond first aid, as defined by in OSHA's directions

---

EXAM ALERT

Familiarize yourself with medical interventions that come under the category of first aid, as well as with those that go beyond first aid.

- ▶ Work-related injuries or illnesses that are considered significant, as defined in OSHA's directions, or that meet specific criteria outlined in those directions

Required Forms

Covered employers must maintain records using OSHA Form 300, OSHA Form 300A, and OSHA Form 301 for each worksite.

OSHA's Form 300: Log of Work-Related Injuries and Illnesses

OSHA's Form 300 is used to record the "what," "how," "when," "where," and "who" of work-related injuries and illnesses. The employer has seven working days from the time it learns of a work-related injury or illness to record it on this form.

NOTE

Work-related deaths and/or inpatient hospitalizations of three or more employees resulting from a work-related incident must be reported to OSHA within eight hours.

> **CAUTION**
>
> Care must be taken to preserve employee privacy when completing these forms. Under certain circumstances—including upon employee request—the words "privacy case" should be substituted for the employee's name. In these cases, a separate document must be maintained matching case numbers with employee names (for identification purposes).

OSHA's Form 301: Injury and Illness Incident Report

A separate Form 301 must be completed for each work-related injury or illness within seven calendar days of the date on which the employer learns of the work-related injury or illness. Completed forms must be maintained by the employee for five years following the year in which the incident or illness occurred.

OSHA's Form 300A: Summary of Work-Related Injuries and Illnesses

Employers use the Form 300A to record a numeric summary of all work-related injuries and illnesses logged in OSHA's Form 300 over the course of each calendar year. This form indicates the number of cases, the number of workdays impacted, and the numbers and types of work-related injuries and illnesses. A worksheet is also available to assist employers in filling out this summary. Each year, a completed Form 300 must be posted conspicuously for three months (between February 1 and April 30).

> **TIP**
>
> Detailed instructions on how to complete these forms, as well as actual downloadable forms, can be found at www.osha.gov.

Optional Calculations

OSHA provides formulas for calculating incidence rates (search www.osha.gov for this information).

An employer would then compare its incidence rate to incidence rates for other employers of similar size, or other employers in their industry.

Posting and Access Requirements

All employers covered by OSHA must display the OSHA 3165 poster (see "Employee Rights Under OSHA").

In addition, all employers covered by OSHA must provide employees, their designated representatives, and OSHA with access to employee exposure and medical records (29 CFR 1910.1020). Exposure records must be maintained for 30 years, and medical records must be maintained for 30 years after the employee's period of employment ends.

Employer Responsibilities—Standards

OSHA's standards, or requirements, apply to one or more of the four industries designated by OSHA:

- ▶ General Industry
- ▶ Maritime
- ▶ Construction
- ▶ Agriculture

OSHA identifies six standards that apply to most general industry employers:

- ▶ *Hazard Communication Standard ("Employee Right-to-Know")*—This standard ensures that employers and employees have knowledge and awareness about hazardous chemicals located in the workplace, and that they know how to protect themselves. This is also referred to as "Employee Right-to-Know." Specifically, this standard requires all employers having hazardous materials at the workplace to implement a written Hazard Communication Program. Four important key elements of this program are Material Safety Data Sheets (MSDS), orientation, training, and container labeling requirements.

- ▶ *Emergency Action Plan Standard*—Although recommended for all employers, an emergency action plan is mandatory only if required by a separate OSHA standard.

- ▶ *Fire Safety Standard*—Although recommended for all employers, a fire safety plan is mandatory only if required by a separate OSHA standard.

- ▶ *Exit Routes Standard*—Mandatory for all employers, the exit route standard defines exit requirements and addresses maintenance, safeguarding, and operational dimensions of exit routes. OSHA defines an exit route as "a continuous and unobstructed path of exit travel from any point within a workplace to a point of safety" (Source: OSHA Fact Sheet, Exit Routes).

- ▶ *Walking/Working Surfaces Standard*—Mandatory in all permanent places of employment (with few exceptions), this standard seeks to minimize or eliminate slips, trips, and falls in the workplace. Its coverage impacts surfaces such as floors, platforms, ladders, and steps.

- ▶ *Medical and First Aid Standard*—OSHA requires employers to provide medical and first aid personnel and supplies in accordance with the hazards of the workplace. The specifics of each program, however, will differ from workplace to workplace, and from employer to employer.

In a list that OSHA specifically describes as "not comprehensive," OSHA identifies nine additional standards that may apply to workplaces. These are described in Table 8.1.

TABLE 8.1   Nine OSHA Standards

Standard	Employers May Be Covered If...
Machine Guarding	Employees operate machinery such as saws, slicers, power presses, and so on.
Lockout/Tagout	Employees work with equipment that can start up without warning, or that release hazardous energy.
Electrical Hazards	Any electrical systems are present.
Personal Protective Equipment (PPE)	Mandatory employer assessment determines that PPE is necessary. If so, the employer must provide, maintain, and require the use of PPE.
Respirators	Respirators are necessary to protect the health of employees. If so, the employer must provide respirators.
Hearing Conservation	Employees are exposed to excessive noise.
Confined Spaces	Employees work in confined spaces, thereby increasing the likelihood of entrapment, and/or placing the employee in close physical proximity to hazards (such as machinery with moving parts).
Bloodborne Pathogens	Employees are exposed to blood or other bodily fluids through the performance of their regular duties.
Powered Industrial Tools	Powered industrial tools, such as forklifts, are used.

The Needlestick Safety and Prevention Act of 2000

The Needlestick Safety and Prevention Act of 2000 was, essentially, a compliance directive for enforcing the Bloodborne Pathogens Standard. The act added three key requirements to the existing standard:

▶ Evaluation and implementation of safer needle devices (as they become available). Reviews of—and searches for—such enhancements must be done annually.

▶ Actively involve employees who actually use needles and needle devices in this evaluation and selection process.

▶ Maintenance of a log of all injuries resulting from contaminated sharps.

EXAM ALERT

The PHR exam may cover any or all of these (or other) standards in greater detail. Increase your knowledge of all of them, especially if they do not apply to your particular industry.

OSHA—Inspections and Investigations

OSHA compliance officers can conduct inspections or investigations without prior notice or warning. Upon showing proper identification, a compliance officer is free to conduct reasonable inspections and investigations during regular working hours.

EXAM ALERT

There are certain limited circumstances under which OSHA may give employers 24-hours advance notice:

▶ In cases of apparent imminent danger, to enable the employer to abate the danger as quickly as possible

▶ In circumstances where the inspection can most effectively be conducted after regular business hours or where special preparations are necessary for an inspection

▶ Where necessary to assure the presence of representatives of the employer and employees or the appropriate personnel needed to aid in the inspection

▶ In other circumstances where the Area Director determines that the giving of advance notice would enhance the probability of an effective and thorough inspection.

Giving advanced notice is an involved process that triggers a series of requirements and guidelines. Visit www.osha.com for more information about these special circumstances.

Employer Rights

Employers have certain rights with respect to inspections, including the right to:

▶ Request proper identification from compliance officers

▶ Ask the compliance officer for the reason for the inspection or investigation—and get an answer

▶ Have an opening conference with the compliance officer

▶ Accompany the compliance officer as he or she conducts the inspection

▶ Have a closing conference with the compliance officer

▶ File a "notice of contest" to dispute the results of the inspection

▶ Request an informal settlement agreement process after an inspection

▶ Protect the confidentiality of trade secrets

▶ Require the compliance officer to obtain a search warrant

OSHA Priorities

OSHA recognizes that its compliance officers can't be everywhere, all the time. For this reason, OSHA has established a tiered priority system for workplace inspections. Listed in order of importance (from highest to lowest), OSHA's priorities are

1. Imminent danger

2. Catastrophes and fatal accidents

3. Employee complaints

4. Planned inspections in high-hazard industries

5. Follow-up inspections

See www.osha.gov for additional information about each of these conditions.

OSHA Inspections

OSHA inspections consist of an opening conference, the physical inspection, and a closing conference.

EXAM ALERT

Familiarize yourself with what an employer might experience during the opening conference, the physical inspection, and the closing conference.

Federal OSHA Complaint-Handling Process

When OSHA receives a complaint, it makes a determination as to whether its investigation will be conducted onsite or offsite. This determination is made on the basis of eight predetermined criteria, at least one of which must be met in order for OSHA to conduct an onsite inspection:

▶ A written, signed complaint by a current employee or employee representative with enough detail to enable OSHA to determine that a violation or danger likely exists that threatens physical harm or that an imminent danger exists

▶ An allegation that physical harm has occurred as a result of the hazard and that it still exists

▶ A report of an imminent danger

▶ A complaint about a company in an industry covered by one of OSHA's local or national emphasis programs or a hazard targeted by one of these programs

▶ Inadequate response from an employer who has received information on the hazard through a phone/fax investigation

▶ A complaint against an employer with a past history of egregious, willful, or failure-to-abate OSHA citations within the past three years

▶ Referral from a whistle-blower investigator

▶ Complaint at a facility scheduled for or already undergoing an OSHA inspection. (www.osha.gov)

Workers who complain have the right to have their names withheld from their employers, and OSHA will not reveal this information.

If none of these criteria is met, or if the employee or employee representative requests, OSHA may investigate via phone/fax method. In such cases, OSHA will telephone the employer, describe the alleged hazards and follow up with either a fax or a letter. According to www.osha.gov:

> The employer must respond within five days, identifying in writing any problems found and noting corrective actions taken or planned. If the response is adequate, OSHA generally will not conduct an inspection. The employee who filed the original complaint will receive a copy of the employer's response. If still not satisfied, the complainant may then request an on-site inspection.

Source: www.ohsa.gov. 2007.

EXAM ALERT

At times, OSHA will investigate an employee complaint with a phone/fax investigation instead of an onsite inspection. Know the circumstances under which this can happen, and know what an employer needs to do.

OSHA Violations and Penalties

OSHA has established five categories of violations—and five levels of accompanying penalties. Table 8.2 highlights these penalties.

TABLE 8.2   OSHA Violations and Penalties

Violation	Description of Violation of Standard	Penalty
Willful	Deliberate and intentional.	Up to $70,000 per violation. Will escalate in the event of employee death. Incarceration is possible.
Serious	Death or serious injury probable. The employer either knew or should have known about the violation.	Up to $7,000 for each violation.
Other-than-serious	Unlikely to result in serious injury or death.	Up to $7,000 for each violation.
De Minimis	No direct or immediate relationship to safety or health	NA. They are documented, but are not included on the citation.
Failure to Abate Prior Violation	Violation continues beyond the prescribed abatement date.	Up to $7,000 per day.
Repeat	Same or substantially similar violation as was found during a previous inspection.	Up to $70,000 for each violation.

> **EXAM ALERT**
>
> With the exception of those that are de minimis, violations result in citations. Know the process that must be followed upon receipt of a citation, and know the appeal process.

Mine Safety and Health Act (MSHA), 1977

The MSH Act is the second piece of legislation created specifically to protect employee health and safety—this time, for underground and surface miners working in coal, as well as noncoal, mines. Unlike OSHA, inspections of mines are mandatory—at least four times a year for underground mines and at least twice a year for surface mines.

> **NOTE**
>
> Check out www.msha.gov for additional information on the MSH Act.

Drug-Free Workplace Act, 1988

The Drug-Free Workplace Act requires federal contractors (with contracts of $100,000 or more) and individuals and organizations who are awarded federal grants (of any size) to agree to maintain a workplace free from drugs. Like the OSH and MSH Acts, the Drug-Free Workplace Act is administered and enforced by the Department of Labor.

Three key requirements that the act imposes on employers are as follows:

► Publish a statement notifying employees that the manufacture, distribution, dispensation, possession, or use of a controlled substance in the workplace is prohibited. This statement must also include a description of the consequences of violating this policy.

► Establish a drug-free awareness program addressing the dangers of drug use in the workplace, the employer's drug-free policy (including the consequences of violating that policy), and information about programs that are available to employees who use drugs.

► Distribute a copy of the workplace substance abuse policy to all employees.

NOTE

Visit www.dol.gov for additional information on the Drug-Free Workplace Act and for other requirements that it imposes on employers.

USA Patriot Act, 2001

Just one month after the terrorist attacks of September 11, 2001, President Bush signed the USA Patriot Act (Uniting and Strengthening America by Providing Appropriate Tools Required to Intercept and Obstruct Terrorism). Each of the titles in the Patriot Act (along with a final title called "miscellaneous"), gives insight into the focus of this act (Wikipedia.com, 2007):

► Title I: Enhancing Domestic Security Against Terrorism

► Title II: Enhanced Surveillance Procedures

► Title III: International Money Laundering Abatement and Anti-Terrorist Financing Act of 2001 (the title's sections primarily amend portions of the Money Laundering Control Act of 1986 and the Bank Secrecy Act of 1970)

► Title IV: Protecting the Border

► Title V: Removing Obstacles to Investigating Terrorism

► Title VI: Providing for Victims of Terrorism, Public Safety Officers and Their Families

► Title VII: Increased Information Sharing for Critical Infrastructure Protection

► Title VIII: Strengthening the Criminal Laws Against Terrorism

► Title IX: Improved Intelligence

► Title X: Miscellaneous

Homeland Security Act, 2002

The Homeland Security Act, passed 13 months after the September 11, 2001, terrorist attacks, established the Department of Homeland Security, a cabinet-level agency composed of 22 previously independent federal agencies.

The vision, mission, and strategic goals of DHS—an entity inextricably linked to risk management of the highest order—are as follows (www.dhs.gov):

Vision

Preserving our freedoms, protecting America…we secure our homeland.

Mission

We will lead the unified national effort to secure America. We will prevent and deter terrorist attacks and protect against and respond to threats and hazards to the nation. We will ensure safe and secure borders, welcome lawful immigrants and visitors, and promote the free-flow of commerce.

Strategic Goals

▶ Awareness: Identify and understand threats, assess vulnerabilities, determine potential impacts and disseminate timely information to our homeland security partners and the American public.

▶ Prevention: Detect, deter and mitigate threats to our homeland.

▶ Protection: Safeguard our people and their freedoms, critical infrastructure, property and the economy of our Nation from acts of terrorism, natural disasters, or other emergencies.

▶ Response: Lead, manage and coordinate the national response to acts of terrorism, natural disasters, or other emergencies.

▶ Recovery: Lead national, state, local and private sector efforts to restore services and rebuild communities after acts of terrorism, natural disasters, or other emergencies.

▶ Service: Serve the public effectively by facilitating lawful trade, travel and immigration.

▶ Organizational Excellence: Value our most important resource, our people. Create a culture that promotes a common identity, innovation, mutual respect, accountability and teamwork to achieve efficiencies, effectiveness, and operational synergies.

Sarbanes-Oxley Act, 2002

On July 30, 2002, President Bush signed into law the Sarbanes-Oxley Act of 2002, which he characterized as "the most far reaching reforms of American business practices since the time of Franklin Delano Roosevelt." The act mandated a number of reforms to increase corporate responsibility, expand financial disclosures, and combat corporate and accounting fraud, and created the Public Company Accounting Oversight Board, also known as the PCAOB, to oversee the activities of the auditing profession. The full text of the act is available at www.sec.gov/about/laws/soa2002.pdf. You can find links to all commission rulemaking and reports issued under the Sarbanes-Oxley Act at www.sec.gov/spotlight/sarbanes-oxley.htm (www.sec.gov).

Occupational Health

At their core, occupational health programs and initiatives help to ensure that workplaces remain healthy. Within that framework, organizations need to consider the physical, psychological, and emotional dimensions of health. Organizations also need to realize that while maintaining a healthy work environment is critical to maintaining a healthy workplace, it isn't enough. Employers also need to address—and be prepared to respond to—health-related issues that can develop in the workplace because of conditions, issues, or problems that don't originate in the workplace.

One area of responsibility related to occupational health involves identifying, preventing, and/or minimizing health hazards in the workplace. Another dimension involves developing appropriate responses in the event that a health hazard or health risk does emerge.

Health Hazards

A health hazard refers to anything in the workplace that creates or increases the possibility of work-related injuries. There are several types of health hazards with which HR professionals must be familiar.

Environmental Health Hazards

Environmental health hazards originate in—and exist because of "something" in the workplace. Environmental health hazards refer to a wide spectrum of conditions, circumstances, objects and/or organisms in the workplace that can create or increase the likelihood of employee illness or injury. In this chapter, we'll cluster environmental health hazards into three categories: physical, chemical, and biological.

Physical Hazards: Objects/Conditions

One type of physical health hazard results from actual, tangible "things" and/or conditions in the workplace that increase the risk of work-related illnesses or injuries. This type of hazard may be caused by or related to a variety of factors. Table 8.3 highlights some of these factors.

TABLE 8.3   Causes of Physical Hazards

Cause/Contributing Factor	Example
Failure to properly maintain or repair equipment or other physical objects	A tear in carpeting is not repaired, increasing the likelihood of trips and falls.
Failure to address and resolve potentially dangerous conditions	A puddle of water collects on the floor because of a leaking freestanding freezer unit, increasing the likelihood of slips and falls.
Poor process design	Bus drivers (such as for rental car companies) who enter information into portable computer terminals while in transit, increasing the likelihood of accidents.
Physical conditions relating to the actual performance of the job	A road paving crew installs or resurfaces asphalt in high heat conditions, increasing the likelihood of dehydration or heatstroke.
Physical conditions resulting from the actual operators who are exposed to high noise	MRI levels, increasing the likelihood of temporary or permanent hearing loss.

Physical Hazards: Design

Physical hazards can also result from the way in which the workplace or workspace is designed (also referred to as ergonomics). Ergonomic problems can result from poor workplace design—for instance, doors in hallways that have no windows increase the likelihood of collisions between employees who don't know that a door is about to swing in their direction. Ergonomic problems can also result from poor workspace design—for instance, LCD monitors that are placed above eye level increase the likelihood of back or neck injury because employees frequently need to look up.

Another significant area of concern involves work-related musculoskeletal disorders (MSDs). MSDs are perhaps better known as repetitive stress injuries (RSIs), cumulative trauma syndrome (CTSs), or cumulative trauma disorders (CTDs). Specific examples of MSDs are the following:

- ▸ Carpal tunnel syndrome
- ▸ Trigger finger
- ▸ Chronic lumbar strain
- ▸ Tendonitis
- ▸ Bursitis

MSDs are caused, or exacerbated, by forceful exertions, awkward postures, repetitive movements, and/or exposure to extreme environmental conditions (for example, heat, cold, humidity, or vibration). MSDs represent a serious and expensive workplace problem. In 1998, the National Academy of Sciences published a report estimating that financial costs from MSDs were in the vicinity of $20 billion annually.

OSHA has adopted a four-pronged approach to address MSDs and other ergonomics-related issues:

- Industry-specific or task-specific guidelines
- Enforcement
- Outreach and assistance (to businesses)
- National Advisory Committee

Chemical Health Hazards

Chemicals represent another potential workplace hazard. Many—perhaps even most—businesses use some type of chemicals in the course of their operations (for instance, gasoline at a service station, acetone at a nail salon, or certain cleaning supplies in an office). As required by the Hazard Communication Standard, employers must have MSDSs for all chemicals located in the workplace.

Material Safety Data Sheets (MSDSs)

In general, the MSDS must provide information about chemical hazards in the workplace, as well as protective measures that are available. Although OSHA does not mandate use of any specific MSDS format (unlike the I-9 form), the agency does provide the following sample MSDS on its website. (This form, OSHA 174, does include and reflect all information that is required to comply with MSDS guidelines.)

Material Safety Data Sheet	U.S. Department of Labor
May be used to comply with OSHA's Hazard Communication Standard, 29 CFR 1910.1200. Standard must be consulted for specific requirements.	Occupational Safety and Health Administration (Non-Mandatory Form) Form Approved OMB No. 1218-0072
IDENTITY (As Used on Label and List)	Note: Blank spaces are not permitted. If any item is not applicable, or no information is available, the space must be marked to indicate that.

SECTION I

Manufacturer's Name	Emergency Telephone Number
Address (Number, Street, City, State, and ZIP Code)	Telephone Number for Information
	Date Prepared
	Signature of Preparer (optional)

SECTION II—HAZARDOUS INGREDIENTS/IDENTITY INFORMATION

Hazardous Components (Specific Chemical Identity; Common Name(s))	OSHA PEL	ACGIH TLV	Other Limits Recommended	%(optional)

SECTION III—PHYSICAL/CHEMICAL CHARACTERISTICS

Boiling Point	Specific Gravity (H_2O = 1)
Vapor Pressure (mm Hg)	Melting Point
Vapor Density (AIR = 1)	Evaporation Rate (Butyl Acetate = 1)
Solubility in Water	
Appearance and Odor	

SECTION IV—FIRE AND EXPLOSION HAZARD DATA

Flash Point (Method Used)	Flammable Limits	LEL	UEL
Extinguishing Media			
Special Fire Fighting Procedures			
Unusual Fire and Explosion Hazards			
(Reproduce locally)	OSHA 174, Sept. 1985		

SECTION V—REACTIVITY DATA

Stability	Unstable	Conditions to Avoid
	Stable	
Incompatibility (*Materials to Avoid*)		
Hazardous Decomposition or Byproducts		
Hazardous Polymerization	May Occur	Conditions to Avoid
	Will Not Occur	

SECTION VI—HEALTH HAZARD DATA

Route(s) of Entry:	Inhalation?	Skin?	Ingestion?
Health Hazards (*Acute and Chronic*)			
Carcinogenicity:	NTP?	IARC Monographs?	OSHA Regulated?
Signs and Symptoms of Exposure			
Medical Conditions Generally Aggravated by Exposure			
Emergency and First Aid Procedures			

SECTION VII—PRECAUTIONS FOR SAFE HANDLING AND USE

Steps to Be Taken in Case Material is Released or Spilled
Waste Disposal Method
Precautions to Be Taken in Handling and Storing
Other Precautions

SECTION VIII—CONTROL MEASURES

Respiratory Protection (*Specify Type*)		
Ventilation	Local Exhaust	Special
	Mechanical (*General*)	Other
Protective Gloves	Eye Protection	
Other Protective Clothing or Equipment		
Work/Hygienic Practices		

* U.S.G.P.O.: 1986 - 491 - 529/45775

EXAM ALERT

Be familiar with required—and suggested—elements of MSDSs.

Chemical Health Hazards: Teratogens

One specific group of chemicals, called teratogens, will not harm pregnant women—but do have the potential to harm fetuses. To deal with this category of chemicals, some organizations have developed fetal protection policies. In some cases these organizations—and policies—are well intentioned; in others, establishing such policies could constitute an attempt to minimize potential legal exposure. Fetal protection policies are intended to protect fetuses from the possibility of being harmed by teratogens. The impact of most (if not all) these policies, as ruled by the Supreme Court, is unlawful gender discrimination.

The landmark case that resulted in this Supreme Court ruling was Automobile Workers v. Johnson Controls (1990). Johnson Controls manufactured batteries, a process that exposed employees to high levels of lead. The Supreme Court ruled that Johnson Controls' policy constituted a violation of Title VII of the Civil Rights Act of 1964, as amended by the Pregnancy Discrimination Act. The Act states that women cannot be discriminated against

> Because of or on the basis of pregnancy, childbirth, or related medical conditions; and women affected by pregnancy, childbirth, or related medical conditions shall be treated the same for all employment-related purposes.

In the Johnson case, Supreme Court Associate Justice Byron White wrote in his opinion that "decisions about the welfare of the next generation must be left to the parents who conceive, bear, support, and raise them, rather than to the employers who hire those parents."

Biological Health Hazards

Biological health hazards can be introduced into the workplace by people—employees, customers, vendors, and so forth. Biological health hazards can also be caused by some factor other than person-to-person transmission.

Under the ADA, infectious diseases are considered to be disabilities. As such, employers must determine what reasonable accommodations—specifically, ones that do not cause undue hardship—must be afforded to individuals with infectious diseases. Infectious diseases also pose unique challenges in that employers must take great care to ensure that the health of all individuals in the workplace is not threatened by possible person-to-person transmission. Essentially, the rights of people with infectious diseases must be balanced against the obligation to protect those who work with them.

> **CAUTION**
>
> Determinations relative to what constitutes "reasonable accommodation," "undue hardship," and "threat" must be made carefully. Such decisions cannot be made on the basis of misinformation or co-workers' irrational—albeit genuine—fears. Employers should educate employees, as appropriate, while protecting the confidentiality of people with disabilities.

HR professionals need to be familiar with certain infectious diseases. In the following sections, we will discuss HIV/AIDS, Hepatitis B and C, tuberculosis, and pandemics.

Biological Health Hazards: HIV/AIDS

Human Immunodeficiency Virus (HIV) and Acquired Immune Deficiency Syndrome (AIDS) are transmitted person to person through blood or other bodily fluids. Transmission of HIV/AIDS is of particular importance in the health care industry, because of the nature of the work performed in that industry.

Employees with HIV/AIDS are afforded protection under the Americans with Disabilities Act. Like any other person with a disability, a person with HIV/AIDS may continue to hold his or her position as long as he or she can perform the essential functions of the position with or without reasonable accommodation (that does not cause undue hardship to the organization).

> **CAUTION**
>
> Bias against individuals with HIV/AIDS may exist in the workplace—and that bias is often based on misinformation. HR professionals must be alert to signs of such bias and must be prepared to take appropriate action.

Biological Health Hazards: HBV

The Hepatitis B virus (HBV) causes Hepatitis B, a potentially serious (and potentially fatal) form of liver inflammation. People with HBV may experience a wide range of symptoms—anything from no symptoms to serious damage to the liver. Like HIV/AIDS, HBV is transmitted through blood and other bodily fluids and is therefore of particular concern to those in the health care industry. Unlike HIV/AIDS, a vaccine for HBV exists—and must be made available to "all occupationally exposed employees." The term "made available" reflects the fact that an employee cannot be required to get an HBV vaccination.

Biological Health Hazards: HCV

The Hepatitis C virus (HCV) causes Hepatitis C, a viral infection of the liver. Transmitted by blood or bodily fluids, HCV has been identified by the Center for Disease Control and Prevention as the most chronic bloodborne infection in the United States.

Although most people with HCV will experience no symptoms for many years, over time that can change. After 10, 20, or as much as 40 years, people with Hepatitis C can develop cirrhosis or cancer of the liver. There is no vaccine for HCV, so the best protection is afforded through prevention, such as PPE (protective personal equipment).

Biological Health Hazards: Tuberculosis

Tuberculosis, or TB, is a highly infectious bacterial disease. Although TB usually affects the lungs, it can also impact other organs.

TB can be spread by sneezing or coughing, and is thus an important workplace issue. An increase in drug-resistant strains of TB in the 1980s—along with an increased population of individuals with suppressed immune systems—led to a renewed focus on TB. The number of cases of TB has decreased dramatically in the last decade; in fact, according to OSHA, the number of cases of TB is now at its lowest level since reporting began in 1953.

Biological Health Hazards: Pandemics

The government defines a pandemic as "a global disease outbreak. A flu pandemic occurs when a new influenza virus emerges for which people have little or no immunity, and for which there is no vaccine. The disease spreads easily person-to-person, causes serious illness, and can sweep across the country and around the world in very short time" (www.pandemciflu.gov). Concerns relative to pandemics currently focus on avian H5N1 virus (commonly referred to as "avian flu" or "bird flu"). The H5N1 virus has raised concerns about a potential human pandemic because

- It is especially virulent.

- It is being spread by migratory birds.

- It can be transmitted from birds to mammals and in some limited circumstances to humans.

- Like other influenza viruses, it continues to evolve.

According to the government, since 2003 a growing number of human H5N1 cases have been reported in Azerbaijan, Cambodia, China, Djibouti, Egypt, Indonesia, Iraq, Lao Democratic People's Republic, Nigeria, Thailand, Turkey, and Vietnam. More than half of the people infected with the H5N1 virus have died, and most of these cases are all believed to have been caused by exposure to infected poultry. Although there has been no sustained human-to-human transmission of the disease, there is concern that H5N1 will evolve into a virus capable of human-to-human transmission.

Avian flu represents, in some ways, a confluence of risk management matters pertaining to infectious disease and emergency preparedness. Although it is critical for organizations to prepare, just as they would do with any sound emergency preparedness plan, it is equally critical that organizations not overreact, or allow fear to fuel their actions, or reactions.

Employee Assistance Programs (EAPs)

Employee assistance programs (EAPs) provide employees with help and resources on a variety of personal issues that can—and often do—have a direct impact on employee job performance. More specifically, the Department of Health and Human Services defines an employee assistance program (EAP) as: "a worksite-based program designed to assist in the identification and resolution of productivity problems associated with employees impaired by personal concerns, including, but not limited to, health, marital, family, financial, alcohol, drug, legal, emotional, stress, or other personal concerns that may adversely affect employee job performance." (Source: Employee Assistance Professionals Association, www.eapassn.org.)

As such, EAPs—which are paid for by organizations—benefit employers as well as employees.

EAPs provide a variety of programs addressing topics that include financial, legal, and health issues. Areas of assistance can range from childcare, to elder care, to substance abuse. EAPs are also available as a resource for workplaces that have experienced difficult incidents, such the death of an employee or an act of workplace violence.

EAPs can be administered within the organization, through vendors who operate outside the organization, or through some combination of the two. Still others are provided through a consortium arrangement.

CAUTION

> The degree to which employees perceive an EAP as confidential will play a key role in determining the degree to which employees will use its services—and, therefore, the degree of success that the EAP will ultimately achieve. Ensuring confidentiality is essential, but—by itself—is not enough. Ensuring that employees recognize and believe in the confidentiality of the program is equally important.

Although EAPs are paid for by organizations, the costs of services of which employees avail themselves are sometimes shared with employees. For instance, an employee might be able to participate in a certain number of fully paid counseling sessions, after which the costs might either be shared, or borne fully by the employee, depending upon how each particular program is structured.

In 1995, the average annual cost of EAP services per eligible employee nationwide was $26.59 for internal programs staffed by company employees and $21.47 for external programs provided by an outside contractor, according to the Research Triangle Institute. These costs, however, pale in comparison to the expenses associated with recruiting and training replacements for employees who have been terminated because substance abuse problems—costs which have been estimated to run up to—and in some cases well beyond—$50,000.

External EAPs are estimated to cost anywhere from $15 to $40 per employee, per year. EAPs, however, can pay for themselves many times over by attaining the following measurable contributions:

- Reduced turnover

- Decreased absenteeism and/or tardiness

- Increased productivity

- Increased employee satisfaction

- Decreased risk of workplace violence

Health and Wellness Programs

Health and wellness programs offer employees the opportunity to enhance the quality of their lives through healthier lifestyle choices. Health and wellness programs take a proactive approach to health of body, mind, and spirit.

Although prevention is a key element, health and wellness programs can also provide assistance to employees who are dealing with existing health issues (for instance, weight problems or smoking).

Wellness programs, however, are not (and should not be) positioned to HR's business partners as something that is "nice to do" for employees. Instead, health and wellness programs constitute a solid business investment that benefits the organization as well as its employees. According to Ron Goetzel, Ph.D., Director of the Cornell University Institute for Health and Productivity Studies, wellness programs have been shown to yield a 3-to-1 return on investment (ROI). In that same article, published in the November/December 2006 edition of the North Carolina Medical Journal, Goetzel references one specific success story, in which Citibank reported a savings of $8.9 million in medical expenditures from their health promotion program after investing 1.9 million in the program—thereby generating an ROI of 4.56 to 1.

> **TIP**
>
> As strategic business partners, HR professionals must be well prepared to present themselves in a manner that addresses the needs and overarching performance of the organization.

EXAM ALERT

Be familiar with types, elements, and benefits of health and wellness programs.

Like EAPs, health and wellness programs benefit employers as well as employees. As with EAPs, HR professionals must be prepared to demonstrate the specific financial and nonfinancial benefits that would accrue to their employers as a result of implementing health and wellness programs.

Chemical Use and Dependency

The statistics regarding costs associated with chemical/substance use, abuse, and dependency—particularly as related to the workplace are economically staggering to workplaces. As published on the DOL website (www.dol.gov):

▶ More than six percent of the population over 12 years of age (13.9 million people) has used drugs within the past 30 days. Rates of use remain highest among persons aged 16 to 25—the age group entering the work force most rapidly (National Household Survey on Drug Abuse. August 1998. U.S. Department of Health and Human Services. Rockville, MD).

▶ Seventy-three percent of all current drug users aged 18 and older (8.3 million adults) were employed in 1997. This includes 6.7 million full-time workers and 1.6 million part-time workers (National Household Survey on Drug Abuse. August 1998. U.S. Department of Health and Human Services. Rockville, MD).

▶ More than 14 percent of Americans employed full- and part-time report heavy drinking, which is defined as five or more drinks on five or more days in the past 30 days. The heaviest drinking occurred among persons between the ages of 18 and 25 years (August 1998. U.S. Department of Health and Human Services. Rockville, MD).

▶ According to a national survey conducted by the Hazelden Foundation, more than sixty percent of adults know people who have gone to work under the influence of drugs or alcohol ("Addiction in the Workplace Survey." October 22, 1996. Hazelden Foundation. Center City, MN).

The Impact of Drug and Alcohol Use in the Workplace

The economic and human costs of drug and alcohol use are staggering. More specifically, the National Institutes of Health recently reported that alcohol and drug abuse cost the economy $246 billion in 1992. In addition, numerous studies, reports, and surveys suggest that substance abuse is having a profoundly negative effect on the workplace in terms of decreased productivity and increased accidents, absenteeism, turnover, and medical costs. The following statistics highlight the impact of substance abuse on the workplace:

▶ In 1990, problems resulting from the use of alcohol and other drugs cost American businesses an estimated $81.6 billion in lost productivity due to premature death (37 billion) and illness (44 billion); 86% of these combined costs were attributed to drinking (*Substance Abuse and Mental Health Statistics Sourcebook*, 5/95, p.3. Substance Abuse and Mental Health Services Administration, U.S. Department of Health and Human Services. Rockville, MD).

▶ Results from a U.S. Postal Service study indicate that employees who tested positive on their preemployment drug test were 77% more likely to be discharged within the first three years of employment and were absent from work 66% more often than those who tested negative (Normand, J., Salyards, S. & Maloney, J. "An Evaluation of Preemployment Drug Testing." *Journal of Applied Psychology*. Vol. 75, No. 6, 1990. pp. 629–639).

▶ A survey of callers to the national cocaine helpline revealed that 75% reported using drugs on the job, 64% admitted that drugs adversely affected their job performance, 44% sold drugs to other employees, and 18% had stolen from co-workers to support their drug habit (National Cocaine Helpline. "1-800-COCAINE." Summit, NJ. 1987).

▶ Alcoholism causes 500 million lost workdays each year. "Treatment is the Answer: A White Paper on the Cost-Effectiveness of Alcoholism and Drug Dependency Treatment." National Association of Treatment Providers. Laguna Hills, CA. March, 1991.

▶ According to the U.S. Department of Health and Human Services, in 1990, problems resulting from the use of alcohol and other drugs cost American businesses an estimated $81.6 billion in lost productivity due to premature death (37 billion) and illness (44 billion)—of which approximately $70 billion was attributed to drinking.

▶ The National Institutes of Health recently reported that alcohol and drug abuse cost the economy $246 billion in 1992.

▶ In 1992, the National Association of Treatment Providers in Laguna Hills, California, estimated that drug abuse results in 500 million lost workdays each year.

▶ According to results of a National Institute on Drug Abuse (NIDA) sponsored survey, employees who use drugs are 2.2 times more likely to request early dismissal or time off, 2.5 times more likely to have absences of eight days or more, three times more likely to be late for work, 3.6 times more likely to be involved in a workplace accident, and 5 times more likely to file a workers' compensation claim.

Substance Abuse Programs

According to the U.S. Department of Labor's Working Partners for an Alcohol- and Drug-Free Workplace initiative, a comprehensive substance program consists of the following five components:

▶ Drug-free workplace policy

▶ Supervisor training

▶ Employee education

▶ Employee assistance

▶ Drug testing

One more critical element (in many ways perhaps the most critical element) must be added to this list: management buy-in and support. Without this, the likelihood that the program will be successful is greatly diminished—and HR is more likely to be seen as an enforcer, rather than as a strategic partner.

As with all workplace initiatives to which HR contributes, it is important to quantify the benefits of establishing a substance abuse program.

Symptoms of Chemical and Substance Abuse

HR professionals need to be able to recognize the warning signs of chemical and substance abuse:

▶ Sudden decline in quality or quantity or work performed, for no apparent reason

▶ Increased errors

▶ Increased accidents

▶ Inconsistent behavior

▶ Emotional unpredictability

It is important to note, however, that any of these symptoms could result from a variety of other factors, so guard against jumping to any conclusions.

Drug Testing

Drug testing in the workplace is a hotly debated topic. Some states restrict certain types of drug testing, and some federal laws require drug testing of certain employees. Drug testing programs must be administered fairly, and consistently, to similarly situated employees.

> **CAUTION**
>
> Consult with senior leadership—and with legal counsel—before implementing or changing a drug-testing program. Such changes can have unforeseen legal and employee relations ramifications.

A variety of types of drug-testing programs exists, each of which has different goals and objectives. Table 8.4 highlights these programs further.

TABLE 8.4 Types of Drug Tests

Type of Drug Test	Purpose/Description
Pre-employment	Decrease the likelihood of hiring someone who is currently using/abusing drugs. To ensure that similarly situated candidates are being treated consistently, it is important to ensure that all candidates applying for a particular position(s) participate in preemployment drug tests. To ensure even greater consistency, conduct the test at the same point in the preemployment process.

(continues)

TABLE 8.4   *Continued*

Type of Drug Test	Purpose/Description
Pre-promotion	Decrease the likelihood of promoting an employee who is currently using/abusing drugs.
Annual physical tests	Drug testing is performed as part of each employee's annual physical exam to identify current drug users/abusers for assistance or disciplinary action.
Reasonable suspicion and for cause	For cause tests are conducted when an employee shows obvious signs of not being fit for duty. Reasonable suspicion tests are conducted when employee has a documented pattern of unsafe work behavior. These tests are conducted to protect the safety and well being of employees and co-workers, and to identify opportunities for rehabilitation.
Random	Unannounced tests are conducted at random, for reasons related to safety or security.
Post-accident	Employees who are involved in an accident or unsafe practice incident are tested to determine whether alcohol or some other drug was a factor. These tests are intended to protect the safety of employees (users and nonusers) and to identify opportunities for rehabilitation.
Treatment follow up	Employees who return to work after participating in an alcohol or drug treatment program are periodically tested to ensure that they remain free of illegal substances.

EXAM ALERT

Be familiar with drug-testing techniques, as well as appropriate intervention strategies.

Work-Related Stress

Stress is a significant workplace issue. In its 1999 report titled "Stress at Work," the National Institute for Public Safety and Health (NIOSH) defined stress as the "harmful physical and emotional responses that occur when the requirements of the job do not match the capabilities, resources, or needs of the worker." Stress can be more than disquieting—it can actually cause illness and injury. And stress is expensive. The American Institute of Stress estimates a $300 billion annual price tag for stress, which includes costs relating to accidents; absenteeism; employee turnover; diminished productivity; direct medical, legal, and insurance costs; workers' compensation awards; and tort and FELA (Federal Employers' Liability Act) judgments. In the book *Stress Costs*, author Ravi Tangri presents a formula for tabulating the actual costs of stress, which he asserts account for

- ► 19% of absenteeism
- ► 40% of turnover
- ► 30% of short- and long-term disability
- ► 10% of drug plan costs
- ► 60% of total workplace accidents

EXAM ALERT

Be familiar with the physical, psychological, and mental manifestations of stress.

HR professionals must also be able to identify, implement, and evaluate interventions designed to prevent or eradicate job stress. NIOSH outlines a valuable three-step approach to this in "Stress at Work," www.cdc.gov/niosh/.

CAUTION

Stress, left unchecked or unresolved, can lead to burnout. Know the symptoms of employee burnout.

Safety

Workplace safety can be defined in many ways. In essence, a "safe workplace" can be defined as one in which employees are free from risks of injury or illness. Call it prevention, or call it avoidance, either way, workplace safety requires that companies take a proactive approach to accidents, injury, and illness:

1. Organizations must minimize the likelihood that work-related injuries or illnesses will occur.

2. Organizations must proactively establish response plans in the event that injuries or illnesses do occur.

EXAM ALERT

Familiarize yourself with different types of safety training and incentive programs, as well as effective ways to implement such programs within the organization.

OSHA and Workplace Safety

OSHA, as its name implies, is the government agency charged with ensuring a safe and healthy workplace. OSHA recommends a four-module approach to safety and health management:

- ▶ *Module 1: Safety and Health Payoffs*—Work-related injuries are expensive, financially and otherwise. According to the National Safety Council, workplace injuries cost society $127.7 billion in 1997. The cost is also human—according to OSHA, nearly 16,000 workers are injured every workday

- ▶ *Module 2: Management System*—Safety and Health Integration—Organizations must create and cultivate a culture of safety. Safety can't be separate from the culture; rather, it must be an integral component of the culture. Within this culture of safety, four specific elements can then be created, and integrated:

    - ▶ Management Leadership and Employee Involvement

    - ▶ Worksite Analysis

- ▸ Hazard Prevention and Control

- ▸ Safety and Health Training

▸ *Module 3: Conducting a Safety & Health Checkup*—Organizations must then assess their own safety and health—take a good hard look at themselves with respect to each of those four areas identified in module 2.

▸ *Module 4: Creating Change*—The roadmap is in place, and the self-analysis has been conducted. The next step is to implement necessary change. In order to do this, obstacles will need to be identified and overcome, and a process implementation strategy—beginning with the buy-in of top management—must be developed and implemented.

Safety Committees

Safety committees provide a means by which employees and managers can collaboratively work toward increasing workplace safety. Safety committees can also support HR professionals as they research, develop, select, and implement safety training and incentive programs.

> **EXAM ALERT**
>
> Familiarize yourself with different types of safety training and incentive programs, as well as effective ways to implement those programs within the organization.

Some of the purposes of safety committees are as follows:

- ▸ Building and maintaining interest in health and safety issues

- ▸ Ensuring that managers and employees recognize that they are primarily responsible for preventing workplace accidents

- ▸ Reinforcing safety as part of the fabric of the organization's culture.

- ▸ Providing a forum for discussing health- and safety-related issues

- ▸ Informing, educating, and training employees about emerging safety-related information and/or guidelines

Functions that safety committees might carry out in support of these objectives could include the following:

- ▸ Analyzing accidents/incidents to identify trends, and to plan corrective action

- ▸ Conducting periodic (such as monthly) safety inspections

- ▸ Planning and carrying out training

- ▸ Reporting and analyzing accomplishments as well as current safety concerns

- ▸ Setting annual safety objectives

- ▸ Ensuring that an effective safety program is in place

> **EXAM ALERT**
>
> Carefully review the specified safety-related responsibilities and knowledge. In addition to reflecting upon your practical experience, seek out as much information as possible—anecdotal and otherwise—relative to each of those topics. This is particularly important if you have had limited practical experience with safety-related issues.

Security

Security refers to protection of the workplace and of the employees who work there. Security threats can come from a wide range of possible sources, just a few of which are

- ▸ Natural disasters, such as earthquakes

- ▸ Theft

- ▸ Workplace violence

- ▸ Terrorism (including biological terrorism)

- ▸ Identity theft

- ▸ Fire

- ▸ Flood

- ▸ Hazardous materials

- ▸ Computer viruses/hackers

HR professionals need a working knowledge of these and other threats that can jeopardize workplace security.

> **EXAM ALERT**
>
> Familiarize yourself with different types of safety training and incentive programs, as well as effective ways to implement those programs within the organization.

A cursory review of the preceding list reinforces the fact that security issues are business issues—ones that can jeopardize an organization's very existence. As such, it is critical for organizations to conduct a SWOT analysis—strengths, weaknesses, opportunities, and threats—of security-related issues.

Threats are often perceived as coming from outside the organization. Overlooking internal threats, however, can be disastrous. For instance, a company's own employees can even present a security threat. Disgruntled employees, departing employees, or former employees can present threats in the form of sabotage, theft, espionage, or violence.

HR must partner with internal and/or external security experts to protect the tangible—and intangible—assets of the organization. Of primary importance are the organization's human assets—its employees. Other assets, such as technology, facilities, and financial assets, must also be protected.

When Prevention Isn't Enough

The criticality of emergency preparedness planning was perhaps among the most painful—and the most valuable—of the many lessons learned from the 9/11 terrorist attacks. On that day, the unthinkable became real. Now, it is a part of our shared history. As HR professionals, however, we must not allow any degree of complacency to creep back into our business operations. HR must work ceaselessly and collaboratively to develop emergency response plans should a situation arise in which security is breached. Although the plans we collaboratively develop may never be utilized, failing to do so will surely place employers, employees, and all other assets at significant risk.

It is here, during a discussion of workplace security, that we are naturally led to where this chapter began—an in-depth review of risk management. Security is, at its core, all about assessing, preparing for, addressing, and in a holistic sense, managing various types of risk. This applies to any imaginable type of asset—technical, human, financial, or physical. The reality is that it is not possible to remove all risk. Nor would that necessarily be advisable, because security so often finds itself perched on the opposite of the pendulum from freedom. In other words, total security might be possible, but there is a cost—a cost that may not represent an acceptable choice to senior leadership. Risk is real—whether it emanates from within or outside the organization, or even from within or outside the nation. It is unavoidable, and whether it takes the form of issues pertaining to health, safety, or security, it must be addressed and managed to the best of the organization's—and our profession's—collective ability.

Chapter Summary

Knowledge and skill in the areas of risk management present another significant opportunity for HR professionals to add value to the organization. As such, HR professionals must understand and be able to respond effectively to OHSS issues relating to risk management.

This holds true even if risk management OHSS does not seem to fall directly within an HR professional's formal job description. HR professionals cannot be prepared to handle only those situations that are predictable or routine. We need look no further than the wake of the terror attacks of 9/11 to see examples of how HR professionals can—and will—be called upon to bring their knowledge and expertise to situations that are predictable, as well as to situations that are unpredictable. Knowledge and skill in the areas of risk management will ensure that we are poised to rise to the challenges with which we will inevitably be presented.

Key Terms

- Fair Credit Reporting Act (FCRA), 1970
- Risk Management
- Occupational Safety and Health Act (OSH Act), 1970
- Privacy Act, 1974
- Employee Polygraph Protection Act (EPPA), 1988
- Americans with Disabilities Act (ADA), 1992
- Mine Safety and Health Act (MSH Act), 1977
- Drug-Free Workplace Act, 1988
- USA Patriot Act, 2001
- Homeland Security Act, 2002
- Sarbanes-Oxley Act, 2002
- Fair and Accurate Credit Transactions Act (FACTA), 2003
- General Duty Clause
- Standards
- OSHA 3165

- Work-Related Injury/Illness
- OSHA Form 300
- Privacy Case
- OSHA Form 300A
- OSHA Form 301
- General Industry
- Hazard Communication Standard
- Material Safety Data Sheets (MSDS)
- Emergency Action Plan Standard
- Fire Safety Standard
- Exit Routes Standard
- Walking/Working Surfaces Standard
- Medical and First Aid Standard
- Machine Guarding Standard
- Lockout/Tagout Standard
- Electric Hazards Standard
- Personal Protective Equipment Standard
- Respirators Standard

- Hearing Conservation Standard
- Confined Spaces Standard
- Bloodborne Pathogens Standard
- Powered Industrial Tools Standard
- The Needlestick Safety and Prevention Act of 2000
- Willful Violation
- Serious Violation
- Other-Than-Serious Violation
- Repeat Violation
- Failure to Abate Prior Violation
- Health Hazards
- Environmental Hazards
- Physical Health Hazards
- Ergonomics
- Musculoskeletal Disorders (MSDs)
- Repetitive Stress Injuries (RSIs)
- Cumulative Trauma Syndrome (CTSs)
- Cumulative Trauma Disorders (CTDs)
- Teratogens
- Fetal Protection Policies
- Automobile Workers vs. Johnson Controls

- Biological Health Hazards
- Infectious Diseases
- HIV/AIDS
- HBV
- HCV
- Tuberculosis (TB)
- Pandemics
- Employee Assistance Programs (EAPs)
- Health and Wellness Programs
- Substance Use/Abuse
- Drug Testing
- Preemployment Drug Testing
- Prepromotion Drug Testing
- Reasonable Suspicion Drug Testing
- For Cause Drug Testing
- Random Drug Testing
- Post-Accident Drug Testing
- Treatment Follow-up Drug Testing
- Stress
- Burnout
- Incident and Emergency Response Plans
- Safety Committees

Apply Your Knowledge

This chapter focuses on risk management issues. Complete the following exercises, review questions, and exam questions as a way of reviewing and reinforcing the knowledge and skills you'll need to perform your responsibilities as an HR professional.

Exercises

1. One of the line managers with whom you consult has decided to terminate an employee for poor performance. This employee has been with the company for five years. A year ago, when a new manager (your internal client) took over the department, she soon realized that the employee's performance was well below expectations (despite what had been written in the employee's earlier performance appraisals). The manager coached, counseled, and gave the employee every opportunity to improve his performance through the progressive disciplinary process. Still, his performance was well below expectations. Now, the manager has asked you to help with the arrangements for the termination meeting. One of the items the manager wants your advice on is what to do about the employee's laptop computer equipment and files. Which of the following approaches would you recommend to the manager?

   A. Arrange for the employee's access to all shared network files and email to be blocked or removed while the termination meeting is actually taking place. Then, out of courtesy to this long-term employee, allow him to take the laptop home overnight to remove any personal, non-network files.

   B. Arrange for the employee's access to all electronic files and information to be blocked or removed while the termination meeting is actually taking place. Immediately after the meeting, retrieve the laptop from the employee.

   C. After the termination meeting, arrange for someone to accompany the employee to his workstation. That person can observe while the employee takes a few minutes to remove personal files from his laptop.

   D. Allow the employee a few minutes to privately copy or remove personal files from his laptop. This way, this long-term employee can "save face" and maintain his dignity during a difficult situation. Then retrieve the laptop from the employee.

2. After putting together a detailed, multiphased proposal—which included an impressive cost-benefit analysis—you have obtained approval to establish an EAP program at your organization. This is the first opportunity you've had to introduce a new initiative at your organization, so you want to do everything possible to ensure its success. Which of the following factors will have the greatest impact on the ultimate success or failure of this EAP program?

   A. Ensuring that employees believe that the program offers absolute confidentiality.

   B. Ensuring that the program offers absolute confidentiality.

   C. Administering the program by an outside vendor.

   D. Ensuring that you conduct a cost-benefit analysis annually to demonstrate the program's ongoing value, and to thereby secure ongoing management support.

3. An employee who just turned 18 two weeks ago—a day before she was hired—drops a box of materials on her foot, is taken to the emergency room, and is diagnosed with several broken bones. Which of the following has to happen?

   A. OSHA must be notified within 8 hours.

   B. The OSHA Form 300 must be completed within seven working days.

   C. The OSHA Form 301 must be completed and posted within seven calendar days of the date on which the employer learns of the work-related injury or illness.

   D. The OSHA Form 300A must be completed within seven calendar days of the work-related injury or illness.

4. You've been selected to become the HR manager for your organization's new facility. This facility is the first satellite location—and in fact the only location other than the organization's very large world headquarters office (WHQ). At WHQ, you operated as a compensation analyst, so this will be your first opportunity to function as a generalist. Because you've always been surrounded by experts from every HR discipline, you're not certain how to go about meeting safety requirements at the new location. You know that you need MSDS sheets, but you're not sure under what conditions. You do some research on the OSHA website, and learn that you must have MSDS sheets in place if

   A. Any chemicals are accessible in the workplace.

   B. Any chemicals are present in the workplace.

   C. Any chemicals are stored in the workplace.

   D. Any chemicals are used in the workplace.

5. You've accepted a position as the HR manager with a small manufacturing organization. You were acquainted with the former HR manager because you were both active in the local SHRM chapter. He has decided to move out of state to be closer to his aging parents, and you're excited to be following in his footsteps at his former company. From everything he has told you, the company "has its act together" with respect to HR-related issues—including safety issues, EEO reports, I-9 documentation, and sound compensation practices, just to name a few. You're surprised, then, when you come across a document stating that the organization was cited for a "Serious Violation" three months earlier. You're concerned, because you know that a serious violation is

   A. Considered by the EEOC to be deliberate and intentional.

   B. Unlikely to result in death, but is likely to result in serious injury.

   C. One that the employer either knew about or should have known about.

   D. The most serious category of violation recognized by the Department of Justice.

Review Questions

1. What three employer requirements were added to the Bloodborne Pathogens Standard by the Needlestick Safety and Prevention Act of 2000?

2. In what way was the Automobile Workers v. Johnson Controls (1990) Supreme Court ruling significant?

3. The General Duty Clause identified three responsibilities: two for employers, and one for employees. What are they?

4. What is the best way to prevent Hepatitis C/HCV from being transmitted in the workplace?

5. What are the six critical components of a comprehensive substance program? Of these, which is the most important?

Exam Questions

1. Which of the following laws was not created specifically to address occupational safety and health issues?

    A. Drug-Free Workplace Act

    B. MSHA

    C. OSHA

    D. WARNA

2. Which of the following is exempt from coverage under OSHA?

    A. Family farms that employ fewer than 11 employees

    B. Federal government employees

    C. Self-employed individuals

    D. Certain low-risk industries specified by OSHA

3. Which of the following statements about health and wellness programs is most true?

    A. They are of primary benefit to employers.

    B. They are of primary benefit to employees.

    C. They take a proactive approach to health and wellness issues.

    D. They take a reactive approach to health and wellness issues.

4. All of the following are likely functions of a safety committee except

    A. Investigating accidents and incidents

    B. Conducting inspections

    C. Instituting PPE enhancements

    D. Identifying safety concerns

5. Which of the following is not a category of workplace drug testing?

    A. Pre-employment

    B. Reasonable Cause

    C. Post-accident

    D. Random

6. Which of the following statements does not reflect a security-related HR responsibility?

    A. Develop/select, implement, and evaluate security plans to protect the company from liability.

    B. Develop/select, implement, and evaluate record-keeping tools for reporting internal and external breaches of security to OSHA.

    C. Develop/select, implement, and evaluate security plans to protect employees (for example, injuries resulting from workplace violence).

    D. Develop/select, implement, and evaluate incident and emergency response plans

7. Which of the following is most likely to cause or contribute to the onset of an MSD?

    A. Improper use of PPE.

    B. Poor ergonomic design.

    C. Poor ventilation.

    D. Improper use of MSDS.

8. An employee who has just learned that he or she is HIV positive

    A. Is entitled to continue performing his or her job as long as he or she can perform the essential functions of that job.

    B. May continue to perform his or her job until he or she begins to develop visible or other outward symptoms.

    C. Should strongly consider informing co-workers about his or her HIV status, so as to address any fears or concerns in a proactive manner.

    D. Constitutes a direct threat to co-workers' health and should therefore be strongly encouraged to take a leave of absence.

9. According to the OSH Act, which of the following statements is true?

   A. Employers must correct workplace hazards by the date indicated on the citation and must certify that these hazards have been reduced or eliminated.

   B. Employees have the right to copies of medical records of co-workers who have been exposed to toxic and harmful substances or conditions.

   C. Employers must submit a plan to reduce or eliminate workplace hazards by the date indicated on the citation.

   D. Employees have the right to review, but not to photocopy, their medical records or records of their exposure to toxic and harmful substances or conditions.

10. Under OSHA, employees enjoy all of the following rights except

   A. The right to notify their employer or OSHA about workplace hazards.

   B. The right to ask OSHA to maintain your confidentiality.

   C. The right to request an OSHA inspection if you believe that there are unsafe and unhealthful conditions in your workplace.

   D. The right to file a complaint with OSHA within 45 days of discrimination by your employer for making safety and health complaints or for exercising your rights under the OSH Act.

Answers to Exercises

1. **Answer B is the best answer.** Employees who are being terminated pose a potentially significant risk to the organization's technological, human, and financial resources—including proprietary information. This holds true for any employee—even long-standing ones. Don't take any chances. With respect to technical considerations, access to all computer-based files and information should be blocked or removed during (but not before) the termination meeting. As appropriate, arrangements can be made for the employee to retrieve personal computer files at a later time. Answer A is not the best answer, since the potential risk posed by terminated employees isn't limited to shared or network resources. Answer C is not the best answer because a great deal of damage can potentially be done under the seemingly "watchful eye" of an observer. In addition, this could be embarrassing to and uncomfortable for the employee, as well. Answer D is not the best answer because a great deal of damage can be exacted in a very short period of time—even by those employees from whom we would not expect such behavior. Once again "better safe than sorry" is the best way to proceed—just ensure you maintain the employee's dignity and privacy to the greatest extent possible.

2. **Answer A is the best answer.** Employees must believe and trust that an EAP provides absolute confidentiality in order to be willing to use it, and an EAP must be used if it is to be truly successful. Answer B is not the best answer; although it is essential that the EAP offer absolute confidentiality, by itself, that isn't enough. The EAP will not be successful if employees do not believe that the EAP offers absolute confidentiality, even if it does. Answer C is not the best answer because the success or failure of an EAP is not contingent upon whether it is administered inside the organization, outside the organization, or by some combination of both methods. Answer D is not the best answer; although it is important to conduct cost-benefit analyses to demonstrate the value of an EAP and to bolster ongoing management support, doing so will not directly impact whether employees choose to trust—and therefore use—a program. If a program isn't used, it's not successful—no matter what the "numbers" indicate.

3. **Answer B is the best answer** because the OSHA Form 300 must be completed within seven working days. Answer A is not the best answer because OSHA must be notified within 8 hours only in the event of a death or the inpatient hospitalization of three or more employees. Answer C is not the best answer because the OSHA form 301 requires a detailed account of each work-related injury or accident. Although it must be completed within seven calendar days, it is not posted. Answer D is not the best answer because the OSHA Form 300A is a summary report of all work-related injuries and illnesses that take place in a calendar year, and which therefore cannot be completed until after the end of each year.

4. **Answer B is the best answer.** The presence of any chemicals in the workplace triggers the requirement for MSDS sheets. This is true even if chemicals are not accessible to employees (Answer A), and even if chemicals are stored—but not used—in the workplace (Answer C). Finally, the requirement is also triggered even if chemicals aren't actually being used in the workplace, but are still physically located or present within the workplace (Answer D).

5. **Answer C is the best answer.** Answer A is not the best answer, because "serious violations" are issued by OSHA, not by the EEOC. In addition, "willful"—not "serious"—violations are considered to be deliberate and intentional. Answer B is not the best answer because a serious violation is likely to result in death or serious injury. Answer D is not the best answer because "willful" violations are issued by OSHA, not by the Department of Justice. In addition, "willful"—not "serious"—violations are considered to be the most serious type of OSHA violation (and are the only type of violation that can result in mandatory imprisonment of an employer).

Answers to Review Questions

1. The Needlestick Safety and Prevention Act of 2000 added the following three employer requirements to the Bloodborne Pathogens Standard:

   ▶ Maintaining a log of all injuries resulting from contaminated sharps.

   ▶ Evaluating—and implementing—safer needle devices (as they become available).

   ▶ Involving employees who use needles and needle devices in the evaluation and selection of needles and needle devices.

2. The Automobile Workers v. Johnson Controls (1990) Supreme Court ruling established that most, if not all, fetal protection policies result in gender discrimination. It also affirmed that parents—not employers—bear the obligation of protecting fetuses from chemical risk.

3. The General Duty clause established that employers are responsible for ensuring a safe workplace and for complying with all current and future OSHA-related standards. It also established that employees are responsible for following all safety and health-related rules stemming from the act.

4. Because no vaccine is available for HCV, the best way to prevent the transmission of Hepatitis C/HCV in the workplace is to ensure the proper use of personal protective equipment (PPEs).

5. The six critical components of a comprehensive substance abuse program are

   ▶ Management buy-in and support

   ▶ Drug-free workplace policy

   ▶ Supervisor training

   ▶ Employee education

   ▶ Employee assistance

   ▶ Drug testing

   Of these, management buy-in and support is the most important.

Answers to Exam Questions

1. **Answer D is the best answer.** WARNA, the Worker Adjustment and Retraining Notification Act, addresses plant closings and mass layoffs. The Drug-Free Workplace Act, MSHA (Mine Safety and Health Act), and OSHA (Occupational Safety and Health Act) were all created specifically to address issues of health and safety in the workplace.

2. **Answer C is the best answer.** Answer A is not the best answer because family farms are exempt from OSHA coverage only if they do not employ anyone who is not a family member. Answer B is not the best answer because federal government employees are covered under the OSH Act (however, state and local government employees are not). Answer D is not the best answer because although OSHA designates certain low-risk industries as exempt from OSHA reporting requirements; those industries are still covered by the OSH Act.

3. **Answer C is the best answer.** Health and wellness programs take a more proactive—rather than reactive—approach. Answer D is not the best answer; although health and wellness programs do address some issues "reactively" (for instance, smoking cessation or weight loss), health and wellness programs are more frequently proactive in nature. Answers A and B are not the best answers because health and wellness programs can significantly benefit employees *and* employers.

4. **Answer C is the best answer.** Although safety committees could very likely formulate recommendations relative to personal protective equipment (PPE) enhancements, they are far less likely to have final decision-making authority. Safety committees, therefore, would not likely find themselves in a capacity to institute their own recommendations. Safety committees, however, do play an essential role relative to investigating accidents and incidents (Answer A), conducting inspections (Answer B), and proactively identifying safety concerns (Answer D).

5. **Answer B is the best answer.** "Reasonable suspicion" is one category of drug test, and "for cause" is another. Preemployment (answer A), post-accident (answer C), and random (answer D) are all categories of drug tests.

6. **Answer B is the best answer.** OSHA requires most employers to maintain records and submit reports relative to work-related injuries and accidents, but not specifically in response to security breaches (unless, of course, those breaches result in work-related injuries or accidents). Answers A, C, and D do represent security-related HR responsibilities.

7. **Answer B is the best answer.** Poor ergonomic design can result in employees assuming awkward postures or having to move in problematic ways. In turn, and over time, this can lead to the development of an MSD (musculoskeletal disorder). Answers A and C are not the best answers because neither use of PPE (personal protective equipment) nor poor ventilation are identified as significant contributing factors to MSDs. Answer D is not the best answer; although MSDS is a similar acronym, it refers to materials data safety sheets, which are generally unrelated to MSDs.

8. **Answer A is the best answer.** A person who is HIV positive or who has AIDS is considered a person with a disability under the ADA (Americans with Disabilities Act) and is therefore entitled to perform the essential functions of his or her job as long as he or she can do so with or without reasonable accommodation (that does not cause undue hardship to the organization). Developing visible or outward symptoms (answer B)—as long as those symptoms are unrelated to the person's ability to perform the essential functions of his or her position—does not preclude an individual from continuing to work. Answer C is not the best answer because an employee who is HIV positive or who has AIDS is entitled to maintain confidentiality relative to either of those conditions. Answer D is not the best answer because the belief that a person who is HIV positive or who has AIDS poses a direct threat to co-workers is unfounded.

9. **Answer A is the best answer.** Answer B is not the best answer; although each employee has a right to copies of his or her own medical records or records of his or her exposure to toxic and harmful substances or conditions, employees do not have the right to copies of co-workers' medical records. Answer C is not the best answer; employers must correct workplace hazards by the date indicated on the citation—not just create or submit a plan to do so. Answer D is not the best answer because an employee does have the right to photocopies of his or her medical records or records of his or her exposure to toxic and harmful substances or conditions.

10. **Answer D is the best answer.** You have 30 days to file a complaint with OSHA if your employer has discriminated against you for making safety and health complaints or for exercising your rights under the OSH Act. Answers A, B, and C are not the best answers because each identifies rights that employees enjoy under OSHA.

Suggested Readings and Resources

Department of Labor. www.dol.gov, 2007.

Employee Assistance Professionals Association. www.eapsassn.org, 2007.

Insurance Information Institute (III). www.iii.org, 2007.

OSHA. www.osha.gov, 2007.

Society for Human Resource Management (SHRM). www.shrm.org, 2007.

Other Internet Resources: Search the Web for "OSH Act," "MSH Act," "Occupational Health, Risk Management," "Occupational Health, Safety, and Security," "Drug-Free Workplace Act," and other related terms.

www.amazon.com: Search for "occupational health," "workplace safety," "workplace security," and "OSHA" to find reference materials, 2007.

Wikipedia.com: www.wikipedia.com, 2007.

Fiorillo, Lorayne. *Financial Fitness in 45 Days*. Irvine, CA: *Entrepreneur Magazine*, 2000.

PART II
Apply Your Knowledge

Practice Exam

Practice Exam Answers

Practice Exam

1. Which of the following is not one of the four categories of modern tort law as it pertains to invasion of privacy?

   ○ **A.** Intrusion of solitude

   ○ **B.** Public disclosure of private and embarrassing facts

   ○ **C.** Unbecoming light

   ○ **D.** Appropriation of identity

2. Which of the following is not mandated by the General Duty Clause?

   ○ **A.** Employers must ensure a safe workplace.

   ○ **B.** Employers must comply with all current and future OSHA-related standards.

   ○ **C.** Employees must report all work-related injuries resulting in hospitalization (emergency room or in-patient) to their employer.

   ○ **D.** Employees must follow all safety and health-related rules stemming from the OSH Act.

3. All of the following statements articulate beliefs that are reflected in the design of the balanced scorecard except

   ○ **A.** Dissatisfied customers will eventually look to others who will meet their needs and expectations.

   ○ **B.** Employees need to continually grow and learn so as to be able to perform in a manner that will truly support the attainment of organizational goals.

   ○ **C.** To remain untainted and objective, measurement systems must be maintained separately from management systems.

   ○ **D.** The business process perspective ascertains performance levels through specific measures that are unique to each particular organization.

4. It's important for HR professionals to understand the differences and interplay between effectiveness and efficiency. Efficiency is

   ○ **A.** The degree to which goals are appropriate

   ○ **B.** Doing things right

   ○ **C.** Doing the right things

   ○ **D.** Impossible to achieve without effectiveness

5. The Retirement Equity Act enacted a number of important provisions, including

  ○ **A.** Increasing the minimum age requirement for pension plan participation

  ○ **B.** Requiring qualified pension plans to provide automatic survivor benefits and allow for waiver of survivor benefits without the consent of the participant or the spouse

  ○ **C.** Clarifying that pension plans are prohibited from obeying qualified domestic relations (court) orders (QDROs) requiring them to make benefit payments to a participant's former spouse (or another alternative payee) if that order violates ERISA's prohibitions against assignment or alienation of benefits

  ○ **D.** Prohibiting plans from counting maternity and paternity leaves as breaks in service for participation and vesting purposes

6. Which of the following is the least important factor in ensuring that an employee survey is a valuable employee involvement strategy?

  ○ **A.** Ensure confidentiality by administering the survey through an external consultant

  ○ **B.** Ensure that the survey input is maintained in a fully confidential manner

  ○ **C.** Ensure that employees believe in the confidentiality of the survey

  ○ **D.** Ensure management buy-in and support

7. Which of the following characteristics is most likely to first manifest itself during the development (or growth) stage in the organizational life cycle?

  ○ **A.** A core group of highly talented employees who focus fixedly on the founder for direction and inspiration

  ○ **B.** Resistance to OD and change initiatives

  ○ **C.** Resistance to the process of formalizing policies and procedures

  ○ **D.** An entitlement mentality toward pay and benefits

8. The scientific method includes all of the following steps except

  ○ **A.** Question and observe

  ○ **B.** Develop a hypothesis

  ○ **C.** Design a method

  ○ **D.** Assimilate existing data

9. Which of the following terms best describes transactional leaders?

   ○ **A.** Enforcers

   ○ **B.** Coaches

   ○ **C.** Captains

   ○ **D.** Directors

10. Of the following four types of pay that an employee could earn, which one would not need to be included in an employee's regular rate of pay?

    ○ **A.** Overtime pay

    ○ **B.** Premium pay (for weekend work)

    ○ **C.** Bonus pay

    ○ **D.** Incentive pay

11. All of the following statements about OD are true except

    ○ **A.** OD refers to the process through which the overall performance, growth, and effectiveness of an organization is enhanced through strategic, deliberate, and integrated initiatives.

    ○ **B.** OD incorporates the following four academic disciplines: psychology, sociology, anthropology, and management.

    ○ **C.** OD helps maintain the organization's focus on the belief that the systems that have been enacted within organizations are ultimately responsible for whether the work of the organization is accomplished.

    ○ **D.** OD interventions are intended to identify an organization's competitive advantages and to ensure the organization's success.

12. Which of the following statements about ULP strikes is untrue?

    ○ **A.** ULP strikes are called during contract negotiations.

    ○ **B.** Striking workers must be returned to their original positions after the strike is over.

    ○ **C.** ULP strikes are called when the employer has committed an unfair labor practice.

    ○ **D.** Employers cannot hire permanent strike replacements during a ULP strike.

13. All of the following are required by the Hazard Communication Standard except

  ○ **A.** Material Safety Data Sheets

  ○ **B.** Signed employee acknowledgement forms

  ○ **C.** Container labeling requirements

  ○ **D.** Training and orientation

14. Which of the following occurs during a jurisdictional strike?

  ○ **A.** Employees who are not directly involved in an economic dispute choose not to cross a picket line out of support for striking workers.

  ○ **B.** A union seeks to pressure an employer to assign particular work to its members, rather than to members of other unions or to nonunion workers.

  ○ **C.** The strike occurs even though the collective bargaining agreement contains a no-strike clause prohibiting striking during the duration of the agreement.

  ○ **D.** A union seeks to pressure an employer to grant some sort of concession from the employer during collective bargaining negotiations.

15. Copyrights are granted for which period of time?

  ○ **A.** The lifetime of the author

  ○ **B.** The lifetime of the author, unless there are heirs to whom the copyright has been deeded

  ○ **C.** The lifetime of the author plus 70 years

  ○ **D.** The lifetime of the author plus 95 years

16. When conducting panel interviews, it is generally advisable to do all of the following except

  ○ **A.** Let the candidate know ahead of time that he or she will be participating in a panel interview.

  ○ **B.** Plan in advance who will ask which questions and in which order, and arrange for "hand offs" from one interviewer to another.

  ○ **C.** Interview in a room that has a round table, if possible.

  ○ **D.** Place all the interviewers on one side of the table and the candidate on the other.

17. According to OSHA, which of the following does not need to be recorded?

  ○ **A.** Days away from work

  ○ **B.** Injuries that result in bleeding

  ○ **C.** Restricted work or job transfer

  ○ **D.** Loss of consciousness

18. If an employee is engaged in protected concerted activity, an employer might be considered to have violated the NLRA if all but which of the following conditions are met?

○ **A.** The employee and/or collective bargaining unit advised the employer of the concerted nature of the employee's activity.

○ **B.** The employer knew of the concerted nature of the employee's activity.

○ **C.** The concerted activity was protected by the NLRA.

○ **D.** The adverse employment action in question (for instance, termination) was motivated by the employee's protected concerted activity.

19. Henry Fayol was a guru in the area of

○ **A.** Quality

○ **B.** Management

○ **C.** Strategic human resources

○ **D.** Human behavior

20. *General Dynamics Land Systems* v. *Cline, 2004*, a case that addressed age discrimination, established/clarified that

○ **A.** The ADEA prohibits favoring the old over the young.

○ **B.** The ADEA prohibits favoring the old over the young, and it also prohibits favoring the young over the old.

○ **C.** Younger employees (even if they are over the age of 40) cannot allege age discrimination because of programs that favor older employees.

○ **D.** Younger employees (even if they are over the age of 40) can allege age discrimination because of programs that favor older employees.

21. What method of job evaluation is this: "A nonquantitative job evaluation technique that categorizes jobs into broad categories, or levels, based on the level—and, ultimately, value to the organization—of the work that is performed by jobs within each level. Each level incorporates specific responsibilities and benchmark statements that describe the nature, complexity, autonomy, and so forth of the work that is performed by positions in that level."

○ **A.** Job classification

○ **B.** Job slotting

○ **C.** Whole job ranking

○ **D.** Factor comparison

22. An organization's total compensation/total rewards program should do all of the following except

○ **A.** Support and reinforce the mission, vision, and values of the organization

○ **B.** Be consistent with the culture of the organization

○ **C.** Be competitive with the total compensation programs offered by labor market competitors

○ **D.** Attract, motivate, and retain targeted/appropriate employees

23. If a case does proceed to court, HR's role varies significantly depending on a host of factors. HR professionals could conceivably find themselves performing any of the following functions except

○ **A.** Testifying

○ **B.** Sitting at the counsel table during the trial

○ **C.** Collecting data during discovery

○ **D.** Responding to the complaint

24. In determining whether outsourcing might be an appropriate option, which of the following considerations is least appropriate to take into consideration?

○ **A.** Vendors' technological resources and capabilities as compared to your project requirements

○ **B.** Internal abilities and talents versus abilities and talents available through outsourcing

○ **C.** The importance and complexity of the function that is being considered for outsourcing

○ **D.** The degree of variability in transaction volume of the function that is being considered for outsourcing

25. Your organization has decided to outsource its payroll function, and you're involved in the process of researching vendors. Which of the following actions would be least valuable to you?

○ **A.** Find out what each vendor's track record is over a long period of time by speaking with clients from several years ago.

○ **B.** Find out about each vendor's most recent performance by speaking with recent and/or current clients.

○ **C.** Find out whether each vendor has related experience, and ascertain how recently the vendor gained that experience.

○ **D.** Find out about each vendor's commitment to quality. Determine how it manifests itself and how can it be measured.

26. Which of these individuals is least likely to create an oral contract?

  ○ **A.** A full-time recruiter

  ○ **B.** A hiring manager who interviews candidates for open positions in his or her area

  ○ **C.** An employee's current supervisor

  ○ **D.** An employee's current co-worker

27. According to equity theory, if an employee feels that he is being treated unfairly at work, he is least likely to take which of the following actions?

  ○ **A.** Encourage others to produce more.

  ○ **B.** Encourage others to produce less.

  ○ **C.** Recognize that life is not always fair, and start looking for a new job.

  ○ **D.** Recognize that life is not always fair, and accept the situation as it is.

28. Which case established the following relative to what constitutes a sexually hostile work environment: "This standard, which we reaffirm today, takes a middle path between making actionable any conduct that is merely offensive and requiring the conduct to cause a tangible psychological injury. Conduct that is not severe or pervasive enough to create an objectively hostile or abusive work environment—an environment that a reasonable person would find hostile or abusive—is beyond Title VII's purview. Likewise, if the victim does not subjectively perceive the environment to be abusive, the conduct has not actually altered the conditions of the victim's employment, and there is no Title VII violation."

  ○ **A.** *Taxman v. Board of Education of Piscataway, 1993*

  ○ **B.** *Meritor Savings Bank v. Vinson, 1986*

  ○ **C.** *St. Mary's Honor Center v. Hicks, 1993*

  ○ **D.** *Harris v. Forklift Systems, 1993*

29. Which of the following is true of Ishikawa's fishbone diagram?

  ○ **A.** Demonstrates how 20% of causes account for 80% of effects

  ○ **B.** Identifies factors that ultimately affect whether a desired outcome will be attained

  ○ **C.** Assesses the potential impact of utilizing quality circles in a particular situation

  ○ **D.** Depicts information about a single factor

30. All of the following statements about the ADEA are true except

○ A. ADEA prohibits discrimination based on age, for individuals age 18 and older (so as to ensure that individuals are not discriminated against based on being too young, as well as based on being too old).

○ B. ADEA covers private employers with 20 or more employees, state and local governments (including school districts), employment agencies, and labor organizations.

○ C. ADEA does not establish an upper cap, or an age at which it once again becomes legal to discriminate against individuals based on age.

○ D. ADEA is subject to certain exceptions and places certain requirements on employers, particularly with respect to benefits plans, coverages, and early retirement incentives.

31. In the acronym KSAs, *A* refers to

○ A. An attitudinal predilection toward the type of work performed in the position

○ B. Specific information that the incumbent either needs to know or with which he or she needs to be familiar

○ C. The ability to perform a particular task

○ D. Specific traits required to successfully perform a position

32. A manager with whom you have not previously worked comes to you for help with implementing solutions she has come up with to address a turnover problem in her department. Your first response should be to

○ A. Communicate your commitment to implementing the manager's solution.

○ B. Offer alternative solutions based on experience you have had with similar situations.

○ C. Ask questions to obtain more information about the problems the manager is experiencing.

○ D. Ask questions to obtain information that will help you implement the manager's solution more effectively.

33. Of the following four options, the best way to avoid or minimize the likelihood of a negligent referral claim against the organization is to

○ A. Refuse to provide any employee references

○ B. Provide only titles, dates of employment, and final salary when providing references

○ C. Outsource the process of providing employee references to a third party

○ D. Require a signed release form from the employee or former employee before providing a reference

34. Which of the following statements about defined contribution plans is untrue?

- ○ **A.** Unlike defined benefit plans, defined contribution plans do not promise a specific monthly benefit (or total benefit) at retirement.

- ○ **B.** Defined contribution plans shift the risk away from the employer (which is where it rests for defined benefit plans) and back onto the employee.

- ○ **C.** Defined contribution plans are decreasing in popularity, while defined benefit plans are increasing in popularity.

- ○ **D.** Examples of defined contribution plans include 401(k) plans, employee stock ownership plans, and profit-sharing plans.

35. In which case did the U.S. Supreme Court rule that, in the absence of underrepresentation as demonstrated and documented through an affirmative action plan, organizations cannot take race into account when making decisions relative to who will be laid off and who will be retained (and that doing so would constitute a violation of Title VII of the Civil Rights Act of 1964)?

- ○ **A.** *Taxman v. Board of Education of Piscataway, 1993*

- ○ **B.** *Meritor Savings Bank v. Vinson, 1986*

- ○ **C.** *St. Mary's Honor Center v. Hicks, 1993*

- ○ **D.** *Harris v. Forklift Systems, 1993*

36. Which law implemented changes in two sections of the United States tax code that resulted in the creation of two new—and ultimately very important—employee benefits?

- ○ **A.** Consolidated Omnibus Budget Reconciliation Act (COBRA), 1985

- ○ **B.** The Revenue Act

- ○ **C.** Health Insurance Portability and Accountability Act (HIPAA)

- ○ **D.** Retirement Equity Act (REA)

37. A cash balance plan is

- ○ **A.** A defined benefit plan that expresses the promised benefit in terms of a stated account balance

- ○ **B.** A defined benefit plan that expresses the promised benefit in terms of a specific monthly benefit

- ○ **C.** A defined contribution plan that expresses the promised benefit in terms of a stated account balance

- ○ **D.** A defined contribution plan that expresses the promised benefit in terms of a specific monthly benefit

38. The balanced scorecard

   ○ **A.** Consists of a variety of nonfinancial measures of success and is intended to be used as a tool to balance out other traditional financial measures of success

   ○ **B.** Consists of a variety of financial measures of success and is intended to be used as a tool to balance out other tools that only incorporate one single financial measure of success

   ○ **C.** Consists of a variety of financial and nonfinancial measures of success and is intended to balance them against each other within the scorecard

   ○ **D.** Consists of a variety of measures that are predicated on the evaluative ratings, or scores, collected from multiple stakeholders pertaining to multiple financial and nonfinancial measures of success

39. Which of the following statements about the Civil Rights Act of 1991 is untrue?

   ○ **A.** It expanded employees' rights.

   ○ **B.** It expanded employees' remedies.

   ○ **C.** It capped damages at $500,000 per employee.

   ○ **D.** It allowed for jury trials for discrimination cases.

40. McClelland's acquired needs theory focuses on one primary motivator, which is

   ○ **A.** Achievement

   ○ **B.** Recognition

   ○ **C.** Equity

   ○ **D.** Rewards

41. Joseph M. Juran's focus on quality addresses three key areas, which include all of the following except

   ○ **A.** Quality planning

   ○ **B.** Quality circles

   ○ **C.** Quality improvement

   ○ **D.** Quality control

42. Strategic planning is a step-by-step process through which an organization does all of the following except:

   ○ **A.** Ensures its individual and organizational readiness for the future

   ○ **B.** Generates a statement that articulates what the organization wants to become in the future

   ○ **C.** Identifies where it wants to be and what it wants to accomplish in the long-term (often 3–5 years)

   ○ **D.** Begins to map out how its vision and mission for the long-term will be attained

43. Which of these is not a type of legislation?

   ○ **A.** Concurrent resolution

   ○ **B.** Compound resolution

   ○ **C.** Joint resolution

   ○ **D.** Simple resolution

44. Which of the following factors is least relevant to creating and sustaining credibility during the implementation of a strategic plan?

   ○ **A.** Securing the support and commitment of senior leadership

   ○ **B.** Clear, complete, and appropriate documentation of the process

   ○ **C.** A commitment to follow through on every step of the process

   ○ **D.** Representative participation from all levels of the organization

45. For the set of numbers 5, 29, 194, 87, 645, 42, 29, 334, and 97, the mean is

   ○ **A.** 162.4

   ○ **B.** 645

   ○ **C.** 29

   ○ **D.** 87

46. A manager within your organization sends you an email asking you to help her with terminating an employee. This is the first time you've heard about the situation. The manager has specifically asked your help with pulling together the COBRA paperwork, calculating the final paycheck, and making sure that the employee turns over his company ID and corporate credit card. The manager tells you how much she needs and appreciates your help and is glad she can count on you.

This manager probably views HR primarily in terms of the following dimension:

○ **A.** Operational/Tactical

○ **B.** Strategic

○ **C.** Administrative

○ **D.** Transformational

47. The difference between job posting systems and job bidding systems is

○ **A.** Job bidding systems deal with jobs that are currently open, whereas job posting systems deal with jobs that might open at some point in the future.

○ **B.** Job bidding systems are directed at internal candidates, whereas job posting systems are directed at external candidates.

○ **C.** Job bidding systems deal with jobs that might open at some point in the future, whereas job posting systems deal with jobs that are currently open.

○ **D.** Job bidding systems are directed at internal candidates, whereas job posting systems are directed at internal as well as external candidates.

48. According to the Older Worker's Benefit Protection Act (OWBPA), individuals are prohibited from waiving their rights or claims under ADEA unless such a waiver is "knowing and voluntary." OWBPA established nine specific criteria for ensuring that such waivers are knowing and voluntary, one of which requires that employers must allow employees time to consider any right-to-sue waivers that the employer offers in exchange for early retirement benefits. How many days must an employer allow?

○ **A.** At least one week

○ **B.** At least two weeks

○ **C.** At least three weeks

○ **D.** At least one week for each year of service

49. The progressive discipline process is predicated on a belief that includes which of the following ideas/assumptions?

○ **A.** An employee decides whether to perform his or her job satisfactorily.

○ **B.** The employee, when hired, was at least minimally qualified for the position.

○ **C.** Both A and B.

○ **D.** Neither A nor B.

50. An organization conducts an employee survey and finds that many employees are bored with their jobs, unhappy with their pay, and feel as though they don't get enough vacation time. If the organization's primary goal is to motivate employees, what is the first step that should be taken?

   ○ **A.** Conduct an external survey to determine pay rates and vacation allotments among labor market competitors.

   ○ **B.** Identify ways in which employees' jobs can be enriched, and implement them.

   ○ **C.** Give everyone an across-the-board raise and an extra week of vacation, and let employees know that you will be conducting a salary/benefits survey to see if further adjustments are needed.

   ○ **D.** Before you take any action, conduct another employee survey to ensure that results of the second survey are consistent with the results of the first survey.

51. According to Hersey and Blanchard's model, effective leaders

   ○ **A.** Identify the leadership style that is best suited to them and use that style consistently.

   ○ **B.** Determine the quadrant into which each employee falls and manage employees in each quadrant according to the corresponding leadership style.

   ○ **C.** Place emphasis on ensuring that an employee has the ability to execute the technical, or functional, skills required to complete a task.

   ○ **D.** Utilize different leadership approaches, with different employees, at different times.

52. Which of the following was not one of Knowles's five key assumptions about how adults learn?

   ○ **A.** The learner's need to know

   ○ **B.** The learner's readiness to learn

   ○ **C.** The learner's self-concept

   ○ **D.** The learner's willingness to change

53. When would a plan provider that offers mental health benefits be exempt from MHPA?

   ○ **A.** If the plan provider is a small employer with fewer than 15 people

   ○ **B.** If a plan provider's costs (measured in terms of actual claims) increase 1% or more because of the application of MHPA's requirements

   ○ **C.** If a plan provider's costs (in terms of insurance premiums) increase 1% or more due to the application of MHPA's requirements

   ○ **D.** Never

54. Under COBRA, plan providers must offer plan participants the opportunity to continue participating in

   ○ **A.** Group health care plans, wellness programs, and long-term disability insurance

   ○ **B.** Group health care plans

   ○ **C.** All health and welfare plans for which the plan participant cannot secure coverage through another individual's group plan

   ○ **D.** All health and welfare plans

55. According to the Equal Pay Act, the substantial equality of job content is assessed based on four factors:

   ○ **A.** Working conditions, effort, skill, and scope

   ○ **B.** Effort, skill, responsibility, and working conditions

   ○ **C.** Scope, accountability, responsibility, and working conditions

   ○ **D.** Responsibility, skills, working conditions, and scope

56. An approach in which an organization chooses to utilize a relatively small number of grades is known as

   ○ **A.** Flattening

   ○ **B.** Growthbanding

   ○ **C.** Broadbanding

   ○ **D.** Gradesharing

57. Which of the following is not one of Philip B. Crosby's four Absolutes of Quality Management?

   ○ **A.** Quality means conformance to requirements, not goodness.

   ○ **B.** Quality is achieved by prevention, not appraisal.

   ○ **C.** Quality has a performance standard of zero defects, not acceptable quality levels.

   ○ **D.** Quality is measured by specific production indexes, not by customer satisfaction.

58. Which of the following statements is least reflective of an organization's statement of vision?

  ○ **A.** It is a descriptive and inspirational statement that articulates where the organization wants to be and what it wants to become in the future.

  ○ **B.** It gives employees an awareness that they have a meaningful opportunity to be part of something bigger than themselves.

  ○ **C.** It motivates and inspires employees to aspire to the legacy that the vision can create and that it ultimately can leave behind.

  ○ **D.** It speaks to the nature of the organization's business or purpose, its customers, and sometimes even its employees and its role in the community.

59. After the House of Representatives and the Senate have approved a bill in identical form, the legislation will die unless

  ○ **A.** The president takes no action for 10 days while Congress is not in session.

  ○ **B.** The president takes no action for 10 days while Congress is in session.

  ○ **C.** The president sends the legislation back for Conference Committee Action.

  ○ **D.** The president overrides Congress.

60. Preemployment medical exams can only be conducted

  ○ **A.** If all candidates who apply for a position are required to partake in a preemployment medical exam

  ○ **B.** If the medical exam is job related and consistent with business necessity

  ○ **C.** If the medical exam is conducted by a physician who is not employed or retained by the employer

  ○ **D.** If the candidate reveals that he or she has a disability that might require a reasonable accommodation

61. EO 11246 requires covered employers to develop and implement an auditing system that periodically measures the effectiveness of its total affirmative action program. This requirement could include all of the following actions except

  ○ **A.** Monitor records of all personnel activity, including referrals, placements, transfers, promotions, terminations, and compensation, at all levels to ensure the nondiscriminatory policy is carried out.

  ○ **B.** Require internal reporting on a scheduled basis as to the number of charges of discrimination that have been filed based on race, gender, and veterans status during the length of each AAP degree to which equal employment opportunity and organizational objectives are attained.

  ○ **C.** Review report results with all levels of management.

  ○ **D.** Advise top management of program effectiveness and submit recommendations to improve unsatisfactory performance.

62. Which of the following statements about trend analysis is true?

   ○ **A.** It can provide information that can be helpful in developing a better understanding of business cycles.

   ○ **B.** It can become the basis for a number of applications, including forecasting staffing needs.

   ○ **C.** It looks at how two variables have changed over time.

   ○ **D.** It looks at the relationship between one dependent variable and more than one independent variable.

63. WARN covers which employers?

   ○ **A.** Employers with 15 or more employees

   ○ **B.** 100 or more full-time employees

   ○ **C.** All private employers

   ○ **D.** Private employers with 20 or more employees

64. Learning organizations are best described as those within which

   ○ **A.** The HRD/training budget is equivalent to (or exceeds) the merit budget.

   ○ **B.** Employees at all levels of the organization commit to attaining knowledge and skills that will enable them to perform better and attain more.

   ○ **C.** Employees at all levels of the organization participate in training initiatives—either individually or through organizational initiatives—at least annually.

   ○ **D.** Each employee's performance appraisal incorporates a goal relative to completing specific training and/or development activities.

65. Which of the following managers is most likely to experience the recency effect?

   ○ **A.** A manager who recently observed a direct report performing his or her position.

   ○ **B.** A manager who recently placed an employee on a performance improvement plan.

   ○ **C.** A manager who maintained consistent documentation during earlier portions of the performance measurement period.

   ○ **D.** A manager who has not consistently documented the direct report's performance during the performance measurement period.

66. For overtime purposes, hours worked includes

  ○ **A.** All hours for which an employee received compensation

  ○ **B.** All hours for which an employee was granted prior to, or subsequent to, approval to work

  ○ **C.** All hours during which an employee performed work

  ○ **D.** All hours during which an employee was required or allowed to perform work

67. The Equal Pay Act prohibits discrimination based on sex in the payment of wages or benefits to men and women who

  ○ **A.** Perform the same work for the same employer

  ○ **B.** Perform substantially equal (but not identical) work for the same employer

  ○ **C.** Perform substantially equal (but not identical) work for different employers within the same relevant labor market

  ○ **D.** Perform the same work for different employers within the same relevant labor market

68. Which of the following statements about job grades is not true?

  ○ **A.** Grades represent a hierarchy of levels into which jobs of similar internal worth are categorized.

  ○ **B.** Jobs within the same grade share a similar level of value or worth to the organization.

  ○ **C.** Jobs within the same grade are paid according to a corresponding compensation range.

  ○ **D.** Grades represent a hierarchy of levels into which jobs of similar external worth are categorized.

69. Which of the following statements about unemployment insurance is not true?

  ○ **A.** Unemployment insurance is a mandatory benefit program.

  ○ **B.** In general, the maximum period for receiving unemployment insurance benefits is 26 weeks.

  ○ **C.** Except in three states (in which only employers contribute), unemployment insurance is funded through employer and employee taxes.

  ○ **D.** Unemployment insurance was established as part of the federal Social Security Act, and is administered at the state level.

70. Which of the following is not a disadvantage of the nonquantitative job evaluation method known as job slotting?

   ○ A. Job slotting is somewhat expensive and difficult to administer.

   ○ B. It is more likely that jobs will be evaluated based on the person, not the position.

   ○ C. Job slotting can be used only when a job structure is already in place.

   ○ D. There is a greater chance that rater error and subjectivity can taint the job evaluation process.

71. Which of the following statements about protected concerted activities is not true?

   ○ A. Protected concerted activity refers to associational rights that are granted to employee through the NLRA.

   ○ B. The NLRA protects associational rights for employees who belong to a union.

   ○ C. The NLRA does not protect associational rights unless an employee belongs to a union.

   ○ D. Employees have the right to refrain from engaging in protected concerted activities.

72. When there is a FEPA, all of the following statements are true except

   ○ A. Charges must be filed with the EEOC within 180 days of the alleged discriminatory act.

   ○ B. The EEOC usually maintains responsibility for handling charges that are filed with it if the basis for the charge is also protected under state or local law.

   ○ C. The FEPA usually maintains responsibility for handling charges that are filed with it if the basis for the charge is also protected under federal law.

   ○ D. A charge may not be filed with the EEOC when state or local EEO law is more protective than the corresponding federal law.

73. COBRA covers employers who employ

   ○ A. 2 or more employees during the prior year

   ○ B. 15 or more employees as of the close of the most recent payroll period

   ○ C. 20 or more employees during the prior year

   ○ D. 50 or more employees as of the close of the most recent payroll period

74. Which of the following statements about Hepatitis B/HBV is untrue?

- ○ **A.** HBV is transmitted through blood and other bodily fluids.

- ○ **B.** A person with HBV is considered to be a person with a disability.

- ○ **C.** A vaccine for HBV exists, and must be administered annually to at-risk employees.

- ○ **D.** People with HBV might experience a wide range of symptoms.

75. The defining case for employment tests and disparate impact was

- ○ **A.** *McDonnell Douglas Corp v. Green, 1973*

- ○ **B.** *Griggs v. Duke Power, 1971*

- ○ **C.** *Meritor Savings Bank v. Vinson, 1986*

- ○ **D.** *Washington v. Davis, 1976*

76. Which of the following activities would be least likely to happen during onboarding?

- ○ **A.** Tour of the facility

- ○ **B.** Background investigation

- ○ **C.** Opportunity to meet with current employees

- ○ **D.** Review of the mission of the organization, and of how that mission relates to the position

77. Three of the following terms refer to the same sort of instrument or tool, and one does not. Which one of these terms means something different from the other three?

- ○ **A.** Employee surveys

- ○ **B.** Multi-rater surveys

- ○ **C.** Attitude surveys

- ○ **D.** Climate surveys

78. The AFL-CIO is an example of a

- ○ **A.** National union

- ○ **B.** Local union

- ○ **C.** Federation

- ○ **D.** International labor organization

79. The LMRA, also known as the Taft-Hartley Act, was an amendment designed to remedy what the Republican Congress saw as two major omissions in the Wagner Act, including:

○ **A.** The identification of behaviors and practices that would be considered ULPs on the part of employers

○ **B.** The identification of behaviors and practices that would be considered ULPs on the part of unions

○ **C.** The identification of behaviors and practices that would be considered ULPs on the part of employees

○ **D.** The identification of behaviors and practices that would be considered ULPs on the part of managers

80. The landmark Supreme Court case that confirmed the legality of mandatory arbitration agreements was

○ **A.** *NLRB v. Phoenix Mutual Life Insurance Co., 1948*

○ **B.** *EEOC v. Waffle House, Inc., 2002*

○ **C.** *Circuit City Stores, Inc. v. Adams, 2001*

○ **D.** *NLRB v. Henry Colder Co., 1990*

81. OSHA did all of the following except

○ **A.** Establish relief for employees who suffer work-related injuries and illnesses.

○ **B.** Establish a means of enforcement.

○ **C.** Encourage and assist states to take steps to ensure safe and healthful workplaces.

○ **D.** Provide for relevant research, information, education, and training.

82. Change interventions that focus on improving what work is done, as well as the ways and processes through which the work is done, are considered

○ **A.** Human processual interventions

○ **B.** Technostructural interventions

○ **C.** Sociotechnical interventions

○ **D.** Organization transformation change interventions

83. Which of the following statements about the PBGC is not true?

   ○ A. PBGC is a government corporation created by ERISA.

   ○ B. PBGC is funded by a combination of employer and employee payroll taxes.

   ○ C. PBGC protects participants in most defined benefit plans and cash balance plans (within certain limitations).

   ○ D. PBGC ensures that participants will receive payments of certain benefits if a covered plan is terminated.

84. In conducting a SWOT analysis, the strengths and weaknesses portion of the analysis is directed

   ○ A. Internally

   ○ B. Externally

   ○ C. Both internally and externally

   ○ D. Neither internally nor externally

85. The landmark case *McKennon v. Nashville Banner Publishing Co., 1995,* established that

   ○ A. An employer will be held accountable for discriminatory employment actions unless it discovers evidence after taking the discriminatory employment action that would have led the employer to that same employment action for legitimate, nondiscriminatory reasons.

   ○ B. An employer will be held accountable for discriminatory employment actions even if it discovers evidence after taking the discriminatory employment action that would have led the employer to that same employment action for legitimate, nondiscriminatory reasons.

   ○ C. An employer will not be held accountable for discriminatory employment actions if it discovers evidence after taking the discriminatory employment action that would have led the employer to that same employment action for legitimate, nondiscriminatory reasons.

   ○ D. An employer will not be held accountable for discriminatory employment actions even if it discovers evidence after taking the discriminatory employment action that would have led the employer to a different employment action for legitimate, nondiscriminatory reasons.

86. FMLA entitles eligible employees (who work for covered employers) up to 12 weeks of unpaid, job-protected leave during any 12-month period for all of the following reasons except

   ○ **A.** For the birth and care of the newborn child of the employee

   ○ **B.** For placement of a son or daughter for adoption or foster care with the employee

   ○ **C.** To care for an immediate family member (spouse, child, sibling, or parent) with a serious health condition

   ○ **D.** To take medical leave when the employee is unable to work because of a serious health condition

87. Which of the following statements about factor comparison is untrue?

   ○ **A.** Factor comparison provides a degree of objectivity and reliability across raters.

   ○ **B.** Factor comparison evaluates each job with respect to each compensable factor.

   ○ **C.** Factor comparison assigns a point value to each level within each factor.

   ○ **D.** Factor comparison involves ranking each compensable factor of each job.

88. The Drug-Free Workplace Act requires all of the following except

   ○ **A.** Establishing an EAP (or equivalent program) to which employees who use drugs can turn for assistance and rehabilitation

   ○ **B.** Publishing a statement notifying employees that the manufacture, distribution, dispensation, possession, or use of a controlled substance is prohibited in the workplace

   ○ **C.** Establishing a drug-free awareness program addressing the dangers of drug use in the workplace and the employer's drug-free policy, and information about programs that are available to employees who use drugs

   ○ **D.** Distributing a copy of the workplace substance abuse policy to all employees

89. Which of the following activities would not constitute an unfair labor practice on the part of an employer during a union organizing campaign?

   ○ **A.** Tell workers that the organization will fire or punish them if they engage in any union activity.

   ○ **B.** Grant workers wage increases or special concessions in an effort to bribe people from joining a union.

   ○ **C.** Require employees to attend presentations to listen to the employer's opinions about the unionization of its operations

   ○ **D.** Tell workers that existing benefits will be discontinued if the workplace is unionized.

90. An employer who makes a hot cargo agreement has done all of the following except

  ○ **A.** Agreed to stop doing business with another entity

  ○ **B.** Refused to stop doing business with another entity

  ○ **C.** Committed a ULP

  ○ **D.** Helped the union

91. Which of the following represents sound advice with respect to dealing with employees who remain with an organization after downsizing?

  ○ **A.** Let the employees who remain know when the final round of layoffs is done (so they can feel more secure and confident).

  ○ **B.** Communicate clearly, frequently, and in a truthful manner with the employees who remain.

  ○ **C.** Encourage the employees who remain to be loyal to the organization, just as the organization has found a way to be loyal to each of them.

  ○ **D.** Minimize the amount and frequency of communication (to avoid the possibility of creating unrealistic expectations or of saying something that might change).

92. All of the following statements about negligent hiring are true except

  ○ **A.** Negligent hiring refers to the process of hiring an employee without engaging in appropriate due diligence.

  ○ **B.** Appropriate due diligence includes looking into items such as the candidate's credentials and prior work experience.

  ○ **C.** An organization can prevent negligent hiring tort claims—or can ensure that it will prevail in any such claim—by performing due diligence on all employees before they are hired.

  ○ **D.** Negligent hiring tort claims might be filed after an employee who was hired through a flawed hiring process inflicts some sort of harm on another person.

93. Which of the following statements about focus groups is least true?

  ○ **A.** Skillfully facilitated focus groups can generate a great deal of valuable data.

  ○ **B.** The synergy of the group dynamics can contribute to a more valuable data collection experience.

  ○ **C.** When facilitated by the same individual, participants across multiple focus groups will have a similar data collection experience.

  ○ **D.** Focus groups can provide a qualitative approach to data collection.

94. Which of the following factors should have the least impact on how base pay for newly hired employees is set?

   ○ **A.** The relative worth of the job to the organization

   ○ **B.** Each incumbent's rate of pay in his or her current/most recent position

   ○ **C.** The market rate for the position in the marketplace

   ○ **D.** Whether the job requires hot skills

95. An agreement between an employer and an employee that states that the employer will give the employee a job, as long as the employee agrees not to join or have any involvement with a labor union is known as a

   ○ **A.** Yellow dog contract

   ○ **B.** Hot cargo agreement

   ○ **C.** Featherbedding agreement

   ○ **D.** Union shop agreement

96. Which of the following is the least likely reason that an organization might want to settle a charge of discrimination?

   ○ **A.** To save money

   ○ **B.** To avoid bad press

   ○ **C.** To avoid a strike

   ○ **D.** Because discrimination might have actually taken place

97. Which of the following would not describe a purpose of a safety committee?

   ○ **A.** Building and maintaining interest in health and safety issues

   ○ **B.** Satisfying the OSHA requirement that covered organizations establish cross-functional safety committees

   ○ **C.** Reinforcing safety as part of the fabric of the organization's culture

   ○ **D.** Providing a forum for discussing health- and safety-related issues

98. Which of the following cases established that gender can be used as a factor in the selection process if there is underrepresentation in a particular job classification, as long as the AAP does not set forth a quota?

   ○ **A.** *Johnson v. Santa Clara County Transportation Agency, 1987*

   ○ **B.** *Martin v. Wilks, 1988*

   ○ **C.** *Harris v. Forklift Systems, 1993*

   ○ **D.** *Taxman v. Board of Education of Piscataway, 1993*

99. Which of the following statements about diversity is true?

   ○ **A.** Diversity is a legally mandated program, similar to affirmative action.

   ○ **B.** Diversity initiatives require the preparation and filing of specific reports to the federal government on an annual basis.

   ○ **C.** Diversity can encompass attributes or characteristics such as communication styles, regional backgrounds, or affiliation with unions.

   ○ **D.** Diversity programs represent an extension of EEO programs and thus should be limited to the same protected classes that are defined by EEO laws.

100. Which of the following statements about Social Security retirement benefits is untrue?

   ○ **A.** The earliest age at which a worker can retire and still receive benefits is 62.

   ○ **B.** Full retirement age ranges between ages 65 and 67.

   ○ **C.** Workers who work beyond their full retirement age will increase their monthly retirement, the more their monthly retirement income will be.

   ○ **D.** There is no requirement to start receiving retirement benefits by any particular age.

101. An employee who was constructively discharged

   ○ **A.** Was forced to quit due to intolerable working conditions

   ○ **B.** Was terminated at the conclusion of a progressive disciplinary process

   ○ **C.** Was afforded the opportunity to resign (instead of being fired)

   ○ **D.** Was laid off through no fault of his or her own and is eligible for rehire

102. Placement goals

   ○ **A.** Must be established for areas in which underutilization exists

   ○ **B.** Must be pursued through good faith efforts

   ○ **C.** Must be set at an annual percentage rate equal to the availability figure for women or minorities

   ○ **D.** Must be established for each specific minority group when underutilization is found to exist

103. McGregor's motivation theory

○ **A.** Is predicated on the idea that most employees will take on additional work if they think that work will be satisfying or rewarding

○ **B.** Is predicated on the idea that employees are uncommitted, uninterested, hesitant to assume any additional responsibility, and are essentially lazy

○ **C.** Assumes that different managers have different perspectives on employees

○ **D.** Laid the foundation for Maslow's hierarchy of needs

104. According to Hersey and Blanchard's situational leadership model, low task and low relationship dimensions correspond to which quadrant?

○ **A.** Telling

○ **B.** Selling

○ **C.** Participating

○ **D.** Delegating

105. Which of the following statements about correlation is true?

○ **A.** A negative correlation indicates that a relationship does not exist between two factors.

○ **B.** Correlation mathematically determines whether there is a demonstrated relationship between two factors or entities.

○ **C.** The correlation coefficient is a number between 0 and 1 that defines the strength of a relationship between two factors.

○ **D.** The closer the correlation coefficient is to 1, the greater the likelihood that there is a causative relationship between the two factors.

106. Which one of the following requirements must be met for an employee to qualify for an administrative exemption under the FLSA?

○ **A.** The employee's primary duty must be the performance of office or nonmanual work directly related to the management or general business operations of the employer or the employer's customers.

○ **B.** The employee's primary duty must be the performance of work requiring advanced knowledge, defined as work which is predominantly intellectual in character and which includes work requiring the consistent exercise of discretion and judgment.

○ **C.** The employee's suggestions and recommendations as to the hiring, firing, advancement, promotion, or any other change of status of other employees must be given particular weight.

○ **D.** The employee may not spend more than 20% of work time performing functions that are non-exempt in nature.

107. FLA established standards affecting full-time and part-time workers in the private sector and in federal, state, and local governments pertaining to the following four areas:

   ○ **A.** Minimum wage, overtime, record keeping, and child labor

   ○ **B.** Minimum wage, overtime, worker's compensation, and unemployment insurance

   ○ **C.** Minimum wage, overtime, child labor, and wage garnishments

   ○ **D.** Minimum wage, overtime, unemployment insurance, and wage garnishments

108. Which of the following is not a requirement under Sarbanes-Oxley (SOX)?

   ○ **A.** Prohibition against insider trading during certain pension plan blackout periods.

   ○ **B.** Establishment of whistleblower protection in a wide variety of situations for employees who report fraud against shareholders.

   ○ **C.** Plan administrators must provide 30-day written notice in advance of blackout periods to individual account plan participants and beneficiaries.

   ○ **D.** Requirement to disclose whether the company has adopted a companywide code of ethics.

109. One key potential problem with employee participation groups is that, under the NLRA, it is possible that employee participation groups could be found

   ○ **A.** To interfere with employees' ability to affiliate with a collective bargaining unit

   ○ **B.** To interfere with employees' associational rights

   ○ **C.** To be company dominated

   ○ **D.** To have an adverse impact upon members of a protected class

110. Which of the following four statements offers the best definition of slander?

   ○ **A.** A statement that damages someone's character or reputation

   ○ **B.** A false statement that damages someone's character or reputation

   ○ **C.** A false spoken statement that damages someone's character or reputation

   ○ **D.** A false written statement that damages someone's character or reputation

111. In the landmark case *Meritor Savings Bank v. Vinson, 1986,* the Supreme Court ruling stated all of the following *except*

    ○ **A.** Unwelcome sexual advances at work create a hostile work environment, which constitutes gender discrimination under Title VII of the Civil Rights Act of 1964.

    ○ **B.** The employer isn't responsible for the sexually harassing behavior of supervisors in its employ even if it didn't know about the behavior.

    ○ **C.** One way for employers to avoid liability is to prove that a sexually harassed employee had reasonable opportunities to take advantage of a good, clear complaint procedure (without fear of retaliation), but had failed to do so.

    ○ **D.** Employers are automatically liable for sexual harassment by their supervisors.

112. All of the following represent advantages of whole job ranking except

    ○ **A.** Whole job ranking is easy to perform.

    ○ **B.** Whole job ranking establishes factors about each job that need to be taken into consideration when comparing jobs to each other.

    ○ **C.** Whole job ranking is relatively inexpensive to maintain.

    ○ **D.** Whole job ranking produces a list that shows which jobs are most and least important.

113. Which of the following four theorists' work most directly impacts (whether knowingly or unknowingly) incentive plan design?

    ○ **A.** Vroom

    ○ **B.** Maslow

    ○ **C.** Skinner

    ○ **D.** Adams

114. There are five management functions, one of which speaks particularly to the ways in which the manager obtains and arranges resources. Those resources could include people, facilities, materials, and the like. While executing this function, the manager must also make decisions about reporting relationships within the organization. In short, the manager must work to establish linkages between people, places, and things. According to Henri Fayol, this management function is known as

    ○ **A.** Organizing

    ○ **B.** Controlling

    ○ **C.** Planning

    ○ **D.** Coordinating

115. An interviewer truly enjoys interviewing because he feels as though it gives him the opportunity to make a difference in the world by helping individuals who are unemployed find gainful employment. Which of the following four interviewer biases/errors might this interviewer be most likely to experience?

    ○ **A.** Compassion

    ○ **B.** Urgency

    ○ **C.** Leniency

    ○ **D.** Recency

116. Title VII of the Civil Rights Act of 1964 was a landmark piece of legislation prohibiting employment discrimination based on

    ○ **A.** Race, color, religion, sex, and national origin

    ○ **B.** Race, color, age, sex, and national origin

    ○ **C.** Race, age, sex, religion, and handicapping status (renamed to disability upon the passage of the ADA)

    ○ **D.** Race, religion, sex, and national origin

117. An undue hardship is one that does all of the following except:

    ○ **A.** Creates significant difficulty (enough to disrupt business operations)

    ○ **B.** Requires a financial outlay that exceeds 25% of the employee's annual salary

    ○ **C.** Changes something about the (essential) nature of the business

    ○ **D.** Results in a significant financial outlay

118. Which of the following statements about teambuilding is *least* true?

    ○ **A.** Building on the idea that there is no *I* in *team*, teambuilding exercises focus primarily on the role of the team, rather than on the role of each team member.

    ○ **B.** Teambuilding is an effective means through which team members can explore issues such as communication, problem solving, and trust.

    ○ **C.** Teambuilding exercises are most effective when they are linked directly and specifically to organizational objectives.

    ○ **D.** Teambuilding exercises can be of value even if the activity itself doesn't seem to bear any immediate resemblance to the actual workplace.

119. Taft-Hartley identified all but which of the following as unfair labor practices that could be committed by unions:

   ○ **A.** Striking or picketing an employer without giving the required notice

   ○ **B.** Picketing for recognition for more than 30 days without petitioning for an election

   ○ **C.** Causing an employer to discriminate against an employee

   ○ **D.** Refusing to bargain with the employer of the employees it represents

120. All but which of the following constitute protections that were instituted through the Labor Management Reporting and Disclosure Act (also known as Landrum-Griffin)?

   ○ **A.** A requirement that unions submit annual financial reporting to the DOL to document how union members' dues were spent

   ○ **B.** A bill of rights for union members guaranteeing them freedom of speech and periodic secret elections

   ○ **C.** The designation of every union official as an agent of the union

   ○ **D.** Even stronger provisions relative to secondary boycotting and organizational and recognition picketing

121. When a company that owns or operates union as well as nonunion operations shifts work to the nonunion operation in an effort to diminish the impact of the strike, this is referred to as

   ○ **A.** Featherbedding

   ○ **B.** Double breasting

   ○ **C.** Yellow dogging

   ○ **D.** Single roofing

122. The following formula calculates:

   $$\frac{\text{Total of all costs associated with the HRD/training initiative}}{\text{Number of individuals who participate in the HRD/training initiative}}$$

   ○ **A.** ROI

   ○ **B.** Cost per trainee

   ○ **C.** Cost per hire

   ○ **D.** Cost/benefit analysis

123. The Computer Employee exemption includes a different pay threshold before an employee might qualify for an exemption under the FLSA. To qualify for the computer employee exemption, the employee must be compensated either on a salary or fee basis (as defined in the regulations) at a rate not less than

○ **A.** The prevailing wage rate paid for comparable positions in the relevant labor market

○ **B.** $400 per week

○ **C.** $455 per week

○ **D.** $500 per week

124. The significance of *Martin v. Wilks, 1988*, was

○ **A.** Current employees who are negatively impacted by consent decrees that were established in an earlier time and which sought to resolve discrimination that was present in an earlier time may not challenge the validity of such decrees.

○ **B.** Current employees who are negatively impacted by consent decrees that were established in an earlier time and which sought to resolve discrimination that was present in an earlier time may challenge the validity of such decrees.

○ **C.** Gender can be used as a factor in the selection process if there is underrepresentation in a particular job classification, as long as the AAP does not set forth a quota.

○ **D.** Gender can be used as a factor in the selection process if there is underrepresentation in a particular job classification, as long as the AAP does not set forth specific good faith efforts in which the organization will engage to attain that quota.

125. Organizations who lead the market

○ **A.** Choose to offer total rewards/total compensation packages that incorporate a variety of indirect compensation components in addition to a competitive direct compensation component.

○ **B.** Choose to offer variable pay components with greater upside potential than those that are being offered by their labor market competitors, and offer base compensation components that are less competitive than what their labor market competitors are offering.

○ **C.** Choose to offer total rewards/total compensation packages that are more generous than the total rewards/total compensation packages being offered by their labor market competitors.

○ **D.** Choose to offer total compensation packages that are more innovative, creative, atypical, and usually nontraditional than packages being offered by their labor market competitors.

126. Employers enjoy all of the following rights with respect to OSHA inspections *except*

   ○ **A.** The right to request proper identification from the compliance officer

   ○ **B.** The right to learn the reason for the inspection or investigation

   ○ **C.** The right to postpone an inspection until senior leadership is available

   ○ **D.** The right to decline admittance to certain areas that contain trade secrets

127. Under FairPay, highly compensated employees must

   ○ **A.** Earn $150,000 or more annually (of which at least $455 per week must be paid on a salary or fee basis)

   ○ **B.** Oversee office or nonmanual work

   ○ **C.** Customarily and regularly perform at least one of the duties of an exempt executive, administrative, or professional employee identified in the standard tests for exemption

   ○ **D.** All of the above

128. Which of the following statements relative to HR's role in ethics is least true?

   ○ **A.** HR must play a leadership role in establishing, encouraging, and ensuring ongoing ethical behavior within organizations.

   ○ **B.** In its unique role as the conscience of the organization, HR should own the organization's ethical initiative.

   ○ **C.** Ethics must be operationalized so that responsibility for ethics is dispersed throughout the organization.

   ○ **D.** The organization's code of ethics needs to address a variety of issues from a variety of perspectives.

129. The five distinct, yet overlapping, project management processes are (in order):

   ○ **A.** Establishing, developing, implementing, evaluating, and controlling.

   ○ **B.** Initiation, planning, controlling, executing, and closing

   ○ **C.** Planning, organizing, coordinating, directing, and controlling

   ○ **D.** Initiation, planning, executing, controlling, and closing

130. An HR audit is likely to yield information about all of the following *except*

   ○ **A.** The usefulness, appropriateness, and effectiveness of the employee handbook

   ○ **B.** Strategies for decreasing noncompliance with legal requirements

   ○ **C.** Grievances, their causes, and their impact

   ○ **D.** The degree to which the organization complies with HR-related legal requirements

131. Which of the following is a mandatory OSHA standard for all covered employers?

  ◯ **A.** Emergency Action Plan Standard

  ◯ **B.** Fire Safety Standard

  ◯ **C.** Exit Route Standard

  ◯ **D.** Hazard Communication Standard

132. Roger Fisher and William Ury, authors of *Getting to Yes: Negotiating Agreement Without Giving In*, assert that a good agreement is one that is wise, efficient, and that improves the overall relationship between the parties who are involved in working out (not hammering out) an agreement with each other. They set forth four principles of principled negotiation. Which one of the following is not one of the principles?

  ◯ **A.** Separate the people from the problem

  ◯ **B.** Focus on relationships rather than positions

  ◯ **C.** Generate a variety of options before settling on an agreement

  ◯ **D.** Insist that the agreement be based on objective criteria

133. The Mine Safety and Health Act (MSH Act)

  ◯ **A.** Applies only to underground mines

  ◯ **B.** Requires that all mines be inspected at least twice a year (and sometimes four times)

  ◯ **C.** Applies only to coal mines

  ◯ **D.** Provides protections in addition to those afforded by OSHA

134. An organization creates affinity groups. Which of the following of Maslow's needs does this initiative primarily address?

  ◯ **A.** Safety and security

  ◯ **B.** Belonging and love

  ◯ **C.** Esteem

  ◯ **D.** Self-actualization

135. Which of the following is not an example of direct compensation?

  ◯ **A.** Hourly wages/base salary

  ◯ **B.** Shift differentials

  ◯ **C.** Flexible spending accounts

  ◯ **D.** Variable pay

136. According to the FairPay guidelines, which of the following individuals cannot be exempted from the overtime provisions of the FLSA?

   ○ **A.** Manual laborers and other blue-collar workers who perform working involving repetitive operations with their hands

   ○ **B.** Law enforcement officers, such as police officers, detectives, deputy sheriffs, state troopers, and highway patrol officers

   ○ **C.** Employees, regardless of rank or pay level, who perform work such as preventing, controlling, or extinguishing fires of any type

   ○ **D.** Employees who detain or supervise suspected and convicted criminals (correctional officers, parole or probation officers, and the like)

137. Which of the following does not represent a potential disadvantage of an employee referral program?

   ○ **A.** If the current organization is not particularly diverse (with respect to gender, age, race, education background, or a host of other factors), employee referral programs might perpetuate that lack of diversity.

   ○ **B.** If the organization needs to fill multiple openings for the same position during a short period of time, using employee referrals has the potential to significantly increase the cost-per-hire.

   ○ **C.** If an affirmative action plan is in place, and if there are areas of underutilization, an employee referral program is not likely to demonstrate good faith efforts to recruit candidates who are women or minorities.

   ○ **D.** If the organization has prior patterns of hiring discrimination, employee referral programs are likely to reinforce those patterns.

138. Job specs can be expressed as all but which of the following?

   ○ **A.** KSAs

   ○ **B.** Credentials (years of experience, educational requirements, and so on)

   ○ **C.** Physical and or mental requirements

   ○ **D.** Qualifications possessed by the best qualified candidate

139. To what dimension of the organization is Edgard Schein referring when he writes "…a pattern of shared basic assumptions that the group learns as it solved its problems of external adaptation and internal integration, that has worked well enough to be considered valid and, therefore, to be taught to new members as the correct way you perceive, think, and feel in relation to those problems."

   ○ **A.** Vision

   ○ **B.** Mission

   ○ **C.** Culture

   ○ **D.** Values

140. Managers who use performance appraisal systems based on rating scales

   ◯ **A.** Rate employees against each other

   ◯ **B.** Rate employees against performance expectations

   ◯ **C.** Identify statements that are reflective of employees' performance

   ◯ **D.** Write a narrative assessment of employees' performance

141. Which of the four cases listed resulted in the following ruling: "Title VII's prohibition in 703 (a) and (d) against racial discrimination does not condemn all private, voluntary, race-conscious affirmative action plans" and "Congress did not intend to limit traditional business freedom to such a degree as to prohibit all voluntary, race-conscious affirmative action."

   ◯ **A.** *United Steelworkers v. Weber, 1979*

   ◯ **B.** *Regents of California v. Bakke, 1978*

   ◯ **C.** *Johnson v. Santa Clara County Transportation Agency, 1987*

   ◯ **D.** *Griggs v. Duke Power, 1971*

142. The key issues in *Albemarle Paper v. Moody, 1975,* were

   ◯ **A.** Job relatedness and validity

   ◯ **B.** Disparate impact and disparate treatment

   ◯ **C.** Reasonable accommodations and undue hardship

   ◯ **D.** Negligent hiring and negligent retention

143. All of the following represent reasons to establish an ethics program except

   ◯ **A.** To prevent or minimize aggression/violence

   ◯ **B.** To prevent or minimize organizational politics

   ◯ **C.** To prevent or minimize the erosion of trust

   ◯ **D.** To prevent or minimize cynicism

144. Which of the following statements about the Uniform Guidelines on Employee Selection Procedures is not true?

   ◯ **A.** One of its key purposes is to address the concept of adverse impact.

   ◯ **B.** One of its key purposes is to address the concept of adverse treatment.

   ◯ **C.** One important objective of the Uniform Guidelines is to ensure that interview and selection processes are reliable.

   ◯ **D.** One important objective of the Uniform Guidelines is to ensure that interview and selection processes are valid.

145. What makes the outside sales exemption under the FLSA different from all the other exemptions under the FLSA?

○ **A.** A maximum salary is imposed.

○ **B.** A minimum salary is not required.

○ **C.** Employers must reapply for the exemption annually.

○ **D.** None of the above.

146. The best way to prevent Hepatitis C/HCV from being transmitted in the workplace is by

○ **A.** Making the HCV vaccine available to all at-risk employees.

○ **B.** Ensuring proper use of PPE.

○ **C.** Encouraging at-risk employees to wear masks over their mouths.

○ **D.** Including testing for HCV as part of the preemployment physical.

147. The Davis-Bacon Act of 1931

○ **A.** Was the first piece of legislation to consider the topic of—and to actually establish—a minimum wage

○ **B.** Was rendered obsolete by the minimum wage provisions of the FLSA of 1938

○ **C.** Applies only to federal contractors and subcontractors with contracts in excess of $20,000

○ **D.** Applies to construction projects that receive federal funding

148. Youth workers (also known as "children") who are 14 or 15 years old may work

○ **A.** Up to 4 hours on a school day

○ **B.** Up to 20 hours during a school week

○ **C.** Up to 7 hours on a nonschool day

○ **D.** Up to 40 hours during a nonschool week

149. Which of these questions is the most appropriate to ask?

○ **A.** "Tell me about any restriction you have that would prevent you from lifting 30-pound metal sheets onto a conveyor belt for about four hours each day."

○ **B.** "This job requires lifting 30-pound metal sheets onto a conveyor belt for about four hours each workday. Do you have any problems doing this?"

○ **C.** "This job requires lifting 30-pound metal sheets onto a conveyor belt for about four hours each workday. Can you meet this requirement of the position?"

○ **D.** "Although it's technically not part of the job, the person who used to hold this job would help out everyone once in a while with lifting 30-pound metal sheets onto a conveyor belt. Can we count on you to follow in her footsteps, and help out if we needed you to do so?"

150. Which of the following statements about the Portal-to-Portal Act is not true?

- ○ **A.** The Portal-to-Portal Act offered a clearer definition of hours worked for purposes of minimum wage and overtime calculations.

- ○ **B.** It established that employers must compensate workers for the time that they spend performing their jobs, but not for time spent on activities that only relate to the performance of their job.

- ○ **C.** It addresses topics such as travel time, pre-shift work, post-shift work, idle waiting time, overnight travel, training time, and the like.

- ○ **D.** The Portal-to-Portal Act was an amendment of the FLSA.

151. Common law refers to a system of law in which all of the following statements are true *except*

- ○ **A.** Traditions, customs, and precedents have the same force of law as existing laws or statutes.

- ○ **B.** Laws and statutes are, quite literally, interpreted and reinterpreted on a case-by-case basis.

- ○ **C.** Contracts, including employment, are eclipsed by the prevailing common law.

- ○ **D.** Each interpretation and each case sets a precedent but can also be reinterpreted, thus setting a new precedent.

152. The key issue in *Griggs v. Duke Power, 1971*, was

- ○ **A.** Replacing striking workers
- ○ **B.** Employment testing
- ○ **C.** Adverse treatment
- ○ **D.** Adverse impact

153. Taken together, the two 1998 landmark Supreme Court cases *Faragher* v. *City of Boca Raton* and *Ellerth* v. *Burlington Northern Industries* established all of the following *except*

   ○ **A.** If an employee is subjected to a tangible adverse employment action because of a supervisor's sexually harassing behavior, the employer is liable.

   ○ **B.** The employer is vicariously liable when its supervisors create a sexually hostile work environment, even if the employee is not subjected to an adverse employment action.

   ○ **C.** If the employee is not subjected to tangible adverse employment action, the employer may be able to raise as a defense that he acted reasonably to prevent and/or promptly correct any sexually harassing behavior, and that the plaintiff unreasonably failed to take advantage of the employer's preventive or corrective opportunities.

   ○ **D.** If the employee is subjected to tangible adverse employment action, the employer may be able to raise as a defense that he acted reasonably to prevent and/or promptly correct any sexually harassing behavior, and that the plaintiff unreasonably failed to take advantage of the employer's preventive or corrective opportunities.

154. To be eligible to take FMLA leave, an employee must meet four requirements. Which of the following does not constitute one of those requirements?

   ○ **A.** The employee must work for a covered employer (public agencies; federal, state, and local employers; local education agencies [schools]; and private-sector employers with 50 or more employees).

   ○ **B.** The employee must have worked for the employer for a total of at least 12 months (this time does not have to have been uninterrupted).

   ○ **C.** The employee must have worked at least 1,250 hours over the previous 12 months.

   ○ **D.** The employee must work at a location in the United States or in any territory or possession of the United States where at least 75 employees are employed by the employer within 50 miles.

155. Which of the following considerations is least likely to factor into an assessment of whether the standard of just cause or good cause was met?

   ○ **A.** Whether the rule or standard that was violated was newly created or long standing

   ○ **B.** Whether a legitimate investigation looking into the totality of the circumstances around the alleged violation was conducted

   ○ **C.** Whether reasonable proof as to the violation existed or was obtained through investigation

   ○ **D.** Whether the punishment is proportionate to the violation

156. The ruling in the landmark case *Automobile Workers v. Johnson Controls, 1990,* determined that

○ **A.** Employers have an obligation to establish policies to protect unborn fetuses from possible harm resulting from chemical exposure.

○ **B.** Most, if not all, fetal protection policies result in gender discrimination.

○ **C.** The government has the obligation to protect unborn fetuses from chemical risk, even if the parents who conceived them do not choose to do so.

○ **D.** Most, if not all, fetal protection policies constitute a legitimate BFOQ.

157. The process of maintaining awareness of opportunities and threats is known as

○ **A.** SWOT analysis

○ **B.** Environmental scanning

○ **C.** Strategic planning

○ **D.** Contingency planning

158. The significance of *Regents of California v. Bakke, 1978,* was

○ **A.** The permissibility of quotas in college admissions affirmative action programs is irrelevant and nontransferable to the workplace.

○ **B.** The permissibility of quotas in college admissions affirmative action programs is relevant and transferable to the workplace.

○ **C.** The impermissibility of quotas in college admissions affirmative action programs is irrelevant and nontransferable to the workplace.

○ **D.** The impermissibility of quotas in college admissions affirmative action programs is relevant and transferable to the workplace.

159. The employment application often requires the candidate to provide information relative to all of the following areas *except*

○ **A.** Personal data (for example, name, address, and contact information)

○ **B.** Gender/race (as required for EEO reporting)

○ **C.** Employment history (including reasons for leaving prior positions)

○ **D.** Names of professional references

160. In the acronym SMART, *M* stands for

○ **A.** Marketable

○ **B.** Meaningful

○ **C.** Measurable

○ **D.** Motivational

161. Generally speaking, what should be the first step in an effective progressive disciplinary process?

   ○ **A.** Verbal warning

   ○ **B.** Coaching

   ○ **C.** Ensuring consistency

   ○ **D.** Counseling

162. Out of the four following choices, which is the most effective way to deal with "the grapevine?"

   ○ **A.** Apply the motivation principle of extinction—in other words, ignore it.

   ○ **B.** Enact policies to prohibit employees from engaging in conversations about their pay and other confidential matters.

   ○ **C.** If you can't beat 'em, join 'em—use the grapevine as a way of disseminating information.

   ○ **D.** If you can't beat 'em, join 'em—use the grapevine as one way of collecting information.

163. During an organizing campaign, unions are permitted to engage in all of the following activities *except*

   ○ **A.** Inside organizing

   ○ **B.** Salting

   ○ **C.** Surface organizing

   ○ **D.** Organizational picketing

164. Which of the following statements about strikes is not true?

   ○ **A.** Employers cannot hire permanent strike replacements during an economic strike.

   ○ **B.** Employers cannot hire permanent strike replacements during a ULP strike.

   ○ **C.** Workers must be returned to their original positions after a ULP strike is over.

   ○ **D.** Workers cannot be terminated for participating in an economic strike.

165. Offshoring refers to

   ○ **A.** Outsourcing to third-party providers whose corporate headquarters are located overseas

   ○ **B.** Another term for outsourcing

   ○ **C.** Outsourcing to third-party providers whose operations are located overseas

   ○ **D.** Outsourcing to firms that primarily conduct business at their own worksite (rather than at the organization's worksite)

166. To best ensure fair and consistent interviews, interviewers should

  ○ **A.** Ask primary and probing questions that ascertain the skills, knowledge, skills, abilities, and behavioral characteristics that the candidate demonstrated in previous positions.

  ○ **B.** Ensure that primary questions remain consistent from interview to interview.

  ○ **C.** Modify primary questions to reflect a candidate's experience, as indicated on his or her résumé.

  ○ **D.** Ensure that probing questions remain consistent from interview to interview.

167. Which of the following statements about focus groups is untrue?

  ○ **A.** A focus group is more of a communication tool than an involvement tool.

  ○ **B.** Focus groups consist of a representative sample of employees.

  ○ **C.** Focus groups need to include enough people to generate a dynamic and synergistic discussion.

  ○ **D.** Focus groups are led by a neutral facilitator.

168. Which of the following laws was not expanded to include employees of the legislative branch of the government through the Congressional Accountability Act?

  ○ **A.** National Labor Relations Act

  ○ **B.** Employee Polygraph Protection Act

  ○ **C.** Worker Adjustment and Retraining Notification Act

  ○ **D.** Americans with Disabilities Act

169. Which of the following considerations would be least valuable to ask while you are preparing to collect market data?

  ○ **A.** What is the relevant labor market for this position?

  ○ **B.** What sources of market data do you already have, and what additional sources could you get?

  ○ **C.** How does the position compare to others within the existing job worth hierarchy?

  ○ **D.** Who are our labor market competitors in general and for specific jobs?

170. A code of ethics is far less likely to be effective if

   ○ **A.** The organization adopts a one-size-fits-all approach.

   ○ **B.** It omits statements relative to how the code will be implemented and upheld.

   ○ **C.** The CEO does not write the introduction to and/or cover letter accompanying the code.

   ○ **D.** It includes components that could be perceived as threatening or punitive.

171. In general, the NLRB will not agree to accept a petition from a union for an election in all of the following situations *except*

   ○ **A.** A union has been certified in the past year but has not successfully negotiated a contract.

   ○ **B.** An election has been held within the past year.

   ○ **C.** There is a valid contract (not to exceed three years) in effect.

   ○ **D.** There is a valid contract (of any duration) in effect.

172. Of the following outputs, which is least likely to be supported by information that is generated from an HRIS?

   ○ **A.** Increasing overall employee productivity

   ○ **B.** Identifying and rewarding top performers

   ○ **C.** Increasing overall employee commitment

   ○ **D.** Placing the right people in the right jobs at the right times

173. You've been hired as the HR manager of a start-up company that produces a new type of alternative fuel. Which of the following conditions are you least likely to experience in your new role?

   ○ **A.** A request to publish an employee handbook

   ○ **B.** The need to develop total rewards packages that lead the market

   ○ **C.** The need to develop total rewards packages that lag the market

   ○ **D.** A high level of excitement and energy

174. To qualify for an executive exemption under the FLSA, an employee must meet all of the following requirements *except*

- ○ **A.** The employee's primary duty must be managing the enterprise or managing a customarily recognized department or subdivision of the enterprise.

- ○ **B.** The employee must customarily and regularly direct the work of at least two or more other full-time employees or their equivalent.

- ○ **C.** The employee's primary duty includes the exercise of discretion and independent judgment with respect to matters of significance.

- ○ **D.** The employee must have the authority to hire or fire other employees, or the employee's suggestions and recommendations as to the hiring, firing, advancement, promotion, or any other change of status of other employees must be given particular weight.

175. An employee who prefers to learn about HR practices by attending a guest lecture series is probably a

- ○ **A.** Visual learner

- ○ **B.** Auditory learner

- ○ **C.** Kinesthetic learner

- ○ **D.** Vicarious learner

176. Which of the following statements does not constitute a consideration for determining what constitutes fair use?

- ○ **A.** Whether the work will be used for commercial purposes or for not-for-profit or educational purposes.

- ○ **B.** The nature or way in which the work will be used.

- ○ **C.** How much of the work is used, both in terms of the aggregate amount of work that is being used, as well as the percentage of the total work that is being used.

- ○ **D.** Specific permissions that the copyright holder has previously granted, if those permissions are deemed to be precedent-setting in nature.

177. The most renowned example of the Mackay Doctrine in use was

○ **A.** In 2005, when President George W. Bush waived the requirement to pay a prevailing wage rate to government contractors and subcontractors involved in the rebuilding of New Orleans.

○ **B.** In 1996, when President William Jefferson "Bill" Clinton signed legislation permitting employers to require all employees to agree to binding arbitration in exchange for the opportunity to be employed with the organization.

○ **C.** In 1992, when President George H. W. Bush passed an executive order that required more than 11,000 troops returning from the (first) Gulf War be reinstated to the positions that they would have held if they had not experienced a break in service due to their military service.

○ **D.** In 1981, when President Ronald Wilson Reagan replaced 12,000 striking air traffic controllers.

178. Which of the following is least likely to be considered an action-oriented program?

○ **A.** Recruiting at colleges or universities traditionally attended by minorities

○ **B.** Increasing the cash awards granted through the organization's employee referral program

○ **C.** Reaching out to professional organizations whose membership criteria is designed to attract women or minorities

○ **D.** Posting job openings at resource centers for displaced homemakers

179. An employee is hired as a telesales representative for a sports apparel company. She performs exceptionally well in that position and is promoted to the position of field sales manager. Two months later, this employee is injured in a serious automobile accident in which she loses both of her legs. To everyone's amazement, she is ready to return to work two months later. She is told, however, that she will not be able to return to her position as sales manager, but that she is welcome to return to her former position as telesales representative. Although she is not initially given a reason, she is finally told "off the record" that although the customers feel very bad for what happened to her, they just aren't comfortable having a wheelchair-bound field sales manager, and that, ultimately, "the customer is always right." Would this decision likely be upheld as legal under EEO law?

○ **A.** Yes, because of the BFOQ exception to EEO laws.

○ **B.** No, because this would not qualify under the BFOQ exception to EEO laws.

○ **C.** Yes, because of the customer preference exception to EEO laws.

○ **D.** No, because there are no exceptions to EEO laws.

180. The following formula:

$$\frac{\text{\# of terminations during a specified period of time}}{\text{The average \# of employees in the workforce during that same period of time}}$$

Calculates which of the following?

○ **A.** Time to hire

○ **B.** Turnover

○ **C.** ROI

○ **D.** Cost per hire

181. All of the following statements offer sound advice to follow relative to offer letters *except*

○ **A.** State that the only agreements or promises that are valid are those that are included in the offer letter.

○ **B.** Use the offer letter as an opportunity to reaffirm that the employment relationship is at-will.

○ **C.** For exempt positions, avoid expressing earnings in weekly, bi-monthly, or monthly terms (depending upon your payroll cycle), so as not to jeopardize the non-exempt FLSA status.

○ **D.** Avoid language that hints of any sort of long-term employment relationship, as well as any statements that indicate that the employer is "like a family."

182. Which of the following types of tests is most frequently considered to be illegal on a preemployment basis?

○ **A.** Agility tests

○ **B.** Aptitude tests

○ **C.** Honesty tests

○ **D.** Polygraph tests

183. FairPay defines highly compensated employees as those who

○ **A.** Earn $100,000 or more annually if single, or who earn $120,000 or more annually if married

○ **B.** Earn $100,000 or more annually (of which at least $455 per week must be paid on a salary or fee basis)

○ **C.** Earn $100,000 or more annually

○ **D.** Earn $150,000 or more annually

184. In order to be concerted, activity must be

  ○ **A.** Undertaken by individual employees who are acting in pursuit of an individual goal.

  ○ **B.** Undertaken by individual employees who are acting in an independent manner.

  ○ **C.** Protected before it can be concerted.

  ○ **D.** Engaged in with or on the authority of other employees.

185. If an employer does not choose to seek a settlement agreement when a charge of discrimination is first filed, the EEOC can handle the charge in all of the following ways *except*

  ○ **A.** Investigate it

  ○ **B.** Settle it

  ○ **C.** Arbitrate it

  ○ **D.** Dismiss it

186. A protected class is best described as

  ○ **A.** A group of individuals who have, historically, experienced discrimination (for instance, women, people of color, people with disabilities, and so on)

  ○ **B.** A group of individuals who share a common characteristic, and who are protected from discrimination and harassment based on that shared characteristic

  ○ **C.** A group of individuals who have filed charges with the NLRB or taking part in any NLRB proceedings

  ○ **D.** Employees who have engaged in an economic strike and who, therefore, under the Mackay Doctrine, cannot be permanently replaced by the employer

187. If you notice a change in a candidate's nonverbal behavior during the interview

  ○ **A.** Probe for more information around whatever question the candidate was answering when that change occurred.

  ○ **B.** Be familiar with what specific nonverbal communication cues mean (for instance, folded arms indicate aloofness), so you know how to interpret the behavior.

  ○ **C.** Without assessing judgment, point out and describe the changed nonverbal behavior, and ask him or her to help you understand what it means.

  ○ **D.** Mirror the candidate's nonverbal behavior, to see if he or she continues to display that behavior.

188. Annual EEO reports must be filed

- ○ **A.** By employers with federal contracts or subcontracts of $100,000 or more
- ○ **B.** By employers with 100 or more employees
- ○ **C.** By federal contractors and subcontractors with contracts in excess of $10,000 during any one-year period
- ○ **D.** By all employers, with the exception of family farms, who do not employee individuals outside the family

189. Recruiting is

- ○ **A.** The process of creating a pool of candidates and selecting the final candidate
- ○ **B.** The process of attracting and creating a pool of qualified candidates
- ○ **C.** The process of identifying the candidate(s) to whom the position will be offered
- ○ **D.** The process of selecting the candidate to whom the position will be offered

190. After you decide that you are going to conduct an employee survey, what is the first step that you should take?

- ○ **A.** Select an internal or external consultant.
- ○ **B.** Determine the survey methodology.
- ○ **C.** Secure management buy-in.
- ○ **D.** Decide upon the survey content.

191. Union deauthorization

- ○ **A.** Is the process of removing the union's rights to represent the employees
- ○ **B.** Revokes the union security clause in the contract
- ○ **C.** Requires that 50% or more of those who vote during the union deauthorization election support the deauthorization
- ○ **D.** Is far more common than union decertification

192. Preemployment realistic job previews can be conveyed and communicated in a number of ways. Which of the following is the least effective way of providing candidates with a realistic job preview?

- ○ **A.** Verbal descriptions of the work, the work environment, and/or the work conditions
- ○ **B.** The opportunity to read the employee handbook
- ○ **C.** The opportunity to speak with current employees, particularly those who would be the incumbent's peers and/or colleagues
- ○ **D.** The opportunity to interact with other candidates and to compare perceptions of the organization with each other

193. On November 13, 2000, 41 CFR Part 60-2 (the portion of the Federal Register that addresses affirmative action) was significantly revised. Which of the following was not addressed or accomplished by these revisions?

   ○ A. Reduced the number of additional required elements of the written AAP from 10 to 4

   ○ B. Reaffirmed that AAPs establish quotas that must be affirmatively pursued through good faith efforts

   ○ C. Granted employers with fewer than 150 employees permission to prepare a job group analysis that uses EEO-1 categories as job groups

   ○ D. Reduced the 8-factor availability analysis to 2 factors

194. Which of the following statements about the nominal group technique is true?

   ○ A. It constitutes a nonmathematical forecasting technique that draws on the insights of subject matter experts.

   ○ B. It is similar to the Delphi technique in that it affords experts the opportunity to interact with each other.

   ○ C. It is self-directing, self-governing, and relies on the facilitative abilities of the experts who are participating in the forecasting process.

   ○ D. It permits and encourages discussion and collaboration throughout the forecasting process.

195. Which of the following statements about IRCA is inaccurate?

   ○ A. IRCA prohibits discrimination against job applicants based on national origin.

   ○ B. IRCA imposes penalties for knowingly committing recordkeeping errors.

   ○ C. IRCA prohibits giving employment preference to U.S. citizens.

   ○ D. IRCA imposes penalties for hiring illegal aliens.

196. Which of the following statements about torts is not true?

   ○ A. Torts are wrongful acts.

   ○ B. Torts are committed against people, not against things.

   ○ C. The commission of a tort infringes on another person's rights.

   ○ D. Tort doctrine is associated with common law.

197. According to Fred Fiedler, all of the following are factors that contribute to determining a situation's level of favorableness for a particular leadership style except

- ○ **A.** Leader-member relations. This factor looks at how strong and how significant relationships between the leader and the team members are. It considers the degree to which those relationships make the leader more or less effective and influential.

- ○ **B.** Experience-expertise. This factor looks at the degree to which a leader's experience with a particular situation or task has contributed to developing true expertise. It also looks at the degree to which that experience-expertise connection is recognized and appreciated by team members.

- ○ **C.** Task structure. This factor ascertains the degree to which the work that the team members perform is structured.

- ○ **D.** Position power. This factor looks at the degree to which the leader's position holds or can exert power or influence. It also looks at the degree to which the leader can ensure accountability for team members' performance, and the degree to which the leader has the authority to delegate.

198. All of the following are valuable guidelines for managing a vendor and a relationship with a vendor *except*

- ○ **A.** Giving the vendor constructive and positive feedback

- ○ **B.** Setting clear and reasonable expectations

- ○ **C.** Converting full-time vendors from independent contractors to employee to foster greater esprit de corps

- ○ **D.** Incorporating upside potential and downside risk into your negotiated agreements with vendors

199. The four Ps refer to

- ○ **A.** Priorities, posting, places, and people (the four Ps of recruiting)

- ○ **B.** Perception, perspective, proportion, and perseverance (the four Ps of employee relations)

- ○ **C.** Prospect, persistence, proposal, and project (the four Ps of project management)

- ○ **D.** Product, place, price, and promotion (the four Ps of marketing)

200. All of the following statements are true of weighted employment applications *except*

    ○ **A.** They are intended to facilitate the process of assessing each candidate's qualifications.

    ○ **B.** They facilitate and support compliance with EEO guidelines.

    ○ **C.** They can be difficult and time consuming to develop and maintain.

    ○ **D.** They assign relative weights to different elements of the employment application.

201. Which of the statements about common situs picketing is not true?

    ○ **A.** Common situs picketing is a type of secondary boycott.

    ○ **B.** Common situs picketing is generally legal.

    ○ **C.** Common situs picketing occurs when members of a labor union picket a workplace in which multiple employers work.

    ○ **D.** Common situs picketing is permissible when double breasting has occurred.

202. All of the following statements about essential functions are true *except*

    ○ **A.** To be considered essential, a function must be inherently fundamental and necessary to a position.

    ○ **B.** To be considered essential, a function must constitute part or all of the reason the job exists.

    ○ **C.** The elimination of an essential function would substantially alter the nature of the job.

    ○ **D.** They must be identified in the job description.

203. *McDonnell Douglas Corp v. Green, 1979*, determined that the initial burden of proof for establishing a prima facie case of discrimination against an employer (or potential employer) under Title VII of the Civil Rights Act of 1964 rests with the employee (or applicant), who must be able to establish four key elements. Which one of these elements is not one of those four elements that the employee must have to establish a prima facie case?

    ○ **A.** The person is a member of a protected class.

    ○ **B.** The person applied for a job for which the employer was seeking applicants.

    ○ **C.** The person was rejected, despite being the most qualified for the position.

    ○ **D.** After this rejection, the employer continued to seek other applicants with similar qualifications.

204. An organization that utilizes the services of an employment agency/search firm must pay

- ❍ **A.** A fee to a contingency employment agency/search firm whether or not an employee is hired through that agency's efforts
- ❍ **B.** A fee to a contingency employment agency/search firm only if an employee is hired through that agency's efforts
- ❍ **C.** A fee to a retained employment agency/search firm only if an employee is hired through that agency's efforts
- ❍ **D.** Fees to a contingency firm as well as retained employment agencies/search firms whether or not an employee is hired through an agency's efforts

205. All of the following are possible reasons to conduct prescreen phone interviews *except*

- ❍ **A.** To identify legitimate job-related factors that could cause the employer to decide to eliminate the candidate from consideration
- ❍ **B.** To share (with every candidate) job-related information that could lead one or more candidates to self-select out of the selection process
- ❍ **C.** To interact with a candidate in a more informal manner so as to ascertain whether he or she is likely to be a good fit with the organization
- ❍ **D.** To ascertain whether the candidate's desired salary/wage rate is close to the salary/wage range that the organization has established for the position

206. Which of the following situations would be least likely to result in disparate impact?

- ❍ **A.** An employer requires all employees to live within a 30-mile radius of an employer so as to ensure quick response in the event that employees need to report to work immediately.
- ❍ **B.** An employer will not hire any candidates who have experienced a gap in employment.
- ❍ **C.** An employer establishes a high potential program, in which all participants are required to relocate every 9–12 months until they have completed five rotational assignments in five different locations.
- ❍ **D.** An employer creates a cross-training program in which all nonmanagement employees who meet or exceed performance expectations of their current positions would be able to participate.

207. Although it is very difficult to establish good measures of validity, it is possible to make a case for validity if the interview process has certain characteristics. Which of these processes/attributes contributes the least to enhancing the validity of an interview process?

   ○ **A.** The same interviewer conducts every interview for a particular job opening.

   ○ **B.** The interview is based on job analysis.

   ○ **C.** The interviewer asks questions that provide evidence about important job-related skills.

   ○ **D.** The information shared, discussed, and collected during an interview relates to a specific job.

208. Skill inventories refer to

   ○ **A.** Preemployment testing that ascertains the degree to which a candidate possesses specific skills required to perform the position.

   ○ **B.** A central database that captures the KSAs possessed by employees.

   ○ **C.** A performance management instrument that ascertains the degree to which the candidate demonstrates the competencies required by the position during the performance measurement period.

   ○ **D.** An online database used to create job descriptions.

209. An employee seems to be working diligently, but has been continually missing deadlines. After a great deal of coaching and counseling, the employee is ultimately warned that she may experience further disciplinary action, up to and including termination, if she does not bring her performance up to standard. Ultimately, this employee starts meeting deadlines—first sporadically, and then on a more consistent basis. The employee is then praised by her supervisor for her performance. This is an example of

   ○ **A.** Negative reinforcement

   ○ **B.** Positive reinforcement

   ○ **C.** Punishment

   ○ **D.** Extinction

210. All of the following are elements of Vroom's expectancy theory except

   ○ **A.** Instrumentality

   ○ **B.** Proclivity

   ○ **C.** Valence

   ○ **D.** Expectancy

211. In behavioral leadership theories, the dimension of leadership behavior known as initiating structure refers to

   - ○ **A.** The interpersonal relationships that managers must first establish with employees before attempting to ensure completion of the actual work

   - ○ **B.** What employees need to do, and how they need to do it, in order to attain objectives

   - ○ **C.** The training in which managers need to participate to develop the skills needed to be an effective leader

   - ○ **D.** The degree to which an individual demonstrates an innate ability to being an effective leader

212. According to the Copyright Act of 1976, which of the following statements is true?

   - ○ **A.** Most of the time, the employer owns/retains the copyright to the work product that an employee generates during the normal course of his or her employment.

   - ○ **B.** Most of the time, an independent contractor owns/retains the copyright to the work product that he or she generates for the organization with which he or she has contracted.

   - ○ **C.** Most of the time, an employee owns/retains the copyright to the work product that he or she generates in the normal course of his or her employment.

   - ○ **D.** Most of the time, a consulting firm owns/retains the copyright to the work product that the consultant generates for the organization with which he or she is consulting.

213. The formative evaluation model

   - ○ **A.** Seeks feedback during and after the development and implementation phases

   - ○ **B.** Uses feedback, analysis, and assessment conducted at one phase of the process to make enhancements in other phases

   - ○ **C.** Was initially developed by Donald L. Kirkpatrick

   - ○ **D.** Measures participants' responses and reactions to the program immediately after the program has been delivered

214. To qualify for the learned professional exemption under the FLSA

   ○ A. The employee's primary duty must be the performance of work requiring advanced knowledge, defined as work that is predominantly intellectual in character and that includes work requiring the consistent exercise of discretion and judgment.

   ○ B. The advanced knowledge must be in a field of science, learning, or other accredited profession.

   ○ C. Both A and B.

   ○ D. Neither A nor B.

215. Which of the following would not be considered a form of indirect compensation?

   ○ A. Legally mandated benefits (such as social security)

   ○ B. Vacation time

   ○ C. Perquisites

   ○ D. Vacation buyout programs

216. Which of the following statements about the MHPA is untrue?

   ○ A. MHPA requires employers that offer health care plans with medical benefits to offer mental health benefits.

   ○ B. Under MHPA, plans can still dictate/define the terms and conditions of benefits provided under mental health plans (for instance, cost-sharing, limits on the number of visits or days of coverage, and so on).

   ○ C. Under MHPA, plans that don't impose annual or lifetime monetary caps on medical and surgical benefits cannot impose annual or lifetime caps on mental health benefits.

   ○ D. Benefits for substance abuse or chemical dependency are excluded from MHPA's requirements relative to annual or lifetime caps.

217. Generally speaking, when an employee handbook is submitted as legal evidence, which of the following factors is usually most important?

   ○ A. EEO/AA statement

   ○ B. Sexual harassment policy

   ○ C. Records retention policy

   ○ D. Employee acknowledgement

218. Which of the following is least likely to be a reason that an organization would conduct an employee survey?

    ○ **A.** To gauge and measure employees' perceptions, viewpoints, and attitudes

    ○ **B.** To take the pulse on specific current and/or potential employee issues

    ○ **C.** To collect information that can be used to address an individual's employee relations issues

    ○ **D.** To collect information that can be used by the organization to help set priorities

219. For a bargaining unit to be established, which of the following has to happen during the election?

    ○ **A.** A simple majority of the voters must cast a vote in favor of the proposed bargaining unit.

    ○ **B.** A simple majority of the individuals who would be members of the proposed bargaining unit must cast a vote in favor of the proposed bargaining unit.

    ○ **C.** When there is more than one bargaining unit competing in the election, a proposed bargaining unit must obtain more votes than other bargaining units obtain.

    ○ **D.** At least 30% of the voters must cast a vote in favor of the bargaining unit.

220. Of the following situations, which one represents the highest priority for OSHA?

    ○ **A.** Referrals from the media

    ○ **B.** Planned inspections in high-hazard industries

    ○ **C.** Employee complaints

    ○ **D.** Catastrophes and fatal accidents

221. With respect to selection procedures, reliability can be defined as

    ○ **A.** The degree to which a selection procedure assesses a candidate's ability to perform representative and significant parts of the job

    ○ **B.** The degree to which incumbents' scores or ratings on a particular selection procedure correlate with their actual job performance

    ○ **C.** The degree to which a selection process or instrument is consistent, and generates consistent information that can be used for decision making

    ○ **D.** The degree to which a clear relationship exists between performance on the selection procedure and performance on the job

222. "The degree of responsibility and accountability which an employer entrusts to— and expects from—a particular position" refers to the definition of which of the four factors used by the Equal Pay Act to assess substantial equality?

   ○ **A.** Skill

   ○ **B.** Trust

   ○ **C.** Accountability

   ○ **D.** Responsibility

223. The Railway Labor Act of 1926 accomplished all of the following *except*

   ○ **A.** Established the grieve now, work later rule

   ○ **B.** Gave management additional tools to make sure the trains ran on time

   ○ **C.** Enabled railroad workers to organize and to have a collective bargaining agent

   ○ **D.** Created the first real win-win scenario for labor and management in American history

224. Taft-Hartley accomplished all of the following *except*

   ○ **A.** Reaffirmed that employers have a constitutional right to express their opposition to unions, so long as employees are not threatened with reprisal for their union activities or promised benefits for refraining from such activities.

   ○ **B.** Prohibited employers from taking adverse employment actions against supervisors who did not support the employer's position.

   ○ **C.** Outlawed closed shops, agreements that stated that employers could only hire individuals who were members of labor unions.

   ○ **D.** Expressly permitted union shops, in which nonunion workers must join the union within a certain amount of time after being hired.

225. The list of the names and addresses of all of the employees who are eligible to vote in the union certification election is known as

   ○ **A.** The Excelsior List

   ○ **B.** The Davis-Bacon List

   ○ **C.** The Hot Cargo List

   ○ **D.** The Waffle House List

Answers to Practice Exam

Answers at a Glance to Practice Exam

1. C	29. B	57. D	85. B
2. C	30. A	58. D	86. C
3. C	31. D	59. B	87. C
4. B	32. C	60. B	88. A
5. D	33. D	61. B	89. C
6. A	34. C	62. A	90. B
7. C	35. A	63. B	91. B
8. D	36. B	64. B	92. C
9. A	37. A	65. D	93. C
10. D	38. C	66. D	94. B
11. C	39. C	67. B	95. A
12. C	40. A	68. D	96. C
13. B	41. B	69. C	97. B
14. B	42. B	70. A	98. A
15. C	43. B	71. C	99. C
16. D	44. A	72. A	100. D
17. B	45. C	73. C	101. A
18. A	46. C	74. C	102. D
19. B	47. C	75. D	103. C
20. C	48. C	76. B	104. D
21. A	49. C	77. B	105. B
22. C	50. A	78. C	106. A
23. D	51. D	79. B	107. A
24. A	52. D	80. C	108. D
25. A	53. B	81. A	109. C
26. D	54. B	82. B	110. C
27. D	55. B	83. B	111. B
28. D	56. C	84. A	112. B

113. A	142. A	171. D	200. B
114. A	143. B	172. C	201. D
115. C	144. B	173. A	202. D
116. A	145. B	174. C	203. C
117. B	146. B	175. B	204. B
118. A	147. A	176. D	205. C
119. A	148. D	177. D	206. D
120. C	149. C	178. B	207. A
121. B	150. B	179. B	208. B
122. B	151. C	180. B	209. C
123. C	152. D	181. C	210. B
124. B	153. D	182. D	211. B
125. C	154. D	183. B	212. A
126. C	155. A	184. D	213. B
127. C	156. B	185. C	214. A
128. B	157. B	186. B	215. D
129. D	158. D	187. A	216. A
130. B	159. B	188. B	217. D
131. C	160. C	189. B	218. C
132. B	161. B	190. C	219. A
133. B	162. D	191. B	220. D
134. B	163. C	192. D	221. C
135. C	164. A	193. B	222. D
136. A	165. C	194. A	223. A
137. B	166. B	195. B	224. B
138. D	167. A	196. B	225. A
139. C	168. A	197. B	
140. B	169. C	198. C	
141. A	170. B	199. D	

Answers with Explanations

1. **Answer C is the best answer.** Unflattering light does not constitute one of the four categories of invasion of privacy; however, false light *does*. Answer A is not the best answer; intrusion of solitude does constitute one of the four categories of invasion of privacy. Answer B is not the best answer; public disclosure of private and embarrassing facts does constitute one of the four categories of invasion of privacy. Answer D is not the best answer; appropriation of identity does constitute one of the four categories of invasion of privacy.

2. **Answer C is the best answer.** Employees must report all work-related injuries to their employer—whether or not the injury results in in-patient hospitalization. Answers A, B, and D are not the best answers because each identifies responsibilities that are mandated by the General Duty Clause.

3. **Answer C is the best answer.** The balanced scorecard manifests the opposite belief; it is, in fact, a management system that turns strategic planning into a hands-on, reality-driven, highly impactful tool. Answers A, B, and D are not the best answers; each reflects a belief that is embodied in the balanced scorecard.

4. **Answer B is the best answer.** Efficiency can be described as doing things right— speaking, therefore, more to *how* something is accomplished than to *what* is accomplished. Answer A is not the best answer; the degree to which goals are appropriate is a statement that is descriptive of effectiveness, not efficiency. Answer C is not the best answer; doing the right things is also a statement that is descriptive of effectiveness, not efficiency. Answer D is not the best answer; it is quite possible to achieve efficiency without achieving effectiveness—in other words, it's possible to do a good job of achieving goals that aren't appropriate (which, in the case of HR, could mean that the goals aren't strategically aligned with the goals of the organization).

5. **Answer D is the best answer.** The Retirement Equity Act did prohibit plans from counting maternity and paternity leaves as breaks in service for participation and vesting purposes. Answer A is not the best answer; REA lowered, rather than increased, the minimum age requirement for pension plan participation. Answer B is not the best answer; REA required qualified pension plans to provide automatic survivor benefits and allow for waiver of survivor benefits *only with the consent of the participant and the spouse*. Answer C is not the best answer; REA clarified that pension plans *may obey* certain qualified domestic relations (court) orders (QDROs) requiring them to make benefit payments to a participant's former spouse (or another alternative payee) *without violating ERISA's prohibitions against assignment or alienation of benefits*.

6. **Answer A is the best answer.** Whether a survey is designed and conducted by someone from inside or outside the organization is not nearly as important as the other considerations that are listed in the other answers. A survey can be successful or unsuccessful whether it is conducted by someone inside, or outside, the organization. How the survey is designed and conducted is generally much more important. Answer B is the not the best answer; ensuring that survey input is maintained in a fully confidential manner is an important determinant of the overall success of an employee survey. Answer C is not the best answer; ensuring that employees believe in the confidentiality of the survey is an important determinant of the overall success of an employee survey. Answer D is not the best answer; ensuring buy-in and support from management is an important determinant of the overall success of an employee survey.

7. **Answer C is the best answer.** Resistance to the process of formalizing policies and procedures is most likely to first manifest itself during the development (or growth) stage in the organizational life cycle. Answer A is not the best answer; having a core group of highly talented employees who focus on the founder is more likely to first manifest itself during stage 1 of the organizational life cycle (introduction or birth). Answer B is not the best answer; resistance to OD and change initiatives is more likely to first manifest itself during stage 3 of the organizational life cycle (maturity). Answer D is not the best answer; an entitlement mentality toward pay and benefits is most likely to first manifest itself during stage 3 of the organizational life cycle (maturity).

8. **Answer D is the best answer.** The scientific method is a form of primary research, not secondary research. Primary research, by definition, goes to the source and, therefore, collects data, rather than assimilates data that been collected by others (existing data is assimilated as part of secondary research). Answers A, B, and C are not the best answers; each represents a step in the scientific method. The only step that is not represented here is the final one, which is to analyze data and reach a conclusion.

9. **Answer A is the best answer.** Transactional leaders use a system built on the carrot and the stick method—and mainly the stick part of it. Answer B is not the best answer; coaching is more characteristic of the transformational leadership style. Answer C is not the best answer; the image of a captain might more closely reflect the role a leader plays in the selling quadrant of Hersey and Blanchard's situational leadership model. Answer D is not the best answer; the image of a director could imply a wider variety of leadership approaches under transactional as well as transformational styles.

10. **Answer C is the best answer.** Bonus pay (which, unlike incentive pay, is discretionary) would not be included in an employee's regular rate of pay.

11. **Answer C is the best answer.** OD helps maintain the organization's focus on the belief that it is the *people* within organizations (not the *systems* within organizations) who perform and accomplish the work of the organization. Answer A is not the best answer; OD does refer to the process through which the overall performance, growth, and effectiveness of the organization is enhanced through strategic, deliberate, and integrated initiatives. Answer B is not the best answer; OD does incorporate psychology,

sociology, anthropology, and management. Answer D is not the best answer; OD interventions are designed to identify an organization's competitive advantages.

12. **Answer C is the best answer.** A ULP is called when a union alleges that an employer has committed a ULP. This does not necessarily mean that the employer actually did, in fact, commit a ULP (the courts would need to subsequently determine that a strike was, in fact, a ULP strike, and not an economic strike in disguise). Answer A is not the best answer; ULP strikes stem from an allegation that the employer has committed a ULP during contract negotiations. Answer B is not the best answer; an employer must return striking workers to their original positions after the strike is over. Answer D is not the best answer; employers cannot hire permanent strike replacements during a ULP strike.

13. **Answer B is the correct answer.** The Hazard Communication Standard has no requirement pertaining to obtaining signed employee acknowledgement forms, although it is always a good idea to obtain signed documentation that participants have attended a training session (especially when such training is required by law). This standard does, however, require MSDS (answer A), container labeling requirements (answer C), and training and orientation requirements (answer D).

14. **Answer B is the best answer.** A jurisdictional strike is one through which a union seeks to pressure an employer to assign particular work to its members, rather than to members of other unions or to nonunion workers. Answer A is not the best answer; employees who are not directly involved in an economic dispute who choose not to cross a picket line out of support for striking workers are engaging in a sympathy strike, not a jurisdictional strike. Answer C is not the best answer; a strike that occurs even though the collective bargaining agreement contains a no-strike clause is a wildcat strike, not a jurisdictional strike. Answer D is not the best answer; a strike used by a union to pressure an employer to grant some sort of concession (namely, an economic concession) from the employer during collective bargaining negotiations is an economic strike, not a jurisdictional strike.

15. **Answer C is the best answer.** Copyrights are granted for the lifetime of the author, plus 70 years (assuming that the work was not created anonymously). Answer A is not the best answer; the copyright does not end when the author dies. Answer B is not the best answer; copyrights cannot be deeded to heirs. Answer D is not the best answer; this answer alludes to copyrights for anonymous works and works that were created under work-for-hire agreements that enter the public domain 95 years after the first year of publication or 120 years after the year in which it was created, whichever comes first.

16. **Answer D is the best answer.** In general, placing all the interviewers on one side of the table and the candidate on the other can unintentionally create an adversarial atmosphere, even if this arrangement makes it easier for the candidate to make eye contact with the interviewers. Answer A is not the best answer; it is a good idea to let the candidate know ahead of time if he or she will be participating in a panel interview to help minimize—or avoid—the anxiety that a surprise of this sort could cause. Answer B is not the best answer; it is a good idea to plan who will ask what questions in advance, and in what order. Answer C is not the best answer; a round table will help create an atmosphere that is conducive to the exchange of information.

17. **Answer B is the best answer.** As long as they fall under the category of "first aid," injuries resulting in bleeding do not need to be recorded unless they also result in death, days away from work (answer A), restricted work or job transfer (answer C), or loss of consciousness (answer D).

18. **Answer A is the best answer.** The question of whether the employee and/or the collective bargaining unit advised the employer of the concerted nature of the employee's activity is irrelevant to whether the employer might be considered to have violated the NLRA. The only three requirements that would need to be met for an employer to be considered to have possibly violated the NLRA are whether the employer knew of the concerted nature of the employee's activity (answer B), whether the concerted activity was actually protected by NLRA (answer C), and whether the adverse employment action in question (for instance, termination) was motivated by the employee's protected concerted activity (answer D).

19. **Answer B is the best answer.** Henry Fayol is known as the father of modern management. Answers A, C, and D are not the best answers; Fayol was not known as a guru in any of these areas.

20. **Answer C is the best answer.** In *General Dynamics Land Systems v. Cline, 2004*, the Supreme Court ruled that younger employees (even if they are over the age of 40) cannot allege age discrimination because of programs that favor older employees. Answer A is not the best answer; *General Dynamics Land Systems v. Cline, 2004*, established that the ADEA does not prohibit favoring the old over the young. Answer B is not the best answer; although the ADEA prohibits favoring the *young over the old*, it has not been interpreted to prohibit favoring the *old over the young*. Answer D is not the best answer; younger employees (even if they are over the age of 40) cannot allege age discrimination because of programs that favor older employees.

21. **Answer A is the best answer.** Job classification is a nonquantitative job evaluation technique that categorizes jobs into broad categories, or levels, based on the level—and, ultimately, value to the organization—of the work that is performed by jobs within each level. Each level incorporates specific responsibilities and benchmark statements that describe the nature, complexity, autonomy, and so forth of the work that is performed by positions in that level. Answer B is not the best answer; job slotting is a nonquantitative job evaluation technique that incorporates, or slots, newly created or revised positions into an existing job hierarchy. Answer C is not the best answer; in whole job ranking techniques (nonquantitative), jobs are ranked, from lowest to highest, according to the importance that each job holds (or, stated differently, the value that each job brings) to the organization. Answer D is not the best answer; factor comparison is a quantitative job evaluation technique that involves the ranking of each compensable factor of each job.

22. **Answer C is the best answer.** The decision whether to lag, match, or lead the market with respect to total compensation/total rewards is just that—a decision. It is not universally true that an organization's total compensation program should be competitive with (in other words, match) the total compensation programs offered

by labor market competitors. Answer A is not the best answer; an organization's total compensation/total rewards program should support and reinforce the mission, vision, and values of the organization. Answer B is not the best answer; an organization's total compensation/total rewards program should be consistent with the culture of the organization. Answer D is not the best answer; an organization's total compensation program should attract, motivate, and retain targeted/appropriate employees.

23. **Answer D is the best answer.** Responding to the complaint is the responsibility of counsel. Although an HR professional might be asked to *assist* in this process, HR is not *primarily* responsible for this activity. This is an important distinction to keep in mind, because HR professionals must be ever-vigilant not to "cross the line" and perform functions that (under the law) can be performed only by an attorney. Answer A is not the best answer; an HR professional may be called on to testify during a trial. Answer B is not the best answer; an HR professional may be called on to sit at the counsel table during the trial, thus being the face of the organization to the judge and jury. Answer C is not the best answer; an HR professional is likely to be called on to collect data during discovery.

24. **Answer A is the best answer.** It would not be advisable or appropriate to consider each vendors' technological resources and capabilities (as compared to the project requirements) until you have ascertained whether outsourcing is an appropriate option. Engaging in those sorts of comparisons at this point in the process is predicated on the assumption (perhaps an implicit one, and perhaps a faulty one) that outsourcing is an appropriate option. Instead, these comparisons should not be made until—and unless—you determine that outsourcing is, in fact, an appropriate option. Answer B is not the best answer; comparing talents and abilities that are available internally to talents and abilities that are available through outsourcing is an appropriate consideration to engage in when determining whether outsourcing might be an appropriate option. Answer C is not the best answer; the importance and complexity of the function that is being considered for outsourcing is an appropriate factor to consider when determining whether outsourcing might be an appropriate option. Answer D is not the best answer; the degree of variability in transaction volume of the function that is being considered for outsourcing is an appropriate factor to consider when determining whether outsourcing might be an appropriate option.

25. **Answer A is the best answer.** Less value can be gleaned from speaking with former clients from several years ago than from the choices offered through the other answers. Answer B is not the best answer; ascertaining a potential vendor's recent performance is more valuable than historical performance because performance can change (or erode) over time. Answer C is not the best answer; information of significant value can be gleaned from comparing each vendor's experience to what is required by the project. Answer D is not the best answer; information of significant value can be gleaned from exploring each vendor's commitment to quality.

26. **Answer D is the best answer.** An oral contract can be created when an agent of the employer promises some benefit or right. The term *agent* is legal, and involved, but of the four individuals listed in the question, the one that is least likely to be considered an agent would be a co-worker. Answer A is not the best answer; a full-time recruiter would be more likely than a co-worker to create an oral contract. Answer B is not the best answer; a hiring manager—even if he or she interviews only for his or her open positions—is more likely than a co-worker to create an oral contract (it only takes one interview, and maybe even one comment, to create an oral contract). Answer C is not the best answer; an employee's current supervisor is more likely to create an oral contract than an employee's current co-worker is.

27. **Answer D is the best answer.** According to equity theory, employees are less likely to accept a situation that they perceive to be inequitable as is than they are to take some sort of action to rectify that inequity. Neither answer A nor answer B is the best answer; according to equity theory, employees who feel they are being treated unfairly might seek to modify their inputs or outputs, or encourage others to modify their inputs or outputs. Answer C is not the best answer; equity theory asserts that people who believe they are being treated unfairly will seek, in one way or another, to make a change that diminishes or eliminates that inequity.

28. **Answer D is the best answer.** *Harris v. Forklift Systems, 1993*, established the reasonable person standard. Answer A is not the best answer; in *Taxman v. Board of Education of Piscataway, 1993*, the Supreme Court ruled that, in the absence of underrepresentation as demonstrated and documented through an affirmative action plan, organizations cannot take race into account when making decisions relative to who will be laid off and who will be retained (and that doing so would constitute a violation of Title VII of the Civil Rights Act of 1964). Answer B is not the best answer; in *Meritor Savings Bank v. Vinson, 1986*, the Supreme Court ruled that a claim of "hostile environment" sexual harassment does constitute a form of sex discrimination actionable under Title VII of the 1964 Civil Rights Act. Answer C is not the best answer; in *St. Mary's Honor Center v. Hicks, 1993*, the Supreme Court ruled that to ultimately prevail in an allegation of discrimination under Title VII of the Civil Rights Act of 1964, the charging party must go beyond a prima facie case and *actually prove* that the employer's reasons for an employment action are, in fact, discriminatory.

29. **Answer B is the best answer.** Ishikawa's fishbone diagram (also known as the cause-and-effect diagram or the Ishikawa diagram) presents a visual representation of factors that impact whether a desired outcome will be obtained. Ishikawa believed that, by presenting all of the possible factors that can contribute to a particular result, any potential process imperfections can be identified in advance and eliminated. Answer A is not the best answer; the Pareto Chart (based on the Pareto Principle) visually depicts the 80–20 rule. Answer C is not the best answer; although Ishikawa dramatically increased worldwide awareness and acceptance of

the idea of quality circles, quality circles are not directly related to his fishbone diagram. Answer D is not the best answer; histograms depict information about a single factor, whereas the Ishikawa diagram depicts information about multiple factors.

30. **Answer A is the best answer.** ADEA prohibits discrimination based on age for individuals age 40 (not age 18) and above. Some states, however, have established age thresholds that are lower. Answer B is not the best answer; the ADEA does cover private employers with 20 or more employees, state and local governments (including school districts), employment agencies, and labor organizations. Answer C is not the best answer; the ADEA does not establish an upper cap, or an age at which it again becomes legal to discriminate against individuals based on age (although it did at one time). Answer D is not the best answer; ADEA is subject to certain exceptions, and does place certain requirements on employers, particularly with respect to benefits plans, coverage, and early retirement incentives.

31. **Answer D is the best answer.** The *A* in KSAs refers to abilities, which can be defined as specific traits required to successfully perform a position. Answer A is not the best answer; the *A* in KSAs does not refer to attitude. Answer B is not the best answer; this answer defines knowledge, the *K* in KSAs. Answer C is not the best answer; this answer defines skill, the *S* in KSAs.

32. **Answer C is the best answer.** HR adds value to this process by asking our clients questions

   ▸ That enable us to collect information.

   ▸ That help us to collaboratively ascertain the underlying problems.

   ▸ That can help us work with managers to distinguish problems from symptoms.

Answer A is not the best answer; although a manager might be convinced of what the problem is and/or of what the solution should be, the manager's assessment is not necessarily 100% complete or correct, so it is not advisable to automatically commit to implementing it. (Instead, find another way to demonstrate your commitment to that manager, to her problem, and—ultimately—to building a relationship with her.) Answer B is not the best answer for a related reason; at this point, you don't truly know what the problem is, so it is not possible to suggest a solution. Additionally, if you use this approach, you are dismissing the manager's opinions and experience, and you risk damaging your relationship with the manager (narcissism won't get you very far in your role as an HR professional). Answer D is not the best answer; it assumes that the manager's assessment of the problem is 100% complete and correct, and that the proposed solution is the best possible intervention.

33. **Answer D is the best answer.** In concert with counsel, develop a policy that requires that current and former employees sign a carefully worded release before information can be released to a third party. This might include designating what information *can* be released, as well as acknowledging what information *must be* released (for instance, to avoid a claim that the organization withheld truthful negative information about the employee). Answer A is not the best answer; refusing to provide any employee references could result in the employer concealing truthful negative information about the employee. Answer B is not the best answer; providing only titles, dates of employment, and final salary information when providing references could still result in a tort claim alleging that the employer concealed truthful negative information about an employee. Answer C is not the best answer; while outsourcing might anesthetize an organization to the fear of litigation, it will not immunize the organization from its consequences.

34. **Answer C is the best answer.** Defined contribution plans are increasing, not decreasing, in popularity. Answer A is not the best answer; it is true that, unlike defined benefit plans, defined contribution plans do not promise a specific monthly benefit (or total benefit) at retirement. Answer B is not the best answer; defined contribution plans do shift the risk away from the employer (which is where it rests for defined benefit plans) and back onto the employee. Answer D is not the best answer; 401(k) plans, employee stock ownership plans, and profit-sharing plans are examples of defined contribution plans.

35. **Answer A is the best answer.** In *Taxman v. Board of Education of Piscataway, 1993,* the Supreme Court ruled that, in the absence of underrepresentation as demonstrated and documented through an affirmative action plan, organizations cannot take race into account when making decisions relative to who will be laid off and who will be retained (and that doing so would constitute a violation of Title VII of the Civil Rights Act of 1964).

36. **Answer B is the best answer.** The Revenue Act of 1978 resulted in the creation of two very important employee benefits: section 125 plans and 401(k) plans. Answer A is not the best answer; passed in 1985, COBRA requires employers who employed 20 or more people during the prior year to offer continuation of group health care coverage to employees and their family members who experience certain qualifying events—events that would have otherwise resulted in the discontinuation of their health insurance benefits. Answer C is not the best answer; HIPAA has two main focuses: the security and portability of health care coverage and privacy considerations. Answer D is not the best answer; an amendment to ERISA, REA incorporated a number of key revisions, many of which addressed the concerns of former spouses (in the event of divorce) and surviving spouses (in the event of death).

37. **Answer A is the best answer.** A cash balance plan is a defined benefit plan that expresses the promised benefit in terms of a stated account balance. Answer B is not the best answer; a cash balance plan is a defined benefit plan, but it doesn't express the promised benefit in terms of a specific monthly benefit (like other defined benefits plans do). Answer C is not the best answer; a cash balance plan is not a defined contribution plan. Answer D is not the best answer; a cash balance

plan is not a defined contribution plan, and it doesn't express the promised benefit in terms of a specific monthly benefit.

38. **Answer C is the best answer.** The balanced scorecard does consist of a variety of financial and nonfinancial measures of success and is intended to balance them against each other within the scorecard. Answers A, B, and D are not the best answers; none of them accurately characterizes a balanced scorecard.

39. **Answer C is the best answer.** The Civil Rights Act of 1991 capped damages at $300,000 per employee, not at $500,000 per employee. Answer A is not the best answer; the Civil Rights of 1991 expanded employees' rights. Answer B is not the best answer; the Civil Rights Act of 1991 expanded employees' remedies. Answer D is not the best answer; the Civil Rights Act of 1991 did allow for jury trials for discrimination cases.

40. **Answer A is the best answer.** McClelland's theory speaks to the need that certain individuals have to achieve. Answers B and D are not the best answers; recognition and rewards both relate to the consequences of achievement, rather than to the achievement itself. McClelland, conversely, asserts that individuals with a high need to achieve are focused more on the act of achieving, rather than on the consequences that result from having attained a particular level of achievement. Answer C is not the best answer; equity is a primary motivator in J. Stacy Adams' equity theory, not McClelland's acquired needs theory.

41. **Answer B is the best answer.** Quality circles were brought to the attention of the world by Ishikawa. Answers A, C, and D encompass Juran's three-point quality focus: quality planning, quality improvement, and quality control.

42. **Answer B is the best answer.** The statement that articulates what the organization wants to become in the future is the vision statement. The vision statement should be one important tool used to guide strategic planning, rather than be a product of strategic planning. Answers A, C, and D are not the best answers; each one makes a true statement about strategic planning.

43. **Answer B is the best answer.** Compound resolution refers to a type of medical imaging, not a type of legislation. Answer A is not the best answer; a concurrent resolution is a type of legislation. Answer C is not the best answer; a joint resolution is a type of legislation. Answer D is not the best answer; a simple resolution is a type of legislation.

44. **Answer A is the best answer.** Securing the support and commitment of senior leadership is critical with respect to *demonstrating commitment to the strategic planning process*, rather than with respect to *creating and sustaining credibility during the implementation of a strategic plan*. Answer B is not the best answer; clear, complete, and appropriate documentation of the process is particularly relevant to creating and sustaining credibility during the implementation of a strategic plan. Answer C is not the best answer; a commitment to following through on every step of the process is particularly relevant to creating and sustaining credibility during the implementation of a strategic plan. Answer D is not the best answer; representative participation from all levels of the organization is particularly relevant to creating and sustaining credibility during the implementation of a strategic plan.

45. **Answer C is the best answer.** Answer A, 162.4, is the mean of the numbers in this set. Answer B, 645, is the highest number in this set. Answer D, 87, is the median of the numbers in this set.

46. **Answer C is the best answer.** The paperwork-type functions described here are administrative and task-oriented in nature and are reflective of the way HR was viewed in the past. Answer A is not the best answer; the functions (as described) do not even rise to an operational or tactical level; they are purely administrative in nature. Answers B and D are the best answers; strategic and transformational dimensions of HR focus on a long-term, future-focused approach to the ways in which HR will work with the organization to attain its organizational mission. It looks at business and organizational issues, rather than more traditional HR issues.

47. **Answer C is the best answer.** Job bidding systems deal with jobs that might open at some point in the future, whereas job posting systems deal with jobs that are currently open. Answer A is not the best answer; job bidding systems deal with jobs that might open at some point in the future, whereas job posting systems deal with jobs that are currently open. Answers B and D are not the best answers; job bidding and job posting systems are both directed solely at internal candidates.

48. **Answer C is the best answer.** Employers must allow at least 21 days to consider any right-to-sue waivers that the employer offers in exchange for early retirement benefits. Thus, answers A, B, and D are incorrect.

49. **Answer C is the best answer.** The progress discipline process is predicated on the belief that (assuming that an employee is at least minimally qualified for the position for which he or she was hired) an employee can choose whether to perform his or her job satisfactorily. It is in this way that we establish the foundation for thinking of progressive discipline as an employee relations initiative. Thus, answers A, B, and D are incorrect.

50. **Answer A is the best answer.** According to Herzberg's motivation-hygiene theory, motivation factors have a positive impact on an employee's motivation level *if, and only if*, hygiene factors are acceptable. In this situation, it appears as though neither motivation nor hygiene factors are acceptable. According to Herzberg's theory, it's important to address hygiene factors first to ensure that motivation factors will have a positive impact. Answer B is not the best answer; it jumps straight to motivation factors. Answer C is not the best answer; it takes a "ready, fire, aim" approach. Although employees have communicated that they are unhappy with their pay, that does not necessarily mean that pay levels are inappropriate, that they need to be increased, or that 5% would be the right number to use. Answer D is not the best answer; although it will probably be necessary to collect more information (perhaps through follow-up meetings), it would not be effective (or even well received) to ask employees to give you the same information, in the same way, through the same type of instrument.

51. **Answer D is the best answer.** Hersey and Blanchard's situational leadership model is predicated on the idea that effective leaders are able to demonstrate different leadership styles, with different employees, at different times, under

different circumstances. Answer A is not the best answer; picking one leadership style and sticking to it in a resolute fashion violates that principle. Answer B is not the best answer; the same employee can fall into two, three, or even four quadrants at the same time because quadrants are determined based on each employee's ability to perform a specific function or task, not based on an employee's overall performance. Answer C is not the best answer; an effective leader focuses on an employee's maturity—the degree to which he or she possesses and demonstrates the nontechnical skills required to bring the task to successful completion—as much as that leader focuses on the technical skills required to perform the function or task.

52. **Answer D is the best answer.** Willingness to change is not one of Knowles's five key assumptions about how adults learn. Answer A is not the best answer; the learner's need to know is one of Knowles's five key assumptions about how adults learn. Answer B is not the best answer; the learner's readiness to learn is one of Knowles's five key assumptions about how adults learn. Answer C is not the best answer; the learner's self concept is one of Knowles's five key assumptions about how adults learn.

53. **Answer B is the best answer.** A plan provider that offers mental health benefits would be exempt from MHPA requirements if actual claims costs increase 1% or more because of the application of MHPA's requirements. Answer A is not the best answer; a plan provider with fewer than 51 people (not 15 people) would be exempt from MHPA requirements. Answer C is not the best answer; a plan provider's costs would need to increase more than 1% in terms of actual claims—not in terms of insurance premiums—for that plan provider to be exempt from MPHA. Answer D—"never"—is not the best answer because answer B provides a legitimate example of when a plan provider that offers mental health benefits would be exempt from MHPA.

54. **Answer B is the best answer.** COBRA requires plan providers to offer plan participants the opportunity to continue participating in the plan provider's group health care plans. Answer A is not the best answer; COBRA does not require plan providers to offer plan participants the opportunity to continue participating in wellness programs or long-term disability insurance. Answer C is not the best answer; a plan participant's ability to join a different group health care plan is irrelevant to the plan provider's obligation to offer the plan participant the opportunity to continue participating in its group healthcare plan. Answer D is not the best answer; COBRA does not require plan providers to offer plan participants the opportunity to continue participating in any benefit programs other than group health care plans.

55. **Answer B is the best answer.** According to the Equal Pay Act, the substantial equality of job content is assessed based on effort, skill, responsibility, and working conditions (more often listed in the order of skill, effort, responsibility, and working conditions). Neither answer A nor answer D is the best answer; scope is not one of the four factors used by the Equal Pay Act to assess substantial equality. Answer C is not the best answer; neither scope nor accountability are among the four factors used by the Equal Pay Act to assess substantial equality.

56. **Answer C is the best answer.** Broadbanding is an approach in which organizations choose to establish and use a relatively small number of grades. Answer A is not the best answer; although one reason that organizations might choose to use broadbands could be to support the implementation of a flatter organization, this process or approach is not known as flattening. Answer B is not the best answer; although one reason that organizations might choose to use broadbands could be to shift employees' focus away from traditional promotions and place it instead on career growth, this process or approach is not known as growthbanding. Answer D is not the best answer; although the institution of broadbanding might result in the collapsing and combining of a large number of grades into a smaller number of grades, this process or approach is not known as gradesharing.

57. **Answer D is the best answer.** Crosby's fourth Absolute of Quality Management states specifically that quality is not measured by production indexes; rather, it is measured by the price of nonconformance. Answers A, B, and C are not the best answers; each one identifies one of Crosby's four Absolutes of Quality Management.

58. **Answer D is the best answer.** It is the mission statement, not the vision statement, that should speak to the nature of the organization's business or purpose, its customers, and sometimes even its employees and its role in the community. Answer A is not the best answer; an organization's statement of vision is a descriptive and inspirational statement that articulates where the organization wants to be and what it wants to become in the future. Answer B is not the best answer; an organization's vision statement should give employees an awareness that they have a meaningful opportunity to be part of something bigger than themselves. Answer C is not the best response; a vision statement should motivate and inspire employees to aspire to the legacy that the vision can create, and that it ultimately can leave behind.

59. **Answer B is the best answer.** If the president takes no action for 10 days while Congress is in session, the legislation automatically becomes law. Answer A is not the best answer; if the president takes no action for 10 days while Congress is not in session, the legislation dies (this is called a pocket veto). Answer C is not the best answer; the president does not have the option of sending legislation back for more committee work. Answer D is not the best answer; if Congress sends a bill to the president, there is nothing to override. In addition, the president cannot override Congress; rather, it is Congress who could override a bill that the president vetoes.

60. **Answer B is the best answer.** Preemployment medical exams can be conducted only if the medical exam is job related and consistent with business necessity. Answer A is not the best answer; an organization cannot require all candidates who apply for a position to take a preemployment medical exam because an employer can only require a candidate to take a medical exam if an offer or conditional offer of employment has already been extended. Answer C is not the best answer; the ADA does not specify who can or cannot conduct a preemployment medical exam. Answer D is not the best answer; a candidate's self-disclosures about a disability

that might require a reasonable accommodation is unrelated to whether and when a preemployment medical exam can be conducted.

61. **Answer B is the best answer.** Employers covered under EO 11246 are not required to file internal reports relative to the number of charges of discrimination that have been filed based on race, gender, and veterans status during the length of each AAP (this might be a good moment to point out, once again, that affirmative action is different from, and should not be confused with, protections against discrimination afforded by EEO laws). Answer A is not the best answer; the internal audit system does require covered employers to monitor records of all personnel activity, including referrals, placements, transfers, promotions, terminations, and compensation at all levels to ensure the nondiscriminatory policy is carried out. Answer C is not the best answer; the internal audit system does require covered employers to review report results with all levels of management. Answer D is not the best answer; the internal audit system does require covered employers to advise top management of program effectiveness and submit recommendations to improve unsatisfactory performance

62. **Answer A is the best answer.** Trend analysis can provide information that can be helpful in developing a better understanding of business cycles. Answer B is not the best answer; ratio analysis, rather than trend analysis, can become the basis for a number of applications, including forecasting staffing needs. Answer C is not the best answer; ratio analysis, not trend analysis, looks at how variables can change over time. Answer D is not the best answer; multiple regression analysis, not trend analysis, looks at the relationship between one dependent variable and more than one independent variable.

63. **Answer B is the best answer.** WARN covers employers with 100 or more full-time employees (this is a somewhat oversimplified explanation; see www.dol.gov for more details). Answer A is not the best answer; the ADA covers employers with 15 or more employees (this is a somewhat oversimplified explanation; see www.eeoc.gov for more details). Answer C is not the best answer; Title VII of the Civil Rights Act of 1964 covers all private employers, among others (this is a somewhat oversimplified explanation; see www.eeoc.gov for more details). Answer D is not the best answer; the ADEA covers private employers with 20 or more employees (this is a somewhat oversimplified explanation; see www.eeoc.gov for more details).

64. **Answer B is the best answer.** In learning organizations, employees at all levels do strive to acquire knowledge and develop skills that will enable them, individually and collectively, to attain higher levels of performance. Answer A is not the best answer; the size of an HRD/training budget does not necessarily correlate to the degree to which an organization is truly a learning organization. Answer C is not the best answer; although learning organizations often manifest their commitment through training, training is not the *only* type of HRD initiative through which an organization can demonstrate that commitment. Answer D is not the best answer; linking performance appraisal to training and development is not the only way in which an organization can demonstrate its commitment to being a learning organization (although it is often a good idea).

65. **Answer D is the best answer.** Managers who have not consistently maintained documentation throughout the entire performance measurement period are more likely to rely upon recent events when preparing an employee's performance appraisal. Answer A is not the best answer; although it *is possible* for a manager who has recently observed a direct report to experience the recency effect, managers who did not maintain consistent documentation throughout the performance measurement period are even more likely to experience the recency effect. Answer B is not the best answer, for a similar reason. Answer C is not the best answer; a manager who maintained documentation during earlier portions of the performance measurement period is less likely to experience the recency effect than a manager who did not maintain such documentation.

66. **Answer D is the best answer.** For overtime purposes under the FLSA, hours worked would include all hours during which an employee was required or allowed (suffered or permitted) to perform work. Answer A is not the best answer; the hours for which an employee receives compensation might include hours during which an employee was not suffered or permitted to work (such as vacation pay, jury duty pay, and so on). Answer B is not the best answer; whether an employee was granted approval to work (prior or subsequent) is irrelevant to calculating hours worked. Answer C is not the best answer; hours worked would include hours that an employee is suffered or permitted to work, not just those hours during which the employee actually performs work.

67. **Answer B is the best answer.** The Equal Pay Act prohibits discrimination based on sex in the payment of wages or benefits to men and women who perform substantially equal (but not identical) work for the same employer and within the same establishment. Answer A is not the best answer; the work in question has to be substantially equal, not the same or identical. Answer C is not the best answer; the work in question must be performed for the same employer and within the same establishment. Answer D is not the best answer; the work in question must be substantially equal (not the same or identical) and must be performed for the same employer and within the same establishment.

68. **Answer D is the best answer.** Grades represent a hierarchy of levels into which jobs of similar internal, not external, worth are categorized. Because of this distinction, answer A is not the best answer; grades do represent a hierarchy of levels into which jobs of similar internal worth are categorized. Answer B is not the best answer; jobs within the same grade do share a similar level of value or worth to the organization. Answer C is not the best answer; jobs within the same grade are paid according to a corresponding compensation range.

69. **Answer C is the best answer.** Unemployment insurance is funded solely through *employer* taxes (except in only three states, where employees contribute as well). Answer A is not the best answer; unemployment insurance is a mandatory benefit program. Answer B is not the best answer; in general, the maximum period for receiving unemployment insurance benefits is 26 weeks (although the federal government may choose to extend the benefit period during difficult economic times). Answer D is not the best answer; unemployment insurance was established

as part of the federal Social Security Act of 1935 and is administered at the state level.

70. **Answer A is the best answer.** Job slotting is not expensive or difficult to administer (in fact, its inexpensive cost and ease of administration are two of its advantages). Answer B is not the best answer; job slotting increases the likelihood that a job will be evaluated based on the person, not the position. Answer C is not the best answer; job slotting can be used only when a job structure is already in place. Answer D is not the best answer; as with any nonquantitative job evaluation method, there is a greater chance with job slotting that rater error and subjectivity can taint the job evaluation process.

71. **Answer C is the best answer.** Section 7 of the NLRA *does* protect associational rights for employees who belong to a union, as well as for those who do not. Employers need to be careful not to interfere with protected concerted activities even in workplaces that are nonunionized. Answer A is not the best answer; protected concerted activity refers to associational rights that are granted to employee through the NLRA. Answer B is not the best answer; the NLRA does protect associational rights for employees who belong to a union. Answer D is not the best answer; employees have the right to refrain from engaging in protected concerted activities.

72. **Answer A is the best answer.** Charges must be filed with the EEOC within 180 days of the alleged discriminatory act when there is no FEPA. Answer B is not the best answer; the EEOC usually maintains responsibility for handling charges that are filed with it if the basis for the charge is also protected under state or local law. Answer C is not the best answer; the FEPA usually maintains responsibility for handling charges that are filed with it if the basis for the charge is also protected under federal law. Answer D is not the best answer; a charge may not be dual filed with the EEOC when state or local EEO law is more protective than the corresponding federal law.

73. **Answer C is the best answer.** Passed in 1985, COBRA covers employers who employed 20 or more employees during the prior year. Thus, answers A, B, and D are incorrect.

74. **Answer C is the best answer.** Although a vaccine for HBV does exist, that vaccine must be made available to at-risk employees; employers may not require employees to be vaccinated against HBV. Answer A is not the best answer; HBV is transmitted through blood and other bodily fluids. Answer B is not the best answer; a person with HBV is considered to be a person with a disability. Answer D is not the best answer; people with HBV might experience a wide range of symptoms.

75. **Answer D is the best answer.** *Washington v. Davis, 1976,* determined that a test that has an adverse impact on a protected class is still lawful, as long as the test can be shown to be valid and job related. Answer A is not the best answer; the key issue in *McDonnell Douglas Corp v. Green, 1973,* was disparate treatment and establishing a prima facie case. Answer B is not the best answer; the key issue in *Griggs v. Duke Power, 1971,* was adverse impact. Answer C is not the best answer; the key issue in *Meritor Savings Bank v. Vinson, 1986,* was sexual harassment.

76. **Answer B is the best answer.** Onboarding refers to the new hire orientation process, and a background investigation is far more likely to occur during the preemployment reference checking phase than during the new hire orientation process. Answer A is not the best answer; the onboarding process often includes a tour of the facility. Answer C is not the best answer; the onboarding process often gives newly hired employees the opportunity to meet with current employees. Answer D is not the best answer; the onboarding process should include a review of the mission of the organization, and of how that mission relates to the position.

77. **Answer B is the best answer.** A multi-rater survey refers to a performance feedback and management tool in which one individual receives feedback on his or her performance from a variety of people, holding a variety of perspectives. A multi-rater, or 360-degree, survey is different from employee surveys (answer A), attitude surveys (answer C), and climate surveys (answer D), all of which refer to surveys that are distributed throughout the organization to collect information on a variety of topics that are relevant to the entire organization—not just to one single person.

78. **Answer C is the best answer.** The AFL-CIO is an example of a federation, which is a group of national unions. Answer A is not the best answer; the AFL-CIO is not a national union. Answer B is not the best answer; the AFL-CIO is not a local union. Answer D is not the best answer; the AFL-CIO is not an international labor organization.

79. **Answer B is the best answer.** One of the two omissions that the Wagner Act sought to address was the identification of behaviors and practices that would be considered ULPs on the part of unions. Neither answer A nor answer D is the best answer; the Wagner Act did identify behaviors and practices that would be considered ULPs on the part of employers/managers. Answer C is not the best answer; an employee cannot commit a ULP unless he or she is acting on behalf of a union or an employer, in which case his or her role in that capacity would eclipse the significance of his or her role as an individual and is therefore already addressed through the Wagner Act.

80. **Answer C is the best answer.** In *Circuit City Stores, Inc. v. Adams, 2001,* the court ruled that requiring employees to sign mandatory arbitration agreements as a condition of employment is legal, and that such agreements are enforceable under the Federal Arbitration Act (FAA). Answer A is not the best answer; in *NLRB v. Phoenix Mutual Life Insurance Co., 1948,* it was confirmed that union and nonunion employees enjoy associational rights afforded under the NLRA. Answer B is not the best answer; less than 10 months after the Circuit City case, the court ruled in *EEOC v. Waffle House, Inc., 2002,* that although the existence of a signed mandatory arbitration agreement precluded the employee from being allowed to file a private lawsuit, it did *not* preclude the EEOC from seeking its own independent action against an employer. Answer D is not the best answer; *NLRB v. Henry Colder, 1990,* was a case in which an employer was found to have committed an unfair labor practice by interfering with protected concerted activities.

81. **Answer A is the best answer.** Workers' compensation programs (not the OSH Act) are designed to enable workers to obtain relief (in particular, monetary relief) for work-related injuries. Answer B is not the best answer; OSH Act did establish a means of enforcement. Answer C is not the best answer; OSH Act did encourage and assist states to take steps to ensure safe and healthful workplaces. Answer D is not the best answer; OSH Act did provide for relevant research, information, education, and training.

82. **Answer B is the best answer.** Technostructural interventions focus on improving what work is done, as well as the ways and processes through which the work is done. This category or OD intervention looks at job design, job redesign, job restructuring, work content, workflow, work processes, and the like. Answer A is not the best answer; human processual interventions seek to effect change and impact relationships within (and between) groups and individuals, on more of an interpersonal level. Answer C is not the best answer; sociotechnical interventions focus on groups in the workplace and the ways in which those groups can become more (or semi) autonomous with respect to the performance and execution of the work. Answer D is not the best answer; organization transformation change interventions focus on the organization as a complex human system that must be continually examined and reexamined.

83. **Answer B is the best answer.** The PBGC (Pension Benefit Guaranty Corporation) is funded by insurance premiums that are paid by plan sponsors, not by tax dollars (payroll or otherwise). Funding for the PBGC also comes from investment income, assets from underfunded pension plans it has taken over, and recoveries from companies formerly responsible for those plans. Answer A is not the best answer; the PBGC is a government corporation created by ERISA. Answer C is not the best answer; the PBGC protects participants in most defined benefit plans and cash balance plans (within certain limitations). Answer D is not the best answer; the PBGC ensures that participants will receive payments of certain benefits if a covered plan is terminated.

84. **Answer A is the best answer.** Assessing strengths and weaknesses is an inward-looking process. Answer B is not the best answer; the external portion of the SWOT analysis refers to assessing opportunities and threats. By default, then, neither answer C nor answer D can be the best answer.

85. **Answer B is the best answer.** *McKennon v. Nashville Banner Publishing Co., 1995,* established that an employer will be held accountable for discriminatory employment actions *even if* it discovers evidence after taking the discriminatory employment action that would have led the employer to that same employment action for legitimate, nondiscriminatory reasons. Thus, answers A, C, and D are incorrect.

86. **Answer C is the best answer.** Although FMLA entitles employees to take job-protected leave to care for an immediate family member, siblings are not included in the definition of an immediate family member. Answer A is not the best answer; FMLA does entitle employees to take job-protected leave for the birth and care of the newborn child of the employee. Answer B is not the best answer; FMLA does entitle employees to take job-protected leave for placement of a son or daughter for adoption or foster care with the employee. Answer D is not the best answer; FMLA does entitle employees to take job-protected leave when the employee is unable to work because of a serious health condition.

87. **Answer C is the best answer.** Factor comparison assigns a monetary value, not a point value, to each level within each factor. Answer A is not the best answer; the factor comparison method of job evaluation does provide a degree of objectivity and reliability across raters. Answer B is not the best answer; factor comparison does evaluate each job with respect to each compensable factor. Answer D is not the best answer; factor comparison involves ranking each compensable factor of each job.

88. **Answer A is the best answer.** The Drug-Free Workplace Act does not require employers to establish an EAP (employee assistance program). In the event an organization does have an EAP (or equivalent program), however, information about that program must be included as part of the employer's drug-free awareness program (answer C). Answer B is not the best answer; the Drug-Free Workplace Act does require employers to establish a drug-free awareness program addressing the dangers of drug use in the workplace and the employer's drug-free policy, and information about programs that are available to employees who use drugs. Answer D is not the best answer; the Drug-Free Workplace Act does require employers to distribute a copy of the workplace substance abuse policy to all employees.

89. **Answer C is the best answer.** Employers can require employees to attend mandatory presentations during which management will present its opinions about unions in general, and about the unionization of its operations. There are certain limitations to this, however, to which the employer must adhere (for instance, these "captive audience meetings" cannot be held within 24 hours of the actual election). It is also worth noting that although an employer can require an employee to attend captive audience meetings, the employer cannot truly require the employee to listen. Answer A is not the best answer; telling workers that the organization will fire or punish them if they engage in any union activity would constitute a ULP. Answer B is not the best answer; granting workers wage increases or special concessions in an effort to bribe people from joining a union would constitute a ULP. Answer D is not the best answer; telling workers that existing benefits will be discontinued if the workplace is unionized would constitute a ULP.

90. **Answer B is the best answer.** An employer who makes a hot cargo agreement has not refused to stop doing business with another entity; instead, it has agreed to stop doing business with another entity (answer A), thus helping to protect union work (answer D) by allowing union members to refuse to handle or process work

produced by nonunion entities. Answer C is not the best answer; an employer who makes a hot cargo agreement has committed a ULP.

91. **Answer B is the best answer.** Make no promises, and offer no assurances—just be open, honest, and credible in the way in which you communicate with the employees who remain. Answer A is not the best answer; there is no way to know whether additional layoffs will occur, and making any statements to that effect could unintentionally create an implied contract with employees. Answer C is not the best answer for the same reason. Answer D is not the best answer; minimizing the frequency or amount of communication in which you engage with employees will only add to their feelings of uncertainty (and, potentially, mistrust).

92. **Answer C is the best answer.** Although it is important to perform due diligence, performing due diligence does not insulate an organization from exposure relating from negligent hiring claims. One way in which this can happen is if stated job requirements for a particular position that are used as a guide through the hiring process do not reflect the skills or credentials that are actually required to perform a particular position. Answer A is not the best answer; negligent hiring does refer to the process of hiring an employee without engaging in appropriate due diligence. Answer B is not the best answer; appropriate due diligence could include looking into items such as the candidate's credentials and prior work experience. Answer D is not the best answer; it is quite possible that negligent hiring tort claims might be filed after an employee who was hired through a flawed hiring process inflicts some sort of harm on another person.

93. **Answer C is the best answer.** It can be challenging to replicate identical conditions across various focus groups, even when focus group meetings are conducted by the same individual. These differences in conditions could taint/affect the consistency of the data that is collected. Answer A is not the best answer; skillfully facilitated focus groups can generate a great deal of valuable data. Answer B is not the best answer; the dynamics that exist in focus groups often can lead to a more synergistic and productive data collection experience. Answer D is not the best answer; focus groups do, in fact, provide a qualitative approach to data collection.

94. **Answer B is the best answer.** Although some organizations do choose to consider each incumbent's most recent salary or wage rate when setting base pay rates for new hires, this should be the least important of the four factors listed (if it is even factored in at all). Many variables could render the newly hired employee's most recent rate of pay irrelevant—for instance, the employee might have held a different position, in a different sector, in a different city, in a different industry, at a different time, and so on. Answer A is not the best answer; the relative worth of the job to the organization is likely to affect how base pay for new hires is set. Answer C is not the best answer; the market rate for the position in the marketplace is likely to affect how base pay for new hires is set. Answer D is not the best answer; whether the job requires hot skills is likely to affect how base pay for new hires is set.

95. **Answer A is the best answer.** A yellow dog contract is a contract or agreement between an employer and an employee that states that the employer will give the employee a job, as long as the employee agrees not to join or have any involvement with a labor union. Answer B is not the best answer; an employer who makes a hot cargo agreement agrees to stop doing business with another entity (thus helping to protect union work by allowing union members to refuse to handle or process work produced by nonunion entities). Answer C is not the best answer; a featherbedding agreement states that the employer will pay wages to union members whether or not their work is needed. Answer D is not the best answer; a union shop agreement exists when an employer agrees that anyone who is hired by the organization must join the union.

96. **Answer C is the best answer.** Neither economic nor ULP strikes are related to the filing of an EEO charge and are not likely to factor into the decision-making process of whether to settle a charge. Answer A is not the best answer; an organization might decide to settle a charge to avoid the costs (financial as well as nonfinancial) of responding to (fighting) that charge. Answer B is not the best answer; an organization might decide to settle a charge to avoid bad press, which can harm business, even when no evidence is found to support the charging party's allegation of discrimination. Answer D is not the best answer; an organization might decide to settle a charge of discrimination if it believes that there is a possibility that unlawful discrimination might have taken place or when evidence exists that strongly supports that possibility.

97. **Answer B is the best answer.** There is no specific OSHA requirement mandating the creation of a safety committee. Many organizations, however, do find that safety committees can make significant contributions toward achieving other health and safety objectives or mandates. Answer A is not the best answer; one purpose of a safety committee is to build and maintain interest in health and safety issues. Answer C is not the best answer; one purpose of a safety committee is to reinforce safety as part of the fabric of the organization's culture. Answer D is not the best answer; one purpose of a safety committee is to provide a forum for discussing health- and safety-related issues.

98. **Answer A is the best answer.** *Johnson v. Santa Clara County Transportation Agency, 1987*, established that gender can be used as a factor in the selection process if there is underrepresentation in a particular job classification, as long as the AAP does not set forth a quota. Thus, answers B, C, and D are incorrect.

99. **Answer C is the best answer.** Diversity can—and, some would argue, should—encompass attributes or characteristics such as communication styles, regional backgrounds, or affiliation with unions, to name just a few examples. Answer A is not the best answer; diversity is not legally mandated (although it makes sound sense from an organizational and business perspective). Answer B is not the best answer; diversity initiatives do not have governmentally mandated reporting requirements. Answer D is not the best answer; diversity can, and should, extend well beyond the boundaries of legally protected classes.

100. **Answer D is the best answer.** Although there is no mandatory retirement age (with few exceptions, such as pilots who must retire from that particular position at age 60), there is a requirement that everyone must start receiving retirement benefits by age 70. Answer A is not the best answer; the earliest age at which a worker can retire and still receive benefits is 62. Answer B is not the best answer; full retirement age ranges between age 65 and age 67, depending on the year of birth. Answer C is not the best answer; workers who work beyond their full retirement age will increase their monthly retirement. The longer they work past their full retirement age, the more their monthly retirement income will be.

101. **Answer A is the best answer.** An employee who was constructively discharged was subjected to such intolerable working conditions that remaining employed with the organization was impossible. Answers B, C, and D are not the best answers because none of those definitions accurately defines constructive discharge.

102. **Answer D is the best answer.** Unless significant underutilization exists, placement goals are set for minorities (in total). If, however, significant underutilization exists (in which case it might be necessary to set goals for particular minority groups). Answer A is not the best answer; placement goals must be established for areas in which underutilization exists. Answer B is not the best answer; placement goals must be pursued through good faith efforts. Answer C is not the best answer; placement goals must be set at an annual percentage rate that is equivalent to the availability figure for women and/or minorities.

103. **Answer C is the best answer.** McGregor's motivation theory—Theory X and Theory Y—is predicated on the assumption that different managers have different perspectives on employees. Answers A and B are not the best answer; McGregor's theory recognizes that managers can ascribe to either of these perspectives; neither is necessarily primary across-the-board. Answer D is not the best answer; Maslow's theory predated McGregor's theory.

104. **Answer D is the best answer.** According to Hersey and Blanchard's situational leadership model, low task and low relationship dimensions correspond to the "delegating" quadrant. Answer A is not the best answer; "telling" corresponds to high task and low relationship. Answer B is not the best answer; "selling" corresponds to high task and high relationship. Answer C is not the best answer; "participating" corresponds to high relationship and low task.

105. **Answer B is the best answer.** Correlation mathematically determines whether there is a demonstrated relationship between two factors or entities. Answer A is not the best answer; a negative correlation *does indicate* that a relationship *does* exist between two factors. Answer C is not the best answer; the correlation coefficient is a number between −1 and 1 that defines the strength of a relationship between two factors. Answer D is not the best answer; the correlation coefficient speaks to the strength of a relationship, not to causative dimensions of that relationship.

106. **Answer A is the best answer.** According to the revised FLSA guidelines, to qualify for an administrative exemption under the FLSA, the employee's primary duty must be the performance of office or nonmanual work directly related to the management or general business operations of the employer or the employer's customers. Answer B is not the best answer; the requirement that "the employee's primary duty must be the performance of work requiring advanced knowledge, defined as work which is predominantly intellectual in character and which includes work requiring the consistent exercise of discretion and judgment" applies to the learned professional exemption, not the administrative exemption. Answer C is not the best answer; the requirement that "the employee's suggestions and recommendations as to the hiring, firing, advancement, promotion, or any other change of status of other employees must be given particular weight" is one portion of one of the requirements under the executive exemption. Answer D is not the best answer; FairPay revisions eliminated references to percentages of time spent performing exempt and non-exempt tasks.

107. **Answer A is the best answer.** The FLSA established minimum standards affecting full-time and part-time workers in the private sector and in federal, state, and local governments pertaining to minimum wage, overtime, record keeping, and child labor. Answer B is not the best answer; the FLSA does not address or establish standards relating to worker's compensation or unemployment insurance. Answer C is not the best answer; FLSA does not address or establish standards relating to wage garnishments. Answer D is not the best answer; the FLSA does not address or establish standards relating to unemployment insurance and wage garnishments.

108. **Answer D is the best answer.** Sarbanes-Oxley (SOX) establishes a requirement to disclose whether the company has adopted a code of ethics that applies to the company's key officers, not to the company as a whole. Key officers include, at a minimum, the company's principal executive officer, principal financial officer, principal accounting officer or controller, or persons performing similar functions. Answer A is not the best answer; SOX does prohibit insider trading during certain pension plan blackout periods. Answer B is not the best answer; SOX does require the establishment of whistleblower protection in a wide variety of situations for employees who report fraud against shareholders. Answer C is not the best answer; SOX does require plan administrators to provide 30-day written notice in advance of blackout periods to individual account plan participants and beneficiaries.

109. **Answer C is the best answer.** One key potential problem that HR professionals need to be aware of is the possibility that employee groups could be found to be company dominated and, therefore, be rendered illegal. Although employee participation groups are neither legal nor illegal by definition, the way in which they are administrated can have a huge impact on whether any particular group is deemed to be legal or illegal. Answers A, B, and D are not the best answers; none of these answers identifies a frequently identified key potential problem with employee participation groups.

110. **Answer C is the best answer.** Of the four choices in this question, slander is best defined as "a false spoken statement that damages someone's character or reputation." Answer A is not the best answer; even if it damages someone's character or reputation, a statement must be false in order to be considered slanderous. Answer B is not the best answer; "a false statement that damages someone's character or reputation" is more general in that it encompasses spoken and written statements and is therefore a better definition of the term *defamation* than it is of the term *slander*. Answer D is not the best answer; "a false written statement that damages someone's character or reputation" constitutes libel, not slander.

111. **Answer D is the best answer.** Answer B is not the best answer; the Supreme Court found that an employer *is* responsible if its supervisors engage in sexually harassing others *even if it didn't know about that behavior*. The court did point out, however, that although it isn't enough for an organization to just have a policy prohibiting discrimination; one way for employers to reduce this liability is to prove that a sexually harassed employee had reasonable opportunities to take advantage of a good, clear complaint procedure (without fear of retaliation), but had failed to do so (answer C). Answer A is not the best answer; in *Meritor Savings Bank v. Vinson, 1986*, the Supreme Court ruled for the first time that sexual harassment (whether quid pro quo or hostile environment) constitutes a violation of Title VII of the Civil Rights Act of 1964. The Supreme Court specifically rejected the lower court's view that employers are not automatically liable for sexual harassment by their supervisors

112. **Answer B is the best answer.** Whole job ranking does not establish factors about each job that need to be taken into consideration when comparing jobs to each other (this is one of the disadvantages of whole job ranking). Answer A is not the best answer; whole job ranking is easy to perform. Answer C is not the best answer; whole job ranking is relatively inexpensive to maintain. Answer D is not the best answer; whole job ranking does produce a list that will show which jobs are most and least important.

113. **Answer A is the best answer.** For incentive programs to be effective, employees need to believe that they can attain the goals that have been set as part of the incentive program and that the reward that they would earn by attaining those goals is worth it. This model dovetails with Victor Vroom's expectancy theory that asserts that people will put forth effort when they believe that it will result in an outcome, and that that outcome is worthwhile. Thus, answers B, C, and D are incorrect.

114. **Answer A is the best answer.** These functions describe the organizing management function, which speaks particularly to the ways in which the manager obtains and arranges resources. Those resources could include people, facilities, materials, and the like. While executing this function, the manager must also make decisions about reporting relationships within the organization. In short, the manager must work to establish linkages between people, places, and things. Answer B is not the best answer; the controlling function is the one through which the manager assumes more of an oversight role and ascertains the degree to which the planning in which he or she engaged actually produced the desired results. Answer C is not the best answer; planning consists of laying the groundwork for how managers will work toward accomplishing the organization's goals. Answer D is the not the best answer; the coordinating function consists of activities through which the manager brings together all the resources that he or she has organized to accomplish the stated plan.

115. **Answer C is the best answer.** In the context of interviewing, the leniency bias/error occurs when an interviewer applies an inappropriately lenient standard to one or more candidates, resulting in a higher overall assessment of the candidate. Neither answer A nor answer B is the best answer; neither is a legitimate and recognized interviewing bias/error. Answer D is not the best answer; the recency error occurs when the interviewer recalls the most recently interviewed candidates more vividly than candidates who were interviewed earlier in the process.

116. **Answer A is the best answer.** Title VII of the Civil Rights Act of 1964 established five areas of protection: race, color, religion, sex, and national origin. Answer B is not the best answer; age did not become a protected class until the passage of the Age Discrimination in Employment Act (ADEA) in 1967. Answer C is not the best answer; Title VII of the Civil Rights Act of 1964 did not address the question of disability (under any appellation). Answer D is not the best answer; Title VII of the Civil Rights Act of 1964 included color as a protected class.

117. **Answer B is the best answer.** The ADA does not define "undue hardship" in terms of a person's salary. Answer A is not the best answer; the ADA does describe an undue hardship as one that creates significant difficulty (enough to disrupt business operation). Answer C is not the best answer; the ADA does describe an undue hardship as one which changes something about the (essential) nature of the business. Answer D is not the best answer; the ADA describes undue hardship as one which requires a significant financial outlay, but it does not specifically define what significant financial outlay means, as answer B asserts.

118. **Answer A is the best answer.** Although teambuilding is team focused, it also recognizes the criticality of addressing and enhancing the role of the individual within the team. Answer B is not the best answer; teambuilding is an effective means through which team members can explore issues such as communication, problem solving, and trust. Answer C is not the best answer; teambuilding exercises are most effective when they are linked directly and specifically to organizational

objectives and/or to the mission, vision, and/or values of the organization. Answer D is not the best answer; parallels between teambuilding scenarios and their relevance to the workplace might not always be immediately apparent. Sometimes teambuilding exercises are intentionally designed so that they are not immediately recognized as being analogous to the workplace, so that participants may gain greater insights after they do identify those similarities.

119. **Answer A is the best answer.** Taft-Hartley was more specific, in that it identified striking or picketing a health care establishment (not just any employer) without giving the required notice as a ULP that could be committed by a union. Answer B is not the best answer; Taft-Hartley did identity picketing for recognition for more than 30 days without petitioning for an election as a ULP that could be committed by a union. Answer C is not the best answer; Taft-Hartley did identify causing an employer to discriminate against an employee as a ULP that could be committed by a union. Answer D is not the best answer; Taft-Hartley did identify refusing to bargain with the employer of the employees it represents as a ULP that could be committed by a union.

120. **Answer C is the best answer.** The Labor Management Reporting and Disclosure Act (also known as the Landrum-Griffin Act) specifically designated every union official as a *fiduciary*, not as an agent of the union. Answer A is not the best answer; the Landrum-Griffin Act did institute a requirement that unions submit annual financial reporting to the DOL, to document how union members' dues were spent. Answer B is not the best answer; the Landrum-Griffin Act did institute a bill of rights for union members guaranteeing them freedom of speech and periodic secret elections. Answer D is not the best answer; the Landrum-Griffin Act did institute even stronger provisions relative to secondary boycotting and organizational and recognition picketing.

121. **Answer B is the best answer.** Double breasting occurs when a company that owns or operates union as well as nonunion operations shifts work to the nonunion operation in an effort to diminish the impact of the strike. Answer A is not the best answer; featherbedding occurs when an employer agrees to pay wages to union members whether or not their work is needed. Answer C is not the best answer; there is no such expression as *yellow dogging* in labor relations (a yellow dog contract, however, is one in which an employer agrees to give the employee a job, as long as the employee agrees not to join or have any involvement with a labor union). Answer D is not the best answer; there is no such expression as single roofing in labor relations.

122. **Answer B is the best answer.** This formula calculates the cost per trainee, also known as the cost per participant. Answer A is not the best answer; this formula does not yield a calculation of return on investment. Answer C is not the best answer; this formula is unrelated to hiring costs. Answer D is not the best answer; this formula does not represent a cost/benefit analysis.

123. **Answer C is the best answer**. The employee must be compensated either on a salary or fee basis (as defined in the regulations) at a rate not less than $455 per week or, if compensated on an hourly basis, at a rate not less than $27.63 an hour. Answer A is not the best answer; computer employees are not covered under the prevailing wage rate provisions of the Davis-Bacon Act. Answer B and D are incorrect; neither $400 per week nor $500 per week is the rate at which an employee must be compensated to qualify for the computer employee exemption.

124. **Answer B is the best answer.** Current employees who are negatively impacted by consent decrees that were established in an earlier time and which sought to resolve discrimination that was present in an earlier time *may* challenge the validity of such decrees. Answer A is not the best answer; it asserts the opposite. Answer C is not the best answer; *Johnson v. Santa Clara County Transportation Agency, 1987*, established that gender can be used as a factor in the selection process if there is underrepresentation in a particular job classification, as long as the AAP does not set forth a quota. Answer D is not the best answer; there is no case that resulted in this finding.

125. **Answer C is the best answer.** The bottom line is this: Organizations that lead the market with respect to total rewards/compensation offer better total rewards/total compensation packages than their competitors do. It's that simple. For purposes of determining whether an organization leads the market in this way, the balance of direct and indirect compensation pay components is not relevant (answer A), nor is the mix of variable and base pay (answer B), nor is the level of innovation or creativity of the total rewards/total compensation package. All that matters is the total (and multifaceted) value of the package. Answer D is not the best answer; organizations that lead the market do not necessarily choose to offer total compensation packages that are more innovative, creative, typical, and nontraditional than packages being offered by their labor market competitors.

126. **Answer C is the best answer.** Although OSHA might give employers 24 hours notice under certain circumstances, employers may not request a postponement of an inspection until senior leadership is available. Answer A is not the best answer; employers do have the right to request proper identification from the OSHA compliance office. Answer B is not the best answer; employers do have the right to learn the reason for the inspection or investigation. Answer D is not the best answer; employers do have the right to decline admittance to certain areas that contain trade secrets.

127. **Answer C is the best answer.** To qualify for the highly compensated employee exemption under FLSA, an employee must customarily and regularly perform at least one of the duties of an exempt executive, administrative, or professional employee identified in the standard tests for exemption. Answer A is not the best answer; to qualify for the highly compensated employee exemption under FLSA, an employee must earn $100,000 (not $150,000) or more annually (of which at least $455 per week must be paid on a salary or fee basis). Answer B is not the best answer; to qualify for the highly compensated employee exemption under FLSA, an employee must perform (not oversee) office or nonmanual work. Thus, answer D—all of the above—is not the best answer.

128. **Answer B is the best answer.** Although it is true that HR is often viewed as the conscience of the organization, this role/reality should not result in HR "owning" the organization's ethical initiatives. (It is important to remember here that leading is different from owning—a key point for HR professionals to keep in mind.) Conversely, responsibility for ethics must be operationalized and dispersed throughout the organization (answer C). Answer A is not the best answer; HR must play a leadership role with respect to establishing, encouraging, and ensuring ongoing ethical behavior within organizations. Answer D is not the best answer; the organization's code of ethics does need to address a variety of issues from a variety of perspectives (for instance, employees, customers, shareholders, suppliers, and the community at large).

129. **Answer D is the best answer.** The five distinct, yet overlapping, project management processes are initiation, planning, executing, controlling, and closing. Answer A is not the best answer; establishing, developing, implementing, and evaluating are the four steps of strategic planning. Answer B is not the best answer; although it cites the five project management processes, they are not presented in the right order. Answer C is not the best answer; planning, organizing, coordinating, directing, and controlling are the five management functions.

130. **Answer B is the best answer.** HR audits cannot yield strategies; conversely, they yield information that the organization can subsequently use to draw conclusions and develop strategies. Answer A is not the best answer; an HR audit is likely to yield information relative to the usefulness, appropriateness, and effectiveness of the employee handbook. Answer C is not the best answer; an HR audit is likely to yield information about grievances, their causes, and their impact. Answer D is not the best answer; an HR audit is likely to yield information about the degree to which the organization complies with HR-related legal requirements.

131. **Answer C is the best answer.** The exit route standard is a mandatory OSHA standard covering all employers. Answers A and B are not the best answers; although the Emergency Action Plan Standard and Fire Safety Standard are both recommended for all employers, they are not mandatory unless required under a separate OSHA standard. Answer D is not the best answer; the Hazard Communication Standard applies only to those workplaces where there are hazardous materials or chemicals.

132. **Answer B is the best answer.** Interest-based bargaining advocates focus on interests rather than position, not on relationships rather than positions. Answer A is not the best answer; interest-based bargaining does advocate separating the people from the problem. Answer C is not the best answer; interest-based bargaining does advocate generating a variety of options before settling on an agreement. Answer D is not the best answer; interest-based bargaining does advocate insisting that the agreement be based on objective criteria.

133. **Answer B is the best answer.** MSH Act requires at least four inspections per year of underground mines and at least two inspections per year of surface mines. Answer A is not the best answer; MSH Act applies to underground and surface mines. Answer C is not the best answer; MSH Act applies to coal and noncoal mines. Answer D is not the best answer; employees who are covered by MSH Act are exempt from OSH Act.

134. **Answer B is the best answer.** Affinity groups bring together people who share common interests, goals, and/or backgrounds. Answer A is not the best answer; affinity groups do not primarily address safety and security needs. Although members might derive benefits that affect their esteem (answer C) or that enable them to self-actualize (answer D), affinity groups primarily address the need for belonging and love.

135. **Answer C is the best answer.** Direct compensation refers to components that are presented to employees in the form of cash, and indirect compensation refers to components that are presented to employees in forms other than cash (noncash). A flexible spending account is an example of a benefit, not an example of direct compensation. Answer A is not the best answer; hourly wages/base salary is a form of direct compensation. Answer B is not the best answer; shift differentials are a form of direct compensation. Answer D is not the best answer; variable pay is a form of direct compensation.

136. **Answer A is the best answer.** According to the FairPay guidelines, manual laborers and other blue collar workers who perform work involving repetitive operations with their hands, physical skill, and energy *cannot be exempted* from the overtime provisions of FLSA, *no matter how much they earn.* Answers B, C, and D cite positions that, although likely to be non-exempt, still require a case-by-case review, and thus, they are not the best answers.

137. **Answer B is the best answer.** Employee referral programs can result in significant savings in cost-per-hire, not significant increases in cost-per-hire. Answers A is not the best answer; one potential disadvantage of an employee referral program is that if the organization is not particularly diverse (with respect to gender, age, race, education background, or a host of other factors), employee referral programs might perpetuate that lack of diversity. Answer C is not the best answer; one potential disadvantage of an employee referral program is that if an affirmative action plan is in place, and if there are areas of underutilization, an employee referral program is not likely to demonstrate good faith efforts to recruit candidates who are women or minorities. Answer D is not the best answer; one potential disadvantage of an employee referral program is that if the organization has prior patterns of hiring discrimination, employee referral programs are likely to reinforce those patterns.

138. **Answer D is the best answer.** Just as it is critical to distinguish between the position and the incumbent, so too it is important not to confuse actual job requirements—such as KSAs (answer A), credentials (answer B), and physical or mental requirements (answer C)—with any particular candidate's or incumbent's qualifications.

139. **Answer C is the best answer.** Schein recognized and appreciated the formal, as well as the informal, dimensions and expressions of culture. As HR professionals, so must we. Thus, answers A, B, and D are incorrect.

140. **Answer B is the best answer.** Performance appraisal tools that use rating scales require managers (or any other appraisers) to evaluate employee performance on a variety of categories using a multiple point scale (often three, four, or five points). Those categories can consist of individual goals, individual competencies, multiple goals, groups of competencies, and the like. Each point on the scale corresponds to a different level of performance against standards. Answer A is not the best answer; performance appraisal systems that require managers to compare employees against each other are called ranking methods, not rating methods. Answer C is not the best answer; the performance appraisal method that requires managers to indicate statements that are reflective of the employee's performance is called a checklist method. Answer D is not the best answer; the performance appraisal method that requires managers to write a narrative assessment of employee's performance is called the essay method.

141. **Answer A is the best answer.** The ruling in *United Steelworkers* v. *Weber, 1979,* was that affirmative action plans that establish voluntary quotas that have been jointly agreed to by an organization as well as its collective bargaining unit do not constitute race discrimination under Title VII of the Civil Rights Act of 1964. More specifically, the court ruled that "…Congress did not intend to limit traditional business freedom to such a degree as to prohibit all voluntary, race-conscious affirmative action." The ruling went on to say, "It is not necessary in these cases to define the line of demarcation between permissible and impermissible affirmative action plans; it suffices to hold that the challenged Kaiser-USWA plan falls on the permissible side of the line. The purposes of the plan mirror those of the statute, being designed to break down old patterns of racial segregation and hierarchy, and being structured to open employment opportunities for Negroes in occupations which have been traditionally closed to them. At the same time, the plan does not unnecessarily trammel the interests of white employees, neither requiring the discharge of white workers and their replacement with new black hires, nor creating an absolute bar to the advancement of white employees since half of those trained in the program will be white. Moreover, the plan is a temporary measure, not intended to maintain racial balance, but simply to eliminate a manifest racial imbalance." Thus, answers B, C, and D are incorrect.

142. **Answer A is the best answer.** The key issues in *Albemarle Paper v. Moody, 1975,* were job relatedness and job validity. This case established that any tests that are used as part of the hiring or promotional decision making process must be job-related. This applies to any instrument that is used as a test, even if that was not its original purpose. This case also established that employment tests must demonstrate predictive validity, consistent with the Uniform Guidelines for Employee Selection Procedures. Thus, answers B, C, and D are incorrect.

143. **Answer B is the best answer.** An ethics program cannot prevent or minimize organizational politics. Let's be realistic; there aren't many things that can prevent or minimize organizational politics. However, an ethics program *can* prevent or minimize *dysfunctional manifestations of organizational politics*—manifestations that can become destructive or even dangerous. Answer A is not the best answer; preventing or minimizing aggression/violence represents one reason to establish an ethics program. Answer C is not the best answer; preventing or minimizing the erosion of trust represents one reason to establish an ethics program. Answer D is not the best answer; preventing or minimizing cynicism represents one reason to establish an ethics program.

144. **Answer B is the best answer.** Adverse treatment was not one of the key topics that the Uniform Guidelines on Employee Selection Procedures was designed to address. Answer A is not the best answer; one of the key purposes of the Uniform Guidelines was to address the concept of adverse impact. Answer C is not the best answer; one important objective of the Uniform Guidelines is to ensure that interview and selection processes are reliable. Answer D is not the best answer; one important objective of the Uniform Guidelines is to ensure that interview and selection processes are valid.

145. **Answer B is the best answer.** A minimum salary is not required to qualify for the outside sales exemption under the FLSA. Answer A is not the best answer; no maximum cap is imposed under the outside sales exemption. Answer C is not the best answer; employers do not need to apply for any FLSA exemption. Thus, answer D—none of the above—is not the best answer.

146. **Answer B is the best answer.** Preventing transmission of HCV by proper use of protective personal equipment (PPE) is the best means of protection. Answer A is not the best answer; there is no vaccine for HCV. Answer C is not the best answer; HCV is transmitted by blood and other bodily fluids, not by airborne particles. Answer D is not the best answer; a person with HCV is covered under the Americans with Disabilities Act and therefore cannot be screened for or eliminated from consideration for employment solely because of HCV status.

147. **Answer A is the best answer.** The Davis-Bacon Act of 1931 was the first piece of legislation to consider the topic of—and to actually establish—a minimum wage. Davis-Bacon, however, was (and still is) limited to federal government construction projects and nonfederal government construction projects in excess of $2,000 that receive federal funding (hence, neither answer C nor answer D is the best answer). Answer B is not the best answer; the Davis Bacon Act was not rendered obsolete by the minimum wage provisions of the FLSA; Davis-Bacon requires that covered contractors and subcontractors are required to provide laborers and mechanics who are employed at the actual worksite with wages and benefits that are equal to (or better than) what workers on similar local projects receive.

148. **Answer D is the best answer.** Children who are 14 or 15 years old may work up to 40 hours during a nonschool week. Answer A is not the best answer; children who are 14 or 15 years old may work up to 3 (not 4) hours on a school day. Answer

B is not the best answer; children who are 14 or 15 years old may work up to 18 (not 20) hours during a school week. Answer C is not the best answer; children who are 14 or 15 years old may work up to 8 (not 7) hours on a nonschool day.

149. **Answer C is the best answer.** As articulated, the question states the requirement in specific, measurable, job-related terms, and asks the candidate (in a closed-ended manner) whether he or she can meet that requirement of the position. Answer A is not the best answer; as phrased, this question seeks information that may reveal the existence or nature of a medical condition and/or disability. Answer B is not the best answer; using the phrase "Do you have any problems doing this" is more likely to elicit information relating to a disability than the closed-ended question, "Can you meet this requirement of the position?" Answer D is not the best answer; as described, it does not appear as though this function would be considered "essential" (in fact, it does not even appear as though this responsibility falls within this function of this position at all). In addition, interview questions should be based on the requirements of the job itself, not on the basis of the performance of prior incumbents.

150. **Answer B is the best answer.** In actuality, the Portal-to-Portal Act clarified that employers are required to compensate workers for working time that they spend performing their jobs and for working time that they spend on activities that relate to the performance of their jobs. Answer A is not the best answer; the Portal-to-Portal Act did offer a clearer definition of hours worked for purposes of minimum wage and overtime calculations. Answer C is not the best answer; the Portal-to-Portal Act did address topics such as travel time, pre-shift work, post-shift work, idle waiting time, overnight travel, training time, and the like. Answer D is not the best answer; the Portal-to-Portal Act was an amendment of the Fair Labor Standards Act.

151. **Answer C is the best answer.** In a common law system, contracts that govern the terms and conditions of employment (including employment contracts and collective bargaining agreements) take precedence over traditions, customs, and precedents. For example, a collective bargaining agreement could modify employment-at-will status, even though that concept exists in common law. Answer A is not the best answer; in common law systems, traditions, customs, and precedents have the same force of law as existing laws or statutes. Answer B is not the best answer; in a common law system, laws and statutes are interpreted and reinterpreted on a case-by-case basis. Answer D is not the best answer; in a common law system, each interpretation and each case sets a precedent that can subsequently be reinterpreted, thus setting a new precedent.

152. **Answer D is the best answer.** *Griggs v. Duke Power, 1971*, established that discrimination did not need to be deliberate or intentional to be real. Instead, it can exist even when a particular policy or practice has a statistically significant adverse impact upon members of a protected class. Thus, answers A, B, and C are incorrect.

153. **Answer D is the best answer.** If the employee is subjected to tangible adverse employment action, the employer may not raise a defense that it acted reasonably to prevent and/or promptly correct any sexually harassing behavior. Answer A is not the best answer; Faragher and Ellerth did establish that an employer is liable if the employee is subjected to an adverse employment action. Answer B is not the best answer; the employer is vicariously liable when its supervisors create a sexually hostile work environment, even if the employee is not subjected to an adverse employment action. Answer C is not the best answer; if the employee is not subjected to tangible adverse employment action, the employer may be able to raise as a defense that he acted reasonably to prevent and/or promptly correct any sexually harassing behavior, and that the plaintiff unreasonably failed to take advantage of the employer's preventive or corrective opportunities.

154. **Answer D is the best answer.** To be eligible to take FMLA leave, an employee must meet four requirements, one of which is that the employee must work at a location in the United States or in any territory or possession of the United States where at least 50 (not 75) employees are employed by the employer within 75 (not 50) miles. Answer A is not the best answer; the employee must work for a covered employer—public agencies, state, local and federal employers, local education agencies (schools), and private—sector employers with 50 or more employees. Answer B is not the best answer; the employee must have worked for the employer for a total of at least 12 months (this time does not have to have been uninterrupted). Answer C is not the best answer; the employee must have worked at least 1,250 hours over the previous 12 months.

155. **Answer A is the best answer.** Just cause or good cause refers to a particular legal standard or test that is used to ascertain whether a specific disciplinary action was appropriate. Of the four items that are listed, whether the particular rule that was violated was newly created is least likely to significantly impact the overall assessment of the level of fairness of the action that was taken (this assumes, of course, that the employee knew about the rule and was warned of the possible consequences before such action was taken). Answer B is not the best answer; whether a legitimate investigation looking into the totality of the circumstances around the alleged violation was conducted is likely to factor into an overall assessment relative to just cause. Answer C is not the best answer; whether reasonable proof as to the violation existed or was obtained through investigation is likely to factor into an overall assessment relative to just cause. Answer D is not the best answer; whether the punishment is proportionate to the violation is likely to factor into an overall assessment relative to just cause.

156. **Answer B is the best answer.** The ruling in the landmark case *Automobile Workers v. Johnson Controls, 1990,* determined that most, if not all, fetal protection policies result in gender discrimination. Answer A is not the best answer; the Supreme Court ruled that these sorts of decisions must be left to parents, not to employers.

Answer C is not the best answer; the Supreme Court ruling rendered the ruling that government does *not* have the obligation to protect unborn fetuses from chemical risk, even if the parents who conceived them do not choose to do so. Answer D is not the best answer; few, if any, fetal protection policies would qualify for a bona fide occupational qualification exception.

157. **Answer B is the best answer.** Environmental scanning refers to the process of maintaining awareness of opportunities and threats. Answer A is not the best answer; although maintaining awareness of opportunities and threats is part of SWOT analysis, SWOT analysis also incorporates maintaining awareness of strengths and weaknesses. Answer C is not the best answer; although conducting a SWOT analysis is an essential part of strategic planning, it does not encompass everything that is involved with strategic planning. Answer D is not the best answer; although an organization's awareness of threats is likely to highlight the need for contingency planning, those two concepts are not synonymous.

158. **Answer D is the best answer.** The Supreme Court ruled in *Regents of California v. Bakke, 1978*, that race could be a factor in college admission decisions, but that quotas are impermissible. Although this case was based on a college admission program, its significance has extended to the workplace. Neither answer A nor answer B is the best answer; those choices both assume that the Supreme Court ruled in *Regents of California v. Bakke, 1978*, that quotas are permissible in college affirmative action programs. Answer C is not the best answer; although it acknowledges that quotas are impermissible in college admission decisions, it asserts that this ruling is not transferable to the workplace.

159. **Answer B is the best answer.** The actual employment application may not request information relative to gender, race, or any other information related to protected-class membership. Pull-out sheets, however, that contain information needed for applicant flow data (for purposes relating to affirmative action reporting) are generally considered acceptable when handled in an appropriate and legal manner. Answer A is not the best answer; employment applications can request personal information such as the candidate's name, address, and contact information. Answer C is the not best answer; employment applications can request information relative to a candidate's employment history, including reasons for leaving prior positions. Answer D is not the best answer; employment applications can request names of professional references.

160. **Answer C is the best answer.** In the acronym SMART, M stands for measurable. Objectives—whether related to performance management or any other HRD (or, for that matter, HR) initiative—must be measurable. Answer A is not the best answer; although goals should be marketable to the degree that they relate to the overarching objectives of the organization and are, therefore, hopefully widely embraced, marketability is not one of the key driving forces behind goal setting. Answers B and D are not the best answers, for similar reasons.

161. **Answer B is the best answer.** If progressive discipline is truly viewed as an employee relations initiative, the process should start with the most foundational element of a relationship—communication. Coaching, or discussing the problem, is an appropriate way, therefore, to initially address a performance issue. Answer A is not the best answer; a verbal warning might be the second step in a progressive disciplinary process. Before you move to this step, give coaching a chance. It just might turn out that coaching, if performed well, can preclude the need to take any additional progressive disciplinary steps. Answer C is not the best answer; when you notice a performance issue, speak to the employee before you do anything else. The employee might even provide you with information that could prove to be very valuable, particularly with the question of consistency. Answer D is not the best answer; counseling resembles a verbal warning more closely than it resembles coaching, and therefore should not be the first step in a progressive discipline process.

162. **Answer D is the best answer.** Don't waste your energy trying to deny that informal communications and methods exist. They do, and they can't be eliminated. Nor should they be as long as they do not become destructive. Instead of trying to wish away the grapevine, consider shifting your perspective. One possible way in which to do this is to be open to gathering information through informal, as well as formal, methods. Answer A is not the best answer; ignoring the grapevine won't make it go away. In fact, if you are not open to gleaning information from time to time through the grapevine, you might find that you don't know about important items—items that you might not have otherwise heard about if you hadn't been open to less formal communication media. Answer B is not the best answer; trying to prohibit employees from engaging in conversations about their pay and other confidential matters might reinforce HR's reputation as the "personnel police." It might also constitute a violation of the NLRA if it is found that your action has interfered with employees' associational rights. Answer C is not the best answer; gleaning information from the grapevine doesn't mean that you should throw fuel on the fire. Starting rumors (let's face it, that's what it is) can seriously damage your credibility, as well.

163. **Answer C is the best answer.** This is the best answer in part because there is no commonly recognized activity known as surface organizing. Rather, *surface bargaining* is an impermissible activity during the bargaining (rather than the organizing) process. Surface bargaining refers to going through the motions of bargaining, with no real intent of ultimately reaching agreement (in other words, keeping bargaining at the surface, without moving toward true agreement). Answer A is not the best answer; unions may engage in inside organizing, an activity through which prounion individuals can seek to influence others at the workplace, unless a valid no-solicitation rule is in effect 100% of the time. Answer B is not the best answer; unions may engage in salting, the process through which a salt (a

union organizer) seeks employment with the organization for the express purpose of actively organizing and campaigning within the organization. Answer D is not the best answer; unions may engage in organizational picketing, which is designed to generate interest on the part of employees to vote for union representation.

164. **Answer A is the best answer.** Employers can hire permanent strike replacements during an economic strike. This is different from ULP strikes, in which employers cannot hire permanent strike replacements (answer B). Answer C is not the best answer; workers must be returned to their original positions after a ULP strike is over. Answer D is not the best answer; workers cannot be terminated for participating in an economic strike.

165. **Answer C is the best answer.** Offshoring refers to the process of outsourcing to third-party providers whose operations are based overseas. Answers A, B, and D all offer inaccurate definitions of offshoring and thus are not the best answers.

166. **Answer B is the best answer.** Primary questions are based on the knowledge, skills, abilities, and behavioral characteristics required of a particular position and therefore should remain consistent from candidate to candidate. Answer A is not the best answer; it is important to ask primary and probing questions that ascertain the candidate's ability to demonstrate the knowledge, skills, and abilities required for the position for which the candidate is applying—whether or not those happen to correlate with the knowledge, skills, abilities, and behavioral characteristics that each demonstrated in his or her previous positions. Answer C is not the best answer; as stated above, primary questions are based on the knowledge, skills, abilities, and behavioral characteristics required of a particular position and therefore should remain consistent from candidate to candidate. Answer D is not the best answer; probing questions are asked in answer to each candidate's answer to primary questions, those probing questions will vary from interview to interview. Interviewers can still ensure consistency, however, by limiting their probing questions to those that relate to the original primary question.

167. **Answer A is the best answer.** A focus group is an employee involvement tool as much as it is a communication tool. Answer B is not the best answer; focus groups consist of a representative sample of employees. Answer C is not the best answer; focus groups need to include enough people to generate a dynamic and synergistic discussion (but not so many people that not everyone has a chance to participate). Answer D is not the best answer; focus groups are led by a neutral facilitator whose role is to elicit feedback and input on a specific topic.

168. **Answer A is the best answer.** The National Labor Relations Act was not included among the 12 laws that were expanded to include employees of the legislative branch through the Congressional Accountability Act. Three of the 12 laws that were included in this expansion were the Employee Polygraph Protection Act (answer B), the Worker Adjustment and Retaining Notification Act (answer C), and the Americans with Disabilities Act (answer D).

169. **Answer C is the best answer.** Asking how the position compares to others within the existing job worth hierarchy is a valuable question, but it pertains to internal, rather than external, considerations. That question is addressed through the job evaluation process, and is not as appropriate to ask when you are preparing to collect market data. Answer A is not the best answer; it is valuable and appropriate to ask about the relevant labor market for a position when you are preparing to collect market data. Answer B is not the best answer; it is valuable and appropriate to ask about what sources of market data you already have, and about what other sources you could get, when you are preparing to collect market data. Answer D is not the best answer; it is valuable and appropriate to ask about labor market competitors in general, as well as for a specific job, when you are preparing to collect market data.

170. **Answer B is the best answer.** Excluding statements relative to how the code of ethics will be implemented and upheld greatly diminishes the likelihood that the code will be effective. Doing so, in effect, robs the code of teeth. Answer A is not the best answer; the code of ethics must be administered consistently if it is to be effective. Calling that a one-size-fits-all approach is just a negative way of saying that everyone will be held to the same standard—and that's a good thing. Answer C is not the best answer; although it is advisable that the CEO write the introduction to and/or the cover letter that will accompanying the code of ethics, the ultimate effectiveness of the code of ethics is less contingent upon that than it is upon the consistent application of the code within the organization. Answer D is not the best answer; it is quite possible that employees or others might perceive certain elements of the code as threatening or punitive. That might simply be, however, another way of saying that the code will hold employees accountable and that there will be consequences for failing to uphold the code—both of which add teeth to the code and increase the likelihood that it will be effective.

171. **Answer D is the best answer.** In general, petitions from a union for an election would not be accepted if there is a valid contract in effect that lasts no longer than three years (answer C). Those circumstances would include situations in which a union has been certified in the past year but has not successfully negotiated a contract (answer A) and situations in which an election has been held within the past year (answer B).

172. **Answer C is the best answer.** Although it is important to recognize and exploit (in the best sense of that word) the benefits that can ultimately accrue from an HRIS, it is equally important to recognize the limitations of an HRIS. There are points at which a line must be drawn, and at which technology becomes far less relevant and effective than human beings; increasing employee commitment is probably one of those points. Answer A is not the best answer; an HRIS should provide information that can be used to increase overall employee productivity. Answer B is not the best answer; an HRIS should provide information that can be used to identify and reward top performers. Answer D is not the best answer; an HRIS should provide information that will support placing the right people in the right jobs at the right time.

173. **Answer A is the best answer.** HR might or might not have a presence during the introduction or birth stage of the organizational life cycle. If you are fortunate enough to have a presence, you might find that the formalization of policies and procedures (as would be found in a handbook) is not the most valued or appreciated dimension of your role (give it time…). Answer B is not the best answer; during the introductory phase of the organizational life cycle, employees might find themselves paid above market rates as a reflection of the founder's desire to lure them on board. Answer C is not the best answer; struggling start-ups often find themselves searching for solid financial footing. In such situations, employees might earn less cash compensation, and have those diminished earnings offset by other noncash rewards (equity, intrinsic rewards, and so on). Answer D is not the best answer; you are likely to find—and experience—a high level of excitement and energy in your new role.

174. **Answer C is the best answer.** The executive exemption does not require that the employee's primary duty include the exercise of discretion and independent judgment with respect to matters of significance (however, this is one of the requirements for an administrative exemption). Answer A is not the best answer; to qualify for an executive exemption under the FLSA, the employee's primary duty must be managing the enterprise, or managing a customarily recognized department or subdivision of the enterprise. Answer B is not the best answer; to qualify for an executive exemption under the FLSA, the employee must customarily and regularly direct the work of at least two or more other full-time employees (or the equivalent). Answer D is not the best answer; to qualify for an executive exemption under the FLSA, the employee must have the authority to hire or fire other employees, or the employee's suggestions and recommendations as to the hiring, firing, advancement, promotion, or any other change of status of other employees must be given particular weight.

175. **Answer B is the best answer.** Auditory learners learn most effectively through their sense of hearing. Answer A is not the best answer; visual learners learn most effectively through their sense of sight/vision. Answer C is not the best answer; kinesthetic (or tactile) learners learn most effectively through their sense of touch (or, in a more general sense, through hands-on experiences). Answer D is not the best answer; vicarious learners are not among the three recognized learning styles. The term *vicarious learner*, however, does exist, and is defined as one who learns best by observing others participating in learning, which is not reflected in the scenario described in the question.

176. **Answer D is the best answer.** When determining what constitutes fair use, any permissions that the copyright holder has previously granted are not relevant to a determination of fair use. Answer A is not the best answer; whether the work will be used for commercial purposes or for not-for-profit or educational purposes does constitute a consideration for determining what constitutes fair use. Answer B is not the best answer; the nature or way in which the work will be used does constitute a consideration for determining what constitutes fair use. Answer C is not the best answer; how much of the work is used, both in terms of the aggregate amount of work that is being used as well as the percentage of the total work that is being used, does constitute a consideration for determining what constitutes fair use.

177. **Answer D is the best answer.** The most famous real-life example of the Mackay Doctrine occurred in 1981 when President Ronald Reagan replaced 12,000 striking air traffic controllers. Answer A is not the best answer; President George W. Bush's decision to waive the requirement to pay a prevailing wage rate to government contractors and subcontractors involved in the rebuilding of New Orleans suspended the Davis-Bacon Act for the first time in its 74-year history (this action was wholly unrelated to the Mackay Doctrine). Answers B and C are not the best answers because actions such as these would not fall under the Mackay Doctrine, and because they never happened.

178. **Answer B is the best answer.** Employee referral programs are not likely to bring in candidates who would address issues of underutilization because employees are less likely to refer candidates who are of a different race or gender than they are to refer candidates who are of the same race or gender. Answer A is not the best answer; recruiting at colleges or universities traditionally attended by minorities is likely to be considered an action-oriented program (if the job group or organization is underutilized with respect to race). Answer C is not the best answer; reaching out to professional organizations whose membership criteria are designed so as to attract women or minorities is likely to be considered an action-oriented program. Answer D is not the best answer; posting job openings at resource centers for displaced homemakers is likely to be considered an action-oriented program (if the job group or organization is underutilized with respect to gender).

179. **Answer B is the best answer.** The BFOQ (bona fide occupational qualification) exception to EEO laws would refer to certain job requirements that are mandated by business necessity that might have an unintended discriminatory (disparate) impact upon applicants or employees on the basis of gender, religion, or national origin. The scenario described in the question would not be likely to fall under that exception. Neither answer A nor answer C is the best answer; this decision would not likely be upheld as legal under EEO law. Answer D is not the best answer; there are certain permissible exceptions to EEO laws (for instance, BFOQ, professionally developed test of skill or ability, seniority systems, and piece rate systems).

180. **Answer B is the best answer.** The formula used to calculate turnover is:

$$\frac{\text{\# of terminations during a specified period of time}}{\text{The average \# of employees in the workforce during that same period of time}}$$

181. **Answer C is the best answer.** It is advisable to express earnings in short-term increments in offer letters; however, this has nothing to do with forfeiting the exempt FLSA status. Instead, this should be done so as not to unintentionally create an implied contract. Answer A is not the best answer; it is advisable to specifically state in an offer letter that the only agreements or promises that are valid are those that are included in the offer letter. Answer B is not the best answer; it is advisable to use the offer letter as an opportunity to reaffirm that the employment relationship is at-will. Answer D is not the best answer; it is advisable to avoid language that hints of any sort of long-term employment relationship, as well as any statements that indicate that the employer is "like a family."

182. **Answer D is the best answer.** With very few exceptions (such as for armored car services or pharmaceutical distributors), it is almost always illegal to administer polygraph tests on a preemployment basis. Answers A (agility tests), B (aptitude tests), and C (polygraph tests) are not the best answers; each can be used, under specific circumstances, within specific prescribed parameters, on a pre-employment basis.

183. **Answer B is the best answer.** FairPay defines highly compensated employees as those who earn $100,000 or more annually (of which at least $455 per week must be paid on a salary or fee basis). Answer A is not the best answer; marital status is irrelevant when determining whether an employee is eligible for the highly compensated employee exemption. Answer C is not the best answer; the highly compensated employee exception incorporates the important stipulation that at least $455 per week of that $100,000 must be paid on a salary or fee basis. Answer D is not the best answer; FairPay sets the highly compensated employee threshold at $100,000, not $150,000.

184. **Answer D is the best answer.** To be concerted, activity must be engaged in with or on the authority of other employees. Neither answer A nor answer B is the best answer; to be concerted, activity must be undertaken by individual employees who are united in pursuit of a common goal. Answer C is not the best answer; activity must be concerted before it can be protected by the NLRA (rather than the other way around).

185. **Answer C is the best answer.** Arbitration is not one of the ways in which the EEOC can handle charges of discrimination. Mediation, however, is one possible option. Answer A is not the best answer; the EEOC can handle a charge of discrimination by investigating it. Answer B is not the best answer; settlement remains one possible, ongoing option, even if this option is not utilized (or successfully utilized) when the charge of discrimination is first filed. Answer D is not the best answer; the EEOC can choose to dismiss the charge of discrimination.

186. **Answer B is the best answer.** A protected class is a group of individuals who share a common characteristic and who are protected from discrimination and harassment on the basis of that shared characteristic. Answer A is not the best answer; antidiscrimination laws protect everyone from discrimination on the basis of a shared characteristic, even if a particular group of individuals has not, historically, experienced discrimination on the basis of that shared characteristic (for instance, women and men are *both* protected from discrimination and harassment based on sex, even though men have experienced gender discrimination far less frequently, on a historical basis). Answer C is not the best answer; although employers may not discriminate against an employee who has filed charges with the NLRB or who has taken part in any NLRB proceeding, as this would be considered an unfair labor practice, these individuals would not, however, be considered members of a protected class as that term is traditionally defined. Answer D is not the best answer; employees who have engaged in an economic strike can be permanently replaced by the employer (according to the Mackay Doctrine); however, this is unrelated to "protected class."

187. **Answer A is the best answer.** A nonverbal communication cue could be an indicator of many things, only some of which might be job related. If you notice a change, use job-related questions to probe for more information about the question that you were asking when you noticed the new or changed nonverbal communication cue. Answer B is not the best answer; there is no one, single "dictionary" of nonverbal behaviors (and, even if someone claims to have written one, it is not advisable to apply it to employment or preemployment interactions). Answer C is not the best answer; it is not advisable to point out and describe the changed nonverbal behavior to the candidate, or to ask him or her to help you understand what it means (it won't do much to build rapport, and it also won't help the interviewer obtain the information he or she needs). Answer D is not the best answer; mirroring the candidate's nonverbal behavior to see if he or she continues to display that behavior will not yield any helpful job-related information and might even create an uncomfortable interpersonal dynamic.

188. **Answer B is the best answer.** EEO reports must be filed by employers with 100 or more employees (and by federal contractors with at least 50 employees and federal contracts of at least $50,000 per year). Answer A is not the best answer; the threshold level for a contract, subcontract, or purchase order is $50,000, not $100,000. Answer C is not the best answer; the filing requirement for federal contractors and subcontractors with contracts in excess of $10,000 during any one-year period refers to requirements established by Executive Order 11246. Answer D is not the best answer; family farms that do not employ individuals outside the family are excluded from coverage under OSHA.

189. **Answer B is the best answer.** Recruiting—a separate and distinct process from selection—is the process of attracting and creating a pool of qualified candidates. Answer A is not the best answer; recruiting does not include the process of selecting the final candidate. Answer C is not the best answer; selection, not recruiting, involves the process of identifying the candidate(s) to whom the position will be offered. Answer D is not the best answer; selection, not recruiting, involves the process of selecting the candidate to whom the position will be offered.

190. **Answer C is the best answer.** The very first thing that needs to be done after you decide to conduct an employee survey is to ensure that you have management support—up through and including top levels of management. Answers A (selecting an internal or external consultant), B (determining the survey methodology), and D (deciding upon the survey content) are not the best answers; although each represents an important step in the survey process, none of these should be the first step in that process.

191. **Answer B is the best answer.** Union deauthorization revokes the union security clause in the contract, thereby effectively creating an open shop. Answer A is not the best answer; the process of removing the union's rights to represent the employee is union decertification, not union deauthorization. Answer C is not the best answer; union deauthorization requires that 50% or more of the members of

the collective bargaining unit (not 50% or more of those who vote in the deautho-rization election) support the deauthorization. Answer D is not the best answer; union deauthorization is far *less* common than union decertification.

192. **Answer D is the best answer.** Providing candidates with opportunities to interact with each other is not an effective way of providing a realistic job preview (gener-ally speaking, it's just not a good idea). Answer A is not the best answer; providing verbal descriptions of the work, the work environment, and/or the work conditions can be a good way of providing candidates with a realistic job preview. Answer B is not the best answer; providing candidates with the opportunity to read the employee handbook can be a good way of providing candidates with a realistic job—and organizational—preview. Answer C is not the best answer; providing candidates with the opportunity to interact with current employees, particularly those who would be the incumbent's peers and/or colleagues, can be a good way of providing candidates with a realistic job preview.

193. **Answer B is the best answer.** The November 2000 revisions confirmed that affirmative action plans *do not* establish quotas. Instead, the revisions confirmed that AAPs establish *goals* that must be affirmatively pursued through good-faith efforts. Answer A is not the best answer; the November 2000 revisions did reduce the number of additional required elements of the written AAP from 10 to 4. Answer C is not the best answer; the November 2000 revisions did grant employers with fewer than 150 employees permission to prepare a job group analysis that uses EEO-1 categories as job groups. Answer D is not the best answer; the November 2000 revisions did reduce the 8-factor availability analysis to 2 factors.

194. **Answer A is the best answer.** The nominal group technique does take a nonmathematical approach to forecasting that draws on the insights of subject matter experts. Answer B is not the best answer; although it is true that the nominal group technique affords experts the opportunity to meet in person and process their ideas from the group, this is not a characteristic that is shared with the Delphi technique (in which the experts do not meet in person). Answer C is not the best answer; the nominal group technique is not self-directing—it is led by a facilitator. Answer D is not the best answer; although the nominal group tech-nique permits collaboration at certain points of the process, collaboration is not permitted at all points in the process. Specifically, at the beginning of the meeting, each expert writes down his or her ideas, after which each expert presents those ideas to the group. Discussion of ideas is not permitted at this point, only presen-tation is acceptable.

195. **Answer B is the best answer.** IRCA imposes penalties for record-keeping errors whether those errors were committed knowingly or unknowingly. Answer A is not the best answer; IRCA does prohibit discrimination against job applicants based on national origin. Answer C is not the best answer; IRCA does prohibit giving employment preference to U.S. citizens. Answer D is the best answer; IRCA does impose penalties for hiring illegal aliens.

196. **Answer B is the best answer.** Although this chapter only talked about torts that can be committed against people, torts can also be committed against a person's property. Answer A is not the best answer; torts are wrongful acts. Answer C is not the best answer; the commission of a tort does infringe upon another person's rights. Answer D is not the best answer; tort doctrine is associated with common law.

197. **Answer B is the best answer.** Fiedler's theory does not address the concept of experience-expertise. Answer A is not the best answer; Fiedler identified leader-member relations as a factor that contributes to determining a situation's level of favorableness for a particular leadership style. Answer C is not the best answer; Fiedler identified task structure as a factor that contributes to determining a situation's level of favorableness for a particular leadership style. Answer D is not the best answer; Fiedler identified position power as a factor that contributes to determining a situation's level of favorableness for a particular leadership style.

198. **Answer C is the best answer.** Vendors, by definition, are not employees. The decision to classify individuals as employees or contractors is a legal determination, not an emotional or psychological one. And although fostering an esprit de corps is essential, that sense of team is separate and distinct from whether an individual is an employee or an independent contractor. Answer A is not the best answer; providing positive and constructive feedback is an important part of effectively managing relationships with vendors. Answer B is not the best answer; setting clear and reasonable expectations is an important part of effectively managing relationships with vendors. Answer D is not the best answer; incorporating upside potential and downside risk into negotiated agreements with contractors is an important part of effectively managing relationships with vendors.

199. **Answer D is the best answer.** The four Ps of marketing (or the *marketing mix*) are product, place, price, and promotion. These refer to the variables that need to be addressed and controlled to best satisfy customers in an organization's target market. Answer A is not the best answer; there are no generally recognized four Ps of recruiting. Answer B is not the best answer; there are no generally recognized four Ps of employee relations. Answer C is not the best answer; there are no generally recognized four Ps of project management.

200. **Answer B is the best answer.** Weighted applications can actually conflict with EEO guidelines (for instance, if extra credit is granted for factors that are not meaningfully related to the job or that are not as related as the weighting might imply). Answer A is not the best answer; weighted employment applications are intended to facilitate the process of evaluating each candidate's qualifications in a consistent and objective manner. Answer C is not the best answer; weighted employment applications are difficult and time consuming to create and maintain because positions are almost constantly evolving and changing in some way. Answer D is not the best answer; weighted employment applications do assign relative weights to different elements of the employment application.

201. **Answer D is the best answer.** Common situs picketing is unrelated to double breasting because the employers in question with double breasting picketing share common ownership, while the employers in question with common situs picketing share a common work location. Answer A is not the best answer; common situs picketing is a type of secondary boycott. Answer B is not the best answer; common situs picketing is legal as long as the picket signs indicate the name of the employer with whom the picketers have a dispute. Answer C is not the best answer; common situs picketing occurs when members of a labor union picket a workplace in which multiple employers work.

202. **Answer D is the best answer.** The ADA states that "consideration shall be given to the employer's judgment as to what functions of a job are essential, and if an employer has prepared a written description before advertising or interviewing applicants for the job, this description shall be considered evidence of the essential functions of the job." So, although the failure to have a job description in place that identifies essential job functions could significantly diminish the strength of the employer's position in defending an allegation that an employee or applicant has been discriminated against based on disability, this does not necessarily equate to a mandatory legal requirement to do so. Answer A is not the best answer; to be considered essential, a function must be inherently fundamental and necessary to the position. Answer B is not the best answer; to be considered essential, a function must constitute part, or all, of the reason the job exists. Answer C is not the best answer; the elimination of an essential function would substantially alter the nature of the job.

203. **Answer C is the best answer.** Although the person must be able to establish that he or she was qualified for the position, he or she does not need to be able to establish that he or she was the *most* qualified for the position in order to establish a prima facie case. Answer A is not the best answer; the person must be able to establish that he or she is a member of a protected class. Answer B is not the best answer; the person must be able to establish that he or she applied for the position for which the employer was seeking applicants. Answer D is not the best answer; the person must be able to establish that the employer continued to seek other applicants with similar qualifications.

204. **Answer B is the best answer.** An organization that utilizes the services of a search firm must pay a fee to a contingency employment agency/search firm only if an employee is hired through that agency's efforts. Answer A is not the best answer; an organization that utilizes the services of a contingency employment agency/search firm does not pay a fee to that agency/firm unless an employee is hired through that agency's efforts. Answer C is not the best answer; an organization that utilizes the services of a retained employment agency/search firm must pay a fee whether or not an employee is hired through that agency's efforts. Answer D is not the best answer; see the explanations for the other answers.

205. **Answer C is the best answer.** Just like in-person interviews, prescreen phone interviews should be professional, consistent, and stick to job-related factors. Any assessment of informal "fit" that is made through informal interactions is more likely to be based on factors that are not specifically related to the job-related knowledge, skills, abilities, and behavioral characteristics that are required for a position. Answer A is not the best answer; a prescreen phone interview can be an effective way to identify legitimate job-related factors that could cause the employer to decide to eliminate the candidate from consideration. Answer B is not the best answer; a prescreen phone interview can be an effective way to share job-related information (with every candidate) that could lead one or more candidates to self-select out of the selection process. Answer D is not the best answer; a prescreen phone interview can be an effective way to ascertain whether the candidate's desired salary/wage rate is close to the salary/wage range that the organization has established for the position.

206. **Answer D is the best answer.** (For this discussion, keep the definition of disparate or adverse impact in mind: Disparate or adverse impact occurs when a seemingly neutral policy or practice has a disproportionately negative impact on a member of a protected class.) Although it is conceivable that this scenario could result in adverse impact, of the four situations described, creating a cross-training program in which all nonmanagement employees who meet or exceed performance expectations of their current positions would be able to participate is the least likely to have an adverse impact on a protected class. Answer A is not the best answer; requiring employees to live within a certain radius of an employer could potentially have an adverse impact if it has the impact of screening out individuals based on membership in a protected class, for instance, race (this policy could also eliminate people from consideration based on socioeconomic status; although socioeconomic status does not constitute a protected class, it could be discriminatory depending on the characteristics shared by individuals who have been eliminated because of this requirement. Employers would be better advised to consult with counsel relative to the appropriateness of requiring specific response times for specific positions). Answer B is not the best answer; excluding candidates who have gaps in employment could potentially have an adverse impact on women (who are more likely to experience a gap in employment than men) and individuals over the age of 40 (who are more likely to have experienced a layoff or other involuntary termination). Answer C is not the best answer; any program that requires people to relocate frequently could potentially have an adverse impact based on gender or age.

207. **Answer A is the best answer.** Of all these factors, having the same interviewer perform every interview contributes the least to ensuring that the interview process will have validity. Why? Because if the interview is not based on job analysis (answer B), if the interviewer (even if it is the same person) does not ask questions that elicit information about important job-related skills (answer C), or if the information that is shared, discussed, and collected during an interview does not relate to a specific job (answer D), having the same person conduct the interview

isn't going to do anything to enhance validity. What *will* contribute to validity is if the interview(s) incorporates these processes/attributes into the interview process.

208. **Answer B is the best answer.** A skill inventory is a central database that captures the KSAs possessed by employees. When a position opens up, the organization can then use the skill inventory system to generate a list of current employees who meet the minimum qualifications for the position. Answers A, C, and D are not the best answers; none of them represents an accurate definition of skill inventories.

209. **Answer C is the best answer.** The employee chooses to stop missing deadlines so as to stop the negative consequences (coaching, counseling, and the possibility of further progressive disciplinary action up to and including termination). Answer A is not the best answer; the employee's behavior is not desired, and the consequences of that behavior are also undesirable. As such, this is not an example of positive reinforcement. Answer B is not the best answer; the employer is trying to discourage the behavior, not encourage the behavior. As such, this is not an example of positive reinforcement. Answer D is not the best answer; the employee's behavior is not being ignored, so this is not an example of extinction.

210. **Answer B is the best answer.** Answers A (instrumentality), C (valence), and D (expectancy) are all elements within Vroom's expectancy theory. Although addressed by certain motivation theories, the concept of proclivity is not specifically addressed by any of the motivation theories in this book.

211. **Answer B is the best answer.** This dimension of leadership relates to the dimensions of leadership that speak specifically to ensuring that employees successfully perform the work associated with the position. Answer A is not the best answer; "the interpersonal relationships that managers must first establish with employees before attempting to ensure completion of the actual work" refers to the dimension identified through behavioral leadership theories, known as *consideration* or *employee-centered*. Answer C is not the best answer; "the training in which managers need to participate to develop the skills needed to be an effective leader" does not reflect one of the two leadership dimensions. Answer D is not the best answer; "the degree to which an individual demonstrates an innate ability to being an effective leader" articulates a belief that is ascribed to the trait leadership theories, not the behavioral leadership theories.

212. **Answer A is the best answer.** Employers do normally own/retain the copyright to work product that is generated by an employee during the normal course of his or her employment. Neither answer B nor answer D is the best answer; independent contractors/consulting firms do not normally own/retain the copyright to the work product generated for the organization for which they are consulting. (From the perspective of the organization, however, it is important to have a signed written agreement that states that a work-for-hire arrangement has been established and that the organization owns/retains all work product that is produced.) Answer C is not the best answer; an employee does not normally own/retain the copyright to the work product that he or she generates in the normal course of his or her employment.

213. **Answer B is the best answer.** The formative evaluation model uses feedback, analysis, and assessment conducted at one phase of the process to make enhancements in other phases. Answer A is not the best answer; the formative evaluation model seeks feedback throughout—rather than at the end of—the development and implementation phases. Answer C is not the best answer; the formative evaluation model was developed by Robert Brinkerhoff. Answer D is not the best answer; it refers to Kirkpatrick's reaction-level analysis (which measures participants' answers and reactions to a program immediately after the program has been delivered).

214. **Answer A is the best answer.** To qualify for the learned professional exemption under the FLSA, the employee's primary duty must be the performance of work requiring advanced knowledge, defined as work that is predominantly intellectual in character and that includes work requiring the consistent exercise of discretion and judgment. Answer B is not the best answer; the advanced knowledge must be in a field of science or learning. Work that requires advanced knowledge in other accredited professions would not qualify under this exemption. Thus, answer C—both A and B—is not the best answer. Thus, answer D—neither A nor B—is not the best answer.

215. **Answer D is the best answer.** A vacation buyout program (a program through which an employer will buy back a certain amount of unused vacation time) constitutes cash compensation and therefore is not a form of indirect compensation. Answer A is not the best answer; whether legally mandated or not, benefits are a form of indirect compensation. Answer B is not the best answer; vacation time (or any program that grants employees paid time off) is a form of indirect compensation. Answer C is not the best answer; perquisites (also known as "perks"), such as a company car, club memberships, financial planning, and the like are a form of indirect compensation.

216. **Answer A is the best answer.** MHPA (the Mental Health Parity Act) does *not* require health plans to offer mental health benefits; rather, it applies only to plans that *do* offer mental health benefits. Answer B is not the best answer; under MHPA, plans can still dictate/define the terms and conditions of benefits provided under mental health plans (for instance, cost sharing, limits on the number of visits or days of coverage, and so forth). Answer C is not the best answer; under MHPA, plans that don't impose annual or lifetime monetary caps on medical and surgical benefits *cannot* impose annual or lifetime caps on mental health benefits, either. Answer D is not the best answer; benefits for substance abuse or chemical dependency are excluded from MHPA's requirements relative to annual or lifetime caps.

217. **Answer D is the best answer.** The single-most important factor that is most likely to impact whether the handbook will support the *employer's* position or the *employee's* position is the presence or absence of a signed employee acknowledgement. Without it, even the most carefully crafted handbook, including one with a carefully (and effectively) written EEO/AA statement (answer A) or sexual harassment policy (answer B), will be less relevant because it cannot be proven that the employee received, read, understood, and had the opportunity to ask questions

about it. Answer C is not the best answer; employee handbooks usually don't include a records retention policy.

218. **Answer C is the best answer.** To collect information that could be used to address an individual's employee relations issues, the employee survey could not remain anonymous, rendering it useless and ineffective. Answer A is not the best answer; an organization would conduct an employee survey to gauge and measure employees' perceptions, viewpoints, and attitudes. Answer B is not the best answer; an organization would conduct an employee survey to take the pulse on specific employee current and/or potential issues. Answer D is not the best answer; an organization would conduct an employee survey to collect information that can be used by the organization to help set priorities.

219. **Answer A is the best answer.** For a bargaining unit to be established, a simple majority of those who choose to vote in the election must vote in favor of the proposed bargaining unit. Answer B is not the best answer; a simple majority of voters (not of potential members) is required for a bargaining unit to be established. Answer C is not the best answer; even when there is more than one bargaining unit competing in an election, a proposed bargaining unit must still obtain a simple majority of the votes (This is significant for two reasons: First, a runoff election might be required. Second, in that runoff election, the bargaining unit could find itself competing either with another bargaining unit or with the option of remaining union-free). Answer D is not the best answer; the relevant distinction here is that at least 30% of the employees who would be in the collective bargaining unit must sign authorization cards before the union can petition the NLRB to hold an election—all of which takes place, of course, long before the actual election.

220. **Answer D is the best answer.** Of the four choices listed in the question, catastrophes and fatal accidents would represent the highest priority, followed by employee complaints (answer C); referrals from the media or other individuals, agencies, or organizations (answer A); and planned inspections in high hazard industries (answer B). Imminent danger, however, poses an even higher priority for OSHA than any of the situations listed in this explanation.

221. **Answer C is the best answer.** The degree to which a selection process or instrument is consistent, and generates consistent information that can be used for decision making, determines the degree to which that instrument is reliable. Answer A is not the best answer; the degree to which a selection procedure assesses a candidate's ability to perform representative and significant parts of the job measures its content validity, not its reliability. Answer B is not the best answer, the degree to which incumbents' scores or ratings on a particular selection procedure correlate with their actual job performance measures its criterion-related validity, not its reliability. Answer D is not the best answer; the degree to which a clear relationship exists between performance on the selection procedure and performance on the job measures (in a more general sense) its validity.

222. **Answer D is the best answer.** With respect to the Equal Pay Act, the definition of responsibility is "the degree of responsibility and accountability which an employer entrusts to and expects from a particular position." Answer A is not the best answer; with respect to the Equal Pay Act, the definition of skill is "the amount or degree of experience, ability, education, and training required to perform the job." Neither answer B nor answer C is the best answer; the Equal Pay Act does not designate trust or accountability as one of the four factors used to assess substantial equality.

223. **Answer A is the best answer.** The Railway Labor Act of 1926 established the work now, grieve later rule (there is no grieve now, work later rule). Answer B is not the best answer; the Railway Labor Act of 1926 did afford management additional tools to make sure the trains ran on time. Answer C is not the best answer; the Railway Labor Act of 1926 did enable railroad workers to organize and to have a collective bargaining agent. Answer D is not the best answer; the Railway Labor Act of 1926 did create the first real win-win scenario for labor and management in American history.

224. **Answer B is the best answer.** Taft-Hartley enacted provisions that permitted (not *prohibited*) employers to fire supervisors who engaged in union activities or who did not support the employer's position. Answer A is not the best answer; Taft-Hartley did reaffirm that employers have a constitutional right to express their opposition to unions, so long as employees are not threatened with reprisal for their union activities or promised benefits for refraining from such activities. Answer C is not the best answer; Taft-Hartley did outlaw closed shops, agreements that stated that employers could only hire individuals who were members of labor unions. Answer D is not the best answer; Taft-Hartley did expressly permit union shops, in which nonunion workers must join the union within a certain amount of time after being hired.

225. **Answer A is the best answer.** The list of the names and addresses of all of the employees who are eligible to vote in the union certification election is also known as the Excelsior List. This nickname comes from the NLRB decision *Excelsior Underwear, Inc. v. NLRB*, 1966, in which the NLRB considered whether "a fair and free election [can] be held when the union involved lacks the names and addresses of employees eligible to vote in that election, and the employer refuses to accede to the union's request…." The NLRB ruled that it could not. As a result, the employer must provide the list of employees' names and addresses within seven days after the NLRB has scheduled an election. Thus, answers B, C, and D are incorrect.

PART III
Appendixes

CD Contents and Installation Instructions

The CD features an innovative practice test engine powered by MeasureUp, giving you yet another effective tool to assess your readiness for the exam.

Multiple Test Modes

MeasureUp practice tests are available in Study, Certification, Custom, Adaptive, Missed Question, and Non-Duplicate question modes.

Study Mode

Tests administered in Study Mode allow you to request the correct answer(s) and explanation to each question during the test. These tests are not timed. You can modify the testing environment *during* the test by clicking the Options button.

Certification Mode

Tests administered in Certification Mode closely simulate the actual testing environment you will encounter when taking a certification exam. These tests do not allow you to request the answer(s) and/or explanation to each question until after the exam.

Custom Mode

Custom Mode allows you to specify your preferred testing environment. Use this mode to specify the objectives you want to include in your test, the timer length, and other test properties. You can also modify the testing environment *during* the test by clicking the Options button.

Adaptive Mode

Tests administered in Adaptive Mode closely simulate the actual testing environment you will encounter taking an adaptive exam. After answering a question, you are not allowed to go back; you are allowed only to move forward during the exam.

Missed Question Mode

Missed Question Mode allows you to take a test containing only the questions you have missed previously.

Non-Duplicate Mode

Non-Duplicate Mode allows you to take a test containing only questions not displayed previously.

Random Questions and Order of Answers

This feature helps you learn the material without memorizing questions and answers. Each time you take a practice test, the questions and answers appear in a different randomized order.

Detailed Explanations of Correct and Incorrect Answers

You'll receive automatic feedback on all correct and incorrect answers. The detailed answer explanations are a superb learning tool in their own right.

Attention to Exam Objectives

MeasureUp practice tests are designed to appropriately balance the questions over each technical area covered by a specific exam.

Installing the Software from the CD

The minimum system requirements for the CD are the following:

- ▶ Microsoft Windows 95, 98, Me, NT4, 2000, XP, or Vista
- ▶ 7MB disk space for the testing engine
- ▶ An average of 1MB disk space for each test

To install the CD, follow these instructions:

> **NOTE**
>
> If you need technical support, please contact MeasureUp at 678-356-5050 or email support@measureup.com. Additionally, you'll find Frequently Asked Questions (FAQ) at www.measureup.com.

1. Close all applications before beginning this installation.

2. Insert the CD into your CD-ROM drive. If the setup starts automatically, go to step 6. If the setup does not start automatically, continue with step 3.

3. From the Start menu, select Run.

4. Click Browse to locate the MeasureUp CD. In the Browse dialog box, from the Look In drop-down list, select the CD-ROM drive.

5. In the Browse dialog box, double-click `Setup.exe`. In the Run dialog box, click OK to begin the installation.

6. On the Welcome Screen, click MeasureUp Practice Questions to begin installation.

7. Follow the Certification Prep Wizard by clicking Next.

8. To agree to the Software License Agreement, click Yes.

9. On the Choose Destination Location screen, click Next to install the software to `C:\Program Files\Certification Preparation`.

> **NOTE**
>
> If you cannot locate MeasureUp Practice Tests through the Start menu, see the section later in this Appendix titled, "Creating a Shortcut to the MeasureUp Practice Tests."

10. On the Setup Type screen, select Typical Setup. Click Next to continue.

11. In the Select Program Folder screen, you can name the program folder your tests will be in. To select the default, click Next and the installation will continue.

12. After the installation is complete, verify that "Yes, I want to restart my computer now" is selected. If you select "No, I will restart my computer later," you will not be able to use the program until you restart your computer.

13. Click Finish.

14. After restarting your computer, select Start, Programs, MeasureUp, and then MeasureUp Practice Tests.

15. On the MeasureUp Welcome Screen, click Create User Profile.

16. In the User Profile dialog box, complete the mandatory fields and click Create Profile.

17. Select the practice test you want to access and click Start Test.

Creating a Shortcut to the MeasureUp Practice Tests

To create a shortcut to the MeasureUp Practice Tests, follow these steps.

1. Right-click your desktop.

2. From the shortcut menu, select New, Shortcut.

3. Browse to C:\Program Files\MeasureUp Practice Tests and select the MeasureUpCertification.exe or Localware.exe file.

4. Click OK.

5. Click Next.

6. Rename the shortcut MeasureUp.

7. Click Finish.

After you have completed step 7, use the MeasureUp shortcut on your desktop to access the MeasureUp products you ordered.

Technical Support

If you encounter problems with the MeasureUp test engine on the CD, contact MeasureUp at 678-356-5050 or email support@measureup.com. Technical support hours are from 8 a.m. to 5 p.m. EST Monday through Friday. Additionally, you'll find FAQs at www.measureup.com.

If you'd like to purchase additional MeasureUp products, telephone 678-356-5050 or 800-649-1MUP (1687) or visit www.measureup.com.

Glossary

Numbers

80–20 rule (also known as the Pareto Principle) A principle that asserts that 80% of effects result from 20% of causes. The 80–20 rule, and the chart that visually depicts it, is intended to help individuals focus their efforts where there is the greatest likelihood of bringing about the desired change

A

acceptable quality levels (AQLs) According to Phil Crosby's zero defect philosophy, acceptable quality levels refer to the acceptable level of errors that are sometimes permitted—and that thus preclude the possibility of fully attaining quality objectives through the "zero defects" standard that Crosby alternatively espoused.

action-oriented programs Programs that are specifically designed to correct any areas of underutilization and, thereby, to attain established placement goals (with respect to affirmative action).

ADDIE A five-phase model (often used within a context of instructional design) that includes analysis/assessment (of needs), design, development, implementation, and evaluation.

administrative exemption An exemption under the FLSA. To qualify for an administrative exemption

- ▶ The employee's primary duty must be the performance of office or nonmanual work directly related to the management or general business operations of the employer or the employer's customers.

- ▶ The employee's primary duty includes the exercise of discretion and independent judgment with respect to matters of significance.

adverse impact (also known as disparate impact) Occurs when a seemingly neutral policy or practice has a disproportionately negative impact on a member(s) of a protected class. Adverse impact that results from policies or practices that are not job-related and that have a statistically significant impact on members of a protected class can constitute unlawful discrimination.

Affirmative Action Plans (AAPs) Programs created under Executive Order 11246 to overcome the effects of past societal discrimination by identifying areas of underutilization. AAPs set forth (and require documentation of) good faith efforts to address and resolve that underutilization. Federal contractors and subcontractors with 50 employees and $50,000 or more in contracts during any 12-month period are also required to design and implement formal AAPs.

affirmative defenses Legitimate explanations that employers can set forth to explain inequities in pay between men and women under the Equal Pay Act of 1963. These arguments can be based on—and must be proven to be—a function of

▸ Seniority

▸ Merit

▸ Quantity or quality of production

▸ Any factors other than sex

Age Discrimination in Employment Act, 1967 A law that prohibits discrimination on the basis of age, for individuals age 40 and above. There is no upper cap on age limit (although there originally was). The ADEA covers private employers with 20 or more employees, state and local governments (including school districts), employment agencies, and labor organizations.

agency shop Employees are not required to join the union. They must, however, pay a monthly fee that is typically equivalent to union dues if they choose not to join the union. Agency shops are illegal in right-to-work states.

agility tests Preemployment tests that are used to ascertain whether the candidate can perform the physical requirements of the position for which he or she is applying.

aging The process of mathematically adjusting market data collected during the market pricing process to a common date (usually the date on which the market analysis is being conducted).

agriculture One of the major industries designated by OSHA.

AIDS (acquired immune deficiency syndrome) An infectious disease that is transmitted from person to person through blood or other bodily fluids.

Albemarle Paper v. Moody, 1975 Key issue: job relatedness and validity of employment tests. Significance: any tests that are used as part of the hiring or promotional decision-making process must be job related. This applies to any instrument that is used as a "test," even if that was not its original purpose. This case also established that employment tests must demonstrate predictive validity, consistent with the Uniform Guidelines for Employee Selection Procedures.

ally doctrine A doctrine that states that a union can expand on its primary picketing activity to include employers who are "allies" of the primary employer. One specific situation that can permit the union to conduct secondary boycott is the ally doctrine.

American Society for Personnel Administration (ASPA) ASPA was renamed Society for Human Resource Management (SHRM) in 1989.

Americans with Disabilities Act (ADA), 1992 A law that guarantees equal opportunity for qualified individuals with disabilities in public accommodations, employment, transportation, state and local government services, and telecommunications.

andragogy The study and science of how adults learn.

aptitude tests Preemployment tests that are used to ascertain whether the candidate possesses the skills and/or knowledge required to perform the position for which he or she is applying.

attitude surveys (also sometimes called employee or climate surveys)   A vehicle through which employees can express their opinions or share their perspectives. Sometimes attitude surveys can even provide a vehicle through which employees can truly contribute in a meaningful and significant way to their organizations by having a voice in shaping the policies, practices, and directions of their organizations.

auditory learners   Those who learn most effectively by processing information that they hear.

authorization cards   Cards that, once signed by employees, demonstrate and confirm employees' interest in joining a union. After 30% of the employees who would be in the collective bargaining unit have signed authorization cards, the union can petition the NLRB to hold an election (the 30% threshold demonstrates a "showing of interest" to the NLRB). Often, however, unions seek to obtain signed authorization cards from 50% or more employees before petitioning the NLRB. In addition, under the NLRA, after 50% or more employees who would be in a collective bargaining unit have signed authorization cards, the employer could choose to recognize the union as the representative of all workers in that bargaining unit (though this process, referred to as a "card check," rarely happens).

Automobile Workers vs. Johnson Controls, 1990   The case in which the Supreme Court ruled that Johnson Controls' fetal protection policy constituted a violation of Title VII of the Civil Rights Act of 1964, as amended by the Pregnancy Discrimination Act.

availability analysis   The section of an affirmative action plan that determines the availability of minorities and women for jobs in their establishments, compares incumbency to availability, declares underutilization, and establishes goals to eliminate the underutilization.

B

background check   A process through which the specifics of an individual's past history are explored and revealed.

balanced scorecard   An approach to strategic management that seeks increased clarity and specificity by offering a clear and unequivocal prescription of what companies should measure to appropriately balance financial measures of success with/against nonfinancial measures of success.

base pay   The fixed rate of pay that an employee receives for performing his or her job. Base pay does not include earnings obtained through shift differentials, benefits, overtime, incentive premiums, or any pay element other than the employee's fixed rate of pay.

BASIC (behavioral, as soon as possible, specific, interactive, consistent)   An acronym that outlines the principles that should be followed when providing feedback to, and discussing feedback with, employees.

Beck Rights   The right for bargaining unit members to pay only that portion of union dues which is attributable to mainline union responsibilities (collective bargaining, organizing in the same industry, contract administration, and the like). It is up to the employee, however, to exercise his or her Beck rights. Beck rights were established by the 1988 Supreme Court decision in Communication Workers of America v. Beck, 1988.

behavior-based interviews   Interviews that require the candidate to describe past experiences that demonstrate the degree to which he or she possesses the knowledge, skills, and abilities required to successfully perform the position for which he or she is applying.

behavior-level evaluation Measures whether participants' on-the-job behaviors have changed in a manner consistent with training objectives. In short, it measures *transfer of training*—the degree to which participants apply the skills and knowledge covered in the training sessions in the workplace. This level of evaluation takes place some period of time (weeks, or perhaps even months) after the training is completed.

behavioral anchored ranking scales (BARS) A performance appraisal method that starts by identifying the most critical responsibilities or requirements of a position. Then, for each responsibility or requirement, "anchor" statements offering a specific description of a particular type of behavior (which corresponds to a particular level of performance) are written.

benefits Noncash, or indirect, rewards provided to employees in recognition of and in exchange for the performance of their jobs.

bills Statutes, in their draft format, while they are on their way to becoming law.

biological health hazards Dangers of a biological origin or nature that are introduced into the workplace.

bona fide occupational qualification (BFOQ) Legitimate job requirements that are mandated by business necessity that can have an unintended discriminatory (disparate) impact on applicants or employees.

Brinkerhoff, Robert Brinkerhoff's evaluation model incorporates "formative evaluation."

broadbanding An approach to pay systems that includes a relatively small number of grades. Organizations might choose to use broadbands to bring about a cultural change (for instance, to support the implementation of a flatter organization) or to shift employees' focus away from traditional promotions and place it instead on professional growth and development. Broadbands typically have range spreads of 100% or more.

business (or organizational) ethics A shared values-based system designed to inculcate within the organization's population a sense of how to conduct business properly, appropriately, and consistently with the underlying values of the organization.

business process perspective One of the four perspectives of the balanced scorecard. This perspective scrutinizes key internal business processes so as to measure and ascertain how well those processes generate business results (that is, products and services) that meet customer expectations. The business process perspective ascertains performance levels through specific measures that are unique to each particular organization.

C

captive audience meeting A mandatory meeting held by management, in the workplace, during regular working hours, during which the employer can share its opinions relative to unions and the unionization of its operations. Captive audience meetings cannot be held within 24 hours of the actual election.

career development The development of individuals within the organization.

case study A training method through which participants are presented with a real-life situation that allows them to apply the knowledge they have learned and practice the skills they have developed during the training session.

cash balance plan A type of defined benefit plan that expresses the promised benefit in terms of a stated account balance (similar to the way a defined contribution plan does).

cause-and-effect diagram (also known as the Ishikawa or fishbone diagram)   An important quality tool developed by Ishikawa that presents a visual representation of factors that impact whether a desired outcome will be obtained. Ishikawa believed that, by presenting all the possible factors that contribute to a particular result, any potential process imperfections can be identified in advance and eliminated.

certification   The process by which HR professionals earn formal recognition by a professional certifying body (HRCI).

change management   Activities involved in: "(1) defining and instilling new values, attitudes, norms, and behaviors within an organization that support new ways of doing work and overcome resistance to change; (2) building consensus among customers and stakeholders on specific changes designed to better meet their needs; and (3) planning, testing, and implementing all aspects of the transition from one organizational structure or business process to another" (as defined by the Government Accounting Office).

change process theory   The theory that looks at the dynamics behind how change happens within organizations.

charge   A formal complaint, submitted to an agency, that alleges unlawful discrimination.

charging party (also called the complainant)   A person who alleges that he or she has experienced unlawful discrimination.

checklist   A rating method type of performance appraisal in which the appraiser reviews a series of statements that could describe an employee's performance and literally checks off those statements that are reflective of the employee's performance during the performance measurement period. Sometimes checklists are weighted (called *weighted checklists*), in which case the weightings are used to generate a mathematically calculated score.

chemical health hazards   Any chemical in the workplace for which evidence exists that acute or chronic health effects may occur in exposed employees.

child labor   The child labor provisions of the FLSA restrict the number of hours (and the times of the day) that children under the age of 16 can work, as well as the types of work that children under the age of 18 can perform.

Circuit City Stores, Inc. v. Adams, 2001   The landmark Supreme Court case that confirmed the legality of requiring employees to sign mandatory arbitration agreements as a condition of employment and that such agreements are enforceable under the Federal Arbitration Act (FAA).

Civil Rights Act of 1991   A law that significantly expanded employees' rights and remedies under Title VII of the Civil Rights Act of 1964. In addition to establishing the right for plaintiffs in Title VII cases to enjoy jury trials, it allowed for plaintiffs to be awarded compensatory and punitive damages.

Clayton Act, 1914   A law enacted to build on and clarify the Sherman Act. The provision of the Clayton Act that is most relevant to labor—and therefore to HR professionals—is that Section 6 of the act specifically exempts labor unions and agricultural organizations from the Sherman Antitrust Act.

cliff vesting   A vesting arrangement in which an employee earns a nonforfeitable right to 100% of his or her employer's contributions after a specified number of years, but forfeits all rights to those contributions if his or her employment is terminated before he or she vests.

climate survey (also sometimes called attitude survey or employee survey) A vehicle through which employees can express their opinions or share their perspectives. Sometimes climate surveys can even provide a mechanism through which employees can truly contribute in a meaningful and significant way to their organizations by having a voice in shaping the policies, practices, and direction of their organizations.

closed shop Employers can hire only employees who are already members of the union. Closed shops were ruled illegal by the Taft-Hartley Act; however, hiring halls do, in one sense, encourage a closed shop arrangement. A hiring hall is a union-operated placement office that refers registered applicants to jobs on the basis of a seniority or placement system.

closing processes Those processes (within project management) that mark the end of the project, including the sign-off process. As part of closing processes, stakeholders must determine whether, and to what degree, the project met its obligations. In general, closing processes are considered the fifth of five project management processes, although there can be considerable overlap between those five distinct processes.

COBRA qualifying event Events that would have otherwise resulted in the discontinuation of health insurance benefits for employees, their spouses, and dependent children.

cognitive ability tests Preemployment tests that are used to assess the candidate's intelligence and/or current skill level with respect to a job-related function. Cognitive tests could be administered to assess skills such as problem-solving, mathematical skill, or numerical ability.

collective bargaining agreement (CBA) The output of a successful collective bargaining process. The CBA contains provisions related to a variety of conditions of employment and outlines the procedures to be used in settling disputes that might arise throughout the duration of the contract.

common law A system of law in which traditions, customs, and precedents have the same force of law as existing laws or statutes that have been enacted as a result of the full legislative process. With a common law system, laws and statutes are, quite literally, interpreted and reinterpreted on a case-by-case basis. In practice, each interpretation (and each case) sets a precedent but can also be reinterpreted, thus setting a new precedent. As it evolves, this process results in rights being granted to employees on an individual basis.

common situs picketing A type of picketing that is actually a type of secondary boycott. Common situs picketing occurs when members of a labor union picket a workplace in which multiple employers work: the employer with whom the labor union has the dispute, as well as one or more employers with whom the labor union does not have a dispute. Common situs picketing is legal as long as the picket signs indicate the name of the employer with whom the picketers have a dispute.

Communication Workers of America v. Beck, 1988 The Supreme Court case that established the right for bargaining unit members to pay only that portion of union dues which is attributable to mainline union responsibilities (collective bargaining, organizing in the same industry, contract administration, and the like). It is up to the employee, however, to exercise his or her Beck rights.

compa-ratio The compa-ratio for each employee is calculated by dividing the employee's pay rate by the range midpoint for his or her position. Compa-ratios can be a particularly valuable measure for organizations that seek to match the market because, in such systems, midpoints are often considered to be a close approximation of the market rate for a position. By calculating the compa-ratio, therefore, it is possible to compare the employee's rate of pay with the market rate for his or her position.

comparative methods   Performance appraisal methods in which the appraiser compares employees to each other.

compensable factors   Skills, abilities, characteristics, or areas of responsibility that an organization values and for which it is willing to pay. Some sample compensable factors include education, experience, financial responsibility, responsibility for contacts, and so on.

compensation   Cash-based rewards provided to employees in recognition of and in exchange for the performance of their jobs.

competencies   Skills or behaviors that reflect how employees are expected to deliver performance goals/objectives.

complainant (also called the charging party)   A person who alleges that he or she has experienced unlawful discrimination.

computer employee exemption   An exemption under the FLSA. To qualify for a computer employee exemption:

▶ The employee must be compensated either on a salary or fee basis (as defined in the regulations) at a rate not less than $455 per week or, if compensated on an hourly basis, at a rate not less than $27.63 an hour.

▶ The employee must be employed as a computer systems analyst, computer programmer, software engineer, or other similarly skilled worker in the computer field performing the duties described next:

▶ The employee's primary duty must consist of:

   1. The application of systems analysis techniques and procedures, including consulting with users to determine hardware, software, or system functional specifications.

   2. The design, development, documentation, analysis, creation, testing, or modification of computer systems or programs, including prototypes, based on and related to user or system design specifications.

   3. The design, documentation, testing, creation, or modification of computer programs related to machine operating systems.

   4. A combination of the aforementioned duties, the performance of which requires the same level of skills.

concerted activities   Any activities undertaken by individual employees who are united in pursuit of a common goal are considered to be concerted activity. For an employee's activity to be concerted, the activity must be engaged in with, or on the authority of, other employees, rather than just on behalf of only himself or herself (Meyers Industries, 281 NLRB 882 [1986]).

concurrent resolutions   A legislative measure that addresses a concern that pertains to the Senate as well as the House of Representatives. Concurrent resolutions, however, are not submitted to the president and thus do not have the force of law.

confidentiality agreement   A type of employment agreement that prohibits employees from revealing any confidential information to which they might be exposed during the course of their employment. This could include trade secrets, patent information, and the like. It also usually prohibits employees from using confidential information in any way other than the purposes for which it was intended, and which is necessary, within the context of their jobs.

Congressional Accountability Act (CAA), 1995

Expanded coverage of the following 12 laws to congressional employees:

- Fair Labor Standards Act (FLSA), 1938
- Title VII of the Civil Rights Act of 1964, as amended
- Age Discrimination in Employment Act of 1967
- Occupational Safety and Health Act of 1970
- Rehabilitation Act of 1973
- Civil Service Reform Act of 1978
- Employee Polygraph Protection Act of 1988
- Worker Adjustment and Retraining Notification Act of 1988
- Americans with Disabilities Act of 1990
- Family and Medical Leave Act of 1993
- Veterans Reemployment Act of 1994
- Uniformed Services Employment and Reemployment Rights Act of 1994

Consolidated Omnibus Budget Reconciliation Act (COBRA), 1985   An amendment to Title I of ERISA that requires employers who employed 20 or more people during the prior year to offer continuation of group health care coverage to employees and their family members who experience certain qualifying events—events that would have otherwise resulted in the discontinuation of their health insurance benefits. COBRA places certain requirements on plan participants who want to extend coverage and places certain requirements on the plan provider, in particular with respect to notification requirements.

construct validity   The degree to which a selection procedure measures the degree to which the test taker possesses a particular psychological trait (if, of course, it can be shown that the trait is required for successful performance of the position).

construction   One of the major industries designated by OSHA.

constructive discharge   An employee who alleges constructive discharge asserts that he or she was subjected to such intolerable working conditions that remaining employed with the organization would be impossible. Essentially, an employee who alleges that he or she was constructively discharged is alleging that he or she was forced to quit.

content validity   The degree to which a selection procedure assesses a candidate's ability to perform significant parts of the job.

contingency employment agencies   Search firms to whom an organization pays a fee only if that firm's efforts result in the organization actually hiring a candidate. The services of this type of agency are more often secured in an effort to fill entry-level professional or supervisory-level positions.

contract doctrines   Another way in which common law directly impacts the employment relationship. A contract is an agreement that is enforceable by law. Employment contracts are made between an employer and an employee and can be either oral or written. They can include topics such as term or length of employment, compensation and benefits, job responsibilities, and termination.

contrast error/bias (interviewing)   An interviewing error/bias that occurs when the interviewer compares candidates to each other instead of comparing them to the requirements of the position.

contrast error/bias (performance management)   A performance management error/bias in which the appraiser compares the performance of each employee to the performance of other employees instead of comparing it to the established performance standards for the position.

controlling function   Identified by Fayol as one of the five management functions, the controlling function is the one during which the manager ascertains the degree to which the planning in which he or she was engaged actually produced the desired results. If the manager determines that there is a gap between the targeted goals and the actual results, the manager must then focus on ways to bridge that gap.

controlling processes   Those processes (within project management) that include managing the scope of the project and ensuring that the project stays in line with the original objectives. A significant degree of follow-up is required to carry out controlling processes. In general, controlling processes are considered the fourth of five project management processes, although there can be considerable overlap between those five distinct processes.

coordinating function   Identified by Fayol as one of the five management functions. Through the coordinating function, the manager brings together all the resources that he or she has organized to accomplish the stated plan.

Copyright Act of 1976   A law protecting the work of authors, artists, and others who create original materials. This law also addresses fair use and public domain questions.

cost per trainee/cost per participant   A formula that calculates:

$$\frac{\text{Total of all costs associated with the HRD/training initiative}}{\text{Number of individuals who participate in the HRD/training initiative}}$$

creative professional exemption   An exemption under the FLSA. To qualify for a creative professional exemption

▶ The employee's primary duty must be the performance of work requiring invention, imagination, originality, or talent in a recognized field of artistic or creative endeavor.

criterion-related validity   The degree to which a selection procedure correlates with employees' subsequent job performance.

critical incident   A narrative performance appraisal method in which the appraiser creates and maintains documentation throughout the year relative to specific situations in which the employee met, and did not meet, the performance expectations of the position.

Crosby, Philip B.   A quality guru known for his zero defects standard (in contrast to acceptable quality levels [AQLs]). This management philosophy asserts that employees will perform at whatever level management sets for them.

cumulative trauma disorders (CTDs) (also known as repetitive stress injuries [RSIs] or cumulative trauma syndrome [CTS])   Injuries that result from placing too much stress (often through overuse) on a part of the body.

cumulative trauma syndrome (CTS) (also known as repetitive stress injuries [RSIs] or cumulative trauma disorders [CTDs])   Injuries that result from placing too much stress (often through overuse) on a part of the body.

customer perspective   One of the four perspectives of the balanced scorecard. This perspective focuses on the criticality of customer focus and customer satisfaction. Dissatisfied customers will eventually look to others who will meet their needs and expectations (often without ever sharing their reasons for doing so), which, if the numbers are large enough, can ultimately lead to organizational decline.

D

Davis-Bacon Act, 1931   The first piece of legislation to consider the topic of, and actually establish, a minimum wage. Davis-Bacon, however, was (and still is) limited to the construction industry, specifically those contractors and subcontractors on

- ▶ Any and all federal government construction contracts.

- ▶ Nonfederal government construction projects in excess of $2,000 that receive federal funding.

Contractors and subcontractors who meet either of these criteria are required to provide laborers and mechanics who are employed at the actual worksite with wages and benefits that are equal to (or better than) what workers on similar local projects receive.

decline   The fourth stage of the organizational life cycle, after which—if inertia has set in and if atrophy has begun—decline will not be far behind.

defamation   A tort doctrine that, in a general and practical sense, refers to making a false statement that damages someone's character or reputation. Defamation that is in written form is referred to as *libel*, and defamation that is made through the spoken word is referred to as *slander*. An employee could sue an employer for libel or slander for a variety of reasons, such as the provision of a false reference to potential employers.

defined benefit plan   A more traditional type of pension plan in which the employer promises to pay the employee a specified monthly benefit at retirement. Under defined benefit retirement plans, employers shoulder more of the risk than employees.

defined contribution plan   A type of retirement plan that does not promise a specific monthly benefit (or total benefit) at retirement. Instead, the employer and/or the employee contribute to the employee's individual retirement savings account. Those contributions are then invested, and these investments can either make money or lose money. In this way, defined contribution plans shift the risk away from the employer (which is where it rests for defined benefit plans) and back onto the employee.

The Delphi Technique   A structured, nonmathematical (qualitative) forecasting technique in which opinions from a variety of experts are sought, distilled, and distilled again. An objective, neutral, uninvolved leader recaps what the experts submit, summarizes that information, and condenses it into a more concise format. (The leader is not one of the experts and does not inject his or her opinions or interpretations into the process.) This happens several times until a final position is identified, one that incorporates the input of many individuals but that does not unduly reflect any one position or viewpoint.

Deming, W. Edwards   A true quality pioneer who, though unappreciated in America until the 1980s, brought his expertise to Japan, where he was revered until—and long after—his death. One of Deming's most noteworthy contributions is his 14-point quality management program.

demonstration   A training method during which the instructor/facilitator literally shows the participants how to perform a particular function, duty, or role.

design patents   Granted for the invention of a new, original, and ornamental design for an article of manufacture.

designation of responsibility   The section of an affirmative action plan that identifies the person who has overall responsibility for ensuring the successful implementation of the affirmative action plan.

development/growth   The second stage of the organizational life cycle, during which the organization grows in so many ways. Market share, facilities, equipment, revenues, and the number of employees are all likely to expand, to varying degrees. Along with that growth, the organization is likely to experience some growing pains.

direct compensation   Components of total compensation that are presented to employees in the form of cash.

directing function   Identified by Fayol as one of the five management functions, the directing function is the one during which the actual work is performed—goods are produced or services are provided. In addition to ensuring that things go smoothly from a technical perspective, in the directing phase, the manager must also focus attention on leading and motivating the human resources who are actually performing the work.

directive interviews   Highly structured interviews in which interviewers maintain control, in significant part by asking consistent questions of all candidates.

disability   A medical condition or disorder that substantially limits a person's ability to perform major life activities.

disability benefits   One of the three primary components of the Social Security Act.

discrimination   Discrimination, in the truest sense of the word, is not necessarily illegal. To discriminate is to make a distinction or to discern. When distinctions or discernments are made on the basis of factors, traits, or characteristics that are protected by law, however, discrimination becomes unlawful.

disparate impact (also known as adverse impact)   Occurs when a seemingly neutral policy or practice has a disproportionately negative impact on a member (or members) of a protected class. Disparate impact that results from policies or practices that are not job-related and that have a statistically significant impact on members of a protected class can constitute unlawful discrimination.

disparate treatment   A type of unlawful discrimination that occurs when an employer intentionally treats one or more applicants or employees differently on the basis of their race, color, sex, religion, national origin, age, disability, or any other characteristic that is protected by law.

distributive bargaining   An approach to collective bargaining in which each side sets forth its position and does its best to stick to it. By the end of the process, one side will have won some (or all) of what it wanted, and one side will have lost some (or all) of what it wanted. Distributive bargaining is essentially adversarial in nature. It assumes that "there's only so much to go around." When you divide up the pie, therefore, one side will end up with more of the pie and one side will end up with less.

diversity   Diversity refers to process of recognizing, valuing, and embracing the many ways in which a group or organization embodies differences and leveraging those differences to enhance the overall performance of individuals and groups.

documentation   Notes maintained relative to an employee's performance.

double-breasting picketing   A type of picketing that is actually a type of secondary boycott. Double-breasting picketing occurs when a company that owns or operates union as well as nonunion operations shifts work to the nonunion operation in an effort to diminish the impact of the strike. In this situation, the nonunion operation to which the business has been shifted can be picketed.

Drug-Free Workplace Act, 1988   A law that requires federal contractors (with contracts of $100,000 or more) and individuals and organizations who are awarded federal grants (of any size) to agree to maintain a workplace free of illegal drugs.

drug testing   Analysis that ascertains whether drugs are present within a person's body.

E

economic strike   Any strike that is not directly tied to the union's allegation that the employer has committed a ULP. Economic strikes are called in an effort to obtain some sort of economic concession from the employer during collective bargaining negotiations—concessions relating to higher wages, better working conditions, lower health insurance premiums, and the like. Economic strikers cannot be terminated except under highly limited situations, such as if they engage in serious misconduct during the strike. (However, note that under the Mackay doctrine, the employer can permanently replace economic strikers.)

effects bargaining   Bargaining that takes place when nonmandatory subjects would have an impact that does fall under the category of required subjects.

effort   One of the four factors used as a basis to assess the substantial equality of job content under the Equal Pay Act of 1963. *Effort* refers to the amount of physical or mental exertion required to perform the job.

Ellerth v. Burlington Northern Industries, 1998 (along with Faragher v. City of Boca Raton, 1998)
Key issue: Sexual harassment. Significance: If an employee is subjected to a tangible adverse employment action because of a supervisor's sexually harassing behavior, the employer is liable. The employer is also vicariously liable when its supervisors create a sexually hostile work environment, even if the employee is not subjected to an adverse employment action. This is true regardless of whether the employer itself was negligent or otherwise at fault. However, if the employee is not subjected to tangible adverse employment action, the employer might be able to raise as a defense that it acted reasonably to prevent and/or promptly correct any sexually harassing behavior and that the plaintiff unreasonably failed to take advantage of the employer's preventive or corrective opportunities.

employee   An individual who has been hired by an organization to perform work for that organization and who is compensated directly on that employer's payroll system.

employee and labor relations   Employee and labor relations encompass every dimension of relationships at the workplace, with the overall objective of balancing employee's needs and rights with the employer's need to attain short-term, long-term, emerging, and strategic objectives.

employee assistance programs (EAPs)   Employee assistance programs provide employees with help and resources on a variety of personal issues that can—and often do—have a direct impact on employee job performance. As such, EAPs (which are paid for by organizations) benefit employers as well as employees.

employee communication strategies   One cornerstone—perhaps *the* cornerstone—of effective employee relations. Effective communication can't happen by accident; it must be strategized and executed. Organizations must be deliberate about communicating with, and not just communicating to, employees.

employee handbooks   An important and frequently used method that organizations use to communicate information about policies, procedures, and rules. Handbooks provide, in a sense, the "rules of the road" in that they ensure that employees are fully informed (in writing) about the obligations and benefits that are associated with being an employee.

Handbooks can vary widely in terms of the information they contain, their length, the topics they cover, and the tone in which they are written. Organizational culture must be taken into consideration when decisions of this sort are made.

employee involvement strategies   Deliberate efforts to actively and meaningfully involve employees in the experience of their own employment. HR professionals must seek to actively and meaningfully involve employees in the experience of their own employment.

employee participation groups Groups through which employees are invited to participate actively in the process of managing the organization by contributing ideas and providing feedback. Employee participation groups can also provide an excellent way of encouraging creative involvement and enhancing commitment. Although employee participation groups are neither legal nor illegal by definition, it is the way in which they are administrated that can have a huge impact on whether any particular employee participation group is deemed to be legal or illegal under the NLRA.

employee referral A recruiting technique through which current employees are used as a source for recruiting external candidates into the applicant pool.

employee relations The way in which an organization responds to, handles, and/or addresses any issue that has impact on employees and their relationships

- ▶ To and with other employees
- ▶ To and with managers
- ▶ To and with those outside the employment in the organization with whom they come into contact as part of their employment experience

Employee Retirement Income Security Act (ERISA), 1974 A law that was established to protect the interests of those who participate, and the beneficiaries of those who participate, in employee benefit plans. ERISA applies only to programs established by private industry employers. ERISA establishes minimum participation and vesting standards for retirement programs and minimum standards for welfare benefit (including health) plans.

employee stock ownership plans (ESOPs) A type of defined contribution plan in which investments to individual accounts are made primarily in the form of employer stock.

employee surveys (also sometimes called attitude surveys or climate surveys) A vehicle through which employees can express their opinions or share their perspectives. Sometimes employee surveys can even provide a vehicle through which employees can truly contribute in a meaningful and significant way to their organizations by having a voice in shaping the policies, practices, and directions of their organizations.

employer branding The process by and through which organizations deliberately and intentionally decide on the marketing strategy that will be used to promote the employer's brand within the labor market.

employment application Documents/forms (paper or electronic) that seek consistent job-related information from candidates relative to their work history, education, and qualifications.

employment-at-will A common-law tort doctrine under which the employer and the employee are both granted broad rights, most of which focus on the right of either party to terminate the employment relationship at any time for any lawful reason. A number of important exceptions to the employment-at-will doctrine exist, including lawful reasons, public policy exceptions, wrongful terminations, and implied contracts.

Although everyone involved in the hiring /employment/termination process shares in this responsibility, HR must be particularly diligent about ensuring that a lawful, legitimate, nondiscriminatory reason exists and can be articulated when a decision to terminate an employee is being contemplated.

employment contracts An agreement that addresses and outlines various aspects of the employment relationship and that is binding on the organization as well as on the employee.

employment testing Preemployment tests, tools, or instruments used to ascertain the degree to which a candidate possesses and can demonstrate the knowledge, skills, and abilities required to successfully perform the position for which he or she is applying.

environmental health hazards A type of health hazard that originates in and exists because of something in the workplace. Environmental health hazards refer to a wide spectrum of conditions, circumstances, objects, and organisms in the workplace that can create or increase the likelihood of employee illness or injury.

environmental scanning The process through which organizations maintain awareness of the opportunities and threats presented by the surroundings—both macro and micro—within which they operate.

Equal Employment Opportunity (EEO) Laws, regulations, structures, and processes that are designed to ensure that all employment-related decisions are based solely on job-related factors and without regard to factors including race, color, religion, sex, age, national origin, disability, or other factors protected by law.

Equal Employment Opportunity Commission (EEOC) The government agency responsible for enforcing Title VII of the Civil Rights Act of 1964 (Title VII), the Equal Pay Act (EPA), the Age Discrimination in Employment Act (ADEA), and the Americans with Disabilities Act (ADA).

Equal Pay Act, 1963 A law that prohibits discrimination on the basis of sex in the payment of wages or benefits to men and women who perform substantially equal (but not identical) work, for the same employer, in the same establishment, and under similar working conditions. (An *establishment* generally refers to one specific physical location.) Similar to the way in which FLSA status is determined, substantial equality is determined by job content, not job titles.

ergonomics The way in which the workplace or workspace is designed.

essay method A narrative performance appraisal method in which the appraiser writes short essays describing and documenting each employee's performance during the performance measurement period.

ethics A shared values-based system that serves to guide, channel, shape, and direct the behavior of individuals in organizations in an appropriate and productive direction that is consistent with the values of the organization.

Excelsior List The list of names and addresses of all employees who are eligible to vote in the union certification election. After the union has obtained recognition, regardless of the way in which that recognition is obtained, the employer must provide the NLRB with this list, which the NLRB will in turn provide to the union. The nickname "Excelsior List" is derived from the 1966 NLRB decision *Excelsior Underwear, Inc. v. NLRB*.

Excelsior Underwear, Inc. v. NLRB, 1966 The NLRB case in which the NLRB considered whether "a fair and free election [can] be held when the union involved lacks the names and addresses of employees eligible to vote in that election, and the employer refuses to accede to the union's request." The NLRB ruled that it could not. As a result, the employer must provide the list of employees' names and addresses within seven days after the NLRB has scheduled an election.

executing processes Those processes (within project management) that "bring everything together," including the project's scope, objectives, and deliverables. In general, executing processes are considered the third of five types of project management processes, although there can be considerable overlap between those five distinct processes.

executive exemption An exemption under the FLSA. To qualify for an executive exemption

- ▶ The employee's primary duty must be managing the enterprise or managing a customarily recognized department or subdivision of the enterprise.

- ▶ The employee must customarily and regularly direct the work of at least two or more other full-time employees or their equivalent.

- ▶ The employee must have the authority to hire or fire other employees, or the employee's suggestions and recommendations as to the hiring, firing, advancement, promotion, or any other change of status of other employees must be given particular weight.

Executive Order 11246 EO 11246, the first employment-related EO, established two key requirements for federal contractors and subcontractors that have contracts in excess of $10,000 during any one-year period:

- ▶ These employers are prohibited from discriminating in employment decisions on the basis of race, creed, color, or national origin. This requirement reconfirmed the nondiscrimination requirements established by Title VII of the Civil Rights Act of 1964.

- ▶ These employers must take affirmative steps or actions in advertising open positions, recruiting, employment, training, promotion, compensation, and termination of employees to ensure the elimination of employment barriers for women and minorities (people who we might refer to today as "people of color").

exempt An employee who is exempt from the overtime (and minimum wage) provisions of the FLSA.

exit interviews Conversations with employees who are leaving the organization in an effort to obtain helpful, fact-based, job-related information about the departing employee's experience with the organization.

external recruiting The process of creating a pool of qualified candidates who are not currently employed with the organization.

F

factor comparison A quantitative job evaluation system that involves the ranking of each compensable factor of each job. A monetary value for each level with each factor is subsequently identified. Similar to the point factor method, each job is evaluated with respect to each compensable factor, and the appropriate level (with an accompanying dollar value) is selected. When all of the levels that have been selected are added together, a pay rate for each job will emerge.

Failure to Abate Prior Violation A violation that continues beyond the prescribed abatement date. OSHA may propose a fine of up to $7,000 per day for each failure to abate prior violation.

fair employment practices agencies (FEPAs) State or local agencies that are responsible for enforcing EEO laws that are specific to their respective jurisdiction.

Fair Labor Standards Act (FLSA) A law that establishes standards with respect to minimum wage, record keeping, child labor standards, and overtime pay.

FairPay The nickname for the 2004 revisions of the FLSA.

fair use The right to use copyrighted works without the permission of the author under certain circumstances, such as "criticism, comment, news reporting, teaching (including multiple copies for classroom use), scholarship, or research."

Family and Medical Leave Act (FMLA), 1993   The Family and Medical Leave Act (FMLA) entitles eligible employees (who work for covered employers) up to 12 weeks of unpaid, job-protected leave during any 12-month period for one or more of the following reasons:

- ▶ The birth and care of the newborn child of the employee

- ▶ Placement with the employee of a son or daughter for adoption or foster care

- ▶ Care for an immediate family member (spouse, child, or parent) with a serious health condition

- ▶ Medical leave when the employee is unable to work because of a serious health condition

Faragher v. City of Boca Raton, 1998 (along with Ellerth v. Burlington Northern Industries, 1998)
Key issue: Sexual harassment. Significance: If an employee is subjected to a tangible adverse employment action because of a supervisor's sexually harassing behavior, the employer is liable. The employer is also vicariously liable when its supervisors create a sexually hostile work environment even if the employee is not subjected to an adverse employment action. This is true whether the employer itself was negligent or otherwise at fault. However, if the employee is not subjected to tangible adverse employment action, the employer may be able to raise a defense that it acted reasonably to prevent and/or promptly correct any sexually harassing behavior, and that the plaintiff unreasonably failed to take advantage of the employer's preventive or corrective opportunities.

Fayol, Henri   Known as the father of modern management, Fayol identified five functions of a manager, now referred to as planning, organizing, coordinating, directing, and controlling.

featherbedding   An agreement that requires the employer to pay wages to union members whether or not their work is needed.

Federal Mediation and Conciliation Service (FMCS)
A resource that maintains lists of qualified arbitrators. FMCS was created by the Labor Management Relations Act (LMRA), also known as the Taft-Hartley Act.

federation   A formal group of national unions that choose to affiliate with each other. Its many members speak with one voice, thus wielding even greater influence and lobbying power. Federations do not, however, get involved with bargaining or contract administration.

feedback   Information that is provided to and discussed with an employee relative to his or her performance and the specific ways in which that performance is meeting or not meeting expectations.

fetal protection policies   Policies that are intended to protect unborn fetuses from the possibility of being harmed by teratogens. The impact of most (if not all) these policies, as ruled by the Supreme Court, is unlawful gender discrimination.

fiduciary   According to ERISA, a fiduciary is a person or entity "who exercise discretionary control or authority over plan management or plan assets, have discretionary authority or responsibility for the administration of a plan, or provide investment advice to a plan for compensation or have any authority or responsibility to do so are subject to fiduciary responsibilities" (www.dol.gov).

Plan fiduciaries could include, for example, plan trustees, plan administrators, and members of a plan's investment committee.

fiduciary responsibility   Fiduciaries are charged with running the plan(s) for which they are responsible solely in the interest of participants and beneficiaries. They must ensure that the sole purpose of the plan is and remains providing benefits to participants and beneficiaries and paying plan expenses. Fiduciaries must also act with skill, care, prudence, and diligence. For instance, they must protect plan participants by diversifying plan investments and must follow the terms of plan documents to the extent that those terms are consistent with ERISA. They also must avoid conflicts of interest, and, many would argue, even the possibility of an appearance of a conflict of interest (the same standard to which HR professionals should hold themselves, as well).

field review   A narrative performance appraisal method in which someone other than the employee's supervisor—someone from HR, for instance—prepares the performance appraisal.

financial perspective   One of the four perspectives of the balanced scorecard. The financial perspective is the most traditional of Kaplan's and Norton's four perspectives.

first-impression error/bias (interviewing)   An interviewing error/bias that occurs when the interviewer places an inordinate level of emphasis on the impression that the candidate makes on him or her during the first few minutes, seconds, or even moments of the interview.

first-impression error/bias (performance management)   A performance management error/bias in which the appraiser forms an impression of the employee's performance early in the performance measurement period (or, even worse, early in the individual's employment) and places an inordinate level of emphasis on that impression.

fishbone diagram (also known as the cause-and-effect diagram or Ishikawa diagram)   An important quality tool developed by Ishikawa that presents a visual representation of factors that impact whether a desired outcome will be obtained. Ishikawa believed that by presenting all the possible factors that contribute to a particular result, any potential process imperfections can be identified in advance and eliminated.

flexible spending accounts (FSAs)   A type of Section 125 plan. Flexible Spending Accounts (FSAs) enable employees to set aside pretax dollars to pay for medical expenses that are not covered by insurance. FSAs can also be set up for dependent care. Employees decide how much money to set aside for the following year, and that amount is automatically deducted from the employee's pay on a pretax basis. After incurring and paying for eligible expenses, employees apply for reimbursement from the FSA.

focus groups   An important vehicle for communicating with and involving employees in the organization. A focus group consists of a small but representative sample of individuals within an organization. Within each focus group, discussions are led by a neutral facilitator who seeks to elicit feedback and input on a specific subject.

for-cause drug testing   Drug testing that is conducted when an employee shows obvious signs of not being fit for duty, in an effort to protect the safety and well being of employees and co-workers, and to identify opportunities for rehabilitation.

forced distribution method (also known as the forced ranking method)   A comparative performance appraisal method in which the appraiser ranks the performance of his or her direct reports so that, overall, the performance levels of all of the employees, when looked at together, reflect a bell-shaped curve.

forced ranking method (also known as the forced distribution method) A comparative performance appraisal method in which the appraiser ranks the performance of his or her direct reports so that, overall, the performance levels of all of the employees, when looked at together, reflect a bell-shaped curve.

formative evaluation A process by which evaluative feedback and input is sought throughout the development and implementation phases in an effort to strengthen the ultimate training initiative through real-time incorporation of evaluative feedback.

four absolutes of quality management Phil Crosby's four absolutes of quality management include

1. Quality means conformance to requirements, not goodness.

2. Quality is achieved by prevention, not appraisal.

3. Quality has a performance standard of Zero Defects, not acceptable quality levels.

4. Quality is measured by the Price of Nonconformance, not indexes.

full cafeteria plan The most comprehensive and administratively burdensome of the three types of Section 125 plans. Employers who offer full cafeteria plans provide their employees with a specific amount of money from which they can use to pick and choose from a variety of benefits programs.

G

gainsharing Incentive plans that are designed to motivate employees to reach specific goals relating to cost cutting or revenue generation, and that share a portion of that savings (or that increased revenue) with the employees who helped to achieve it. Gainsharing plans are based on team/group performance, not individual performance.

General Duty Clause Part of the Occupational Health and Safety Act (OSHA) that identifies two primary duties for employers (ensuring a safe workplace, and complying with all current and future OSHA-related standards), and one for employees (following all safety and health-related rules stemming from the act).

General Dynamics Land Systems v. Cline (2004) Key Issue: Age Discrimination (Relative). Significance: Younger employees (even if they are over the age of 40) cannot allege age discrimination because of the establishment of programs or decisions that favor older employees. As Justice David Souter wrote in the opening of his opinion, "The Age Discrimination in Employment Act of 1967 (ADEA or Act), 81 Stat. 602, 29 U.S.C. [section] 621 et seq., forbids discriminatory preference for the young over the old. The question in this case is whether it also prohibits favoring the old over the young. We hold it does not."

general industry One of the major industries designated by OSHA.

Global Professional in Human Resources (GPHR) The Global Professional in Human Resources certification, granted by and issued through HRCI.

goals/objectives Statements that express and communicate performance expectations in terms of "what" is expected to be produced.

good faith bargaining Refraining from behaviors during the collective bargaining process that could constitute bad faith bargaining. The following behaviors, when demonstrated by either the union or the employer, could constitute bad faith bargaining:

▶ Failing to agree to meet at reasonable and convenient places and/or times.

▶ Failing to show up at the agreed-upon places and/or times.

▶ Repeatedly canceling meetings.

▶ Failing to maintain an "open mind" during negotiations.

▶ Surface bargaining: Going through the motions of bargaining, with no real intent of ultimately reaching agreement (in other words, keeping bargaining "at the surface," without moving toward true agreement).

▶ Repeatedly withdrawing previous positions/concessions.

▶ Refusing to bargain on mandatory items, insisting on bargaining on permissive items, or attempting to bargain on illegal items.

▶ Committing any sort of ULP(s).

graded vesting   A vesting arrangement in which an employee earns a nonforfeitable right to an increasing percentage of his or her employer's contributions over a period of years.

grades (also referred to as pay grades or job grades)   "Levels" into which jobs of similar internal worth can be categorized. Jobs within the same grade share a similar level of value or worth to the organization. Different organizations will have different numbers of pay grades, with differing degrees of distinction between each of those grades.

Griggs v. Duke Power, 1971   Key issue: adverse impact. Significance: Discrimination need not be deliberate or observable to be real. Rather, it can exist if a particular policy or practice has a statistically significant adverse impact upon members of a protected class. This is true even when the same requirement applies to all employees or applicants, as was the situation in this case. When a particular requirement does have an impact on members of a protected class, the burden of proof rests with the employer to demonstrate that the requirement is, in fact, job related and consistent with business necessity.

Grutter v. Bollinger and Gratz v. Bollinger (2003)   Barbara Grutter was applying for admission to the University of Michigan Law School, and Jennifer Gratz was applying for the University of Michigan as an undergraduate student. Lee Bollinger was the president of the University of Michigan.

Key issue: Affirmative action. Significance: Race can be taken into account as an admissions factor because it furthers the establishment of diversity—a "compelling state interest"—as long as the admissions process is "narrowly tailored" to achieve the objective of achieving a diverse student body.

Interestingly, Supreme Court Justice Sandra Day O'Connor indicated that cases of this sort will likely be ruled differently in the future: "Race-conscious admissions policies must be limited in time. The Court takes the Law School at its word that it would like nothing better than to find a race-neutral admissions formula and will terminate its use of racial preferences as soon as practicable. The Court expects that 25 years from now, the use of racial preferences will no longer be necessary to further the interest approved today."

These cases fall under the category of "reverse discrimination" because they alleged race discrimination and were brought by people who were not minorities/people of color.

H

halo error/bias (interviewing)   An interviewing error/bias that occurs when the interviewer evaluates the candidate positively on the basis of one outstanding qualification or characteristic.

halo error/bias (performance management)   A performance management error/bias in which the appraiser evaluates the employee positively on the basis of one outstanding qualification or characteristic.

Harris v. Forklift Systems, 1993 Key Issue: Sexual harassment. Significance: The court clarified the standard relative to what constitutes a sexually hostile work environment: "This standard, which we reaffirm today, takes a middle path between making actionable any conduct that is merely offensive and requiring the conduct to cause a tangible psychological injury. Conduct that is not severe or pervasive enough to create an objectively hostile or abusive work environment—an environment that a reasonable person would find hostile or abusive—is beyond Title VII's purview. Likewise, if the victim does not subjectively perceive the environment to be abusive, the conduct has not actually altered the conditions of the victim's employment, and there is no Title VII violation."

hazard communication standard (also known as employee right-to-know) Ensures that employers and employees have knowledge and awareness about hazardous chemicals located in the workplace, and that they know how to protect themselves. Specifically, this standard requires all employers having hazardous materials at the workplace to implement a written hazard communication program. Four important key elements of this program are Material Safety Data Sheets (MSDS), orientation, training, and container labeling requirements.

HBV (hepatitis B virus) The virus that causes Hepatitis B, a potentially serious (and potentially fatal) form of liver inflammation.

HCV (hepatitis C virus) The virus that causes Hepatitis C, a viral infection of the liver.

health and welfare benefits A variety of nonretirement, nonmandatory benefits that can be effective ways of attracting, motivating, and retaining employees.

health and wellness programs Programs that offer employees the opportunity to enhance the quality of their lives (usually proactively, but also reactively) through healthier lifestyle choices.

health hazards Anything in the workplace that creates or increases the possibility of work-related injuries.

Health Insurance Portability and Accountability Act (HIPAA), 1996 An amendment to ERISA that has two primary focuses: the security and portability of health care coverage, and privacy considerations.

With respect to the security and portability of health care coverage, HIPAA was intended to help workers experience greater security and portability with respect to health care coverage, even when an employee changes jobs. HIPAA also afforded significantly greater protections for employees who have or who have a family member with a preexisting medical condition.

health maintenance organization (HMO) A managed care model of health care and health insurance. In an HMO, each participant chooses a primary care physician, or PCP, who serves as a gatekeeper. Participants must see their PCPs first, and the PCP then decides whether to refer the patient to a specialist or for additional tests.

highly compensated employee exemption An exemption under the FLSA. To qualify for a highly compensated employee exemption, an employee must

▸ Earn $100,000 or more annually (of which at least $455 per week must be paid on a salary or fee basis)

▸ Perform office or nonmanual work

▸ Customarily and regularly perform at least one of the duties of an exempt executive, administrative, or professional employee identified in the standard tests for exemption

HIPAA covered entity   One of three groups of individuals or corporate entities (health plans, health care providers, and health care clearinghouses) that are covered by HIPAA's privacy rule, which thus requires specific actions regarding protected health information (PHI):

- ▶ Enact written PHI privacy procedures

- ▶ Designate a privacy officer

- ▶ Require business associates to sign agreements stating that they will respect the confidentiality of PHI

- ▶ Train all employees in HIPAA privacy rule requirements

- ▶ Establish a complaint handling and resolution process for issues related to the HIPAA privacy rule

- ▶ Ensure that PHI is not used for making any employment-related decisions

HIPAA privacy rule   Designed to protect patients and other consumers of health care services from the unauthorized disclosure of any personally identifiable health information (protected health information, or PHI). Health information is considered to be personally identifiable if it relates to a specifically identifiable individual.

histogram   A graph that depicts information about a single factor. In addition to being used to graphically communicate information, histograms can also sometimes help identify patterns or explanations.

HIV (human immunodeficiency virus)   The virus that causes AIDS (acquired immune deficiency syndrome).

Horns error/bias (interviewing)   An interviewing error/bias that occurs when the interviewer evaluates the candidate negatively on the basis of one poor characteristic or dimension of performance.

Horns error/bias (performance management)   A performance management error/bias in which the appraiser evaluates the employee negatively on the basis of one poor qualification or characteristic.

hostile work environment   A form of sexual harassment that occurs when unwelcome sexual conduct unreasonably interferes with an individual's job performance or creates a hostile, intimidating, or offensive work environment. Hostile work environment harassment can be found to exist whether the employee experiences (or runs the risk of experiencing) tangible or economic work-related consequences. By definition, hostile work environments can be created by virtually anyone with whom an employee might come in contact in the workplace.

hot cargo agreements   An agreement entered into by an employer in which the employer agrees to stop doing business with another entity. Hot cargo agreements can thus help to protect union work by allowing union members to refuse to handle or process work produced by nonunion entities. Hot cargo agreements were made illegal by the Landrum-Griffin Act.

hours worked   "Hours worked" means "hours worked," not "hours paid." In other words, according to the FLSA, hours that have been paid but not worked (vacation time, sick time, holiday time, jury duty time, and the like) do not count toward the 40-hour overtime threshold (although some organizations may voluntarily choose to count these hours toward the 40-hour threshold). "Hours worked" also doesn't mean "hours approved to work." If an employer "suffers or permits" a non-exempt employee to work, that employee must be compensated for that time. So, whether the employer requires the employee to work or simply allows the employee to work, the time counts as "hours worked" and must be compensated appropriately.

HR audit   The primary tool that many HR departments use to assess their own effectiveness and efficiency with respect to ascertaining how well they have aligned themselves with the organization's strategic objectives.

HRIS   An integrated computer-based system that collects, processes, analyzes, stores, maintains, and retrieves information relating to all dimensions of the HR function.

human processual interventions   OD interventions that seek to effect change and impact relationships within (and between) groups and individuals.

Human Resource Certification Institute (HRCI)   An affiliate of SHRM, HRCI is the credentialing organization of the HR profession.

human resource development   Human resource development employs effective training, development, change management, and performance management functions and initiatives to ensure that the skills, knowledge, abilities, and performance of the workforce will meet the short-term, long-term, emerging, and strategic objectives of the organization.

I

I-9   The form (mandated by IRCA) that documents an employee's identity and eligibility to legally work in the United States.

Identification of Problem Areas   The section of an affirmative action plan that provides an in-depth analysis of its total employment process to determine whether and where impediments to equal employment opportunity exist.

illegal subjects   Topics that simply cannot be the subject of collective bargaining. These would include items that would constitute a violation of the NLRA, subsequent labor laws, or (for that matter) any law.

Immigration Reform and Control Act (IRCA), 1986   A law that prohibits employers from discriminating against job applicants on the basis of national origin and from giving preference to U.S. citizens. IRCA also established penalties for those who knowingly hire illegal aliens (people who are referred to, by some individuals and organizations, as "undocumented workers," rather than "illegal aliens").

imminent danger   OSHA's highest priority for investigation, and defined in the act as "any conditions or practices in any place of employment which are such that a danger exists which could reasonably be expected to cause death or serious physical harm immediately or before the imminence of such danger can be eliminated through the enforcement procedures otherwise provided by this Act."

implementation theory   A theory that focuses on carrying out specific strategies—in this case, OD interventions—that are designed to bring about the unfreezing, moving, and refreezing through Lewin's change process theory.

implied contracts   A tort doctrine under which an employee can allege that a promise of employment has been created, even when that promise is not explicitly written or articulated. Sometimes, the language that is used within employer-published documents (electronic or hardcopy) can actually be sufficient to create a contract between the employer and the employees. An oral contract can be created when an "agent" of the employer "promises" some benefit or right. The term "agent" is legal and involved, but the point is this—be careful what your supervisors, recruiters, and others say to current, and especially to potential, employees.

incentive plans   Variable compensation plans that establish specific financial and nonfinancial goals and targets for individuals, groups, and organizations. For incentive programs to be effective, employees need to believe that they can attain the goals that have been set as part of the incentive program and that the reward that they would earn by attaining those goals is sufficiently worthwhile.

indemnity insurance   The most traditional type of medical insurance plan. Indemnity plans provide participants with (virtually) unrestricted choices relative to their doctors, hospitals, and other health care providers. Health care providers are paid a fee for the services they actually provide and perform.

independent contractor   An individual who has been retained by an organization to perform work for that organization and who is not compensated directly on that employer's payroll system.

indirect compensation   Components of total compensation that are presented to employees in forms other than cash.

individual, small group, or large group activities/applications   A training method during which the instructor provides participants with an opportunity to immediately apply the knowledge they have learned or the skills they have developed through hands-on application.

industrial relations   One of the earlier monikers by which the HR profession was known.

infectious diseases   Viral or bacterial diseases that can be transmitted from person to person.

initiating processes   Those processes (within project management) that secure approval and/or authorization to undertake the project. In general, initiating processes are considered the first of five project management processes, although there can be considerable overlap between those five distinct processes.

Injury and Illness Incident Report (also known as the OSHA Form 301)   A form that must be completed for each work-related injury or illness within seven calendar days of the date on which the employer learns of the work-related injury or illness, and which must be maintained by the employee for five years following the year in which the incident or illness occurred.

integrative bargaining   An approach to collective bargaining that looks at multiple issues as a whole. Instead of just splitting up the pie, it creatively considers how it might be able to "make the pie bigger." It looks at how the needs of both sides can be better met when looked at in their entirety, and at how a "win-win" solution can be explored, rather than settling for the "win-lose" scenario that will almost invariably result from distributive bargaining. In essence, advocates of integrative bargaining believe that an agreement that renders one side "better off" does not necessarily have to result in the other side being "worse off." Instead, through creativity and cooperation, "trade offs" are sought that will ultimately benefit both sides.

integrity, or honesty, tests   Preemployment tests that are used to ascertain the degree to which a candidate would be likely to engage in behavior that is dishonest or that reflects a potential lack of integrity.

internal audit and reporting system   An auditing system that periodically measures the effectiveness of an organization's total affirmative action program.

internal recruiting   The process of creating a pool of qualified candidates from individuals who are already employed with the organization. Two primary mechanisms for seeking internal candidates for positions within the organization are job posting and job bidding.

international labor organizations   A formal group of labor organizations that operates on the international level in much the same manner as federations operate on the national level, only bigger.

interviewing error/bias   Factors that are not related to a job that (when not identified and managed) can taint or impact an interviewer's assessment of a candidate.

introduction/birth   The first stage of the organizational life cycle, during which excitement and energy are high, and cash flow may be low. Struggling start-ups often find themselves searching for solid footing, financially as well as operationally. The core group of highly talented employees who join the organization during the introduction/birth stage of the organizational life cycle may focus fixedly on the founder as a source of direction, wisdom, and inspiration.

invasion of privacy   The right to privacy is a key issue in the workplace and "workspace" (meaning the electronic dimensions of the workplace as well as the physical ones). Modern tort law includes four categories of invasion of privacy, all of which employers need to be aware:

▶ Intrusion of solitude

▶ Public disclosure of private and embarrassing facts

▶ False light

▶ Appropriation of identity

involuntary terminations   A decision, initiated by the employer, to end the employment relationship.

Ishikawa diagram (also known as the "cause-and-effect" diagram or "fishbone" diagram)   An important quality tool developed by Ishikawa that presents a visual representation of factors that impact whether a desired outcome will be obtained. Ishikawa believed that, by presenting all of the possible factors that contribute to a particular result, any potential process imperfections can be identified in advance, and eliminated.

Ishikawa, Kaoru   A quality guru committed to the idea of continued customer service, even after the customer purchases the product. Ishikawa also believed strongly in the criticality of securing top-level management support, and dramatically increased worldwide awareness and acceptance of the idea of quality circles, originally a Japanese philosophy.

J

job analysis   The process by which information about a specific position is collected, and through which (up to) three important outputs are generated: a job description, job specifications, and job competencies.

job bidding   A system that invites employees to express interest in any internal position at any time, even if a position is not currently available.

job classification   A whole job evaluation technique that categorizes jobs into broad categories, or "levels," based on the level—and, ultimately, value to the organization—of the work that is performed by jobs within each job level. Each level incorporates specific responsibilities and benchmark statements that describe the nature, complexity, autonomy, and so on of the work that is performed by positions in that level.

job competencies   Broad categories of behavioral characteristics that are required to perform successfully in a particular position, department or organization. They are often referred to by organizations as "key success factors," "competencies for success," or "performance factors." They could include things such as "communication skills," "teamwork," and/or "judgment."

job description   A document that contains information about a job, such as the essential functions, expected outputs, key accountabilities, requirements, and so forth of the position. This information is collected through the job analysis process.

job evaluation   The process through which every job in an organization is assessed and compared to other jobs in the organization. At the conclusion of the job evaluation process, it will be possible to knowledgeably ascertain the relative worth of each job within the organization. When this is done for positions, an overall job worth hierarchy has been created.

job group analysis   The section of an affirmative action plan that is used by nonconstruction contractors to begin the process of comparing the employer's representation of women and minorities to the estimated availability of qualified women and minorities who are available to be employed.

job match   An external position to which an internal job is compared during the market pricing process.

job posting   A system that announces position openings to current employees within the organization.

job slotting   A whole job evaluation technique that incorporates or "slots" newly created or revised positions into an existing job hierarchy. This process of slotting is accomplished by comparing the new or revised job descriptions to job descriptions of positions that have already been evaluated and assigned within the hierarchy.

job-specific employment applications
Employment applications that are tailored to seek highly specific and relevant information pertaining to one specific position.

job specifications   The skills, knowledge, abilities, behavioral characteristics, and other credentials and experience necessary to perform a position successfully.

Johnson v. Santa Clara County Transportation Agency, 1987   Key issue: Affirmative action. Significance: Gender can be used as a factor in the selection process if there is underrepresentation in a particular job classification, as long as the AAP does not set forth a quota.

This case falls under the category of "reverse discrimination" because it alleged sex discrimination and was brought by a man.

joint resolutions   A resolution passed by the Senate as well as the House of Representatives that has the force of law after it has been either signed by the president, or passed over the veto of the president.

Juran, Joseph M.   A giant in the area of quality who focused on the perspectives and the needs of customers, and whose quality management ideas focused on three key areas: quality planning, quality improvement, and quality control.

jurisdictional strikes   A strike through which a union seeks to pressure an employer to assign particular work to its members, rather than to members of other unions or to nonunion workers.

K–L

Kirkpatrick, Donald L.   Kirkpatrick's theory takes a "summative" approach to evaluation in that it is predicated on the interpretation of data that is collected after the initiative has been implemented. Kirkpatrick's approach, therefore, allows for a complete analysis of the entire initiative on four levels: reaction, learning, behavior, and results.

Knowles, Malcolm   Identified five key assumptions about how adults learn:

- ▶ Learner's need to know
- ▶ Learner's self-concept
- ▶ Role of learner's experience
- ▶ Readiness to learn
- ▶ Orientation to learning

Kolstad v. American Dental Association, 1999
Key Issue: Punitive damages under the Civil Rights Act of 1991. Significance: Punitive damages can be awarded only when the employer has acted with malice and reckless indifference to the employee's federally protected rights. This subjective standard was considered to be easier to establish than the more objective standard that would be required if employees had to prove that the nature of the actual behavior to which they had been subjected reached a level where it would be considered "egregious."

KSAs   The minimally acceptable levels of knowledge, skills, and abilities required to successfully perform a position.

Labor Management Relations Act (also known as the Taft-Hartley Act), 1947   An amendment designed to remedy what the Republican Congress saw as two major omissions in the NLRA (Wagner Act): first, the identification of behaviors and practices that would be considered ULPs on the part of unions, and second, a provision that would allow the government to issue an injunction against a strike that threatened national interests. The Labor-Management Relations Act identified the following unfair labor practices that could be committed by unions:

- Restraining or coercing employees in the exercise of their rights or an employer in the choice of its bargaining representative

- Causing an employer to discriminate against an employee

- Refusing to bargain with the employer of the employees it represents

- Engaging in certain types of secondary boycotts

- Requiring excessive dues

- Engaging in featherbedding

- Picketing for recognition for more than 30 days without petitioning for an election

- Entering into hot cargo agreements

- Striking or picketing a health care establishment without giving the required notice

Labor Management Reporting and Disclosure Act (also known as the Landrum-Griffin Act), 1959   A law that created additional labor-management guidelines, including

- A requirement that unions submit annual financial reporting to the DOL, to document how union members' dues were spent

- A bill of rights for union members guaranteeing them freedom of speech and periodic secret elections

- The designation of every union official as a fiduciary

- Even stronger provisions relative to secondary boycotting and organizational and recognition picketing

labor market competitors   Other employers with whom you are competing for talent.

labor relations   Labor relations speaks to the many dimensions and facets of the relationship between management and groups of workers who happen to be represented by a labor union. In some ways, labor relations can be thought of as a subset of employee relations (see the definition for *employee relations*).

lag the market   A compensation approach in which an organization chooses, by design, or simply because of budgetary constraints, to offer total compensation packages that are less competitive than the total compensation packages that are being offered by their labor market competitors. Organizations that lag the market might offset this potential disadvantage by reinforcing and maximizing the intrinsic rewards that it offers—long-term potential growth opportunities, the ability to contribute to a particularly significant organizational mission, and so on.

Landrum-Griffin Act (also known as the Labor Management Reporting and Disclosure Act), 1959   A law that created additional labor-management guidelines, including

- A requirement that unions submit annual financial reporting to the DOL, to document how union members' dues were spent

- A bill of rights for union members guaranteeing them freedom of speech and periodic secret elections

- The designation of every union official as a fiduciary

- Even stronger provisions relative to secondary boycotting and organizational and recognition picketing

lead the market   A compensation approach in which an organization offers total compensation packages that are "better" than packages being offered by their labor market competitors. Organizations that lead the market may believe that higher compensation packages will attract higher-performing employees who will, in turn, pay for themselves, and then some. In short, these organizations want the best of the best and are willing to pay for it.

leadership development   The strategic investment in the managers and leaders who work within the organization.

leafleting   The onsite or offsite distribution of leaflets and flyers.

learned professional exemption   An exemption under the FLSA. To qualify for a learned professional exemption

  ▶ The employee's primary duty must be the performance of work requiring advanced knowledge, defined as work which is predominantly intellectual in character and which includes work requiring the consistent exercise of discretion and judgment.

  ▶ The advanced knowledge must be in a field of science or learning.

  ▶ The advanced knowledge must be customarily acquired by a prolonged course of specialized intellectual instruction.

learning and growth perspective   One of the four perspectives of the balanced scorecard. This perspective looks at employee training, as well as attitudes toward individual and corporate growth. It emphasizes the criticality of the knowledge worker, of people as the organization's primary resource, and of the need for employees to continually grow and learn so as to be able to perform in a manner that will truly support the attainment of organizational goals.

learning level evaluation   Measures whether and to what degree participants have mastered the skills or acquired the knowledge explored through the learning objectives. "Pre-tests" and "post-tests," which are frequently seen in e-learning applications, are one means of assessing skills development and knowledge acquisition.

learning organization   Ones in which individuals at all levels strive to acquire knowledge and develop skills that will enable them, individually and collectively, to attain higher levels of performance. The concept of a learning organization is fundamental to HRD and is often supported through training initiatives.

learning styles   Different ways that people learn and process ideas and information. There are three different learning styles: visual, auditory, and tactile/kinesthetic.

lecture/lecturette   A training method that includes presenting information to participants. Lecturettes are simply shorter versions of lectures.

leniency error/bias (interviewing)   An interviewing error/bias that occurs when the interviewer applies an inappropriately lenient standard to one or more candidates, resulting in a higher overall assessment of the candidate(s).

leniency error/bias (performance management)   A performance management error/bias in which the appraiser applies an inappropriately lenient standard to one or more employees, resulting in a higher overall assessment of the employee's (or employees') performance.

Lewin, Kurt   Lewin first described the change process as one that involves three stages: unfreezing, moving, and refreezing.

life insurance   A health and welfare benefit that helps employees to provide their beneficiaries and loved ones with income in the event of their deaths. Many employers offer a certain amount of life insurance at no cost to employees and offer optional supplemental life insurance, as well.

lobbying   The process of reaching out to elected officials to express beliefs and opinions with the hope of influencing a governmental body.

local union   A specific level of a union organization that is largely responsible for the day-to-day administration of the labor agreement and relationship with union members. "Locals" generally have an elected president and elected stewards who represent the workers in the workplace. Larger local unions might have a full-time paid business agent. Most locals belong to and are chartered by a larger national union.

Log of Work-Related Injuries and Illnesses (also known as the OSHA Form 300)   A form used to record the "what," "how," "when," "where," and "who" of all work-related injuries and illnesses and must be completed within seven calendar days from the time the organization learns of a work-related injury or illness.

long-form employment applications   Employment applications that require candidates to provide more detailed and comprehensive information about their work history, education, and qualifications.

long-term disability insurance (LTD)   A health and welfare benefit that provides employees with the opportunity to replace a designated percentage of an employee's income that is lost through illness or injury.

long-term incentive programs   Incentive programs that area usually more than one year in duration.

M

Mackay Doctrine   The doctrine that grants employers the right to permanently replace workers who strike during an economic strike. This right and this nickname are derived from the 1938 Supreme Court decision in *NLRB v. Mackay Radio and Telegraph Co.*

maintenance of membership   Employees who voluntarily choose to join a union must maintain their individual memberships for the duration of the labor contract. Each employee then has a 30-day window at the beginning of the next contract period during which he or she may terminate membership. Maintenance of membership arrangements are illegal in right-to-work states.

major life activities   Include but are not necessarily limited to walking, seeing, hearing, breathing, caring for oneself, performing manual tasks, sitting, standing, lifting, learning, and thinking.

major restorative care   A category of dental care or coverage that includes more involved procedures such as bridgework and crowns, and that usually have a lower reimbursement percentage (perhaps 50%).

management by objectives (MBO)   A goal-centered OD intervention that focuses primarily on collaboratively generating individual employee objectives that align with organizational objectives. Measurement is an essential element of an MBO program. As follows logically, MBO is often used as a performance appraisal method because of its strong orientation toward goal establishment and attainment.

management by walking around (MBWA)   A management approach where a manager makes a commitment to spend a dedicated amount of time with employees on a regular basis. By increasing his or her visibility, the manager creates opportunities to provide feedback to and receive input from employees. Management by walking around also helps ensure that employees have increased access to "the boss," thereby increasing the potential for spontaneity, creativity, and synergy.

mandatory arbitration agreements   A type of employment agreement that stipulates that, in return for the opportunity to be employed by the organization, the employee agrees to resolve employment-related issues through a neutral third party (the arbitrator/s) instead of filing a private lawsuit against the employer.

maritime   One of the major industries designated by OSHA.

market data   Data that is collected through the process of market pricing. Market data can be obtained about a number of benchmark positions as part of a larger initiative, and can be used in a number of ways. For instance, market data can help in the building of a job-worth hierarchy, around which other positions can be placed using a whole job slotting technique. Market data can also be used to obtain information for one particular job, in combination with other job evaluation techniques that might be used.

market pricing   A process of looking at the relevant labor market to ascertain what the going rate or market rate is for a particular position. Market pricing can yield valuable pay data about "benchmark" jobs—jobs for which close matches can be identified in the relevant labor market.

Martin v. Wilks, 1988   Key Issue: Affirmative action. Significance: Current employees who are negatively impacted by consent decrees that were established in an earlier time and which sought to resolve discrimination that was present in an earlier time may challenge the validity of such decrees.

This case falls under the category of "reverse discrimination" because it alleged race discrimination and was brought by individuals who were not minorities/people of color.

mass layoff   Occurs (under WARN) when one of the following two events happens within a 30-day period at a single worksite: 500 full-time employees are laid off, or at least 33 percent of the workforce is laid off (if and only if that 33% includes between 50 and 499 full-time employees).

match the market   A compensation approach in which an organization chooses to offer total compensation packages that are comparable to the total compensation packages being offered by their labor market competitors. Organizations that match the market make a conscious choice to be "externally competitive" with respect to total compensation.

material safety data sheet (MSDS)   Required (by the Hazard Communication Standard) for all chemicals located in the workplace.

maturity   The third stage of the organizational life cycle, during which the growing pains have passed and the culture is well-established. It's important to ensure that certain elements of the culture do not become a bit too well-established. If this were to happen, an "entitlement mentality" could begin to emerge relative to pay and/or benefits. The organizational structure could evolve in a somewhat rigid manner, and resistance to OD and change initiatives could be high.

McDonnell Douglas Corp v. Green, 1973   Key issue: Disparate treatment/prima facie. Significance: The initial burden of proof for establishing a prima facie (Latin for "at first view") case of discrimination against an employer (or potential employer) under Title VII of the Civil Rights Act of 1964 rests with the employee (or applicant), who must be able to establish four key elements:

- ▶ The person is a member of a protected class.

- ▶ The person applied for a job for which the employer was seeking applicants.

- ▶ The person was rejected, despite being qualified for the position.

- ▶ After this rejection, the employer continued to seek other applicants with similar qualifications.

After the employee establishes a prima facie case for disparate treatment, the burden of proof then shifts to the employer, who must then provide a nondiscriminatory reason for its decision.

McGehee and Thayer Identified three levels of HRD/training needs analysis and assessment: organizational analysis, task or work (operations) analysis, and individual or person (man) analysis.

McKennon v. Nashville Banner Publishing Co., 1995 Key issue: After-acquired evidence. Significance: An employer will be held accountable for discriminatory employment actions even if it discovers evidence after taking the discriminatory employment action that would have led the employer to that same employment action for legitimate, nondiscriminatory reasons.

medical tests Preemployment medical tests, or exams, that can be conducted only if the exam is job-related and consistent with business necessity, and even then only after an offer (or a conditional offer) of employment has been extended to the candidate.

Medicare An amendment to the Social Security Act that provides hospital and medical insurance for the elderly and people with disabilities. There are three parts to Medicare: Hospital Insurance (sometimes called Part A); Medical Insurance (sometimes called Part B); and Prescription Benefits (sometimes called Part D).

Medicare—Part A The portion of Medicare that helps pay for inpatient hospital care, skilled nursing care, and other services.

Medicare—Part B The portion of Medicare that helps pay for items such as doctor's fees, outpatient hospital visits, and other medical services and supplies.

Medicare—Part C The portion of Medicare available to persons who are eligible for Part A and enrolled in Part B through which private health insurance companies can contract with the federal government to offer Medicare benefits through their own policies.

Medicare—Part D The portion of Medicare that added prescription drug benefits for all individuals eligible for Medicare Part A and enrolled in Medicare Part B.

Mental Health Parity Act (MHPA), 1996 A law that prohibits group health plans providers, insurance companies, and HMOs that offer mental health benefits from setting annual or lifetime dollar limits on mental health benefits that are lower than any such dollar limits for medical and surgical benefits.

Meritor Savings Bank v. Vinson, 1986 Key issue: Sexual harassment. Significance: This was the first ruling to establish that sexual harassment (whether quid pro quo or hostile environment) constitutes a violation of Title VII of the Civil Rights Act of 1964. In addition, the court ruled that it isn't enough for an organization to have a policy prohibiting discrimination. Instead, the ruling stated that "reasonable care requires effective communication of policies and training. The employer has the burden of proof."

Mine Safety and Health Act (MSH Act), 1977 The second piece of legislation created specifically to protect employee health and safety—this time, for underground and surface miners working in coal as well as non-coal mines.

minimum wage The lowest hourly rate of pay that an employer can legally pay an employee.

mission A statement that articulates, in essence, the reason why the organization is in existence. It may speak to the nature of the organization's business or purpose, its customers, and sometimes even its employees and its role in the community. A mission statement should be broad (but not overly generalized), brief, clear, unambiguous, and designed to last for "the long haul."

moving The second stage in Lewin's change process theory. Through the moving stage, people are brought to accept the change and experience the "new state" that the change was designed to bring about.

multiple linear regression A mathematical technique that examines the past relationship between several variables, determines the statistical strength of that relationship, and, on the basis of that analysis, projects future conditions.

musculoskeletal disorders (MSDs)   Work-related illnesses and/or injuries that affect one or more parts of the musculoskeletal system.

N

narrative method   Performance appraisal method in which the appraiser uses a narrative format to write and record observations and assessments of each employee's performance.

National Industrial Recovery Act, 1933   A law that guaranteed laborers the right to organize and bargain collectively (Title I). The act also established that employees could not be required, as a condition of employment, to join or refrain from joining a labor organization. In May of 1935, the National Industrial Recovery Act was held unconstitutional by the U.S. Supreme Court (*Schechter Poultry Corp. v. United States*). Although this decision was wholly unrelated to labor and collective bargaining, the Supreme Court decision rendered the labor-related provisions illegal, as well. The right to organize and bargain reverted, once again, back to railway workers, and no one else. This would not, however, be the case for long.

National Labor Relations Act (also known as the Wagner Act), 1935   A law that guaranteed "the right to self-organization, to form, join, or assist labor organizations, to bargain collectively through representatives of their own choosing, and to engage in concerted activities for the purpose of collective bargaining or other mutual aid and protection." Certain groups or categories of employees are excluded under the NLRA from membership in a bargaining unit. Examples would include managers, supervisors, confidential employees (essentially secretaries and administrative assistants to managers who can make labor relations decisions), and several others.

National Labor Relations Board (NLRB)   A federal agency created by the NLRA that is responsible for administering and enforcing the rights established by the NLRA. As stated on its website, the NLRB has two principle functions:

- To determine, through secret-ballot elections, the free democratic choice by employees whether they wish to be represented by a union in dealing with their employers and if so, by which union

- To prevent and remedy unlawful acts, called unfair labor practices, by either employers or unions

national union   A specific level of a union organization that brings together all the union locals for a particular group that are scattered across the country. There are usually different hierarchical levels in between the local union and the national union. National unions have far more power with respect to bargaining and political influence than the union locals could have on their own. National unions also advise and guide local unions and may also manage nationwide benefits programs (such as retirement programs and health insurance plans).

The Needlestick Safety and Prevention Act of 2000   A compliance directive for enforcing the Bloodborne Pathogens Standard that added three key requirements to the existing standard:

- Evaluation and implementation of safer needle devices (as they become available). Reviews of and searches for such enhancements must be done annually.

- Actively involve employees who actually use needles and needle devices in this evaluation and selection process of safer needle devices.

- Maintenance of a log of all injuries resulting from contaminated sharps.

negligent hiring   A tort doctrine that speaks to an employer's decision to hire an individual without engaging in appropriate "due diligence" into that candidate's credentials, prior work experience, and the like. In essence, negligent hiring claims arise after an individual is hired through a flawed hiring process. A hiring process can be flawed for a number of reasons. For instance, a sound hiring process that is applied in an unsound manner would be flawed, as would a hiring process that is designed in a flawed manner. Flaws could relate to inadequate or poorly conducted reference checks, job requirements that do not reflect the skills or credentials that are truly required for a position, and the like.

negligent referral   A tort doctrine that speaks to the failure of an organization to reveal truthful, negative information about an employee (or former employee) to a potential employer.

negligent retention   A tort doctrine that speaks to the continued employment of an individual who is performing in an unfit manner and, therefore, should have been terminated. Negligent retention tort claims might be filed when an employee who should have been terminated, but was not, inflicts some sort of harm on another person. Negligent retention claims are often filed in conjunction with other tort claims, such as negligent training, intentional infliction of emotional distress, and the like.

negligent training   A tort doctrine that refers to an employer's failure to provide proper training to an employee, when that failure results in some sort of unfit performance by the employee.

Negligent training can emerge as an issue either when an employee who was hired for one position assumes another position for which he or she may not be fully and appropriately trained, or when an employee's job duties and responsibilities change over time, thus requiring additional training if the employee is to continue performing the job in a fit manner.

NLRB v. Mackay Radio and Telegraph Co., 1938   The Supreme Court case that established that employers have the right to permanently replace workers who strike during an economic strike.

NLRB v. Weingarten, 1975   Weingarten Rights, derived from the Supreme Court decision in *NLRB v. Weingarten*, 1975, established the right of unionized employees to have union representation at an investigatory interview with management if the employee reasonably believes that discipline might result from that meeting. Although the NLRB reversed this decision in 2000 (Epilepsy Foundation of Northeast Ohio, 331 NLRB 676) and held that nonunion employees also have the right to have a representative present at a meeting of this sort, in 2004 the NLRB returned to its original determination and held that nonunion employees do not have the right to have a co-worker or other representative present in a meeting when the employee reasonably believes it might result in discipline.

nominal group technique   A nonmathematical, qualitative forecasting technique that calls upon the expertise and predictive ability of experts who meet in person and process their ideas as a group. Led by a facilitator, the meeting begins with each expert writing down his or her ideas, after which each expert presents those ideas to the group. The group then comes together to discuss everyone's ideas, after which each individual group member is called upon to independently rank the ideas. The meeting facilitator will then combine all of the individual rankings to determine which are the most important to the group.

noncompete agreements   A type of employment agreement that prohibits current and (within stated limitations) former employees from competing against the employer. "Competing" can manifest itself in a number of ways and must be defined within the agreement.

nondirective interviews   Relatively unstructured interviews through which the candidate, not the interviewer, guides and controls the flow and content of information discussed.

non-exempt An employee who is covered by the overtime (and minimum wage) provisions of the FLSA.

nonquantitative job evaluation techniques Job evaluation techniques that determine the relative value of jobs within the organization without using mathematical techniques. Instead, these methods focus on the "whole job" (which is why these techniques are also referred to as "whole job" methods).

nontraditional staffing alternatives Work arrangements that do not fall clearly within "internal" or "external" recruiting methods, because they could be used as a retention tool for existing employees, as a way to attract candidates, or as a way to outsource current assignments. Examples of nontraditional staffing alternatives could include the use of temporary help, temp-to-hire arrangements, or consultants. Current or newly hired employees can also participate in flexible staffing programs through part-time employment, telecommuting, job sharing arrangements, or seasonal employment.

nonverbals Also known as "body language" or "nonverbal communication cues", nonverbals refer to communication that is not based on spoken language.

Norris-LaGuardia Act, 1932 A law that strengthened unions even more by establishing the rights of labor unions to organize and to strike. It also prohibited federal courts from enforcing "yellow dog" contracts or agreements.

O

occupational health, safety, and security Occupational health, safety, and security promotes employees' physical and mental well-being while maintaining a safe and nonviolent work environment, all in support of the employer's short-term, long-term, emerging, and strategic objectives.

Occupational Safety and Health Act (OSH Act), 1970 The first law to establish consistent health and safety standards for the workplace.

Occupational Safety and Health Administration (OSHA) The federal agency created to administer and enforce the Occupational Safety and Health Administration Act (OSH Act).

offshoring A specific type of outsourcing that uses vendors that are located overseas.

Old Age, Survivors, and Disability Insurance (OASDI) (also known as the Social Security Act) Old Age, Survivors, and Disability Insurance program (OASDI) is a social insurance program (although some would define it differently) that is funded through payroll taxes. Its three primary components are retirement income, disability benefits, and survivor's benefits.

Older Worker's Benefit Protection Act (OWBPA), 1990 An amendment to the ADEA that makes it illegal to discriminate against older workers with respect to benefits, or to target older workers for layoffs.

onboarding (also known as orientation) The process by which a new employee transitions into the organization.

open door policy A "standing invitation," and a genuine one, for employees to raise their concerns with managers and/or human resources, face to face. The use of an "open door" cannot result in penalties, formal or otherwise, against those employees who avail themselves of this resource.

open shop Employees are required neither to join the union nor to pay union dues. This is the only type of union security clause that is legal in right-to-work states (and for federal government employees).

operational/tactical HR   Somewhere in between the administrative functions that must be performed to keep our organizations going and the inventive and creative life force that is part of strategic management lies the operational or tactical dimension of the HR function. The operational, tactical, or day-to-day performance and execution of the HR role can be accomplished in many ways, some of which do more to define us toward the administrative end of the spectrum, and others that demonstrate more vividly how and whether the overarching strategic objectives of HR (and, therefore, of the organization) are being brought to life. Operational/tactical level HR is one leg of the HR stool—the other two legs are strategic HR and transformational HR.

organization development (OD)   The planned and structured process through which the overall performance, growth, and effectiveness of an organization is enhanced through strategic, deliberate, and integrated initiatives. The interesting and complex area of OD incorporates four academic disciplines: psychology, sociology, anthropology, and management.

organization transformation change   OD interventions that focus on the organization as a complex human system that must be continually examined and reexamined.

organizational culture   The "way things are done around here"; the formal and informal manifestation of what the organization "is all about." Organizational culture encompasses historical events, current events, and future events (whether potential, likely, or simply rumored). More specifically, organizational culture reflects and embodies the norms, mores, values, beliefs, customs, and attitudes of the organization and of those who work within the organization.

organizational display   The section of an affirmative action plan that essentially provides an organization chart that depicts the contractor's workforce in terms of incumbents' race, gender, and wages. The organization display is the newer, shorter, and simpler version of the "workforce analysis."

organizational (or business) ethics   A shared values-based system designed to inculcate within the organization's population a sense of how to conduct business properly.

organizational-level analysis   Level 1 of McGehee and Thayer's three levels of HRD/training needs analysis and assessment. Organizational-level analysis determines where HRD/training can and should be used within the overall organization.

organizational life cycle   Four evolutionary stages of birth, growth, maturity, and decline experienced by organizations over the course of time. These phases or stages are roughly approximate to the phases of life experienced by humans, thereby further bolstering the perspective of the organization as a living, breathing entity. Each phase of the organizational life cycle will warrant different HR systems or interventions.

organizational picketing   Picketing that is designed to generate interest on the part of employees to vote for union representation.

organizational structure   The various ways in which organizations can be designed to as to attain maximum levels of effectiveness and efficiency.

organizing function   Identified by Fayol as one of the five management functions, organizing speaks to the ways in which the manager obtains and arranges the resources that he or she needs to implement the plans (the output of the "planning" function). Those resources could include people, facilities, materials, and so on.

orientation (also known as onboarding)   The process by which a new employee is supported as he or she transitions into the organization.

orthodonture   A specialty type of dental coverage that is often covered at a relatively low percentage (perhaps 50%) and that often has a lifetime cap per covered employee.

OSHA 3165 A poster that lists each employee's rights related to health and safety. This poster must be displayed in a conspicuous place that is easily visible to employees and applicants for employment.

OSHA Form 300 (also known as the Log of Work-Related Injuries and Illnesses) A form used to record the "what," "how," "when," "where," and "who" of certain work-related injuries and illnesses, and that must be completed within seven calendar days from the time the organization learns of a work-related injury or illness.

OSHA Form 300A (also known as the Summary of Work-Related Injuries and Illnesses) A form used to record a numeric summary of all work-related injuries and illnesses logged in OSHA's Form 300 over the course of each calendar year. This form indicates the number of cases, the number of workdays impacted, and the numbers and types of work-related injuries and illnesses. A worksheet is also available to assist employers in filling out this summary. Each year, a completed Form 300 must be posted conspicuously for three months (between February 1 and April 30).

OSHA Form 301 (also known as the Injury and Illness Incident Report) A form that must be completed for each work-related injury or illness within seven calendar days of the date on which the employer learns of the work-related injury or illness, and that must be maintained by the employee for five years following the year in which the incident or illness occurred.

other-than-serious violation A violation that is unlikely to result in serious injury or death. OSHA may propose a fine of up to $7,000 for each other-than-serious violation.

outside sales exemption An exemption under the FLSA. Unlike the other types of exemptions, a minimum salary is not required to establish an exemption on the basis of outside sales. The following criteria, however, must be met:

▶ The employee's primary duty must be making sales (as defined in the FLSA) or obtaining orders or contracts for services or for the use of facilities for which a consideration will be paid by the client or customer

▶ The employee must be customarily and regularly engaged away from the employer's place or places of business

outsourcing The reassignment of responsibilities, functions, or jobs that had been performed within the organization to now be carried out by resources that are outside the organization ("third-party contractors").

overtime Hours worked in excess of 40 per week.

P

paired comparison method A comparative performance appraisal method in which the appraiser compares every employee in the group, one at a time, to every other employee in the group.

panel interviews Interviews in which more than one person interviews a candidate at the same time.

Pareto Principle (also known as the 80–20 rule) A principle that asserts that 80% of effects result from 20% of causes. The Pareto principle and the chart that visually depicts it are intended to help individuals focus their efforts where there is the greatest likelihood of bringing about the desired change.

pay for time not worked Programs that pay employees for time that they did not actually work (for instance, sick days, vacation days, jury duty, personal time, designated holidays, floating holidays, bereavement leave, and the like).

pay grades (also referred to as grades or job grades)   Levels into which jobs of similar internal worth can be categorized. Jobs within the same pay grade share a similar level of value or worth to the organization. Different organizations will have different numbers of pay grades, with differing degrees of distinction between each of those grades.

pay structures   The "building blocks" that are used to create compensation systems that will support the total compensation philosophy of the organization, and that will, in turn, support the attainment of the organization's objectives.

pedagogy   The study and science of how children learn.

Pension Benefit Guaranty Corporation (PBGC)   A government corporation created by ERISA that functions as an insurer that provides a minimum guaranteed benefit for certain pension plans. PBGC protects participants in most defined benefit plans and cash balance plans (within certain limitations). PBGC is funded by insurance premiums that are paid by plan sponsors, not by general tax dollars. Funding also comes from investment income, assets from underfunded pension plans it has taken over, and recoveries from companies formerly responsible for those plans.

performance appraisal   The form that is reviewed during the meeting that takes place at the end of the performance measurement period, during which the manager and the employee review the employee's performance during the prior year and look ahead to the next year.

performance management   Day-to-day activities in which managers engage with their employees as they work to collaboratively accomplish organizational objectives.

performance standards/expectations   The expectations that an organization has for an employee with respect to what he or she is responsible for accomplishing, and/or the ways in which the employee executes his or her position.

permissive subjects (also known as voluntary subjects)   "Permissive" subjects of bargaining are topics that can be submitted to collective bargaining if and only if the employer and the employees' representative are willing to do so. Attempting to force bargaining on a voluntary or permissive subject constitutes a ULP.

perpetuating past discrimination   Unlawful discrimination that occurs when an employer's past discriminatory practices are perpetuated through current policies or practices, even those that appear to be nondiscriminatory. When linked in some way with past discrimination, seemingly nondiscriminatory practices can have a discriminatory effect.

person (man) level analysis   Level 3 of McGehee and Thayer's three levels of HRD/training needs analysis and assessment. Person (man) level analysis assesses performance of a particular individual.

personality tests   Preemployment tests that are used to gather information about a candidate's personality traits, motivation, discipline, and other characteristics.

phone interviews   A telephone-based prescreen interview that is used as one important tool to determine which candidates will be invited in for a face-to-face interview.

physical hazards—design   A physical hazard that results from the way in which the workplace or workspace is designed (also referred to as ergonomics).

physical health hazards   A type of health hazard that results from actual, tangible things and/or conditions in the workplace that increase the risk of work-related illnesses or injuries.

picketing   An expression of free speech that takes place when people congregate outside a workplace. To be considered protected concerted activity, picketing must remain nonviolent.

piece-rate systems   Compensation programs under which individuals are paid according to their production volume.

pilot programs   A training program that is generally delivered to a subsection of the population of individuals who would ultimately be expected to participate in the training initiative. Others who might also participate in a pilot program could be decision makers, senior management (from whom you wish to secure buy-in), and other key stakeholders.

placement goals   The section of an affirmative action plan that establishes goals for areas in which underutilization exists.

plaintiff   A party who files a lawsuit alleging unlawful discrimination.

planning function   Identified by Fayol as one of the five management functions, planning lays the groundwork for how managers will work toward accomplishing the organization's goals. Through planning, managers decide what needs to get done, when it needs to get done, who will do it, how it will get done, and where it will be done.

planning processes   Those processes (within project management) through which objectives are established, along with the best alternatives that will support the attainment of those objectives. In general, planning processes are considered the second of five project management processes, although there can be considerable overlap between those five distinct processes.

plant closing   Occurs (under WARN) when a facility or operating unit is shut down for more than six months or when 50 or more employees at a worksite lose their jobs during any 30-day period.

plant patents   Granted for the invention, discovery, or asexual reproduction of any distinct and new variety of plant.

point factor   A quantitative job evaluation system that first identifies specific compensable factors and then establishes levels of performance within each of those compensable factors. The relative importance of each compensable factor to the organization is "weighted," and a different point value is then assigned to each level within each compensable factor.

point of service (POS)   A type of managed healthcare plan that is a combination of the HMO and PPO managed care models. Like the PPO model, there is a network of physicians and health care providers who have agreed to provide services at a discounted rate. Like the HMO model, there is a gatekeeper, a primary care physician who must provide plan members with referrals to specialists and for other services. Unlike the HMO model, however, referrals can be made to physicians who are either inside or outside the network. Although out-of-network referrals will cost participants more, they are permissible.

Portal to Portal Act, 1947   An amendment to the FLSA that offered clearer definitions of "hours worked" for purposes of minimum wage and overtime payments. According to the act, employers are only required to compensate workers for working time that they spend on activities that relate to the performance of their job.

postaccident drug testing   Drug testing that is conducted for employees who are involved in an accident or unsafe practice incident to determine whether alcohol or some other drug was a factor, to protect the safety of employees (users and nonusers), and to identify opportunities for rehabilitation.

predictive validity   The degree to which the predictions made by a selection procedure actually manifest themselves through future performance.

preemployment drug testing   Drug testing that is conducted to decrease the likelihood of hiring someone who is currently using/abusing illegal drugs.

preexisting condition   Under HIPAA, a condition for which medical advice, diagnosis, care, or treatment was recommended or received during the six-month period prior to an individual's enrollment date.

preferred provider organization (PPO)   A managed care health care plan that offers a network of health care providers who band together to offer services at a discounted rate to plan participants. PPOs resemble indemnity plans, in that network providers are paid when they render services and plan participants can choose which doctors they want to visit and when they want to visit them. Plan participants can also choose to avail themselves of doctors or other health care providers who are outside the network; however, the costs to the member will be higher than they would have been if the member had chosen a doctor within the network.

Pregnancy Discrimination Act, 1978   A law that amended Title VII of the Civil Rights Act of 1964 to specifically prohibit discrimination on the basis of pregnancy, childbirth, or related medical conditions.

premium-only plans (POPs)   The simplest and most transparent (from employees' perspectives) of the three Section 125 plans. With POPs, employees pay for their portion of certain insurance premiums on a pretax basis. The net effect is that each employee's taxable income is reduced, which is how employers and employees can reduce taxes and save money.

pre-promotion drug testing   Drug testing that is conducted to decrease the likelihood of promoting someone who is currently using/abusing illegal drugs.

prescreen interviews   An interview used early in the selection process to determine which candidates meet specific predetermined job requirements.

prescription drug coverage   A health and welfare benefit that affords employees with discounted or (less frequently) free prescription drugs. Some employers provide prescription drug coverage as part of their medical plan, whereas others provide this coverage under a separate plan. Plan members may be required to pay a copay, to purchase their prescriptions at certain pharmacies, to use generic drugs (when available), or to use mail order services for maintenance drugs (prescriptions that are prescribed for chronic, long-term conditions and that are taken on a regular, recurring basis).

preventive care   A category of dental care or coverage that includes things such as regular dental checkups, exams, cleanings, and sometimes X-rays. It is often reimbursed at 100% of cost or at 100% of reasonable and customary (R&C) expenses, so as to encourage plan members to take advantage of measures that encourage good oral health and that potentially decrease long-term costs.

primary care physician (PCP)   A member's primary physician, who in HMO and POS models is the "gatekeeper" who must provide plan members with referrals to specialists and for other services.

primary duty   The principal, main, major, or most important duty that the employee performs. Determination of an employee's primary duty must be based on all the facts in a particular case, with the major emphasis being on the character of the employee's job as a whole.

primary questions   Questions that are asked of all candidates for a particular position during a particular interview process. They are designed to elicit relevant information about how well the candidate possesses and would demonstrate the skills, knowledge, abilities, behavioral characteristics, and other requirements of the position.

primary research   A process that involves collecting data firsthand from the original source from which it emanates.

privacy case   In an effort to preserve privacy, under certain circumstances (including upon employee request), the words "privacy case" should be substituted for the employee's name in the OSHA Form 300 (also known as the Log of Work-Related Injuries and Illnesses). In these cases, a separate document must be maintained that matches case numbers with employee names (for identification purposes).

probing questions   The questions that an interviewer asks as a way of following up to the candidate's response to primary questions. Because they are asked in response to each candidate's initial response to the primary question, probing questions will vary from interview to interview. Interviews can still ensure consistency, however, by asking probing questions that relate only to each original primary question.

Professional in Human Resources (PHR)   The Professional in Human Resources certification, granted by and issued through HRCI.

profit sharing   Organizationwide incentive plans that establish an organizationwide profit goal. If the goal is reached, the profits are shared with employees. Profits can either be shared immediately (cash profit-sharing plans) or later (deferred profit-sharing plans).

profit sharing plans   A type of defined contribution plan under which the organization contributes to its employees' accounts. These contributions often come from profits and thus serve as an incentive to performance.

progressive discipline   A system that incorporates a series of steps—each more progressively "involved," advanced, or serious, than the last—for addressing performance or behavior that does not meet expectations. Progressive discipline provides multiple opportunities, at multiple decision points, for employees to make decisions that will result in them maintaining their employment. When applied appropriately, therefore, progressive discipline can be an empowering process as well as an employee relations initiative.

project management   "The application of knowledge, skills, tools, and techniques to a broad range of activities in order to meet the requirements of a particular project" (Project Management Institute).

protected class   A group defined by a common characteristic that is protected from discrimination and harassment on the basis of law. People who share a common characteristic and who are protected from discrimination and harassment on the basis of that shared characteristic are said to belong to a protected class.

protected concerted activity   Protected concerted activity refers to associational rights that are granted to employees through Section 7 of the NLRA. Protected concerted activity can include activity aimed at improving employees' terms and conditions of employment. Through this language, the NLRA protects associational rights for employees who do not belong to a union as well as for employees who are unionized. This interpretation was confirmed by 1948. As such, employers need to be careful not to interfere with protected concerted activities even in workplaces that are nonunionized.

public domain   Copyrights eventually expire, upon which the work enters the public domain. This means that the work is available and free for all to use. In addition, many federal government works are also considered to be in the public domain.

Q

qualified domestic relations order (QDRO)   Court orders that require employers to make benefit payments to a participant's former spouse (or another alternative payee) without violating ERISA's prohibitions against assignment or alienation of benefits.

qualified person   A candidate who meets minimum job requirements (education, experience, licenses, and so on) and can perform the essential functions of the position with or without reasonable accommodation.

quantitative job evaluation techniques   Job evaluation techniques that determine the relative value of jobs within the organization without using mathematical techniques. Quantitative (or "factor-based") job evaluation methods identify the degree to which each position is responsible for or requires specific "compensable factors."

quid pro quo A form of sexual harassment that occurs when an individual's submission to or rejection of sexual advances or conduct of a sexual nature is used as the basis for employment-related decisions. Quid pro quo harassment, by nature, originates from a supervisor or from others who have the authority to influence or make decisions about the terms and conditions of the employee's employment.

R

Railway Labor Act, 1926 A law that provided what was perhaps the first "win-win scenario" for labor and management. Railroad management wanted to keep the trains moving, which meant they needed to end "wildcat" strikes. Railroad workers wanted to organize, to be recognized as the exclusive bargaining agent in dealing with the railroad, and to negotiate and enforce agreements. The Railway Labor Act addressed both issues. The Railway Labor Act is also significant in that it is where the "work now, grieve later" rule originated. In an effort to keep the rails running, which Congress felt was in the public's interest, Congress mandated that when disputes arise in the workplace, transportation workers covered by the RLA must "work now and grieve later" (with a few exceptions, such as for safety).

The Railway Labor Act applied only to interstate railroads and their related undertakings—at the time, the most critical element of the nation's transportation infrastructure. In 1936, it was amended to include airlines engaged in interstate commerce.

random drug testing Unannounced drug tests that are conducted at random, for reasons related to safety or security.

range spread The percentage that is calculated by subtracting the minimum of the range from the maximum of the range and dividing that number by the minimum of the range. Range spreads allow organizations to recognize and compensate employees within the same job and within jobs that are in the same grade, for different levels of skill, experience, or performance.

ranges A range of compensation rates that correspond to grades and that guide the pay rates for jobs within that grade. Ranges specify the lowest (minimum) and the highest (maximum) compensation rates for which positions within each grade are generally paid. The halfway point between those two figures is known as the midpoint.

ranking method A comparative performance appraisal method in which the appraiser literally "ranks" his or her direct reports, in terms of overall performance, from "best" to "worst."

rapport The process of helping a candidate to relax and feel comfortable and welcome at the beginning of the interview.

rating methods Performance appraisal methods in which the appraiser compares the performance of the employee against the expected behavior.

rating scales A type of performance appraisal in which the appraiser rates the employee on a variety of different categories using a three-, four-, or five-point scale. Those categories can consist of individual goals, individual competencies, multiple goals, groups of competencies, and the like. Each point on the scale corresponds to a different level of performance against standards.

ratio analysis A mathematical technique that examines changes, movements, and trends over a period of time. Instead of looking at just one variable alone, however, it looks at two variables and how the relationship between those two variables has evolved over time.

reaction level evaluation   Measures participants' responses and reactions to a program immediately after it has been delivered. This level of evaluation often takes the form of a short survey that participants are asked to complete at the end of a training session.

reading   A training method during which the instructor/facilitator directs the participants to read specific printed materials.

realistic job preview   A realistic picture of the position and the organization (that is provided to candidates). This, in turn, will help the candidate make a realistic and accurate assessment of whether he or she will be willing and/or able to function effectively within the day-to-day realities of the position, the department or unit, and the organization.

reasonable accommodation   A change in the way that one (or more) responsibilities relating to the execution of a position is performed, so as to enable a person with a disability to perform the essential functions of the position. Accommodations do not necessarily have to be adopted if they are unreasonable—in other words, if they cause undue hardship to the organization.

reasonable cause   A determination made by the EEOC relative to whether discrimination has occurred. If the EEOC determines that there is no reasonable cause, the case is closed, the parties are notified, and the charging party is given a "right to sue" letter. The charging party then has 90 days to file a private lawsuit.

If the EEOC determines that there is reasonable cause, the EEOC will attempt conciliation with the employer in an effort to develop a remedy for the discrimination. If the EEOC cannot conciliate the case, the EEOC will decide whether to take the case to court (this happens in a very small percentage of cases). If the EEOC does not take the case to court, it will close the case and issue the charging party a "right to sue" letter.

reasonable suspicion drug testing   Drug testing that is conducted when an employee has a documented pattern of unsafe work behavior in an effort to protect the safety and well being of employees and co-workers, and to identify opportunities for rehabilitation.

recency error/bias (interviewing)   An interviewing error/bias that occurs when the interviewer recalls recently interviewed candidates more vividly than candidates who were interviewed earlier in the process.

recency error/bias (performance management)   A performance management error/bias in which the appraiser places undue emphasis on the employee's most recent performance, rather than considering performance demonstrated throughout the entire performance measurement period.

recertification   The process by which HR professionals who have earned PHR, SPHR, and/or GPHR certification maintain the currency of that status.

recruiting   The process of attracting and creating a pool of qualified candidates.

refreezing   The third and final stage in Lewin's change process theory. Through the refreezing stage, people come to experience that what once represented a change has now become, in simplest terms, the norm.

Regents of California v. Bakke, 1978   Key issue: Affirmative action. Significance: The Supreme Court ruled that while race could be a factor in college admission decisions, quotas could not be established.

Although this case was based on a college admissions program, its significance extended to workplace affirmative action programs.

This case falls under the category of "reverse discrimination" since it alleged race discrimination and was brought by someone who was not a minority/person of color.

regular rate of pay   An employee's regular rate of pay includes more than just his or her hourly rate of pay; it would also include any incentives and commissions. It would not, however, include bonuses (which, unlike incentive programs, are discretionary), pay for time not worked, premium pay for weekend or holiday work, and the like.

Rehabilitation Act, 1973   A law that prohibits discrimination on the basis of physical and mental disabilities.

Section 503 of the act requires affirmative action and prohibits employment discrimination by federal government contractors and subcontractors with contracts of more than $10,000.

Section 504 of the act states that "no otherwise qualified individual with a disability in the United States shall be excluded from, denied the benefits of, or be subjected to discrimination under" any program or activity that either receives federal financial assistance or is conducted by any executive agency or the United States Postal Service.

Section 508 requires that federal agencies' electronic and information technology is accessible to people with disabilities, including employees and members of the public.

relevant labor market   The size and scope of the geographic area within which an organization would seek to attract qualified candidates for a particular position(s). Even within the same organization, the relevant labor market for different positions can vary widely depending upon the skills, knowledge, abilities, and behavioral characteristics required to perform each position successfully. Other factors that impact how an organization defines the relevant labor market might be the degree of competition that exists among employers for particular skills and/or knowledge, and the degree to which certain skills and/or knowledge requirements are industry specific.

reliability   The degree to which a selection process or instrument is consistent.

relief   When a plaintiff prevails in an EEO lawsuit, he or she may be awarded various forms of "relief" or remedies.

relocation   The process of moving a current or existing (or, less frequently, newly hired) employee's primary residence from one location to another.

remedies   When a plaintiff prevails in an EEO lawsuit, he or she may be awarded various forms of remedies or "relief."

repeat violation   A violation that is the same or substantially similar to a violation that was found during a previous inspection. OSHA may propose a fine of up to $70,000 for each repeat violation.

repetitive stress injuries (RSIs) (also known as cumulative trauma syndromes [CTSs] or cumulative trauma disorders [CTDs])   Injuries that result from placing too much stress (often through overuse) on a part of the body.

replacement charts   Tools that identify names of individuals who could potentially fill a particular position in the event that an opening were to occur.

request for proposal (RFP)   A request to potential vendors to propose solutions to address specific requirements (which are identified in the RFP document, and to which potential vendors respond in writing).

required subjects   Subjects that must be bargained in good faith if either the employer or the employees' representative requests it. Examples of required subjects include pay, wages, hours of employment, pensions for present employees, bonuses, group insurance, grievance procedures, safety practices, seniority, procedures for discharge, layoff, recall, or discipline, and union security.

research   Finding answers to questions.

respondent   The person or party against whom a charge of unlawful discrimination has been filed.

responsibility   One of the four factors used as a basis to assess the substantial equality of job content under the Equal Pay Act of 1963. "Responsibility" refers to the degree of responsibility and accountability that an employer entrusts to and expects from a particular position.

restorative care   A category of dental care or coverage that refers to oral "repairs" that are usually of a relatively minor nature, such as cavities or root canals. The reimbursement for restorative care is generally less than the reimbursement rate for preventive care (perhaps 80% instead of 100%).

results level evaluation   Looks specifically at whether the business or organizational results that were expected to occur as a result of training did in fact occur. This level of results-based evaluation is measurable, concrete, and usually of keen interest to the leaders of the organization because results speak volumes.

retained employment agencies   Search firms to whom an organization pays a fee whether or not the organization actually hires a candidate referred by the firm. The services of this type of agency are more often secured in an effort to fill executive-level positions.

retirement benefits   One of the three primary components of the Social Security Act.

Retirement Equity Act, 1984   An amendment to ERISA that incorporated a number of key revisions, many of which addressed the concerns of former (in the event of divorce) and surviving (in the event of death) spouses.

Revenue Act, 1978   Among many other changes, the Revenue Act added two sections to the tax code that essentially resulted in the creation of two new and ultimately very important employee benefits: Section 125 plans and 401(k) plans.

right-to-know (also known as the employee hazard communication standard)   Ensures that employers and employees have knowledge and awareness about hazardous chemicals located in the workplace, and that they know how to protect themselves. Specifically, this standard requires all employers having hazardous materials at the workplace to implement a written Hazard Communication Program. Four important key elements of this program are Material Safety Data Sheets (MSDS), orientation, training, and container labeling requirements.

right to sue letter   A letter issued by the EEOC that entitles the recipient (the charging party) to bring a private lawsuit within the specified time frame.

right-to-work states   States in which union shops and closed shops are illegal. In a right-to-work state, no employee has to join the union.

role play   A training method that is similar to case studies and can even be designed to be the natural "culmination" of a case study. Role plays, in one sense, take case studies one step farther, in that participants actually "act out" the ways in which they would apply the knowledge and practice the skills in particular situations.

S

safe harbor provisions   Provisions under which an employer that has made improper salary deductions can protect itself from losing the exemption. To do so, the employer would be required to

- Have a clearly communicated policy prohibiting improper deductions and including a complaint mechanism

- Reimburse employees for any improper deductions

- Make a good faith commitment to comply in the future

safety committees   A vehicle through which employees and managers can collaboratively work to increase workplace safety.

salary   A predetermined amount of compensation that an employee will be paid per week.

salting   Activity engaged in by a "salt," a union organizer who seeks employment with the organization for the express purpose of actively organizing and campaigning within the organization.

Sarbanes-Oxley Act (SOX), 2002   A law designed to protect investors, SOX enacted reforms designed to enhance corporate responsibility and financial disclosures, and to combat corporate and accounting fraud.

Schechter Poultry Corp. v. United States, 1935   A Supreme Court case that rendered the National Industrial Recovery Act unconstitutional. Although this decision was wholly unrelated to labor and collective bargaining, the Supreme Court decision rendered the labor-related provisions illegal, as well. The right to organize and bargain reverted, once again, back to railway workers, and no one else. This would not, however, be the case for long.

scientific method   A form of primary research that consists of a systematic approach of testing hypotheses and using the knowledge generated to strengthen the degree to which HR can support the overall objectives of the organization.

secondary boycott   Efforts to convince others to stop doing business with a particular organization that is the subject of a primary boycott.

secondary research   A process that involves collecting information "secondhand," meaning not directly from the original source of the data. Secondary research assimilates data that has already been collected by others, and thus allows the secondary researcher to "stand on the shoulders" of those who conducted the primary research.

Section 125   The tax code created by the Revenue Act of 1978 that created flexible benefits plans (often referred to as "cafeteria" plans). Section 125 plans can help employers as well as employees save money by reducing payroll taxes.

Section 401(k)   The second employee benefit that was created by the Revenue Act. A type of defined contribution plan, 401(k) plans allow employees to set aside pre-tax dollars to save for their retirement. This can be done through salary deduction, which may or may not be matched in part or (less frequently) in whole by employer contributions. 401(k) dollars can also be set aside through deferral of profit sharing income.

security   Protection of the workplace, and of the employees who work there.

selection   The process of choosing the candidate(s) to whom the position will be offered.

selection criteria   The "shopping list" of what you're looking for in the individuals who will populate your candidate pool (and, ultimately, the employees who will join the organization). This could and often will include KSAs, job specifications, behavioral characteristics, required credentials, and specific requirements stemming from job competencies.

Senior Professional in Human Resources (SPHR)   The Senior Professional in Human Resources certification, granted by and issued through HRCI.

seniority systems   Bona fide seniority or merit-based systems that are not intended or designed to discriminate unlawfully.

serious violation   A violation that the employer either knew about or should have known about, and from which death or serious injury is probable. OSHA may propose a fine of up to $7,000 per serious violation.

sexual harassment   A form of sex discrimination rendered illegal by Title VII of the Civil Rights Act of 1964. There are two categories of sexual harassment: quid pro quo and hostile work environment.

Sherman Antitrust Act, 1890   A law passed in an effort to curb the growth of monopolies. Under the act, any business combination that sought to restrain trade or commerce would from that time forward be illegal. Specifically, the act states that

▶ Section 1: "Every contract, combination in the form of trust or otherwise, or conspiracy, in restraint of trade or commerce among the several States, or with foreign nations, is declared to be illegal."

▶ Section 2: "Every person who shall monopolize, or attempt to monopolize, or combine or conspire with any other person or persons, to monopolize any part of the trade or commerce among the several States, or with foreign nations, shall be deemed guilty of a felony."

The Sherman Antitrust Act also placed responsibility for pursuing and investigating trusts on government attorneys and district courts.

short-form employment applications   Shorter versions of an organization's standard employment application.

short-term incentive programs   Incentive programs that are usually one year or less in duration.

short-term incentives—individual   Variable incentive programs (usually one year or less in duration) that are used to motivate employees to attain specific individual financial or nonfinancial objectives.

short-term incentives—team/group   Variable incentive programs (usually one year or less in duration) that are used to motivate teams/groups to attain specific team/group financial or nonfinancial objectives. Short-term team/group incentive programs are intended to foster collaborative efforts and synergy among employees who are pursuing a common goal.

similar-to-me error/bias (interviewing)   An interviewing error/bias that occurs when the interviewer evaluates a candidate on the basis of how much a candidate is similar to, or different from, him or her.

similar-to-me error/bias (performance management)   A performance management error/bias in which the appraiser evaluates an employee's performance on the basis of how much a candidate is similar to, or different from, him or her.

simple linear regression   A mathematical forecasting technique that examines the past relationship between two factors, determines the statistical strength of that relationship, and, on the basis of that analysis, projects future conditions.

simple resolutions   A legislative measure that pertains to either the Senate or the House of Representatives. Simple resolutions offer a nonbinding opinion, are not submitted to the president, and do not have the force of law.

simplified employee pension plan (SEP)   A defined contribution plan that allows employers to contribute on a tax-favored basis to individual retirement accounts (IRAs) that employees set up for this purpose.

simulations   A mathematical forecasting technique that creates scenarios through which different "realities" can be tested out to see what could happen under a variety of changing conditions.

skill   One of the four factors used as a basis to assess the substantial equality of job content under the Equal Pay Act of 1963. Skill refers to the amount or degree of experience, ability, education, and training required to perform the job.

skill inventories   A central database that captures the many KSAs possessed by its employees, even when those KSAs are not being used by an employee in his or her current position.

small group discussions/instructor-facilitated large group discussions   A training method during which the facilitator encourages learning by drawing upon the experiences and insights of the participants. This is used as a way of reinforcing the adult learning principle that says that adult learners believe that they have a significant amount of valuable experience from which they can draw to enhance their own learning, and from which others can learn, as well.

SMART   An acronym that can be applied to performance management (as well as other objectives that are developed and used within HR). The acronym speaks to the following attributes: specific, measurable, action-oriented, realistic, and time-bound.

Social Security Act (SSA), 1935 (also known as Old Age, Survivors and Disability Insurance [OASDI])   Social security is a social insurance program (although some would define it differently) that is funded through payroll taxes. Social security has three primary components, which are now referred to as retirement income, disability benefits, and survivor's benefits.

sociotechnical interventions   OD interventions that focus on the ways in which groups can become more (or semi) autonomous with respect to the performance and execution of the work.

St. Mary's Honor Center v. Hicks, 1993   Key Issue: Burden of proof. Significance: To prevail in an allegation of discrimination under Title VII of the Civil Rights Act of 1964, an employee goes beyond a prima facie case and actually proves that the employer's true reasons for an employment action are, in fact, discriminatory.

standards   Requirements created by the Occupational Health and Safety Administration (OSHA) as a way of ensuring the health and safety of employees.

strategic HR   The transactions, the tasks, the procedural functions that need to be done. Strategic-level HR is one leg of the HR stool—the other two legs are operational/tactical HR and transformational HR.

strategic management   Strategic HR management speaks to HR's overall commitment, in both word and deed, to meeting the ever-evolving short-term, long-term, and strategic objectives of the organization.

stress   According to Public Safety and Health (NIOSH), the "harmful physical and emotional responses that occur when the requirements of the job do not match the capabilities, resources, or needs of the worker."

stress interviews   Interviews in which the interviewer(s) deliberately creates a high-stress environment in an effort to ascertain how the candidate would respond in a similarly stressful situation in the workplace post hire.

strictness error/bias (interviewing)   An interviewing error/bias that occurs when the interviewer applies an inappropriately harsh and demanding standard to one or more candidates, resulting in a lower overall assessment of the candidate(s).

strictness error/bias (performance management)   A performance management error/bias in which the appraiser applies an inappropriately harsh and demanding standard when evaluating the performance of one or more employees, resulting in a lower overall assessment of the employee(s).

substance use/abuse programs   A comprehensive program that consists of a drug-free workplace policy, supervisor training, employee education, employee assistance, and drug testing.

suggestion programs   Programs that invite employees to submit their ideas (often anonymously) relative to any work-related topic, such as improving work systems, identifying or eliminating safety concerns, or even exposing unethical (or criminal) behavior. Questions submitted through suggestion programs or "boxes" need to be responded to quickly, regardless of whether the suggestion is implemented. Employees must be heard and feel heard for any suggestion program to be successful.

Summary of Work-Related Injuries and Illnesses (also known as the OSHA Form 300A)   A form used to record a numeric summary of all work related injuries and illnesses logged in OSHA's Form 300 over the course of each calendar year. This form indicates the number of cases, the number of workdays impacted, and the number and types of work-related injuries and illnesses. A worksheet is also available to assist employers in filling out this summary. Each year, a completed Form 300 must be posted conspicuously for three months (between February 1 and April 30).

summary plan description (SPD)   A document that employees (or beneficiaries) who become participants in a retirement plan that is covered under ERISA are entitled to receive, at no cost, from the plan administrator. The SPD describes what the plan provides and how it operates. It also provides information relative to when an employee can begin to participate in the plan, how service and benefits are calculated, when benefits becomes vested, when and in what form benefits are paid, and how to file a claim for benefits.

summative evaluation   An approach that it is predicated on the interpretation of data that is collected after the initiative has been implemented. Summative evaluation allows for a complete analysis of the entire initiative on four different levels: reaction, learning, behavior, and results.

survivor's benefits   One of the three primary components of the Social Security Act.

SWOT analysis (strengths, weaknesses, opportunities, threats)   An analysis that is conducted to ascertain the strengths and weaknesses that are inherent to an organization, as well as the opportunities and threats that it faces from external forces.

sympathy strikes   A type of strike that occurs when employees who are not directly involved in an economic dispute choose not to cross a picket line out of support for striking workers. Sympathy strikers do not need to be employed by the same employer as the employees who are actually on strike in order to engage in a sympathy strike. A sympathy strike is considered protected concerted activity.

T

tactile/kinesthetic learners   Those who learn most effectively by processing information with which they can interact in a "hands on" manner, in the most literal sense of the word. They like to touch, to feel, to explore, and to experience the world around them.

Taft-Hartley Act (also known as the Labor Management Relations Act), 1947   An amendment designed to remedy what the Republican Congress saw as two major omissions in the NLRA (Wagner Act): first, the identification of behaviors and practices that would be considered ULPs on the part of unions, and second, a provision that would allow the government to issue an injunction against a strike that threatened national interests. Taft-Hartley identified the following unfair labor practices that could be committed by unions:

- Restraining or coercing employees in the exercise of their rights or an employer in the choice of its bargaining representative

- Causing an employer to discriminate against an employee

- Refusing to bargain with the employer of the employees it represents

- Engaging in certain types of secondary boycotts

- Requiring excessive dues

- Engaging in featherbedding

- Picketing for recognition for more than thirty days without petitioning for an election

- Entering into hot cargo agreements

- Striking or picketing a health care establishment without giving the required notice

task or work (operations) level analysis   Level 2 of McGehee and Thayer's three levels of HRD/training needs analysis and assessment. Task or work (operations) level analysis collects and addresses data about a particular job or group of jobs.

Taxman v. Board of Education of Piscataway, 1993
Key issue: Affirmative action. Significance: The U.S. Court of Appeals for the Third Circuit ruled that, in the absence of underrepresentation as demonstrated and documented through an affirmative action plan, organizations cannot consider race when making decisions relative to who will be laid off and who will be retained. Doing so would constitute a violation of Title VII of the Civil Rights Act of 1964.

This case falls under the category of "reverse discrimination" because it alleged race discrimination and was brought by a person who was not a minority/person of color.

teambuilding   Exercises and initiatives that seek to help the team learn to function more effectively so that it can attain its overall objective (which must link, of course, to overall organizational objective).

technostructural interventions   OD interventions that focus on improving what work gets done, as well as the ways and processes through which the work gets done. It looks at job design, job redesign, job restructuring, work content, workflow, work processes, and the like.

teratogens   A specific group of chemicals that will not harm pregnant women, but that do have the potential to harm unborn fetuses.

third-party vendor   An entity or person outside the organization to whom work can be outsourced.

Title VII of the Civil Rights Act, 1964   A landmark piece of legislation prohibiting employment discrimination the basis of race, color, religion, sex, and national origin.

tort doctrines   Torts are wrongful acts committed against another individual's property or person. By definition, the commission of a tort infringes on another person's rights.

Some of the major tort doctrines that affect individual employee rights in the absence of an employment or labor contract are

- Employment-at-will
- Wrongful termination
- Implied contracts
- Defamation
- Invasion of privacy
- Negligent hiring
- Negligent training
- Negligent retention
- Negligent referral

total compensation   All of the "rewards" that an organization gives, grants, or otherwise bestows upon its employees in exchange for the services those employees have rendered through their employment. It includes more obvious items, such as wages and salaries, that would fall under the subheading "compensation," as well as mandatory and optional benefits such as social security contributions, health and welfare programs, and the like. It also includes items that some but not all employees enjoy, such as incentives, bonuses, stock options, and so on.

total quality management (TQM)   An OD intervention that is ultimately aimed at meeting or exceeding customer expectations through the commitment of everyone in an organization (often through a team-based approach) to continuous improvement of products and/or services.

total rewards   Total rewards speaks to HR's responsibility to ensure that the organization's total compensation and benefits programs, policies, and practices reinforce and support the short-term, long-term, and emerging and strategic objectives of the organization.

transformational HR   Takes a long-term, future-focused approach to the ways in which HR will work with the organization to attain its organizational mission. It looks at business and organizational issues, rather than "HR issues." It fosters and cultivates change and is dynamic, impactful, and ever-evolving.

treatment follow-up drug testing   Drug testing that is conducted periodically for employees who return to work after participating in an alcohol or drug treatment program to ensure that they remain substance-free.

trend analysis   A mathematical technique that looks at and measures how one particular factor changes over a period of time.

tuberculosis (TB)   A highly infectious bacterial disease that usually affects the lungs and that can also affect other organs.

turnover analysis   Measures the percentage of the workforce that has left the organization during a specified period of time.

U

ULP strike   A strike called by a union that alleges, correctly or incorrectly, that the employer has committed an unfair labor practice during contract negotiations. Employers cannot hire permanent strike replacements during a ULP strike, and the striking workers must be returned to their original positions after the strike is over.

undue hardship   A hardship created by a requested accommodation that creates significant difficulty (enough to disrupt business operations), results in a significant financial outlay, or changes something about the (essential) nature of the business.

unemployment insurance   A program intended to help employees financially "bridge" the gap between positions when an employee has lost his job through no fault of his own. Unemployment insurance was established as part of the federal Social Security Act of 1935, but is administered at the state level. Unemployment insurance is funded through employer taxes (except in three states, where employees contribute as well).

unfair labor practice (ULP)   Unlawful acts that can be committed by either employers or unions. The NLRA (Wagner Act) identified five categories of employer unfair labor practices:

- To "interfere with, restrain, or coerce employees" in the exercise of their rights to engage in concerted or union activities or refrain from them
- To dominate or interfere with the formation or administration of a labor organization
- To discriminate against employees for engaging in concerted or union activities or refraining from them
- To discriminate against an employee for filing charges with the NLRB or taking part in any NLRB proceedings
- To refuse to bargain with the union that is the lawful representative of its employees

Unfair labor practices that could be committed by unions were identified in 1947, in the Labor Management Relations Act (also known as the Taft-Hartley Act).

unfreezing   The first stage in Lewin's change process theory. Through the unfreezing stage, everyone who is involved with and impacted by the change must be brought to the point where he or she can understand and accept that a particular change will happen.

Uniform Guidelines on Employee Selection Procedures, 1978   A law that establishes a uniform set of principles relative to all elements of the selection process, including but not limited to interviewing, preemployment testing, and performance appraisal. A key purpose of the Uniform Guidelines is to deal with the concept of "adverse impact" (also known as "disparate impact") as it pertains to the employment process, and to ensure that interview and selection processes are reliable (consistent) and valid.

Uniformed Services Employment and Reemployment Rights Act (USERRA), 1994   A law that provides reinforcement rights for individuals who miss work because of "service in the uniformed services," which is defined as voluntary or involuntary uniformed service.

union deauthorization   The revocation of the union security clause in the contract, which thereby creates an "open shop." Deauthorization requires a majority vote of the entire bargaining unit, not just the members of the unit who vote in the deauthorization election.

union decertification   The process by which employees vote to remove the union's rights to represent the employees. This process is similar to certification, only in reverse. Decertification requires a 50% (or more) of individuals who vote in the decertification election.

union security clauses   Articles that are included in some agreements in an effort to protect the interests, strength, and security of the union. Union security clauses regulate membership in the union and, consequently, relate to the payment of dues. Some of the more common types of union security clauses include

- ▶ Open shop
- ▶ Closed shop
- ▶ Union shop
- ▶ Agency shop
- ▶ Maintenance of membership

union shop   Newly hired employees must join the union within a specified period of time, usually 30 days, and must remain a member of the union as a condition of employment. In a union shop, employers must terminate employees who are not union members. Union shops are illegal in "right to work" states.

United Steelworkers v. Weber, 1979   Key issue: Affirmative action. Significance: Affirmative action plans that establish voluntary quotas that have been jointly agreed to by an organization as well as its collective bargaining unit do not constitute race discrimination under Title VII of the Civil Rights Act of 1964 if they are designed to remedy past discrimination that has resulted in current underutilization.

This case falls under the category of "reverse discrimination" because it alleged race discrimination and was brought by someone who was not a minority/person of color.

U.S. Patent Act   Patents confer certain rights upon the individual to whom the patent is granted. Specifically, a patent holder has "the right to exclude others from making, using, offering for sale, or selling" the invention in the United States or "importing" the invention into the United States.

utility patents   Granted for the invention or discovery of any new and useful process, machine, article of manufacture, or composition of matter, or any new and useful improvement thereof.

utilization analysis   The section of an affirmative action plan that compares the percentage of qualified women and minorities available to be employed in a particular job group to the percentage of women and minorities who are actually employed in that job group.

V

validity   The degree to which selection processes measure skills that relate meaningfully and clearly to the skills that are required to perform a particular job.

values   Beliefs on which the organization has been built. They are the tenets that shape and guide strategic and day-to-day decision making, as well as the behaviors that are exhibited in the organization. Organizations identify values, in part, as a way to clearly guide those decisions and behaviors. Values are often represented in terms and principles such as integrity, honesty, respect, and so on.

variable pay   Also known as "at risk" pay, variable pay is cash compensation that fluctuates and is tied, in some way, to the employee's performance.

vesting   The process by which an employee earns a nonforfeitable right to the employer's contribution of his or her defined benefit/defined contribution plan.

VETS-100   The Federal Contractor Veterans' Employment Report that must be filed annually by those having federal contracts or subcontracts of $100,000 or more.

Vietnam Era Veterans' Readjustment Assistance Act (VEVRAA), 1974   A law that requires employers with federal contracts or subcontracts of $25,000 or more to provide equal opportunity and affirmative action for Vietnam era veterans, special disabled veterans, and veterans who served on active duty during a war or in a campaign or expedition for which a campaign badge has been authorized.

vision   A brief yet comprehensive descriptive and inspirational statement that articulates where the organization wants to be and what it wants to become in the future.

vision coverage   A type of health and welfare benefit. An employer will typically offer vision coverage as a discount program (generally around 10%). Vision coverage generally includes items such as exams, contact lenses, and glasses.

visual learners   Those who learn most effectively by processing information that they see.

voluntary subjects (also known as permissive subjects)   Voluntary subjects of bargaining are topics that can be submitted to collective bargaining if and only if the employer and the employees' representative are willing to do so. Attempting to force bargaining on a voluntary or permissive subject constitutes a ULP.

voluntary terminations   A decision initiated by the employee to end the employment relationship.

W–X

Wagner Act (also known as the National Labor Relations Act), 1935   A law that guaranteed "the right to self-organization, to form, join, or assist labor organizations, to bargain collectively through representatives of their own choosing, and to engage in concerted activities for the purpose of collective bargaining or other mutual aid and protection." Certain groups or categories of employees are excluded under the Wagner Act from membership in a bargaining unit. Examples would include managers, supervisors, confidential employees (essentially secretaries and administrative assistants to managers who can make labor relations decisions), and several others.

Walsh-Healey Public Contracts Act, 1936   The Walsh-Healey Public Contracts Act requires contractors who have contracts with the federal government that exceed $10,000 to pay an established minimum wage to workers employed through that contract. In addition to minimum wage, Walsh-Healey PCA also addressed issues including overtime pay and safe and sanitary working conditions.

Washington v. Davis, 1976   Key issue: Employment tests and disparate impact. Significance: A test that has an adverse impact on a protected class is still lawful, as long as the test can be shown to be valid and job related.

weighted employment applications   Employment applications that assign relative weights to different portions of the application in an effort to facilitate the process of evaluating candidates' qualifications in a consistent and objective manner.

Weingarten Rights   The right of a unionized employee to have union representation during a potential disciplinary interview.

whole job methods   Nonquantitative job evaluation techniques that determine the relative value of jobs within the organization without using mathematical techniques.

whole job ranking   A whole job evaluation technique that ranks, from lowest to highest, according to the importance that each job holds (or, stated differently, the value that each job brings) to the organization. In essence, a whole job ranking is a list that reflects which jobs are more important to the organization, and which jobs are least important to the organization, in rank order.

wildcat strikes   A type of strike that occurs when a strike is called even when a collective bargaining agreement contains a no-strike clause that prohibits striking during the duration of the agreement. Wildcat strikes are not protected concerted activity.

willful violation   A violation that is deliberate and intentional. OSHA may impose a fine of up to $70,000 per willful violation (more in the event of the employee's death), and possibly incarceration.

Worker Adjustment and Retraining Notification Act (WARN), 1988   A law that mandates employer notification requirements under specific circumstances involving mass layoffs and plant closings, thus giving displaced workers time to make arrangements for other employment. WARN covers employers with 100 or more full-time employees.

worker's compensation   State laws intended to provide medical care to injured employees and death benefits to families of those who died. Worker's comp is a "no fault" system—injured workers receive medical and/or compensation benefits regardless of who caused the job-related accident.

workforce analysis   The section of an affirmative action plan that essentially depicts the contractor's workforce in terms of incumbents' race, gender, and wages. The workforce analysis is the older, longer, and more complex version of the "organizational display."

workforce planning and employment   Workforce planning and employment speaks to HR's responsibility to ensure integrated, seamless, and effective recruitment, hiring, orientation, and exit processes that support the short-term, long-term, emerging, and strategic objectives of the organization.

working conditions   One of the four factors used as a basis to assess the substantial equality of job content under the Equal Pay Act of 1963. Working conditions refer to the physical surroundings of the position, as well as any hazards that are associated with a particular position.

work-life programs   Programs that provide employees with the opportunity to combine or "balance" professional and nonprofessional dimensions of their lives, including flexible schedules, job sharing, telecommuting, and compressed work weeks. Work-life programs offer advantages for employees as well as employers who want to market themselves in the relevant labor market.

work-related illness   Illnesses resulting from an event or condition in the work environment that fall into any one of the following four categories: skin diseases or disorders, respiratory conditions, poisoning, hearing loss, or "all other illnesses."

work-related injury   Any wound or damage to the body resulting from an event in the work environment.

workweek   A workweek is any fixed and regularly recurring period of 168 hours (24 hours in a day, seven days a week).

wrongful termination   A tort doctrine that speaks to the employer having ended the employment relationship for wrongful reasons. One possible basis for wrongful termination could exist if an employee was terminated in violation of an individual employment contract. Others could apply as well, and would vary from state to state.

Y–Z

"yellow dog" contract   A contract or an agreement between an employer and an employee in which the employer agrees to give the employee a job as long as the employee agrees not to join or have any involvement with a labor union.

zero defects   Phil Crosby's philosophy, which asserts that employees will perform at whatever level management sets for them. For that reason, settling for "goodness," rather than the full attainment of objectives, would effectively preclude the possibility of attaining those objectives.

zipper clause   A collective bargaining article through which both parties agree that the agreement is an exclusive and complete "expression of consent"—in other words, that the only items that can be collectively bargained until the expiration of the agreement are the ones that are actually included in the agreement. After the agreement is signed, new subjects cannot be added, and existing subjects cannot be reopened for negotiation. The contract has been zipped closed.

Index

Federal Mediation and Concilation Service (FMCS), 440

grievance handling procedures, collective bargaining agreements (CBAs), 439-440

panels, 440

permanent, 440

ASPA (American Society for Personnel Administration)

AAI (ASPA Accreditation Institute), 24-26

Cornell University conference on personnel, 24

name change to SHRM (Society for Human Resource Management), 23

assessment exams, PHR versus SPHR certification, 33-34

attitude versus behavior, 236

auditory learners, 262

audits, human resources, 110

Authorization to Test (ATT) letters, 36

automatic feedback, practice tests, 614

Automobile Workers v. Johnson Controls (1990), fetal protection policies, 479

availability analysis, affirmative action plans (AAPs), 143

avoidance (risk management), 456

B

B.F. Skinner's Operant Conditioning (1957), 48-49

background checks, 199-200

balanced scorecard system (strategic management), 106-107

base pay, compensation, 325

Beck rights, union dues, 435

behavior

attitude versus, 236

interviews based on, 187

leadership, theories on, 53

behavioral anchored rating scales (BARS), performance appraisals, 280

biases, interviews

contrast errors, 192

first-impression errors, 193

halo errors, 193

horn errors, 193

leniency errors, 193

managing, 192-193

recency errors, 193

similar-to-me errors, 194

strictness errors, 193

bills (legislation), hearing and voting process, 115-116

binding arbitration, grievance handling procedures, 439-440

biological health hazards (occupational health), 479-481

Blake and Mouton's Situational Leadership Theory, 55

Bloodborne Pathogens Standard (OSH Act, 1970), 469

break schedules, training sessions, 268-269

break-even analysis, measuring human resources effectiveness, 110

Brinkerhoff's Stages of Evaluation theory, 252-253

broadbanding, pay grades, 329

bumping rights clauses, collective bargaining agreements (CBAs), 432

bursitis, 476

business continuity plans, 457-458

business process perspective, balanced scorecard system (strategic management), 107

C

C&B (Compensation and Benefits)

base pay, 325

employees versus independent contractors, 302-303

exams

answers, 370-372

questions, 365-367

exempt status, 304

administrative type, 306

computer employees, 307

creative professional type, 307

executive type, 306

highly compensated employees, 307

learned professional type, 306

non-exempt status versus, 304

outside sales employees, 307

safe harbor provisions, 308

salary basis, 305

exercises, 362-364, 367-369

independent contractors versus employees, 302-303

job evaluation, 321-323

legislation

COBRA Act of 1985, 335-336

Davis-Bacon Act of 1931, 314

Employee Retirement Income Security Act (ERISA) of 1974, 330-334

Equal Pay Act of 1963, 320

Fair Labor Standards Act of 1938, 314-319

Family and Medical Leave Act of 1993 (mandatory benefit program), 347-351

Federal-State Unemployment Insurance Program (mandatory benefit program), 344-345

Health Insurance Portability and Accountability Act of 1996, 337-338

Medicare (mandatory benefit program), 342-344

Mental Health Parity Act of 1996, 339

Older Worker's Benefit Protection Act of 1990, 336

Portal-to-Portal Act of 1947, 319

Retirement Equity Act of 1984, 334

Revenue Act of 1978 (optional benefit program), 345-347

Sarbanes-Oxley Act of 2002, 339-340

Social Security (mandatory benefit program), 340-342

D

I

K - L

N

O

P

Q - R

S

U - V

W

X - Y - Z

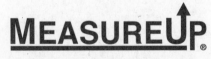